To the memory of Kurt Lewin, whose contributions continue to instruct and inspire generations of social psychologists.

The SAGE
# Handbook of Methods in Social Psychology

Edited by

## Carol Sansone
University of Utah

## Carolyn C. Morf

and

## A.T. Panter
University of North Carolina, Chapel Hill

**SAGE** Publications
*International Educational and Professional Publisher*
Thousand Oaks ■ London ■ New Delhi

*For information:*

Sage Publications, Inc.
2455 Teller Road
Thousand Oaks, California 91320
E-mail: order@sagepub.com

Sage Publications Ltd.
6 Bonhill Street
London EC2A 4PU
United Kingdom

Sage Publications India Pvt. Ltd.
B-42, Panchsheel Enclave
New Delhi 110 017  India

Printed in the United States of America

**Library of Congress Cataloging-in-Publication Data**

The Sage handbook of methods in social psychology /
Carol Sansone, Carolyn C. Morf, A. T. Panter, editors.
    p. cm.
Includes bibliographical references and index.
ISBN 0-7619-2535-X (Cloth) — ISBN 0-7619-2536-8 (Paper)
    1. Social psychology—Methodology. I.  Sansone, Carol. II.  Morf, Carolyn C.
III.  Panter, A. T.
HM1019.S24 2004
302′.01—dc21

                                          2003004673

This book is printed on acid-free paper.

03  04  05  06  10  9  8  7  6  5  4  3  2  1

| | |
|---|---|
| *Acquisitions Editor:* | Jim Brace-Thompson |
| *Editorial Assistant:* | Karen Ehrmann |
| *Copy Editor:* | A. J. Sobczak |
| *Production Editor:* | Diane S. Foster |
| *Typesetter:* | C&M Digitals (P) Ltd, |
| *Proofreader:* | Penny Sippel |
| *Indexer:* | Juniee Oneida |
| *Cover Designer:* | Michelle Kenny |

# Brief Contents

# Detailed Contents

## 14. Measuring Individuals in a Social Environment: Conceptualizing Dyadic and Group Interaction

RICHARD GONZALEZ AND DALE GRIFFIN

# Preface

The genius of social psychology as a field has been its ability to investigate the seemingly unstudiable, complex behaviors that characterize humans as social creatures. The field has a rich history of methodological innovation with strong contributions to basic and applied research. However, it is sometimes difficult for both new and seasoned researchers to keep up with innovations that allow a greater diversity in the kinds and levels of research questions that can be addressed. As a result, the nature of the questions asked by many researchers may be unnecessarily constrained. Conversely, a rush to embrace newer approaches can lead to a less-than-thorough consideration of fundamental issues that transcend any particular approach.

We believe that the decision to use a particular methodological approach is optimally made when grounded in careful considerations of the "big picture" of a program of research. Thus, methodological decisions are tied inextricably to what the researcher, ultimately, wants to know. Our major purpose in editing this handbook was to create an integrated collection of conceptually guided chapters that address the common and unique methodological decisions that researchers must make when using both traditional and cutting-edge research paradigms. Based on our "top-down" perspective, chapters in this volume emphasize the conceptual basis of the methodology, with an explicit focus on the meaning of data when obtained via a particular methodology. Our thinking has been heavily influenced by the writings of Kurt Lewin, to whose memory we dedicate this book. Lewin believed firmly that theory and method are completely intertwined and that we should use our questions to come up with creative methodologies to address them. To Lewin, "research is the art of taking the next step" (Lewin, 1949/1999, p. 25). We believe we have captured this art as well as the science with the present collection of chapters.

We implemented the top-down perspective in two ways. First, the overall organization of the handbook parallels what we see as the "big picture" of the overall research process. Beginning chapters address issues related to selecting and identifying research questions and populations, middle chapters address issues related to design and analysis issues, and later chapters address issues related to expanding the original social psychological questions to other disciplines within and outside psychology. Statistical analysis is considered a process in service of research design, and it is included to the extent that it helps to illuminate the distinct meaning of data obtained through a particular methodological approach or design. Thus, the focus is on the conceptual meaning of the data and analysis, rather than on microlevel "how to" guidance through analytical issues.

Second, we have attempted to maintain the top-down perspective within each chapter. All contributors were asked to follow a general template in which they first describe a concrete and relevant social psychological research problem (or problems) and then discuss relevant methodological issues in the context of that problem. Contributors to this volume were selected because they have developed expertise on particular methodological approaches or issues in social psychology—and, more important, they did so in response to attempting to discover the best way to understand the psychological phenomena that interested them. Thus, these researchers fit the "Lewin model" in that they have let the research questions guide their methods, rather than the reverse. These expert researchers discuss traditional and state-of-the-art methodological advances by first outlining concrete research phenomena and related questions of interest and then showing how these questions may be best answered through design and analysis decisions.

Adopting the top-down perspective led to several features of this handbook that set it apart from other methods books. In addition to traditional methodological areas relevant for social psychologists, the book includes innovative chapters such as those on ethics, culture and diversity, and individual differences. Moreover, the handbook captures social psychology's increasing emphasis on research that crosses disciplines both within and outside psychology (e.g., social neuroscience, social development, and social psychology and the Internet). Also included is a section on some applications of social psychology and its methods to other domains (e.g., program evaluation, health, education, and organizations). It was impossible to include all possible domains of application, but we chose domains that we thought would have the broadest interest and that would have common issues as well as unique challenges. In reading these chapters, it is evident that there are many similarities across areas of application; thus, our hope is that these diverse samplings will also allow for translations to other areas.

We intend the audience for this handbook to be active researchers interested in using social psychological approaches to address their research questions. This audience includes graduate students and advanced undergraduates who are being introduced to the methods of social psychology. It futher includes more advanced behavioral scientists in academic and research settings who are interested in learning about modern perspectives on classic approaches as well as newer methodological approaches in social psychology.

Our hope is that readers will come away with an appreciation for the complexity of the field's phenomena along with a sense of excitement about the fun and value of the research methods that can be used to unravel these phenomena. As editors of this volume, we have learned a lot from the authors and their chapters, and we hope that readers do the same!

## ACKNOWLEDGMENTS

We wish to thank our colleagues Irwin Altman, Walter Mischel, Monisha Pasupathi, and Bert Uchino for their sage advice and thoughtful feedback at critical points throughout this process. We are also grateful to Angela Newman at the University of Utah for her critical help in bringing order out of chaos as we tried to keep track of all the various versions of files and other paperwork associated with developing and finalizing the book. Jim Brace-Thompson, senior editor at Sage Publications, provided both the initial enthusiasm and constant support for this project, and he helped to make our vision of the book a reality. We thank him for that. We also thank A. J. Sobczak for his extraordinarily thoughtful and critical work as copy editor and Diane Foster for all her efforts as production editor. Finally, we would each like to note some personal acknowledgments. Carol Sansone would like to thank her family, friends, and students for their patience and support during the several years she devoted to completion of the book. She would also like to thank her younger brother, Don, for allowing her to publicly confess her past misdeed in Chapter 1. Carolyn C. Morf would like to acknowledge with gratitude the help and support of her family and friends during the preparation of this volume. Finally, A. T. Panter would like to express her sincere thanks to her major supports during this project: George Huba, Nechama and Yaakov Huba, Sarajane Brittis, and her family, especially Danielle, Michaela, and Gideon Panter.

Carol Sansone
Carolyn C. Morf
A. T. Panter

## REFERENCE

Lewin, K. (1999). Cassirer's philosophy of science and the social sciences. In M. Gold (Ed.), *The complete social scientist: A Kurt Lewin reader* (pp. 23-36). Washington, DC: American Psychological Association. (Original work published 1949)

# Part I

# INTRODUCTION AND OVERVIEW

## CHAPTER 1

# The Research Process

## Of Big Pictures, Little Details, and the Social Psychological Road in Between

CAROL SANSONE

*University of Utah*

CAROLYN C. MORF

A. T. PANTER

*University of North Carolina, Chapel Hill*

When 6 years old, one of us [CS] hit her younger brother on the head with a rock. He was bending over to look into a basement window, and a rock was on the ground next to him. Curious about what would happen if the rock hit his head, she was unprepared (given a steady diet of Looney Tunes cartoons) for the result: It hurt him. Though long forgiven and mostly forgotten (except at holidays), this episode illustrates both the motivation behind most science—the need to know what happens, and why—and the potential negative consequences of allowing available methods to shape our questions, rather than the reverse.

Formal training in research methods and design can mask this elemental problem, but the problem remains. In social psychology, it is easy to see why the problem occurs. Social psychologists study very complex behaviors, which are simultaneously connected with a host of contextual features and of internal, not directly observable, processes (e.g., perceiving, construing, feeling, goal-striving). Considerable creativity and thought have gone into creating methodological approaches that allow the researcher to focus in on subsets of these complex, interrelated features and processes.

An early example of this creativity was the work by Kurt Lewin and his students. At the time that psychodynamic and behaviorist approaches were emphasizing motivation defined in terms of instincts or reward outcomes, Lewin and colleagues proposed that motivation is attached to the *process* of goal-striving. From both psychodynamic and behaviorist perspectives, this proposal would have been neither worthwhile nor feasible to examine. In contrast, Lewin and colleagues developed a methodological approach in which the researcher creates a situation in the laboratory that should trigger the unobservable psychological process (e.g., goal-striving) and compares it to a situation that should not. Furthermore, these researchers proposed that the relative motivational differences created in these situations, which could not be measured directly, should be reflected in related variables that could be measured. For example, Zeigarnik (1927, as cited in Lewin, 1951) developed a method for testing the hypothesis that motivation attached to goal-striving is reflected at the thinking level; the method involved measuring the relative memory for completed and uncompleted tasks. Her approach led to the identification of the "Zeigarnik effect" (remembering roughly twice as many of the uncompleted tasks)—an objectively measured, empirical finding that reflects a hidden, dynamic psychological process. This ability to test hypotheses involving complex, unobservable processes created a foundation for the laboratory science of social psychology that followed. In addition, Lewin and colleagues investigated these processes in "real world" settings, translating hypotheses and developing creative ways to test their predictions in organizations facing change, among housewives dealing with wartime rationing, and so on.

The work by Lewin and his group represents one of the earliest examples of the methodological creativity found in social psychology, but it certainly is not the last. In fact, many of the early "classics" in social psychology research are known for the creation of novel methodologies in addition to the ideas that led to them. Many of these methodologies are still used. Just a few examples of this include the work by Hovland and his colleagues at Yale (e.g., Hovland, Janis, & Kelley, 1953) investigating persuasion and

attitude change (e.g., measuring attitudes about a topic after individuals read persuasive messages), Asch's (1946) work on impression formation (e.g., measuring people's impressions of a hypothetical individual after they are given a list of traits that ostensibly describe the individual), Festinger's (e.g., Festinger & Carlsmith, 1959) work on cognitive dissonance (e.g., the insufficient justification paradigm), and Schachter's (e.g., Schachter & Singer, 1962) work on emotion (e.g., the misattribution paradigm).

When methodological paradigms are created that seem to capture, at least to some extent, the complex behaviors and processes involved in social psychological phenomena, the paradigms usually include a typical setting (e.g., lab), participant population (e.g., college students), operationalizations, procedures, and analyses. All these aspects of the paradigm tend to be repeated in subsequent applications. And it is here that the problem can occur—that is, the methodological paradigm can start to guide *and* constrain the questions that researchers ask. For example, instead of continuing to ask questions about the nature of the goal-striving process, researchers may begin to limit their investigations to factors that affect memory for novel tasks completed in a lab. Although knowledge gained about the memory process may be useful in its own right, these studies may take us away from the original phenomenon of the goal-striving process (which is reflected in, but not limited to, memory for these tasks). Perhaps a more recent example of this problem may be seen in the rise of studies that employ cognitive neuroscience paradigms without first considering whether these paradigms are the best way to study the phenomena. (For a discussion of this problem, see Cacioppo, Lorig, Nusbaum, and Berntson, Chapter 17, this volume.)

Figure 1.1 illustrates the idealized research process. The figure shows a process of research that is relatively linear, stagewise, and iterative.

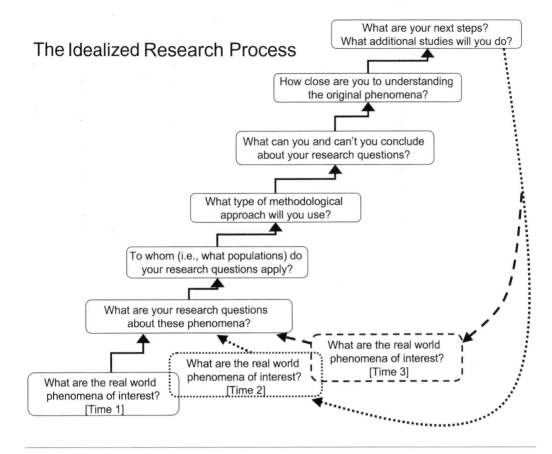

**Figure 1.1** A Schematic Drawing of the Idealized Research Process

The process starts with our identifying the phenomena that we want to understand. We then generate specific questions and hypotheses, as well as decide if these questions or hypotheses should be universal. We next operationalize our hypothesized constructs in some more concrete way that invoke important measurement principles, select an appropriate research design, analyze the results, and decide to what extent our initial hypotheses were supported. Depending on the evidence we gather and our conclusions about the patterns in our data, we hope that we gain some increased understanding of our phenomena of interest— and probably have even more questions than when we began. We then cycle through the process again with revised questions or questions that arose as consequences of our research findings. At some point, we may converge at some broader set of conclusions, and in some cases we may shift our emphasis on a given question. Thus, over time, with empirical studies, samples, and methodologies, we gradually build a knowledge base about the phenomena—perhaps broad enough so that we can apply this knowledge to treat, change, or alleviate important social problems.

If the process is so clear and is agreed upon, then why do we believe that allowing one's methods to drive the research question is an elemental problem? In the following section, we describe how this idealized research process can be affected by the very social psychological processes that social psychologists study. We will also briefly outline what we see as the consequences of these effects, consequences that can contribute to this elemental problem. We then describe this handbook, which we have organized according to these ideas about the research process.

## THE RESEARCH PROCESS

### The Starting Point: The Phenomena

Often, the phenomena we focus on come from observing the world around us: the experiences we have, the curious patterns that we see in people's behaviors, the social problems we would like to be able to alleviate. Whatever the specific phenomenon, what we actually focus on for our research efforts is necessarily only one small part, filtered through our own construal processes. As we identify and define what aspects of the phenomena are of particular interest to us, then, we have begun to make decisions that will limit what we discover about the phenomena.

This reality argues in favor of having a diverse group of scientists identifying the phenomena, because different experiences, backgrounds, and contexts will lead to identifying different phenomena, or in focusing on different aspects of the phenomena, or in defining those aspects from a different perspective (Sue, 1999). For example, suppose a researcher is interested in the phenomena of how people react when a supervisor provides different feedback to two subordinates when, objectively, their work products seem to be the same. A researcher from a majority perspective (e.g., being white or male) may define the phenomena in terms of watching someone else (a member of a minority group) get more positive feedback for the same work because the other person is being given special treatment. In contrast, someone from the minority perspective (e.g., being African American or female) may define the phenomena in terms of watching

someone else (a member of the majority group) being given more positive feedback for the same work product because the person is being held to a lower standard. In one sense, these two perspectives of the phenomena are the same: People believe that the supervisor is using different standards to evaluate performance as a function of the worker's group membership. The different takes on the phenomena, however, will lead to very different directions in the subsequent research process. If we assume that the phenomena have existence outside our perceptions (see Gergen, 2001, for a different perspective), then each researcher, no matter what methodological approach is used or how many attempts are made, can only approximate the phenomena, just as a single measurement can never fully define a latent construct. Furthermore, phenomena are not static; they (and our perspectives on them) evolve and change as illustrated in Figure 1.1 by the gradual shift in the "phenomena of interest" over time.

Discussing the potential effects only of the individual researchers' construal processes would be misleading, however. Decisions about what phenomena are considered important to study, and how they are defined, are often shaped by the social context that the "field" represents. The field can (and should) positively affect the research process. Reading the past literature provides researchers with other perspectives on phenomena, perhaps supporting but also challenging the individual researcher's perspective (and any biases he or she might have). Moreover, the literature provides information and suggestions about various ways to examine the phenomena empirically, allowing the individual researcher to build on what others have done, rather than having to "re-invent the wheel."

In addition to the positive effects that the larger research community can have on the research process, however, there may also be some negative effects. For example, in our work as editors, reviewers, and advisers, the broader significance of the topic being studied is a key dimension for our judgments of proposals and manuscripts. It is natural to think that topics in which we are already interested and invested are important to research (e.g., Renninger, 2000). Thus, this human tendency can create a gateway through which phenomena already being researched (with an established methodological paradigm) are evaluated as more important by the "field." One consequence of this is that when phenomena are identified and defined from perspectives that are not a major part of the status quo, they may be less likely to make it through the gateway. For example, a meta-analysis of editorial decisions at *Personality and Social Psychology Bulletin* found that articles submitted by women as lead authors were less likely to be accepted for publication (Petty, Fleming, & Fabrigar, 1999); one possible explanation for this finding is that during the period studied, women were relatively more likely to choose phenomena to research that were not considered as central to the field.

A second consequence of peer review is that by maintaining the status quo in terms of the research topics that are considered important, it also tends to maintain established methodological paradigms. Of course, there is nothing inherently wrong with using established methodological paradigms: They often become established precisely because they have been very useful in testing research questions. Established paradigms become a problem only when they start to constrain the kinds of questions asked.

## The Research Question

Once the phenomena of interest are identified, the next step in the process is to articulate more specific research questions. That is, what about the phenomena, more specifically, are you trying to understand or predict? Although the terms "research questions" and "research hypotheses" often are used interchangeably in discussing the research process, they can be distinct—that is, a hypothesis proposes an answer to the research question. As such, hypotheses include the question (sometimes implicitly), but the question does not necessarily have to include hypotheses—as the rock episode at the beginning of the chapter illustrates. Moreover, the same research question may lead a researcher to plan multiple studies that together address the question, whereas hypotheses are more specific to a given study. Because it is broader and more inclusive, therefore, we use "research question" in our discussion.

Sometimes the question is only a small step from the original observation. At other times, however, the research question may be a number of steps removed. In the supervisor feedback example discussed previously, a researcher may ask whether the effect of experiencing differential feedback on a worker's motivation depends on the worker's beliefs about why it happened. In this case, the researcher has taken a complex phenomenon that may be tied to a particular context and time (see Altman, 1988) and has abstracted out one small dimension about which to ask questions. Just as in identifying and defining the phenomena, then, the researcher makes choices of what to ask about the phenomena, and these choices are guided by his or her perspective as well as that provided by the field. These research questions guide as well as limit subsequent methodological choices and what we can eventually learn.

## To Whom Does the Question Apply?

Once we have decided on what question or questions we want to ask, we should then decide *to whom* the question or questions apply. Traditionally, social psychologists have been very good at identifying situational parameters for their questions, and they often see this identification as progress in understanding the phenomena. Identifying potential population parameters, however, is often an overlooked step in the research process. Does the research question ask about a psychological process or outcome that we assume is universal to all humans? To all living creatures? Or is it particularly relevant to some cultures, or to some groups within cultures (e.g., majority or minority, male or female, individuals high or low in narcissism)?

In fact, when we first start to investigate a particular research question, we probably do not know how widely the question should apply. Even at this point, however, we believe it is essential to ask the question because the "I don't know" response is important to acknowledge when making subsequent decisions about operationalizations and designs, as well as when interpreting findings. By making sure to ask the question before conducting a study, we are in a better position to discover important information about the boundaries of a particular methodological approach as well as insights into the phenomena itself. For example, by asking this question, we may discover that older women are less likely than college-age women to conform to a unanimous majority (Pasupathi, 1999), or that lack of choice is less likely to negatively affect children's motivation when they come from Asian American backgrounds (Iyengar & Lepper, 1999). These "limitations" to the assumption of universality may in fact lead to a better understanding of the underlying psychological process.

## Operationalizations and Design

Only after these earlier steps have been considered can the researcher make final decisions about which measures will reflect the most appropriate operationalizations of their constructs, and relatedly, about the best methodological setting in which to collect the data. Decisions about how to operationalize

constructs and the design to use are often made concurrently because these decisions typically constrain each other. For example, how closely does the researcher in our supervisor feedback example want to capture the original phenomena? Does he or she want to investigate the question in a real organizational setting where a supervisor gives feedback to subordinates? Or create an analog to the original situation, assuming that the relevant psychological processes generalize beyond that setting? These decisions are likely to be affected by whether (and to what degree) the researcher's goal is to draw causal inferences about the phenomena.

In social psychology, this goal typically means using an experimental design in which people are randomly assigned to conditions—and this often means (but does not have to mean) creating an analog for the situation. These decisions should be guided by consideration of what approach will allow the researcher to most clearly address the research question. In fact, however, the emphasis on experimental lab studies often precludes a careful consideration of whether this approach provides the best match for the question. For example, if the research question involves what happens as the result of real interpersonal interactions, the research design should include these interactions. If the research question asks about what happens over time, the design needs to include or reflect some kind of longitudinal component. Because designs incorporating such elements as interactions and passage of time are difficult and expensive to implement, as well as more complicated to analyze, researchers often settle for questions that can be answered by more typical methods—and perhaps miss the aspect of their research questions that is most interesting, important, or critical.

These early steps in the research process can easily be transposed, with researchers starting to generate their research questions or research hypotheses *after* deciding on an existing methodological paradigm. When using an existing paradigm, the researcher necessarily constrains what questions can be asked. These constraints are a problem to the extent that the researcher ends up drifting away from the phenomena he or she wants to understand.

For example, many theorists suggested that intrinsic motivation is based on feelings of competence that result from effectively controlling one's environment (e.g., White, 1959). To test this idea, pioneer researchers in the area (e.g., Deci, 1975) created a paradigm to study the effects of competence feedback. In this paradigm, college students are asked to play a skill game or puzzle, then receive competence feedback that differs in terms of valence or the manner in which it is conveyed. Much of the subsequent research used this paradigm as the starting point. As one result, the research questions drifted from asking about the nature of intrinsic motivation itself to questions about the parameters of the effects of competence feedback.

Sansone (1986) proposed that the role of competence may have been overemphasized in our understanding of intrinsic motivation because this typical paradigm used activities in which doing well was the goal of engagement, and it compared receiving competence feedback with no feedback. Over several studies using tasks and feedback that varied in their emphasis on personal competence (i.e., that differed from the established paradigm), Sansone and colleagues found that feelings of competence enhanced intrinsic motivation primarily when competence goals were salient at the outset of the task (Sansone, 1986, 1989; Sansone, Sachau, & Weir, 1989). By using a different methodological paradigm, therefore, this research led to some different conclusions about the nature of intrinsic motivation, which ultimately led to different questions being asked and different models being constructed (e.g., Sansone & Harackiewicz, 2000; Sansone & Smith, 2000).

Without a firm sense of the research question (or questions), it also becomes difficult to select the best method of analysis. Unfortunately, it can be easy to select analyses for reasons other than that they are the best fit to the research question. For example, researchers may use traditional, easily available approaches because they are the approaches with which they (and most reviewers) are most familiar. Conversely, researchers may choose state-of-the-art analyses just because they are the latest trend. The optimal match of design to analytic method emerges from a careful consideration of the best way to answer the basic research question in a direct and comprehensible way (Wilkinson & the APA Task Force on Statistical Inference, 1999).

The mismatch between research question and data analysis is one reason that Tukey (1961; reprinted in 1986) advised that the standard dissertation research process for doctoral students be readjusted and reevaluated. He suggested that a more effective approach when graduate students are developing ideas for dissertation projects is for them to begin by thoroughly analyzing a previously collected data set relevant to the phenomenon of interest. Only then would they be encouraged to generate specific research questions, presumably with a much clearer understanding of what kinds of analysis are most appropriate to particular questions. In that way, one's initial research question would be fully informed by data analysis (especially of the exploratory type), and the typical data analysis stage of a dissertation project would be less prone to being minimized and rushed, as often happens when the overriding focus is on completing the project.

## Can We Answer the Question?

A critical stage in the research process is interpreting what we have found. Can we answer our original research question? To what extent do the data support our more specific hypotheses (assuming that we have them)? It is only if we have clearly articulated the research question that we can know how well our question has been answered. Assuming that we have used operationalizations, designs, and analyses appropriate to our question, any answer is valuable. In fact, in discovering that a hypothesis was not supported, we often find a different (and sometimes more interesting) answer (or question), one that helps understand the original phenomena beyond our initial filter. Thus, having clearly articulated research questions does not mean that we overlook serendipitous findings or effects that we did not foresee. In fact, we believe the reverse. Unless the unexpected finding is dramatic (or draws blood, as in our opening example), it is only when we know what we are looking for that we recognize that we have found something else. Otherwise, our confirmation biases can sweep findings into our "model" and miss information suggesting something different.

Ultimately, the question is this: What have we learned about the original phenomena as the result of this research? Does what we have learned lead us to redefine the phenomena? Focus on different aspects of the phenomena? Expand to whom it applies? It is at this point that the cycle begins again, as we further differentiate the phenomena of interest, perhaps moving to different, related phenomena, or perhaps changing what we see as the phenomena. We believe it is critically important that researchers recognize that at this point in the process, they have learned only as much as their methodological decisions allowed them to. We tend to recognize this important fact only when we are using innovative methodologies (e.g., functional magnetic resonance imaging [fMRI], Implicit Associations Test [IAT])—it is then that we tend to become aware that the nature of our research questions is shaped by the possibilities of a particular method.

What we conclude about our question will determine the next steps that we take. As made

clear by Lewin's (1951) emphasis on "gradual approximation" and by Cronbach and Meehl's (1955) seminal paper on construct validation, a psychological phenomenon becomes best understood in depth through bridging levels of analysis and through the use of multiple methodologies. At this point in the research process, therefore, a researcher can choose multiple directions in which to go. He or she may follow up some finding using the same methodological paradigm (e.g., to identify potential moderators or mediating processes) but can also make connections to other settings, populations, disciplines, and researchers. As noted by Cronbach and Meehl (1955), the deeper the construct analysis of the phenomenon goes, the more extensive and interconnected to related work the validation becomes.

For example, Morf and Rhodewalt (2001a, 2001b) described the paradoxical lives of narcissists, who, in their continual efforts to construct and maintain a grandiose self, engage in behaviors that continually undermine and erode these efforts. The internal logic and coherence of these paradoxical behaviors became clear only in the course of conducting a program of research involving different measures and methodological approaches. By employing this programmatic approach, Morf and Rhodewalt were able to identify how narcissists' thoughts, feelings, and motivations interrelate within their self-system to create the prototypic, self-defeating behavioral patterns observed in this personality syndrome.

Although the idealized process involves cumulative and programmatic research that casts the nomological net wider and wider, making connections to other disciplines within and outside psychology typically involves knowledge of methodological paradigms and analysis strategies that are not part of our usual training. Making these necessary connections therefore may necessitate multidisciplinary collaboration. Moreover, as reviewers of others' work, we are usually ill equipped to evaluate the quality and level of contribution made by this research. As one result, researchers tend to stick to their familiar paradigms, particularly when they are concerned about getting (or keeping) a job. Nevertheless, researchers should be encouraged to spread their wings and venture beyond their home territory. The potential benefits we reap from applying different epistemological and methodological lenses to our phenomena of interest can be great—as can the fruits of multidisciplinary collaborations, no matter how difficult they are initially to establish. Science at its best is not a solitary enterprise; it is cumulative, as each investigation adds its unique contribution to the puzzle of understanding a phenomenon (or interrelated set of phenomena).

## ORGANIZATION OF THIS HANDBOOK

### Organizing Principles

As we hope is clear at this point, we believe that the decision to use a particular methodological approach is optimally made when grounded in careful considerations of the "big picture" of a program of research. Thus, methodological decisions are tied inextricably to what the researcher, ultimately, wants to know. We have used this "top-down" perspective to develop and organize this handbook in two ways. First, the overall organization of the handbook parallels the picture of the research process that we have discussed. As a result, the beginning chapters address issues related to identifying and defining phenomena, research questions, and populations. Middle chapters address issues related to design and data analysis, and later chapters address issues related to expanding the original social psychological questions to other disciplines within and outside psychology. Because of this top-down approach, the book includes innovative chapters such as those on ethics, culture and diversity, and individual differences as well as chapters that have an interdisciplinary (e.g., social neuroscience, social development, social psychology and the Internet) and applied (e.g., program evaluation, health, education, organizations) focus.

Second, we have attempted to maintain the top-down perspective within each chapter. Thus, all contributors were asked to follow a general template in which they first describe a concrete and relevant social psychological research problem (or problems) and then discuss relevant methodological issues in the context of that problem. Chapters emphasize the conceptual basis of the methodology, with an explicit focus on the meaning of data when obtained via a particular methodology. Statistical analysis is considered a process in service of research design, and it is discussed to the extent that it helps to illuminate the distinct meaning of data obtained through a particular methodological approach or design.

Contributors to this volume were selected because they have developed expertise on particular methodological approaches or issues in social psychology—and, more important, they did so in response to their attempts to discover the best way to understand the psychological phenomena that interested them. Thus, these researchers have let the research questions guide the methods, rather than the reverse. These expert researchers discuss traditional and state-of-the-art methodological advances by first outlining concrete research phenomena and related questions of interest and then showing how these questions may be best answered through design and analysis decisions.

### Specific Organization

#### Part II: Fundamental Issues in Social Psychological Research

In the next part, chapters highlight the set of decisions that must be made no matter the particular type of methods chosen. One set of decisions involves the initial assumptions upon which all subsequent methodological issues rest, including the role of theory in guiding the research questions, whether one believes that "testing" research questions involves objective or constructive processes, the level of analysis at which researchers choose to examine their research questions, and so on. Thus, in the first chapter in this section, Cook and Groom address some of the issues associated with these kinds of decisions and suggest that there is a gap between how social psychologists *should* make these decisions and how they typically do so, posing some challenges for researchers to consider. Chapter 3, by Kimmel, addresses the important ethical issues surrounding the decisions about particular research questions and associated methodological approaches in social psychology. For example, how do and should ethical considerations shape the nature of the research questions it is possible to ask? How do these ethical considerations change as the methodological approach changes, and what are some of the important ethical considerations for the future? In Chapter 4, Fiske considers how to make these decisions in the context of generating a long-term program of research, rather than focusing on a single study. She also discusses the balance between generating a long-term program, publication and funding issues, and the importance of following one's own interests or passions.

*Part III: Design and Analysis*

Part III focuses on the set of design and analysis decisions researchers must make when they adopt given methodological approaches. Section A of this part—"Implications of a Heterogeneous Population: Deciding for Whom to Test the Research Question(s), Why, and How"—addresses issues surrounding the study populations and the implications of assuming an "average response" when the population is not homogeneous. Chapters in this section also consider the reverse: that is,

the implications of explicitly acknowledging and incorporating the heterogeneity of a population through research design and measurement of key constructs. Miller's chapter on cultural sensitivity addresses these issues in the context of potential variability among different populations and among subgroups within populations, and it provides important insights about why diversity of participant populations is often ignored in social psychological research. Shoda's Chapter 6, on personality and individual differences, addresses these issues in the context of potential individual variability within groups. This chapter also discusses different ways to conceive of and measure the interactions between individual differences and various aspects of situations.

Section B—"Operationalizing the Constructs: Deciding What to Measure, Why, and How"—addresses the decisions related to operationalizing constructs, both as predictors (e.g., manipulated or naturally occurring) and as outcomes. These chapters address the strengths and the weaknesses associated with different kinds of measures to help readers choose optimal measures for testing a given research question or questions for a given population. These chapters cover some of the more traditional ways to operationalize constructs as well as address some newer distinctions that have emerged as important in the field. For example, Wegener and Fabrigar's Chapter 7, on quantitative measures, focuses on traditional psychometric approaches to capturing social psychological phenomena in terms of the amount of the construct in question. Thus, this chapter includes discussions of self-report (e.g., scales) as well as nonself-report (e.g., behavioral, archival) quantitative measures and addresses key lessons from the survey methodological literature about scale construction and design. In contrast, the second chapter on qualitative measures (King, Chapter 8) focuses on attempts to capture social psychological phenomena through more open-ended data sources. King addresses issues related to using self-report and nonself-report qualitative measures (e.g., behavioral acts, narratives, interviews), as well as issues relevant to transforming these measures through coding. Kihlstrom's Chapter 9 addresses the distinction between implicit and explicit measures of an underlying construct, and what that distinction might mean for understanding the construct. It also discusses this distinction in light of current popular implicit measures (e.g., IAT and reaction times). In the final chapter in this subsection, Hoyle and Robinson (Chapter 10) address the distinctions related to understanding moderation and mediational processes when describing the link between a variable and an outcome, as well as discussing key design decisions that affect interpretation of these processes.

Section C of Part III—"Research Designs: Deciding the Specific Approach for Testing the Research Question(s), Why, and How"— addresses decisions concerning the specific research design. This subsection includes consideration of the more traditional approaches but also includes emerging, state-of-the-art perspectives. For example, Chapter 11, by Haslam and McGarty, addresses traditional experimental designs as a way to test social psychological research questions. The strength of these kinds of designs is the ability to identify causation. Haslam and McGarty include discussion of issues related to that goal (e.g., demand characteristics, random assignment, experimental control) but also include discussion of the necessary trade-offs made between internal and external validity. Similarly, Chapter 12, by Mark and Reichardt, also includes a discussion of trade-offs between internal and external validity, but it does so in the context of quasi-experimental and correlational designs as means of testing social psychological questions. The strength of these kinds of designs lies in the ability to identify predictive relationships among sets of variables that may not lend themselves to

traditional experimental manipulations. The chapter includes discussion of issues relevant to that goal.

In contrast to these more traditional approaches, the next three chapters discuss newer approaches that often involve some combination and extension of traditional approaches. Thus, Chapter 13, by West, Biesanz, and Kwok, addresses designs, assumptions, and related analytic strategies for experiments whose focus is on examining people within contexts and over time. Chapter 14, by Gonzalez and Griffin, describes conceptual issues and data-analytic options related to designs that involve people interacting, primarily with one other person. The final chapter in Part III covers the empirical aggregation of results across studies using meta-analysis (Wood and Christensen, Chapter 15). In this case, the focus is on examining studies across people, time, and contexts.

### Part IV: Emerging Interdisciplinary Approaches

The chapters in Part IV address how the sets of decisions described previously play out in some of the newer, cutting-edge topics and interdisciplinary approaches in social psychology. These chapters highlight recent attempts to expand beyond traditional social psychology questions and methods to incorporate emerging technologies and methodological approaches from other areas both inside and outside psychology. Although they do not present an exhaustive list, these chapters highlight the benefits of cross-fertilization when the strengths of different disciplines are combined and integrated. For example, Birnbaum's Chapter 16 addresses research that combines social psychology with the technological world of the Internet. Birnbaum addresses how traditional social psychology questions may be addressed through data collected online, and he explicitly compares studies conducted via the Internet with traditional lab-based studies in terms of likely populations, procedures, and ethical considerations. Chapter 17, by Cacioppo, Lorig, Nusbaum, and Berntson, focuses on the biological bases of and connections to social psychological phenomena. The authors consider some of the newer neuroimaging and other neuroscience techniques and how these may be used to inform social psychological questions or issues. This chapter also includes a consideration of how our understanding of biological systems may be enhanced by including social psychological phenomena. Chapter 18, by Pomerantz, Ruble, and Bolger, addresses the inclusion of developmental questions when examining social psychological phenomena, using the metaphor of the video camera. The authors address the implications of the continuity and discontinuity of social psychological phenomena across the life span. They also address how including social psychological approaches to developmental questions forces a shift in thinking about development as an intraindividual process to thinking about development as embedded in the social dynamics that make up our everyday life.

*Part V: The Application
of Social Psychology and Its
Methods to Other Domains*

In the final part of the book, chapters address the applications of social psychology methods and knowledge to "real world" settings and domains outside social psychology. These relatively shorter chapters include discussion of issues relevant to the typical populations, measures, designs, and analyses used in each domain. These chapters also briefly discuss the added requirement that is often an important part of applying social psychology approaches to the "real world": that is, the need to create and maintain relationships with outside agencies and organizations. For example, program evaluation allows researchers to study the effectiveness of treatments or programs and often involves a delicate balance between the goals of the organization conducting the program and the social psychologist researcher (Maruyama, Chapter 19). Typically, evaluation of these programs requires combining knowledge from multiple areas within and across disciplines, and these combinations are rarely tested in laboratories.

The other three chapters in Part V focus on particular domains of applications, rather than on a given methodological approach such as program evaluation. These chapters provide an overview of the application of social psychology questions and methods to important and highly relevant domains: clinical and health psychology (Salovey & Steward, Chapter 20), organizations (Thompson, Kern, & Loyd, Chapter 21), and education (Harackiewicz & Barron, Chapter 22). Taken together, these chapters highlight the commonalities across applications while also addressing the challenges and contributions unique to each area of application.

## CONCLUSION

We are inherently social beings, and as such the goal of understanding how a person can affect and be affected by others often captures our attention, our thoughts, our feelings, and our concern. That goal is the subject matter of great (and little) books, movies, television shows, computer games, and advice columns. Clearly, social psychologists study things that we want to know about each other *and* ourselves, and do so in creative ways.

In that context, we hope that this handbook will allow the field to continue its strong tradition but also to grow to include newer methodological developments and approaches. Even more important, we hope that this book helps social psychologists consider different kinds of research questions from the ones they may typically ask by tying the discussion of methodological details to the "big picture" of a research program. In addition, we believe that the chapters in this handbook provide an excellent starting point for researchers who want to pursue these newer questions by helping them to become aware of the critical methodological decisions that must be made in pursuit of those questions. We have learned a lot ourselves from the many wonderful chapters in this volume—and we know younger brothers everywhere will sleep more soundly!

## REFERENCES

Altman, I. (1988). Process, transactional/contextual, and outcome research: An alternative to the traditional distinction between basic and applied research. *Social Behavior, 3,* 259-280.

Asch, S. E. (1946). Forming impressions of personality. *Journal of Abnormal and Social Psychology, 41,* 258-290.

Cronbach, L. J., & Meehl, P. E. (1955). Construct validity in psychological tests. *Psychological Bulletin, 52,* 281-302.

Deci, E. L. (1975). *Intrinsic motivation.* New York: Plenum.

Festinger, L., & Carlsmith, J. M. (1959). Cognitive consequences of forced compliance. *Journal of Abnormal and Social Psychology, 58,* 203-210.

Gergen, K. J. (2001). Psychological science in a postmodern context. *American Psychologist, 56,* 803-813.

Hovland, C. I., Janis, I. L., & Kelley, H. H. (1953). *Communication and persuasion.* New Haven, CT: Yale University Press.

Iyengar, S. S., & Lepper, M. R. (1999). Rethinking the value of choice: A cultural perspective on intrinsic motivation. *Journal of Personality and Social Psychology, 76*(3), 349-366.

Lewin, K. (1951). *Field theory in social science: Selected theoretical papers* (D. Cartwright, Ed.). New York: Harper & Row.

Morf, C. C., & Rhodewalt, F. (2001a). Unraveling the paradoxes of narcissism: A dynamic self-regulatory processing model. *Psychological Inquiry, 12,* 177-196.

Morf, C. C., & Rhodewalt, F. (2001b). Expanding the dynamic self-regulatory processing model of narcissism: Research directions for the future. *Psychological Inquiry, 12,* 243-251.

Pasupathi, M. (1999). Age differences in response to conformity pressure for emotional and nonemotional material. *Psychology and Aging, 14,* 170-174.

Petty, R. E., Fleming, M. A., & Fabrigar, L. R. (1999). The review process at *PSPB*: Correlates of interreviewer agreement and manuscript acceptance. *Personality and Social Psychology Bulletin, 25,* 188-203.

Renninger, K. A. (2000). Individual interest and its implications for understanding intrinsic motivation. In C. Sansone & J. M. Harackiewicz (Eds.), *Intrinsic and extrinsic motivation: The search for optimal motivation and performance* (pp. 375-407). San Diego: Academic Press.

Sansone, C. (1986). A question of competence: The effects of competence and task feedback on intrinsic interest. *Journal of Personality and Social Psychology, 51,* 918-931.

Sansone, C. (1989). Competence feedback, task feedback, and intrinsic interest: An examination of process and context. *Journal of Experimental Social Psychology, 25,* 343-361.

Sansone, C., & Harackiewicz, J. M. (Eds.). (2000). *Intrinsic and extrinsic motivation: The search for optimal motivation and performance.* San Diego: Academic Press.

Sansone, C., Sachau, D. A., & Weir, C. (1989). Effects of instruction on intrinsic interest: The importance of context. *Journal of Personality and Social Psychology, 57,* 819-829.

Sansone, C., & Smith, J. (2000). Interest and self-regulation: The relation between having to and wanting to. In C. Sansone & J. M. Harackiewicz (Eds.), *Intrinsic and extrinsic motivation: The search for optimal motivation and performance* (pp. 341-372). San Diego: Academic Press.

Schachter, S., & Singer, J. E. (1962). Cognitive, social and physiological determinants of emotional state. *Psychological Review, 69,* 379-399.

Sue, S. (1999). Science, ethnicity, and bias: Where have we gone wrong? *American Psychologist, 54,* 1070-1077.

Tukey, J. W. (1961). Statistical and quantitative methodology. In D. P. Ray (Ed.), *Trends in social science* (pp. 84-136). New York: Philosophic Library.

Tukey, J. W. (1986). Statistical and quantitative methodology. In L. V. Jones (Ed.), *The collected works of John W. Tukey: Vol. III. Philosophy and principles of data analysis, 1949-1964* (pp. 143-186). Belmont, CA: Wadsworth.

White, R. W. (1959). Motivation reconsidered: The concept of competence. *Psychological Review, 66,* 297-333.

Wilkinson, L., & the APA Task Force on Statistical Inference. (1999). Statistical methods in psychology journals: Guidelines and explanations. *American Psychologist, 54,* 594-604.

# Part II

# FUNDAMENTAL ISSUES IN SOCIAL PSYCHOLOGICAL RESEARCH

## CHAPTER 2

# The Methodological Assumptions of Social Psychology

## The Mutual Dependence of Substantive Theory and Method Choice

THOMAS D. COOK

*Northwestern University*

CARLA GROOM

*University of Texas, Austin*

> *Assume . . . 1. To take up or adopt. . . . 2. To undertake. . . . 3. To arrogate to oneself. . . . 4. To take for granted; suppose to be a fact. . . . What a debater postulates he openly states and takes for granted without proof; what he assumes he may take for granted without mention.*
>
> —*Webster's Comprehensive Dictionary: International Edition* (1984)

## INTRODUCTION

If you open any edition of the *Handbook of Social Psychology* or any recent textbook on social psychology, you will almost certainly find G. W. Allport's 1954 definition of the field as "an attempt to understand and explain how the thought, feeling, and behavior of individuals are influenced by the actual, imagined, or implied presence of others" (p. 5). As widespread and useful as Allport's description is, it provides only part of an answer to the question

"What is social psychology?" This is because it does not prioritize among its constitutive elements, even though different components have been emphasized at different times in the history of social psychology. More fundamentally, a full account of any scientific community's belief system will likely reveal some purposes that are latent and thus not amenable to explicit definition (Polanyi, 1958).

A more complete understanding of social psychology is achieved through inductive inspection of the research practices of those who call themselves social psychologists. According to Kuhn (1970), the effective boundaries of all fields are delimited by the tacit agreements that a specific community of scholars makes about the norms regulating how research practice should be carried out. Some of the preferences are explicit, but others are implicit. This chapter discusses the most salient explicit postulates about how to do social psychology while also trying to force out some of the field's more latent assumptions about method.

Identifying who social psychologists are is tricky. There are several social psychology communities, and they only partially overlap. The most distinctive consists of researchers belonging to professional societies such as the Society for Experimental Social Psychologists, the Society for Personality and Social Psychology, the Society for the Psychological Study of Social Issues, and Division 8 of the American Psychological Association. These individuals are mostly located in North American psychology departments, and their work is the main focus of this chapter.

Their operating assumptions, however, are not identical with the assumptions of researchers who call themselves social psychologists and who work in American sociology departments or business schools or even those who work in psychology departments in Europe. Although it would be instructive to explore the differences among these various communities, we do not have the space to do so here.

Restricting ourselves to the practice of social psychologists working in American psychology departments leads to an unfortunate solipsism. Both authors of this chapter are social psychologists working in the United States and so are immersed in the field's assumptions. We cannot hope to take the methodological temperature of the subdiscipline as well as future historians of science will.

To add to this complication, scientific practice is heterogeneous even within the target community of social psychologists. To take full account of this heterogeneity would entail discussing all the forms of research practice found in social psychology today—from basic to applied research, from lab to field settings, from quantitative to qualitative work, and from single studies to research syntheses. It would also have to consider generational differences in how social psychology is pursued. Space limitations preclude doing any of this with integrity.

An alternative would be to analyze only elite and/or cutting-edge methodological practice—the strategy adopted by many writers of chapters in this volume. Although this would be interesting and important, it would not capture what most contemporary social psychologists actually do in most of their work. They are journeymen and -women, not pioneers in the construction or use of novel methods.

The approach we eventually adopted is to identify and explore *modal* methodological practice, hoping that more readers will recognize themselves and their work in such an account. We acknowledge that the account we offer depends on an ideal type characterization of methodological practice, so there are legitimate exceptions to every generalization we make.

There is a second reason to focus on modal practice. The distribution of methodological practices within social psychology seems quite leptokurtic—that is, the proportion of researchers using what we later describe as modal practices seems to be very high relative to the proportion working in the tails of the distribution, where practice is more idiosyncratic. To illustrate this, consider the number and heterogeneity of method chapters in the various *Handbooks of Social Psychology*. There were 9 such chapters in the 1954 edition (Lindzey, 1954), covering many different kinds of method. There were 10 in Lindzey and Aronson (1969), just as varied, but there were only 6 in the 1985 edition and 4 in Gilbert, Fiske, and Lindzey (1998)—one each on experimentation, surveys, measurement, and data analysis. Missing by that fourth edition were chapters on observational methods, content analysis, program evaluation, and many other topics. Many social psychologists aspire to methodological eclecticism, but most of the research programs that are achieved employ a restricted set of methods.

Our description of the methods constituting modal practice relies in part on the method chapters in recent editions of the *Handbook of Social Psychology*. But we rely even more on our own analysis of research reports from the most widely read journals—the *Journal of Personality and Social Psychology* (*JPSP*) and the *Personality and Social Psychology Bulletin* (*PSPB*)—as well as on content analyses of these reports where available (e.g., Rozin, 2001).

But given the editorial policies and the system of rewards in science today, journals cannot provide perfect data on the method practices actually used in a particular field. Journal writers have to impress gatekeeping editors and reviewers. In part, they seek to do this by illustrating their knowledge of and adherence to the community's currently dominant methodological norms and theoretical forms. From these incentives follow sins of omission and commission that inadvertently distort accounts of the original intentions of a research project and of the procedures actually used in it.

Well-constructed random surveys that ask social psychologists about their practice would provide a useful supplement to analyses of the methods detailed in individual journal articles, but to our knowledge, these surveys have not been done recently. We are forced, therefore, to supplement the journal analysis with our own firsthand experience of social psychologists' behavior (inevitably including our own), with other social psychologists' informal accounts of their own behavior, and with published critiques of the field—even those with somewhat of a whistle-blowing flavor.

A further difficulty arises in seeking to define methodology. Is it simply method, a group of techniques for data collection and analysis? Or does it enter into a chicken-and-egg relationship with substantive theory, making their analytic separation unfruitful?

Individual methods were designed to answer specific types of questions that implicitly place a higher priority on some forms of theory than others. Thus, scientific surveys were created to generate multi-attribute descriptions of well-defined populations, thus privileging theories that compare population groups along racial, gender, class, or even national lines. Experiments were designed to describe the effects of manipulable causal agents, originally in agricultural research, where the pragmatic goal was to identify whether something worked better than something else—a purpose for which substantive theory need not play any role. Although experiments always privilege causal questions of an "if-then" kind, they are theory-relevant only to the extent that they can help distinguish between competing theories or otherwise illuminate a single theory.

Path analysis was designed to ascertain the degree of correspondence between a substantive theory of a phenomenon and data collected about that same phenomenon—with the theory usually being specified in the form of multiple, causally ordered determinants of the outcome. Path analysis seeks to identify the complexly ordered causes of a given effect, in contrast to experiments, which seek to describe some of the effects of a given cause.

Other purposes have accreted to each of the general methods above, yet the original purposes still remain dominant and linked to a unique form of substantive theory. The kinds of research questions posed are partial products of the tools at hand. The implication of this is that if a given tool is not in the repertoire of a researcher or her circle of professional acquaintances, then the type of question corresponding to that tool is not likely to be asked. And if asked, the question certainly will be answered poorly. The assumptions behind the dominant forms of theory in a field thus are inextricably tied to the assumptions behind its most widely used methods. New researchers are routinely taught that theoretical questions precede and determine method choices, but in actual research practice the reverse causal flow is also to be found—method capabilities determine the kinds of questions that get tested and hence the kinds of theory that are generated.

## THE HYPOTHETICO-DEDUCTIVE METHOD

### The Types of Theory That Social Psychologists Construct

If "theory" were easy to explicate, philosophers would not study meta-theory. But because they do, and because social psychology is intimately involved with substantive theory and its testing, we must explore what kind of theory social psychologists test. This is not easy.

"Grand" theories of the reach of, say, Weber or Durkheim in sociology or of the neoclassical model in economics have had a short life in psychology. This was true of psychoanalytic theory, systems theory, and behaviorism, and it is likely to be the fate of a pure cognitive science that excludes biology and culture.

To be relevant to social psychology, any grand theory has to be adapted to social referents. Doing so has prompted the development of the various theory types with which social psychologists have worked over the years. Cognitive consistency theories are one such type, with their emphasis on tension states that demand resolution, as with dissonance or balance theory. Another type consists of social learning theories, with their emphasis on social modeling and other ways of acquiring social knowledge, as with research on attitude formation and change. Another type of theory deals with group dynamics, emphasizing how small social systems evolve, respond to their internal and external environments, and then change their borders and operations. Finally, also borrowed from psychology, writ large, were theories of social cognition. Variously, these emphasize individuals as rational knowers, as cognitive misers, as cognitive tacticians, or as quasi-automata programmed to respond to social primes.

Social psychology places strong normative emphasis on testing hypotheses deduced from substantive theory (Aronson, Wilson, & Brewer, 1998). The most commonly tested theories come from *within* theory classes such as those described above. Thus, Higgins's self-discrepancy theory (1989) is part of a broader class of social comparison theories, postulating that people's goals motivate their actions, not directly, but via observed discrepancies between these goals and one's present state. Sherman's encoding flexibility model of stereotype function (e.g., Sherman, Lee, Bessenoff, & Frost, 1998) suggests ways in which stereotypes regulate the processing of information that is or is not consistent with the stereotype—all in the service of maximizing information gain. Sherman's theory is best categorized as coming from within the broader class of cognitive theories and even from within the subclass of theories emphasizing human limits to information processing.

At first glance, evolutionary psychology seems to be a much broader type of theory than the theory of Higgins or Sherman. It proceeds by identifying key social problems that our ancestors must have faced before deducing from these problems the kinds of psychological mechanisms that might have evolved to solve them. For example, did women's need to choose mates who could provide sufficient resources to rear a child lead to hard-wired sex differences in mate preference that can then be experimentally tested for in 21st-century men and women? On grounds like these, evolutionary psychology has been offered as a unifying "meta-theory" for all of social psychology (Buss & Kenrick, 1998). Yet to do this, evolutionary psychology would have to subsume or otherwise explain theories within the other theory types such as cognitive consistency, social learning, and social cognition, not to speak of all the exemplars that fall within each of them. But it does not and cannot do that. In practice, therefore, evolutionary psychology functions just like any other lower-order theory in social psychology—as a source of hypotheses about the validity of parts of that theory.

One striking feature of theories in social psychology is how many of them postulate a linear flow of influence, irrespective of how many variables are thought to intervene between a causal agent and its distal effect. (The mode, by the way, seems to be one, though some path analytic models have more.) With its multiple connections, feedback loops, and other dynamic properties, systems theory involves quite different assumptions about the course of influence. But social psychologists rarely use systems theory as the explicit meta-theory organizing relationships among constructs.

It is not clear why the linear flowchart is at the heart of most substantive models in social psychology, but it may have to do with social psychologists' distinct preference for the experiment. The experiment was designed to assess how one deliberately manipulated variable marginally affects some measured outcome. Systems' notions are more multivariate. They depend on longer time lines and reciprocal causal relations, and they do not necessarily privilege a single causal agent. This raises a question: Does the method social psychologists use most often inadvertently constrain the form of theory that gets tested?

Does it also affect a second salient difference between theory in social psychology and the other social sciences—the relative paucity of theories that seek to detail the multiple sources of influence on a given outcome? Theories of the determinants of the cause are much less prevalent in psychology than are theories of the effects of this same cause. As a result, little attention is given to providing a full explanatory model of any single aspect of social behavior, thought, or emotion. Does X affect Y? is the question; not What are all the causes of Y?

Some critics (e.g., Rozin, 2001) have argued that social psychology suffers not from testing too narrow a form of theory, but from too much theory altogether. Preoccupation with theory can block exploratory research, and exploratory research is certainly not modal in social psychology. Such preoccupation can also encourage perseveration and confirmation bias long after a particular theory is no longer productive (Greenwald, Pratkanis, Leippe, & Baumgardner, 1986), particularly when investigators persist with failing ideas to which their names are publicly linked. When theories are of limited generality, preoccupation with them can retard the development of broader theories that might reconcile disparate findings and theories within some new overarching theory (Moscovici, 1972). Thus, the preoccupation with testing theory of a particular type may not be cost-free.

These issues aside, normative practice in social psychology is clear. Social psychologists use and apotheosize substantive theory. They construct it at some level that is certainly not "grand" and probably is not "middle level" if the latter is understood as theory at the level of, say, social learning, cognitive consistency, or group dynamics. Most of the specific theories that social psychologists examine come from within such broad theory classes. Thus, theories of rational actors, cognitive misers, cognitive tacticians, or semi-automata reacting to primes are all examples from within the class of cognitive theories. Tests of social cognition as a class are rare. To our knowledge, no one has yet conditioned varying numbers or constellations of social attributes to a neutral stimulus in order to examine how they affect subsequent information processing.

Instead, the theories typically tested are those of modest generality, at what we might roughly call a "lower middle" level.

## The Theory-Hypothesis Link

Popper's (1934/1959) formulation of the hypothetico-deductive method requires deducing a clear hypothesis from some theory (whatever its reach), and then validly testing this hypothesis. The preferred hypotheses are those that probe the theory's core postulates; and the preferred tests of such hypotheses depend on setting up a situation so that no other theory predicts the same pattern of data as the hypothesis under test. The explicit task therefore is to differentiate the target theory from other theories by virtue of the closeness of the fit between the data obtained and the data uniquely predicted by the target theory (Cook & Campbell, 1979).

Doing all this requires highly explicit theory with prioritized postulates and, hence, prioritized hypotheses. Basing hypothesis formulation on abstract language, insight, or intuition alone is not enough; nor is it enough to claim that a hypothesis tests some part of a theory. At issue is testing the central assumptions that identify a given theory and make it substantively unique.

Most journal studies report tests of theory-derived hypotheses, but these are rarely the most identity-conferring hypotheses from that theory. In part, this is because most theories are not that explicit. In part also, it is because time and experience sometimes are needed to decide which theoretical postulates are key. As a result, the modal journal study does not seek to validate (or invalidate) an entire theory. Instead, it probes whether the obtained results are consonant with some part of a theory, or it elucidates some of the boundary conditions under which the theory does and does not hold.

The modal hypothesis that gets tested is causal in the activity theory sense (Shadish,

Cook, & Campbell, 2002); that is, it specifies what should happen to Y if X is deliberately varied. This preference entails that Y is validly measured and X validly manipulated. Of these two tasks, the manipulation of X usually is more problematic. To illustrate why this is the case, consider priming subjects to elaborate on a persuasive message. It is inevitable that priming will be imperfectly linked to elaborated information processing. Some members of the experimental group may not do any elaborating at all, while others may do little elaborating or not the kind that is under test. Moreover, some of the control subjects may spontaneously elaborate even if not the same message content on which members of the treatment group elaborate.

In ordinary language, naming a cause (X) requires using abstract language to describe those components within a treatment manipulation that, on theoretical grounds, are thought to bring about an effect. However, in experimental practice (and logic), the causal agent is always a contrast and not what happens in a single group. Usually, it is the contrast between the theoretically specified components of a treatment and whatever happens to controls. Given that the components of the treatment and control interventions can overlap, false negative conclusions about cause can ensue if researchers insist on describing the active causal agent with recourse only to what happens in the treatment group. The situation is even more complicated if the control group includes components that are irrelevant to the theory under test but that are correlated with both the outcome and knowledge of being included in a study. Then, both false positive and false negative causal conclusions can result from describing the causal agent exclusively in treatment group terms.

To avoid these causal pitfalls requires (a) carefully explicated substantive theory about the cause and how it is related to the presumed effect, (b) planned treatment contrasts that are as large as possible, (c) valid (and hence also reliable) measures to assess whether the experimental manipulation is varying what it is supposed to vary, and (d) collecting data on these measures across all the study groups, including no-treatment controls. The era of "black box" experimentation is over. At a minimum, researchers need to realize that all causes are comparative and to demonstrate that only small shortfalls occur between the comparative cause as it is conceptualized, implemented, and measured.

The preference for an activity theory of cause also entails an implicitly negative valuation of certain other kinds of theory, especially theory about demographic variables that cannot be manipulated directly. Race, gender, class, and age are examples of this. Sometimes, though, theory is specific enough to detail the individual or social processes that are thought to mediate a demographic variable's suspected effects. In this case, knowledge of these mechanisms can be used to collect data that test hypotheses about the conditions under which a demographic variable varies in the size or direction of its relationship to a given outcome. Essentially, this involves testing a statistical interaction hypothesis that specifies how the demographic variable and mediator mutually influence the outcome. Formulating more complex contingency hypotheses is a strategy that is also heavily used in evolutionary psychology, another field in which researchers cannot manipulate variables easily.

The key to the method's success is familiar, however. Hypotheses still need to be made that are so novel in their implications that no other theory makes these same predictions. It is not enough merely to demonstrate a correspondence between hypothesis and data: No alternative interpretations must remain viable. With demographic variables (and evolutionary theory), the hope is to achieve such uniqueness of prediction by specifying a complex theory-derived data pattern rather than through a simple comparison of values derived from groups that are initially identical except for the presence of the treatment under test.

After a correlation has been demonstrated between a demographic variable and some possible mediator of an "effect," the preferred practice in social psychology is not to derive the complex statistical interaction predictions mentioned above. Rather, it is to create a theory of the mediator and then to turn this mediator into an independent variable. Thus, if data indicate that younger teachers are more effective than older ones, this might lead to the hypothesis that the younger teachers have higher expectancies for their students and to the corollary hypothesis that it is these expectancies that drive greater learning. Both of these hypotheses can then be tested directly in order to develop a more complete substantive theory of teacher expectancies.

One rationale for turning presumed mediating variables into tested independent variables is that most mediators are manipulable whereas demographic variables are not. Another rationale is that theories of mediators are more general because the same mediator often can be activated many ways, both in the laboratory and in the real world. Going back to expectancies for student performance, many older teachers have high expectancies for their students even if younger teachers have higher expectancies on the average. In addition, teachers are not the only ones with education-relevant expectancies—most parents also have them. Thus, as a causal agent, educational expectancies have a potentially broader reach than teacher age.

A third rationale is that theories featuring individual-level psychological mediators generally are more interesting to psychologists than are theories featuring demographic variables such as age, race, and gender. There are many reasons for this, but one is surely that the mediators typically examined are more causally proximal to outcomes that psychologists value than are demographic variables.

The preference for simple hypotheses that transform theoretical mediators into manipulated causes goes beyond the demographic context. The main explanatory constructs in psychology are nearly all specified at the individual level and are hypothetical rather than ostensive—that is, they cannot be directly pointed to and so are rarely amenable to direct manipulation or measurement. Indeed, experiments are designed in the expectation that the observed manipulation (let us call it X) will impact on the outcome (Y) because the explanatory variable (Z) followed from X and affected Y. Sometimes, this chain of reasoning is advanced without any measurement of Z or of proxies for it. Then, interpretation depends heavily on the face validity of X as well as on the theoretical uniqueness of the X-to-Y prediction and on how closely the data fit that prediction.

Sometimes, though, a measure of Z is possible, albeit usually in proxy form rather than as a truly direct measure. Thus, in an experiment on whether elaborated message processing mediates attitude change, students can be asked to write down their reactions to a persuasive message during exposure to it. These thoughts can then be content-analyzed. Alternatively, brain scans might be used to see which local areas of the brain experience blood flow changes when the message is being processed. A test of causal mediation then entails seeing if the relationship between X and Y decreases when Z is statistically controlled (Hoyle & Robinson, Chapter 10, this volume; Judd & Kenny, 1981).

But two problems stand out here: Is Z validly measured? And, does the link from Z to Y entail a threat to internal validity from selection because individuals were not randomly assigned to their Z scores? The preferred way around this last problem is to turn the Z into an X in the next study, directly manipulating elaborated processing by priming individuals to process with and without elaboration or even (within ethical limits)

manipulating brain blood flows, though it is difficult to imagine experimentally re-creating an exact pattern of earlier observed changes in multisite cranial blood flow. But given social psychology's broad use of hypothetical explanatory variables specified at the individual level, it is obvious that such manipulation is not easy. A different, effective, and entirely statistical way to get around the selection problem is, in some circumstances, to use random assignment as an instrumental variable in order to examine the effect of a measured Z variable (Angrist, Imbrens, & Rubin, 1996).

This last strategy requires a measure of Z, though, and most researchers cannot wait for the next study in order to turn their suspected Z into an X. So in actual research practice, proxy measures of theoretically specified mediators often are used to complement the treatment manipulation. But these measures inevitably entail validity and selection problems, leading to a serious conundrum: How can experiments be used to test multivariate explanatory theory about Z variables when experiments were designed to test causal connections between two (but rarely more) observed (and not even hypothetical) X and Y variables? Theory-based explanation requires prior knowledge of the determinants of the cause (for selection purposes) and correct specification of the processes mediating between the cause and effect. Yet experiments were not designed for either of these purposes.

Transforming causal explanations into independent variables becomes increasingly difficult the more elaborate the causal explanatory theory is. Consider dual process models within the social cognition domain. They postulate two forms of processing: (a) controlled or "systematic" processes that are resource demanding, intentional, controllable, and subject to awareness; and (b) automatic or "heuristic" processes that generally are efficient, unintentional, uncontrollable, and out of awareness (see Bargh, 1994). As noted, priming methods can be used to induce each of these, albeit within limits; and MRI scans can discriminate between the two. But what to do with theories that postulate how these two processes operate together—whether in parallel, as with Eagly and Chaiken's Heuristic Systematic Model of persuasion (1998), or as alternatives, as with Petty and Cacioppo's Elaboration Likelihood Model (1986)? How can one practically test a hypothesis that requires simultaneously manipulating the two presumptively unique processes? Human ingenuity being what it is, the task may not be impossible, but it is extremely difficult.

Meta-scientists such as Kuhn (1970) remind us that all theories inevitably are underspecified, so that no hypothesis is capable of definitive refutation. When disconfirming data are generated, the validity of the deduction and/or of the data can be questioned. It is also possible to claim that the theory is true, but under circumstances different from those tested to date. This is why certainty-seeking philosophers disparage the substantive theories scientists work with, seeing them as etched more in putty than in the stone required for definitive refutation.

A more charitable epistemological position is that all practical theories are works in progress (Cook, 1985). Thus, when a theory first seems to be disconfirmed, this should lead to its revision rather than to claims it has been refuted, and so on, as each succeeding theoretical revision is itself tested and perhaps again empirically disconfirmed, generating yet another version of the original theory. As the conditions under which the theory is demonstrably invalid continue to grow, enthusiasm for the theory is likely to wane in the relevant community of scholars. Although the theory might be true under some as yet still untested circumstances, these may be so limited that scholars no longer see any point to persisting with the theory. It is therefore rejected on pragmatic grounds, not because logic nor data has shown it to be false under all conditions.

## Form of Data Collection

From Popper's falsificationist perspective, social psychologists should collect data about hypotheses that can prove a theory wrong. The social psychology of social psychological practice suggests, however, that researchers are more likely to want to show that their theory is right. From this arises the concern with possible biases emanating from the researcher's own wishes, hopes, expectations, and dreams. Related to this are setting biases, especially in the laboratory, where respondents might try to second guess situational norms in order to conform with them and help the researcher through how they react to them.

To disconfirm hypotheses, data have to be theory-free; otherwise they cannot function as neutral adjudicators between truth claims. But epistemologists remind us that all data are fallible, and therefore no single hypothesis test can carry the adjudicatory weight Popper assigns it. However, studies that self-consciously incorporate the discipline's recognized mechanisms of bias control can help better approximate the generation of theory-neutral data. So can independent research programs that vary the source and direction of bias. Facts may not be logically possible, but many observations are stubbornly replicated, whatever the theory used to generate them. They have great facticity and provide the bedrock from which novel theories are developed. A theory that fails to subsume the relevant facts of the past is not going to get much respect.

Even so, individual researchers are capable of less self-criticism about the quality of data and results than is provided by the social system of science that editors and reviewers represent. It is they who begin the process of determining what level of merit should be assigned to an article, serving as precursors to a process of public discussion of merit that develops after the article is published. Data never provide perfect tests of the empirical claims a hypothesis makes, though some forms of data are stronger than others. The ultimate warrant for claims about data quality reside in a complex mix of social consensus, logic, and the results of past empirical research on biases.

In social psychology, a supreme value is accorded to data that confirm or disconfirm an a priori hypothesis. Data that do not make this kind of contribution are judged to be less worthy of journal space. This preference for hypothesis-testing has some unintended consequences.

First, it has encouraged some researchers whose data do not fit the hypothesis to reframe their hypothesis so that they can write up the results as though they had been predicted. Kerr (1998) calls this "HARKing: Hypothesizing After the Results are Known." The reality is that many studies produce results at odds with the original prediction. To abandon the work at this point entails a considerable waste of time and effort and can endanger a career. HARKing has evolved as an uneasy compromise between the goals and structure of the hypothetico-deductive method and the needs of individual scientists for whom publication is a major goal. Beginning social psychologists soon learn of this mismatch between formally and informally sanctioned epistemology and practice. Indeed, in his guide to professional issues in social psychology, Bem (1987) explicitly advocates retrospective hypothesis creation. In contrast, Kerr laments the capitalizing on chance that inevitably results.

Another consequence of fallible hypothesis tests is the growing editorial demand for single articles that present the results from multiple experiments linked into a small research program. Wegner (1992) has pointed out the consequences of this practice for effective alpha rates. Across two experiments, each with an alpha rate of .05, the true rate is .0025. Does the field really want a level of stringency that culls out even more ideas than those already abandoned by the current .05 rate? Moreover, social psychologists are trained in experimental,

and not multi-experimental, design. The latter is not fully worked out yet, even in a theory of method sense, let alone practically.

So, what are the goals of a multistudy strategy? One is surely to achieve some form of replication; and another is to extend the theory under test by examining more of its implications. Theories of multi-experimental design will require subtle distinctions among types of replication (exact, partial, conceptual, etc.) as well as realistic analyses of the conditions under which each is most useful. It will also require discussions about what constitutes a sufficiently close replication to allay fears of a Type I error. Also needed will be elaboration of what constitutes a theoretical elaboration that is sufficiently distinctive to advance the research program conceptually, as well as discussion of the relative value of independent and non-independent replications. Finally, statistical wisdom on combining results will be needed, especially when experiments are few and not independent.

Meta-analysis is the best developed form of multi-experimental design and analysis, and its use is common in social psychology (see Wood & Christensen, Chapter 15, this volume). Its virtues include (a) more statistical power than single studies typically achieve; (b) the ability to probe potential biases associated with measured design features; (c) the empirical assessment of how robust results are across measured setting, person, and time variables, as well as across coded ways of operationalizing the cause and effect; and (d) the chance to examine more of the causal explanatory theories about processes mediating between a cause and effect. For all these reasons, reviews of empirical findings constitute the dominant unit of progress in science, though path-breaking single studies get all the glamour. Reviews are not part of modal practice in social psychology, however, except as part of the perfunctory narrative introduction to an article. Single studies, or small programs of research bundled into a single article, constitute modal practice.

Although such bundling is an advance over a single report of a single study, it is still far from being a literature review or meta-analysis.

To judge by mainstream journals, modal practice in social psychology also places little value on exploratory research, whether as the original study goal or as an overt attempt to discover why the data failed to confirm with prior expectations (Kenny, 1985). Exploration should be more prevalent in social psychology and done so as not to capitalize on chance (Tukey, 1977). Exploration brings to the surface novel issues that are worth further study, and it is a central function of ethnography.

But ethnography makes other claims, including some that directly link it to the hypothetico-deductive method that social psychologists prefer and that, at first sight, seems so antithetical to ethnographic practice. Yet, as explicated by Becker (1958), ethnography involves formulating a hypothesis from observations, thinking through the implications of this hypothesis, and then going out into the field to collect data to examine these implications. When the data and theoretical implications fit imperfectly, the earlier hypothesis about implications is revised and new implications are then developed and tested. If the next round of data still fails to fit the new implications, then the hypothesis is revised again, new implications are developed, and new data are collected. This iterative hypothetico-deductive process continues until closure is reached.

Few social psychologists know about this correspondence between epistemology and practice in ethnography and social psychology. But we suspect few of them would appreciate the correspondence, largely because the data ethnographers collect are mostly qualitative. Yet the data are clearly empirical, and they are products of the same disciplined process of theory development, hypothesis deduction, and empirical data collection that drives so much of social psychological practice.

## THE DUAL HEGEMONY OF ANOVA AND THE LABORATORY EXPERIMENT

The overwhelming majority of social psychology studies are conducted in a laboratory setting, use undergraduate participants, last no longer than an hour, and involve random assignment to two or more experimental conditions. Rozin (2001) examined articles in the Attitudes and Social Cognition and the Interpersonal Relations and Group Processes sections of *JPSP*, volume 66 (1994), and found that 73% of the 44 articles used North American undergraduate samples, 95% used analysis of variance (ANOVA), and just 7% used observation or interview methods.

Fortunately, data from randomized laboratory experiments analyzed by ANOVA constitute one of the strongest frameworks for a certain kind of causal inference-making in the social sciences today. Heavy reliance on the experiment makes the description of causal relationships of an if-then kind (Cook & Campbell, 1979) the dominant framework for constructing research problems and organizing thinking in social psychology today (Kenny, 1985). But causal description is not necessarily causal explanation, and science values explanation over description. To make the transition from description to explanation requires selecting for study only those causal hypotheses that have been deduced as central postulates from an explicit and overarching theory that seeks to explain a given phenomenon. Hence, in the method section of their journal articles, researchers give considerable attention both to describing and to justifying their independent and dependent variables in terms of some broader theory as well as to illustrating just how the selected if-then causal proposition will be tested.

Other types of question are relatively neglected, whether about the prediction of an outcome, about the form of structural relationships among the multiple causes of an outcome, or about the exploration of new ideas emanating from outside established theoretical boxes. Cause of an if-then kind is paramount, and ANOVA is responsive to this primacy. So is the laboratory setting, which is designed to keep competing alternative interpretations out of the explanatory system so that the hypothesized cause-effect relationship can play out without perturbation from irrelevant outside forces.

The ANOVA emphasis privileges the search for simple main effects caused by few causal variables. One manipulation (relative to no-treatment controls) seems to be as common as two manipulations of explicit theoretical interest. Higher-order factorial experiments are rare, as are parametric experiments that vary many levels of the independent variable in order to identify the functional form of the cause-effect relationship. So, the central question is whether there is a causal relationship from A to B and not identifying the form of this relationship.

It is still rare to find effect sizes being reported in order to characterize the size of a causal relationship, though meta-analysis and the 2001 APA publications manual are changing this, as is the requirement by some journals to report them. Even so, greater use of effect sizes probably will engender further methodological discussion. One likely topic is the desirability of using dependent variables with grounded metrics that are easily communicable and do not need to be standardized (such as time or money). Another is the comparability of effect sizes when certain choices exist for computing them. One is when they can be computed with or without covariates. Using covariates increases effect sizes, but not all studies have them or the same set of them. Another is when effect sizes can be computed as a difference between means or between slopes. With repeated measures, the effect size of a final point difference might be much less than the effect size for the contrast between the slopes. But not all studies have repeated measures or the same number of them. It is progress indeed to move beyond statistical significance testing as a flawed way to compute the size of an effect. But standardized effect sizes, although superior, are far from perfect for carrying out the comparative mission to which they speak. Fields such as economics choose not to use them, preferring instead to frame their questions around effects that are measured in easily understood interval scale metrics so that results can be reported out as unstandardized regression coefficients. Dealing with variables that are more hypothetical, psychology does not have the same luxury.

The dominance of ANOVA also means that it is rare to find social psychological theories explicitly constructed around interactions between different treatments or between a given treatment and either person or setting variables. Rozin's review of *JPSP* revealed that fewer than 10% of the articles reported participants' social class *or* race *or* religion *or* the year *or* season in which data were collected. Researchers did report participant sex in 72% of the articles; however, they did not necessarily report the relationship between sex and the observed outcome. It is as though respondents are considered interchangeable or simply sources of error variance, not sources of information about the possible boundaries of a causal connection.

The reason for this neglect is that most social psychologists seem willing to believe that most cause-effect relationships are general across persons and settings. If one believes this assumption to be true, then there is no reason to search for interactions between independent variables and person or setting characteristics. To do so would entail the hassle of constructing a different kind of theory, building a different kind of design, and then collecting and analyzing data differently, all without any guarantee that one will learn anything important about restrictions to the generality of a causal claim. Campbell (1969) asserted that physical scientists also assume that any independently replicated finding is universal until subsequent research shows otherwise. Given that, and because the value of a substantive theory is widely held to be contingent on its reach, why should social psychologists assume that their theories are not universal? To do so denigrates the very theory they are about to test.

In this connection, consider the contact hypothesis. As a simple main effect, it asserts that increasing the amount of contact between individuals from different groups will reduce any intergroup conflict between them. This idea was of great interest in social psychology 50 years ago, but research on it almost petered out once it emerged that such contact worked only under a large number of quite disparate circumstances that still cannot be integrated into a novel, parsimonious theory (Hewstone, 1996). Researchers abandoned the contact hypothesis as overly contingent.

The validity of the ontological assumption that most causal relationships are universal is of great moment. On it depends the utility of simple ANOVA designs rather than more complicated designs that entail different kinds of theory and more extensive or more representative sampling designs, measurement, and analysis. Social psychologists are conscious of relying on college samples, stripped down laboratory settings, few and short-lasting interventions, and simple data-analytic procedures like ANOVA. In this regard, Sears (1986) outlined some special properties of student populations that can be inferred from other psychological work. Among other things, he noted that their late-adolescent status probably makes them especially susceptible to social influence. However, most psychologists (e.g., Mook, 1983) do not worry that individual differences of person, setting, or time might affect levels of compliance. Their concern is only whether such differences condition how the manipulation and compliance are related, thus creating a different list of causal factors than would emerge if a different population,

setting, or time had been used. Causal relationships constitute the key theoretical issues in the field, not preexisting group mean differences. The latter is the province of personality theory and research.

Even if a causal relationship should turn out to be contingent, some types of contingency have more serious theoretical implications than others. Moderator variables that reverse the sign of a causal connection clearly restrict causal generalization. So, if this were the preferred criterion for inferring that effects are non-universal, then the technical stringency of meeting the sign-reversal criterion makes it reasonable to surmise that causal effects in social psychology generally are universal and that overgeneralization is not much of a problem. However, the case is murkier with a less stringent generalization criterion, such as differences in slopes without a necessary difference in their sign. Using this criterion, we would be more likely to discover that the world is more complicated than simple main effects.

It would therefore be useful to assess the frequency of stable statistical interactions in social psychology that involve person, setting, and time features, both with and without sign reversals. However, this enterprise would be fraught with perils. It is notoriously difficult to conduct statistically powerful tests of interactions and to uncover stable ones that replicate. To achieve this requires (a) strong theory specifying the exact form of the interaction, (b) reliably measured samples of persons and settings that manifestly include the tails of the distributions, (c) samples that are large, (d) causal variables that are not truncated, (e) dependent variables without floor or ceiling effects, and (f) dependent variables whose theoretical meanings would change if their interval scales were arithmetically transformed. Meeting these requirements is difficult in all social research but clearly more so in laboratory than survey work.

Although the incidence of interactions cannot be tested sensitively, indirect evidence suggests that stable interactions are quite rare and that the world might be organized according to many broad main effects. Few of the meta-analyses conducted to date of which we are aware have resulted in many stable interactions between a treatment class and either person, setting, or time variables. Moreover, Cronbach and Snow (1977) tried to develop a list of replicated interactions involving some kind of teaching intervention and student or teacher characteristics. They met with what we judge to be little success. In addition, many social psychologists are proud that ordinary Americans seem to recognize themselves in reports about laboratory studies that get into the media, suggesting that these reports speak to Everyman's experience, or at least to the experience of the North American Everyman. (However, a selection factor would operate here if journalists choose to feature a result because it seems to them to be general.) In any event, the empirical evidence on the universality assumption is far from complete and difficult to evaluate. Such as it is, that evidence does not seem to seriously invalidate the assumption.

Two things are clear, though. Just as the logic of designing multi-experiment studies is different in subtle and important ways from the logic of designing single studies, so the logic and practice of testing interaction predictions is subtly different from the logic of testing main effects. Few social psychologists seem to realize this, perhaps because they need not do so as long as they continue to assume that the majority of interesting causal connections are universal.

The belief in causal universality that allows social psychologists to rely on college sophomores, laboratory settings, and short-lasting interventions is not shared by other social scientists or policy actors. Social psychology is routinely criticized for an overreliance on the laboratory that seems to undermine the face validity of results. This is not to deny that some social psychological findings are commented on beyond the field, particularly field study results like those of Milgram (1974), Latané and Darley (1970), and Zimbardo, and those laboratory results that are counterintuitive or otherwise provocative. Even so, laboratory results do not seem to command as much respect in the human sciences as do results from surveys, field experiments, and longitudinal studies, a verdict that would be unfair if laboratory results do indeed routinely generalize to other settings and kinds of respondents. But the criticism is nonetheless made and, because of its laboratory and undergraduate emphasis, social psychology does less well in the public relations domain than many other social sciences.

## SPECIFIC THEORETICAL CONCERNS AND THEIR METHODOLOGICAL IMPLICATIONS

### The Social Cognitive Revolution

If ANOVA and the laboratory experiment are the knife and fork of social psychology, then cognitive explanatory variables are currently its bread and butter. Indeed, the centrality of information processing and mental representations led Markus and Zajonc (1985) to remark that social psychology has essentially become the study of the social *mind*. They suggested that social cognition is no longer concerned with an "O-S-O-R" (i.e., stimulus-organism-response) formulation that privileges how attributes of the organism mediate causal relationships. Instead, they prefer an "O-S-O-R" formulation because it makes causally central the organism's subjective construal of the world, not the world itself.

In the 1970s and 1980s, social psychologists unearthed or resurrected many biases that testify to the mismatch between external reality and human perception of it, including unrealistic optimism (Irwin, 1944) and the actor-observer attributional bias (Jones & Nisbett,

1972). Once the key influence on a person's thought, feeling, and behavior was recognized not to be reality but to be the perception thereof, then the mental processes that created and reacted to these perceptions became the proper focus of social psychology. The objective nature of the world assumed a lesser status.

By the time this turn was being made in social psychology, cognitive psychologists had already been exploring perception, reasoning, categorization, mental representation, and other ways in which the mind imposes structure on the world. Their concepts and methods were now keenly explored by social psychologists, who borrowed them and applied them to the social domain. Social cognition was born. Sixteen years later, Tesser and Bau (2002) set out to review the current themes in the field and concluded that social cognition was still dominant. Indeed, they characterized the 1990s as "the decade of social cognition" (p. 81). The perceiver's "black box" had become the central concern of social psychology, in sharp contrast to the stimulus-response approach.

The methodological implications of this shift included a need to develop ways to tap hidden cognitive processes (e.g., via reaction times, error rates, and other alternatives to introspection). Also implied was less emphasis on the precise characteristics of the independent variable because the primary aim of experimental stimuli was now to activate a relevant mental representation. Whether it was specifically conceived of as a stereotype or trait category, the mental representation was usually held to be an abstraction (Sherman, 1996). Because an abstraction is, by definition, a synthesis across multiple, partially different stimuli, the precise characteristics of independent variables are no longer crucial. It hardly matters whether a stereotype is activated through unscrambling a stereotype-related sentence (e.g., Banaji, Hardin, & Rothman, 1993), through subliminal priming of a stereotyped category (e.g., Macrae,

Milne, & Bodenhausen, 1994), or through presenting the face of a member of a stereotyped group (e.g., Fazio, Jackson, Dunton, & Williams, 1995). All are valid operational definitions of the same latent construct, of the same psychologically active mechanism.

Other examples of the relative lack of concern with operational specifics can be found within social cognition. Researchers have demonstrated that the accessibility of a representation (e.g., a stereotype) shapes information processing in basically the same way regardless of whether the accessibility results from a chronic traitlike tendency to have that representation accessible or from a temporary priming of that representation in the laboratory (Bargh, Bond, Lombardi, & Tota, 1986). Belief that there are many ways to manipulate the same underlying process has the fortunate advantage of enhancing construct validity, especially when it can be empirically shown that several different manipulations all activate the same measured mechanism and have the same relationship with the outcome. When this pattern of results emerges, it is clear that the particular form of the manipulation is an irrelevancy and that causal potency may well lie with the common mechanism each manipulation elicits.

Pursuing a strategy that assigns secondary status to observable independent variable attributes requires considerable care. For instance, awareness of the prime, however induced, does matter, and it can produce contrast effects in judgment as the person attempts to correct away from its influence (Schwarz & Bless, 1992). So, the theoretically mundane and merely vehicular components of independent variables should not be decided on lightly.

Moreover, the assumption is made that external environments do not affect individuals other than through individuals' perception of them. Is this universally true of neighborhood, school, family, peer, media, and work influences (Cook, Herman, Phillips, & Setterston,

2002), let alone true of the influence of more distal social events such as city and national politics? It is true that perceptions of neighborhoods are more strongly correlated with adolescent outcomes than are objective neighborhood attributes (Jessor & Jessor, 1973), but this does not mean that the objective characteristics play no independent role (Cook, Herman, et al., 2002; Furstenberg, Cook, Eccles, Elder, & Sameroff, 1999).

## The Relative Neglect of Theories of Interpersonal Dynamics

Given the dominance of social cognition and laboratory settings, modal research practice pays little attention to theories of interpersonal dynamics. Pennebaker (2002) noted that there is no APA division devoted to language even though language "is the basis of most human communication and is the filter through which we understand and learn about ourselves and others" (p. 9). The Interpersonal and Group Processes section of *JPSP* often has the least journal space devoted to it, and the articles published there tend to focus on phenomena like social comparison that involve social cognition about a specific (but not necessarily present) person or group of people. Identity negotiation researchers who focus directly on the dynamic exchange between a perceiver and target, for example in the case of self-fulfilling prophecies (e.g., Swann, 1987), are the exception rather than the rule.

Admittedly, it is difficult to capture interpersonal dynamics in a short-term lab study. In the early years of social psychology, when theories about interpersonal relations were more prevalent, field studies were conducted that allowed participants to interact relatively freely over a significant period of time, during which the researchers observed and administered interventions. For example, Sherif, Harvey, White, Hood, and Sherif (1961) arranged a summer camp where they assigned boys randomly to teams, observed the resulting intergroup conflict, and, when tensions escalated, intervened with cooperative tasks. It would not be possible to collect such long-term data in a conventional laboratory setting using paid undergraduates.

However, confederates can be used in the laboratory to manipulate controlled interpersonal events, as they have since the days of Asch's (1952) conformity studies. Even so, many interpersonal events are rather resistant to experimental control, and even when they can be brought into the lab, it can be difficult to analyze the data they provide within ANOVA. This is because people influence each other in complex ways through time, entailing observations that rarely are independent. As Kenny (1985) noted, this violates the independent errors assumption of ANOVA and forces researchers to use more complicated hierarchically ordered statistics that few social psychologists now know (Bryk & Raudenbush, 1992; Gonzalez & Griffin, Chapter 14, this volume). So, for quite different reasons, interpersonal interdependence is a tepid topic in social psychology today, left to an intrepid but perhaps increasing few. When preferences are clustered around a dominant theory class (such as social cognition), this limits not just the form of preferred theory but also method choices. There is little immediate need to venture into the novel methodological territories that different kinds of theoretical framing require.

## The Neglect of High-Impact Manipulations and the Kinds of Theory They Promote

In social psychology's history, the words "lab" and "experiment" did not automatically go together as they do today. Involvement in both non-experiments and field experiments was more common. When researchers are willing to proceed on the basis of a direct relationship between objective situations and overt behavior, field experiments are enabled. Thus, to take one from many examples,

Milgram, Bickman, and Berkowitz (1969) induced varying numbers of confederates to stare up at the sixth floor of an arbitrarily chosen New York building. As predicted, the percentage of passersby joining in the "gawking" was a diminishing function of the number of confederate "gawkers."

It is not the purpose of experiments to re-create reality. Rather, it is to decompose and recombine what is in the world, often heightening it but always clarifying it—in Bacon's words, "Twisting Nature by the Tail." High-impact treatments push the boundaries of human experience, as in Milgram's work and in the laboratory simulation of prison life by Haney, Banks, and Zimbardo (1973) that had to be terminated prematurely because of the sadistic tendencies that developed among the "guards" toward their "prisoners." But since then, few other laboratory experiments can be offered as examples of high impact. Motivationally, most operate in a lower key, as short-term analogs to deeper and longer lasting experiences.

Ironically, it was probably ethically questionable attempts to construct high-impact manipulations in the laboratory that helped crown the low-impact laboratory study as sovereign and that hastened the move toward explicitly analog, nondeceptive approaches (e.g., Prisoner's Dilemma games to study cooperation, lists of traits to study impression formation). Jones (1985) has even opined that Milgram's obedience study and Festinger's dissonance experiments bear partial responsibility for "the range of available procedures [being] restricted by ethical concerns enforceable by human subjects committees" (p. 98). What we want to note here is that the timing of these ethical concerns (Baumrind, 1964) coincided with the rise of an information-processing paradigm that rarely requires high-impact manipulations (see also Kimmel, Chapter 3, this volume). Thus, there were both theoretical and ethical reasons why social psychologists moved away from the study of "hot" motivated behavior and toward "colder" social cognition.

## The Average Person as the Locus of Explanation

Both Asch (1952) and Lewin (1951) regarded the interaction between person and situation as the critical subject matter of social psychology. Neither one nor the other claimed special status, but their intersection did. When one considers modern practice in social psychology, it is apparent that the field does not share this interactionist emphasis. Instead, it places most emphasis on the individual, more accurately the average individual studied, leaving less room for supra-individual phenomena as explanatory constructs. The field seems to have reasserted F. H. Allport's (1924) reductionist view that collective phenomena are understood properly with reference only to the minds of individuals—primarily as these individuals perceive the social world and process information about it.

Individual differences are rarely part of the modern story, though they would be required for a full interactionist perspective (see Shoda, Chapter 6, this volume, for a detailed discussion of different possible approaches to including individual differences). There are both moral and ideological reasons why individual differences have lost their appeal. The assumption of universal responsivity to causal agents is compatible with the egalitarian, meritocratic ideology of the West. Moreover, social psychologists have tried to avoid the mistakes of individual difference researchers, whose early work (say, on group differences in intelligence) seemed to support questionable political actions (Kamin, 1974). Also psychologists may be sensitive to their own proclivity as laypersons to overlook situational explanations of behavior in favor of dispositional ones, the fundamental attribution error (Nisbett & Ross, 1980). Fears like these probably have helped reinforce the field's move toward assigning a major causal role to individual psychological constructions of situations rather than to individual dispositions or objective situations or to the interplay between the two.

Unfortunately perceptions of social situations are not always anchored in a broad range of comparative experience and so may be quite unstable. They certainly run the risk of overlooking stable structural forces that might have serious long-term repercussions. Eagly's social role theory of sex differences in psychological functioning (Eagly, Wood, & Diekman, 2000) is sensitive to this last dilemma, being an attempt to sketch how social structure creates power and resource inequalities that have perpetuated stable but learned sex differences in psychological functioning. Her perspective on objective and sustained social contexts is much more like what sociologists assume in their studies of how family, school, and neighborhood forces sustain cross-generational stability in social class standing. For them, as for Eagly, perceived contexts count; but actual contexts also do.

Even cross-cultural psychologists locate culture in the individual mind, with Bond (2002) recently criticizing cross-cultural researchers for falling prey to the ecological fallacy of ascribing to the person properties that are only demonstrably true of the group (as with the construct of individualism). A similar reluctance is evident when it comes to reciprocal causation between the person and environment. For instance, prejudice tends to be studied either in terms of perceiver bias and representations (e.g., Devine, 1989) or in terms of the consequences of stigma for the target (e.g., Crocker & Major, 1989; Steele & Aronson, 1995). But Shelton (2000) recently asked why psychologists are not examining the actual interactions between, say, African Americans and European Americans in order to explain prejudice. Like culture, prejudice seems to be "psychologized," restricted to being a property of individuals.

Attempts by European social psychologists to explore supra-individual explanatory constructs are evident in notions such as depersonalization, according to which the person actually takes on a different self when acting as a group member (e.g., Turner & Onorato, 1999). The contrast here is with American cousins to these ideas, such as the interdependent self-construal of Markus and Kitayama (1991) that again places most conceptual focus on the individual.

Moving away from an individual focus has methodological repercussions. For instance, data analyses would have to take account of how social systems are hierarchically ordered, with individuals nested within groups and groups within larger aggregates like schools or neighborhoods or universities. This would move analysis toward hierarchical linear modeling (HLM) rather than ANOVA (see Gonzalez & Griffin, Chapter 14, this volume; West, Biesanz, & Kwok, Chapter 13, this volume). How individuals are conceptualized also has methodological repercussions. Most social psychologists prefer a variable-centered conceptualization of individuals, invoking concepts such as race, age, and gender or single personality attributes such as neuroticism or degree of loneliness. In contrast, some developmental psychologists are experimenting with person-centered approaches to individual differences (e.g., Magnusson & Bergmann, 1990) that require tricky multivariate techniques such as cluster analysis to construct multivariate profiles of types of individuals. Knowledge of ANOVA will not suffice for anyone studying either interpersonal relationships or individual differences conceived as multivariate profiles.

Most social psychologists like to believe they are studying the "average human" or at least "the average North American," but they actually study the average person in whatever sample they have at hand. This sample is rarely randomly selected from a clearly designated and theoretically justified population, a preferred strategy for generalization in science. Purposive samples are the order of the day. These can sometimes promote generalization, but only when accompanied by ancillary information and analyses (Cook, 1993). Furthermore, even with purposive samples, detailed description of the sample is very important for generalization, but social psychologists rarely provide such description in detail. True, there are some researchers with interests in more circumscribed populations, for instance the average neurotic, the average shy, or the average African American person. At a minimum, these researchers need to show that the persons they sample in their studies belong in the target class, even if they were not randomly selected from that class and even if the correlates of class membership (and hence potential confounds for interpretation) have not been described as fully as they might have been. Sample description is rudimentary in social psychology because practitioners generally believe that individual differences do not matter much and that theories about specific populations are less important than theories about people in general. So why go to all the trouble?

Given this belief system, social psychologists do not develop theories about individual differences that might interact with an intervention. Nor, in general, do they test many interaction possibilities in post hoc fashion. Of course, with the small samples and truncated distributions they typically use (because of who is recruited into experiments), the statistical power of the interaction tests they do conduct is limited. This points to a serious inferential difficulty that would ensue if interaction predictions were more common in the field, as well as to the need for social psychologists to be more knowledgeable about the design and sampling modifications that serious interaction testing requires. In any event, believing that social psychology deals with the reactions of the average person helps promote the field's status as a cumulative science that does not have to worry much about the population dependence of results.

Of course, individual differences are not completely ignored; nor are statistical interactions with treatments. However, when they occur, the focus is mostly on those individual difference factors that might moderate psychological mechanisms assumed to be universal. For example, Oyserman, Kemmelmeier, and Coon (2002) depict cross-cultural psychology as seeking to "identify cultural contingencies that moderate general processes of human cognition, affect, and behavior" (p. 110). These "cultural contingencies" are nearly always framed in terms of psychological processes such as values and traditions rather than in terms of sociological or political processes such as class inequality or the distribution of resources. When national differences are demonstrated, most social psychologists are then inclined to move to a more abstract level of theory that subsumes the differences by invoking some novel underlying commonality. Jahoda (1986) has argued against this, however, contending that it is better to stay with the national particulars and to construct different psychologies for different countries. In his view, it is better to gain a full and data-based psychological understanding that is applicable in at least *some* national contexts than it is to create some universalist explanation framed in exclusively individualistic terms.

### The Assumption of Irrelevant Domains and Hence the Generation of Theories With Minimal Grounded Content

For the modal social psychologist, the processes acting upon mental representations are construed to be essentially similar, not only across all human beings but also across all domains of content. Evolutionary psychologists (e.g., Tooby & Cosmides, 1992) do not share this view, believing that the human mind is an evolved set of tools specialized for discrete domains of life that were important to survival (e.g., face perception, mate preferences). They postulate that some psychological processes will therefore be domain-specific, an assumption otherwise rarely shared in social psychology.

The opposite assumption—of cross-domain generalizability—is more widespread and has several important implications. First, it effectively erases the line between social and nonsocial cognition (Hastie & Carlston, 1980). This justifies the construction of social cognition as an enterprise concerned more with a standard cognitive analysis applied to social phenomena than with the generation of unique analyses designed to identify how cognitive performance differs because a social versus nonsocial object is being appraised. This last emphasis is clear in early social psychological work on the symbolic properties of objects, such as Bruner and Goodman's (1947) demonstration that the value associated with (heavily socially imbued) coins influenced people's judgments about the size of circles—a social cognitive cause of a seemingly nonsocial perception.

Second, social psychologists who assume cross-domain generalization can avoid studying such problematic domains as divorce, bereavement, parenting, cults, and so on, so long as they can plausibly argue that the same social, cognitive, and emotional processes account for most of the variance found between these domains. But how can this assumption be tested (better, "probed") except through a laborious process of measurement, experimentation, and synthesis across these various domains? Until empirical research on domain specificity is done, social psychology will seem rather content-free to most outside observers, not imbued with deep insider knowledge of the behaviorally grounded phenomena to which its theories and results are thought to apply.

Third, G. W. Allport's (1954) description of social psychology invokes social contexts that are real, implied, or imagined, without differentiating between the three. Given domain generality, the need to differentiate is reduced. In this regard, consider the diverse ways that social rejection has been operationalized. Manipulations include (a) using live confederates who exclude the participant from a game of catch (Nezlek, Kowalski, Leary, Blevins, & Holgate, 1997), (b) using "internet chat rooms" that remove face-to-face contact but not the perceived reality of the interaction (Gardner, Pickett, & Brewer, 2000), and (c) asking participants to imagine being rejected (e.g., Craighead, Kimball, & Rehak, 1979). Using Immersive Virtual Environment Technology, Blascovich et al. (in press) studied the conditions under which participants would show social influence effects such as maintaining interpersonal distance or conforming to the level of bets placed by others in a virtual casino. Results showed differences depending on whether the respondents thought they were interacting with figures or with "avatars" that either possessed photographic realism (e.g., were represented by a computerized person rather than a beach ball), *or* corresponded to a real person rather than a simple computer program.

These results all suggest that the assumption of stimulus-independent processes is not always appropriate, that artificial stimuli cannot be used willy-nilly in lieu of more realistic ones. Similarly, real and perceived neighborhoods are not always substitutable.

Social psychologists seem to believe that nature is structured with important general truths (laws?) at its center, and with less important specific qualifications at its periphery. There is no obvious reason why the social psychological world should be organized around general laws rather than around a vast collection of *n*-way interactions that would be detected if research were more sensitively designed so as to detect interactions rather than main effects.

Even so, epistemologists value parsimony more than complexity, and the prestigious physical sciences employ a law-oriented view of knowledge growth. They have generally prospered believing that one independent replication justifies the assumption that results are general until subsequent research proves otherwise. Given these realities, we cannot envisage social psychologists mounting a serious attack to describe a more complex ontological structure than they now assume.

## CONCLUSION

Methodological practice in social psychology has changed over time and will continue to do so. The rigid impression of research methods one finds in most introductory textbooks is an illusion. From the way the questions are formulated to the way data are collected, analyzed, and interpreted, empirical work involves hundreds of choices at every stage. Some of these choices are not conscious because the alternatives are not known, or are rendered invisible or inappropriate by the collective decision of the social psychology community to do things a particular way. But the alternatives are still there.

Although this chapter is a plea for greater diversity of method choice in social psychology, we acknowledge that taking the position of the modal social psychologist has limited our account of the variation that already exists in the field. Fortunately, the chapters following this one put some of this variation back into play, as they seek to introduce social psychologists to newer techniques and hence to extend their options.

However, we see no virtue to methodological pluralism per se. The key need is for researchers to get their questions or issues straight and then to use the best available tools for collecting relevant data. Sometimes, a single method will suffice, like use of the sample survey when a population description is called for. More often, though, multiple methods will be needed, given the limitations of many individual methods. Even then, though, there is no justification for using multiple methods willy-nilly. An explicit justification is required for the several methods chosen because they have to differ in their imperfections and in the direction of any biases presumed to attend these imperfections (Cook, 1985).

The main problem for a field is when commitment to a particular style of research inadvertently precludes theoretical growth by restricting the kinds of questions asked. Compared both to its own past and to social psychology as it is practiced in Sociology departments, the social psychology we have described here runs that risk. Seen meta-theoretically, it rarely deals with systems notions, including multivariate and reciprocal causation. It rarely deals with the social and individual determinants of the social factors it varies. It rarely probes the person, setting, and time factors that might condition a causal relationship, instead assuming a routine generalization of findings that individual studies can rarely test, given the small and homogeneous samples typically used. In addition, field research is rare relative to laboratory research; research with populations other than university students is also rare; and exploratory research is much rarer than hypothesis testing. Cognitive theories are still dominant, though interpersonal, emotional, biological, and cultural concepts are gaining in currency, albeit often linked to cognition, as in cognitive neuroscience. The best case for methodological pluralism in the field is not that better answers can be provided to traditional questions; it is that a wider range of questions can be asked that will encourage a wider range of theory development.

## REFERENCES

Allport, F. H. (1924). *Social psychology*. Boston: Houghton Mifflin.

Allport, G. W. (1954). The historical background of modern social psychology. In G. Lindzey (Ed.), *The handbook of social psychology* (Vol. 1, pp. 3-56). Cambridge, MA: Addison-Wesley.

American Psychological Association. (2001). *Publication manual of the American Psychological Association* (5th ed.). Washington, DC: Author.

Angrist, J. D., Imbrens, G. W., & Rubin, D. B. (1996). Identification of causal effects using instrumental variables. *Journal of the American Statistical Association, 91*, 444-455.

Aronson, E., Wilson, T. D., & Brewer, M. B. (1998). Experimentation in social psychology. In D. T. Gilbert, S. T. Fiske, & G. Lindzey (Eds.), *The handbook of social psychology* (4th ed., Vol. 2, pp. 99-142). New York: McGraw-Hill.

Asch, S. E. (1952). *Social psychology*. New York: Prentice-Hall.

Banaji, M. R., Hardin, C., & Rothman, A. J. (1993). Implicit stereotyping in person judgment. *Journal of Personality & Social Psychology, 65*(2), 272-281.

Bargh, J. A. (1994). The four horsemen of automaticity: Awareness, intention, efficiency, and control in social cognition. In R. S. Wyer & T. K. Krull (Eds.), *Handbook of social cognition* (Vol. 1, pp. 1-40). Hillsdale, NJ: Lawrence Erlbaum.

Bargh, J. A., Bond, R. N., Lombardi, W. J., & Tota, M. E. (1986). The additive nature of chronic and temporary sources of construct accessibility. *Journal of Personality and Social Psychology, 50*(5), 869-878.

Baumrind, D. (1964). Some thoughts on ethics of research: After reading Milgram's "Behavioral Study of Obedience." *American Psychologist, 19*(6), 421-423.

Becker, H. S. (1958). Problems of inference and proof in participant observation. *American Sociological Review, 23*, 652-660.

Bem, D. J. (1987). Writing the empirical journal article. In M. P. Zanna & J. M. Darley (Eds.), *The compleat academic: A practical guide for the beginning social scientist* (pp. 171-201). New York: Random House.

Blascovich, J., Loomis, J., Beall, A. C., Swinth, K. R., Hoyt, C. L., & Bailenson, J. N. (in press). Immersive virtual environment technology as a methodological tool for social psychology. *Psychological Inquiry*.

Bond, M. H. (2002). Reclaiming the individual from Hofstede's ecological analysis—A 20-year odyssey: Comment on Oyserman et al. (2002). *Psychological Bulletin, 128*(1), 73-77.

Bruner, J. S., & Goodman, C. C. (1947). Value and need as organizing factors in perception. *Journal of Abnormal & Social Psychology, 42*, 33-44.

Bryk, A. S., & Raudenbush, S. W. (1992). *Hierarchical linear models*. Newbury Park, CA: Sage.

Buss, D. M., & Kenrick, D. T. (1998). Evolutionary social psychology. In D. T. Gilbert, S. T. Fiske, & G. Lindzey (Eds.), *The handbook of social psychology* (4th ed., Vol. 2, pp. 982-1026). New York: McGraw-Hill.

Campbell, D. T. (1969). Prospective: Artifact and control. In R. Rosenthal & R. L. Rosnow (Eds.), *Artifact in behavioral research* (pp. 351-382). New York: Academic Press.

Cook, T. D. (1985). Post-positivist critical multiplism. In R. L. Shotland & M. M. Mark (Eds.), *Social science and social policy* (pp. 21-62). Beverly Hills, CA: Sage.

Cook, T. D. (1993). A quasi-sampling theory of the generalization of causal relationships. In L. Sechrest & A. G. Scott (Eds.), *New directions for program evaluation: Vol. 57. Understanding causes and generalizing about them* (pp. 39-82). San Francisco: Jossey-Bass.

Cook, T. D., & Campbell, D. T. (1979). *Quasi-experimentation: Design and analysis issues.* Boston: Houghton Mifflin.

Cook, T. D., Herman, M., Phillips, M., & Setterston, R. J., Jr. (2002). Some ways in which neighborhoods, nuclear families, friendship groups and schools jointly affect changes in early adolescent development. *Child Development, 73*(4), 1283-1309.

Craighead, W. E., Kimball, W. H., & Rehak, P. J. (1979). Mood changes, physiological responses, and self-statements during social rejection imagery. *Journal of Consulting & Clinical Psychology, 47*(2), 385-396.

Crocker, J., & Major, B. (1989). Social stigma and self-esteem: The self-protective properties of stigma. *Psychological Review, 96*(4), 608-630.

Cronbach, L. J., & Snow, R. E. (1977) *Aptitudes and instructional methods: A handbook for research on interactions.* New York: Irvington.

Devine, P. G. (1989). Stereotypes and prejudice: Their automatic and controlled components. *Journal of Personality and Social Psychology, 56*(1), 5-18.

Eagly, A. H., & Chaiken, S. (1998). Attitude structure and function. In D. T. Gilbert, S. T. Fiske, & G. Lindzey (Eds.), *The handbook of social psychology* (4th ed., Vol. 1, pp. 269-322). New York: McGraw-Hill.

Eagly, A. H., Wood, W., & Diekman, A. B. (2000). Social role theory of sex differences and similarities: A current appraisal. In T.T.H.M. Eckes (Ed.), *The developmental social psychology of gender* (pp. 123-174). Mahwah, NJ: Lawrence Erlbaum.

Fazio, R. H., Jackson, J. R., Dunton, B. C., & Williams, C. J. (1995). Variability in automatic activation as an unobtrusive measure of racial attitudes: A bona fide pipeline? *Journal of Personality and Social Psychology, 69*(6), 1013-1027.

Furstenberg, F. F., Jr., Cook, T. D., Eccles, J., Elder, G. H., & Sameroff, A. (1999). *Managing to make it: Urban families in high-risk neighborhoods.* Chicago: University of Chicago Press.

Gardner, W. L., Pickett, C. L., & Brewer, M. B. (2000). Social exclusion and selective memory: How the need to belong influences memory for social events. *Personality and Social Psychology Bulletin, 26*(4), 486-496.

Gilbert, D. T., Fiske, S. T., & Lindzey, G. (Eds.). (1998). *The handbook of social psychology* (4th ed.). New York: McGraw-Hill.

Greenwald, A. G., Pratkanis, A. R., Leippe, M. R., & Baumgardner, M. H. (1986). Under what conditions does theory obstruct research progress? *Psychological Review, 93*(2), 216-229.

Haney, C., Banks, C., & Zimbardo, P. (1973). Interpersonal dynamics in a simulated prison. *International Journal of Criminology & Penology, 1*(1), 69-97.

Hastie, R., & Carlston, D. E. (1980). Theoretical issues in person memory. In R. Hastie, T. M. Ostrom, E. B. Ebbesen, R. S. Wyer, Jr., D. L. Hamilton, & D. E. Carlston (Eds.), *Person memory: The cognitive basis of social perception* (pp. 1-53). Hillsdale, NJ: Erlbaum.

Hewstone, M. (1996). Contact and categorization: Social psychological interventions to change intergroup relations. In C. N. Macrae, C. Stangor, & M. Hewstone (Eds.), *Stereotypes and stereotyping* (pp. 323-368). New York: Guilford.

Higgins, E. T. (1989). Self-discrepancy theory: What patterns of self-beliefs cause people to suffer? In L. Berkowitz (Ed.), *Advances in experimental social psychology* (Vol. 22, pp. 93-136). San Diego: Academic Press.

Irwin, F. W. (1944). The realism of expectations. *Psychological Review, 51*, 120-126.

Jahoda, G. (1986). Nature, culture and social psychology. *European Journal of Social Psychology, 16*(1), 17-30.

Jessor, R., & Jessor, S. L. (1973). The perceived environment in behavioral science. *American Behavioral Scientist, 16*(6), 801-827.

Jones, E. E. (1985). Major developments in social psychology during the past five decades. In G. Lindzey & E. Aronson (Eds.), *Handbook of social psychology* (3rd ed., Vol. 1, pp. 47-107). New York: Random House.

Jones, E. E., & Nisbett, R. E. (1972). The actor and the observer: Divergent perceptions of the causes of behavior. In E. E. Jones, D. E. Kanouse, H. H. Kelley, R. E. Nisbett, S. Valins, & B. Weiner (Eds.), *Attribution: Perceiving the causes of behavior* (pp. 79-94). Morristown, NJ: General Learning Press.

Judd, C. M., & Kenny, D. A. (1981). Process analysis: Estimating mediation in treatment evaluations. *Evaluation Review, 5*, 602-619.

Kamin, L. J. (1974). *The science and politics of I.Q.* Potomac, MD: Lawrence Erlbaum.

Kenny, D. A. (1985). Quantitative methods for social psychology. In G. Lindzey & E. Aronson (Eds.), *The handbook of social psychology* (3rd ed., Vol. 1, pp. 487-508). New York: Random House.

Kerr, N. L. (1998). HARKing: Hypothesizing after the results are known. *Personality & Social Psychology Review, 2*(3), 196-217.

Kuhn, T. S. (1970). *The structure of scientific revolutions:* Chicago: University of Chicago Press.

Latané, B., & Darley, J. M. (1970). *The unresponsive bystander: Why doesn't he help?* New York: Appleton-Crofts.

Lewin, K. (1951). *Field theory in social science: Selected theoretical papers* (D. Cartwright, Ed.). New York: Harpers.

Lindzey, G. (Ed.). (1954). *The handbook of social psychology* (1st ed.). Cambridge, MA: Addison-Wesley.

Lindzey, G., & Aronson, E. (Eds.). (1969). *The handbook of social psychology* (2nd ed.). Reading, MA: Addison-Wesley.

Lindzey, G., & Aronson, E. (Eds.). (1985). *The handbook of social psychology* (3rd ed.). New York: Random House.

Macrae, C. N., Milne, A. B., & Bodenhausen, G. V. (1994). Stereotypes as energy-saving devices: A peek inside the cognitive toolbox. *Journal of Personality and Social Psychology, 66*(1), 37-47.

Magnusson, D., & Bergman, L. R. (1990). A pattern approach to the study of pathways from childhood to adulthood. In L. N. Robins & M. Rutter (Eds.), *Straight and devious pathways from childhood to adulthood* (pp. 101-115). Cambridge, UK: Cambridge University Press.

Markus, H. R., & Kitayama, S. (1991). Culture and the self: Implications for cognition, emotion, and motivation. *Psychological Review, 98*(2), 224-253.

Markus, H., & Zajonc, R. B. (1985). The cognitive perspective in social psychology. In G. Lindzey & E. Aronson (Eds.), *The handbook of social psychology* (3rd ed., Vol. 1, pp. 137-230). New York: Random House.

Milgram, S. (1974). *Obedience to authority*. New York: Harper & Row.

Milgram, S., Bickman, L., & Berkowitz, L. (1969). Note on the drawing power of crowds of different size. *Journal of Personality and Social Psychology, 13*(2), 79-82.

Mook, D. G. (1983). In defense of external invalidity. *American Psychologist, 38*(4), 379-387.

Moscovici, S. (1972). Society and theory in social psychology. In J. Israel & H. Tajfel (Eds.), *The context of social psychology: A critical assessment* (pp. 17-81). London: Academic Press.

Nezlek, J. B., Kowalski, R. M., Leary, M. R., Blevins, T., & Holgate, S. (1997). Personality moderators of reactions to interpersonal rejection: Depression and trait self-esteem. *Personality and Social Psychology Bulletin, 23*(12), 1235-1244.

Nisbett, R. E., & Ross, L. (1980). *Human inference: Strategies and shortcomings of social judgment.* Englewood Cliffs, NJ: Prentice-Hall.

Oyserman, D., Kemmelmeier, M., & Coon, H. M. (2002). Cultural psychology, a new look: Reply to Bond (2002), Fiske (2002), Kitayama (2002), and Miller (2002). *Psychological Bulletin, 128*(1), 110-117.

Pennebaker, J. W. (2002). What our words can say about us: Toward a broader language psychology. *Psychological Science Agenda, 15*, 8-9.

Petty, R. E., & Cacioppo, J. T. (1986). *Communication and persuasion: Central and peripheral routes to attitude change.* New York: Springer-Verlag.

Polanyi, M. (1958). *Personal knowledge.* London: Routledge & Kegan Paul.

Popper, K. (1959). *The logic of scientific discovery.* London: Hutchinson. (Original work published 1934)

Rozin, P. (2001). Social psychology and science: Some lessons from Solomon Asch. *Personality & Social Psychology Review, 5*(1), 2-14.

Schwarz, N., & Bless, H. (1992). Constructing reality and its alternatives: An inclusion/exclusion model of assimilation and contrast effects in social judgment. In L. L. Martin & A. Tesser (Eds.), *The construction of social judgments* (pp. 217-245). Hillsdale, NJ: Lawrence Erlbaum Associates.

Sears, D. O. (1986). College sophomores in the laboratory: Influences of a narrow data base on social psychology's view of human nature. *Journal of Personality and Social Psychology, 51*(3), 515-530.

Shadish, W. R., Cook, T. D., & Campbell, D. T. (2002). *Experimental and quasi-experimental designs for generalized causal inference.* Boston: Houghton Mifflin.

Shelton, J. N. (2000). A reconceptualization of how we study issues of racial prejudice. *Personality & Social Psychology Review, 4*(4), 374-390.

Sherif, M., Harvey, O. J., White, B., Hood, W., & Sherif, C. (1961). *Intergroup conflict and cooperation: The Robber's Cave experiment.* Norman: Institute of Group Relations, University of Oklahoma.

Sherman, J. W. (1996). Development and mental representation of stereotypes. *Journal of Personality and Social Psychology, 70*, 1126-1141.

Sherman, J. W., Lee, A. Y., Bessenoff, G. R., & Frost, L. A. (1998). Stereotype efficiency reconsidered: Encoding flexibility under cognitive load. *Journal of Personality and Social Psychology, 75*(3), 589-606.

Steele, C. M., & Aronson, J. (1995). Stereotype threat and the intellectual test performance of African Americans. *Journal of Personality and Social Psychology, 69*(5), 797-811.

Swann, W. B. (1987). Identity negotiation: Where two roads meet. *Journal of Personality and Social Psychology, 53*(6), 1038-1051.

Tesser, A., & Bau, J. J. (2002). Social psychology: Who we are and what we do. *Personality & Social Psychology Review, 6*(1), 72-85.

Tooby, J., & Cosmides, L. (1992). The psychological foundations of culture. In J. Barkow, L. Cosmides, & J. Tooby (Eds.), *The adapted mind: Evolutionary psychology and the generation of culture* (pp. 19-136). New York: Oxford University Press.

Tukey, J. W. (1977). *Exploratory data analysis.* Reading, MA: Addison-Wesley.

Turner, J. C., & Onorato, R. S. (1999). Social identity, personality, and the self-concept: A self-categorizing perspective. In T. R. Tyler R. M. Kramer, & O. P. John (Eds.), *The psychology of the social self: Applied social research* (pp. 11-46). Mahwah, NJ: Lawrence Erlbaum.

Wegner, D. M. (1992). The premature demise of the solo experiment. *Personality and Social Psychology Bulletin, 18*(4), 504-508.

## CHAPTER 3

# Ethical Issues in Social Psychology Research

## ALLAN J. KIMMEL

*ESCP-EAP, European School of Management*

It is now commonly understood within social psychology that decisions about particular research questions and associated methodological issues are inextricably bound to a wide range of ethical considerations. This understanding, however, has not always been as evident as it might have been, but rather grew out of an extended process of self-reflection and debate. Focused attention on ethical issues within the discipline also developed amid fears that future research necessarily would be restricted as a result of the growing influence of external regulation by governmental and other regulatory bodies. Although ethical considerations played a minor role, if any role at all, in the research process during social psychology's formative period, today they have a formidable influence on most of the decisions relative to the planning and conduct of investigations, from the recruitment of participants to the subsequent application of research findings.

It is impressive to recognize the relative rapidity by which the moral imperatives of research practices have entered into the collective psyche of investigators within the discipline. Less than 50 years ago, research ethics rarely, if ever, represented a formal component of the training and practice of social psychologists. As Kelman (1996) has noted, prior to the 1960s the idea had not yet taken hold that systematic attention to researchers' moral obligations to research participants and to society as a whole represented an integral element of the research process. The fact that today these matters are considered as a matter of course suggests that social psychologists have taken great strides in terms of acknowledging and responding to their ethical and moral responsibilities. Nonetheless, it is understandable that the ethical dimension can be seen as a source of added complications in the actual conduct of a research investigation. Confronted by an increasingly daunting array of ethical guidelines, governmental regulations, and institutional review, investigators often are compelled to weigh methodological and ethical requirements in order to choose

AUTHOR'S NOTE: The author thanks the volume editors for their constructive comments during the preparation of this chapter.

whether and how to pursue particular research questions. The practical difficulties imposed by attempts to cope with these two sets of demands often are linked to the recognition that the most methodologically sound study is not necessarily the most ethical one, and vice versa.

In retrospect, much of the impetus for ethical progress in social psychology was sparked by a significant increase in the implementation of ethically questionable research practices. For example, by the mid-1970s, the practice of deceiving research participants in social psychology studies had become commonplace. According to various estimates, the percentage of studies using deception in the *Journal of Personality and Social Psychology* (*JPSP*) rose from around 20% in 1960 to nearly 70% in 1975 (e.g., Adair, Dushenko, & Lindsay, 1985; McNamara & Woods, 1977). When psychological journal editors were asked to nominate studies they considered to be empirical landmarks in social psychology, the five most frequently nominated involved elaborate laboratory deceptions of the studies' purpose and procedures (Diamond & Morton, 1978). It is possible that most of, if not all, these studies would not have been approved (at least in their original form) by contemporary ethical review boards, reflecting the necessity to bear in mind the impact of the prevailing ethical climate on judgments pertaining to research issues.

Although deception arguably has proven to be the most pervasive ethical issue in social psychology research, other practices also have aroused considerable concern, including the invasion of participants' right to privacy, failure to protect the anonymity of respondents or the confidentiality of data, unobtrusive observations of unsuspecting participants, and the use of psychological or physically risky manipulations in experimental studies. In addition to the possibility that research practices may pose a risk of harm directly to individual participants, issues pertaining to the implications of research that go beyond the immediate data-collection setting also have been addressed. For example, research findings might be exploited for various political or personal ends to the detriment of certain societal groups; ethical misconduct could reduce public trust in psychologists or negatively influence perceptions of the scientific process; and mass-mediated accounts of unethical social psychological research could tarnish the discipline's public image and ultimately jeopardize community support and funding for the research enterprise. Indeed, it is essential that judgments pertaining to an investigation's moral dimension take into account the possible effects of the research on all those implicated by it, whether directly or indirectly.

## CHAPTER OVERVIEW

This chapter focuses on ethical issues in social psychology pertaining to decisions about particular research questions and associated methodological approaches. The discussion begins with a consideration of the evolution of ethical debate and regulation in the discipline. Next, an overview is provided of the ethical issues that emerge in the conduct of experimental, field, and applied research, including a focus on problems related to the use of deception. At various points, I refer to my own ongoing research on rumors in order to illustrate some of these issues. The last section of the chapter addresses issues related to ethical safeguards and the impact of ethical review.

## THE EVOLUTION OF ETHICAL DEBATE AND REGULATION IN SOCIAL PSYCHOLOGY

Developments toward ethical regulation often tend to follow in the wake of disclosures of ethical misconduct and the reporting of studies involving the mistreatment of research participants (Kuschel, 1998). For example, in sociology, Humphrey's (1970) "tearoom trade" study of homosexual behavior in public restrooms aroused considerable controversy and prompted sociologists to reevaluate their discipline's formative ethical code. Humphrey did not inform the participants who congregated in the restrooms that he was observing their conduct for research purposes; later, he altered his appearance and presented himself as a health service worker in order to interview the men at their homes for the purpose of obtaining information about homosexual lifestyles. In political science, a study that aroused extensive controversy was Project Camelot, a 1964 research project conducted under the auspices of the U.S. government that was intended to study counterinsurgency in Latin America (Horowitz, 1967). The project was quickly condemned on ethical grounds as a blatant attempt by the project sponsors to identify means for suppressing popular revolts in foreign countries.

These and similar studies added fuel to the fire of public and professional discourse on matters related to scientific ethics and the treatment of research participants. This also was the case in psychology, most notably as a result of experimentation involving deception. In a series of field experiments conducted during the early 1960s, young military recruits unknowingly were subjected to bogus life-threatening emergencies (such as the apparent imminent crash landing of their aircraft) in order to study their reactions to psychological stress (Berkun, Bialek, Kern, & Yagi, 1962). In another controversial study, alcoholic volunteers were led to believe they were participating in an experiment to test a possible treatment for alcoholism but instead were injected with a drug that caused a terrifying, albeit temporary, respiratory paralysis, leading many of the participants to believe that they were dying (Campbell, Sanderson, & Laverty, 1964).

No doubt the most widely known and controversial example of deceptive research in

social psychology is Milgram's (1963) obedience studies, a series of laboratory investigations conducted from 1960 to 1964 involving research volunteers who were led to believe they were administering dangerous electric shocks to an innocent victim. Although ostensibly presented as a study about learning, the experiment's intent was to observe the extent to which the participants would obey the orders of a malevolent authority (the experimenter). What aroused great concern in the scientific community, in addition to the fact that 65% of all participants in the standard experiments administered the strongest "shocks" in response to the authority's commands, was that participants apparently experienced intense psychological upset and physical distress as a function of the experimental guise. Despite the lack of direct evidence that anyone suffered lasting harm as a result of the research, the obedience experiments remain at the forefront of most discussions of research ethics in social psychology and related disciplines. Although the target of scathing ethical and methodological attacks for many years, Milgram's research has received renewed attention by those who have praised its insights into obedient behavior (Miller, Collins, & Brief, 1995).

Social psychology experiments rarely elicit the sorts of intense reactions in participants as in the studies described here; nonetheless, the latter were instrumental in providing an impetus for ethical scrutiny within the discipline and the public domain.

## Governmental Regulations for Behavioral Research in the United States

Federal safeguards concerning the rights and welfare of human research participants have been in place as part of U.S. Public Health Service (PHS) policy since 1966, although the initial focus was limited to clinical research in medical fields. In 1969, PHS policy was extended to cover all research involving human participants, including biomedical and behavioral investigations. The concept of consent was emphasized in these initial governmental regulations as well as the necessity for committee review of research that put participants at risk. In July, 1974, following Senate hearings on some prominent cases of research abuses, Congress signed into law the National Research Act (1974), which led to the creation of the National Commission for the Protection of Human Subjects of Biomedical and Behavioral Research.

Following an extended period of review, the National Commission (1979) issued its final recommendations in 1978 along with the two-volume *Belmont Report*, which proposed norms for ethical conduct in various areas, including competence of the researcher, identification of risks and benefits, appropriate selection of participants, voluntary informed consent, and compensation for injury. Formal regulations were published by the Department of Health and Human Services (DHHS) in the January 26, 1981, issue of the *Federal Register*. Most noteworthy among the regulations were requirements mandating proper review by institutional review boards (IRBs) for the approval of DHHS-funded research projects, including the exemption of broad categories of research that posed little or no risk of harm. The current DHHS regulations governing the implementation of the National Research Act, which have been amended over the years, are available in the Code of Federal Regulations issued by the Office for Protection From Research Risks (OPRR) (1991).

## Professional Ethical Standards

By the mid-1960s, a growing number of critics had begun to question the proliferation of deceptive and potentially harmful manipulations in psychological research. For example, Baumrind (1964), largely in reaction to Milgram's obedience research,

argued that deceptive procedures pose certain psychological risks to participants, including loss of self-esteem and dignity and a possible loss of trust in legitimate authority. In view of the methodological drawbacks of some deception studies, she further questioned whether such studies held much potential for serious benefit. According to other prominent critics, deception had become a commonplace procedure that increasingly was being employed even in research situations where it was unnecessary (Kelman, 1967).

Largely in response to the changing nature of research in the discipline, the American Psychological Association (APA) has taken steps to codify and periodically modify ethical principles for human participant studies. These principles have served as a model for other professional associations around the world and are unique in that they were derived largely through an empirical approach based on a survey of critical incidents pertaining to ethical dilemmas experienced by the association's members. The current version of the code (APA, 2002), is the result of a 50-year history of development and revision and is presumed to reflect the values of APA members as well as the moral growth of the discipline of psychology (Jones, 2001).

The APA research principles became substantially more stringent in the 1973 version of the code (American Psychological Association, Ad Hoc Committee on Ethical Standards in Psychological Research, 1973), as well as in subsequent versions, in light of the controversy surrounding the dramatic increase in deception experiments and criticisms regarding the broadly stated and qualified nature of some of the principles. Many apparently perceive the current principles to be more exacting than they were intended to be, as they were meant to be applied within a cost-benefit framework that permits the researcher to consider whether the benefits of the research outweigh possible harm to participants. This utilitarian approach has continued to fuel further debates over interpretation of the principles and their implementation.

The current principles emphasize voluntary participation and informed consent as fundamental prerequisites for human participant research. The principle of voluntary informed consent was most notably introduced in the *Nuremberg Code* (1949), a general set of standards formulated to prevent atrocities like those perpetrated by Nazi researchers during World War II and the forerunner to all subsequent guidelines governing experimentation with human participants (Schuler, 1982). Following increasing disclosures of objectionable research in the social and behavioral sciences, it became apparent that the Nuremberg Code (along with the subsequent Helsinki declarations for guiding the conduct of health and medical researchers) was insufficient to ensure the safety and well-being of research participants (Kuschel, 1998).

Consistent with U.S. federal guidelines and some scientific journals (e.g., *Psychological Science*), the APA standards require informed consent for nearly all human research. When obtaining informed consent from prospective research participants, social psychologists are expected to communicate the following types of information (APA, 2002): (a) the purpose of the research, expected duration, and procedures; (b) the right to decline to participate and to withdraw from the research once participation has begun; (c) the foreseeable consequences of declining or withdrawing; (d) reasonably foreseeable factors that may be expected to influence willingness to participate, including potential risks, discomfort, or adverse effects; (e) any prospective research benefits; (f) limitations on confidentiality; (g) incentives for participation; and (h) whom to contact for questions about the research and participants' rights. For guidance as to the design, administration, and evaluation of valid consent forms and procedures, see Fischman (2000), Grundner (1986), and Kimmel (1996).

Exceptions to informed consent are allowed under federal regulations and professional standards when certain conditions are met, such as the research involves no more than minimal risk to participants; the study could not practically be carried out with informed consent; the research consists of anonymous questionnaires, naturalistic observations, or archival research for which disclosure of responses would not result in negative consequences for participants; and so forth (see APA, 2002; OPRR, 1991). Obtaining partially or fully informed consent in practice can be difficult, particularly when the cognitive capacity of participants is limited or impaired. Such is the case when participants are selected from vulnerable groups, such as children, the elderly, the mentally disabled and handicapped, and underprivileged persons.

The primary ethical concerns for persons from vulnerable groups consist of whether they understand what they are told about the nature and purpose of a study, are able to weigh the risks that a study may entail for them, and can consent on their own, without the agreement of a legal guardian. There also is the possibility that they may have a lower tolerance for potentially risky or deceptive manipulations. Professional ethics codes are consistent in specifying that research involving children and participants with impairments that will limit their understanding requires special safeguarding procedures. A common approach to dealing with the issue of consent is to use parental or proxy consent as a substitute for, or in addition to, obtaining consent from the vulnerable participant (e.g., British Psychological Society, 1995).

A related issue that emerges in considerations of informed consent pertains to the potential coercion (and related forms of exploitation) of individuals for research participation. This issue has been most widely discussed in terms of the use of students for research purposes. University subject pools typically comprise students who are encouraged (and sometimes required) to participate in campus research in order to obtain some sort of incentive. Although the incentive may be monetary in nature, it is more likely to take the form of course credit or fulfillment of a prerequisite to obtaining a course grade (Lindsay & Holden, 1987). Despite college recruits representing a convenient, inexpensive study population, several ethical concerns have been voiced about the use of this population (e.g., Korn, 1988). Specifically, there are fears that alternative means of satisfying course requirements may not be offered or else are excessively time-consuming or noxious; that students may receive little if any educational debriefing; and that readily accessible complaint procedures are not available. Several guidelines have been proposed for the ethical use of student subject pools (see, for example, APA, 1982), and in recent years students have been offered an increasing array of alternatives to the research requirement (McCord, 1991; Raupp & Cohen, 1992).

Keeping in mind individuals' freedom to decline to participate, several strategies for recruiting research participants have been proposed, including financial inducements, lotteries, gifts, or the simple promise to provide a summary of the study's results. Perhaps the most serious ethical concern related to recruitment involves the point at which offers of inducements to participate become coercive, thereby threatening one's right not to participate or one's freedom to withdraw from an ongoing study. As of yet, there are no clear ethical standards for obtaining guidance in such cases beyond the necessity for researchers to maintain a sensitivity to the possibility that they are exerting excessive pressure on targeted participants to enhance recruitment. For example, the APA code recommends that "reasonable efforts" be made to avoid offers of excessive or inappropriate inducements to potential participants that "are likely to coerce participation" (APA, 2002, p. 11). The use of monetary incentives, which has been recommended as an effective practice for maximizing response rates (American Association for Public Opinion Research [AAPOR], 2002; Bearden, Madden, & Uscategui, 1998), has increased in psychology over the past decade as psychologists have made a more concerted effort to include nonstudent adult participants in their samples (Kimmel, 2001).

With regard to deception, the APA code dictates that deception should be used only if a study's results are likely to be sufficiently important, an alternative nondeceptive procedure is not feasible, the research is not likely to cause physical pain or severe emotional distress, and the deception is to be explained to participants as early as possible. In short, the critical determinant of the acceptability of deception is that it is "justified by the study's significant prospective scientific, educational, or applied value" and that the only way the study feasibly could be carried out is by introducing deception as an integral aspect of the research procedure (APA, 2002, p. 11). The criterion of value has proven contentious for critics who point to the subjective nature inherent in the researcher's determination of a study's prospective benefits. However, in recent years, the federal requirement that scientists obtain institutional approval prior to conducting research has evolved as an important component of the APA code.

In addition to governmental regulations and the APA code, social psychologists can obtain guidance for research conduct by consulting standards that have been promulgated by other professional groups. For example, codes of ethics for survey research have been developed by organizations such as the International Chamber of Commerce/European Society for Opinion and Marketing Research (ICC/ESOMAR) (2001), the Council of American Survey Research Organizations (CASRO) (1995), the American Association for Public Opinion Research (AAPOR) (2002), and the Council for Marketing and Opinion Research (CMOR) (1999). As well as clarifying the rights of respondents, clients, or sponsors and the professional responsibilities of researchers, these codes offer extensive ethical principles in the conduct of public opinion research and in the use of such research for policy and decision making in the public and private sectors. The codes vary in specificity with regard to the range of major ethical issues involving research participants, including deceptive practices, invasion of privacy, and lack of consideration/concern for respondents (N. C. Smith & Klein, 1999). Bearing in mind that many social psychologists are employed in applied settings, it is important to note that corporate codes of conduct have been implemented by a number of companies in North America and Europe (Berenbeim, 1992; Chonko, 1995).

Finally, professional codes of ethical conduct have been developed by a number of psychological associations around the world, including the Australian Psychological Society (1986), the Canadian Psychological Association (1991), the British Psychological Society (1995), the German Association of Professional Psychologists (1986), the French Psychological Society (1976), the Netherlands Institute of Psychologists (1988), the General Assembly for the Scandinavian Psychological Associations (European Federation of Psychology Associations, 1998), the Psychological Association of Slovenia (1982), the Spanish Psicólogo (Colegio Oficial de Psicólogos, 1987), and the Swiss Federation of Psychologists (Fédération Suisse des Psychologues, 1991). Each of these codes emphasizes and promotes an overriding high regard for the well-being and dignity of research participants, as reflected in the attention given to such topics as informed consent, protection from harm, and privacy issues (including confidentiality) (Kimmel, 1996). Nonetheless, the codes differ in terms of the degree of specificity with which principles are formulated and in the basic ethical positions taken, with stronger emphasis placed either on research benefits or risks to research participants. Such differences are reflective of cultural variations in value systems, moral judgments, and approaches to ethical decision making. Consequently, social psychologists should be particularly sensitive to foreign ethical guidelines during the conduct of cross-cultural research, as different standards of acceptable and unacceptable conduct are likely to prevail in different country contexts.

## ETHICAL DILEMMAS IN SOCIAL PSYCHOLOGICAL RESEARCH

Investigations into widely researched social psychology subject areas such as attitudes, aggression, prejudice, intimate relationships, group dynamics, impression formation, and social identity commonly touch upon a variety of interests and values that are prerequisite and central to ethical decision making. Because of the sensitive nature of much social psychological research, the question is not whether ethical dilemmas will be encountered, but rather when and under which circumstances they are likely to pose the most difficult problems for the researcher (and other parties) involved, how such dilemmas can be anticipated before they emerge, and what steps can be taken by the researcher to either avoid or satisfactorily resolve the dilemmas. At the core of most of the ethical conflicts encountered within social psychology are the sometimes opposing interests of science and the protection of others. This point was emphasized in an insightful early critique of deceptive psychology experiments by Vinacke (1954), who raised important questions about the "proper balance between the interests of science and the thoughtful treatment of the persons who, innocently, supply the data" (p. 155).

### Defining "Ethics," "Morality," and "Ethical Dilemma"

A first step in being able to anticipate an ethical dilemma is knowing what this and related terms represent in the context of research decisions. The word "ethics" is derived from the Greek *ethos*, meaning a person's character or disposition, whereas "morality" is derived from the Latin *moralis*, meaning custom, manners, or character. As it has evolved in common usage, the term *morality* has come to pertain to questions about whether specific acts are consistent with accepted notions of right or wrong. The term *ethical* is more likely to be used to connote rules of behavior or conformity to a code or set of principles (Frankena, 1973; Reynolds, 1979).

For example, we have seen that the APA research principles condone the use of deceit under certain specified circumstances, meaning that an investigator who deceives research participants could be considered as acting within the bounds of ethical propriety. However, we still may feel that the researcher's behavior was not right in a moral sense by applying the deontological principle that deceiving others can never be justified. As is apparent, deception in this case might be viewed as proper according to one set of principles (those by which professional psychologists are guided), but not according to another more general set of principles derived from a particular moral reasoning approach.

Choices for conduct in each research situation are related to the decision maker's values, and these values must be weighed carefully when important decisions are to made. An *ethical dilemma* is apparent in research situations in which two or more desirable values present themselves in a seemingly mutually exclusive way, with the values suggesting different courses of action that cannot be maximized simultaneously. Many ethical issues that arise in social psychology research result from conflicting sets of values involving the goals, processes, or outcomes of an investigation.

Deception often lies at the core of ethical dilemmas for social psychology researchers, who must weigh the scientific requirements of validity (i.e., in obtaining an objective and valid measure of behavior) against the ethical imperative of informed consent. The decision to opt for deception in an attempt to maximize the validity of a study runs counter to the obligation to be forthcoming with research participants. In one form or another, arguments against deception claim that because it involves lying and deceit, its use in research is morally reprehensible and may have potentially harmful effects on each of the parties implicated by it (e.g., Ortmann & Hertwig, 1997). Adair et al. (1985) clearly summarized some of the key concerns about its use in psychology by suggesting that deception

> violates the individual's right to voluntarily choose to participate, abuses the basic interpersonal relationship between experimenter and subject, contributes to deception as a societal value and practice, is a questionable base for development of the discipline, is contrary to our professional roles as teachers or scientists, and will ultimately lead to a loss of trust in the profession and science of psychology. (p. 61)

When considering the potential dilemmas involving the use of deceptive research practices, it is important to recognize that the effects of deception may be positive (i.e., beneficial to recipients) or negative (i.e., harmful to recipients), short or long term, and immediate or delayed. For example, a research participant may be initially unaffected by the awareness of having been duped into believing that a fictitious organization had sponsored the study but may experience a short-term loss of self-esteem when later reading a magazine article about how easily people are deceived by researchers. In this case, the deception effects are negative, delayed, and short term. Although deception is most readily thought of as a practice that is employed during the data collection stage, in fact it may be used at each stage of the research process (see Table 3.1). Specific issues linked to the use of deception are considered in detail below.

**Table 3.1**    Use of Deception at Various Stages of the Research Process

| Subject Recruitment | Research Procedure | Postresearch/Application |
|---|---|---|
| Identity of researcher and/or sponsor | Misrepresentation of purpose | Violation of promise of anonymity |
| Purpose of research | False information about procedures, measures, etc. | Breach of confidentiality |
| Participation incentives | Withholding information | Misrepresenting implications of research results |
| Involving people in research without their knowledge | Concealed observation | False feedback during debriefing session |

SOURCE: Adapted from Kimmel and Smith (2001).

## ETHICAL ISSUES IN THE CONDUCT OF LABORATORY, FIELD, AND APPLIED RESEARCH

We next turn our attention to some of the ethical considerations that emerge in the use of specific methodological approaches commonly employed in the investigation of social behavior. The degree of control over a study's circumstances and the characteristics of one's role obligations are two of the more important factors likely to engender a variety of unique ethical dilemmas in laboratory, field, and applied settings. I have recognized some of these varying dilemmas at first hand in the context of my research on marketplace rumors, as described in the following sections.

### Laboratory Research Issues

Issues related to deception have dominated ethical concerns linked to social psychological research conducted in laboratory settings. The controlled conditions of the laboratory offer the experimenter a ready opportunity to actively mislead participants about the true nature of the situation and purpose of the investigation. Other *active deceptions* in laboratory settings have included the use of research "confederates" who act out predetermined roles, untrue statements about the researcher's identity, incorrect information

about research procedures and instructions, false feedback given to the participant, and misleading information about the timing or setting of the investigation (e.g., when the study actually begins and ends or related studies presented as unrelated).

The primary justification for using deception in laboratory settings is that if researchers conformed to the letter of the law regarding informed consent and did not deceive participants at all, then many investigations either would be impossible to conduct or would result in biased findings. Consistent with this point, it has been shown that informing participants of the true purpose and procedures of a study can exacerbate the problem of research artifacts, distorting participant responses and severely jeopardizing the tenability of inferred causal relationships (see Broder, 1998). One can readily imagine how a completely informed consent obtained during investigations into social psychological phenomena such as altruism and prejudice could cause participants to behave differently in order to present a more socially acceptable (as opposed to a natural or typical) image to the researcher. In this way, informed consent essentially operates as an independent variable—studies conducted with or without it may come up with vastly different results (Resnick & Schwartz, 1973). Thus, for some intended investigations, the decision to be made is not whether to use deception, but whether the research is necessary. The decision *not to do* a study because it would require deception is perhaps as morally problematic as the decision *to do* a study involving deception when one considers the potential loss of knowledge involved (Haywood, 1976; Rosenthal & Rosnow, 1984).

In addition to eliciting more spontaneous behavior from participants than otherwise might be the case, deception can increase the researcher's degree of methodological control over the experimental situation. These advantages were evident in some of the classic studies of helping behavior carried out by Latané and Darley (1970) in order to determine whether the number of bystanders present during an emergency would influence the likelihood of intervention by any one bystander. Clearly, the researchers could not have expected an emergency to occur repeatedly in a natural setting under precisely the same circumstances with a different number of onlookers present during each occurrence. Instead, it was more feasible for them to conduct their studies in the laboratory, where the number of bystanders present could be systematically manipulated in a series of carefully contrived "emergencies" (such as an apparent fire in an adjoining room or an epileptic seizure experienced by a research confederate). By creating such fictional environments in the laboratory, investigators can manipulate and control the variables of interest with much greater facility than if deception is not used.

One might legitimately question whether the extreme deceptions used in the helping experiments can be justified. In addition to moral concerns about misleading research participants, it can be argued that the research paradigm exposed participants to psychological risks, including guilt and a threat to their self-esteem for not helping, stress during the emergency itself, and embarrassment at being duped by the researchers. However, one might defend the procedures by contending that the

risks were far outweighed by the importance of the subject matter and potential gain in knowledge about helping behavior during emergencies. Deceiving participants about the true nature of the project may have been the only feasible way to collect data to test the causal hypotheses under study.

By contrast, I have chosen to eschew the laboratory setting in my own research on the factors that give rise to marketplace rumors and the efficacy of strategies to offset their effects. Although the rumor process has effectively been investigated in some ingenious laboratory experiments (e.g., Kamins, Folkes, & Perner, 1997; Tybout, Calder, & Sternthal, 1981), I chose to study the circumstances surrounding naturally occurring rumors using non-experimental field approaches (such as in-depth consumer interviews and mail surveys involving brand managers). In so doing, I was willing to sacrifice a large degree of methodological control that the laboratory setting would have provided. Moreover, I did not want to exacerbate the rumor problem by creating false information in the laboratory and running the risk that (even debriefed) participants might spread it to others once their involvement in the study had ended.

Criticisms of deception have been directed to the very core of the methodological assumptions upon which the use of the procedure depends: (a) that the level of naivete among research participants is high, (b) that the procedure does not produce cues that suggest to participants that deception is taking place, and (c) that participant suspiciousness of deception does not alter the experimental effect. Doubt has been raised that deception adequately serves its methodological purpose in many research situations, that of preventing participants from discovering the study's true purpose or certain aspects of the procedure that could influence their natural response to experimental variables. For example, some evidence suggests that Milgram's obedience experiments lacked experimental realism because several participants may have seen through the deception (Orne & Holland, 1968; Patten 1977). One difficulty in assessing the degree to which a deception study possesses experimental realism has to do with the "pact of ignorance" that may develop between the researcher and participants (Orne, 1959). Participants may conceal that they saw through a deception scenario because it would compromise the value of their participation, and researchers may make little effort to uncover information that would invalidate a participant's data and thereby delay completion of the study.

With regard to the potential consequences of deception, the degree of severity of any negative effects must enter into decisions about whether or not to proceed with a study as planned. "Severe deceptions" are those that create false beliefs about central, important issues related to participants' self-concept or personal behavior, as when an experimental manipulation leads participants to believe they lack self-confidence. "Mild deceptions" are those that create false beliefs about relatively unimportant issues peripheral to participants' self-concept, such as misleading them about the research sponsor or study purpose (Toy, Olson, & Wright, 1989). Severe deceptions can be expected to create negative effect both during and after actual participation in the research (e.g., upset or anxiety linked to a reduced self-image), whereas mild deceptions are unlikely to create negative beliefs and effect until the debriefing session at the end of the study (e.g., disappointment that the study was not really supported by an environmental protection group).

The fact that social psychologists are more likely to employ severe deceptions that are relevant to the fundamental beliefs and values of research participants than are investigators in related fields, such as consumer research, to some extent explains why deception has been such a central issue in social psychology. Studies involving severe deceptions are harder to justify when ethical principles are applied and are more likely to encounter problems when subjected to committee review. However, although mild deceptions are unlikely to cause harm to participants, they still can be morally problematic (N. C. Smith, Klein, & Kimmel, 2002). Some of the possible consequences of deception for each of the parties involved in the research process are summarized in Table 3.2.

Another set of related potential problems particularly salient in laboratory research pertains to the levels of suspiciousness that participants bring to the research setting, especially for individuals who have been deceived in previous studies, and the effects of suspiciousness and deception on subsequent experimental performance. Some persons come to the laboratory setting unaware that deception may take place or else have only a vague knowledge that it is a possibility. In such cases, suspicions may be aroused by demand characteristics (i.e., various task-orienting hints and cues), such as certain comments in the instructions which suggest that something is going on that is different from the experimenter's description. Others may already harbor suspicions as a result of information obtained elsewhere (such as in the recruitment appeal or campus scuttlebutt).

Additionally, there is some evidence that research participants who have been debriefed may communicate the true purpose and other details of studies to future participants, a tendency referred to as "leakage" (Diener, Matthews, & Smith, 1972). Expectations about a study could have a counterproductive effect on the results, motivating participants to behave in ways that do not reflect their natural behaviors or compelling them to behave in uncooperative ways in order to undermine the research.

There has not been much research on the extent of suspiciousness or leakage in the research setting, and researchers do not routinely probe levels of participant suspiciousness.

**Table 3.2**    Potential Costs and Benefits of Deception Studies

| Recipient | Benefits | Costs |
|---|---|---|
| Participant | Increased understanding of science and the research process<br>Feeling of having contributed to science<br>Self-insight (from personal content revealed by deceptive probes) | Inflicted insight<br>Embarrassment<br>Image of science lowered<br>Mistrust of others |
| Researcher | Capacity to elicit spontaneous behavior from participants<br>Increased degree of methodological control<br>Enhanced reputation from successful endeavors | Legal sanctions (e.g., if confidentiality breached)<br>Undermines integrity and commitment to the truth<br>Tarnished image |
| Profession | Facilitates attempts to determine validity of theories, previous research, and assessment instruments | Exhausts pool of naïve participants<br>Jeopardizes community and industry support for the research enterprise |
| Society | Scientific advancement and progress<br>Increased understanding of behavior<br>Insight into applications toward the betterment of humanity | Undermines trust in expert authorities and science<br>Increased suspiciousness (e.g., self-consciousness in public) |

SOURCE: Adapted from Kimmel and Smith (2001).

Estimates of the overall percentage of participants identified as suspicious in social psychology laboratory studies have ranged from only 1.8% to 3% (Adair et al., 1985; Kimmel, 2001). These results may be somewhat suspect given that participants cannot be counted on to be totally forthcoming in revealing their suspicions or knowledge about research procedures and hypotheses. Along these lines, Taylor and Shepperd (1996) have offered the following suggestions: (a) the simple admonishment to participants not to discuss the details of an experiment among themselves is inadequate, (b) the experimenter should not leave participants unsupervised during a deceptive experiment in situations where information about the study could be discussed, and (c) investigators should more carefully evaluate the procedures they use to assess perceptions of the study and levels of participant suspiciousness.

Perhaps the issue that has raised the greatest concern among researchers regarding the problem of suspiciousness is its potential for influencing research performance. Research results on the effects of participant distrust are somewhat inconsistent (e.g., Epstein, Suedfeld, & Silverstein, 1973; Stricker, Messick, & Jackson, 1967) and have led some behavioral scientists to conclude that in general there are no major differences between the data of suspicious and reportedly naive participants (Kimmel, 1996; Schuler, 1982). The effects of suspicion on behavior in an experiment is likely to be mediated by several factors, including the participant's perceptions of the situation, motivations for acting on the suspicions, and the possibility that suspicion can operate differentially across different conditions of a study (Rosnow & Aiken, 1973).

A final set of considerations pertaining to the use of deception has to do with societal attitudes regarding its use, participant reactions to having been deceived and, in a broader sense, the impact of deception on perceptions of the discipline and science in general. Surveys intended to assess reactions to deception have shown that individuals in the general population do not have serious objections to its use for psychological research purposes (Collins, Kuhn, & King, 1979; Sullivan & Deiker, 1973) and that attitudes toward behavioral science research have not been negatively affected by the continued use of deception by psychologists (Sharpe, Adair, & Roese, 1992). Further, studies have revealed that individuals who have participated in deception experiments versus nondeception experiments reported that they did not mind being deceived and viewed the deception research as having greater educational benefit (e.g., Christensen, 1988; C. P. Smith, 1981). Overall, it appears that researchers and regulators tend to be more severe critics of deception than are current or potential research participants.

Evidence suggests that deception rates in social psychology have declined in recent years as researchers respond to ethical guidelines, review mechanisms, and social pressure. Concurrently, social psychologists have become more inclined to utilize alternative procedures that circumvent some of the ethical issues, such as nondeceptive field research (Kimmel, 2001; Nicks, Korn, & Mainieri, 1997; Vitelli, 1988).

## Field Research Issues

A substantial amount of behavioral science research is conducted "in the field"—that is, outside the artificial setting of the laboratory. Although laboratory research continues to be the preferred choice for a majority of social psychologists, many now recognize the potential value of field research, and there is evidence that its use in social psychology has gradually increased over recent decades (Adair et al., 1985; Kimmel, 2001). This includes a rise in use of some of the developing research approaches that serve as the focus of the chapters by King (Chapter 8) and

Miller (Chapter 5) in this book, including archival and cross-cultural research.

Field research offers investigators a ready alternative to ameliorate some of the ethical issues that arise in the laboratory context. Many social psychological research problems can be studied in everyday reality without necessitating the deception or manipulation of participants. For example, I was able to gather a wealth of information about the ways companies treat rumors about their consumer offerings by having brand managers respond to a mail questionnaire in the very settings where the rumors were naturally being encountered (Kimmel & Audrain, 2002).

Unlike the approach used in my rumor research, in which managers could choose whether or not to respond to a questionnaire, in some field investigations participants are unaware that they are being observed or otherwise taking part in a research study. For example, early investigators obtained samples of ongoing conversation among unsuspecting people in such natural settings as railroad stations, college campuses, restaurants, and streets in residential and commercial areas (e.g., Landis & Burtt, 1924; Moore, 1922). One obvious difference between naturalistic field investigations and laboratory research is that it is evident to participants in the latter that they are participating in a research study; in fact, the very act of entering a psychology laboratory implies a certain degree of tacit consent to undergo scientific procedures and experiences that may involve something more than what is readily apparent.

Although many ethical issues emerge in non-laboratory settings, two major areas of concern stand out. The first has to do with the privacy rights of participants. Because the inherent nature of much field research is to elude the awareness of those who are observed, the possibility that participants' privacy will be invaded must be fully considered. The second area of concern involves the informed consent of participants. As in laboratory studies, informed consent can be problematic in the field because much research simply could not be carried out with the full awareness of research participants.

### Privacy

The circumstances characterizing participation in field research are such that the individual's determination of whether or not to participate frequently is violated. This occurs when people are not informed of their role as research participants and are unaware that a study is in progress. A social contract has not been established with the researcher—informed consent cannot be given, and individuals cannot choose to refuse to participate or leave once the study is in progress. In many cases, it will not be possible to debrief participants or inform them of the results once the study has been completed. (These points also are relevant to the use of archival data for research purposes.) Under such circumstances, if researchers obtain or reveal (wittingly or unwittingly) information about attitudes, motivations, or behavior that a participant would prefer not to have revealed, the latter's basic right to privacy will have been breached (see Allen, 1997, for an example from field research on special cultures).

At least four dimensions underlie the placement of different research situations on an invasion of privacy continuum, a continuum that ranges from situations in which privacy could not be said to be violated (e.g., observations of the public behavior of public figures) to situations in which privacy could be said to be violated (e.g., nonpublic figures who presumably are unaware of the possibility they are being observed) (Webb, Campbell, Schwartz, Sechrest, & Grove, 1981). First, there is the element of publicness in the location of behavior under study. People can lay less claim to privacy protections for behavior that takes place in public settings (shopping malls, airports, etc.) as opposed to behavior in private settings (such as

their own homes). A second dimension is the publicness of the person—public personalities regularly are subject to observations and reporting that would be considered invasions of privacy by less public individuals. Third, the degree of anonymity provided must be considered. Privacy clearly is maintained when the linkage between the individual and the information obtained for research has been completely severed; conversely, the risk of privacy invasion is high when information can be linked to identifiable persons. The aforementioned conversation studies can be justified on ethical grounds by the public and anonymous nature of the observations, as well as by the fact that the risks posed (in this case, having information of a private nature revealed to others) were no greater than those encountered in daily experience.

A final factor in privacy considerations is the nature of the information disclosed during a study. Certain information (e.g., income level, alcohol and drug use, birth control practices) can be expected to raise privacy issues. Ethical judgments must take into account the possibility that disclosed information, particularly when it can be associated with individual participants, may be perceived as an invasion of privacy.

### Informed Consent

It is difficult to consider the ethical issues pertaining to privacy fully without taking into account the principle of informed consent. Even the most private settings can be studied without raising ethical concerns if the people within those settings freely consent to observation once sufficiently informed. However, much field research involves situations in which informed consent either is not feasible or is detrimental to the interests of the research. On the other hand, informed consent will be irrelevant for many research activities that involve observations of ongoing public behavior or the analysis of public records and archives.

Field investigations are less likely to involve the direct presentation of mistruths to participants than are laboratory studies. Unlike active deceptions, where false information is provided to the participant, *passive deceptions* involve truths that are left unspoken (i.e., withholding key information about the study). When I obtained the consent of consumers for an interview study on rumors related to electricity that I was conducting for the French national electric company (EDF), I chose to inform participants that the study pertained to their usage behavior and concerns related to electricity (which, in part, it did), but not that we specifically were interested in rumors. This was to see if participants would spontaneously mention rumors on their own prior to our asking direct rumor-related questions. In our judgment, the use of passive deception during the recruitment stage was justified because it did not pose any identifiable risks and we presumed that the decision to participate would not have been different had participants known that the study focused on rumors. It would have been more difficult to justify withholding information about the study sponsor, as many of our French participants may have been upset at having learned after the fact that the research was sponsored by the national utility company.

### Social Psychology Research and the Internet

As an increasing number of social psychologists begin to exploit the potential of the Internet and other emerging technologies for research purposes, it is likely that new ethical dilemmas will emerge and some familiar ones will be recast in a different light (see Birnbaum, Chapter 16, this volume). In their analysis of issues pertaining to Internet-based research, Nosek, Banaji, and Greenwald (2002) identified three key differences between Internet and standard laboratory research: the physical absence of a researcher, the questionable adequacy of informed consent and debriefing procedures, and the potential loss of participant anonymity or confidentiality.

The absence of an investigator to a certain extent reduces the potential for coercion and thus represents an ethical benefit of Internet-based research. However, it also means that the researcher likely will be unable to respond to participant concerns or adverse reactions once the study is under way. Moreover, should the participant choose to withdraw early from a study, this will undermine the possibility that an adequate debriefing can be carried out. Thus, special care should be taken to ensure that the informed consent process is thorough and includes clear instructions that will enable debriefing for those persons who leave the study early (see Nosek et al., 2002, for more specific recommendations). Researchers also should take all steps necessary to protect against the possibilities that data may be intercepted by a third party or accessed once stored in files on an Internet-connected server (see Sharf, 1999).

### Applied Research Issues

Applied research is oriented toward the acquisition of information that will prove relevant to some practical problem, defined as such from the perspective of the researcher, society, or a specific group (such as a government agency, community association, or business organization) (see Part V of this volume). The goals of applied research are oriented toward modifying or improving the present situation, as would be the case for a study intended to develop an effective advertising campaign for the use of condoms in an attempt to control the spread of AIDS. Many social psychologists are employed as applied researchers in industrial settings, market research firms, advertising agencies, treatment facilities, and government agencies to evaluate the effectiveness of current policies and programs, or to design new ones.

Among the more serious ethical issues in the context of applied research are those involving the misuse of new scientific knowledge or the improper implementation of widely accepted procedures and principles. The inappropriate utilization of research findings outside clearly stated limiting conditions can have serious and far-reaching consequences, and such utilization raises some important ethical questions when social researchers consult with and report their data to organizations, human service and community agencies, legal and educational officials, and the like. Granted, these considerations also are relevant within the realm of more theoretical (or so-called "basic") research, despite the often-expressed position that non-applied research is value free and morally neutral (see Kimmel, 1988). Ethical dilemmas pertaining to the use of research findings are more likely to emerge, however, when the research is conducted in collaboration with others whose goals, interests, and values may be at odds with those of the researcher or, more generally, those of the scientific discipline (Mirvis & Seashore, 1982).

Researchers must fulfill the obligation to treat research participants fairly; in addition, they should attempt to fulfill the expectations of the client or research user. The investigator also has a responsibility to protect the well-being of the public when the results are put into action. Ethical conflicts may arise as the researcher recognizes that certain duties and responsibilities toward one group are inconsistent with those toward some other group or with one's own values. For example, it may be that the only way to obtain reliable data that will satisfy certain obligations to a client is by deceiving respondents about the true nature of a study. It thus becomes one's responsibility as a researcher to clarify and openly communicate from the outset one's own role in the situation and to establish limits in terms of assisting the organization in meeting its anticipated goals.

To illustrate, we can consider how ethical dilemmas might have arisen during the conduct of my rumor study for EDF. One of the company's overriding interests in electricity-related rumors was to identify the kinds of beliefs and fears prevalent among the French consuming public relative to electromagnetic fields (EMFs) emanating from outdoor power plants. When company representatives explained to me prior to data collection that their goal was to better inform consumers and reduce anxieties linked to distorted beliefs about EMFs, I recognized that the company's expectations were consistent with my own. The project enabled me to gain further insight into the social-psychological dynamics underlying the emergence and spread of rumors in the context of an ongoing problem situation, while the company searched for more effective means of communicating with its customers. We shared mutual interests in ultimately being able to reduce public misconceptions and the spread of fear-inducing rumors.

By contrast, imagine how opposing interests or role conflicts could have led to ethical dilemmas in this case. If I had suspicions that the company intended to use the results of the research to scare homeowners away from areas where the company planned to erect new power stations or to foment the spread of rumors so as to increase the purchase of electrical safety devices, I would not have been able to continue my involvement with the research project. The company's goals would have conflicted with my own moral values and with the ethical standards of my profession, which clarify that research findings should not be applied to the detriment of individuals or groups.

Ethical dilemmas involving conflicting role expectations should be anticipated prior to carrying out an investigation, especially when entering a relationship with a client whose priorities may subsequently change. As an alternative to forgoing involvement with a troublesome study altogether, a determination should be made as to whether a more ethical research approach for obtaining the desired information or outcomes is available. With regard to the potential misuse of scientific knowledge, it is important to consider such a possibility as one weighs potential costs and anticipated benefits prior to conducting the research. To be sure, scientists should not be considered responsible for a misreading or misinterpretation of their work as long as special care has been taken, when publicizing the research, to state boundary conditions pertinent to the usefulness of the research in applied contexts.

## ETHICAL SAFEGUARDS AND INSTITUTIONAL REVIEW

Whereas formal review and external monitoring originally were limited mostly to large, funded research projects, nowadays most human participant studies are subjected to some kind of external review process. In fact, the proliferation and increased role of ethics committees, professional standards, legalities, and other external restrictions have already subjected psychologists to a higher level of professional ethical accountability than is found in many other professions (including law, politics, and marketing), where both passive and active forms of deception are commonplace (Rosnow, 1997). Over time, participation in research has become much safer than many of the everyday activities in which people engage (Diener, 2001).

Although there are a number of safeguards in place for preventing most of the serious breaches of ethics that might occur in social psychology research, the first line of defense for the protection of the various interests involved in and affected by the research process consists of researchers themselves. This point has been emphasized in most ethics codes, which point out that researchers have a professional responsibility to evaluate carefully and thoroughly the ethics of their investigations (e.g.,

APA, 2002). Ethical decision making involves balancing a set of considerations as to how best to contribute to science and human welfare. Important aspects of this decision-making process are the recognition that most research questions in science can be pursued in more than one manner and that the ethical researcher is one who selects the methodological approach that is most likely to satisfy research goals while minimizing potentially negative consequences.

## *Debriefing and Other Safeguards*

Ethical guidelines typically necessitate that all deceived participants be fully debriefed within a reasonable period following their involvement in a study. This requirement is often cited as an important safeguard against some of the potential risks inherent in the use of deception. The debriefing session can serve a variety of functions, foremost of which are to provide researchers with a means of assessing whether participants were adversely affected by the research procedures and to serve as an opportunity to eliminate any harm or lasting false impressions about the study. It is during the debriefing period that psychologists should refer a participant to an appropriately trained provider if something problematic (such as severe depression) has been revealed about that person during the study. Moreover, in special cases in which confidentiality must be breached (e.g., studies in which it is learned that certain individuals are suicidal or intend to harm others), participants can be reminded about any limitations to confidentiality that were agreed upon during the consent procedure, if feasible (see Behnke & Kinscherff, 2002, for additional recommendations).

The effectiveness of debriefing in successfully correcting a participant's misconceptions resulting from deception is questionable, particularly in cases where the debriefing procedure involves only a cursory attempt by the researcher to inform participants that they were deceived. Effective debriefing may require both "dehoaxing" (i.e., convincing deceived participants that the information they had been given was in fact fraudulent and relieving any anxiety resulting from that information) and "desensitizing" (i.e., helping deceived participants to deal with new information about themselves acquired as a consequence of their behavior during the study). It is possible that the realization that one has been deceived could result in a loss of self-esteem and embarrassment, in addition to creating a negative attitude toward the researcher or science (e.g., Baumrind, 1985). In this light, it is important to recognize that the debriefing process, although designed to resolve ethical problems and provide a methodological check on research methods, paradoxically can have unintended adverse effects on research participants (Toy, Wright, & Olson, 2001). In some cases, for example, it may be appropriate to withhold certain information during the debriefing (e.g., about individual differences) when it is judged that awareness could cause more harm than good to participants.

Unless debriefing is carried out with "care, effort, and vigilance" (Holmes, 1976, p. 867), there is the possibility that persons already deceived once may question the validity of the information provided during the debriefing. This is one reason that deceptive debriefings are especially ill-advised. The so-called "perseverance process," whereby perceptions and beliefs created during a study continue long after they have been discredited, also may cast doubt on the effectiveness of debriefings in undoing the effects of deceptive manipulations. It has been shown that self-relevant and nonself-relevant perceptions (e.g., created by deceptive feedback following experimental tasks) may become cognitively detached from the evidence that created them; as a result, even after the basis for the perceptions is disconfirmed (via a debriefing), individuals may tend to cling to the original beliefs (Ross, Lepper, & Hubbard, 1975). It is for these reasons that some researchers have recommended a process approach to debriefing, focusing on the psychological processes that underlie the effects of deception and debriefing and structuring postexperimental procedures accordingly (see Aronson & Carlsmith, 1968; Mills, 1976; and Toy, Wright, et al., 2001, for specific suggestions for designing thorough process-oriented debriefings).

Given these points, it is clear that an effective debriefing interview should be treated seriously as an essential element of the research process. The researcher should bear in mind its functions as an educational tool as well as a method for identifying and ameliorating any adverse effects. Initially, the researcher should explain the procedures and reasons for them in language that is understandable to participants (this may require pilot testing), including a discussion of the importance of the study and its relevance to understanding social behavior. When deception is revealed, the researcher should sensitively explain that the procedure was selected as a last resort, apologize for having used it, and fully explain how the deception was carried out, perhaps by displaying and explaining specific research materials. During the entire process, one needs to carefully monitor and appropriately respond to the participant's affective reactions and comments while encouraging honest feedback about the study.

As previously discussed with respect to research using the Internet, debriefing tends to be more difficult to carry out in nonlaboratory settings, especially in cases where participants initially are unaware that they have been studied for research purposes, are no longer accessible to the researcher, or are unwilling to pay attention to the debriefing. In certain situations, such as the naturalistic studies of conversations described above, debriefing participants once the observations have been made could do more harm than good. There is not much a researcher can do if a participant indicates displeasure at having been secretly observed, given that the observation already has been carried out. Moreover, the debriefing could serve to raise levels of discomfort or paranoia in other public settings and could have a negative impact on the image of scientists in general.

Another somewhat more uncertain remedy for some of the potential adverse effects of deception is *forewarning*, whereby researchers take steps to brief participants about the study at the outset, informing them that certain information may have to be withheld until the end of the investigation and that they are free to withdraw at any time. The researcher then can carry out the study only with those individuals who are willing to continue. As a form of limited consent, forewarning may be seen as ethically preferable to not obtaining consent at all because individuals essentially agree to be deceived and the researcher will not have directly misled them (Diener & Crandall, 1978). However, some participants may be sensitized by the forewarning to engage in problem-solving behavior aimed at identifying the nature of the deception (Geller, 1982).

In addition to forewarning, other alternative procedures to deception in the laboratory setting have been proposed, such as role playing and simulations (see Greenberg, 1967, and Geller, 1982, for a discussion of these procedures). In general, these procedures appear to have only limited potential and are unlikely to supersede the use of deception in the foreseeable future.

## Institutional Review

Beyond the decision-making responsibilities of the individual researcher, whose objectivity may come into question as a result of a vested interest in conducting a study guided more by methodological and theoretical concerns than ethical ones, there now exists an extensive system of external review for overseeing the ethicality of research. The review process consists of a set of mechanisms, including IRB evaluations of research proposals near the beginning of a study and continuing through journal editor scrutiny of the procedures in research reports submitted for publication.

The ethical review of proposals now is required at nearly all American and Canadian research institutions before researchers are given a green light to proceed with planned investigations. (External review of human participant research varies greatly outside North America; see Kimmel, 1996). Certain additional hurdles may have to be cleared prior to reaching the review board stage (e.g., departmental approval in academic and organizational settings; parental consent; school, hospital, or prison board approval), and further review may occur at various intervals once data collection has begun.

To ensure the protection and welfare of participants, review boards typically attempt to ascertain that the anticipated benefits of an investigation are greater than any risks posed and that informed consent procedures are adequate. Whereas at one time this formal review process emphasized the protection of participants from "extraordinary risks," the identification of even everyday risk now is obligatory for all proposals. During such a review, the investigator is required to present detailed information about all aspects of a proposed study, including specifics about the characteristics of participants, the procedure and research materials, the nature of any deceptions, confidentiality, risks, and method of debriefing.

Over the years, membership requirements and review criteria for IRBs have undergone several changes (Gray & Cooke, 1980; Hansen, 2001). The initial U.S. federal regulations requiring IRB review stipulated that an IRB was to consist of at least five members with varying backgrounds and fields of expertise, at least one member who was not affiliated with the institution, and representation from each gender (Department of Health, Education, and Welfare, 1975). The composition of review boards now has broadened so that a majority of the participants may not be researchers, but rather members of the clergy, lawyers, medical professionals, and the like who have minimal familiarity with the methodological intricacies of the research process and perhaps little appreciation of the potential merits of scientific research. The efficiency and fairness of an IRB no doubt can be maximized when it consists of a diversity of members whose expertise is commensurate with the types of research that the committee typically reviews. Diversity is essential in light of evidence suggesting that differences in individual background characteristics (such as gender, age, professional experience, culture, and moral philosophy) lead to predictable biases in ethical judgments (Kimmel, 1991; Schlenker & Forsyth, 1977).

## Impact and Effectiveness of the Review Process

The expanded influence of external review has brought with it a growing concern that review boards are overstepping their intended role in an overzealous effort to force behavioral and social research into a biomedical mold, thereby making it increasingly difficult for many researchers to proceed with their studies. Considerations that are not specifically related to the rights and welfare of research participants, such as the study design and methodology, now are routinely included in evaluations of research proposals. Because a poorly designed study can have serious ramifications and costs, one might argue that the technical elements of a proposed investigation in fact should be included as a dimension of ethical review (Rosenthal, 1994). Nonetheless, there remains widespread disagreement over

whether the scientific aspects of investigations ought to be taken into account by IRBs, especially by members who lack scientific expertise (e.g., Colombo, 1995; Diener, 2001).

Evidence regarding the effectiveness of ethical review committees in protecting research participants from risk and the impact of such committees on research is somewhat mixed. Mueller and Furedy (2001) have pointed out some of the difficulties inherent in attempts to assess review board performance, including the probability that unscrupulous researchers will bypass the review process entirely; the built-in inadequacies of considering number of incidents (e.g., participant complaints) over time as an indicator of effectiveness; and the misconception that "a problem found" with a research proposal equates with "an incident avoided." Further, a growing body of evidence suggests that there may be important deficiencies in the performance of some IRBs (Ceci, Peters, & Plotkin, 1985; Mordock, 1995; Prentice & Antonson, 1987; Shea, 2000), particularly in terms of inconsistencies in the application of decision standards and subsequent recommendations.

Several suggestions for improving the review process have been offered. For example, to sensitize IRB members to the costs and benefits of doing and not doing research, a casebook of actual research protocols that have received extensive review and analysis by both investigators and participants can be provided (Rosnow, Rotheram-Borus, Ceci, Blanck, & Koocher, 1993). For unique research cases, an advisory board could be created within a discipline's professional association, and that board would be charged with analyzing and reviewing an IRB decision when disagreements emerge. Another approach to improving the review process is to take steps to minimize problems of communication between IRB members and investigators and to encourage regular communication between IRBs (see

Hansen [2001] and Tanke and Tanke [1982] for further discussion).

Among other recommendations for tempering review panel evaluations of research, especially research posing minimal risk (e.g., Ilgen & Bell, 2001), Diener (2001) has proposed that (a) exemptions should be granted with greater frequency for research without true risk of harm; (b) prototypes of certain types of research protocols can be given approval, with subsequent research fitting these prototypes granted expedited review; (c) review boards should recognize their obligation to foster potentially beneficial research, in addition to protecting research participants; and (d) compensation assistance should be provided to researchers to offset the costs accrued as a result of lengthy and unreasonable delays and demands (e.g., help in completing forms; advice for getting the research approved). (See Azar [2002] for an overview of several ongoing projects oriented toward the rewriting of current IRB regulations, education of researchers and review board members, and standardization of the system.)

## CONCLUSION: ETHICAL CHALLENGES AND OPPORTUNITIES

It is understandable that many social psychologists react with trepidation when confronted with the maze of apparently cumbersome rules and regulations that have evolved over the years to respond to research issues. As described by Rosnow (1997), "even experienced researchers often find themselves caught between the Scylla of methodological and theoretical requirements and the Charybdis of ethical dictates and moral sensitivities" (p. 345). Nonetheless, these developments are typical of ethical progress and are essential for providing a common set of values by which scientific discovery can proceed. Moreover, whenever ethical sensitivities have been raised as a result of an increased attention to moral issues within society or because of unfortunate research abuses, many positive changes within the scientific disciplines have followed, including innovative procedures that conform to both scientific and ethical standards.

## REFERENCES

Adair, J. G., Dushenko, T. W., & Lindsay, R. C. L. (1985). Ethical regulations and their impact on research practice. *American Psychologist, 40,* 59-72.

Allen, C. (1997). Spies like us: When sociologists deceive their subjects. *Lingua Franca, 7,* 30-39.

American Association for Public Opinion Research. (2002). *Code of professional ethics and practices.* Retrieved February 15, 2003, from www.aapor.org

American Psychological Association. (1982). *Ethical principles in the conduct of research with human participants* (Rev. ed.). Washington, DC: Author.

American Psychological Association. (2002). Ethical principles of psychologists and code of conduct 2002. Retrieved February 17, 2003, from www.apa.org/ethics/code2002.html

American Psychological Association, Ad Hoc Committee on Ethical Standards in Psychological Research. (1973). *Ethical principles in the conduct of research with human participants.* Washington, DC: Author.

Aronson, E., & Carlsmith, J. (1968). Experimentation in social psychology. In G. Lindzey & E. Aronson (Eds.), *The handbook of social psychology* (Vol. 2, pp. 1-79). Cambridge, MA: Addison-Wesley.

Australian Psychological Society. (1986). *Code of professional conduct*. Parkville, Victoria, Australia: Author.

Azar, B. (2002). Ethics at the cost of research? *Monitor on Psychology, 33*, 38-40.

Baumrind, D. (1964). Some thoughts on ethics of research: After reading Milgram's "Behavioral study of obedience." *American Psychologist, 19*, 421-423.

Baumrind, D. (1985). Research using intentional deception: Ethical issues revisited. *American Psychologist, 40*, 165-174.

Bearden, W. O., Madden, C. S., & Uscategui, K. (1998). The pool is drying up. *Marketing Research, 10*, 26-33.

Behnke, S. H., & Kinscherff, R. (2002). Must a psychologist report past child abuse? *Monitor on Psychology, 33*, 56-57.

Berenbeim, R. E. (1992). *Corporate ethics practices*. New York: The Conference Board.

Berkun, M., Bialek, H. M., Kern, P. R., & Yagi, K. (1962). Experimental studies of psychological stress in man. *Psychological Monographs: General and Applied, 76*, 1-39.

British Psychological Society. (1995). *Code of conduct, ethical principles and guidelines*. Leicester, UK: Author.

Broder, A. (1998). Deception can be acceptable. *American Psychologist, 53*, 85-86.

Campbell, D., Sanderson, R. E., & Laverty, S. G. (1964). Characteristics of a conditioned response in human subjects during extinction trials following a single traumatic conditioning trial. *Journal of Abnormal and Social Psychology, 68*, 627-639.

Canadian Psychological Association. (1991). *Canadian code of ethics for psychologists* (Rev. ed.). Old Chelsea, Quebec: Author.

Ceci, S. J., Peters, D., & Plotkin, J. (1985). Human subjects review, personal values, and the regulation of social science research. *American Psychologist, 40*, 994-1002.

Chonko, L. B. (1995). *Ethical decision-making in marketing*. Thousand Oaks, CA: Sage.

Christensen, L. (1988). Deception in psychological research: When is its use justified? *Personality and Social Psychology Bulletin, 14*, 664-675.

Colegio Oficial de Psicólogos. (1993). *Código deontológico del psicólogo* [Deontological code of the psychologist]. Madrid: Author.

Collins, F. L., Jr., Kuhn, I. F., Jr., & King, G. D. (1979). Variables affecting subjects' ethical ratings of proposed experiments. *Psychological Reports, 44*, 155-164.

Colombo, J. (1995). Cost, utility, and judgments of institutional review boards. *Psychological Science, 6*, 318-319.

Council for Marketing and Opinion Research. (1999). *Respondent bill of rights*. Retrieved February 15, 2003, from www.cmor.org

Council of American Survey Research Organizations. (1995). *Code of standards for survey research*. Port Jefferson, NY: Author.

Department of Health and Human Services. (1981, January 26). Final regulations amending basic HHS policy for the protection of human research subjects (45 CFR, Pt. 46). *Federal Register, 46*(16), 8366-8391.

Department of Health, Education, and Welfare. (1975, March 13). Protection of human subjects: Technical amendments (45 CFR, Pt. 46). *Federal Register, 40*, 11854-11858.

Diamond, S. S., & Morton, D. R. (1978). Empirical landmarks in social psychology. *Personality and Social Psychology Bulletin, 4*, 217-221.

Diener, E. (2001). Over-concern with research ethics. *Dialogue, 16*, 2.

Diener, E., & Crandall, R. (1978). *Ethics in social and behavioral research*. Chicago: The University of Chicago Press.

Diener, E., Matthews, R., & Smith, R. (1972). Leakage of experimental information to potential future subjects by debriefed subjects. *Journal of Experimental Research in Personality, 6*, 264-267.

Epstein, Y. M., Suedfeld, P., & Silverstein, S. J. (1973). The experimental contract: Subjects' expectations of and reactions to some behaviors of experimenters. *American Psychologist, 28*, 212-221.

European Federation of Psychology Associations. (1998). *Ethical principles for Scandinavian psychologists*. Brussels: Author.

Fédération Suisse des Psychologues. (1991). *Code déontologique*. Lausanne, Switzerland: Author.

Fischman, M. W. (2000). Informed consent. In B. D. Sales & S. Folkman (Eds.), *Ethics in research with human participants* (pp. 35-48). Washington, DC: American Psychological Association.

Frankena, W. K. (1973). *Ethics* (2nd ed.). Englewood Cliffs, NJ: Prentice-Hall.

French Psychological Society. (1976). *Code de déontologie*. Paris: Author.

Geller, D. M. (1982). Alternatives to deception: Why, what, and how? In J. E. Sieber (Ed.), *The ethics of social research: Surveys and experiments* (pp. 39-55). New York: Springer-Verlag.

German Association of Professional Psychologists. (1986). *Professional code of ethics for psychologists*. Bonn: Author.

Gray, B., & Cooke, R. A. (1980). The impact of institutional review boards on research. *Hastings Center Report, 10*, 36-41.

Greenberg, M. (1967). Role playing: An alternative to deception? *Journal of Personality and Social Psychology, 7*, 152-157.

Grundner, T. M. (1986). *Informed consent: A tutorial*. Owings Mills, MD: National Health Publishing.

Hansen, C. (2001). Regulatory changes affecting IRBs and researchers. *APS Observer, 14*(7), 13-14, 25.

Haywood, H. C. (1976). The ethics of doing research . . . and of not doing it. *American Journal of Mental Deficiency, 81*, 311-317.

Holmes, D. S. (1976). Debriefing after psychological experiments. *American Psychologist, 31*, 858-867.

Horowitz, I. L. (1967). *The rise and fall of Project Camelot*. Cambridge: MIT Press.

Humphrey, L. (1970). *Tearoom trade*. Chicago, IL: Aldine.

Ilgen, D. R., & Bell, B. S. (2001). Informed consent and dual purpose research. *American Psychologist, 56*, 1177.

International Chamber of Commerce/European Society for Opinion and Marketing Research. (2001). ICC/ESOMAR international code of marketing and social research practice. Retrieved February 14, 2003 from www.esomar.nl

Jones, S. E. (2001). Ethics code draft published for comment. *Monitor on Psychology, 32*(2), 76.

Kamins, M. A., Folkes, V. S., & Perner, L. (1997). Consumer responses to rumors: Good news, bad news. *Journal of Consumer Psychology, 6*, 165-187.

Kelman, H. C. (1967). Human use of human subjects: The problem of deception in social psychological experiments. *Psychological Bulletin, 67*, 1-11.

Kelman, H. C. (1996). Foreword. In A. J. Kimmel, *Ethical issues in behavioral research: A survey* (pp. xiii-xv). Cambridge, MA: Blackwell.

Kimmel, A. J. (1988). *Ethics and values in applied social research*. Newbury Park, CA: Sage.

Kimmel, A. J. (1991). Predictable biases in the ethical decision making of American psychologists. *American Psychologist, 46,* 786-788.

Kimmel, A. J. (1996). *Ethical issues in behavioral research: A survey.* Cambridge, MA: Blackwell.

Kimmel, A. J. (2001). Ethical trends in marketing and psychological research. *Ethics & Behavior, 11,* 131-149.

Kimmel, A. J., & Audrain, A.-F. (2002, August). *Rumor control strategies within French consumer goods firms.* Paper presented at the 110th annual convention of the American Psychological Association, Chicago.

Kimmel, A. J., & Smith, N. C. (2001). Deception in marketing research: Ethical, methodological, and disciplinary implications. *Psychology & Marketing, 18,* 663-689.

Korn, J. H. (1988). Students' roles, rights, and responsibilities as research participants. *Teaching of Psychology, 15,* 74-78.

Kuschel, R. (1998). The necessity for code of ethics in research. *Psychiatry Today: Journal of the Yugoslav Psychiatric Association, 30,* 247-274.

Landis, M. H., & Burtt, H. E. (1924). A study of conversations. *Journal of Comparative Psychology, 4,* 81-89.

Latané, B., & Darley, J. M. (1970). *The unresponsive bystander: Why doesn't he help?* New York: Appleton-Century-Crofts.

Lindsay, R.C.L., & Holden, R. R. (1987). The introductory psychology subject pool in Canada. *Canadian Psychology, 28,* 45-52.

McCord, D. M. (1991). Ethics-sensitive management of the university human subject pool. *American Psychologist, 46,* 151.

McNamara, J. R., & Woods, K. M. (1977). Ethical considerations in psychological research: A comparative review. *Behavior Therapy, 8,* 703-708.

Milgram, S. (1963). Behavioral study of obedience. *Journal of Abnormal and Social Psychology, 67,* 371-378.

Miller, A. G., Collins, B. E., & Brief, D. E. (1995). Perspectives on obedience to authority: The legacy of the Milgram experiments. *Journal of Social Issues, 51,* 1-19.

Mills, J. (1976). A procedure for explaining experiments involving deception. *Personality and Social Psychology Bulletin, 2,* 3-13.

Mirvis, P. H., & Seashore, S. E. (1982). Creating ethical relationships in organizational research. In J. E. Sieber (Ed.), *The ethics of social research: Surveys and experiments* (pp. 79-104). New York: Springer-Verlag.

Moore, H. T. (1922). Further data concerning sex differences. *Journal of Abnormal and Social Psychology, 17,* 210-214.

Mordock, J. B. (1995). Institutional review boards in applied settings: Their role in judgments of quality and consumer protection. *Psychological Science, 6,* 320-321.

Mueller, J. H., & Furedy, J. J. (2001). Reviewing for risk: What's the evidence that it works? *APS Observer, 14*(7), 1, 26-28.

National Commission for the Protection of Human Subjects of Biomedical and Behavioral Research. (1979). *The Belmont report: Ethical principles and guidelines for the protection of human subjects of research.* Washington, DC: Government Printing Office.

National Research Act, Public Law 93-348, Title II—Protection of Human Subjects of Biomedical and Behavioral Research (Part A). (1974).

Netherlands Institute of Psychologists. (1988). *Professional code for psychologists.* Amsterdam: Author.

Nicks, S. D., Korn, J. H., & Mainieri, T. (1997). The rise and fall of deception in social psychology and personality research, 1921 to 1994. *Ethics & Behavior, 7,* 69-77.

Nosek, B. A., Banaji, M. R., & Greenwald, A. G. (2002). E-research: Ethics, security, design, and control in psychological research on the Internet. *Journal of Social Issues, 58*, 161-176.

Nuremberg Code. (1949). In *Trials of war criminals before the Nuremberg military tribunals under Control Council Law No. 10, 2* (pp. 181-182). Washington, DC: Government Printing Office.

Office for Protection From Research Risks, Protection of Human Subjects. (1991, June 18). Protection of human subjects: Title 45, Code of Federal Regulations, Part 46 (GPO 1992 O-307-551). *OPRR Reports*, pp. 4-17.

Orne, M. T. (1959). The nature of hypnosis: Artifact and essence. *Journal of Abnormal and Social Psychology, 58*, 277-299.

Orne, M. T., & Holland, C. H. (1968). On the ecological validity of laboratory deceptions. *International Journal of Psychiatry, 6*, 282-293.

Ortmann, A., & Hertwig, R. (1997). Is deception acceptable? *American Psychologist, 52*, 746-747.

Patten, S. C. (1977). Milgram's shocking experiments. *Philosophy, 52*, 425-440.

Prentice, E. D., & Antonson, D. L. (1987). A protocol review guide to reduce IRB inconsistency. *IRB: A Review of Human Subjects Research, 9*, 9-11.

Psychological Association of Slovenia. (1982). *Code of ethics for psychologists*. Ljubljana, Slovenia: Author.

Raupp, C. D., & Cohen, D. C. (1992). "A thousand points of light" illuminate the psychology curriculum: Volunteering as a learning experience. *Teaching of Psychology, 19*, 25-30.

Resnick, J. H., & Schwartz, T. (1973). Ethical standards as an independent variable in psychological research. *American Psychologist, 28*, 134-139.

Reynolds, P. D. (1979). *Ethical dilemmas and social science research*. San Francisco: Jossey-Bass.

Rosenthal, R. (1994). Science and ethics in conducting, analyzing, and reporting psychological research. *Psychological Science, 5*, 127-134.

Rosenthal, R., & Rosnow, R. L. (1984). Applying Hamlet's question to the ethical conduct of research: A conceptual addendum. *American Psychologist, 39*, 561-563.

Rosnow, R. L. (1997). Hedgehogs, foxes, and the evolving social contract in psychological science: Ethical challenges and methodological opportunities. *Psychological Methods, 2*, 345-356.

Rosnow, R. L., & Aiken, L. S. (1973). Mediation of artifacts in behavioral research. *Journal of Experimental Social Psychology, 9*, 189-201.

Rosnow, R. L., Rotheram-Borus, M. J., Ceci, S. J., Blanck, P. D., & Koocher, G. P. (1993). The institutional review board as a mirror of scientific and ethical standards. *American Psychologist, 48*, 821-826.

Ross, L., Lepper, M. R., & Hubbard, M. (1975). Perseverance in self-perception and social perception: Biased attributional processes in the debriefing paradigm. *Journal of Personality and Social Psychology, 32*, 880-892.

Schlenker, B. R., & Forsyth, D. R. (1977). On the ethics of psychological research. *Journal of Experimental Social Psychology, 13*, 369-396.

Schuler, H. (1982). *Ethical problems in psychological research*. New York: Academic Press.

Sharf, B. F. (1999). Beyond Netiquette: The ethics of doing naturalistic discourse research on the Internet. In S. Jones (Ed.), *Doing Internet research: Critical issues and methods for examining the Net* (pp. 243-256). Thousand Oaks, CA: Sage.

Sharpe, D., Adair, J. G., & Roese, N. J. (1992). Twenty years of deception research: A decline in subjects' trust? *Personality and Social Psychology Bulletin, 18*, 585-590.

Shea, C. (2000). Don't talk to the humans: The crackdown on social science research. *Lingua Franca, 10*, 26-34.

Smith, C. P. (1981). How (un)acceptable is research involving deception? *IRB: A Review of Human Subjects Research, 3*, 1-4.

Smith, N. C., & Klein, J. G. (1999). *Ethics in marketing research and the use of remedial measures to mitigate the deception of respondents.* Unpublished manuscript, McDonough School of Business, Georgetown University.

Smith, N. C., Klein, J. G., & Kimmel, A. J. (2002). *The ethics of deception in consumer research.* Unpublished manuscript, London Business School.

Stricker, L. J., Messick, S., & Jackson, D. N. (1967). Suspicion of deception: Implications for conformity research. *Journal of Personality and Social Psychology, 5*, 379-389.

Sullivan, D. S., & Deiker, T. A. (1973). Subject-experimenter perceptions of ethical issues in human research. *American Psychologist, 28*, 587-591.

Tanke, E. D., & Tanke, T. J. (1982). Regulation and education: The role of the institutional review board in social science research. In J. E. Sieber (Ed.), *The ethics of social research: Fieldwork, regulation, and publication* (pp. 131-149). New York: Springer-Verlag.

Taylor, K. M., & Shepperd, J. A. (1996). Probing suspicion among participants in deception research. *American Psychologist, 51*, 886-887.

Toy, D., Olson, J., & Wright, L. (1989). Effects of debriefing in marketing research involving "mild" deceptions. *Psychology & Marketing, 6*, 69-85.

Toy, D., Wright, L., & Olson, J. (2001). A conceptual framework for analyzing deception and debriefing effects in marketing research. *Psychology & Marketing, 18*, 663-689.

Tybout, A. M., Calder, B. J., & Sternthal, B. (1981). Using information processing theory to design marketing strategies. *Journal of Marketing Research, 18*, 73-79.

Vinacke, W. E. (1954). Deceiving experimental subjects. *American Psychologist, 9*, 155.

Vitelli, R. (1988). The crisis issue assessed: An empirical analysis. *Basic and Applied Social Psychology, 9*, 301-309.

Webb, E. J., Campbell, D. T., Schwartz, R. D., Sechrest, L., & Grove, J. B. (1981). *Nonreactive measures in the social sciences* (2nd ed.). Boston: Houghton Mifflin.

## CHAPTER 4

# Developing a Program of Research

SUSAN T. FISKE

*Princeton University*

A prospective graduate student yesterday asked me how I ended up doing the work I do. This question appears with alarming frequency—a sign, one fears, of becoming a Fixture in the Field. Fixtures are fixed, and science is moving, so in the spirit of motion, let's consider the process of developing, growing, maintaining, and refreshing a program of research. My own entry into the field was motivated by both nature and nurture (my father a psychologist, my mother a community volunteer), both of which suited me to puzzle over experiences with people in social contexts. The influences of the social context, of course, are what social psychology is all about, so it makes sense that a social psychologist would believe that the nature of a person's social contexts shapes that person's research program. Whatever your own social contexts and resulting research puzzles, I will suggest in this chapter that the processes of developing a research career are knowable, manageable, and even fun.

Consider four cases of social contexts that produced creative puzzles, for at least one budding social scientist. As a kid in the 1950s on the South Side of Chicago, I calibrated a certain level of ethnic diversity as natural and

appropriate, much the way one calibrates a certain amount of snow as appropriate for a proper winter. I don't claim that the neighborhood's integration was flawless, but it was deep and abiding, and the adults I knew seemed proud of it. Moving to Boston for college, I was struck by an absence that took me a while to place. Although there was the right amount of fluffy white stuff, the people were far too white. The lack of ethnic variety in the Boston I encountered—the result of heavy de facto segregation—seemed odd to me. Probably primed by my mother's interest in communities, I couldn't figure out why people would want to live that way. Probably primed by my father's orientation to research, I realized there must be empirical answers. Puzzle number one gave rise to my research on stereotyping, about which more later.

Some time later, I observed up close some organizations with few women in high places, though plenty in low places. Some women who were extremely competent, by all reasonable standards, simply were not promoted. None were obvious cases of gender discrimination because some women—a very few—seemed to be getting ahead. But the proportions and the standards were off. One case in point was Ann

Hopkins, a would-be partner in a top accounting firm, who brought in millions of business dollars but was faulted for lacking interpersonal skills. Because the advice from her supporters included the exhortation to be more feminine, gender clearly played some role, according to the Supreme Court, where her case ended up. This setting (in which I testified as the plaintiff's expert witness) was not an isolated instance of the phenomenon. In various organizations, women who behaved like doormats apparently had a better chance of being promoted than women who did not, so some combination of gender and personality was at play. Clearly, personality matters a lot to men's success as well, but it was mattering more for some unarguably competent women. Probably primed to notice because of my suffragist grandmother and great-grandmother, I couldn't figure out why organizations would shoot themselves in the foot by depriving themselves of such considerable talent. Puzzle number two gave rise to my research on ambivalent sexism.

Puzzle number three came from a more directly personal experience. At the time, I couldn't figure out why, as an assistant professor, I was glued to my department head's every gesture and expression. It was a hierarchical place, and the department head held a lot of power over my fate. Outcomes such as salary, promotion, teaching, and research funds all depended heavily on this person's opinion of me. I wasn't the only one who analyzed his every twitch. In a heavily vertical organization, attention seemed to be directed upward. Spurred by this observation, reflecting back on graduate school, I recalled a similar phenomenon among all the graduate students, whereby we all overanalyzed our advisers' every reaction. As a professor rising in the field, I began to notice students who overreacted to my slightest irrelevant grimace or tired sigh. Later, in a more democratic, horizontal department, I noticed much less of that vigilance. This kind of puzzle motivated my research on outcome dependency.

Finally, puzzle number four resulted from a continuing sense of wonder about people as unbelievably complex. How in the world do we manage to make sense of each other? As an adolescent, it's a normal developmental task to think about your peers' opinions. Like my peers, I worried especially about how people made sense of me and what they thought of me. Later, I became more concerned about how I and others made sense of other people, and whether we were being fair. In particular, I worried about whether people were putting too much emphasis on often inappropriate aspects of each other: appearance, ethnicity, gender, and the like. Puzzle number four led to an abiding interest in social cognition.

This chapter takes us from scattered real-world phenomena of personal and social interest to a long-term program of research. Topics will include how to generate the following: a personal perspective, compelling hypotheses, convincing research, readable write-ups, appropriate outlets, programmatic approaches, and a willingness to be wrong. The chapter will also address critically important sideshows to performing research: collaboration, teaching, funding, and service. All of this intends to suggest that the processes of developing a long-term research program are knowable, and one can manage one's progress toward a research program by becoming and remaining aware of choices one makes at each step—and still solve some personal puzzles along the way.

## START BY KNOWING THAT MANY PERSPECTIVES ARE NOT YET REPRESENTED

A social psychologist straddles the domain between social sciences, which have clear political and social implications, and most of psychology, which deals with parts of the person. Social psychology, because it deals with the whole person in a social context, has implications for our own perspectives not only as scientists and intellectuals, but also as insightful people with group identities, politics, and even moral beliefs. Empirically examining a variety of perspectives through social psychological research deepens and tests our own perspectives. Because each of us brings a unique combination of perspectives, each of us has a particular starting point for a research program. Social psychology needs a variety of perspectives to be a healthy science precisely because it deals with people in social context. Competing perspectives, with solid empirical evidence, will better approximate the truth.

As a college senior, I recall auditing a course on gender differences and thinking that the differences all seemed to put women at a disadvantage. For example, it certainly sounded better to be field independent than field dependent (guess which gender and which race are field dependent). Then I wondered: What if one called the variable "field sensitivity" instead? Likewise, internal control or primary control sounded better than succumbing to external control or secondary control (again, with gender, ethnicity, and cultural differences going in one direction). But what if one called it "social harmony control" instead? Clearly, I realized, people's values inform the research questions they bother to ask, the methods they use, the interpretations they make, and certainly what they name their variables. It seemed important, then, to have researchers with a variety of perspectives compete in the contest of ideas. I also realized that one cannot have a credible voice without the corresponding methodological expertise. So one has to take one's puzzles into more systematic conceptualizations and operationalizations.

## COMPELLING, COHERENT HYPOTHESES: WHAT'S THE BIG PICTURE?

The sources of one's research ideas can be intellectual, personal, group, or worldview. Some

might argue for a hierarchy here, but to the extent that one can combine these levels of insight, my experience and perception are that one does better acknowledging all these sources. In my view, one does not have to choose among theoretical sophistication, social problems, and everyday appeal. What's important is keeping in mind ideas that are interesting from a big-picture perspective. (For another perspective on big-picture sources of ideas, read McGuire's [1973] "The Yin and Yang of Progress in Social Psychology: Seven Koan.")

### Intellectual Sources

The most common intellectual fount of ideas is a theoretical discontent. Existing perspectives simply prove inadequate. Perhaps they do not explain the existing data. Perhaps they possess internal contradictions. Perhaps they omit important aspects of the phenomena. Perhaps they explain everything, so they are untestable.

Just as one may move forward by rejecting current theory, one may progress by reviving old theories viewed through modern lenses. For example, the Zajonc (1994) theory of emotions as regulating cerebral blood flow came in part from an older theory proposing similar ideas, but without modern techniques to test it. Historical revival also underlies some of my own work on the continuum model of impressions (S. T. Fiske, Lin, & Neuberg, 1999; S. T. Fiske & Neuberg, 1990), which partly came from contrasting Solomon Asch's (1946) two processes of impression formation. More generally, William James (1890) and Fritz Heider (1958) are rich sources of ideas to be newly framed and tested afresh.

A general meta-theoretical perspective can provide ideas as well. For example, a pragmatic approach (James's "thinking is for doing"; S. T. Fiske, 1993b) can provide hypotheses about why people think, feel, or do what they do, by testing people's reactions against the practical functions served. Similarly, an evolutionary standpoint, a cultural contrast, a consistency theory perspective, or a self-enhancement assumption each can shape hypotheses.

Synthesis across areas also provides a rich source of ideas. One can work across similar literatures within social psychology—for example, competing models of impression formation or attitude change, which may turn out to be two equally valid modes that operate under different circumstances (Chaiken and Trope, 1999, collected 35 theories that combine two modes in this way). Or one can read or talk to other social scientists—such as political scientists, sociologists, or economists—who operate at a more macro level but may make assumptions about psychological processes that seem psychologically undeveloped or implausible but salvageable for new theory nonetheless. Some of the most innovative work occurs at the boundaries between disciplines and subdisciplines.

One also may develop theory by critiquing the theory of specific other viewpoints. More often than not, though, pure critique does not go far. Building hypotheses merely as a reaction to someone else's hypotheses leaves limited ground to explore. One ends up by picking at the toenails of giants. Better to stand on their shoulders.

### Personal Sources

Intuition, hunches, and personal experience also can inform one's hypotheses. People often will develop a sense that their own experiences, or those of people they know well, represent a more widespread phenomenon that has been overlooked. Case studies can come from real people or even from literature, songs, and movies. Psychological insight is many people's hobby, though only well-trained methodologists know how to formulate a logical series of testable propositions from it. In Heider's (1958) view, commonsense psychology was a foundation

for systematic analyses by theoreticians of interpersonal perception processes.

### Group Sources

In parallel, one's perspective on the existing viewpoints may be informed by one's social group identity. My budding insights into the ways that values inform the research process were fueled no doubt by the fact that most of the researchers whose theories I studied were men. When I graduated from college, the editorial board of the *Journal of Personality and Social Psychology* included 1 woman and 20 men, the reviewers for each issue averaged about 1 woman and 20 men, the senior authors averaged about 1 woman per issue, and the editors included none. Social psychology as a field began to include women more rapidly than many areas of psychology and more than many areas of science (see Berscheid, 1992, for a compelling discussion). My point here is simply this well-worn one: If certain socially significant groups do not participate, then the field loses the variety of perspectives needed for a healthy set of dialogues. An underrepresented point of view can counter unconscious biases in prior work or in the dominant approach.

### Worldview Sources

People's explicit value systems—religious, ethical, political—can create a conviction that a fundamental truth is being missed. Whatever value-driven basis one may have (the good Samaritan study of Darley and Batson, 1973, comes to mind), the research itself must be logically reasoned and methodologically rigorous in order to survive the scientific review process, which looks with justifiable suspicion on research with a value-based agenda. Nonetheless, if one can conceptually articulate and operationally define one's predictions, a value-inspired agenda remains a valid perspective for informing empirical tests.

## General Principles, Regardless of Source

Whether the source is intellectual, personal, group, worldview, or—most likely—a combination, several principles contribute to uncovering an idea. First, one must mind the gap, in any of the preceding sources. While reading, hearing, or teaching the research literature, listen to the still, small voice of discomfort, disturbance, or disruption. It takes a subtle inner ear to hear that voice, but cultivate it. When you do hear the voice, ponder what's wrong or missing, make a note, and then work with it later.

Some people keep a folder of ideas. If you do, you'll be surprised at how often the same or similar ideas occur to you. This is your perspective. Follow it. Patterns in what tends to annoy you will turn into a program of research.

In sorting through your ideas, pick perspectives that are underrepresented. A fresh idea creates an excited following. Few ideas, however, start a procession of follow-up studies. If you can't lead the parade, at least anticipate the parade route and get there early to point the way. Watch smart, interesting people and see what they are beginning to consider, before most people have noticed. Think about the implications of their work and the probable directions in which it will move the field. Don't imitate those you observe, but apply their general direction to your own interests.

Beware, however, of runaway bandwagons. Once a trend has swelled beyond a certain size, you won't have that much to add to it. Avoid crowds: You won't stand out, and your pocket is likely to get picked. If you work in an area after it becomes too crowded, it is hard to say anything new, and it is all too easy to be scooped.

See whether your idea has general appeal. The "cocktail party test" is whether you can explain your idea to a nonspecialist in a way that is clear, brief, and interesting. If the listener immediately develops an urge for hors d'oeuvres, you may not have focused enough on the most compelling aspect of your hypotheses. Your idea should be simple enough that a neophyte can remember the main point the morning after. One journal editor told me that he would read manuscripts in the evening and see whether he could remember the main idea during his next-morning jog. If so, the author had made a lasting impression. As Jacob Cohen (1990) put it, in promoting simplicity, "less is more."

Wallow in a reliable effect, to generate compelling hypotheses. Especially if you yourself have uncovered a reliable, original effect, pursue its moderators. See what other theoretically interesting independent variables shape it. Boundary conditions ultimately define any phenomenon. If you can make an effect come and go at will, then you begin truly to understand it. Besides moderators, pursue mediators. What underlying psychological mechanisms explain your effect? What process comes between your main independent and dependent variables? If your effect matters, then its moderators and mediators will matter too. Consider stereotype threat (Steele, Spencer, & Aronson, 2002). The first generation of research demonstrated that black people and women could underperform in contexts that made salient the relevant negative stereotypes about their groups, even when their performance would otherwise be equivalent. The second wave of research addressed generalizability (defining moderators and boundaries), showing that a variety of groups are vulnerable to stereotype threat in domains where they have negative reputations: men on emotional sensitivity, lower classes on academic performance, whites in sports, whites in academics relative to Asians, and more. The second wave of research also tackled potential mediators such as anxiety, distraction, vigilance, and effort. Second-generation research can create those all-important publications at certain career stages, but I wouldn't make a career of tweaking someone else's finding. When you tweak your own original finding, it's called programmatic research on a series of compelling hypotheses.

Whatever you work on, follow your passion. Enjoy it. Study what intrigues you. Why else put up will all the grief associated with research?

## CONVINCING RESEARCH: READ THIS BOOK

Many problems in research design are most easily solved by conversation and feedback—early and often. All of us think we should go it alone without help. Graduate students and junior faculty often think help-seeking will (a) bother the busy important senior faculty or (b) reflect badly on them when they are evaluated. Au contraire. When you are evaluated, someone (preferably several someones) will have to be your advocate(s), or else the cynical critics (of which academia has many) will win and you will lose. To be an advocate, the person has to know your research intimately. If the person has talked with you about your formative decisions, the person will be a far more credible advocate than if he or she reads your work one night before the meeting. This does not require you to collaborate and coauthor with more senior people—a little of this is OK, but too much leads to obvious problems in attributing credit. All you need to do is seek advice sometimes. People love to give advice; they love to feel invested in your work and your career. Benjamin Franklin once said something to the effect of "ask a favor, gain a friend; do a favor, lose a friend." Even older faculty want to feel appreciated and valued. All social psychologists know about reciprocity:

If you indicate that you value colleagues' intellect, they are more likely to value yours, assuming the dialogue is equal. If you approach a senior colleague with a draft of a research design or a grant proposal, they cannot plausibly claim later that it was all their idea. But it's fine if they later say they had an influence on some aspect of it. Consider their suggestions without being defensive, and use the useful ones. Find a comfortable balance on the continuum from being overly isolated to being collegial to being overly dependent. Chances are, you'll err on the side of being too independent, so don't be embarrassed about asking whether someone might have time to give you feedback. Better too early than too late.

Having to talk about your research also puts it into perspective. You have to explain first why you are conducting this particular research, and that will keep your eye on the big picture. I have noticed a pattern among my students, especially undergraduates, over the years. When we first discuss doing research together, or when they describe their research to someone else, they almost always start with the method and forget to mention the hypothesis. This is like deciding whether to drive, bike, walk, or swim—before you know where you want to go. There may be times when the ride is the point, but typically not in science. Different destinations require different modes of transport. Different hypotheses suggest different methods. If you want to go for a bike ride, with no destination in mind, that's fine, but don't conduct an experiment just because you thought of a clever procedure. Probably, if you have a method in mind, a hypothesis may be lurking in a mental corner somewhere. Some searching probably will uncover the implicit hypotheses, which then need to be specified and developed. But do wait to choose a method until after the concepts are clear (novices tend to seize on a method too early).

Moving from concept to operation, from hypothesis to method, disciplines the mind.

For example, to create a working definition of aggression for an experiment, the researcher must decide what kinds of aggression count: Indirect as well as direct? Passive as well as active? Nonverbal as well as verbal? How does aggression differ from assertiveness? After having decided on a particular kind (e.g., physical violence), what levels are appropriate for the hypothesis, the participants, and the setting? What is ethical and feasible? Will it be possible to study people blasting another person with noise? Shocking another person? Hitting another person? Any area poses challenges of operationalization: Being forced to specify, for instance, what specific activities are interesting or boring, what is discrimination versus prejudice, what is the affective versus cognitive aspect of an attitude, all helps one to think more clearly about the concepts involved.

Besides the conceptual discipline involved in operationalization, practical discipline accompanies the working definitions. Most of the concerns are obvious: The procedure must be feasible and plausible, in all the ways you will know for your specific setting. Probably the most common but not obvious issues involve trying to do too much at once. More focused questions invite more careful operationalizations, so they are more likely to yield results. One can't do everything well. Moreover, the first time you run a study, it may not work, so you will have to fine-tune the method, which is more difficult with too many variables simultaneously in play. Simple and elegant is more effective than complex and baroque. You'll just have to give up testing some of the side issues right away.

Because of all the uncertainties in blazing new trails, it can be helpful to build on established paradigms that have worked in the past for you, your collaborators, or others in the field. The method you know has certain established strengths and weaknesses. Inventing a new method will almost certainly (a) take more time, (b) invite more criticism, and (c) not work out exactly as planned. One has

to choose one's battles. Sometimes, inventing a new procedure is worthwhile, if that is the focus of one's contribution, but sometimes effort and energy must go elsewhere. Make a conscious choice.

In general, many impactful social psychology experiments display drama in the dependent variable and subtlety in the independent variable. Small changes in the situation (such as an experimenter merely saying "the experiment requires that you continue") cause dramatic changes in the participants' behavior (e.g., shocking someone else to death; Milgram, 1965). This advice, credited to Stanley Schachter (L. Ross & Nisbett, 1991), fits other famous studies' seemingly trivial independent variables ($1 versus $20 payment, many or few bystanders, having retirees water their own houseplants or not) and dramatic dependent variables (liking a patently boring task, rescuing an accident victim, mortality rates).

Whatever your variables, multiple methods matter. Whatever method you choose, it will have drawbacks. Only by converging operations can researchers know whether the effect is true and not simply an artifact. The same effect across methods is more compelling than the same method applied to many different phenomena. For example, the bogus pipeline (E. E. Jones & Sigall, 1971) is one method for getting at people's true racial attitudes, beyond the socially desirable response. If other methods (subliminal priming, response times, nonverbal indicators) also show that people have racial prejudices that they fail to admit, then the converging result, across methods, is compelling. In personality psychology, this idea—first expressed by Campbell and D. W. Fiske (1959)—holds that a researcher more reliably assesses personality traits by using multiple measures across multiple traits. In the multitrait-multimethod matrix, one looks for traits that emerge reliably across methods, and one can detect methods that have their own effects, regardless of particular traits. For example, one might find that questionnaire methods all contain a common element (acquiescence bias), whereas response time measures all contain another (age bias). For both personality and social psychology, methodological pluralism allows researchers to triangulate on the same phenomenon from the perspective of different methods with different strengths and weaknesses.

Having collected the data, attack the analyses with enthusiasm. Let your data do the talking. At the first stage, the researcher becomes a detective, in Abelson's (1995) terms, analyzing the data in every conceivably useful way. No analysis is forbidden. Try anything, and see what happens. Having poked, squeezed, pulled, opened, shaken, and inverted the data, you will see that some patterns keep appearing and some seem elusive. The data are trying to tell you what the robust results really are. Trust the ones that don't disappear when the analytic assumptions change slightly.

Having played the detective, the researcher moves to the next role, as a lawyer advocating a particular interpretation of the evidence. The lawyer must play according to certain procedural rules, agreed-upon methods, statistical techniques, and ethical obligations. Nevertheless, having a certain perspective to argue, one tries to make the best scientific case, within the rules. To keep you honest, the judge and jury are editors and reviewers, as well as other readers.

## READABLE WRITE-UPS READERS WILL READ

Readers are busy, distracted people: Why should they bother with your article? To paraphrase Dahl (1961), science is a sideshow in the great circus of life. People read your articles because they thereby acquire nuggets of knowledge, insight, entertainment, ideas, and clues. To assume that people will read your work because it is good for them is to assume

that people read like they take vitamins. Some people will do it dutifully, but they won't ask for seconds and they won't successfully recommend it to others. Presenting your work effectively is more than mere showiness; it allows your ideas to communicate clearly what they can contribute.

Some great advice about writing psychology articles comes from Bem (2003) and Sternberg (1993). One particular highlight includes the ideal hourglass shape of an article, starting with the broadest context; becoming progressively more specific through the introduction; leading into the most concrete, narrow specifics of method and results; then again broadening outward to the end of the discussion, which takes the reader back to the widest context.

Considering the article's overall flow, one wants to create tension and suspense: Will the hypotheses hold up? Will the alternative interpretation win out? Where will it all end? Suspense can be arranged by making a plausible case for the competing alternative to your favored hypothesis. Otherwise, with hindsight bias (Fischhoff, 1975), your hypothesis and results will seem all too obvious to the reader, who will fail to be impressed.

The single most important principle of writing anything is to make an argument for something. The argument in this chapter was stated at the outset: The processes of developing a long-term research program are knowable, and one can manage one's progress toward a research program by becoming and remaining aware of choices one makes at each step—and enjoy it. In any kind of writing, always make an argument and have a point to make, but play by the rules. People forget this basic premise with surprising predictability. What do you want to say? What is the take-home message? When my students (both graduate and undergraduate) read research articles for class, I always insist that they tell me what the author(s) were trying to do. It is surprisingly hard to find the hypothesis in many research articles and harder still to find the argument in a review article. Having collected all that data and read all those articles, what did you learn and what do you want to tell us? A well-written article of any sort has a thesis. It does not read like a string of note cards joined as a string of paragraphs. Instead, use specific aspects of specific studies to support each point.

To make a strong empirical article, which is a data-based argument, go with the strongest studies. Most researchers are tempted—having gone to enormous trouble to run each study, having tended it through conception, realization, and analysis—to include every last one, with every last measure that might be relevant. Unfortunately, several weak studies do not equal one strong study. Readers do not sum the quality of evidence over studies; they average it, so weak data dilute strong data. Try not to become so attached to each study that you cannot evaluate it with a cold, hard eye, and know when it is time to leave it aside.

More generally, admit your limits. Know the strengths of your data (that part is easy), but also anticipate the reviewers' criticisms, however unreasonable. Then, explain their possible criticism ("A critic might argue . . .") and show why it is wrong or at least not deadly. Readers are more impressed when authors do not oversell their work. Many reviewers are impressed when they can say, "Every time I thought of a flaw or potential problem, the authors addressed it on the next page."

Finally, do pay attention to the basic rules of good writing. Learning to write is a lifelong project. You can get a leg up from Strunk and White's slim classic, *The Elements of Style* (2000, currently priced at about $6.95). The most common problems in writing psychology are passive voice and needless words. Learn to excise the fat, leaving only the lean, muscular, healthy prose. If this proves difficult, try editing on paper as well as on the computer screen, and try coming back to

your work after a break. Both lend an outside perspective to the too-familiar prose. Better still, find an honest friend and heed the person's advice. However annoying, the reader is always right (or at least diagnostic). That is, if one reader has a problem, others will too. It is better to hear the bad news from a friend, who may save you a round of rejection and revision.

## OUTLETS: VISIBLE AND INVISIBLE

Assess the market value of your research. It almost all hinges on the quality of your data, no matter how elegant your theory. You may have a hypothesis that deserves to be true, but reviewers are trained to attack at the sign of any weakness, and editors go with the most negative review (Fogg & Fiske, 1993). Be ruthless with the quality of your evidence; don't waste your time and reviewers' time with outlets that simply won't work. If you are too close to your product to judge it yourself, ask some colleagues. It is better to hear bad news from allies than critics.

Develop a thick skin: The criticisms are not directed at you personally, no matter how nasty they may seem. It's not you; it's this particular version of this particular set of studies. Of all the people I've known well enough to trade rejection stories, practically none receives an immediate acceptance for any study, no matter how brilliant. (This says nothing about my choice of friends!) Most of us make person-specific attributions for our rejections: This editor or suspected reviewer hates me, I am a foreigner, I am unknown, I am too famous, my ideas are too mainstream, my ideas are too new. The more parsimonious explanation is the 90% rejection rate for the best journals. Rejection is part of the ritual, so get used to it. Most of us cope by going through stages of grief: first shock, then anger at the stupid *#@&^% reviewers, then sadness (maybe I should sell shoes), then (after a decent interval) the gradual realization that maybe the reviewers made a few reasonable points. As one considers how to address their criticisms, one begins to feel relieved that they didn't accept the article with all its glaring flaws.

If your article is rejected, heed your own clarion call for more research: Consider doing it. Alternatively, you may decide that you are willing to settle for a lesser outlet. There is almost always a trade-off between time and quality; it takes longer to get into the best journals. One professor publishes only in the best journals, jettisoning studies and doing new ones until the reviewers cave in. This may be hard on graduate students and junior faculty, however, who may not get publications in time to find or keep a job. Another equally successful professor used to have the envelope ready for the next journal even before receiving feedback from the first one, on the grounds that reviews are arbitrary and non-overlapping, so revision to suit one bunch of reviewers is futile. I take a slightly different tack, having learned that editors recruit reviewers with differing expertise (D. W. Fiske & Fogg, 1990), so of course they don't agree; they are evaluating the article on different dimensions. So, one can learn from the reviews, and can collect new data or not, but the ultimate decision rests on the timing/quality trade-off, which may depend on the stage of your career (how important is it to get stuff out quickly) and the trendiness of your research topic (which also may determine how important it is to get stuff out quickly).

If you are scooped, don't panic. Chances are, the other person did the research differently than you did. Being scooped is annoying at best and deeply wounding at worst (though I know one professor who claims to be relieved not to have to complete a study when someone else does it first). Especially at the start of one's career, when one has not yet had many ideas, each idea is even more precious. Nevertheless, people do not really own ideas; they own the work. Ideas are in the air, and people often acquire them unconsciously from others, or perhaps because those ideas are the next plausible step in the progress of science. What you do own is your work on the idea, developing it and operationalizing it. No two people work in precisely the same way, so you should have some new angle to contribute. Besides, any one study is only one small part of a research program. Keep your eye on the big picture.

## PROGRAMMATIC APPROACH: FOLLOW YOUR BLISS

The research program itself should be your passion, so do not allow a few rejections to set you back too far. Follow whatever interests you the most; this enterprise is too much work to tolerate anything less. Caring about what you do will carry you over the bumps in the road. If you don't know for sure what you want to pursue, you can discover your own preferences as revealed by the patterns of your chosen research problems. It won't take you long to discover the pattern, and then you can build on it.

Above all, as mentioned earlier, treasure a reliable effect when you find it. Domesticate it by trying it in different theoretically interesting contexts and variations. Teach it new tricks by making it come and go at will. If you can make an effect appear and disappear, as noted, then you really understand it. In effect, knowing the moderator variables explains much about the effect. Also, learn what's inside it: What are the mediating variables that link the primary cause to the primary effect?

Having played awhile with your treasured effect, don't fully housebreak it. Let it outside, for others to take for a walk. If you clean up all the mess from your effect, no one else will be interested. Let other people do something with it—unless, of course, you are utterly driven to know every last detail of its nature.

Some researchers believe in letting others housebreak their discoveries, whereas other researchers are more possessive. In general, what Bob Abelson calls the "neats" like to clean up every detail, whereas the "scruffies" like to propose an idea and let others clean up.

Researchers who belong to the neats and the scruffies differ also in their willingness to be wrong. Scruffies generally believe it is better to be wrong than boring, to flame out in a burst of fireworks, pick up, and start over after making a great but misguided show. Neats generally believe it is better to be careful and cautious, building an argument brick by brick. Both perspectives have some merit, and each of us has to calibrate our own willingness to be wrong. Research requires taking some risks, trying on new ideas to see how they fit, and being willing to discard them if they don't, but high-risk, high-gain research can leave you with nothing at the end of the day. Balance is key.

Besides individual differences in the willingness to be wrong or to take risks, one's situation matters, of course. It is easier to take risks after achieving tenure; that's the whole point of lifelong job security. It is easier to take risks with one's left hand if one is already maintaining a more reliable research program with one's right hand. It is easier to take risks if you have some solid publications already. Staking the initial stages of your career on one high-risk, high-gain project probably is not a good idea.

Evaluators do look for both quantity and quality. That is the hard truth. Most departments want to know what your own particular phenomenon is. I was once told to find a "Fiske effect." But most departments also have an implicit expectation for sheer number of publications per year (I've heard the number two, in one of the top few journals, but it varies a lot). The trick is to try to keep projects in the pipeline—some things at the planning stage, others piloting, others running, other analyzing, others (one hopes) writing, and others under review.

What about fillers? Many evaluators discount chapters in edited volumes. It can be good to do one or two as a graduate student, if your adviser asks you to collaborate, because the writing and literature review experience can be useful. But if you are going to do all that work, why not do it for a review journal? If you are going to do all that work, why be second author? Within the bounds of maintaining a good relationship with your adviser, discuss the issues of costs and benefits for you to do a chapter together. For junior faculty, there are likely to be fewer invitations, either from editors or from more senior collaborators, but that is probably just as well. For graduate students, chapters may be evidence of some form of low-level activity, but for junior faculty, that isn't much help. Look up the citation rates for someone's chapters, compared to articles. The chapters are low, low, low.

So why do chapters at all? First, for fun. If you have something you want to say, and you don't want to have to deal with reviewers (only the editors who invited you, probably for the perspective they know you have), a chapter is a good outlet. Second, for prestige. Some very few volumes, of course, carry a lot of prestige, and you will know which ones and presumably accept those invitations. Third, for a particular audience who may not otherwise see your work. Fourth, for a literature review you have written for another purpose. One of my more cited chapters was prepared originally as a grant proposal. It is the rare edited book, however, that has much impact, and likewise the chapters therein.

Chapter invitations are gratifying, as a sign to you and your evaluators that you've had an impact on the field in a particular area. The key is weighing the opportunity to be associated with a particular collection of editors and authors, to be able to speculate and go beyond the data, to make a controversial argument, and to support the editors' enterprise, on one hand, with the opportunity costs, on the other hand, such as sacrificing time that could be spent on articles and grants.

When in doubt, concentrate on research articles. If you do chapters, do them as a second priority, not a first priority. Save your best hours in the day for research writing. Some people write chapters at home on weekends or during the evenings, when they have nothing more pressing to do. But if you put your name on it, you still have to do a good job. It should not be too far afield from your research program, so you do have something intelligent to say, without undertaking a whole new line of inquiry, and then other people can see why you bothered. Otherwise and overall, all else being equal, stick with the journal articles.

## COLLABORATION: BESIDE EVERY GOOD RESEARCHER STANDS A TEAM

In each arena—coming up with ideas, forming hypotheses, designing research, analyzing it, writing it, dealing with rejection, and doing programmatic research—good collaborators are priceless. In finding collaborators, as in finding romantic partners, be open to serendipity but be choosy. Each of us has research interests and talents that form a template; this template can mesh with a variety of other templates, but not all. The point is that no one adviser or collaborator is the be-all and end-all. You can work happily with various people. Your template is at the ready; various prospects can fit. So choose what works, but don't agonize over the perfect match.

Interdisciplinary collaborations in particular matter right now, given both the complexity of some paradigms and the potential for creativity at the boundaries of disciplines (see Cacioppo, Lorig, Nusbaum, and Berntson, Chapter 17, this volume, and Part V of this handbook). As noted, some of the more macro social sciences make strong psychological assumptions that they do not test; political psychology and behavioral economics come out of such collaborations. Some of the latest work in cognitive neuroscience has discovered that it needs social psychologists to help interpret the pesky intrusiveness of emotion and other social variables. Social psychologists need neuroscientists, physicists, and statisticians to do social neuroscience. Health psychologists need collaborators with medical expertise. Psychologists and lawyers have much to share. Many funding agencies are particularly excited by interdisciplinary collaborations. Cross-boundary collaborations glue our field together at a time when it is threatening to fly apart into tiny specialized pieces. Building bridges is useful in sticking psychology together.

Cross-boundary collaboration also carries some risks, as I've recently suggested (S. T. Fiske, 2002): The more micro ("harder") sciences look down on the more macro ("softer") sciences; both may resent the intrusion or defection; neither side owes allegiance to you, so resources, alliances, and identity may be at risk; and lack of expertise is a real issue. On the other hand, collaboration cures many of these problems, and some of the most creative work emerges from this kind of project.

Once you have agreed to collaborate, interdependence can work marvels if each of you contributes in areas where the other one is learning. Managing the collaboration requires deliberate attention. Sometimes it is important to have authorship discussions up front, to avoid later misunderstandings. Having the idea is not enough to merit first authorship. As with strangers in the field, so too with collaborators. No one can really own the free-floating idea; only the work establishes ownership. Some researchers refrain from discussing their ideas with anyone except a collaborator, to avoid being scooped. But even with a collaborator, the ideas are likely to develop in ways that are difficult to track, so explicit discussions are key.

In discussing the work that does establish ownership, people typically award authorship to the person who did more work. But beware the self-serving bias here: Your collaborator(s) probably did more than you think. Add together each person's estimate of his or her own contribution, and the total will be more than 100% (M. Ross & Sicoly, 1979). Even if you agree that one person did more, you each are likely to underestimate the other(s). Respect for the self-serving bias suggests giving the other person benefit of the doubt. Include research assistants, staff, and younger collaborators as coauthors, whenever possible and appropriate. That is, people deserve authorship for scholarly input, but they do not deserve authorship just for running participants for pay or providing technical assistance. It is better to be direct, honest, and blunt than to be perceived as exploitative, unethical, or unfair. Although I usually err on the side of inclusiveness, each new coauthor dilutes the perceived impact of the prior authors. In general, communicate, communicate. (See Fine and Kurdek, 1993, for some other reflections on faculty-student coauthorship, and Zanna, 2003, on mentoring graduate students.)

Responsibility for other people's training suggests letting go of some control, letting the less experienced people try their hand at the next step for which they might be ready. Even if you could do the work more efficiently yourself, you are responsible for training those who work with you. The care and feeding of junior collaborators entails not exploiting them or taking them for granted, but making the research experience at whatever level a learning experience in the conduct of science. Both good teaching and research quality control require close supervision. Horror stories abound. I once told undergraduate research assistants to follow a particular telephone sampling procedure to obtain a stratified random sample. When I called the participants later, for an unexpected follow-up, I discovered that the students had not called whom they said they had called; they simply spoke to the first person available. This was a failure of teaching and motivating on my part, as well as irresponsibility on the RAs' part. Had they understood the importance of random sampling, one hopes they would not have cut corners.

## TEACHING: A PIECE OF THE RESEARCH ENTERPRISE

From the research perspective, teaching indeed is a form of collaboration. But of course it is more, because one person clearly has more knowledge and authority, not to mention power to evaluate, than the other. Some departments recognize the teaching that goes on in one-to-one supervision and lab meetings. Most departments do not, perhaps because they view research and teaching as orthogonal.

But are they? One could argue that research and teaching should be negatively correlated, based on scarcity of time and energy, differing personality requirements, and divergent rewards. One could also argue that the relationship should be positive, based on conventional wisdom and the shared requirement for intelligence. One could even argue that the relationship should be zero, because they are different enterprises and the relevant personality dimensions are unrelated. Meta-analysis shows that the overall effect is ever so slightly positive, if anything, but it depends heavily on the evaluative dimension (Feldman, 1987; Hattie & Marsh, 1996). Active researchers rate high on knowledge, commitment, enthusiasm, and organization. Research conveys little or no advantage in facilitating interaction or managing the course. Contrary to popular assumption, teaching and research quality are correlated somewhat more at liberal arts colleges than at universities, perhaps because the variance on research productivity is greater. The small positive relationship holds especially in the social sciences, compared to natural sciences and humanities. Across moderators of the effect size, the relationship is always slightly positive, though typically small. (Oddly enough, time spent on teaching does not correlate with teaching quality.) The relevant point here is that time spent on research does not undermine quality of teaching, but it does predict articles published. Log those research hours, even when you are busy teaching. Set aside time for course prep, meetings with students, and research. Protect each of those spots on your schedule, to keep control of your time.

Given that our jobs entail both teaching and research, and that the two are at best loosely coupled, how can we help teaching improve the quality of our research? Teaching upper-level courses provides a built-in incentive to keep up, whether your students are graduates or undergraduates. Everyone knows that teaching a seminar in your specialty is a plum assignment, but even lower-level survey courses can provide opportunities to scan the literature for readable articles and pithy, up-to-date examples for lecture. Having to become expert on the topic and explain it to students can provide insights into unanswered research questions. Also, some courses have a research component. One professor has students with different accents collect local housing discrimination data by making phone inquiries about rental listings and coding the agency's responsiveness (i.e., whether they even call back). Another professor has students collect questionnaire data from family members and analyzes the data for class. Thinking about your own research goals can enrich your teaching, and vice versa.

In survey courses, keep an eye out for the best, most enthusiastic students. Let them know that they can do research with faculty, as an independent study, research assistantship, or senior thesis. When I was an undergraduate, it never occurred to me that faculty would want to work with me because I knew I didn't know anything. One of my roommates pointed out that I would be free labor, which motivated me to go volunteer to work on a faculty member's research. Many a research career has started that way. As a faculty member or graduate student, be choosy about your individual students. If you can, find people who will work on projects of mutual interest. Point out that they will get more enthusiastic and expert help if it's a topic you're pursuing yourself. (Specific tips on how to teach lie outside the scope of the current volume, but see Bernstein, 2003.)

## FUNDING: AHA! PLUS . . .

Funding your students—especially graduate students—lies in both your and their best interest, because if they are funded, they are less distracted from research by having to earn money in other less useful ways. Fundable research ideas occur in all the ways indicated for any piece of research. The difference is that you have to plan it all in advance. In fact, even if you don't get funded right away, having to plan a plausible research program is not a bad idea. In the stress and overload of the semester, when a new student is ready to work with you, you can pull one of your proposed studies off the shelf (or at least out of the proposal) and develop it together. At least you will know that it fits well with your research program.

Fundable research, in my experience, requires an interesting idea and proof of feasibility. The interesting idea maybe highly innovative, or it may be the next logical step of an old idea. Whichever it is, the good idea is evaluated the way any of our research ideas are evaluated for publication; all the same criteria apply. Perhaps with funding more than other enterprises, the fine line between a great new idea and credibility established by a track record is particularly delicate. Some proposals get rejected for promising what reviewers claim is nothing new. Others are rejected for being so new that they are completely untried. The best combination is a fresh new idea, convincing pilot data, and systematic development of the approach over a series of studies. Methods and statistics have to be credible, so one must prove one's expertise by compulsively specifying all the tiresome details in advance. (For more thoughts on grant writing, see Steinberg, 2003; Sternberg, 2003.)

All the advice about rejection by journals applies here as well. The difference is that you often get to try again (at least a couple of times) with the same funding agency and therefore the same reviewers. In the words of the *I Ching*, perseverance furthers. At a minimum, the reviewers build some cognitive dissonance if they initially said the basic idea was worthy, and then you keep doing every revision they ask. They can still reject your proposal, but at least it requires more mental gymnastics than if you are less responsive to their feedback. It is important to remember that the reviewers are people like us, only they are doing their bit for the field by plowing through other people's grant proposals. Which brings us to . . .

## SERVICE: GIVING IT AWAY

Some wise colleagues pointed out that service is the least useful tool for acquiring tenure (Roediger, 2003; Taylor, 2003). Nevertheless, tenure, promotion, and collegiality require that each person carries some of the shared load. Generosity presumably is owed from the inside out, in concentric circles.

In your own program, service helps to build team spirit and facilitate your colleagues' lives. It is to everyone's advantage to be part of a lively, active program, which requires some effort on behalf of the group. Be generous, but don't be a chump. People

sometimes fail to get their own research done because they do more than their share: being everyone else's favorite statistical consultant, advising all the minority students, advising all the women, advising all the athletes, or running the best meetings. Nevertheless, building your program builds your home away from home where you spend all your days (and some of your evenings). If you want it to be a place you enjoy, you have to contribute whatever you do best.

In your department, also do your share, but no more, unless you are building an administrative vita. Notice what other people at your level do, and strive for equity. If you do less, people will resent you. If you do more, people may be grateful, but you won't get your own research done, and they won't, ultimately, promote you out of gratitude.

In your university, of course, you can also build an administrative vita, if that is your career trajectory, but make it a deliberate choice, not an accident. Active researchers can do well by doing good: Offer your particular forms of expertise above all. (Let the less productive people offer the general administrative labor that runs the university.) Your particular expertise can serve for its intrinsic usefulness. For example, social psychologists know a lot about affiliation, which is useful for student retention; about identity, which is useful for student affairs and housing; about diversity, which is useful on a multicultural campus; about persuasion, which is useful in marketing the university; and so on. In addition, social psychologists are trained to analyze a social situation for the variables that matter, to measure them, and to interpret data. Few other specialties prove as useful in academic management. The other benefits to offering your expertise to the university, besides being the right thing to do, are that it earns you respect among your colleagues and gives you ideas for research.

Service to our national organizations keeps psychology healthy. Grant and journal reviewing is the most obvious, common form of service. Do your share: You will learn a lot about current work in the field by people most relevant to your own areas of expertise. You'll learn a lot about what it takes to get published or funded. You'll keep the enterprise going. You'd be surprised at how controversial peer review can be, outside modern scientific circles. It's a privilege for us to monitor ourselves, to uphold scientific standards, and to teach each other. One professor called it on-the-job training. When you write reviews, write about the manuscript or the proposal, not the researcher as a person. Be direct but sensitive to the other person's feelings. Don't use reviews to show how smart you are, at the other person's expense. Do use reviews as a teachable moment. For grant reviews, especially, be sure to mention the strengths of the proposal. Social psychologists have a reputation for killing each other off, leaving no one alive to be funded. Offer some praise, in case this imperfect proposal is nevertheless one of the better ones and the program officer wants to fund it. Whether you do journal and proposal reviewing at home or as part of a review panel that requires travel may depend in part on your family situation or career stage. Weigh all the factors, but do your share somehow, sometime.

The mid-range organizations (Society for Personality and Social Psychology, Society of Experimental Social Psychology) help all of us by running journals and conferences. Typical stints on these committees are short, perhaps 3 years, and you're off. If asked, you should do it once in your career. The largest psychological organizations (American Psychological Association, American Psychological Society) help all of us by lobbying Congress for research funding. No one else can do it as effectively as they can, and two organizations are better than one. Consider your dues to be your contribution to the lobbying effort, which is expensive but vital. Consider any national service to be your bit in protecting

psychological science from the talk-show crazies, who wield considerable power and influence. They must not be the only voices telling Americans about psychology. Ditto granting interviews to the media.

Service to the larger community is a matter of conscience. Many of us have active social consciences. Our field is biased to select idealists because we believe the interesting variance lies in the situation. The situation is more mutable than variance that allegedly lies wholly within the individual (e.g., narrow interpretations of genetics, personality, prior development). If you believe that the situation influences people, then the answer to social problems lies in public policy that changes the situation. This is a liberal bias. (If you believe that the interesting variance lies within individuals, then public policy that changes the situation is fruitless; it would be better to minimize interventions because people are responsible for their own outcomes. This is a conservative bias.) Social psychologists tend to favor social change; the largest constituency of the Society of the Psychological Study of Social Issues is social psychologists. The practical use of good theories (Lewin, 1943) dates back to the origins of our field, for good reason.

Ethnic minorities and women tend to feel some obligation to give back to their own communities and to help vulnerable in-group members navigate the academic system. (For more on being an academic from one of these groups, see J. M. Jones [2003] and Park [2003].) People from underrepresented groups also get asked to serve on committees precisely so that their group is represented. This combination of factors can increase demands for service. In addition are all the informal networks that increase advising demands. Especially if you are yourself from an underrepresented group, keep an eye on people at comparable rank. If you are doing a lot more, go to your chair and discuss the issue. If the person won't help you cut back, do it yourself by saying no to additional commitments. If you sink under an untenable load of service, you are doing no one any long-run favors.

In department and university service, remember that service is not portable. Research is portable from job to job, and research reputations are the ticket to the next job. Teaching is somewhat portable—the class you prep one place may serve in another place. Service, however, is not especially portable, again unless you want to build an administrative career. Although service may earn you local gratitude and help you to network in the field, you can't live on gratitude, so keep a balance.

## CONCLUSION: FROM MADNESS TO THE METHODS

Offering generic advice about building a research program is a bit mad. I have argued here that the processes of developing a research career are knowable, manageable, and even fun. In doing this, I have drawn on my own experience, observations made, and advice received. I have definitely drawn from one particular perspective, and others will disagree. (For another perspective on beginning a program of research, see Zacks [2003]; for several wise perspectives on being an academic, see the collection of chapters in Darley, Zanna, and Roediger [2003].)

Research careers are highly idiosyncratic, and none is a universal example. As noted at the outset, my own research interests admittedly derive from a social issues perspective: experiences with neighborhood diversity, job-related sexism, organizational dynamics, and sheer wonder. My theoretical approaches have tended to emphasize the importance of social structure in understanding these phenomena. Whether people stereotype or individuate each other depends on situation-driven interaction goals (S. T. Fiske, Lin, et al., 1999; S. T. Fiske & Neuberg, 1990). Attention focuses up the power hierarchy in organizations because people's goals depend on people who

control resources. People higher up are less outcome-dependent on those lower down, so they are free to attend less carefully. Hence, they are vulnerable to stereotype others (S. T. Fiske, 1993a, 2000; Goodwin, Gubin, Fiske, & Yzerbyt, 2000). Men and women have particular kinds of power relations, as well as interdependence, which results in sexism having more than one dimension, sexist male benevolence directed toward cooperative female subordinates, and sexist male hostility directed toward competitive female peers and superiors superiors (both measured by the Ambivalent Sexism Inventory or ASI) (Glick & Fiske, 1996, 2001). Social structure shapes reactions to a variety of out-groups, depending on perceived status and competition, with predictable effects on perceived traits and emotional prejudices (S. T. Fiske, Cuddy, Glick, & Xu, 2002). I give these examples in an effort both to illustrate my own social issues perspective and to illustrate how different lines of work end up connecting.

How do all these personal-intellectual-social research puzzles become programmatic? Some of the links among these lines of research are deliberate, such as Peter Glick and me thinking hard about the nature of male-female interdependence and power relations, partly as a result of the prior work on outcome dependency. Some of the links are serendipitous, such as being convinced that out-groups include more texture than simple antipathy, and consequently thinking about envious prejudice against groups all over the world who immigrate as entrepreneurs (Jews in Europe, Indians in East Africa, Chinese in Indonesia, Koreans in Los Angeles), as well as paternalistic prejudice toward traditional women and people with disabilities; only later did we make the link to subtypes of women and the fit to the ASI. Some of the links are accident, pure and simple: My adviser in graduate school studied attention in social situations (Taylor & Fiske, 1975), so I became interested in that as a dependent variable. Probably an undergraduate degree in interdisciplinary social relations set the stage for these intellectual interests. People not only are shaped by their environments but also choose them. And this is only one person's story. It is OK to have multiple passions, to enter new areas, and to learn throughout one's career as one moves through different environments and areas of concern. Seemingly separate lines of work are likely to intersect over the course of one's career.

Whatever trajectory you create in building, maintaining, or refreshing a research program, doing what you love to do figures prominently on the agenda. One of the joys and challenges of being an academic is that you do set your own research agenda, largely planning your own use of time and energy. You can control your time and your research life, to some extent, so managing your research career can be deliberate to some extent. At a minimum, being aware of some of the processes in developing a research program makes you more aware of the choices.

## REFERENCES

Abelson, R. P. (1995). *Statistics as principled argument.* Hillsdale, NJ: Lawrence Erlbaum.

Asch, S. E. (1946). Forming impressions of personality. *Journal of Abnormal and Social Psychology, 41,* 258-290.

Bem, D. J. (2003). Writing the empirical journal article. In J. M. Darley, M. P. Zanna, & H. L. Roediger III (Eds.), *The compleat academic: A career guide* (2nd ed.). Washington, DC: American Psychological Association.

Bernstein, D. (2003). Tips for effective teaching. In J. M. Darley, M. P. Zanna, & H. L. Roediger III (Eds.), *The compleat academic: A career guide* (2nd ed.). Washington, DC: American Psychological Association.

Berscheid, E. (1992). A glance back at a quarter century of social psychology. *Journal of Personality and Social Psychology, 63,* 525-533.

Campbell, D. T., & Fiske, D. W. (1959). Convergent and discriminant validation by the multitrait-multimethod matrix. *Psychological Bulletin, 56,* 81-105.

Chaiken, S., & Trope, Y. (Eds.). (1999). *Dual process theories in social psychology.* New York: Guilford.

Cohen, J, (1990). Things I have learned (so far). *American Psychologist, 45,* 1304-1312.

Dahl, R. A. (1961). *Who governs? Democracy and power in an American city.* New Haven, CT: Yale University Press.

Darley, J. M., & Batson, C. D. (1973). "From Jerusalem to Jericho": A study of situational and dispositional variables in helping behavior. *Journal of Personality and Social Psychology, 27,* 100-108.

Darley, J. M., Zanna, M. P., & Roediger, H. L., III. (Eds.). (2003). *The compleat academic: A career guide* (2nd ed.). Washington, DC: American Psychological Association.

Feldman, K. A. (1987). Research productivity and scholarly accomplishment of college teachers as related to their instructional effectiveness: A review and exploration. *Research in Higher Education, 26,* 227-298.

Fine, M. A., & Kurdek, L. A. (1993). Reflections on determining authorship credit and authorship order on faculty-student collaborations. *American Psychologist, 48,* 1141-1147.

Fischhoff, B. (1975). Hindsight is not equal to foresight: The effect of outcome knowledge on judgment under uncertainty. *Journal of Experimental Psychology: Human Perception and Performance, 1,* 288-299.

Fiske, D. W., & Fogg, L. F. (1990). But the reviewers are making different criticisms of my paper! Diversity and uniqueness in reviewer comments. *American Psychologist, 45,* 591-598.

Fiske, S. T. (1993a). Controlling other people: The impact of power on stereotyping. *American Psychologist, 48,* 621-628.

Fiske, S. T. (1993b). Social cognition and social perception. In M. R. Rosenzweig & L. W. Porter (Eds.), *Annual review of psychology* (Vol. 44, pp. 155-194). Palo Alto, CA: Annual Reviews.

Fiske, S. T. (2000). Interdependence reduces prejudice and stereotyping. In S. Oskamp (Ed.), *Reducing prejudice and discrimination* (pp. 115-135). Mahwah, NJ: Erlbaum.

Fiske, S. T. (2002). A case for lumping—neatly: Building bridges within and outside psychological science. *American Psychological Society Observer, 15*(7), 5, 37.

Fiske, S. T., Cuddy, A. J., Glick, P., & Xu, J. (2002). A model of (often mixed) stereotype content: Competence and warmth respectively follow from perceived status and competition. *Journal of Personality and Social Psychology, 82,* 878-902.

Fiske, S. T., Lin, M. H., & Neuberg, S. L. (1999). The Continuum Model: Ten years later. In S. Chaiken & Y. Trope (Eds.), *Dual process theories in social psychology* (pp. 231-254). New York: Guilford.

Fiske, S. T., & Neuberg, S. L. (1990). A continuum model of impression formation, from category-based to individuating processes: Influence of information and motivation on attention and interpretation. In M. P. Zanna (Ed.), *Advances in experimental social psychology* (Vol. 23, pp. 1-74). New York: Academic Press.

Fogg, L., & Fiske, D. W. (1993). Foretelling the judgments of reviewers and editors. *American Psychologist, 48,* 293-294.

Glick, P., & Fiske, S. T. (1996). The Ambivalent Sexism Inventory: Differentiating hostile and benevolent sexism. *Journal of Personality and Social Psychology, 70,* 491-512.

Glick, P. & Fiske, S. T. (2001). Ambivalent sexism. In M. P. Zanna (Ed.), *Advances in experimental social psychology* (Vol. 33, pp. 115-188). New York: Academic Press.

Goodwin, S. A., Gubin, A., Fiske, S. T., & Yzerbyt, V. (2000). Power can bias impression formation: Stereotyping subordinates by default and by design. *Group Processes and Intergroup Relations, 3,* 227-256.

Hattie, J., & Marsh, H. W. (1996). The relationship between research and teaching: A meta-analysis. *Review of Educational Research, 66,* 507-542.

Heider, F. (1958). *The psychology of interpersonal relations.* New York: Wiley.

James, W. (1890). *The principles of psychology.* Cambridge, MA: Harvard University Press.

Jones, E. E., & Sigall, H. (1971). The bogus pipeline: A new paradigm for measuring affect and attitude. *Psychological Bulletin, 76,* 349-364.

Jones, J. M. (2003). The dialectics of race: Academic perils and promises. In J. M. Darley, M. P. Zanna, & H. L. Roediger III (Eds.), *The compleat academic: A career guide* (2nd ed.). Washington, DC: American Psychological Association.

Lewin, K. (1943). Psychology and the process of group living. *Journal of Social Psychology, SPSSI Bulletin, 17,* 113-131.

McGuire, W. J. (1973). The yin and yang of progress in social psychology: Seven koan. *Journal of Personality and Social Psychology, 26,* 446-456.

Milgram, S. (1965). Some conditions of obedience and disobedience to authority. *Human Relations, 18,* 57-76.

Park, D. (2003). Women in academia. In J. M. Darley, M. P. Zanna, & H. L. Roediger III (Eds.), *The compleat academic: A career guide* (2nd ed.). Washington, DC: American Psychological Association.

Roediger, H. L., III. (2003). Managing your career: The long view. In J. M. Darley, M. P. Zanna, & H. L. Roediger III (Eds.), *The compleat academic: A career guide* (2nd ed.). Washington, DC: American Psychological Association.

Ross, L., & Nisbett, R. E. (1991). *The person and the situation: Perspectives of social psychology*. New York: McGraw-Hill.

Ross, M., & Sicoly, F. (1979). Egocentric biases in availability and attribution. *Journal of Personality and Social Psychology, 37,* 322-336.

Steele, C. M., Spencer, S. J., & Aronson, J. (2002). Contending with group image: The psychology of stereotype and social identity threat. In M. P. Zanna (Ed.), *Advances in experimental social psychology* (Vol. 34, pp. 379-440). San Diego: Academic Press.

Steinberg, J. (2003). Obtaining a research grant: The view from the granting agency. In J. M. Darley, M. P. Zanna, & H. L. Roediger III (Eds.), *The compleat academic: A career guide* (2nd ed.). Washington, DC: American Psychological Association.

Sternberg, R. J. (1993). *The psychologist's companion: A guide to scientific writing for students and researchers* (3rd ed.). New York: Cambridge University Press.

Sternberg, R. J. (2003). Obtaining a research grant: The applicant's view. In J. M. Darley, M. P. Zanna, & H. L. Roediger III (Eds.), *The compleat academic: A career guide* (2nd ed.). Washington, DC: American Psychological Association.

Strunk, W., & White, E. B. (2000). *Elements of style* (4th ed.). Boston: Allyn & Bacon.

Taylor, S. E., & Fiske, S. T. (1975). Point of view and perceptions of causality. *Journal of Personality and Social Psychology, 32,* 439-445.

Taylor, S. E. (2003). The academic marathon: Controlling one's career. In J. M. Darley, M. P. Zanna, & H. L. Roediger III (Eds.), *The compleat academic: A career guide* (2nd ed.). Washington, DC: American Psychological Association.

Zacks, J. (2003). Setting up your lab and beginning a program of research. In J. M. Darley, M. P. Zanna, & H. L. Roediger III (Eds.), *The compleat academic: A career guide* (2nd ed.). Washington, DC: American Psychological Association.

Zajonc, R. B. (1994). Emotional expression and temperature modulation. In S.H.M. van Goozen & N. E. Van de Poll (Eds.),. *Emotions: Essays on emotion theory* (pp. 3-27). Hillsdale, NJ: Lawrence Erlbaum Associates.

Zanna, M. P. (2003). Mentoring: Managing the faculty-graduate student relationship. In J. M. Darley, M. P. Zanna, & H. L. Roediger III (Eds.), *The compleat academic: A career guide* (2nd ed.). Washington, DC: American Psychological Association.

# Part III

# DESIGN AND ANALYSIS

## Section A

### Implications of a Heterogeneous Population: Deciding for Whom to Test the Research Question(s), Why, and How

## CHAPTER 5

# Culturally Sensitive Research Questions and Methods in Social Psychology

JOAN G. MILLER

*New School University*

Social psychology is distinguished by its attention to the power of the situation and to the dynamics of social groups. It also is highly sensitive to the active role of the observer in making sense of experience. However, even with this sensitivity to context and to processes of individual construal and meaning making, the field gives little weight to culture in its theories and methods. The present chapter offers methodological strategies for enhancing the cultural sensitivity of social psychology, strategies that are critical in increasing the field's theoretical power and explanatory breadth, as well as its applied relevance. While involving design decisions, entailing such issues as sampling, choice of procedure, and interpretation of findings, the strategies also involve key conceptual issues, with strategies for enhancing the cultural sensitivity of research methods in social psychology depending on understanding the theoretical role of culture in informing the field's core conceptual notions. It must be recognized that psychological experience always occurs in and is, in part, constituted by sociocultural processes, resulting in a need to take culture into account in all research designs, even in work conducted with single populations.

There are many answers to the question of why cultural considerations must be considered in social psychological research. It is perhaps most commonly recognized that we need to attend to culture for *methodological control purposes*. It is critical to take into account culturally related differences in individuals' background, knowledge, experiences, or outlooks that may differentially affect their understandings of methodological procedures and lead to such procedures not having equivalent meaning for different subgroups. Thus, for example, populations that are unfamiliar with certain research stimuli may perform poorly on some of the standard items included on intelligence tests (Laboratory of Comparative Human Cognition, 1983). Likewise, even such mundane methodological strategies as tapping background information at the start of a questionnaire can have detrimental effects on performance for certain subgroups, as research on stereotype threat has documented (Steele & Aronson, 1995).

A second motive for attending to cultural issues is for *theory-testing purposes*. This type of effort is guided by concerns with assessing the assumed universality of existing psychological theories through sampling culturally diverse populations, as well as with identifying mediating or moderating variables that affect the manifestation of particular psychological effects. An example of this type of approach may be seen in comparative research that has tested the universality of Baumrind's highly influential model of parenting, a framework that was developed initially based on data from middle-class samples (Baumrind, 1996). This research has uncovered the important phenomenon that authoritarian parenting practices that had been found to have negative effects in middle-class environments tend to have positive effects in the context of dangerous and impoverished neighborhoods, in which they are associated with the provision of higher levels of support and supervision (Baldwin, Baldwin, & Cole, 1990).

Notably, culturally based research is also increasingly guided by *theory construction goals*, with this aim central to the newly reemerging perspective of cultural psychology (e.g., Fiske, Kitayama, Markus, & Nisbett, 1998; Markus, Kitayama, & Heiman, 1996; Miller, 1997, 1999; Shweder, 1990). This type of approach is concerned not merely with uncovering diversity in modes of psychological functioning but also with identifying the previously unrecognized cultural dependence of existing psychological theories. It was this type of agenda, for example, that motivated my early cross-cultural developmental investigation contrasting the everyday social explanations of samples of Euro-American and Hindu Indian adults and children (Miller, 1984). Previous developmental research had documented an age increase in dispositional inference (Damon & Hart, 1982; Livesley &

Bromley, 1973), a trend not only believed to be universal but also assumed to result from developmental changes in young children's cognitive facilities in abstraction and in the range of their experiences. My research documented that Hindu Indians do not display the age increase in dispositional inferences observed among U.S. respondents. Rather, they show an age increase in their emphasis on contextual factors—an age effect notably not observed among U.S. children. This work was important in offering a new explanation of the processes underlying developmental change in social attribution. It became clear that previous cognitive and experiential interpretations of age changes were incomplete and that it was critical to recognize that enculturation processes contribute to such age changes. It also became clear that the direction of developmental change in social attribution is culturally variable rather than universal, as previously assumed.

In sum, taking cultural considerations into account in social psychological research is needed not only for the methodological reasons of ensuring the validity of assessment techniques but also for the theoretical reasons of testing the universality of psychological theories and of formulating new conceptual models. Extending beyond merely an understanding of diversity in psychological functioning, such attention can provide new process understandings of the psychological functioning of widely studied Western populations.

## DOWNPLAYING OF CULTURAL ISSUES IN SOCIAL PSYCHOLOGY

Although recent years have seen a renewed interest in cultural issues in social psychology, such considerations nonetheless remain in a peripheral position in the field. Whereas increasing efforts are being made to sample culturally diverse subgroups, most contemporary social psychological research centers on the predominantly middle-class Euro-American college populations that historically have constituted the prototypic population for social psychological inquiry. Within the major textbooks and substantive handbooks in the field, basic theory tends to be presented in universal terms. Thus, in some illustrative examples, recent major handbooks of social psychology include only a single chapter devoted to cultural psychology, with the indexes revealing relatively few references to culture in the other chapters in the volumes (e.g., Gilbert, Fiske, & Lindzey, 1998; Higgins & Kruglanski, 1996).

To give increasing weight to sociocultural considerations in social psychology, it is critical to understand the reasons why culture tends to be downplayed in the field. It is these types of concerns that can be addressed through gaining a greater understanding of the nature of cultural processes and their role in psychological phenomena as well as through the adoption of more culturally sensitive methodological strategies.

## Key Reasons for Downplaying of Culture

The reasons for the downplaying of culture in social psychology are both conceptual and empirical. They reflect long-standing assumptions in the field about the nature of social psychological explanation as well as disappointment with the findings from various traditions of culturally based social psychological research.

### Culture-Free Approach to Situations

One of the landmark contributions of social psychology is that it has highlighted the power of situations in affecting behavior. It is this insight that underlies some of the early groundbreaking programs of research documenting ways in which situational influences can lead to antisocial behavior, such as in the Milgram conformity experiments (Milgram,

1963) or in the prison simulation study of Zimbardo and his colleagues (Haney, Banks & Zimbardo, 1973). In another example, this type of insight also informs contemporary research on priming and on the mere exposure effect, work that is documenting the power of situations to influence behavior in ways that are outside individuals' conscious awareness (e.g., Bargh, 1996; Bornstein, Kale, & Cornell, 1990). As approached within this dominant perspective, the situation is treated as presenting a veridical structure that can be known through inductive or deductive information processing. No consideration is given to culture as necessarily implicated in the definition of the situation or to cultural presuppositions as constituting prerequisites of what is considered objective knowledge. It is assumed that variability in judgment arises from differences in the information available to individuals or from differences in their informative processing, resulting in certain judgments being more or less cognitively adequate or veridical than others (Nisbett & Ross, 1980).

This realist view of situations gives rise to explanatory frameworks focused on factors in the situation and in the person. Within such frameworks, culture is viewed merely as a distal causal factor with impacts on psychological effects through its influences on proximal situational or person factors, rather than as a factor that itself contributes additional explanatory force. Thus, for example, in certain early models in cross-cultural psychology, such as the eco-cultural model developed by Berry (1976), the situation is treated as presenting varied resources and constraints that are seen as making varied forms of psychological response adaptive, such as field dependence being linked to agricultural modes of subsistence and field independence being linked to hunting and gathering modes (Berry, 1976; Witkin & Berry, 1975). This type of treatment of the situation, it should be emphasized, is important in taking into account that individuals from different backgrounds may be exposed to different ecological experiences. However, it treats culture merely as a consideration that is already accommodated in the social psychological focus on situational factors.

Equally, culture may be treated as an individual difference factor, a stance that is seen, for example, in the enthusiasm shown for assessing culture through individual difference approaches, such as scale measures of individualism/collectivism (e.g., see the recent review by Oyserman, Coon, & Kemmelmeier, 2002). From such a perspective, cultural group membership is viewed as giving rise to individual differences in attitudes, understandings, and available information. Thus, it is viewed as a consideration that already is taken into account in social psychological explanation, through the field's present attention to individual differences or person factors.

*Physical Science*
*Ideals of Explanation*

The tendency to downplay cultural considerations in social psychology also stems from the field's embrace of an idealized physical-science model of explanation. As Higgins and Kruglanski (1996) recently explained, this type of stance involves a view of psychological science as the search for deep structural explanatory mechanisms:

> A discovery of lawful principles governing a realm of phenomena is a fundamental objective of scientific research. . . . A useful scientific analysis needs to probe beneath the surface. In other words, it needs to get away from the "phenotypic" manifestations and strive to unearth the "genotypes" that may lurk beneath. (p. vii)

From this perspective, psychological processes are viewed as resembling the laws of physical science in being timeless, ahistorical, and culturally universal. In adopting this vision as its dominant research paradigm, social psychology has a tendency to consider cultural considerations as mere content effects and thus as factors that ideally should be held constant in order to focus on isolating more fundamental underlying psychological mechanisms (Malpass, 1988).

*Apparent Universality*
*and Explanatory Breadth*
*of Psychological Theories*

The limited interest shown in cultural research within social psychology also reflects the sense within the discipline that social psychological findings, in fact, have been documented in most cases to be cross-culturally robust and to have considerable explanatory scope. It is thus concluded that no significant cross-cultural variation exists in basic psychological phenomena (Brown, 1991).

The conclusion of apparent universality in cross-cultural research is linked with methodological strategies of administering existing research instruments in diverse cultural settings, after making only minor changes in their content to ensure familiarity, and narrowing the scope of the phenomena being investigated in ways that exclude possibly significant cultural variation. An example of the first type of approach may be seen in the extensive body of cross-cultural research that tested the universality of Kohlberg's theory of moral development, through administering standardized Kohlbergian research protocols in more than 45 different societies (Snarey, 1985). Although the results revealed that the distribution of the highest levels of moral development were highly skewed and the highest levels tended to be found primarily in Western urbanized cultures, Kohlberg and his colleagues interpreted the results as confirming the universality of his stage model, because all responses could be seen as either higher or lower stages of Kohlbergian moral stage development (Kohlberg, 1984; C. Levine,

Kohlberg, & Hewer, 1985). In turn, an example of the strategy of adopting methodological procedures that arguably exclude potentially significant sources of variation may be seen in research on the coding of emotional facial expressions. The widely accepted conclusion of fundamental similarity in basic emotion concepts that has emerged from the extensive cross-cultural research conducted on this topic (e.g., Ekman, 1992; Izard, 1992) stems, at least in part, from the use of procedures that tend to gloss over potentially significant sources of variation in emotion concepts, such as differences in how emotion concepts are expressed in everyday language usage, and that downplay the significance of lexicalized emotion terms whose translation into English-language concepts is inexact (see critique in Russell, 1994).

Indirect evidence for the universality of psychological theories also comes from the high levels of intercorrelation observed between psychological constructs. To illustrate, support for the universality of the theory of self-determination developed by Deci, Ryan, and their associates (Deci & Ryan, 1985, 1990) is based not only on research indicating that scales of autonomy support show the same empirical relationships in a country such as Bulgaria as they do in U.S. samples (Deci, Ryan, Gagne, et al., 2001) but also through studies demonstrating that self-determination constructs predict psychological functioning in related domains. In this regard, for example, it is demonstrated that self-determined motivation is related empirically to such variables as adaptive parenting, higher self-esteem, and higher stages of Kohlbergian moral development (e.g., Deci, Ryan, Gagne, et al., 2001; Grolnick, Deci, & Ryan, 1997; Grolnick & Ryan, 1989).

### Disappointment With Recent Cultural Traditions of Research

Finally, the downplaying of the significance of cultural research also reflects certain disillusionment with cultural research that was stimulated by Markus and Kitayama's (1991) groundbreaking article on culture and the self, with its introduction of the distinction between independent and interdependent cultural self-construals. One of the most widely cited articles ever in social psychology, this work has given rise to extensive research that has been inspired by this latter construct, with the focus on examining the extent to which variation in psychological functioning can be predicted by scale measures of this construct (Singelis, 1994; Triandis, 1995).

However, as recent criticisms of this rapidly growing literature make clear, the results observed utilizing scale measures of interdependent/independent self-construals have been disappointing (Hong, Morris, Chiu, & Benet-Martinez, 2000; Matsumoto, 1999; Oyserman et al., 2002). Much of the work has been associated with a stereotypical stance that glosses over important distinctions between and within cultures and that gives insufficient attention to the impact of context on behavior. The same type of sophisticated understanding of situational influences that is evident in mainstream social psychological research is not evident in this type of social psychological work, which much of is focused on cultural questions. Notably, work in this tradition is also yielding findings that, in some cases, appear to contradict directly the claims of the interdependent/independent self-construal paradigm, such as the findings reported by Oyserman et al. (2002), based on their extensive meta-review, that "relationship and family orientation are not empirically closely linked to collectivism" (p. 43).

### CONCEPTUAL ISSUES IN GIVING MORE ATTENTION TO CULTURE

The remainder of this chapter focuses on specific methodological research strategies that are important to adopt in enhancing the cultural sensitivity of social psychological research. Before turning directly to these methodological strategies, however, attention first focuses briefly on some of the conceptual issues that must inform such methodological efforts and that respond to some of the reasons for the field's downplaying of culture noted above. These considerations bear on the nature of culture and its influences on psychological processes.

## Views of Culture

From an ecological perspective, culture is understood as adaptations to the varying requirements of contrasting physical and social structural environments (e.g., Bronfenbrenner, 1979; Whiting & Whiting, 1975). Ecological approaches to culture are of value in highlighting the varied resources and constraints that individuals from different sociocultural communities experience and that influence their behavior. For example, ecological frameworks have informed most contemporary psychological studies with U.S. minority populations, and this work is calling attention to ways in which individuals' access to differential resources and their experiences of bias and discrimination affect important intellectual, social, and health outcomes (e.g., McLoyd & Flanagan, 1990; Neighbors & Jackson, 1996). It may be noted, however, that whereas ecological approaches to culture extend the dominant social psychological models in their recognition that the adaptive context for psychological development is culturally variable, rather than universal, these approaches retain a view of the context as an objective environment. In this respect, then, while essential, such approaches do not challenge the traditional social psychological explanatory focus on features of the person and of the objective situation. For this reason, it is critical to complement ecological approaches to culture with approaches that are symbolically grounded.

Symbolic approaches treat culture as shared meanings that are embodied in artifacts and practices and that form a medium for human development (e.g., Cole, 1995; D'Andrade, 1984; R. A. LeVine, 1984; Shore, 1996). It is recognized that cultural meanings and practices not only represent experience but also are constitutive of experience, in serving to create socially constituted realities (Bartlett, 1932). For example, not only do social categories and institutions depend on cultural definitions (e.g., "bride," "marriage"), but even psychological concepts are recognized to be, in part, culturally based. Thus, as seen in the example of the Japanese concept of *amae*[1] (Doi, 1992; Russell, 1991), even psychological phenomena, such as emotions, depend in part on cultural distinctions embodied in natural language categories, discourse, and everyday social practices (Shweder, 1984; Wierzbicka, 2002).

Challenging the identification of cultural processes exclusively with the situational factors taken into account in social psychological explanation, a symbolic approach to culture highlights the need to recognize that cultural meanings do not bear a one-to-one relationship to objective aspects of the situation. Culture then cannot be understood merely by consideration of the objective affordances and constraints of particular contexts but instead requires taking into account cultural beliefs, values, and practices that are not purely functionally based. To give an example, research has shown that Japanese teachers consider the ideal teacher/student ratio in preschools to be considerably higher than do their U.S. counterparts (Tobin, Wu, & Davidson, 1989). The decisive consideration notably is not the consideration of higher cost in teacher salaries but the value of socializing children to be competent members of social groups. As one Japanese teacher explained, "Children need to have the experience of being in a large group in order to learn to relate to lots of kinds of children in lots of kinds of situations" (Tobin et al., 1989, p. 37).

## Integrating Cultural Considerations With Situational and Person Factors

Finally, it must be recognized that cultural considerations complete but do not replace the focus on situational and person factors in social psychological explanation. This implies that hypotheses involving cultural influences need to be formulated in ways that take into account both contextual variation and individual differences. Equally, it must be recognized that in many cases the impact of individual difference and of contextual factors may themselves be culturally variable. For example, research has shown that whereas U.S. respondents utilize more abstract self-references in a task context that is abstract as compared with concrete, Japanese respondents display the opposite effect of context (Cousins, 1989).

In sum, the key to enhancing the cultural sensitivity of social psychology is understanding culture and its role in psychological functioning. Attention must be paid to culture as an ecological context that presents certain objective affordances and constraints, as well as to culture as a symbolic environment that entails certain meanings and practices that are not entirely functionally based. It must be recognized that a consideration of culture does not replace an attention to person and situational factors but contributes an additional dimension to social psychological explanation.

## METHODOLOGICAL STRATEGIES FOR ENHANCING CULTURAL SENSITIVITY

Building on the conceptual issues discussed above, this section identifies methodological strategies that are valuable to adopt in efforts to enhance the cultural sensitivity of social psychology. The strategies discussed include considerations that are important not only in comparative research designs but also in research that does not focus explicitly on cultural questions and/or on tapping culturally

diverse populations. Given the reality of psychological experience always occurring in specific cultural contexts, sensitivity to cultural issues is needed in all social psychological investigations.

## Cultural Understanding

As a field, social psychology bases many of its research hypotheses, in part, on informal observations made by researchers about behavioral effects that they have observed or personally experienced. In this regard, it is not uncommon for social psychologists to draw on informal personal anecdotes as a preliminary way of communicating to readers the nature of a particular effect. In fact, it has even been argued that much of the success of social psychology, in terms of the generative nature of its ideas and its applied relevance, reflects this interplay between lay understandings and formal scientific inquiry. As Moscovici once commented:

> The real advance made by American social psychology was . . . in the fact that it took for its theme of research and for the content of its theories the issues of its own society. Its merit was as much in its techniques as in translating the problems of American society into sociopsychological terms and in making them an object of scientific inquiry. (1972, p. 19)

A concern that may be raised about this type of stance, however, entails its cultural boundedness. The assumptions that make the research questions and hypotheses of social psychology compelling for North American psychologists, because they speak to issues that are familiar and socially meaningful, contribute to making them less significant for researchers from other cultural groups who may not share these same cultural experiences and outlooks. As conveyed in the following firsthand account by a Chinese psychologist, individuals from other cultural backgrounds may find that their own assumptions and concerns are not adequately taken into account:

> I found the reasons why doing Westernized psychological research with Chinese subjects was no longer satisfying or rewarding to me. When an American psychologist, for example, was engaged in research, he or she could spontaneously let his or her American cultural and philosophical orientations and ways of thinking be freely and effectively reflected in choosing a research question, defining a concept, constructing a theory and designing a method. On the other hand, when a Chinese psychologist in Taiwan was conducting research, his or her strong training by overlearning the knowledge and methodology of American psychology tended to prevent his or her Chinese values, ideas, concepts and ways of thinking from being adequately reflected in the successive stages of the research process. (Yang, 1997, p. 65)

As Yang suggests, there is a sense in which culturally specific themes influence all phases of the research process, often unintentionally excluding certain other cultural sensibilities.

The present considerations highlight the importance, as part of the initial phase of any program of psychological research, of researchers working to enhance their understanding both of their own cultural backgrounds and of those of their participant populations and of challenging the tendency within psychology to privilege the perspectives of middle-class Euro-Americans. As Reid (1994) observed:

> Culture has not so much been ignored in mainstream research as it has been assumed to be homogeneous, that is, based on a standard set of values and expectations primarily held by White and middle-class populations. The research literature across the subdisciplinary areas in psychology demonstrates clearly this assumption of cultural homogeneity. For example, in developmental psychology, *children* means White children (McLoyd, 1990); in psychology of women, *women* generally refers to White women (Reid, 1988). When we mean other than White, it is specified. (Reid, 1994, p. 525)

It must be recognized that there is no single human population that can serve as a normative baseline for understanding human development (see also Miller, 2001a; Shweder & Sullivan, 1993).

In working to gain an understanding of cultural sensibilities that differ from the researcher's own background, it is important to seek cultural knowledge that, as far as is feasible, is nuanced and specific to the particular group under consideration. This implies that researchers should avoid turning to the widely utilized scale measures of individualism/collectivism to provide this type of insight, because of the limited cultural sensitivity of such measures (Miller, 2002). Fortunately, whereas some commitment is required on the part of the researcher to make the necessary effort to acquire a greater understanding of other cultural viewpoints, many strategies are available for achieving this goal.

One valuable strategy for obtaining knowledge about other cultures involves drawing from relevant research literature in related fields, such as anthropology and sociolinguistics, work that in many instances may be ethnographic in nature. In the case of my own research in India, for example, I was able to develop insight into Hindu Indian culture through reading available anthropological and philosophical literature on Hindu Indian beliefs, practices, values, and everyday family life. Notably, one can see the same kind of stance as having informed the perspective adopted by Markus and Kitayama (1991) in their seminal article on culture and the self. Thus, although they proposed a global distinction linked to individualism/collectivism, the references cited in the article are grounded primarily in interdisciplinary research focused specifically on Japan.

Collaborating with a member of the comparison cultural community under consideration represents another valuable strategy for gaining cultural knowledge, one that may be particularly useful in cases in which there is little or no available research literature on a particular community. Ideally, such collaborations should include researchers who have both insider and outsider knowledge of the cultures under consideration (Greenfield, 1997a). Collaborations of this type have been extremely generative in recent cultural research in social psychology, as illustrated by the growing numbers of studies being conducted involving researchers drawn from the United States and from various East Asian cultural groups (e.g., Ji & Nisbett, 2000; Peng & Nisbett, 1999).

Greater cultural understanding also may be obtained through building into research projects, as a prelude to formal data collection, activities and procedures that focus on gaining insight into the outlooks and practices of particular cultural populations. This can entail spending time in such communities conducting informal observations. For example, in the case of my first series of studies in India, I lived for several months in Mysore, India, prior to initiating any formal data collection, as a means of gaining insight into the culture through observing and participating in everyday life. In cases in which it is not feasible to undertake informal preliminary observations of this type, focus group techniques provide a highly valuable approach that may be utilized to gain cultural insight (Hughes & DuMont, 1993; Knodel, 1993). A form of organized small-group discussions, focus groups constitute small groups that investigators assemble and engage in processes of informal group discussion, as a means of tapping participants' personal experiences and reactions to particular topics (Powell & Single, 1996, p. 499). The goal of focus groups is to make possible the gathering of qualitative information regarding the attitudes, beliefs, and feelings of participants, as expressed within a group context. Focus groups offer the advantage of being highly flexible and can be employed effectively both to explore general cultural concerns and to tap respondents' open-ended reactions to issues identified as of theoretical interest in a particular research program.

## Sampling

Attention needs to be given to the cultural implications of different types of sampling strategies. In this regard, effort should be made to go beyond the present tendency for most social psychological research to be conducted on convenience samples of college students. In fact, the need to go beyond convenience samples has been emphasized in the National Institutes of Health's recent mandate to address minority inclusion (or scientifically justify exclusion) explicitly as part of all currently submitted grant proposals.

### Noncomparative "Prototypic" Sampling Strategies

The prototypic sampling strategy in social psychology is noncomparative, with such research experimentally manipulating situational effects or assessing individual differences, while tapping a population (generally college students) that is treated as though it is homogeneous and can provide grounds for making universal claims. In efforts to increase the cultural sensitivity of this type of sampling practice, it is essential not only for researchers to acknowledge potential limitations on the generality of their findings from this type of design but also to give greater conceptual attention to the nature of these limitations. Thus, qualifications on the generality of results should not be issued in a perfunctory way. Rather, it is important for researchers to address in what *specific* respects a claim may be anticipated to be culturally bound or, alternatively, the question of for what *specific* reasons it is likely to prove universal. In short, serious attention needs to be given to the cultural meaning of research findings, even when employing sampling designs that are noncomparative in nature and not explicitly focused on cultural questions.

Equally, greater effort must be paid to unplanned sources of cultural heterogeneity that exist within particular research samples and that are commonly overlooked in the default stance of treating populations as though they are culturally homogeneous. Thus, whenever there are sufficiently large numbers of participants in different cultural subgroups to make this feasible, effort should be made to conduct separate analyses of effects within subgroups to observe empirically whether similar results obtain in all cases. It is recommended that subgroups be analyzed at levels that are linked with cultural traditions and that attend as well to issues of socioeconomic status. It is important that analyses of this type be undertaken in ways that are sensitive to areas of overlap and intermixing between subgroups. As theorists have emphasized (Hermans & Kempen, 1998; Phinney, 1999), cultures assume hybrid forms as a result of the many interconnections and transformations occurring between populations, and thus it is problematic to conceptualize cultures as discrete geographically defined entities. Nonetheless, taking group membership into account provides a vehicle for giving "voice" to the outlooks of different communities, perspectives that may be obscured in stances[2] that deny the possibility of making any distinctions between groups on cultural grounds (Jahoda, 1986; Miller, 1997).

### Noncomparative Cultural Sampling Strategies

Sampling of noncomparative cultural populations also may be utilized effectively in research that is focused explicitly on cultural questions. These projects generally are motivated either by a concern with obtaining normative data or by the methodological requirements of particular research methodologies, such as ethnographic or case study approaches.

Sampling of single cultural populations is increasingly being adopted in research as a means of working to expand the normative baseline for psychological theory, with such efforts encouraged by major U.S. funding organizations, such as the National Science Foundation (NSF) and National Institutes of Health (NIH), in their issuing of specific calls for research with underrepresented minority populations. It is recognized that psychological theory can effectively be made more culturally inclusive only when its descriptive base is broadened to include information about psychological functioning in diverse cultural samples. This type of sampling approach, it may be noted, also is occurring through the increasing internationalization of social psychology, with new journals, such as the *Asian Journal of Social Psychology*, supporting work on exclusively Asian samples, even as the journal also publishes comparative studies.

Sampling of single cultural populations represents the strategy of choice in ethnographic or case study research, in which the focus is on a single cultural setting, if not on a single population from that setting. To illustrate, ethnographic work conducted with inner-city African American families is providing highly informative and in-depth accounts of the multiple environmental stresses experienced within such communities and of the complex patterns of coping observed (e.g., Burton, Allison, & Obeidallah, 1995; Jarrett, 1995), whereas recent ethnographic work among urban street gangs is affording access to study populations and settings that generally remain untapped by questionnaire or survey approaches (e.g., Heath, 1996). In another example, ethnographic case study techniques are adopted commonly in work by sociocultural theorists (e.g., Cole, 1996) in their examination of how use of cultural tools or modes of cultural social organization affect cognition.

## Comparative Cultural Sampling Strategies

Comparative cultural sampling designs are employed commonly in research that tests the universality of particular psychological effects or that examines cultural variation in basic psychological constructs and theories. In such work, it is important for sampling decisions to be culturally nuanced.

In utilizing comparative studies to examine cultural influences on social psychological phenomena, greater consideration must be given to the distinctive nature of cultural orientations (e.g., Dien, 1999; Harkness, Super, & van Tijen, 2000). Equally, greater attention needs to be paid to the overlap and heterogeneity of cultural perspectives. To illustrate, cultural research is pointing to fundamental variation in psychological processes that is subtler in form than is captured in the individualism/collectivist dichotomy. Thus, for example, the concern with affection and respect that Robin Harwood, Nydia Irizarry, and I (Harwood, Miller, & Irizarry, 1995) have found to be central to the outlooks on attachment emphasized by Puerto Rican mothers differs not only from the focus on balancing autonomy and connectedness emphasized among Euro-Americans and assumed within attachment theory (e.g., Ainsworth, 1978) but also from the concern with *amae* identified within Japanese populations (Rothbaum, Weisz, Pott, Miyake, & Morelli, 2000; Yamaguchi, 2001). Equally, the voluntaristic outlook on interpersonal morality that is assumed in Carol Gilligan's morality of caring model (Gilligan, 1982) differs not only from the interpersonal moral outlooks based on *dharma*[3] that tend to be emphasized among Hindu Indian and Buddhist populations (Huebner & Garrod,

1991; Miller, 1994) but also from the focus on maintaining good interpersonal relations that is more central in Japan (Shimizu, 2001). Notably, these examples do not imply that distinct psychological theories need to be formulated for every cultural or subcultural group (see arguments for generality in Miller, 2001b, 2002); however, they caution against the tendency, which is reflected in the contemporary widespread reliance on measures of independent/interdependent self-construals, to adopt comparative designs that gloss over this type of significant variation.

As emphasized in recent anthropological work on culture (e.g., Shore, 1996; Strauss & Quinn, 1997), it also is important to give more attention to within-culture variation in perspectives related to factors such as socioeconomic status and even place. This implies adopting more fluid outlooks on cultural boundaries and avoiding the common tendency in psychology to identify cultures with nation states or even larger units, as when speaking of "East Asian" or "North American" cultures. Illustrating the informative nature of such a stance, research has uncovered variation in individualism across different regions of the United States (Plaut, Markus, & Lachman, 2002; Vandello & Cohen, 1999) as well as documented qualitative variation in forms of individualism linked to socioeconomic status (Kusserow, 1999).

## Representativeness and Equivalence in Sampling

Although it is important to address concerns about the anticipated cultural generality of results, it also must be recognized that representative sampling is not an essential feature of culturally based research designs and, with the exception of large-scale surveys, it is rarely achieved in social psychology. Just as there is no expectation that researchers who are sampling U.S. college students need to tap a representative sample of college students from across the nation, much less the world, there should be no expectation that researchers who may be comparing the responses of U.S. and Japanese college students need to tap populations that are representative of all Americans, much less of all Japanese. This implies that reviewers should not utilize representative sampling as a criterion in evaluating culturally based psychological research because such a standard would lead to all such work being appraised negatively, with the exception of large-scale survey designs.

In lieu of the criterion of samples being representative, however, concern needs to be given to achieving equivalence in the populations tapped in comparative studies and in individuals' responses to research stimuli. Given the skewing of samples that can result, matching samples on preexisting background characteristics should be avoided or utilized only to a minimal extent. Rather, it is preferable, to the extent feasible, to identify naturally occurring samples that are as comparable as possible, in terms of background characteristics salient in the particular study (Cole & Means, 1986). To control for possible confounding preexisting group differences, use also may be made of such statistical control techniques as covariate analysis or the partialing out of variance. To illustrate, in one study in which we assessed U.S. and Indian respondents' moral appraisals of hypothetical research vignettes, we observed that the two groups differed in their perceptions of the commonness of the vignettes portrayed (Bersoff & Miller, 1993). To control for this a priori difference, we utilized a regression procedure to partial out the variance predicated by participants' commonness ratings from their moral reasoning responses (Bersoff & Miller, 1993).

The inclusion of control samples in research designs is a valuable strategy that may be employed in efforts to rule out alternative interpretations of particular effects related to sampling—a technique that is particularly valuable in two-group research designs, given the many uncontrolled sources of variation that may influence any effect (Cook & Campbell, 1979). Use of this type of comparative sampling is illustrated in my early cross-cultural research on social attribution (Miller, 1984). In that investigation, the central cross-cultural comparisons involved middle-class Hindu Indian and middle-class Euro-American samples. However, to evaluate potential alternative interpretations of the results, additional sampling was undertaken both of a lower-class Hindu Indian sample and of a Westernized middle-class Christian Anglo-Indian sample. The finding that no effects of socioeconomic differences were observed within the two Hindu subgroups provided evidence to suggest that differences in wealth could not explain the attributional variation observed in the main U.S./India cross-cultural comparison. The finding that Anglo-Indians displayed a pattern of social attribution that was intermediate between that observed among the middle-class Hindu Indian and middle-class U.S. samples lent support to the claim that a tendency to emphasize personality factors in social attribution is related to Westernization.

### Culture as Process

Within contemporary social psychology, widespread use is made of the scale measure of independent/interdependent self-construals developed by Singelis (1994) as well as of other measures of individualism/collectivism developed by researchers in the tradition of cross-cultural psychology (see, e.g., Triandis, 1995). Interest also is shown in priming as a way of simulating cultural effects under experimentally controlled conditions (e.g., Hong et al., 2000; Oyserman et al., 2002). However, serious limitations exist in both of these strategies, leaving a need to adopt more dynamic methodological approaches.

As critics have noted (e.g., Miller, 2002; Strauss, 2000), scale measures of individualism/

collectivism and of independent/interdependent self-construals subsume cultural variation into two fundamental types, a stance that glosses over variation in outlooks that exists between and within different cultural communities. Furthermore, individual items on these scales tend to portray collectivist cultures in somewhat pejorative terms and to lack adequate construct validity. Such characteristics may be seen in the inclusion of items that portray the self as subordinate to the group in collectivist outlooks.[4] As recent research has shown, however, the self may be experienced as satisfied and fulfilled, rather than as subordinated, in the fulfillment of the types of role expectations emphasized in various collectivist communities (e.g., Iyengar & Lepper, 1999; Miller, in press-b; Miller & Bersoff, 1994). Measures of individualism/collectivism also are problematic in treating psychological processes as bearing a one-to-one relationship to cultural outlooks, a stance that fails to recognize the extent to which behavior is normatively based rather than reflective of individual attitudes or personality (Shweder, 1979; Takano & Osaka, 1999). Given these many weaknesses, it is not surprising that many results obtained utilizing individualism/collectivism scales are of questionable validity (Matsumoto, 1999; Oyserman et al., 2002; Takano & Osaka, 1999). For example, whereas findings within the United States based on individualism/collectivism scales show Latinos as no higher in collectivism than Euro-Americans (Coon & Kemmelmeier, 2001), such a finding does not accord with the conclusions stemming from research that does not rely on individualism/collectivism measures (e.g., Delgado-Gaitan, 1994; Harwood et al., 1995).

It also is problematic to utilize priming approaches to simulate cultural processes and to measure individualism/collectivism. As discussed elsewhere (Miller, 2002), it is not possible to interpret a particular behavioral response, such as a dispositional inference, that might be primed as reflective of an individualistic or collectivist outlook without understanding other cultural meanings to which the response is linked. Dispositional and situational inferences are generated in all cultural groups, with their display affected by contextual factors. Thus, when individuals make a dispositional or situational inference in a priming task, this may be merely because the prime is serving as a contextual manipulation and not because it represents a manipulation of cultural outlook per se.

In lieu of utilizing scale measures to assess individualism/collectivism or priming approaches to tap cultural processes,[5] it is recommended that researchers adopt process-oriented approaches to culture (Greenfield, 1997a). This includes tapping more directly the psychological processes that are implicated in particular culturally variable psychological responses as well as assessing the everyday cultural routines and practices that support such responses.

Methodological approaches that tap the psychological processes underlying particular effects include such strategies as assessing online processing as well as identifying culturally variable patterns of functional relationships (Kitayama, 2002). Online processing involves evaluating information immediately as it is encountered and contrasts with cognitive processing based on long-term memory The use of online processing to explore cultural influences is illustrated in a recent comparative study on the correspondence bias, an attributional tendency in which an individual's dispositions are seen as corresponding to his or her behavior even when the behavior is socially constrained (Miyamoto & Kitayama, 2002). This investigation not only demonstrated that Japanese respondents are less vulnerable to this bias than are U.S. respondents but also importantly showed that this difference is linked to contrasting types of online attitudinal inferences. Thus, it was demonstrated that, in contrast to the U.S. respondents, the Japanese respondents were more situationally focused in their online inferences. In turn, the approach of identifying culturally variable patterns of functional relationships is illustrated in cross-cultural research highlighting the contrasting cultural meanings accorded to shyness. Thus, it has been demonstrated that whereas social reticence tends to be linked to negative outcomes in family and school contexts within North American cultural settings (Kagan, 1994), it is linked to positive family and school outcomes within China (Chen, Rubin, & Li, 1995).

Greater effort also needs to be paid to assessing cultural practices (see, e.g., Greenfield, 1997a; Markus, Mullally, & Kitayama, 1997; Phinney & Landin, 1998; Shweder, Goodnow, Hatano, LeVine, Markus, & Miller, 1998). The value of this type of approach is illustrated in recent research by Evans (2001) which showed that differences in the receptivity to creationist beliefs among fundamentalist vs. nonfundamentalist U.S. Christian families could be explained, in part, by the families' everyday social practices such as having books on dinosaurs in their homes and attending church regularly. Likewise, in a different example, it has been by focusing on differences in everyday social practices in schools and homes, such as time spent on academic tasks and styles of teaching, that Stevenson and his colleagues have been able to identify the cultural processes that underlie the dramatic differences in mathematics achievement that distinguish U.S. from Chinese and Japanese schoolchildren (Stevenson & Lee, 1990; Stigler, Lee, & Stevenson, 1987). (For work utilizing situation sampling techniques to assess cultural practices, see, e.g., Kitayama, Markus, Matsumoto, & Norasakkunkit, 1997.)

## Culturally Appropriate Measures

Finally, it is critical that the procedures that are adopted in social psychological research be culturally sensitive. Presupposing cultural understanding, this sensitivity is a matter of ensuring both that measures are equivalent in meaning for different populations and that they are culturally informative. The first issue represents a long-standing concern in cross-cultural psychology and bears fundamentally on issues of reducing bias in comparative research designs (for extended discussion of these issues, see, e.g., Greenfield, 1997a, 1997b; van de Vijver, 2001; van de Vijver & Leung, 1997). In turn, the second issue, which to date has received more limited attention, bears on ensuring that the constructs tapped in psychological measuring instruments are sufficiently culturally inclusive to accommodate diverse outlooks.

In terms of ensuring the equivalence of measuring instruments in different cultural or subcultural populations, it is critical not merely to adopt such conventional strategies as the use of back translation but also to take into account the contrasting expectations, social knowledge, values, and modes of communication maintained by individuals of different sociocultural backgrounds. To illustrate, certain populations may be unfamiliar with the convention that psychological tests are not designed to measure socially useful information and thus may respond to an IQ-type measure with an answer that is pragmatically useful but that is scored as incorrect according to the norms of the test (e.g., Greenfield, 1997b). For example, village populations have been observed to respond spontaneously in object-sorting cognitive tasks by grouping items into functionally meaningful pairings (e.g., grouping a knife and potato together because the knife is used to cut the potato) rather than into the taxonomic groupings expected by the researchers (e.g., grouping all implement items together, all food items together) (Cole, Gay, Glick, & Sharp, 1971). Interestingly, this type of difference can lead, in certain cases, to various populations experiencing difficulty in responding to multiple-choice questions. Thus, in research among the

Zinacantecan Maya, Greenfield and Childs (1977) observed that respondents with limited schooling treated the multiple options provided in multiple-choice questionnaires as patterns to be put together to create a larger meaning, rather than as discrete options whose only function is to test understanding. The social context of the test situation also may affect the level of comfort that individuals experience in testing situations and their readiness to respond. Thus, for example, Mexican-immigrant parents within the United States spontaneously use questioning less frequently as a conversational strategy at home than do Euro-American parents, a cultural difference that is reflected in the former being more reluctant to answer questions in standard interviewing situations (Delgado-Gaitan, 1994; Greenfield, 1997b).

Notably, in working to ensure the cross-group appropriateness of measures, equivalence needs to be achieved at the level of meaning, a feature that may require utilizing somewhat different objective procedures in different groups. As Greenfield (1997b) observed, "the use of *parallel* procedures across cultures . . . works best when cultures are not too different . . . the use of *qualitatively different* procedures across cultures works best when the cultures are very different" (p. 308). To illustrate use of this type of strategy, in my early cross-cultural attribution research (Miller, 1984), my decision to have individuals explain events from their own experiences, rather than to respond to identical experimentally constructed event situations that I supplied to them, was motivated by a sense that greater equivalence in meaning could be obtained in this way, since the behaviors being explained would have greater ecological validity for all cultural and age groups.

In turn, to ensure the cultural inclusiveness of research methods, it is critically important to recognize that many assessment instruments currently in use embody culturally

specific assumptions and need to be broadened conceptually to accommodate the diverse outlooks of contrasting cultural and subcultural populations. Until this is done, the field will continue to yield results that, while identifying apparent universals, are based on methods that lack sufficient cultural sensitivity to succeed in tapping the cultural variability that exists. It is this property of present psychological research methodology, in fact, that leads psychological research to form somewhat of a closed system, in which it becomes difficult to produce findings that challenge the explanatory scope of existing theoretical models and in which results on diverse psychological measures tend to be highly intercorrelated (Miller, in press-a). Thus, for example, it was only when researchers developed new conceptual models for understanding morality, such as in Gilligan's (1982) morality of caring framework and in various cultural approaches (e.g., Miller, 1994; Snarey, 1985), as well as provided methodologies that were sensitive enough to tap this variation, that the conclusion of the universality of the Kohlbergian model of moral development was challenged effectively.

The present considerations highlight the need for researchers to be more aware of the extent to which the response options provided on standard questionnaires or coding schemes may lack sufficient cultural sensitivity to succeed in tapping the outlooks of diverse cultural populations. Thus, for example, in the scales utilized in research on self-determination theory (e.g., Deci & Ryan, 1987), the "external" motivational orientation is conceptualized as a stance involving the fear of external sanctions, as reflected in items such as "Because I will get in trouble if I don't do well," whereas the "identified" and "intrinsic" motivational stances are conceptualized as involving autonomous individual interest, as reflected in items such as "Because I want to understand the subject" and "Because it's important to *me* to do my homework." These types of response alternatives, however, do not capture the endogenous view of social expectations emphasized in a culture such as Hindu India, in which the motive to uphold duty relates to spiritual fulfillment, not fear of sanctions or mere social conformity (Miller, in press-b). To give another example, the emphasis on training (*chiao shun*) observed among Chinese Americans, as Chao (1994) points out, includes an emphasis on positive affect in conjunction with highly directive parental behavior. It then is not accommodated in the theoretical framework of parenting developed by Baumrind, which presents a scheme for conceptualizing and coding parental behavior into alternatives that link parenting either to an affectively harsh stance ("authoritarian" parenting) or to stances that are much less directive (i.e., either "authoritative" or "permissive" parenting).

To address the issue of the insufficient culturally inclusive nature of the constructs tapped in many existing psychological measuring instruments, the constructs embodied in our methods need to be expanded. Thus, to give an example, cultural researchers have argued for including the construct of relationship harmony and not only the construct of self-esteem in tapping the predictors of life satisfaction (Kwan, Bond, & Singelis, 1997). It is also valuable to utilize assessment instruments that are less constraining of response options and more accommodating to diverse cultural viewpoints. Thus, in my own programs of research, for example, I have tended to rely heavily on methodological approaches that are less directive than standardized questionnaires, such as tapping responses to the projective measure of hypothetical vignette situations (e.g., Miller & Bersoff, 1998) and utilizing open-ended questioning to explore individuals' reasoning (Miller & Bersoff, 1995) (see also King, Chapter 8, this volume; Peng, Nisbett, & Wong, 1997).

## CONCLUSIONS

In conclusion, bringing culture more centrally into the methods of social psychology is integrally related to bringing culture more centrally into the constructs and theories of the field. As has been argued here, the relative invisibility of culture in social psychology, and in psychology more generally, stems in part from the limited attention that we give it in our theories, as well as from our adoption of methods that are insufficiently sensitive to the impact of cultural processes on psychological phenomena. As Matsumoto (2001) recently commented, "all psychologists are cross-cultural in some way; the only difference is in whether they are aware of the cultures being studied, and whether this comparison is explicit or implicit in their work" (p. ix).

The effort to make social psychology more culturally inclusive must build on the complexity and sophistication of the discipline, with the onus on cultural researchers to develop approaches to culture that, in their attention to the nuances of cultural outlooks and to the contextual dependence and often implicit nature of psychological phenomena, embody the rich insights of contemporary social psychology. Equally critical, however, is the need to overcome the complacency of social psychology, which has resulted in relegating culture to a peripheral role as a mere descriptive enterprise with little implication for basic theory. As has been shown, the conceptual stances, sampling practices, and methodological approaches that constitute the mainstream perspective of the discipline have, in many cases, obscured significant cultural variation, yielding findings of universality that may be more apparent than real.

Notably, taking cultural considerations into account more centrally in social psychology promises to yield a richer understanding of basic psychological processes and of the diversity of outlooks that characterize human psychological functioning. Such an effort, which needs to be integrated with efforts to identify brain and other biological foundations for psychological behavior, stands to produce a discipline that is not only more truly universal but also more theoretically sophisticated in its process accounts of psychological phenomena and in its applied implications.

---

## NOTES

1. Experienced in the context of close relationships that entail both attachment and dependence, the Japanese concept of *amae* involves feelings of being able "to depend and presume upon another's love or bask in another's indulgence" (Doi, 1992, p. 8). Individuals experience *amae* in close relationships in being able to presume that their inappropriate behavior will be accepted by their counterpart (Yamaguchi, 2001).

2. Within social psychology, stances that deny the possibility of distinguishing between cultural traditions have been adopted by theorists associated with such postmodern perspectives as social constructionism and discursive psychology (e.g., Edwards, 1995; Gergen, 1992, 1994; Shotter, 1993). As Gergen commented:

We are not speaking . . . of the blending of all, the emergence of monoculture, but rapid and continuous transformations in cultural forms, as they are subject to multiple influences. . . . If there is a continuous blending, appropriation, dissolution, and the like, how are we to draw distinctions among cultural processes? (Gergen, as interviewed in Gulerce, 1995, pp. 149-150)

3. The concept of *dharma* denotes both moral duty and inherent character and is based on perceived spiritually based laws of nature (Marriott, 1990).

4. This type of assumption can be seen, for example, in the following items that appear on the widely used Singelis (1994) measure of independent vs. interdependent self construals: "I will sacrifice my self-interest for the group that I am in" and "I will stay in a group if they need me, even when I'm not happy with the group."

5. The present recommendation applies only to the use of priming for purposes of simulating cultural effects. There are many other important purposes for which it is appropriate to use priming in culturally based research that assesses cognitive processing.

---

## REFERENCES

Ainsworth, M. D. (1978). *Patterns of attachment: A psychological study of the strange situation.* Hillsdale, NJ: Lawrence Erlbaum.

Baldwin, A. L., Baldwin, C., & Cole, R. E. (1990). Stress-resistant families and stress-resistant children. In J. Rolf, A. Masten, D. Cicchetti, K. Neuchtherlin, & S. Weintraub (Eds.), *Risk and protective factors in the development of psychopathology* (pp. 257-280). Cambridge, UK: Cambridge University Press.

Bargh, J. A. (1996). Automaticity in social psychology. In E. T. Higgins & A. W. Kruglanski (Eds.), *Social psychology: Handbook of basic principles* (pp. 169-183). New York: Guilford.

Bartlett, F. C. (1932). *Remembering: An experimental and social study*. Cambridge, UK: Cambridge University Press.

Baumrind, D. (1996). The discipline controversy revisited. *Family Relations: Journal of Applied Family and Child Studies, 45*(4), 405-414.

Berry, J. W. (1976). *Human ecology and cognitive style*. New York: Sage-Halsted.

Bersoff, D. M., & Miller, J. G. (1993). Culture, context, and the development of moral accountability judgments. *Developmental Psychology, 29*(4), 664-676.

Bornstein, R. F., Kale, A. R., & Cornell, K. R. (1990). Boredom as a limiting condition on the mere exposure effect. *Journal of Personality and Social Psychology, 42*, 239-247.

Bronfenbrenner, U. (1979). *The ecology of human development: Experiments by nature and design*. Cambridge, MA: Harvard University Press.

Brown, D. E. (1991). *Human universals*. Philadelphia: Temple University Press.

Burton, L. M., Allison, K., & Obeidallah, D. (1995). Social context and adolescence: Perspectives on development among inner-city African-American teens. In L. Crockett & A. C. Crouter (Eds.), *Pathways through adolescence: Individual development in relation to social context* (pp. 118-138). Hillsdale, NJ: Lawrence Erlbaum.

Chao, R. K. (1994). Beyond parental control and authoritarian parenting style: Understanding Chinese parenting through the cultural notion of training. *Child Development, 65*(4), 1111-1119.

Chen, X., Rubin, K. H., & Li, B. (1995). Social and school adjustment of shy and aggressive children in China. *Development and Psychopathology, 7*(2), 337-349.

Cole, M. (1995). Culture and cognitive development: From cross-cultural research to creating systems of cultural mediation. *Culture and Psychology, I*, 25-54.

Cole, M. (1996). *Cultural psychology: A once and future discipline*. Cambridge, MA: Harvard University Press.

Cole, M., Gay, J., Glick, J., & Sharp, D. W. (1971). *The cultural context of learning and thinking*. New York: Basic Books.

Cole, M., & Means, B. (1986). *Comparative studies of how people think: An introduction*. Cambridge, MA: Harvard University Press.

Cook, T. D., & Campbell, D. T. (1979). *Quasi-experimentation: Design and analysis issues for field settings*. Chicago: Rand McNally.

Coon, H. M., & Kemmelmeier, M. (2001). Cultural orientations in the United States: (Re)Examining differences among ethnic groups. *Journal of Cross-Cultural Psychology, 32*(3), 348-364.

Cousins, S. D. (1989). Culture and self-perception in Japan and the United States. *Journal of Personality and Social Psychology, 56*, 124-131.

Damon, W., & Hart, D. (1982). The development of self-understanding from infancy through adolescence. *Child Development, 53*, 323-338.

D'Andrade, R. G. (1984). Cultural meaning systems. In R. A. Shweder & R. A. LeVine (Eds.), *Culture theory: Essays on mind, self, and emotion* (pp. 88-119). New York: Cambridge University Press.

Deci, E. L., & Ryan, R. M. (1985). *Intrinsic motivation and self-determination in human behavior*. New York: Plenum.

Deci, E. L., & Ryan, R. M. (1987). The support of autonomy and the control of behavior. *Journal of Personality and Social Psychology, 53*(6), 1024-1037.

Deci, E. I., & Ryan, R. M. (1990). A motivational approach to self: Integration in personality. In R. A. Dienstbier (Ed.), *Nebraska Symposium on Motivation: Vol. 38: Perspectives on motivation* (pp. 237-287). Lincoln: University of Nebraska Press.

Deci, E. L., Ryan, R. M., Gagne, M., Leone, D. R., Usunov, J., & Kornazheva, B. P. (2001). Need satisfaction, motivation, and well-being in the work organizations of a former Eastern Bloc country. *Personality and Social Psychology Bulletin, 27*(8), 930-942.

Delgado-Gaitan, C. (1994). Socializing young children in Mexican-American families: An intergenerational perspective. In P. M. Greenfield & R. R. Cocking (Eds.), *Cross-cultural roots of minority child development* (pp. 55-86). Hillsdale, NJ: Lawrence Erlbaum.

Dien, D. S. (1999). Chinese authority-directed orientation and Japanese peer-group orientation: Questioning the notion of collectivism. *Review of General Psychology, 3*(4), 372-385.

Doi, T. (1992). On the concept of *amae. Infant Mental Health Journal, 13,* 7-11.

Edwards, D. (1995). A commentary on discursive and cultural psychology. *Culture and Psychology, 1,* 55-66.

Ekman, P. (1992). Are there basic emotions? *Psychological Review, 99,* 550-553.

Evans, E. M. (2001). Cognitive and contextual factors in the emergence of diverse belief systems: Creation vs. evolution. *Cognitive Psychology, 42*(3), 217-266.

Fiske, A. P., Kitayama, S., Markus, H. R., & Nisbett, R. E. (1998). The cultural matrix of social psychology. In *The handbook of social psychology* (4th ed., Vol. 2, pp. 915-981). Boston: McGraw-Hill.

Gergen, K. J. (1992). Psychology in the postmodern era. *The General Psychologist, 28,* 10-15.

Gergen, K. J. (1994). *Realities and relationships: Soundings in social construction.* Cambridge, MA: Harvard University Press.

Gilbert, D. T., Fiske, S. T., & Lindzey, G. (Eds.). (1998). *The handbook of social psychology* (4th ed.). New York: McGraw-Hill.

Gilligan, C. (1982). *In a different voice: Psychological theory and women's development.* Cambridge, MA: Harvard University Press.

Greenfield, P. M. (1997a). Culture as process: Empirical methods for cultural psychology. In J. W. Berry, Y. H. Poortinga, & J. Pandey (Eds.), *Handbook of cross-cultural psychology: Vol. 1. Theory and method* (2nd ed., pp. 301-346). Boston: Allyn & Bacon.

Greenfield, P. M. (1997b). You can't take it with you: Why ability assessments don't cross cultures. *American Psychologist, 52*(10), 1115-1124.

Greenfield, P. M., & Childs, C. P. (1977). Understanding sibling concepts: A developmental study of kin terms in Zincantan. In P. Dasen (Ed.), *Piagetian psychology: Cross-cultural contributions* (pp. 335-338). New York: Gardner.

Grolnick, W. S., Deci, E. L., & Ryan, R. M. (1997). Internalization within the family: The self-determination theory perspective. In J. E. Grusec & L. Kuczynski (Eds.), *Handbook of parenting and the transmission of values* (pp. 135-161). New York: Wiley.

Grolnick, W. S., & Ryan, R. M. (1989). Parent styles associated with children's self-regulation and competence in school. *Journal of Educational Psychology, 81*(2), 143-154.

Gulerce, A. (1995). Culture and self in postmodern psychology: Dialogue in trouble? [Interview with K.J. Gergen]. *Culture and Psychology, 1,* 147-159.

Haney, C., Banks, C., & Zimbardo, P. (1973). Interpersonal dynamics in a simulated prison. *International Journal of Criminology and Penology, 1,* 69-97.

Harkness, S., Super, C. M., & van Tijen, N. (2000). Individualism and the "Western mind" reconsidered: American and Dutch parents' ethnotheories of the child. In *Variability in the social construction of the child* (New Directions for Child and Adolescent Development No. 87) (pp. 23-39). San Francisco: Jossey-Bass.

Harwood, R. L., Miller, J. G., & Irizarry, N. L. (1995). *Culture and attachment: Perceptions of the child in context.* New York: Guilford.

Heath, S. B. (1996). Ruling places: Adaptation in development by inner-city youth. In R. Jessor, A. Colby, & R. A. Shweder (Eds.), *Ethnography and human development: Context and meaning in social inquiry* (pp. 225-251). Chicago: University of Chicago Press.

Hermans, H., & Kempen, H. (1998). Moving cultures: The perilous problem of cultural dichotomies in a globalizing society. *American Psychologist, 53,* 1111-1120.

Higgins, E. T., & Kruglanski, A. W. (1996). *Social psychology: Handbook of basic principles.* New York: Guilford.

Hong, Y.-Y., Morris, M. W., Chiu, C.-Y., & Benet-Martinez, V. (2000). Multicultural minds: A dynamic constructivist approach to culture and cognition. *American Psychologist, 55*(7), 709-720.

Huebner, A., & Garrod, A. (1991). Moral reasoning in a Karmic world. *Human Development, 34,* 341-352.

Hughes, D., & DuMont, K. (1993). Using focus groups to facilitate culturally anchored research. *American Journal of Community Psychology, 21*(6), 775-806.

Iyengar, S. S., & Lepper, M. R. (1999). Rethinking the value of choice: A cultural perspective on intrinsic motivation. *Journal of Personality and Social Psychology, 76*(3), 349-366.

Izard, C. E. (1992). Basic emotions, relations among emotions, and emotion-cognition relations. *Psychological Review, 99,* 561-565.

Jahoda, G. (1986). Nature, culture and social psychology. *European Journal of Social Psychology, 16,* 17-30.

Jarrett, R. L. (1995). Growing up poor: The family experiences of socially mobile youth in low-income African-American neighborhoods. *Journal of Adolescent Research, 10,* 111-135.

Ji, L.-J., Peng, K., & Nisbett, R. E. (2000). Culture, control, and perception of relationships in the environment. *Journal of Personality and Social Psychology, 78*(5), 943-955.

Kagan, J. (1994). *Galen's prophecy: Temperament in human nature.* New York: Basic Books.

Kitayama, S. (2002). Culture and basic psychological processes—Toward a system view of culture: Comment on Oyserman et al. (2002). *Psychological Bulletin, 128*(1), 89-96.

Kitayama, S., Markus, H. R., Matsumoto, H., & Norasakkunkit, V. (1997). Individual and collective processes in the construction of the self: Self-enhancement in the United States and self-criticism in Japan. *Journal of Personality and Social Psychology, 72*(6), 1245-1267.

Knodel, J. (1993). The design and analysis of focus group studies: A practical approach. In D. Morgan (Ed.), *Successful focus groups: Advancing the state of the art* (pp. 35-50). Newbury Park, CA: Sage.

Kohlberg, L. (1984). *The psychology of moral development: The nature and validity of moral stages.* San Francisco: Harper & Row.

Kusserow, A. S. (1999). De-homogenizing American individualism: Socializing hard and soft individualism in Manhattan and Queens. *Ethos, 27*(2), 210-234.

Kwan, V.S.Y., Bond, M. H., & Singelis, T. M. (1997). Pancultural explanations for life satisfaction: Adding relationship harmony to self esteem. *Journal of Personality and Social Psychology, 73*(5), 1038-1051.

Laboratory of Comparative Human Cognition. (1983). Culture and cognitive development. In W. Kessen (Ed.), *Handbook of child psychology: History, theory and method* (pp. 295-356). New York: Wiley.

Levine, C., Kohlberg, L., & Hewer, A. (1985). The current formulation of Kohlberg's theory and a response to critics. *Human Development, 28*(2), 94-100.

LeVine, R. A. (1984). Properties of culture: An ethnographic view. In R. A. Shweder & R. A. LeVine (Eds.), *Culture theory: Essays on mind, self, and emotion* (pp. 67-87). New York: Cambridge University Press.

Livesley, W. J., & Bromley, D. B. (1973). *Person perception in childhood and adolescence*. London: Wiley.

Malpass, R. S. (1988). Why not cross-cultural psychology?: A characterization of some mainstream views. In M. H. Bond (Ed.), *The cross-cultural challenge to social psychology* (Cross-Cultural Research and Methodology Series) (pp. 29-35). Beverly Hills, CA: Sage.

Markus, H. R., & Kitayama, S. (1991). Culture and the self: Implications for cognition, emotion, and motivation. *Psychological Review, 98*(2), 224-253.

Markus, H. R., Kitayama, S., & Heiman, R. J. (1996). Culture and "basic" psychological principles. In E. T. Higgins & A. W. Kruglanski (Eds.), *Social psychology: Handbook of basic principles* (pp. 857-913). New York: Guilford.

Markus, H. R., Mullally, P. R., & Kitayama, S. (1997). Selfways: Diversity in modes of cultural participation. In *The conceptual self in context: Culture, experience, self-understanding* (pp. 13-61). New York: Cambridge University Press.

Marriott, M. (1990). *India through Hindu categories*. New Delhi: Sage.

Matsumoto, D. (1999). Culture and self: An empirical assessment of Markus and Kitayama's theory of independent and interdependent self-construals. *Asian Journal of Social Psychology, 2*, 289-310.

Matsumoto, D. (Ed.). (2001). *The handbook of culture and psychology*. New York: Oxford University Press.

McLoyd, V. C., & Flanagan, C. A. (Eds.). (1990). *Economic stress: Effects on family life and child development*. San Francisco: Jossey-Bass.

Milgram, S. (1963). The behavioral study of obedience. *Journal of Abnormal and Social Psychology, 67*, 467-472.

Miller, J. G. (1984). Culture and the development of everyday social explanation. *Journal of Personality and Social Psychology, 46*(5), 961-978.

Miller, J. G. (1994). Cultural diversity in the morality of caring: Individually oriented versus duty-based interpersonal moral codes. *Cross-Cultural Research: The Journal of Comparative Social Science, 28*(1), 3-39.

Miller, J. G. (1997). Theoretical issues in cultural psychology. In J. W. Berry, Y. H. Poortinga, & J. Pandey (Eds.), *Handbook of cross-cultural psychology: Vol. 1. Theory and method* (2nd ed., pp. 85-128). Boston: Allyn & Bacon.

Miller, J. G. (1999). Cultural psychology: Implications for basic psychological theory. *Psychological Science, 10*(2), 85-91.

Miller, J. (2001a). The cultural grounding of social psychological theory. In A. Tesser & N. Schwarz (Eds.), *Blackwell handbook of social psychology: Vol. 1. Intrapersonal processes* (pp. 22-43). Malden, MA: Blackwell.

Miller, J. G. (2001b). Culture and moral development. In D. Matsumoto (Ed.), *The handbook of culture and psychology* (pp. 151-169). New York: Oxford University Press.

Miller, J. G. (2002). Bringing culture to basic psychological theory: Beyond individualism and collectivism: Comment on Oyserman et al. (2002). *Psychological Bulletin, 128*(1), 97-109.

Miller, J. G. (in press-a). The cultural deep structure of psychological theories of social development. In R. Sternberg & E. Grigorenko (Eds.), *Culture and competence*. Washington, DC: American Psychological Association.

Miller, J. G. (in press-b). Culture and agency: Implications for psychological theories of motivation and social development. In V. Murphy-Berman & J. Berman (Eds.), *Nebraska Symposium on Motivation: Vol. 49. Cross-cultural differences in perspectives on the self*. Lincoln: University of Nebraska Press.

Miller, J. G., & Bersoff, D. M. (1994). Cultural influences on the moral status of reciprocity and the discounting of endogenous motivation. *Personality and Social Psychology Bulletin, 20*(5), 592-602.

Miller, J. G., & Bersoff, D. M. (1995). Development in the context of everyday family relationships: Culture, interpersonal morality, and adaptation. In M. Killen & D. Hart (Eds.), *Morality in everyday life: Developmental perspectives* (pp. 259-282). New York: Cambridge University Press.

Miller, J. G., & Bersoff, D. M. (1998). The role of liking in perceptions of the moral responsibility to help: A cultural perspective. *Journal of Experimental Social Psychology, 34*(5), 443-469.

Miyamoto, Y., & Kitayama, S. (2002). Cultural variation in correspondence bias: The critical role of attitude diagnosticity of socially constrained behavior. *Journal of Personality and Social Psychology, 83*(5), 1239-1248.

Moscovici, S. (1972). Society and theory in social psychology. In J. Israel & H. Tajfel (Eds.), *The context of social psychology: A critical assessment* (pp. 17-69). New York: Academic Press.

Neighbors, H. W., & Jackson, J. S. (Eds.). (1996). *Mental health in Black America.* Thousand Oaks, CA: Sage.

Nisbett, R., & Ross, L. (1980). *Human inference: Strategies and shortcomings of social judgment.* Englewood Cliffs, NJ: Prentice-Hall.

Oyserman, D., Coon, H., & Kemmelmeier, M. (2002). Rethinking individualism and collectivism: Evaluation of theoretical assumptions and meta-analyses. *Psychological Bulletin, 128*(1), 3-72.

Peng, K., & Nisbett, R. E. (1999). Culture, dialectics, and reasoning about contradiction. *American Psychologist, 54*(9), 741-754.

Peng, K., Nisbett, R. E., & Wong, N. Y. C. (1997). Validity problems comparing values across cultures and possible solutions. *Psychological Methods, 2*(4), 329-344.

Phinney, J. S. (1999). An intercultural approach in psychology: Cultural contact and identity. *Cross-Cultural Psychology Bulletin, 33*(2), 24-31.

Phinney, J. S., & Landin, J. (1998). Research paradigms for studying ethnic minority families within and across groups. In V. C. McLoyd (Ed.), *Studying minority adolescents: Conceptual, methodological, and theoretical issues* (pp. 89-109). Mahwah, NJ: Lawrence Erlbaum.

Plaut, V. C., Markus, H. R., & Lachman, M. E. (2002). Place matters: Consensual features and regional variation in American well-being and self. *Journal of Personality and Social Psychology, 83*(1), 160-184.

Powell, R. A., & Single, H. M. (1996). Focus groups. *International Journal of Quality in Health Care, 8*(5), 499-504.

Reid, P. T. (1994). The real problem in the study of culture. *American Psychologist, 49*(6), 524-525.

Rothbaum, F., Weisz, J., Pott, M., Miyake, K., & Morelli, G. (2000). Attachment and culture: Security in the United States and Japan. *American Psychologist, 55*(10), 1093-1104.

Russell, J. A. (1991). Culture and the categorization of emotions. *Psychological Bulletin, 110,* 426-450.

Russell, J. A. (1994). Is there universal recognition of emotion from facial expression? A review of the cross-cultural studies. *Psychological Bulletin, 115*(1), 102-141.

Shimizu, H. (2001). Japanese adolescent boys' senses of empathy (*omoiyari*) and Carol Gilligan's perspectives on the morality of care: A phenomenological approach. *Culture and Psychology, 7*(4), 453-475.

Shore, B. (1996). *Culture in mind: Cognition, culture and the problem of meaning.* New York: Oxford University Press.

Shotter, J. (1993). *Cultural politics of everyday life: Social constructionism, rhetoric and knowing of the third kind.* Buckingham, UK: Open University Press.

Shweder, R. A. (1979). Rethinking culture and personality theory Part I: A critical examination of two classical postulates. *Ethos, 7*(3), 255-278.

Shweder, R. A. (1984). Anthropology's romantic rebellion against the enlightenment, or there's more to thinking than reason and evidence. In R. A. Shweder & R. A. LeVine (Eds.), *Culture theory: Essays on mind, self, and emotion* (pp. 27-66). Cambridge, UK: Cambridge University Press.

Shweder, R. A. (1990). Cultural psychology—What is it? In J. W. Stigler, R. A. Shweder, & G. Herdt (Eds.), *Cultural psychology: Essays on comparative human development* (pp. 27-66). New York: Cambridge University Press.

Shweder, R. A., Goodnow, J., Hatano, G., LeVine, R. A., Markus, H., & Miller, P. (1998). The cultural psychology of development: One mind, many mentalities. In W. Damon (Ed.), *Handbook of child psychology* (Vol. 1, pp. 865-937). New York: John Wiley & Sons.

Shweder, R. A., & Sullivan, M. A. (1993). Cultural psychology: Who needs it? *Annual Review of Psychology, 44*, 497-527.

Singelis, T. M. (1994). The measurement of independent and interdependent self-construals. *Personality and Social Psychology Bulletin, 20*(5), 580-591.

Snarey, J. R. (1985). Cross-cultural universality of social-moral development: A critical review of Kohlbergian research. *Psychological Bulletin, 97*(2), 202-232.

Steele, C. M., & Aronson, J. (1995). Stereotype threat and the intellectual test performance of African Americans. *Journal of Personality and Social Psychology, 69*(5), 797-811.

Stevenson, H. W., & Lee, S.-Y. (1990). Contexts of achievement: A study of American, Chinese, and Japanese children. In *Monographs of the Society for Research in Child Development* (Serial No. 221, vol. 55, Nos. 1-2). Chicago: University of Chicago Press.

Stigler, J. W., Lee, S.-Y., & Stevenson, H. W. (1987). Mathematics classrooms in Japan, Taiwan, and the United States. *Child Development, 58*(5), 1272-1285.

Strauss, C. (2000). The culture concept and the individualism-collectivism debate: Dominant and alternative attributions for class in the United States. In *Culture, thought, and development* (pp. 85-114). Mahwah, NJ: Lawrence Erlbaum Associates.

Strauss, C., & Quinn, N. (1997). *A cognitive theory of cultural meaning*. New York: Cambridge University Press.

Takano, Y., & Osaka, E. (1999). An unsupported common view: Comparing Japan and the U.S. on individualism/collectivism. *Asian Journal of Social Psychology, 2*, 311-341.

Tobin, J. J., Wu, D. Y. H., & Davidson, D. H. (1989). *Preschool in three cultures: Japan, China, and the United States*. New Haven, CT: Yale University Press.

Triandis, H. C. (1995). *Individualism and collectivism*. Boulder, CO: Westview.

van de Vijver, F. (2001). The evolution of cross-cultural research methods. In D. Matsumoto (Ed.), *The handbook of culture and psychology* (pp. 79-97). New York: Oxford University Press.

van de Vijver, F. J. R., & Leung, K. (1997). Methods and data analysis of comparative research. In J. W. Berry, Y. H. Poortinga, & J. Pandey (Eds.), *Handbook of cross-cultural psychology* (pp. 257-300). Boston: Allyn & Bacon.

Vandello, J. A., & Cohen, D. (1999). Patterns of individualism and collectivism across the United States. *Journal of Personality and Social Psychology, 77*(2), 279-292.

Whiting, B. B., & Whiting, J. W. (1975). *Children of six cultures: A psycho-cultural analysis*. Cambridge, MA: Harvard University Press.

Wierzbicka, A. (2002). Right and wrong: From philosophy to everyday discourse. *Discourse Studies, 4*(2), 225-252.

Witkin, H. A., & Berry, J. W. (1975). Psychological differentiation in cross-cultural perspective. *Journal of Cross-Cultural Psychology, 6,* 4-87.

Yamaguchi, S. (2001). Culture and control orientations. In D. Matsumoto (Ed.), *The handbook of culture and psychology* (pp. 223-243). New York: Oxford University Press.

Yang, K.-S. (1997). Indigenizing westernized Chinese psychology. In M. H. Bond (Ed.), *Working at the interface of culture: Eighteen lives in social science* (pp. 62-76). London: Routledge.

## CHAPTER 6

# Individual Differences in Social Psychology

## Understanding Situations to Understand People, Understanding People to Understand Situations

YUICHI SHODA

*University of Washington*

> *[G]eneral laws and individual differences are merely two aspects of one problem; they are mutually dependent on each other and the study of the one cannot proceed without the study of the other.*
>
> —Lewin (1946, p. 794)

People think, feel, and do different things in different situations, and the changes and variations from situation to situation are not all random. Understanding the nature of such variations, of course, is one of the main missions of social psychology. The goal is to figure out what processes and mechanisms underlie the observed variations. This handbook is full of examples of thoughtful and ingenious ways to pursue that goal. This chapter will focus on providing a broad framework for the role of individual differences in the

AUTHOR'S NOTE: Preparation of this chapter was supported in part by Grant MH39349 from the National Institute of Mental Health. I am grateful to the editors of this volume for their encouragement to embark on this chapter initially and for their extremely careful and thorough reading of multiple drafts throughout its development as well as their constructive suggestions. Kathy Cook, Scott LeeTiernan, Jason Plaks, Vivian Zayas, and Naomi Zavislak provided many opportunities for productive brainstorming sessions. In addition, Kathy Cook provided many of the historical materials cited in this chapter. I am deeply grateful for their support. Correspondence concerning this article should be addressed to Yuichi Shoda, Department of Psychology, University of Washington, Box 351525, Seattle, WA 98195-1525. Electronic mail may be sent to yshoda@u.washington.edu.

investigation of the effects of situations and individuals' social information processing systems that mediate them. One might ask, Why focus on stable individual differences? Surely some people may be more likely on average to display a certain behavior than others, but what does that have to do with the effects of situations? Why does one need to take individual differences into account? This chapter begins by addressing this "why" question (part I), followed by a discussion of "what" questions, namely the nature of individual difference variables that interact with situations (part II); an overview of the issues relating to "how" questions, such as identifying individual difference constructs that interact with situations (part III); and operationalizing them in actual experiments in the form of measures (part IV).

## WHY STABLE INDIVIDUAL DIFFERENCES NEED TO BE TAKEN INTO ACCOUNT

Almost half a century ago, Lee Cronbach, in his APA presidential address, observed that there had been two largely independent research traditions in psychology, which he called the experimental and correlational (Cronbach, 1957). In the experimental tradition, one varies the aspects of situations hypothesized to influence the behavior of interest, while holding constant all other factors. The focus is on the variation created by the experimenter and isolating the effects of it. In contrast, the correlational approach focuses on the already existing variations "presented by Nature" (Cronbach, 1957, p. 671), embedded in a complex web of interrelated variables, only a small fraction of which are observable. Cronbach argued then, as well as 20 years later in his APA distinguished scientist award address (Cronbach, 1975), that neither alone is likely to be sufficient, and that one must focus on the *interactions* between manipulated situational factors and naturally existing individual differences. Why might that be? This chapter approaches that question from the point of view of social psychologists, whose mission is to understand the effects of situations and the psychological mechanisms that underlie those effects.

Consider experiments in which people are exposed to conditions that differ on a situational factor of interest, producing differences in their thoughts, feelings, or behaviors on average. If we do experiment after experiment in which all sorts of situational factors are manipulated, singly and jointly, we will arrive at an understanding of the mechanism that underlies social information processing, resulting in essence in a giant regression equation in which the additive and interactive effects of all variables whose effects have been studied are represented. Or will we?

This chapter argues that there is a potential problem in this strategy. The problem is not simply that it is difficult to manipulate some variables of importance. To be sure, it is unfortunate if the field relies solely on situational manipulation and as a result risks excluding factors whose variations are largely "presented by Nature" rather than created in laboratories. But some variables can be manipulated; so, can't their effects, at least, be established confidently? That may be the case if the effects of those variables don't depend on other variables that are not manipulated. But what if the effects of the situational manipulation critically depend on some unobserved variables? Then effects of situations can differ from one person to another. Might averaging the effects across people at least represent the effects of the situation on the average person? Unfortunately, the "average" person may exist only in statistical abstraction (see Cook and Groom, Chapter 2, this volume).[1]

In summary, (a) many important psychological variables cannot easily be manipulated, (b) even those that can be manipulated may interact with those that cannot, and (c) behaviors may reflect the emergent properties of person-situation systems. Consequently, if one does not take individual differences into account, a sole focus on the "effects" of the manipulated variables on people "in general" may result in at best a partial, and at worst, a misleading, understanding of the process underlying the behavior of interest.

## Lewin's Equation, B = f(P, E)

Although Cronbach's plea to combine the experimental and correlational traditions was more from the point of view of research paradigms, the need to consider both the situations and persons was also central to Kurt Lewin's theory in which the behavior is conceptualized as a function of the *field*, the whole gestalt consisting of persons (or the "object" in the following quotation) and situations involved: "Only by the concrete whole which comprises the object and the situation are the vectors which determine the dynamics of the event defined" (Lewin, 1931, p. 165).

*P = An Individual's Dynamic
Social Information Processing
System: An Example*

How can persons be conceptualized in order to help understand the effects of situations, and how they may vary meaningfully from one person to another? To account for such person × situation interactions, it is helpful to conceptualize personality as a dynamical system (Shoda, LeeTiernan, et al., 2002). In such a system, stability is expected in the underlying structure that generates the thoughts, feelings, and behaviors which themselves can change from one moment to the next in response to situations. The stability of the underlying structure will be reflected not in the constancy of thoughts, feelings, and behaviors, but rather in the way they change, in the way the thoughts and affects come and go.

To illustrate, Figures 6.1 and 6.2 depict differences between two types of individuals

in the cognitions and affects identified from a literature review as relevant for the decision and actual performance of a breast self-examination (BSE) and the network of relations that guides their activation (Miller, Shoda, & Hurley, 1996). Examples of cognitive and affective "units" relevant to BSE are illustrated schematically inside the large ovals in Figures 6.1 and 6.2. A solid arrow connecting one cognitive-affective unit to another indicates that the activation of the first increases the activation of the second. Broken arrows show that the activation of the first reduces the activation of the second. The thoughts, the affects, and the connections that characterize each type are shown in boldface type.

For a woman whose network resembles Figure 6.1, health-risk information is highly likely to activate the thought, "I may develop breast cancer," as indicated by the thick solid arrow (Figure 6.1, Arrow 1). In contrast, for a woman whose network resembles Figure 6.2, with a thin Arrow 1, the objective risk information is less likely to activate this thought.

With regard to observable behavioral responses, depending on whether a woman's cognitive-affective processing network resembles Figure 6.1 or Figure 6.2, the risk information can have potentially opposite outcomes. For example, how an individual mentally represents the information influences the level of arousal and anxiety (Arrow 28). Thus, whether she focuses more on the information itself (e.g., "Now I need to look for changes in this area," Arrow 20) or on a more emotion arousing aspect (e.g., "If I find a lump, that means hundreds of thousands of cancer cells are already there," Arrow 21) has very different impacts on the continued practice of BSE.

*Studying Person ×
Situation Interactions*

With this example in mind, consider the question we asked at the outset of this chapter: How would one investigate the

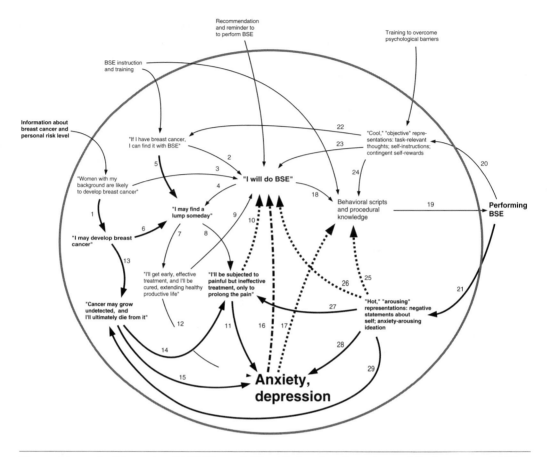

**Figure 6.1** An Illustrative CAPS Network That Undermines Intention and Performance of BSE

SOURCE: Based on, and adapted from, Figure 5 of Miller, Shoda, and Hurley (1996), p. 83.

NOTE: Situational features activate specific subsets of the mediating units, which in turn activate other mediating units. The network of connections is considered stable and characterizes the individual. Arrows indicate activation relationships, such that when one unit is activated, other units that receive solid arrows from it will receive activation proportional to the weight associated with each arrow. The weight may be positive (solid arrows) or negative (dashed arrows).

mechanisms that underlie people's responses to the situational input? Consider these possibilities in the BSE example. If all women more or less fit the processing structure shown in Figure 6.1, one may perform a series of experiments in which each situation feature and cognitive-affective unit is manipulated, and their effects on other cognitive-affective units are assessed. For those mediating units that are difficult or unethical to manipulate, if they are measurable, one may apply statistical approaches and assess evidence that they

mediate the effects of manipulated variables, following Baron and Kenny's (1986) guidelines, also as discussed by Hoyle and Robinson (Chapter 10, this volume). But what if Figure 6.1 described only a small proportion of women, while other women fit Figure 6.2, and yet another group of women were characterized by cognitive-affective dynamics that neither Figure 6.1 nor Figure 6.2 describes? Does heightened awareness increase or decrease the intention to perform BSE? This is analogous to the question that Gordon Allport (1937,

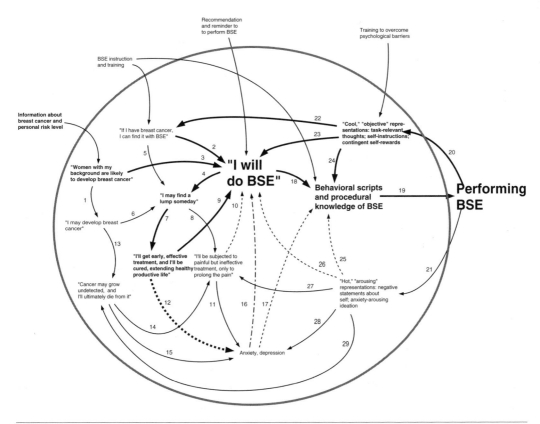

**Figure 6.2**    An Illustrative CAPS Network That Enhances Intention and Performance of BSE

SOURCE: Based on, and adapted from, Figure 6 of Miller, Shoda, and Hurley (1996), p. 84.

p. 102) posed: What is the effect of cooking heat on foods—does it harden or soften them? The question is meaningless unless one specifies the type of food. It results in one answer if the food is a raw egg, but another if the food is a stick of butter.

To summarize, in order to understand the psychological mechanisms that underlie behaviors, one must go beyond examining the responses of people *on average*, a statistical abstraction. To borrow Lewin's phrase, one needs to examine "the *concrete whole* which comprises the object and the situation" [emphasis added], of which Figure 6.1 may be one and Figure 6.2 may be another. It includes potentially numerous components, many of which may not be manipulable or even observable. Most important, a

critical aspect is its structure, or the set of relationships among its components, constituting a distinctive *system* of information processing for each individual.

## WHAT INDIVIDUAL DIFFERENCES?

How does one find the particular aspects of an individual's processing dynamics that are relevant for the behavior one wishes to understand? The rest of this chapter seeks to provide at least the beginning of an answer to this question: This question can be approached both in a top-down, deductive fashion, as well as in a bottom-up, inductive fashion. In a deductive approach, one starts with an individual difference construct chosen on the basis of researchers' informal observations and intuition, or on previous studies or a theory. The inductive approach, on the other hand, focuses on discovering the construct to begin with. Its goal is to systematize the process of discovery and identification of the construct.

Whether one follows the deductive or the inductive path, just what are the important ways in which people differ from one another? As Allport and Odbert (1936) found, the English language has some 18,000 words describing characteristics of a person, and people potentially can differ on all of them. Are there any guidelines to help narrow the search?

Of course, the search for the individual difference construct must be guided by its relevance to the particular behavior one is interested in understanding. But for the purposes of understanding the effects of situations and the mechanisms underlying them, one general guideline applies: The types of individual differences one needs to understand for that purpose are those that *interact* with situation characteristics or situationally induced internal states. Stated differently, one can relatively safely ignore individual difference variables that simply increase or decrease the level of behavioral response while not affecting the impact of situational variables. A "division of labor" of sorts might be achieved, in which the study of such individual differences is considered the subject matter of personality psychologists while social psychologists focus on the effects of situations. In fact, that is often how the fields of personality psychology and social psychology, or "correlational" and "experimental" approaches, are divided, with the consequence that one field's main variance is considered by the other as "that outer darkness known as 'error variance'" (Cronbach, 1957, p. 674). However, to the extent that situational variables interact with individual difference variables, as discussed, social

psychologists can no longer afford to ignore individual differences, and personality psychologists can no longer ignore situations. Just as studying the effects of individual differences in *situations in general* can be misleading, studying the effects of situations on *people in general* can be misleading.

## Individual Differences That Interact With Situations

What individual difference constructs interact with situational factors? What kinds of personal characteristics serve as the "P" in Person × Situation interactions, that is, "P" × "S" interactions? Unfortunately, the question has rarely been addressed directly in standard compilations of measures. In this section, some general characteristics of individual difference variables that interact with situations are identified, based on reviews of the literature as well as an informal e-mail survey sent to members of the Society of Personality and Social Psychology asking them to nominate "individual difference constructs that have been shown to interact with situations."[2]

### Processing Dynamics Type and Diagnostic Situations

A major type of individual difference variables that interact with situations is those that characterize individuals by their particular processing dynamics. The nature of the dynamics in turn identifies "diagnostic situations" that engage the dynamics, situations in which that group of individuals is expected to respond distinctively. As an example of individual difference constructs that identify processing dynamics, consider uncertainty orientation (Sorrentino & Roney, 2000), which distinguishes people who are relatively comfortable dealing with uncertainty and strive to resolve it from those who are more uncomfortable with uncertainty and are likely to avoid situations that increase a subjective sense of uncertainty.

Uncertainty orientation has been shown to be important in answering diverse questions such as the following: Would instructional techniques that involve a cooperative situation (e.g., the Jigsaw classroom) be better than a traditional expository technique? and Would experiencing lack of control in a situation make a person seek new information? It turns out that the answers to these questions depend on an individual's uncertainty orientation. For those who are high in uncertainty orientation, the answer is yes. But for those who are low in uncertainty orientation, the answer was the opposite: Traditional instructions work better than cooperative ones (Huber, Sorrentino, Davidson, & Epplier, 1992); and experiencing uncontrollability makes it more likely that these people, especially if depressed, will avoid new information (Walker & Sorrentino, 2000).

Although the particular situation features that interact with uncertainty orientation differ widely, they have one theme in common, namely the activation of a subjective feeling of uncertainty. Situations that contain this feature trigger the processing dynamics that are characteristic of those who are low, and those who are high, in uncertainty orientation. There are many examples of processing dynamics that interact with situations. To name a few, for individuals with achievement-oriented processing dynamics, competitive situations with externally assigned performance goals enhance the engagement and enjoyment, but for those who are low in achievement motivation, noncompetitive situations with mastery optimize their engagement and enjoyment (Barron & Harackiewicz, 2001). Opportunities for bolstering their grandiose self-concepts define situations in which narcissists exert much effort toward providing evidence of their superiority, even if doing so may offend or hurt others (e.g., Morf & Rhodewalt, 2001; Rhodewalt & Morf, 1998). For people who are characterized by racial rejection sensitivity dynamics (Mendoza-Denton, Purdie, Downey, & Davis, in press), diagnostic situations are ones in which rejection on the basis of one's race is perceived as possible or likely. Many of the individual difference constructs that interact with situations function in a similar way. They describe people who are characterized by a particular type of processing dynamics, which in turn specifies the diagnostic situations that trigger the characteristic dynamics.

A notable subset of this type of interaction involves situations that are generally more demanding, taxing, and stressful. For example, those who are high versus low on neuroticism differ most in their negative affect in situations high in stress (Bolger & Zuckerman, 1995; Mroczek & Almeida, 2002). People scoring high on the measure of Behavior Inhibition System (BIS) were most distinctive in their responses to negative daily events (Carver & White, 1994; Gable, Reis, & Elliot, 2000). J. Crocker, Thompson, McGraw, and Ingerman (1987) found that threats to self-concept served as a diagnostic situation that differentiated individuals high in self-esteem from those low in self-esteem in their tendency to derogate outgroups.

Another type of diagnostic situation involves public versus private settings. Morf and Rhodewalt (1993) found that narcissists' tendency to derogate those who outperformed them was more distinctive in public compared to private settings. Schütz and DePaulo (1996) found that in private settings, people with low self-esteem did not differ from those high in self-esteem in how they evaluated others' artwork, but in public settings people with low self-esteem were more positive than people with high self-esteem. Chen, Shechter, and Chaiken (1996) found that people who are high versus low in self-monitoring did not differ in their expressed opinions in private, but they differed in public, such that when they expected to have a discussion with their partner on a topic, high self-monitors adjusted their expressed attitudes to be more in line with their partner's.

*Types of Person Variables*
*That Affect Processing Dynamics*

Are there any commonalities among the individual difference variables that interact with situations? Those that alter the nature of the effect of situations are likely to influence the way in which individuals process social information. Of course, *how* social information is processed is one of the basic questions addressed by social psychology, so it would not be surprising that the same type of variables that have proven useful for characterizing the effects of situations may also be useful in understanding individual differences. That, of course, is what Lewin proposed more than half a century ago and what is practiced in contemporary research when, for example, operationalizing individual differences in terms of the *chronic* activation of knowledge structures (e.g., Higgins, 1999). These process-oriented constructs were proposed as the basis for characterizing individuals by Mischel (1973), who called them "cognitive social person variables." A closer analysis (Shoda, 1999) found that the primary effects of these variables often are not to increase or decrease any given behavior in general, but rather their behavioral manifestation is in the form of *if . . . then . . .* profiles that characterize the *relationship* between situations and behaviors, as mediated by the individuals in their characteristic ways.

In addition to the activation of concepts, in recent years research in social cognition has turned to the *associations* among concepts, particularly those that operate automatically. Such implicit associations have been the target of both theorizing and empirical assessment, as detailed by Kihlstrom (Chapter 9, this volume). Individuals may differ not only in the chronic accessibility of these mediating cognitions and affective reactions but also in how specific thoughts are associated with each other. Consider the two hypothetical "minds" depicted in Figures 6.1 and 6.2.

These individuals may not differ in the chronic activation of the thought "I may find a lump someday." But they may differ in its association to another thought, "I'll get early, effective treatment, and I'll be cured" compared to its association to the thought "I'll be subjected to painful but ineffective treatment." In short, individuals' social information processing systems may differ (a) in the availability and chronic accessibility of domain-relevant cognitions and affects and (b) in the network of associations among them (Mischel & Shoda, 1995; Shoda, LeeTiernan, et al., 2002). Many of the variables that have been shown to interact with situations refer to either one or more of the component cognitions and affective reactions (e.g., self-efficacy, perceived social support, self-esteem) as well as an entire configuration or system (e.g., neuroticism, shyness).

*Interactions May Involve*
*Highly Content-Specific Personal*
*and Situation Characteristics*

The personal and situational characteristics that interact may be highly content-specific. One example of this is seen in studies of the self-evaluation maintenance model (e.g., Beach et al., 1998), which examines people's emotional responses upon observing that their partner did particularly well in a task. It turns out that whether the participants felt happier, basking in the reflected glory, or instead felt threatened by their partner's superior performance depends on the specifics of the task. In particular, when the partner's superior performance was in a domain (e.g., math) highly central to the participants' self-concept, the effect was an increased sense of threat. On the other hand, when the partner's superior performance was in a domain (e.g., music) less central to the participants, it was more likely they felt happier as a result. Note that the relevant constructs are not the partner's level of performance in general or the participants' global self-evaluation. Rather, it was the particular domain (e.g., math, music) of performance and the particular aspects of self-concept (centrality of math or music) that constituted the *active ingredients*, so to speak, of the situations and persons that produced the crossover interaction.

## Going Beyond the Bandwidth-Fidelity Trade-off

One of the lasting dilemmas a social psychologist faces is the trade-off between the accuracy of predictions (fidelity) and the generality of findings (bandwidth). Ideally, one would like to be able to understand the psychological processes of a given individual so well that it becomes possible to accurately predict that person's behavior in a given situation. On the other hand, unless one is studying significant historical figures (e.g., Runyan, 1983), knowing the specifics of a given person and situation does not contribute much to the field.

How can this dilemma be solved? In addressing this question, it may be useful to consider the historical tendency for psychology to model itself after physics, striving to describe individuals and situations by a small number of quantitative variables, and establishing general laws that specify the relationships among them. If we insist on applying the same framework to psychology, the range of socially and personally significant behaviors that can be understood sufficiently well may be quite limited. It is often the specifics that matter, as in the example above concerning the effect of partners' superior performance. Instead, other sciences might provide a better model, and they may also provide a solution to the accuracy vs. generality dilemma. Take, for example, organic chemistry or geology. There are thousands of different geological locations, and there are even greater numbers of organic compounds one might be interested in learning more about (e.g., just how far

below the surface bedrock lies, what that bedrock consists of, etc.). The specific findings about the bedrock under a particular hill might not merit publication in a top geology journal; however, the principles that were used and new principles that emerge from studies of many specific hills, or chemical compounds, do merit publication. Similarly, in a given study of the self-evaluation maintenance process, for example, there may be a large number of individuals representing a specific configuration of self-concepts. But it is possible to discover general principles that characterize the *relationship* between the specific self-concept of a participant and the domain of her partner's excellent performance. This is worth reporting, as it has generality. In addition, although the general principle does not say anything about whether a specific individual will feel threatened by the superior musical performance of his partner, it spells out a recipe of sorts for what one needs to find out from a person (i.e., the domain of performance central to self) and a situation (i.e., the domain of the partner's superior performance) to predict their interaction with a high degree of accuracy. The challenge is to identify the relationships among the specifics that warrant generalization, and that in turn will indicate what one needs to assess in a person and in a situation to predict their interaction at a specific, non-abstract, level.

## Behavioral Signatures of Personal Types Guide an Inductive Approach to Discovering Individual Difference Constructs

Focusing on individual difference constructs that specify particular types of processing dynamics—and in particular those that speak to individuals' beliefs, goals, and values, as well as emotions and personal strivings, for example—can help narrow the search a little. But that still leaves the question of what beliefs, what goals, and what kinds of processing dynamics are most relevant in understanding behaviors of interest.

The basic principle discussed so far, that one needs to seek individual difference constructs that interact with situations, suggests a route. Individuals' *behavioral signatures*, or the set of *if* to (situation) *then* (behavior) patterns (Shoda, Mischel, & Wright, 1994) reflect the individuals' characteristic ways of processing social information. Behavioral signatures reflect the features of situations an individual notices, the social categories that become activated to encode situations, and the beliefs, values, goals, and affective reactions that in turn become activated (Shoda, 1999). Thus, if one finds groups of individuals who share similar behavioral signatures, there is a good chance that the resultant groups represent distinct types of processing dynamics. Computational tools that make such typologies possible have become available, as has research showing that groups of individuals with similar behavioral signatures in fact shared similar cognitive and affective responses to situations (e.g., Vansteelandt & Van Mechelen, 1998).

Note that this strategy requires one to shift to a more inductive approach to examine within-individual variations before group trends are addressed. Doing so requires having an experimental design in which participants are exposed to multiple situations. (For further discussion of this issue, and in particular on the question of how one goes from the individual's response to the group response, see West, Biesanz, and Kwok, Chapter 13, this volume.)

Such a strategy is not new in other fields of psychology. As early as 1946, Cattell envisioned a research strategy in which one conceptualized behaviors as a function of the person, situation, and occasion, discussed in detail by Cronbach (1984). A full design would fill each cell of a three-dimensional data array, or "Cattell's data box," in which each "slice" represents a person, and the columns and rows of each slice represent situations and

occasions. In this framework, Cattell discussed six distinct types of correlations one can compute: R, Q, P, O, S, and T. The correlations reported in the overwhelming majority of studies in social and personality represent the R-type, which indicates the similarity or dissimilarity in the rank ordering of individuals with regard to their behavior observed in one situation (e.g., one test) with the rank ordering observed in another situation (another test). In contrast, the strategy needed for the inductive approach discussed above represents the Q-type analysis, which focuses on the pattern of variations observed within each person and seeks to index the similarity or dissimilarity among individuals with regard to their pattern of situation-to-situation variation.

Although the Q-type analysis is rare in social and personality psychology, in memory and perception research, it is not uncommon for a participant to return day after day for literally hundreds of trials in which stimuli are presented under different conditions. A publication reporting a new perceptual phenomenon may be based on only a dozen participants. The small number of participants used in these studies might invoke a chorus of reactions among social psychologists, "with such a small N, how can one be sure the results are reliable?" But for these types of experiments, the relevant N is *not* the number of participants but the number of trials. In the extreme, one participant may be enough to establish a psychological phenomenon (e.g., Ebbinghaus, 1885). The purpose of multiple participants in this design is to test if the effects seen in one individual can generalize to other individuals. In so doing, this framework does not assume that the effects of the experimental conditions are the same for all individuals, although in many cases that does turn out to be true in the kinds of studies that employ this type of experimental design. Ironically, this design is rarely employed in social psychology even though that is when the effects are most likely not the same for all individuals.

In light of these observations, when it is possible to operationalize the experiments using a within-subjects design, an inductive, bottom-up strategy becomes available for identifying individual differences construct(s) relevant for a behavior of interest. To illustrate, consider as an analogy a drug trial study. Imagine that an experimental drug and placebo are given to each participant at various times, and the degree of symptom alleviation (and side effects) are observed. After extensive trials to ensure a reliable assessment of response to the drug and placebo conditions, it is possible to determine the effectiveness of the drug vs. the placebo for *each* individual separately. Suppose the following results were obtained when each person's data were analyzed separately. For 50% of the people, there was a statistically significant symptom reduction due to the drug (where the $N$ for a statistical test is the number of repeated trials each individual encountered and $p$ indexes the significance of the effects of the drug *for a given individual*). For another 50% of the people, there was a statistically significant negative effect of the drug, either a worsening of the symptoms or serious side effects emerging. If the study was done as a between-subjects study, the result would have been precisely no overall effect. And unless the particular personal factor that interacts with the drug is identified a priori, it would not be possible to test for interactions with that variable.

But if the study is designed to allow establishing for each person, then the fact that 50% of the patients reliably respond positively to the drug while another 50% reliably respond negatively to it is a significant finding that merits reporting. More important, publication of such a finding can then lead to studies to identify the critical factors that differentiate individuals for whom the drug is effective and those for whom it is detrimental. That, in turn, can prove highly informative in discovering the mechanisms of the drug action. Similarly, in social psychological research, if one adopts an "establish the effects of situational factors in each person first" approach, then one can find clusters of individuals who are similar in their pattern of responses to the situational factors, that is, those with similar behavioral signatures, and systematically look for factors that differentiate among these groups of people.

## Methodological Challenges for Intensive Within-Subject Analyses

It is of course not an accident that experiments in social psychology have not widely adopted the kinds of intensive within-subject analysis described above. The nature of many classical experimental manipulations in social psychology precludes repeated exposures. The elaborate staging needed to create experimental conditions often makes it too time-consuming to expose participants repeatedly to each of the conditions. Furthermore, exposing subjects to exactly the same situation multiple times is often not a viable option. However, there are a number of ways to minimize the factors that sometimes result in drawbacks for within-subject designs, and to take advantage of the intrinsic benefit of them (e.g., Greenwald, 1976). Technological advances have made it possible to present realistic stimuli (e.g., virtual reality technology) in an engaging, interactive way, in which multiple virtual situations may be created and programmed to interact with participants. Research suggests that reactions observed in such "simulated" situations converge with those obtained in real situations (M. D. Robinson & Clore, 2001). Furthermore, many of the research agenda in the field have shifted to make use of repeatedly presented simple stimuli, such as the brief presentation of primes and targets on computers. These advances and changes make examination and establishment, beyond statistical doubt, of the experimental effect *for each participant* an increasing possibility.

In addition, in the past, statistical procedures available for social psychologists have largely been designed with between-group experiments in mind, in part reflecting, and at the same time influencing, the training, assumptions, and common practices in the field. However, more powerful statistical frameworks, algorithms, and most important, easily accessible computer packages that implement them, are becoming increasingly accessible (e.g., see Gonzalez & Griffin, Chapter 14, this volume). For example, the multilevel analysis framework (e.g., Moskowitz & Hershberger, 2002) allows fitting linear models within each individual, whereas the parameter estimates for each individual (e.g., beta weights indicating the effect of a situational variable on a given behavior *for that person*) can in turn be predicted from other variables such as individual differences. Computer implementations of these statistical procedures are available, such as the Hierarchical Linear Model (HLM) (Raudenbush & Bryk, 2002; see www.ssicentral.com/hlm/hlm.htm), SAS Proc Mixed (SAS Institute), and the NLME (nonlinear mixed effects) package (Pinheiro & Bates, 2000; see http://cm.bell-labs.com/cm/ms/departments/sia/project/nlme) available for S-Plus and for the freely available and rapidly maturing statistical software called R (www.r-project.org). Highly related to the multilevel framework is growth-curve modeling and the Mplus software that implements it (B. O. Muthén, 2002; L. Muthén & B. Muthén, 1998–2001; www.statmodel.com). These statistical models make it more natural to design and analyze experiments in which individuals' responses to a variety of experimental stimuli are analyzed and conceptualized at an individual level first. Even without adopting these new comprehensive statistical frameworks, a simple statistic such as the percentage of participants for whom the situational factors had the expected effect can be reported, and its statistical significance can be tested. Doing so naturally draws one's attention to looking at the phenomena at an individual level, rather than in the aggregate, in turn leading to discovering important differences among individuals in the effects of situational factors (i.e., person × situation interactions).

## FINDING, EVALUATING, AND USING MEASURES OF INDIVIDUAL DIFFERENCES

Given the importance of taking individual differences into account in social psychology research particularly and the availability of strategies for identifying potential aspects of individual differences in an inductive, bottom-up process, how does one actually operationalize individual differences and use them in testing models of social behavior?

### What Makes a "Good" Measure: The Intertwined Nature of Reliability and Validity

Fortunately, throughout the history of social and personality psychology in the last century, a large number of measures have been developed. They do not, of course, exhaust all the important ways in which people differ, and no doubt new measures will be devised, as models of individuals as dynamic social information processing systems evolve. Nonetheless, a bewildering array of measures already exists. For example, the volume by J. P. Robinson, Shaver, and Wrightsman (1991) has chapters covering measures of response bias, subjective well-being, self-esteem, social anxiety and shyness, depression and loneliness, alienation and anomie, interpersonal trust and attitudes toward human nature, locus of control, authoritarianism, sex roles (masculinity, femininity, and androgyny), and values. Well over a dozen particular measures are described in each chapter.[3] How do we choose?

First, a good measure must reflect the target construct. Despite the voluminous work on this topic,[4] the ultimate goals are simple: to minimize noise in the measurement and to be sure that the measure reflects what is intended to be measured and not something else. If the measures were a radio, the reception should be clear, and it should be tuned to the right station. But of course the plot thickens as one actually starts tuning the research radio. Reliability can be shown in a variety of ways that do not always produce the same conclusion. Different measures of the same thing may be highly related, for example, different halves of the multi-item questionnaire (split-half reliability), indicating that the items that make up a scale reflect something in common (internal consistency). But the same measure filled out to describe the same person by different raters (interrater reliability), or on different occasions (test-retest reliability), may result in the conclusion that the measure is not reliable.[5] To untangle this, one needs to address a fundamental conceptual issue: What is noise, and what is signal?

Often the issues of reliability and validity are considered in a sequential fashion. First establish reliability, to make sure that the measure is reliably measuring *something*, then worry about validity, to make sure that the *something* is in fact what one intended to measure. But what "noise" is depends on the nature of what is intended to be measured (see Fiske, 2002). For example, observer ratings of how often a woman spontaneously smiles while talking to a particular person may be a fairly reliable measure of how she is feeling in that particular situation, but it may be an unreliable measure of her friendliness or her attitude toward the person. Too often, reliability is considered a property of a particular measure, independent of the construct it is intended to measure. Many an apparent contradiction between studies that report high reliability of a measure and those that report the measure as unreliable stems from the difference in the constructs researchers intended to measure using the same instrument. Relatedly, it is important "to remember that a test is not reliable or unreliable. Reliability is a property of the scores on a test for a particular population of examinees" (Wilkinson & the APA Task Force on Statistical Inference, 1999, p. 596).

## Bootstrapping Upward in the Evolution of Constructs, Theories, and Measures

So, a first step is to be clear about the construct the measure is intended to measure. But in most cases, the quality being "measured" is not something that can be seen or felt, let alone directly measured, but rather a hypothetical construct. An attitude, a belief, a self-concept—these are all qualities that are hypothesized to characterize an individual. When the target of measurement is a hypothetical quality that cannot be observed directly, how does one even ask the question of whether a measure reflects it accurately? How does one address the validity of a measure? That is precisely the question addressed by the APA Committee on Psychological Tests half a century ago (Cronbach & Meehl, 1955), which introduced the notion of *construct validity*. Constructs are defined by the theory or model in which they are embedded. They are an integral part of a model of phenomena one wishes to understand, and they evolve as the model evolves from a crude approximation to a more accurate representation of the processes that give rise to observed phenomena.

Cronbach and Meehl (1955, p. 286) illustrated the construct validation process by the evolution of the construct and measure of temperature. Neither perceived warmth nor expansion of mercury is intrinsically more valid than the other, but the theories in physics relate the latter to a construct that is hypothesized to underlie a wider range of phenomena, which were in fact predicted more accurately by mercury thermometer readings than observers' judgments of the warmth of an object. Thus, what is more "valid" is not the measure alone but rather the whole system consisting of the theory relating multiple constructs (e.g., temperature, pressure) and the measures of the constructs. Cronbach and Meehl noted that the "whole process of conceptual enrichment begins with what in retrospect we see as an extremely fallible 'criterion'—the human temperature sense. That original criterion has now been relegated to a peripheral position. We have lifted ourselves by our bootstraps, but in a legitimate and fruitful way" (Cronbach & Meehl, 1955, p. 286).

The theory and measures evolve when predictions based on them fail. When they fail, one asks: Is it because the measure is faulty, or because the theory, in which the construct is embedded, is faulty? What needs to be fixed? If alternative measures of the same construct can accurately predict the phenomena expected by the theory, then perhaps the theory is fine and the particular measure is at fault. On the other hand, if phenomena predicted by other theories could be predicted accurately using the measure in question, but not those predicted by the first theory, then it's the theory that is faulty, particularly if that theory continues to fail to receive support when using other measures.

### An Example of Construct Validation Research: The Multitrait-Multimethod Matrix

The construct validation process discussed above is particularly important for psychological constructs and theories, and a general discussion of construct validation research can be found, for example, in Messick (1989, 1995). One major aspect of such programs that has received much attention is the pattern of intercorrelations among alternative measures of the same construct, as well as those of different constructs, examined systematically in light of the commonalities in the method of measurement (Campbell & Fiske, 1959). In this approach, called the multitrait-multimethod matrix (MTMM), the "theory" being tested is that measures of the same construct should correlate with each other even if they employ different methods (i.e., convergent validity), and that measures of different constructs should not correlate with each other even if they employ the same method (i.e., discriminant validity). With the development of structural equation modeling and, in particular, confirmatory factor analysis, methods for quantitative analyses of MTMM are now available (e.g., Kenny & Kashy, 1992) and are described in accessible form (e.g., Kenny, 1995; Marsh & Grayson, 1995).

The MTMM is only one specific, and perhaps the simplest, example of general approaches to construct validity. The theories in which the constructs are embedded can be more substantive in nature than simply expecting measures of the same construct to be more strongly correlated than measures of different constructs. With confirmatory factor analysis and structural equation modeling in general, it should be possible to test the fit of a theoretical model with an empirically obtained pattern of correlations. The general principle remains the same: If the fit of the theory and the data is good, then keep both the theory and the measures used to operationalize the theory. If not, revise either the theory or the measure, or both, taking into account the success of the theory using other measures and/or the success of the measures when used to test other theories.

### Construct Validation of Individual Differences Measures via Experiments

Most important for social psychologists, there is no reason for the theories being tested to be confined to patterns of intercorrelations among different types of individual differences. On the contrary, a more decisive test of the measure comes from testing theories that make predictions about the effects of situations. If a measure in fact measures a particular attitude, then it should change as a function of situational manipulations known to induce attitude change. More relevant for the present chapter, if a measure identifies individuals with different processing dynamics, then individual differences are expected to interact with situational factors in ways predicted by the theory of the particular dynamics. In short, a particularly relevant question for those evaluating the construct validity of a measure of individual differences for understanding social psychological phenomena is this: Has it been shown to interact with theoretically relevant situational factors?

## A VALID MEASURE HAS BEEN FOUND! WHAT SHOULD WE DO WITH IT? IMPLICATIONS FOR DATA ANALYSIS AND EXPERIMENTAL DESIGN

### Continuous or Categorical? It Can Matter

Let us suppose that a measure has been found with a great track record for producing theory-predicted patterns of interactions. What, then, would be the next step? What considerations apply as one plans to actually use the measure?

Numerous guides have been written on this topic, both for social psychology research in particular (e.g., Judd, 2000) and in textbooks that provide an integrative and unified framework for analyzing continuous and categorical variables, within- and between-subject designs, and fixed and random effects (e.g., Aiken & West, 1991; Judd & McClelland, 1989; also see J. Cohen, Aiken, West, & Cohen, 2002). Most relevant for the analysis

of interactions between individual difference variables and situational factors, the approaches described in these publications allow one to avoid the need for artificially forming discrete groups (e.g., by dichotomizing via median-split), which not only reduces statistical power but also can result in spuriously significant results (e.g., MacCallum, Zhang, Preacher, & Rucker, 2002; Maxwell & Delaney, 1993).

At the same time, as is the case for most statistical models used to compute statistical significance, the accuracy and appropriateness of conclusions based on these regression-based frameworks also depend on the basic assumptions made by the model. This is particularly relevant as one takes advantage of the power of data-analytic frameworks examining quantitative relationships among interval measurement scales, as compared to the more traditional analysis of variance approaches based on categorical variables that are either nominal or at most ordinal. It is all the more important to examine relatively model-independent "raw" summaries of data. Specifically, it is useful to complement regression-based analyses with exploratory analyses (e.g., Behrens, 1997, Tukey, 1969, 1977, 1980), to observe data without the lens of parametric statistical models. Models that do not rely on assumed linear relationships are also becoming available, such as the regression analyses, as well as to become aware of developments in nonlinear regression (e.g., Huet, 1996), nonparametric regression (e.g., Fox, 2000), and other nonparametric and robust methods (e.g., Hettmansperger & McKean, 1998; Sprent, 2001).

### To Block or Not to Block on Individual Difference Measures?

Although a variety of publications discuss data-analytic methods, a small sample of which are mentioned above, there is yet another issue that merits attention in considering the role of individual differences in social psychological research. That is, how should one take individual differences into account in *designing* a study (compared to what to do once data are collected)? Similar to many data-analytic issues involving measures of individual differences, this also stems from the fact that, unlike experimentally manipulated variables operationalized by random assignment into conditions, aspects of observed as well as unobserved individual differences are correlated with each other. This simple and obvious fact has an important implication for the design of experiments investigating the effects of situations as well, as discussed in some detail below.

Suppose one wishes to determine if making salient one's risk for gender-specific types of cancer would either increase or decrease health-protective behaviors (e.g., frequency of breast self-examination for women or testicular self-examination for men). To study this, students enrolled in an introductory psychology course are randomly assigned to a "risk salience" condition in which they are reminded of their risks, or to a "reassurance" condition that de-emphasizes the risk while encouraging self-examination. Suppose also that students' expectation that they might develop breast or prostate cancer had been assessed in a mass testing session at the beginning of the term and was found to be quite low, reflecting the fact that they were typical young adults. Should one simply randomly assign all students who sign up for this study to one of the two conditions? Or, because we know that those who expect to develop cancer are underrepresented in this sample, should we try to recruit an equal number of participants high vs. low in this expectation? That is, should we block on the expectation variable, to employ a randomized block design?

The question is relatively inconsequential if the effects of subject characteristics and the situational manipulation (salience of risk) do not interact, such that the effects of the manipulation do not vary systematically across individuals. If so, findings about the *effects* of the manipulation obtained for one individual should apply to another individual as well. But what if the cognitive-affective dynamics of 80% of the study participants resemble Figure 6.2, and what if risk salience facilitates self-checking behavior only among those with a low expectation of developing cancer, while it interferes with self-checking among those with higher expectations? In that case, if we do the study with a random sample of students in this population, we are likely to conclude that risk salience on the whole facilitates self-checking.

The conclusion from this low-risk population, of course, could be misleading when generalizing the findings to a population of older adults who come for their annual checkups at a clinic. Blocking on the cancer expectation to ensure adequate representation of the entire range of risk expectation, therefore, would increase the likelihood of detecting the interaction. Of course, after such blocking, the sample is no longer representative of the Psychology 101 population. However, the information about the interaction would make it less risky to extrapolate to populations of older adults with a higher expectation of risk.

Is blocking, then, an ultimate answer? Not necessarily. Consider the possibility that health risk expectations may be correlated with other variables. For example, suppose, thanks to the successful breast cancer risk consciousness–raising campaigns, that breast cancer risks are more salient to women than prostate cancer risks are to men. Then blocking on the expectation of gender-specific cancer risk would result in more women in the high risk expectation block. The observed interaction with the risk salience manipulation may therefore be, in reality, an interaction with gender. That is, risk expectation may be confounded with gender. One may, of course, further block on gender as well, sampling an equal number of women and men within high risk expectation and low risk expectation blocks respectively. But there are potential pitfalls in doing so as well. For example, male college students who are high in their health risk expectation may have some unusual characteristics not found in other men, such as being more pessimistic, or even hypochondriacal, while female college students with a comparable level of health risk expectation may be no more pessimistic than average for female students. One could statistically examine and remove the effects of these subject variables in a multiple regression framework, but that would require appreciable and meaningful variations in risk expectations in the sample of participants studied and being able to safely assume that the effects of these variables are linear and can be extrapolated beyond the range observed in the particular sample. These are big assumptions.

In the end, for every measured individual difference characteristic, there can be many more unobserved characteristics that are correlated with it, and that interact with situations significantly. Blocking on all these variables is not practical, because to the extent that two variables are correlated positively, it would be difficult to obtain samples that are high on one variable and low on the other, and if one does, that sample may have some particular characteristics associated with being rare. For example, would the values, expectations, and professional experience of female professors of engineering be understood simply by virtue of their being female and being professors of engineering? A regression-based estimation of the "effects" of being female and of being a professor of engineering observed in a typical random sample, which is likely to contain only a few, if any, actual female professors of engineering, could be a tenuous exercise in extrapolation. Furthermore, measurement error in the scores used for blocking results in a differential regression to the mean, especially when

one group is sampled from the high end of a distribution and the other is from the low end. (For excellent discussions of this and other methodological issues, see Cook and Campbell [1979, pp. 175-182].)

## *Recasting the Problem: Going Beyond Individual Differences as a Poor Person's Substitute for an Experiment*

How might one solve this dilemma? As for many tough problems, the "solution" may require recasting the problem. What is the nature of the problem, and what are the assumptions that lead us to it? The ultimate source of the "problem" is this: Individual difference characteristics are correlated with each other. In addition to the problem of confounding—not being sure exactly which of the correlated variables are *really* responsible for the phenomenon—there is the issue that it is often not possible to find people who represent certain combinations of variables, making it again more difficult to isolate the effects of each variable. One fundamental assumption, or a conceptual framework, that led us to this quandary is that our goal is to study the effects of individual *variables*, and we are approaching individual differences as a way to operationalize the *variables*. But it is a poor person's operationalization at best, as there is no random assignment.

### *Understanding the Effects of Situations for Each Person First*

What if, instead, we view each individual's social processing system, each with a distinctive configuration of bundles of variables "presented by Nature" (Cronbach, 1957), as a natural unit, and study its functioning? To the extent that individuals' genetics, life experiences, and culture shapes their relatively unique social information processing systems, it may not be entirely unreasonable to liken the role in social psychology of individual differences among people to the role in biology of differences among species. Biologists don't view species as an operationalization of variables—size, shape, number of limbs, presence of feathers, and so on—and examine the "effects" of each of these characteristics in a regression equation. Rather, they take each species one at a time and study the functions of their structure—large-scale structures as well as the molecular structure, as encoded by the unique DNA sequence that defines the species. In their work, it is clear that it does not even make sense to speak of the function of a gene independent of the context of the rest of the species's genome and the cellular chemical environment. That is, the behaviors of an organism, as well as the effect of a particular gene, are a function of the Gestalt, the whole configuration of the genome and the micro (cellular) and macro (ecological) environment.

If one likens species to individual persons with their unique configuration of beliefs, expectations, values, goals, and competencies, the fact that it is difficult to find people with every possible combination of characteristics should not be disconcerting, just as not being able to find a species with feathers and gills does not pose a problem for biologists. People need not be seen as an operationalization of variables one would rather manipulate via random assignment. Instead, it may be more fruitful to see each individual as a distinctive social information *system* that dynamically interacts with the situations and generates thoughts, feelings, and behaviors. In this framework, one route for pursuing generalizable knowledge, rather than knowledge specific to a single individual, may be to identify types of individuals who are similar in their social information processing system. That is, it may be more fruitful to frame our mission in a less variable-centered, and more person- and type-centered, way (e.g., Anderson & Sedikides, 1991; Magnusson, 1998; Robins, John, & Caspi, 1998; Shoda & LeeTiernan,

2002). The "confounding" of variables stops being a "problem" if we seek to understand the functioning of the type of system characterized by the specific configuration of the variables, "as presented by Nature."

*Trading Instant Generalizability for Ultimate Generalizability: The Implications of a Person- and Type-Centered, More Inductive, Approach*

This way of approaching science has some practical implications for social psychology. First, it should not be necessary to fret too much that the results of any given experiment may be limited to the population of individuals studied, not because it's not true, but because of a frank acknowledgment that that is the case in *every* study one ever conducts. Integral for the proposed release from "generalizability fretting," however, is a shift in how one conceptualizes empirical research. Instead of trying to achieve generality in any given study, an alternative goal is a commitment to making every empirical study a part of a cumulative scientific endeavor. This is based on faith, for lack of a better word, in the ultimate success by the scientific community in identifying regularities and generalizable patterns and principles, as studies conducted with different populations of individuals accumulate. But "faith" alone is not sufficient, of course. It requires that any single study *not* claim to have found a "general law" of social psychology that is independent of the characteristics of the individuals serving as participants. In turn, such a claim should not be required as a criterion for publication. Instead, the burden on researchers is to find ways to make available as much information as possible about the individuals who served as participants, for future use in meta-analysis. At least, one can do better than describing study participants as "students enrolled in an introductory psychology class at a large Western university," which presupposes that all that matters is the subject of the class and the size and general geographical location of the university. Without any increase in word count, one could name the university, potentially conveying a lot more information.

Second, the use of a within-subject design, whenever it is possible, would potentially allow for at least a rough assessment of the extent to which there are individual differences that can moderate the effects of the situations. If, for example, the effects of situations vary reliably across participants, then, even if it is not known what individual difference characteristic is relevant, one at least knows there is a need to be particularly cautious in localizing the findings to the population studied and to report as much potentially relevant information about the population as is available. Such a finding is also an indication that it would be fruitful to launch a concerted effort to identify the important differences in the social information processing systems underlying the behavior being studied, which in turn may lead to identifying common types of processing systems. Advancement in the statistical models, such as the multilevel analyses, and practical computer packages that implement them, such as HLM, Mplus, and NLME (discussed earlier in this chapter), would make it possible to characterize the effects of situations for each individual, and then consider variations among individuals in the nature and magnitude of such effects.

## CONCLUDING THOUGHTS: UNDERSTANDING SITUATIONS TO UNDERSTAND PEOPLE, UNDERSTANDING PEOPLE TO UNDERSTAND SITUATIONS

Studies of situations and persons go hand in hand. Predictable patterns of an individual's behavior variation across situations suggests that the distinctions among the situations are important for the individual, engaging the natural distinctions among situations that the person's information processing system makes. If seeing George, Dick, or Don in charge of a situation makes a person more nervous than when others are in charge, then situations involving George, Dick, and Don share some important features that the observer's social information processing system picks up, and that in turn activate certain thoughts and feelings. But what is it about the situations involving George, Dick, and Don that are different from others? To achieve a better understanding of the individual's processing system, and to go beyond observations made in any given situation and predict responses to novel situations (would a situation involving Colin at the helm of an organization make the observer nervous too? Or what if Madeline is in charge?), it is necessary to understand what it was about the situations that made each person respond in his or her characteristic manner. That is, situations need to be understood at the level of their *psychological features*, rather than at the *nominal* level (Shoda, Mischel, et al., 1994).

One concrete example of this approach is a recent systematic attempt at generating a typology of both situations and persons (Kelley et al., 2002). The effort primarily focused on "situations of interdependence," in which the behavior of one partner in a dyad influences the rewards, such as pleasure and gratification, as well as the costs, such as physical or mental effort, pain, embarrassment, or anxiety, for the other partner. For example, a situation may be characterized as one in which the basic features of the Prisoner's Dilemma situation apply, so that if reciprocation is assured, cooperative behavior results in the best outcome for both, but one stands to lose much if the partner does not reciprocate with cooperative behavior. In turn, for each type of situation characteristic, a type (or types) of persons could be identified who share distinctive ways of responding to them.

Patterns of interdependence are, of course, only one aspect of situations. For a given behavior of interest, and for a given domain of life, there are likely to be a relatively small number of key psychological features of situations that are particularly important. Identifying them can in turn lead to identifying types of persons who share distinct dynamics, as discussed earlier. For example, if for an individual a major distinction among social situations is the presence or absence of opportunities for demonstrating his or her superiority, it seems likely that the individual may be characterized by narcissistic processing dynamics (e.g., Morf & Rhodewalt, 2001). If the presence or absence of the possibility of rejection on the basis of race is a major distinguishing feature of situations for another person, then it seems likely that the individual may be characterized by the processing dynamics of racial rejection sensitivity (Mendoza-Denton et al., in press). The analysis of the situations thus facilitates the identification of distinctive personal characteristics. And the analysis of the processing dynamics that characterize an individual in turn leads one to situation features that characterize diagnostic situations. Thus, in order to truly understand people, one needs to understand situations, and to really understand situations, one needs to understand people.

## NOTES

1. Furthermore, although for brevity and clarity the present chapter focuses on the immediate effects of situations, the role of individual differences of course is not limited to people's immediate responses to situations. Naturally occurring situations may differ in the kinds of people they attract, and people's reactions to situations in turn affect the future situations they encounter. Thus it may be necessary to understand the *system* consisting of the particular combination of the person and the environment, rather than each of them separately. That is, the behaviors of individuals may be the emergent properties of the *system* consisting of the individual and the environment, rather than simply a sum of the effects of situations, or persons, that can be observed in isolation. For further discussion of examples of such person-situation interactions, see Shoda, LeeTiernan, and Mischel (2002) as well as Zayas, Shoda, and Ayduk (2002).

2. The results of the survey are summarized in a table available at the following URL: http://depts.washington.edu/pxs/. It lists (a) The "P"—the individual difference, (b) The "S"—the situational dimension/feature with which the "P" construct interacted, and (c) The "B" in B = $f$ (P × S)—the dependent variable on which the "P" and "S" interacted. It is intended as a continuously evolving table; readers who would like to contribute additional constructs are encouraged to send e-mail to P × S@u.washington.edu, a dedicated e-mail account checked periodically to update the table.

3. In addition, a publication of the American Psychological Association, *The Directory of Unpublished Experimental Mental Measures* (Goldman, Mitchel, & Egelson, 1997), lists 2,078 measures that appeared in 37 journals in psychology, education, and sociology from 1991 to 1995. Literally thousands of measures are listed in such publications as *Tests in Print V* (Murphy, Impara, & Plake, 1999), *Tests: A Comprehensive Reference for Assessments in Psychology, Education, and Business* (Maddox, 1997), and *The ETS Test Collection Catalog* (Educational Testing Service, 1993).

4. For excellent discussions of this topic, see the Robinson, Shaver, and Wrightsman (1991) chapter titled "Criteria for Scale Selection and Evaluation," the John and Benet-Martinez (2000) chapter titled "Measurement: Reliability,

Construct Validation, and Scale Construction," and textbooks such as Aiken (1997), Anastasi and Urbina (1997), R. J. Cohen and Swerdlik (1999), Gregory (1996), and Kaplan and Saccuzzo (1997). The generalizability theory (Cronbach, Gleser, Nanda, & Rajaratnam, 1972) provides a unifying framework in which the many "types" of reliability can be thought of as a facet and is covered in Marcoulides (1999).

5. Discussions of various types of reliability and the ways of estimating them are readily available in other more in-depth treatments such as L. Crocker and Algina (1986), Feldt and Brennan (1989), and Nunnally and Bernstein (1994).

## REFERENCES

Aiken, L. R. (1997). *Psychological testing and assessment* (9th ed.). Boston: Allyn & Bacon.

Aiken, L. R., & West, S. G. (1991). *Multiple regression: Testing and interpreting interactions.* Newbury Park, CA: Sage.

Allport, G. W. (1937). *Personality: A psychological interpretation.* New York: Holt, Rinehart & Winston.

Allport, G. W., & Odbert, H. S. (1936). Trait-names: A psycho-lexical study. *Psychological Monographs: General and Applied, 47,* 1-171.

Anastasi, A., & Urbina, S. (1997). *Psychological testing* (7th ed.). Englewood Cliffs, NJ: Prentice Hall.

Anderson, C. A., & Sedikides, C. (1991). Thinking about people: Contributions of a typological alternative to associationistic and dimensional models of person perception. *Journal of Personality and Social Psychology, 60,* 203-217.

Baron, R. M., & Kenny, D. A. (1986). The moderator-mediator variable distinction in social psychological research: Conceptual, strategic, and statistical considerations. *Journal of Personality and Social Psychology, 51,* 1173-1182.

Barron, K. E., & Harackiewicz, J. M. (2001). Achievement goals and optimal motivation: Testing multiple goal models. *Journal of Personality and Social Psychology, 80,* 706-722.

Beach, S.R.H., Tesser, A., Fincham, F. D., Jones, D. J., Johnson, D., & Whitaker, D. J. (1998). Pleasure and pain in doing well, together: An investigation of performance-related affect in close relationships. *Journal of Personality and Social Psychology, 74,* 923-938.

Behrens, J. T. (1997). Principles and procedures of exploratory data analysis. *Psychological Methods, 2,* 131-160.

Bolger, N., & Zuckerman, A. (1995). A framework for studying personality in the stress process. *Journal of Personality and Social Psychology, 69,* 890-902.

Campbell, D. T., & Fiske, D. W. (1959). Convergent and discriminant validation by the multitrait-multimethod matrix. *Psychological Bulletin, 56,* 81-105.

Carver, C. S., & White, T. L. (1994). Behavioral inhibition, behavioral activation, and affective responses to impending reward and punishment: The BIS/BAS Scales. *Journal of Personality and Social Psychology, 67,* 319-333.

Cattell, R. B. (1946). Personality structure and measurement. I. The operational determination of trait unities. *British Journal of Psychology, 36,* 88-103.

Chen, S., Shechter, D., & Chaiken, S. (1996). Getting at the truth or getting along: Accuracy-versus impression-motivated heuristic and systematic processing. *Journal of Personality and Social Psychology, 71,* 262-275.

Cohen, J., Aiken, L. S., West, S. G., & Cohen, P. (2002). *Applied multiple regression-correlation analysis for the behavioral sciences.* Mahwah, NJ: Lawrence Erlbaum.

Cohen, R. J., & Swerdlik, M. E. (1999). *Psychological testing and assessment: An introduction to tests and measurement* (4th ed.). Mountain View, CA: Mayfield.

Cook, T. D., & Campbell, D. T. (1979). *Quasi-experimentation: Design and analysis issues for field settings*. Chicago: Rand McNally.

Crocker, J., Thompson, L. L., McGraw, K. M., & Ingerman, C. (1987). Downward comparison, prejudice, and evaluations of others: Effects of self-esteem and threat. *Journal of Personality and Social Psychology, 52,* 907-916.

Crocker, L. M., & Algina, J. (1986). *Introduction to classical and modern test theory.* New York: Holt, Rinehart & Winston.

Cronbach, L. J. (1957). The two disciplines of scientific psychology. *American Psychologist, 12,* 671-684.

Cronbach, L. J. (1975). Beyond the two disciplines of scientific psychology. *American Psychologist, 30,* 116-127.

Cronbach, L. J. (1984). A research worker's treasure chest. *Multivariate Behavioral Research, 19,* 223-240.

Cronbach, L. J., Gleser, G. C., Nanda, H., & Rajaratnam, N. (1972). *The dependability of behavioral measurements: Theory of generalizability for scores and profiles.* New York: Wiley.

Cronbach, L. J., & Meehl, P. E. (1955). Construct validity in psychological tests. *Psychological Bulletin, 52,* 281-302.

Ebbinghaus, H. von. (1885). *Über das Gedächtnis. Untersuchungen zur experimentellen Psychologie.* Leipzig: Duncker & Humblot.

Educational Testing Service. (1993). *The ETS test collection catalog.* Phoenix, AZ: Oryx Press.

Feldt, L. S., & Brennan, R. L. (1989). Reliability. In R. L. Linn (Ed.), *Educational measurement* (3rd ed., pp. 105-145). Washington, DC: American Council on Education/Oryx.

Fiske, D. W. (2002). Validity for what? In H. I. Braun & D. N. Jackson (Eds.), *The role of constructs in psychological and educational measurement* (pp. 169-178). Mahwah, NJ: Lawrence Erlbaum.

Fox, J. (2000). *Nonparametric simple regression: Smoothing scatterplots.* Thousand Oaks, CA: Sage.

Gable, S. L., Reis, H. T., & Elliot, A. J. (2000). Behavioral activation and inhibition in everyday life. *Journal of Personality and Social Psychology, 78,* 1135-1149.

Goldman, B. A., Mitchel, D. F., & Egelson, P. E. (1997). *The directory of unpublished experimental mental measures* (Vol. 7). Washington, DC: American Psychological Association.

Greenwald, A. G. (1976). Within-subjects designs: To use or not to use? *Psychological Bulletin, 83,* 314-320.

Gregory, R. J. (1996). *Psychological testing: History, principles, and applications* (2nd ed.). Boston: Allyn & Bacon.

Hettmansperger, T. P., & McKean, J. W. (1998). *Robust nonparametric statistical methods.* New York: Wiley.

Higgins, E. T. (1999). Persons or situations: Unique explanatory principles or variability in general principles? In D. Cervone & Y. Shoda (Eds.), *The coherence of personality: Social-cognitive bases of consistency, variability, and organization* (pp. 61-93). New York: Guilford.

Huber, G. L., & Sorrentino, R. M., Davidson, M. A., & Epplier, R. (1992). Uncertainty orientation and cooperative learning: Individual differences within and across cultures. *Learning and Individual Differences, 4,* 1-24.

Huet, S. (1996). *Statistical tools for nonlinear regression : A practical guide with S-PLUS examples.* New York: Springer.

John, O. P., & Benet-Martinez, V. (2000). Measurement: Reliability, construct validation, and scale construction. In H. T. Reis & C. M. Judd (Eds.), *Handbook of research methods in social and personality psychology* (pp. 339-369). New York: Cambridge University Press.

Judd, C. M. (2000). Everyday data analysis in social psychology: Comparisons of linear models. In H. T. Reis & C. M. Judd (Eds.), *Handbook of research methods in social and personality psychology* (pp. 370-393). New York: Cambridge University Press.

Judd, C. M., & McClelland, G. H. (1989). *Data analysis: A model-comparison approach*. San Diego: Harcourt Brace Jovanovich.

Kaplan, R. M., & Saccuzzo, D. P. (1997). *Psychological testing: Principles, applications, and issues* (4th ed.). Wadsworth, CA: Brooks/Cole.

Kelley, H. H., Holmes, J. G., Kerr, N. L., Reis, H. T., Rusbult, C. E., & van Lange, P. A. M. (2002). *An atlas of interpersonal situations*. New York: Cambridge University Press.

Kenny, D. A. (1995). The multitrait-multimethod matrix: Design, analysis, and conceptual issues. In P. E. Shrout & S. T. Fiske (Eds.), *Personality research, methods, and theory: A festschrift honoring Donald W. Fiske* (pp. 111-124). Hillsdale, NJ: Lawrence Erlbaum.

Kenny, D. A., & Kashy, D. A. (1992). Analysis of the multitrait-multimethod matrix by confirmatory factor analysis. *Psychological Bulletin, 112,* 165-172.

Lewin, K. (1931). The conflict between Aristotelian and Galileian modes of thought in contemporary psychology. *Journal of General Psychology, 5,* 141-177.

Lewin, K. (1946). Behavior and development as a function of the total situation. In L. Carmichael (Ed.), *Manual of child psychology* (pp. 791-844). Oxford, UK: Wiley.

MacCallum, R. C., Zhang, S., Preacher, K. J., & Rucker, D. D. (2002). On the practice of dichotomization of quantitative variables. *Psychological Methods, 7,* 19-40.

Maddox, T. (1997). *Tests: A comprehensive reference for assessments in psychology, education, and business*. Austin, TX: Pro-Ed.

Magnusson, D. (1998). The logic and implications of a person-oriented approach. In R. B. Cairns, L. R. Bergman, & J. Kagan. (Eds.), *Methods and models for studying the individual: Essays in honor of Marian Radke-Yarrow* (pp. 33-64). Thousand Oaks, CA: Sage.

Marcoulides, G. A. (1999). Generalizability theory: Picking up where the Rasch IRT model leaves off? In S. E. Embretson & S. L. Hershberger (Eds.), *The new rules of measurement: What every psychologist and educator should know* (pp. 129-152). Mahwah, NJ: Lawrence Erlbaum.

Marsh, H. W., & Grayson, D. (1995). Latent variable models of multitrait-multimethod data. In R. H. Hoyle (Ed.), *Structural equation modeling: Concepts, issues, and applications* (pp. 177-198). Thousand Oaks, CA: Sage.

Maxwell, S. E., & Delaney, H. D. (1993). Bivariate median splits and spurious statistical significance. *Psychological Bulletin, 113,* 181-190.

Mendoza-Denton, R., Purdie, V., Downey, G., & Davis, A. (in press). Sensitivity to race-based rejection: Implications for African-American students' transition to college. *Journal of Personality and Social Psychology.*

Messick, S. (1989). Validity. In R. L. Linn (Ed.), *Educational measurement* (3rd ed., pp. 13-103). New York: Macmillan.

Messick, S. (1995). Validity of psychological assessment. *American Psychologist, 50,* 741-749.

Miller, S. M., Shoda, Y., & Hurley, K. (1996). Applying cognitive social theory to health protective behavior: Breast self-examination in cancer screening. *Psychological Bulletin, 119,* 70-94.

Mischel, W. (1973). Toward a cognitive social learning reconceptualization of personality. *Psychological Review, 80,* 252-283.

Mischel, W., & Shoda, Y. (1995). A cognitive-affective system theory of personality: Reconceptualizing situations, dispositions, dynamics, and invariance in personality structure. *Psychological Review, 102,* 246-268.

Morf, C. C., & Rhodewalt, F. (1993). Narcissism and self-evaluation maintenance: Explorations in object relations. *Personality and Social Psychology Bulletin, 19,* 668-676.

Morf, C. C., & Rhodewalt, F. (2001). Unraveling the paradoxes of narcissism: A dynamic self-regulatory processing model. *Psychological Inquiry, 12,* 177-196.

Moskowitz, D. S., & Hershberger, S. L. (2002). *Modeling intraindividual variability with repeated measures data: Methods and applications.* Mahwah, NJ: Lawrence Erlbaum.

Mroczek, D. K., & Almeida, D. M. (2002). *Age differences in the effect of stress and personality on negative affect.* Unpublished manuscript, Fordham University.

Murphy, L. L., Impara, J. C., & Plake, B. S. (1999). *Tests in print V: An index to tests, test reviews, and the literature on specific tests.* Lincoln, NE: Buros Institute of Mental Measurements.

Muthén, B. O. (2002). Beyond SEM: General latent variable modeling. *Behaviormetrika, 29,* 81-117.

Muthén, L., & Muthén, B. (1998-2001). *Mplus user's guide.* Los Angeles: Muthén & Muthén.

Nunnally, J. C., & Bernstein, I. H. (1994). *Psychometric theory* (3rd ed.). New York: McGraw-Hill.

Pinheiro, J. C., & Bates, D. M. (2000). *Mixed-effects models in S and S-PLUS.* New York: Springer-Verlag.

Raudenbush, S. W., & Bryk, A. S. (2002). *Hierarchical linear models: Applications and data analysis methods* (2nd ed.). Newbury Park, CA: Sage.

Rhodewalt, F., & Morf, C. C. (1998). On self-aggrandizement and anger: A temporal analysis of narcissism and affective reactions to success and failure. *Journal of Personality and Social Psychology, 74,* 672-685.

Robins, R. W., John, O. P., & Caspi, A. (1998). The typological approach to studying personality. In R. B. Cairns, L. R. Bergman, & J. Kagan. (Eds.), *Methods and models for studying the individual:* Essays in honor of Marian Radke-Yarrow (pp. 135–160). Thousand Oaks, CA: Sage.

Robinson, J. P., Shaver, P. R., & Wrightsman, L. S. (1991). Criteria for scale selection and evaluation. In J. P. Robinson, P. R. Shaver, & L. S. Wrightsman (Eds.), *Measures of personality and social psychological attitudes* (pp. 1-16). San Diego: Academic Press.

Robinson, J. P., Shaver, P. R., & Wrightsman, L. S. (Eds.). (1991). *Measures of personality and social psychological attitudes.* San Diego: Academic Press.

Robinson, M. D., & Clore, G. L. (2001). Simulation, scenarios, and emotional appraisal: Testing the convergence of real and imagined reactions to emotional stimuli. *Personality and Social Psychology Bulletin, 27,* 1520-1532.

Runyan, W. M. (1983). Why did Van Gogh cut off his ear? The problem of alternative explanations in psychobiography. *Journal of Personality and Social Psychology, 40,* 1070-1077.

Schütz, A., & DePaulo, B. M. (1996). Self-esteem and evaluative reactions: Letting people speak for themselves. *Journal of Research in Personality, 30,* 137-156.

Shoda, Y. (1999). Behavioral signatures of personality: Perception and generation of coherence. In D. Cervone & Y. Shoda (Eds.), *The coherence of personality: Social-cognitive bases of personality consistency, variability, and organization* (pp. 155-181). New York: Guilford.

Shoda, Y., & LeeTiernan, S. (2002). What remains invariant?: Finding order within a person's thoughts, feelings, and behaviors across situations. In D. Cervone &

W. Mischel (Eds.), *Advances in personality science* (Vol. 1, pp. 241-270). New York: Guilford.

Shoda, Y., LeeTiernan, S., & Mischel, W. (2002). Personality as a dynamical system: Emergence of stability and constancy from intra- and inter-personal interactions. *Personality and Social Psychology Review, 6,* 316-325.

Shoda, Y., Mischel, W., & Wright, J. C. (1994). Intra-individual stability in the organization and patterning of behavior: Incorporating psychological situations into the idiographic analysis of personality. *Journal of Personality and Social Psychology, 67,* 674-687.

Sorrentino, R. M., & Roney, C. J. (2000). *The uncertain mind: Individual differences in facing the unknown.* London: Psychology Press.

Sprent, P. (2001). *Applied nonparametric statistical methods.* Boca Raton, FL: Chapman & Hall.

Tukey, J. W. (1969). Analyzing data: Sanctification or detective work? *American Psychologist, 24,* 83-91.

Tukey, J. W. (1977). *Exploratory data analysis.* Reading, MA: Addison-Wesley.

Tukey, J. W. (1980). We need both exploratory and confirmatory. *The American Statistician, 34,* 23-25.

Vansteelandt, K., & Van Mechelen, I. (1998). Individual differences in situation-behavior profiles: A triple typology model. *Journal of Personality and Social Psychology, 75,* 751-765.

Walker, A. M., & Sorrentino, R. M. (2000). Control motivation and uncertainty: Information processing or avoidance in moderate depressives and nondepressives. *Personality and Social Psychology Bulletin, 26,* 436-451.

Wilkinson, L., & the APA Task Force on Statistical Inference. (1999). Statistical methods in psychology journals: Guidelines and explanations. *American Psychologist, 54,* 594-604.

Zayas, V., Shoda, Y., & Ayduk, O. (2002). Personality in context: An interpersonal systems perspective. *Journal of Personality, 70,* 851-898.

# Part III

# DESIGN AND ANALYSIS

## Section B

### Operationalizing the Constructs: Deciding What to Measure, Why, and How

## CHAPTER 7

# Constructing and Evaluating Quantitative Measures for Social Psychological Research

## Conceptual Challenges and Methodological Solutions

DUANE T. WEGENER

*Purdue University*

LEANDRE R. FABRIGAR

*Queen's University*

From social psychology's earliest days, researchers have based their theories and empirical investigations on the study of latent psychological constructs (e.g., Thurstone, 1928). Concepts such as attitudes, attributions, stereotypes, and interpersonal attraction are all hypothetical constructs that cannot be directly observed but are nonetheless presumed to play an important role in social behavior. One of the great challenges to and successes of social psychology has been the development of reliable and valid approaches to measuring such unobservable constructs. Without such approaches, the empirical examination of social psychological theories would not be possible.

Consider the following example. Attitude researchers have long been interested in understanding why persuasive appeals sometimes fail. One reason may be that messages often fail to target the underlying basis of an attitude. Specifically, researchers have proposed that attitudes (i.e., relatively enduring and global evaluations) can be based on two distinct types of information: affect and cognition. The affective basis refers to emotions and mood states that a person associates with the attitude object. For example, a person might form a positive attitude toward a Porsche based in part on the emotions the car elicits (e.g., excitement). The cognitive basis refers to beliefs about attributes of the attitude object. For instance, a person might develop a positive attitude toward a Porsche based on beliefs about the car's many positive features (e.g., superior handling and performance). It has been proposed that some attitudes may be based on affect whereas others may be based on cognition (e.g., Katz & Stotland, 1959) and that attitudes will be differentially susceptible to persuasive appeals that match versus mismatch the basis of the attitude (e.g., Edwards, 1990; Fabrigar & Petty, 1999).

Any empirical investigation of such matching effects requires measures for a variety of unobservable constructs. First, one must have some way of measuring attitudes. Second, a researcher must be able to determine if attitudes are based predominantly on affect or on cognition. This requires the development of measures of affective and cognitive bases. Such measures could be used either to confirm the success of an experimental manipulation or as a means of categorizing naturally occurring attitudes. Finally, this research question requires confirmation that manipulations of the affective and cognitive nature of the persuasive appeals were successful. Such confirmation requires measures to assess the nature of the evaluative responses produced by the messages.

In this chapter, we review a variety of issues related to the construction and evaluation of quantitative measures of latent psychological constructs. We begin by defining what quantitative measures are and contrasting them with other types of measures. We then summarize the major steps and key issues in constructing quantitative measures (primarily within the context of direct self-report measures of attitudes and related constructs). Next, we review procedures for evaluating the quality of a quantitative measure. Finally, we turn our attention to the development and assessment of indirect or nonself-report measures, emphasizing the applicability of traditional psychometric procedures to these alternative measures.

## DEFINING QUANTITATIVE MEASURES

Quantitative measures typically represent in numerical form the standing of people or objects on some construct of interest. Quantitative measures are intended to produce scores that at least approximate an interval level of measurement (i.e., units of measurement represent equal intervals). Thus, quantitative measures can be contrasted with measures intended to reflect categorical distinctions among people or objects (i.e., nominal scale measures) or simple rank ordering of people or objects on a construct of interest (i.e., ordinal scale measures). There are two potential advantages to having measures with interval level properties (see Gaito, 1980; Townsend & Ashby, 1984). Such measures provide information not only about the relative standing of people on a construct (as in nominal or ordinal data) but also about the magnitude of the difference between people. Also, whether a measure has interval level properties can have implications for the appropriateness of particular statistical procedures. For example, ANOVA, multiple regression, and factor analysis are more likely to be appropriate when measures at least approximate the interval level.

## STAGES IN CONSTRUCTING QUANTITATIVE MEASURES

Constructing quantitative measures can be thought of as occurring in three major stages. First, the researcher must specify the goals of the measure and formulate the theoretical assumptions that guide its construction. Second, a pool of potential items must be generated. Finally, the performance of the individual items must be evaluated and items for the final scale selected. In the sections that follow, we outline key challenges that occur at each stage and discuss strategies for dealing with these challenges. Throughout, we discuss these issues primarily within the context of self-report measures. We do so because such measures are the most widely used type of measure in social psychology. However, nearly all the challenges we discuss as well as many of the strategies for dealing with them are applicable to the construction of quantitative measures that do not involve self-reports.

## Specifying Measurement Goals and Theoretical Assumptions

### Specifying One's Goals for the Measure

Successful measurement begins with specifying the intended goals for the measure (e.g., see Aiken, 1997; Friedenberg, 1995). Obviously, the researcher must determine the domain the measure is intended to assess. For instance, in our example involving attitude bases, the domain of interest includes the constructs of attitudes, affective bases, and cognitive bases. However, outlining the relevant constructs is not sufficient. One should also consider the specificity of the measures that will be used. For instance, does the researcher wish to create general measures of attitude, affect, and cognition that can be used across a range of attitude objects (Crites, Fabrigar, & Petty, 1994; Eagly, Mladinic, & Otto, 1994), or does the researcher wish to design measures for a single attitude object or a specific class of attitude objects (Abelson, Kinder, Peters, & Fiske, 1982; Breckler, 1984)? Another issue is the population for which the measure will be used. This has implications for later decisions such as the wording of instructions and of items as well as the overall length of the measure. For example, a measure designed for children might require simpler wording, fewer items, and simpler response options than a measure designed for adults. Finally, the context in which the measure will be used should also be considered. Is

the measure intended for use in laboratory settings, mass testing sessions, or telephone surveys? For example, a measure designed for telephone surveys might have to be relatively brief because survey respondents often must interrupt ongoing activities to complete the measure and might need to consist of items with relatively few response options because respondents must hold these response options in memory.

### Specifying Theoretical Assumptions

All too often, social psychologists fail to recognize the interdependence of theory and measurement (Crites et al., 1994; Ostrom, 1989). Any time a researcher uses a particular measure, that researcher is implicitly accepting certain assumptions regarding the construct of interest. Consider a measure of attitude basis that asks people to directly report how much their attitudes are based on emotions versus beliefs. Such a measure requires the researcher to accept the assumption that people can successfully introspect about the extent to which their attitudes are based on affect versus cognition. Another approach might be to ask people to report their emotions, beliefs, and attitudes. The researcher could then use statistical procedures to assess the extent to which the two bases are associated with the overall attitude. This measurement strategy does not require the assumption that people can successfully introspect but would require the researcher to accept that people can provide valid self-reports of the content of the bases of their attitudes.

Researchers should explicitly acknowledge the interdependence of measurement and theory and thus clearly delineate their fundamental assumptions before constructing the actual measure (e.g., see Crites et al., 1994). Specification of assumptions should address a variety of issues. Obviously, it should include precise definitions of constructs. For example,

Jackson (1971) suggested that researchers should write behavioral descriptions of people who score high and low on the construct of interest. Assumptions regarding the structural properties of the key constructs might also be important. For example, one might consider attitude, affect, and cognition to be strictly bipolar or to be conceptually independent, with potential for coexisting positive and negative responses within each construct. One would also want to address whether the measures are intended to apply to many objects or whether new measures would be necessary for each new object. Finally, one should specify assumptions regarding how the constructs will manifest themselves. For instance, an attitude measure based on overt behaviors rests on the assumption that attitudes and overt behaviors should be strongly associated. Self-report measures of attitude, affect, and cognition require the assumption that these constructs should manifest themselves in differential responses to specific semantic stimuli.

Articulating theoretical assumptions prior to constructing measures can translate into a number of practical advantages. First, it encourages careful evaluation of assumptions. Implicit assumptions are seldom questioned, whereas explicit assumptions can be critically considered for potential flaws. Theoretical assumptions also can provide a set of standards capable of guiding item generation and evaluation. Precise definitions help to clarify whether the items generated are appropriate in their content and comprehensive in their coverage. For example, imagine that we defined the affective basis of attitudes as comprising specific emotional states associated with an object that are evaluative in nature. This definition could help determine which content would be appropriate for items. For instance, it suggests that terms should reflect specific emotions rather than undifferentiated positive or negative affect. It also suggests that the emotion terms should be clearly positive

or negative. Stating assumptions also can guide decisions regarding measurement features such as question format. For example, if one assumes positive and negative emotions can coexist, one might choose to present emotional states in a unipolar scale format rather than presenting opposing affective states in a bipolar scale format. A final benefit of specifying assumptions is that it communicates information to users of the measure that can assist in proper interpretation. One problem in social psychology has been that different researchers often have set out to study the same construct but have used measures that implicitly suggest very different conceptualizations of the construct (see Crites et al., 1994, for discussion of this in the context of affective and cognitive attitude bases).

## Item Generation

### Creating Items

*Item Content and Wording.* Perhaps the most fundamental issue in creating items is determining the content and wording of items. Although writing items requires subjective judgment and creativity, there are strategies that can assist in the process. First, if conceptual assumptions underlying the measure have been specified, items can be written to have good face validity with respect to the stated assumptions. Consider our definition of the affective basis of attitudes as comprising specific evaluative emotional states associated with an object. One might begin the process of constructing items by generating a list of words commonly used to convey particular positive or negative emotional states. This list could be further expanded by using a thesaurus.

Another complementary strategy is to examine related theories and measures.[1] For example, theories of emotion (e.g., Izard, 1977; Russell, 1980) could be a source for generating items for the measure of the affective basis. Previously constructed measures also can be used. Obviously, in drawing on past theory and measures, researchers should not blindly accept what has been proposed or used in the past. Instead, items drawn from these sources should be assessed in light of the stated assumptions for the current measure. For instance, consider the Circumplex Model of Affect (e.g., Russell, 1980). This theory states that affective states comprise differing amounts of two underlying dimensions: evaluation and arousal. Thus, in the context of this theory, it is possible to have some affective states with little evaluative content. Such emotions do not fit within the stated theoretical assumptions of our example. Hence, in using this theory as a source for items, one would want to select only the subset of affective states that fit the theoretical assumptions.

Generating items also requires consideration of how the items will be worded (e.g., see Janada, 1998; Krosnick & Fabrigar, in press; Schuman & Presser, 1981). Researchers should minimize ambiguity. Obscure words that are unlikely to be recognized by most respondents should be avoided, as should complex wording structures (e.g., items with double negatives or double-barreled items). Researchers should also avoid wording that introduces subtle biases in responses. For instance, item wording should not convey a preference for one response option over another.

*Number of Items.* Multiple-item measures are more likely to provide satisfactory psychometric properties than are single-item measures. This expectation is based on the fact that even well-designed items have some ambiguities and biases, but these sources of error tend to cancel out when items are aggregated. Furthermore, many constructs are broad in scope, making it difficult to represent them adequately with a single item. Thus, researchers should generate a large pool of initial items. Specification of theoretical assumptions can provide guidance regarding whether appropriate coverage has been achieved. Also, because even a carefully implemented item generation process is likely to produce some poor items, "content saturation" of the construct is advisable. That is, the researcher should have multiple items designed to represent each aspect of the construct. For instance, an initial pool of affective items would need to be sufficiently large and diverse such that one could argue that each basic category of emotion was represented by multiple items.

*Response Scale Format.* Respondents usually rate items on some underlying bipolar or unipolar continuum. One key design issue is how many scale points should be provided. This decision requires balancing two competing concerns (see Krosnick & Fabrigar, 1997, in press). A response scale with many scale points can potentially capture subtle distinctions in ratings. However, there may be a maximum level of refinement at which respondents can make their ratings. Scales exceeding this level may provide no additional information or even lead to poorer measurement as a result of increased random error in respondents' ratings. Because the optimum number of scale points is likely to vary with respondent characteristics and the constructs being assessed, there probably is no single number of scale points that will always be ideal. Nonetheless, studies examining the impact of scale point number on item reliability and validity have suggested that the optimum number of scale points is usually five to seven (see Krosnick & Fabrigar, 1997, in press).[2]

Yet another decision is how to label the scale. At a minimum, a rating scale's endpoints must be defined with verbal labels. However, intermediate intervals can be specified in a number of ways. Some scales use boxes; others use numerical values. Some scales use verbal labels for all scale points (often in conjunction with boxes or numbers). Interestingly, such design features can influence responses. For example, the numerical values used in the response scale can convey subtle differences regarding the nature of the construct being assessed. Schwarz and his colleagues (Schwarz & Hippler, 1991; Sudman, Bradburn, & Schwarz, 1996) conducted a series of studies on the impact of numerical values of response scales. They found that respondents interpreted the 11-point rating scale as unipolar when the numerical values were 0 to 10, but as bipolar when the values were −5 to +5.

Studies also have examined the impact of verbal labels for each scale point versus labels only for endpoints. Most studies have found that reliability and validity are increased when fully labeled scales are used (Krosnick & Fabrigar, 1997, in press). However, use of verbal labels for all scale points is likely to be feasible only when a modest number of scale points is used (i.e., seven points or less) and is likely to improve item quality only when appropriate labels are chosen. Thus, when selecting labels, researchers should choose labels that have precise meanings, reflect the full range of the continuum of judgment, and represent relatively equal intervals along the continuum. See Krosnick and Fabrigar (in press) for a description of studies aimed at determining the scale values of particular verbal labels.

*Response Option Order and Item Order.* The order of response options can influence the likelihood of options being selected (Krosnick & Fabrigar, in press; Schuman & Presser, 1981; Sudman et al., 1996). Most of this work has been done with questions using categorical response options rather than rating scales. These studies have indicated that either primacy effects (i.e., selecting earlier options rather than later options) or recency effects (i.e., selecting later options rather than earlier options) can occur depending on whether questions are presented orally or visually and on the plausibility of the options

(Krosnick & Fabrigar, in press; Sudman et al., 1996). Thus, when categorical response options are used and the distribution of responses for these questions is of specific interest, it is advisable to rotate the order of options. Fewer studies have examined the impact of response option order for rating scale questions. Given the ordinal nature of response options for these types of items, only two orders are generally sensible. To date, research suggests that there is a tendency for primacy effects to occur with rating scales (Krosnick & Fabrigar, in press). Thus, if researchers have an interest in interpreting the distribution of responses across the options, it is advisable to counterbalance the order of the rating scale options.

Researchers must also specify the order in which they will present the items. Such decisions can influence the distribution of item responses as well as the correlation between items. Predicting the nature of these effects is difficult because a variety of cognitive processes can play a role in item order effects (see Krosnick & Fabrigar, in press; Schuman & Presser, 1981; Sudman et al., 1996). Nonetheless, there are some practices with respect to item ordering that generally will be appropriate. When using several multiple-item measures, it is best to present the items associated with each measure as a clearly defined block of items rather than intermingling items from different measures. A block presentation is less likely to confuse respondents and can even more effectively communicate the intent of the measure, thereby increasing reliability (Knowles, 1988). In addition, when one measure assesses a more general construct than another, it is best to present the general measure prior to the specific measure. Finally, when measures are of comparable generality, counterbalancing order is advisable when feasible. Thus, in the context of our example, it would be sensible to present the items from the attitude, affective basis, and cognitive basis measures as three sets of items. The attitude measure should be presented first, with the affective and cognitive measures counterbalanced.

## Traditional Scaling Procedures for Item Generation

Thus far, we have discussed numerous procedures for creating items. These procedures can be used in a number of combinations to construct items that best suit the research objectives. However, it is worth noting that a number of formal scaling procedures for generating and presenting items have been developed. These procedures were developed to measure attitudes, but the logic of each approach can be adapted to measure a variety of other constructs. In the sections that follow, we discuss item generation for three of the most widely used of these scaling procedures. Later, we will return to these approaches when discussing methods of item selection.

*Thurstone Equal-Appearing Intervals.* The Thurstone Equal-Appearing Interval (EAI) method (see Mueller, 1986; Thurstone & Chave, 1929) begins the item generation process by specifying the attitude object to be evaluated. A pool is generated that includes approximately 50 statements reflecting varying levels of positivity and negativity toward the object. The goal of this stage is to create statements that represent all levels of the evaluative continuum. Statements are subsequently rated by judges (usually 10 or more) on an 11-point scale indicating the extent to which each statement reflects a positive or negative evaluation of the object. The average scale values across judges are calculated for each statement. The final EAI measure consists of two statements with average scale values at each of the 11 levels of the evaluative continuum. These statements (in random order) are presented in a checklist format in which respondents place a check next to any statements with which they agree and place

an "X" next to any statements with which they disagree. The final score is computed by averaging the scale values of the statements endorsed by the respondent. Although developed for assessing attitudes, the procedure can be used for a wide range of constructs. For example, Breckler (1984) used it to assess affective and cognitive bases of attitudes. He generated statements reflecting varying levels of positive and negative emotional reactions to the attitude object (i.e., snakes) that he then had judges rate according to the level of positivity/negativity these statements reflected. Similarly, he developed statements reflecting beliefs about varying levels of positive and negative attributes of the object that judges also rated in terms of positivity/negativity.

*Likert Summated Ratings.* The Likert Method of Summated Ratings (Likert, 1932; Mueller, 1986) also begins by defining the attitude object of interest. The researcher then generates approximately 30 statements reflecting positive or negative evaluations of the object. Unlike the EAI method, half of the statements should be clearly positive and the other half clearly negative. Statements are then presented (in random order) with 5-point response scales ranging from *strongly agree* to *strongly disagree*. Respondents indicate levels of agreement with each statement. The score is computed by assigning a value of 5 for "strongly agree" responses to positive statements, a value of 4 for "agree" responses to positive statements, and so on. Negative items are reverse-scored. The sum of item responses reflects the attitude. As discussed later, items are chosen for the final attitude measure based on the correlation of individual items with the total score.

*Semantic Differentials.* The semantic differential approach (Mueller, 1986; Osgood, Suci, & Tannenbaum, 1957) usually consists of 4 to 10 bipolar rating scales. These scales typically are 7-point scales with scale points represented by boxes (numerical values are sometimes used) that the respondent checks to indicate his or her rating. The endpoints are labeled with adjectives that reflect opposite meanings and are highly evaluative in nature (e.g., good/bad, positive/negative). Respondents rate the attitude object on each of these bipolar scales. The attitude is typically computed by assigning a value of 7 for maximally positive ratings, a value of 6 to the next most positive ratings, and so on. The overall score is the sum or average of ratings. This approach could be used to assess any construct for which it is possible to find word pairs that reflect the opposite ends of the continuum of interest. Breckler (1984) and Crites et al. (1994) constructed semantic differential scales to assess the affective bases of attitudes (e.g., happy/sad) and the cognitive bases of attitudes (e.g., safe/unsafe).

## Item Evaluation and Selection

Even when constructed with care, it is unlikely that all items generated will be satisfactory. Thus, it is necessary to evaluate the quality of items and discard those that are inadequate. Various approaches have been proposed for accomplishing this goal. These procedures are not mutually exclusive, and thus item selection is most effective using some combination of procedures.[3]

### Judge's Ratings

Judges' ratings can be examined to see how well items reflect the desired properties. Perhaps the best-known example of this approach is the Thurstone EAI procedure. As noted earlier, judges rate each item on the extent to which that item implies a negative or positive evaluation of the attitude object. Descriptive statistics are then computed for each item. Optimal items are those items that have a mean rating very close to one of the 11-scale points (e.g., a mean value of 3.1 versus 3.4) because they allow a researcher to select items at equal intervals. Optimal items also have relatively little variance in judges' ratings because low variance suggests high consensus among judges on the location of that item on the evaluative continuum. Thus, selection of items for a Thurstone EAI scale typically involves choosing two items to represent each of the 11 equally spaced intervals. These two items for each point are the two items that come closest to that point in their mean scale values and have the smallest variances in ratings.

Although judges' ratings usually have been used to select items for Thurstone EAI attitude scales, there is nothing precluding use of this approach to select items assessing other constructs (e.g., see Breckler, 1984). One could have judges rate any set of statements on some underlying dimension of judgment and use these ratings for item selection. Furthermore, if items needed to possess several properties, one could obtain ratings on multiple dimensions. For instance, for scales assessing affective and cognitive bases of attitudes, one might have judges rate where the statements fall on the evaluative continuum. The same or different judges could also rate the extent to which the statements reflected emotional reactions to or beliefs about the attitude object. The final scales would consist of items that reflect equal intervals along the evaluative continuum and that were seen as either clearly emotional in nature (for the affective scale) or clearly object attributes (for the cognitive scale).

### Between-Group Differentiation

Another strategy for selecting items is to examine if items can detect between-group differences (e.g., see Aiken, 1997; Janada, 1998). This strategy involves identifying two groups of people for which there is a strong basis to assume differences on the construct of interest. Items are administered to both groups, and statistical tests for mean item differences across the groups are conducted. Items that fail to show significant differences in the expected direction are discarded. Obviously, the utility of this approach rests on the soundness of the groups selected. Group differentiation approaches have been used widely in the development of psychological measures. For example, within social/personality psychology, the Need for Cognition Scale was partially developed using this approach (Cacioppo & Petty, 1982). Need for cognition is the dispositional tendency to engage in and enjoy effortful cognitive activity. One method by which items were selected was to examine differences in items between university faculty members (a group presumed to be high on this trait) and assembly-line workers (a group assumed to be low on this trait).

## Item Descriptive Statistics

Descriptive statistics also can be used to identify problematic items (e.g., Allen & Yen, 1979). Some methodologists have suggested that items with mean response levels near the endpoints of the scale should be discarded because nearly everyone responds similarly to these items (e.g., agrees or disagrees). These items are unlikely to differentiate among people. Likewise, items with little variance are unlikely to differentiate among respondents. Of note, this concerns variance in ratings of agreement. This is a separate issue from the identification of items low in variance on judges' ratings of item favorability in construction of the Thurstone scales.

## Item-Total Correlations

Researchers often assess items by computing the correlation between each item and the total score or the corrected total score (i.e., the total score on the measure except for the item being correlated with it). Those items that fail to show sizable item-total correlations in the expected direction are discarded. This approach is based on the logic that such items do not differentiate between high and low scorers on the overall measure. Thus, these items contribute little to the overall score and are likely to assess a different construct from the majority of items in the measure (Friedenberg, 1995). The item-total correlation is integral to the Likert summated ratings method of attitude measurement (Likert, 1932; Mueller, 1986) and is discussed in most texts on psychological measurement (e.g., see Friedenberg, 1995; Janada, 1998).

## Factor Analysis

One of the most widely used and informative selection procedures is exploratory factor analysis (EFA). This approach was the basis for the semantic differential method of attitude measurement (Osgood et al., 1957), and it has been used in constructing numerous other measures (Floyd & Widaman, 1995). EFA is a set of statistical procedures designed to uncover the number and nature of latent factors underlying a set of items. Implementing EFA involves a multistep process in which researchers have a choice of a variety of different procedures to accomplish each step. For this reason, conducting EFA can be confusing, and it is not unusual for errors to be made (Fabrigar, Wegener, MacCallum, & Strahan, 1999). A discussion of the key issues involved in implementing EFA is beyond the scope of this chapter. However, reviews of these issues are available (Fabrigar, Wegener, et al., 1999; Finch & West, 1997; Floyd & Widaman, 1995; Wegener & Fabrigar, 2000).

An EFA provides several types of information useful for constructing measures.[4] First, EFA indicates how many factors (latent constructs) are needed to account for the correlations among items. Thus, the predicted dimensionality of a set of items can be tested. For example, imagine a pool of items assessing the affective and cognitive bases of attitudes. It would be expected that these items should tap two distinct dimensions. EFA could be used to test if two factors underlie this pool of items. If this did not occur, this would suggest either that the items had been poorly constructed or that the researcher's assumptions regarding these constructs were in error. Second, EFA provides information regarding the magnitude and direction of relations of the factors with each item (i.e., factor loadings). Thus, for any given factor, a researcher can determine which items that factor influences as well as which items it does not. The factor loadings can then provide insight into the nature of each factor. For instance, in our example, a researcher would expect to find two factors, one primarily influencing the affect items and the other primarily influencing the cognition items. If not, this would suggest poorly constructed items or erroneous theoretical assumptions.

Factor loadings also allow a researcher to identify problematic items. Affect items ideally should show substantial factor loadings on the affect factor (in the theoretically expected direction) but show low loadings on the cognition factor. An affect item that fails to load on the affect factor is not assessing its intended construct. In contrast, an affect item that substantially loads on both the affect factor and the cognition factor is assessing a construct in addition to what it was designed to assess.

An EFA generates two other useful pieces of information. When oblique rotations are used, a matrix of correlations among the factors is provided. This indicates the extent to which factors are distinct from one another and can assist in interpreting the nature of the factors. For example, this information would indicate the extent to which the affective and cognitive bases of attitudes are distinct from one another. EFA also produces communality estimates for items. These estimates indicate the proportion of variance in the item explained by the factors. Items with low communalities are problematic because such items

contain substantial random measurement error and/or are strongly influenced by constructs specific to only that item (which presumably go beyond the construct that the set of items was designed to assess).

Although EFA has long been used to develop measures, confirmatory factor analysis (CFA) has become increasingly popular. CFA is based on the same underlying mathematical model as EFA but involves a somewhat different set of procedures. EFA presumes that a researcher does not have precise prior knowledge of the underlying structure of items. Thus, the number of factors and the relations of factors to items is determined empirically rather than specified a priori. In contrast, CFA assumes relatively precise knowledge and requires a researcher to specify a priori how many factors exist as well as which items these factors will and will not influence.

In recent years, a number of researchers have advocated the use of CFA rather than EFA (e.g., John & Benet-Martinez, 2000). One possible reason is that some methodologists have criticized the seemingly arbitrary nature of EFA. However, many of these criticisms stem from improper implementation of EFA rather than inherent flaws in the method (Fabrigar, Wegener, et al., 1999; Wegener & Fabrigar, 2000). Indeed, when selecting items, it is often more appropriate to use EFA than CFA because the items being examined are often newly constructed items whose properties are not well established. Also, assumptions regarding the structure of the items generally have not been tested. Strong assumptions regarding underlying structure are especially tentative when large pools of items are examined because of the increased possibility that unexpected factors could emerge. Thus, when items are initially evaluated, there is often insufficient basis to confidently specify one or a small subset of a priori models as required in CFA. For example, if items are being developed for a unidimensional measure, there is often little theory to guide development of multifactor models (including the number and nature of alternative factors and the specific items most affected by them). Yet, EFA could identify when multiple factors influence the items, thereby identifying complexities and problems within the item set.

Some researchers might also prefer CFA because of the presumed precision of being able to test the goodness of fit for alternative models and of being able to statistically compare the fit of nested models (as one typically would have when differing numbers of factors are hypothesized to influence the same items). Because EFA and CFA are based on the same statistical model, it is possible to conduct the same sorts of model tests and statistical comparisons of models that differ in the number of factors (see Fabrigar, Wegener, et al., 1999). In fact, some indices of model fit that are popular for CFA were originally developed for use with EFA (e.g., Tucker & Lewis, 1973).

Another strength of EFA is that it provides information that CFA is not well suited to provide. Most notably, EFA can confirm not only that an item loads on the factor it is intended to load on but also that it does not load on factors it should not load on (Gorsuch, 1983). Examining possible cross-factor loadings in CFA is much more cumbersome. Because cross-factor loadings are unexpected, they are often not specified a priori in a CFA. Thus, a researcher may fail to detect items that are problematic because of cross-factor loadings. Alternatively, if each item is specified to load on multiple factors in a CFA, the researcher may encounter model identification problems or produce a solution that is difficult to interpret because it has not been rotated for simple structure (as done in EFA).[5]

We do not wish to imply that CFA is not useful. Instead, our position is that EFA is often more appropriate when initially selecting items. Once items have undergone some evaluation and refinement, it is often sensible to conduct a CFA in a subsequent study to provide more precise tests of the measure's underlying structure. Thus, the development of a measure often begins with EFA and moves to CFA at later stages in the research program (Fabrigar, Wegener, et al., 1999; Gorsuch, 1983).

### Item Response Theory

One increasingly popular approach to item evaluation is item response theory (IRT) (Embretson & Reise, 2000; McKinley & Mills, 1989; Steinberg & Thissen, 1995). IRT is a class of procedures examining the relationship of people standing on some latent construct to responses on a set of items. The heart of IRT is the "item information curve." This is a graphical depiction of the relation between a person's standing on a construct and the probability of selecting a particular response on an item. A wide range of procedures exists for IRT. Although detailed discussion is beyond the scope of this chapter, it is useful to distinguish among certain basic features.

The best known IRT models were developed for dichotomous response items where the items are presumed to reflect a single latent construct. One feature that distinguishes among these models is the number of parameters in the model. One-parameter models represent differences among items solely in terms of a "threshold" parameter. This parameter indicates at what level on the construct there is a .50 probability of endorsing the item. Two-parameter models also include an "item discrimination" parameter. This additional parameter represents differences in the extent to which items are related to the underlying construct. Three-parameter models add a "lower-asymptote" parameter. The lower-asymptote parameter reflects the probability of endorsing an item at the lowest level of the construct. In the context of objective tests, this parameter indicates how likely it is that a person will correctly guess the answer in the absence of any knowledge. In social psychology, the two-parameter model is likely to be the most conceptually sensible (Embretson & Reise, 2000; Finch & West, 1997; Steinberg & Thissen, 1995). Although unidimensional IRT models for dichotomous response items have been most common, models have been developed to deal with a broader range of situations (Embretson & Reise, 2000). For example, one- and two-parameter unidimensional models for items using rating scale formats have been developed.

Two-parameter rating scale models seem best suited for the items social psychologists usually examine. Like dichotomous response item models, these models produce item information curves. However, rather than producing a single item curve, these models produce a set of curves. Each curve reflects the probability of selecting one of the response options as a function of the level of the construct. For example, in a 5-point *strongly agree/strongly disagree* scale, there would be a curve for the probability of selecting the "strongly agree" response, a curve for the probability of selecting the "agree" response, and so on. These curves indicate how well the item discriminates among people along the range of the construct and the extent to which each scale point contributes information regarding the construct (see Embretson & Reise, 2000; Steinberg & Thissen, 1995). This allows the researcher to assess whether respondents are making full use of the response scale or whether the researcher can simplify the response scale (e.g., reduce from seven to three options) without loss of information.

When using IRT to select items, two types of information can guide decisions (Embretson & Reise, 2000). First, it is possible to compute item-fit indices. One should discard items demonstrating poor fit based on the logic that poor item fit is often a function of items not reflecting the construct of interest, being influenced by unintended constructs, or relating to the construct of interest in a manner different from that of other items. A second type of information that can guide item selection is the estimates of item parameters, which can be used to generate item information curves for each item. As noted earlier, these curves (in a two-parameter model) convey information regarding the threshold of endorsement for a particular response and how well the item differentiates among people on the construct. Selection of items using information curves depends on the goals of the measure.

Imagine that the goal is to develop an affective basis measure capable of effectively discriminating among people at all levels of the construct. In the case of rating scale response formats, it is possible for items to differentiate among people along the full range of the affect. Thus, items with high discrimination values and for which each of the response options contributes useful information should be selected (see Steinberg & Thissen, 1995). In other cases, the measure may not need to discriminate at all levels of the construct. For instance, if the construct is normally distributed in the population, the majority of respondents will tend to fall within the moderate range of the continuum. In such a situation, it may not be necessary to select items that can differentiate at the extremes. Instead, one might place an emphasis on items capable of differentiating people in the middle of the continuum. In contrast, if a researcher wishes to differentiate people at one of the extremes, emphasis should be placed on items that discriminate at that end of the continuum. Thus, another benefit of IRT is its ability to construct measures designed to assess a specific portion of the dimension of interest.

## EVALUATING MEASURE QUALITY

Once items have been selected, a researcher must evaluate the quality of the measure. Many of the considerations involved in selecting items also relate directly to evaluation. For example, dimensionality often determines the utility of the measure (e.g., if the purpose is to measure a unidimensional construct). As discussed in the following sections, the general issues of validity and generalizability cross the traditional boundaries between measure construction and evaluation. In many ways, evaluation (traditionally described as reliability and validity) comes down to the all important match between the theoretical construct and the specific items intended to tap the construct. Some questions about the items relate to the consistency of the items with one another. This is partly assessed by factor-analytic or other inductive methods of item selection (e.g., item-total correlations). But the items must also relate closely to the intended construct, and that assessment involves questions of validity rather than reliability. We begin this section by discussing traditional issues of reliability along with an assessment of the most common index of reliability (i.e., Cronbach's alpha) (Cronbach, 1951). We continue by describing a broad structure for thinking about (and organizing) the various types of evidence one might garner in the process of validating a proposed measure.

## Reliability

As noted when discussing item selection, it is likely that nearly all psychological measures are influenced, in part, by error. Techniques such as factor analysis explicitly incorporate random and systematic errors into the measurement model. That is, responses to items can be influenced by random events (such as unexpected noise in the environment that temporarily distracts the respondent from the item) or by factors that influence only that item (such as reactions to a word that appears only in that item, even if the reaction to that word is not the intended construct to be measured).

The concept of random error is central to a classical test theory view of measures (in which a response is conceived as "true score plus error") (e.g., Lord & Novick, 1968). These random errors should not, in principle, be reproduced across multiple responses (i.e., either multiple items or multiple responses to the same item). This would be one reason to construct measures consisting of multiple rather than single items. Even a measure consisting of multiple items ultimately would have some amount of error, however. From this point of view, reliability is defined as the proportion of variance that can be attributed to true scores rather than random error. If all the variance in responses is due to the true score (i.e., to differences in levels of the construct of interest), then reliability would be 1. If all the variance is due to random error, reliability would be zero. The correlation between the observed response and the true score would be the square root of the reliability of the measure.

Evidence for reliability traditionally has taken many forms, including test-retest (stability), internal consistency (split-half), and equivalence reliability.[6] Of course, these different types of reliability address different sources for error in measures. Test-retest (stability) reliability addresses variation in individuals' responses (generally to the same items) across occasions. Internal consistency addresses errors that occur because of different specific items used to represent the construct of interest. Similarly, equivalence addresses errors associated with the sampling of items used in two alternative forms of the same measure.[7]

### Internal Consistency

Reports of internal consistency of measures are ubiquitous in social psychology. Perhaps the presentation of information about internal consistency is so frequent because internal consistency is easily assessed using only the responses of interest in the study itself. Although there are a variety of indices of internal consistency (see Rosenthal & Rosnow, 1991), the most frequently used index is Cronbach's alpha (Cronbach, 1951). Alpha can be used any time the same people respond to multiple items intended to assess the same construct. It does not require two or more testing occasions (as in assessments of test-retest reliability), nor does it require construction of alternative forms of the measure (as in tests of equivalence). The coefficient alpha is often the only evidence given that the items in the measure sufficiently "hang together." Related to this, a large alpha is sometimes interpreted as evidence that the items all index a common construct.

Unfortunately, such inferences go far beyond the information actually provided by coefficient alpha. Alpha is influenced by both the interrelatedness of the items and the number of items in the measure (see John & Benet-Martinez, 2000). This means that one could have equally high alpha coefficients from one measure with many items but low interitem correlations and from another measure with few items but higher interitem correlations. As formalized in the Spearman-Brown prophecy formula (see Lord & Novick, 1968; Rosenthal & Rosnow, 1991), alpha always increases as additional items are added (assuming similar interitem correlations), though this is less the case as the number of items increases and as the overall interitem correlations increase. Because coefficient alpha represents the mean of the reliabilities computed from all possible split halves, this also means that alpha does not measure the homogeneity of the interitem correlations; nor does it reflect the unidimensionality of the scale. That is, the mean reliability could increase by introducing pockets of highly intercorrelated items. In effect, alpha could increase by making the measure multidimensional rather than unidimensional (if added items from a second dimension raise the average intercorrelation of the items) (e.g., see Schmitt, 1996). Because alpha does not address the dimensionality of the measure, other methods (such as exploratory factor analysis or confirmatory factor analysis) are necessary. As has been noted for some time, Cronbach's alpha should not be used if a measure is found to be multidimensional (Cronbach, 1951; Schmitt, 1996); instead, one should create unidimensional subscales and then use alpha separately for each subscale (John & Benet-Martinez, 2000).

It should also be noted that extremely high internal consistency can sometimes signal potential problems with a measure. Imagine that a person uses multiple items to measure cognitive bases of attitudes, but every item uses the same attribute of the object. The only difference across items in this example is the use of different but equivalent names for the attitude object. Such items undoubtedly would have extremely high interitem correlations (and a high Cronbach alpha), but they would also represent a much more narrow representation of the construct than if the items assessed different attributes.

### Stability (Test-Retest)

Test-retest reliability generally is examined by computing the correlation between two different administrations of the same measure. The magnitude of the correlation is presumed to reflect the reliability of the measure. However, it is important to recognize that test-retest correlations reflect not only the reliability of the measure but also the stability of the construct it assesses, the similarity of the contexts in which the measure is administered, and the degree to which there were intervening influences on the construct. Thus, there are a number of limitations with use of simple correlations between two administrations of the same measure or parallel measures (see also Bollen, 1989).

One might argue that the Pearson correlation represents a reasonable index of reliability per se only if there was either perfect stability of the theoretical construct over time or if the shift in the construct were identical for all individuals responding to the measure (so the relative standing of people on the construct should, with a perfectly reliable measure, be the same at each point in time). However, if anything influences the construct between measurements such that some people increase on the construct whereas others decrease, then the correlation coefficient would treat as unreliability (due to measurement error in the classic test theory approach) variance that is actually the result of changes in the construct of interest. Whenever one attempts to assess test-retest reliability, there is a balance between allowing enough time to elapse that consistency of response is not due to memory of previous responses (and attendant consistency pressures) and yet not so much time that there have been substantial changes in the construct of interest (e.g., see Remmers, 1963).

In interpreting test-retest correlations, one must take into account the extent to which one would theoretically expect the construct to be stable versus malleable. For example, if one is assessing overall attitudes or the affective or cognitive bases of attitudes about products that are commonly encountered in television ads, it should not be surprising if there are substantial changes in the attitudes or in the bases over time (if the delay between assessments is sufficiently long). One might actually consider variables as falling along a continuum of theorized stability, with variables such as cognitive abilities or personality traits expected to be quite stable over time, with variables such as attitudes or beliefs expected to be relatively stable but capable of change, and with variables such as concept accessibility or focus of attention expected to be quite malleable, even from moment to moment. Of course, even within a single type of construct, there might be great variability in how stable or malleable the variable should be. For example, attitudes toward political

parties tend to be quite stable over periods of years, whereas attitudes toward particular policy stands are much more variable (e.g., Converse, 1964). Recent research also has shown that attitudes based on effortful cognitive processing are more likely to persist over time than are equally extreme attitudes formed or changed with lower levels of processing (e.g., see Petty, Haugtvedt, & Smith, 1995). Therefore, when examining stability as a form of reliability, it is less than meaningful to provide or seek global recommendations for levels of "acceptable" test-retest reliability. One would clearly expect different levels for different constructs or even with different testing procedures for the same construct.

Whereas changes in the construct can lead to correlations that underestimate reliability, the test-retest correlation could also overestimate reliability if the "errors" at each occasion are positively correlated. That is, if the same omitted factors influence both measures, the simple correlation could overestimate the reliability of the measure of the intended construct. Of course, this would also threaten the validity of inferences about the measure when the measure is interpreted solely in terms of the intended construct (see later sections on different forms of validity evidence).

Because correlations across two time periods can conflate instability of the measure with unreliability, it might often be useful to employ methods that can separate instability of the construct from unreliability of the measure. One example procedure combines latent growth curve analysis with latent state-trait models to derive separate indices of stability and reliability (Tisak & Tisak, 2000; for an application in social psychology, see Cunningham, Preacher, & Banaji, 2001). Similar to the earlier discussion, Tisak and Tisak assume that most psychological constructs include both "state" (malleable) aspects and "trait" (stable) aspects. Therefore, one might construct indices of reliability that are appropriate for different types of variables (e.g., including the malleable component as "true score" if the construct is thought to have "state" aspects; see also Steyer and Schmitt [1990]).

## Validity

Traditional views of validity specify a number of types of validity, including content validity (i.e., items fully representing the construct of interest), face validity (i.e., appearance of the items as assessing the intended construct), and criterion (or external) validity (i.e., ability of the measure to predict related judgments or behaviors or to correlate with conceptually related constructs). Even from rather early on, however, researchers began to talk about the various sources of validity as all relating to the general (and encompassing) notion of construct validity (see Cronbach & Meehl, 1955; Loevinger, 1957). As John and Benet-Martinez (2000) put it, "what seemed like different types of validity are just different sources of evidence that address particular questions of construct validity" (p. 351; see also Messick, 1989). A construct validity approach to measures refocuses one's attention on systematic errors in measures that might occur when a measure taps unintended constructs, in addition to any random error of the type emphasized in discussions of reliability. Therefore, similar to issues of confounding in experimental design, issues of "purity" of the measure are paramount in measurement validation (see Wegener, Downing, Krosnick, & Petty, 1995).

Of course, questions of whether the measure sufficiently taps (and only taps) the construct of interest already have been discussed as being important considerations in the generation and selection of items. Therefore, one often addresses many aspects of construct validity in the process of constructing measures. Once one has developed a measure, a number of types of data might be brought to

bear on what the measure does and does not assess. In the following sections, we organize these types of data using a scheme that seems somewhat more straightforward than the sometimes overlapping types of validity that have been discussed previously as components of construct validity. For example, Messick (1989) specified six types of validity that are represented in the concept of construct validity (see also John & Benet-Martinez, 2000; Loevinger, 1957). When all is said and done, however, one might usefully organize the various types of validity into two simple types of validity evidence: "associative" and "dissociative" forms of evidence.

### "Associative" and "Dissociative" Forms of Validity Evidence

Associative forms of validity evidence support the utility of the measure by showing that the measure is associated with factors and outcomes that would be predicted by relevant theory. These associations make the case for "what the measured construct is." In contrast, "dissociative" forms of validity evidence distinguish the construct from theoretically distinct constructs, thereby making the case for "what the measured construct is NOT." The "associative" and "dissociative" categories are similar, but not identical, to the Campbell and Fiske (1959) categories of "convergent" and "discriminant" validity. The following sections describe these relations in some detail.

*Associative Forms of Validity.* Many types of associations can support that a measure assesses the construct it is intended to assess. In general, however, these associations can be divided into three types: correlations with alternative measures of the same construct, concurrent correlations with related constructs, and correlations with antecedents and/or consequences of the construct. Correlations with alternative measures of the construct have long been referred to as reflecting "convergent validity" (e.g., Campbell & Fiske, 1959). Some alternative measures are quite similar to each other (as when parallel forms of the same questionnaire are used to test equivalence reliability), whereas other alternatives are quite dissimilar. For example, one could imagine measuring the affective bases of attitudes through two different sets of self-reports (see Crites et al., 1994) or through both self-reports and physiological measures of facial muscle groups (see Cacioppo, Martzke, Petty, & Tassinary, 1988). Although Campbell and Fiske (1959) recommended "maximal distinctiveness" of methods used in multitrait-multimethod (MTMM) tests of convergent validity, use of markedly different types of measures might often result in people describing the evidence as falling into "criterion validity" or "external validity" categories. Of course, use of measures that diverge in methodology push generalizability farther than the use of similar methods (see John & Benet-Martinez, 2000). The basic form of evidence is the same, however—that of associations between the measure and some alternative form of measure of the same construct.

Researchers also commonly make the case for construct validity by examining associations between the construct of interest and theoretically related constructs. For example, Weary and Edwards (1994) supported the "causal uncertainty" construct (measured by the Causal Uncertainty Scale, or CUS) by correlating the CUS with the related concepts of intolerance for ambiguity (Budner, 1962) and preference for order (Webster & Kruglanski, 1994). Sometimes people use the term "convergent validity" for such correlations, although Campbell and Fiske (1959) limited the use of this term to the associations among alternative measures of the same (rather than related) constructs.

A closely related type of validity evidence would be obtained when the theoretically related construct can also be conceived as either an antecedent or a consequence of the construct of interest. For example, Weary and Edwards (1994) conceived causal uncertainty as following, in part, from chronic perceptions of loss of control. This notion was consistent with the obtained significant positive correlation between CUS and external locus of control (Rotter, 1966). Of course, evidence of this type becomes even stronger when the antecedent is measured some time in advance of the occasion at which the dependent measure is completed. Although the proposed measure is treated as the criterion in this case, the longitudinal nature of the evidence would have much in common with traditional "predictive validity" studies in which the construct of interest is used to predict future judgments or behavior (i.e., proposed consequences of the construct).

Attitudes have been treated as both antecedents and consequences, often including some separation in measurement between the predictor and the criterion. For example, attitudes have often been conceptualized as antecedents of behavior in studies of attitude-behavior consistency. In such studies, attitudes often are measured at one point in time, and then behaviors are observed or reported either relatively soon thereafter (e.g., Fazio & Zanna, 1981) or after a substantial delay (e.g., Davidson & Jaccard, 1979). As one might expect, the ability of earlier measures of attitudes to guide later behaviors depends, in large part, on the ability of the attitude to remain stable between the measurements of attitude and behavior (e.g., Doll & Ajzen, 1992). There are also contexts in which behaviors can be antecedents rather than consequences of attitudes. For example, when a person lies to someone about the pleasantness of an activity, this can then influence attitudes toward the activity (e.g., Festinger & Carlsmith, 1959). Relations between antecedents and consequences not only address forms of "concurrent" and "predictive" validity but also address what Messick (1989) referred to as "substantive validity" (i.e., evidence reflective of theoretically related processes). For example, if one finds that people with attitudes primarily based on affect are later more persuaded by affective rather than cognitive messages (e.g., Fabrigar & Petty, 1999), this would support the hypothesized "persuasion matching" processes (e.g., Edwards, 1990; Katz & Stotland, 1959).

When validity evidence takes the form of a naturally occurring correlation, one must be particularly aware of the possibility of "third variable" effects. That is, a third variable might create both the antecedent and the consequence. Stronger inferences about the antecedent or consequence status of a construct can be obtained when experimental manipulations are used. For example, evidence of affective attitude bases serving as antecedents to facilitated persuasion by "affective" messages is strongest when the bases are manipulated (see Fabrigar & Petty, 1999). Similarly, one can use manipulations to provide evidence that a measure assesses its intended construct, while markedly decreasing concerns about possible third variables. This has been done with measures of affective versus cognitive bases of attitudes. One could easily imagine that such measures might tap factors such as the amount of prior experience with the attitude object, instead of, or in addition to, tapping the affective or cognitive nature of the prior experience. One way to increase confidence that the measures are assessing "pure" affect or cognition is to create new attitudes based on equal amounts of experience toward a novel attitude object, but experience that differs regarding its affective or cognitive nature (e.g., Crites et al., 1994, Study 2). If the measures are altered by this experimental manipulation in the expected way, this provides support for their validity.

*Dissociative Forms of Validity.* Just as it is important to support the nature of a construct by examining associations with related constructs, one must not ignore the limits to the construct's domain. To continue with our example of affective versus cognitive bases of attitudes, an understanding of affective bases would not only suggest that such measures should correlate with related concepts (such as manipulations of affective experience—an antecedent—or persuasion by affectively framed information—a consequence). This same theoretical approach also would suggest that affectively based attitudes should not be as highly related to previous cognitive experience with the attitude object or with persuasion by cognitively oriented persuasive messages. More generally, a measure of a construct should not only relate to conceptually similar variables; it also should relate less or not at all with variables that are conceptually unrelated to the construct of interest. Campbell and Fiske (1959) addressed this relative "lack of relation" under the rubric of "divergent validity." In their classic MTMM approach, one would include not only alternative measures for each construct of interest but also constructs that varied in their theoretical relations, in order to allow for evidence of differences (i.e., divergence) across the constructs.

It would make little sense for dissociative forms of validity evidence to include relations between alternative forms of the same measure (used for convergent validity in the MTMM terminology), but the other forms of dissociative validity directly parallel those for the associative category. Whereas associative validity evidence comes from relations with like constructs, dissociative validity comes from relative lack of relation with unlike constructs. For example, in the Weary and Edwards (1994) work on causal uncertainty, dissociative (divergent) validity was shown by failing to find any relation between causal uncertainty and social desirability or general intelligence. Similarly, the exploratory factor analyses reported in the Crites et al. (1994) article on affective and cognitive bases of attitudes (in which affective and cognitive items often load on separate factors) imply (and the original correlation matrices support) that the affective items correlate more highly with other affective items than they do with the cognitive items. In addition, the cognitive items correlate more highly with the other cognitive items than with the affective items.

Dissociative forms of validity evidence also appear in examinations of antecedents and consequences. For example, exposure to affective experience with the attitude object (a presumed antecedent of affective attitudes) results in attitudes that are more strongly reflective of affect than of cognition. In contrast, exposure to cognitive information about the attitude object results in attitudes more reflective of cognition than affect. Regarding consequences of affective and cognitive bases, Fabrigar and Petty (1999) found that affective attitude bases resulted in responsiveness to affective but not cognitive persuasive messages. In contrast, cognitive attitude bases resulted in relatively more responsiveness to cognitive rather than affective messages.

*The MTMM Approach.* Since Campbell and Fiske's (1959) seminal paper, researchers have used the MTMM design (crossing two or more traits—constructs—with two or more methods) as a way to address the generalizability of a construct across different methods (i.e., convergent validity) and the relative distinctiveness of any one construct when compared with the other constructs (i.e., divergent validity). One would recognize convergent validity as one of a number of forms of associative validity evidence. Divergent validity is clearly of the dissociative variety.

In the original Campbell and Fiske (1959) approach, inferences about convergent and discriminant validity were based on relatively informal inspection of measures of the same construct using different methods as compared with measures of different traits using the same methods or measures of different traits using different methods. Although the inspection of individual bivariate correlations

is relatively straightforward, the assessment of the conditions laid out by Campbell and Fiske is inherently subjective. In part, this is because there is no clear metric for how much any two correlations should differ in order to "satisfy" the conditions; also, there are often many correlations involved in a given assessment. An additional limitation of the Campbell and Fiske approach is that there is no accounting for measurement error in the bivariate correlations forming the MTMM matrix.

In an effort to provide more parsimonious summaries of MTMM matrices while incorporating measurement error in the model, a variety of analysis procedures have been developed that use some form of confirmatory factor analysis (see Marsh & Grayson, 1995; Visser, Fabrigar, Wegener, & Browne, 2003; Widaman, 1985). The classic confirmatory factor analysis model (Jöreskog, 1974) treats each measure as a function of the relevant construct, the relevant method, and error. Unfortunately, this model suffers from problems with both estimation and interpretation, because the model includes a large number of parameters compared with the number of measures used to estimate the model, and the free parameters include some potential logical inconsistencies (see Visser et al., 2003). Some revised versions of the CFA model attempt to solve the problem of too many parameters by fixing certain paths in the model (e.g., Kenny & Kashy, 1992; Millsap, 1992), but at the expense of being able to address certain questions of interest in MTMM designs (see Visser et al., 2003). Although most of the MTMM models have been conceptualized as additive models (i.e., with traits and methods independently influencing responses), some methodologists have argued that traits and methods often interact. For example, Campbell and O'Connell (1967) found that when two traits were highly correlated, sharing the same method of measurement resulted in a substantial inflation in intertrait correlations. This did not occur to the same extent, however, when the two traits were less correlated. Though less frequently used in the social psychological literature, multiplicative models exist that allow for these variations in method effects across traits and vice versa. In fact, free downloadable software exists to run one such model, the composite direct product model (CDP) (Browne, 1984). This software is comparatively easy to program, and it provides information that relates quite directly to questions of convergent and divergent validity in MTMM studies (see Visser et al., 2003). The CDP model also requires fewer free parameters than the traditional CFA model, thereby running into far fewer estimation problems. Finally, the CDP puts fewer restrictions on the types of questions that can be asked when compared with the revisions of the traditional CFA model that place constraints on the model in an attempt to decrease the number of free parameters.

Limits to the CDP approach certainly exist. For example, as with some of the additive approaches, the CDP output provides little information regarding the performance of individual observed variables. Although useful summaries across methods or traits are provided, the output does not provide direct information about whether methods converged best for certain traits or vice versa. It is also not entirely clear when the additive versus multiplicative assumptions underlying the various CFA approaches are most appropriate or consequential. In our estimation, however, the CDP is currently the most generally useful of the CFA approaches to MTMM data (see Visser et al., 2003).

## BEYOND SELF-REPORT MEASURES

Throughout much of the current chapter, we have dealt with measures that fall squarely into the category of "direct" self-report measures. Such measures are quite frequent in

the attitudes domain in particular and in social psychology more generally. Undoubtedly, this is partly because of the ease with which such responses can be obtained. In addition, for many if not most constructs assessed in social psychology, there is little concern about respondents' ability and/or motivation to provide their perceptions of the judgment target and/or construct. It is worth noting that this in no way conflicts with the oft-cited limitations on people's reports of psychological *process* (e.g., Nisbett & Wilson, 1977). In most areas of social psychology, people are not asked to report on process, but rather on content. For example, in classic studies of information processing in attitude change, message recipients are simply asked to report the content of their attitudes (e.g., to what extent does the advocated policy seem good or bad). The message recipients are not asked to report the extent to which they processed the available information "centrally" versus "peripherally" (Petty & Cacioppo, 1986) or "systematically" versus "heuristically" (Chaiken, Liberman, & Eagly, 1989).

Of course, there are some situations in which one might question the ability or motivation of people to report the true content of their attitudes. Such concerns have been the motivating factors behind "indirect" and "implicit" measures of attitudes, and these types of measures often have been employed in studies of prejudice. For example, researchers have inferred the positivity or negativity of attitudes toward social groups by measuring how close the participant sits to a person from that group (e.g., Fazio, Jackson, Dunton, & Williams, 1995; Macrae, Bodenhausen, Milne, & Jetten, 1994). Also, a variety of measures have been based on speed of responding. For example, participants have been asked to evaluate unrelated words following race primes. To the extent that a person's view of the target (stigmatized) group is negative, responses are facilitated to negative targets that follow group primes (e.g., Fazio, Jackson, et al., 1995; also see Greenwald, McGhee, & Schwartz, 1998). Of course, other indirect measures have been developed as well. For example, Hammond (1948) developed the information error (error choice) technique in which respondents answer seemingly factual questions, with none of the provided answers being correct. The direction of errors is taken as an indication of the person's attitude. Also, physiological measures have a rich history as indirect measures. Some recent and useful approaches include use of Event-Related Potentials (i.e., electrical activity in the brain when a target object differs in valence from a set of preceding items) (Cacioppo, Crites, Gardner, & Berntson, 1994; see Cacioppo, Lorig, Nusbaum, & Berntson, Chapter 17, this volume) and facial electromyography (Cacioppo & Petty, 1979; see Petty & Cacioppo, 1996, for discussion of other traditional indirect measures). Though less used in the attitudes area, social psychologists also use "nonself-report" data of the archival (e.g., see Kerr, Aronoff, & Messe, 2000), observational (e.g., see Bakeman, 2000), and qualitative varieties (e.g., see King, Chapter 8, this volume).

By way of wrapping up this chapter, we would like to emphasize that the construction and validation of indirect or implicit measures can and should follow the same basic steps outlined for direct measures. That is, the construction of such measures would begin with the specification of the goals of the measure and the theoretical assumptions about the qualities of the construct. As noted earlier, the conceptualization of direct self-report measures includes both ability and willingness on the part of respondents to report the content of their views of a target. In contrast, the call for indirect measures (especially in areas such as stereotyping and prejudice) generally has been motivated by concerns about both ability and motivation to report certain attitudes, especially toward controversial social groups (e.g., Greenwald & Banaji, 1995). As noted

by Wegener and Petty (1998), however, one's choice of type of measure would depend a great deal on the type of "implicit cognition" one wishes to investigate. Some conceptions of "implicit cognition" question the ability of respondents to report the content of their views. One possible situation where this might be suspected is if a person high in internal motivation to avoid prejudice privately reports low levels of prejudice on explicit (direct) measures but still shows prejudice on implicit (indirect) measures (see Nosek, 2002). When inability to report content is suspected, one would likely choose one or more implicit (indirect) measures designed to tap into the suspected prejudiced associations in memory. In other instances, however, one could still often use explicit (direct) measures to study "implicit cognition." This is because many studies of "implicit cognition" address the inability of people to realize what has *influenced* their views, even if the content of their views is readily reportable. For example, Greenwald and Banaji (1995) described halo effects as implicit when people fail to realize that the evaluation of a novel attribute (e.g., character) is influenced by a known attribute (e.g., physical attractiveness). In such a case, one could often identify "implicit halo effects" even if one were to measure both the attributes using explicit (direct) measures, because the "implicit" aspect is whether or not people realize the *influence* of one attribute on the other, not in whether people can report the content of the attributes. In fact, it is interesting to note that most of the examples of implicit cognition provided by Greenwald and Banaji (1995)—at a time before many of the most recent "implicit" measures of content were fully developed— actually utilized direct self-report measures of content. If one is truly interested in implicit content (rather than implicit influence), however, direct measures of content would not suffice (see Wegener & Petty, 1998; see also Kihlstrom, Chapter 9, this volume).

Construction of indirect measures has all too often stopped with specification of the goals and theory. That is, the generation and evaluation of specific items have not played the same kind of central role in development of indirect measures that they have for traditional self reports. Yet, there is little reason for this to be the case. For example, as aptly noted by Himmelfarb (1993), although behavioral indices have often been constructed from aggregated sets of behaviors (e.g., Tittle & Hill, 1967), these indices "would ideally be subjected to the item analysis procedures associated with the traditional attitude scaling techniques" (p. 64) (such as Thurstone's use of judge ratings, Likert's use of item-total correlations, or Osgood's use of factor analyses). Indeed, reviews of many of the older indirect attitude measures concluded that these measures left much to be desired. For example, Kidder and Campbell (1970) noted that "of all our imperfect measures, these are apparently not the least impure" (p. 336). Yet, it is not clear that many of even the older indirect measures have gone through the typical item selection and evaluation procedures that have been typical for the direct measures. It stands to reason, for example, that an error choice technique (Hammond, 1948) would perform much better if one were to start with a larger pool of items that are then put through traditional types of item analysis. Given the theoretical conceptions of targets or settings in which indirect measures are needed (e.g., in studies of stereotyping or prejudice), one would also want to seek validity evidence that goes beyond between-group differentiation (as shown by Hammond, 1948). That is, one would want to explicitly address the ability of the error choice items to overcome social desirability concerns. Addressing associative and dissociative forms of validity, one could also assess relations between the information error measure and existing implicit versus explicit scales (perhaps using a full MTMM design) (see Visser et al., 2003).

One of the great successes of social psychology has been the development of valid and reliable measures of a wide variety of psychologically meaningful constructs. As these measures continue to expand in exciting and interesting ways, traditional methods of measure development and evaluation form a firm foundation on which the new measures can be built and tested.

## NOTES

1. Sometimes researchers adapt items, complete measures, or methods of administration for their current purposes. When making such changes, one must recognize that these alterations can influence the psychometric properties of the items. Therefore, one should conduct the same types of evaluations of items with these modified measures as with newly constructed items.

2. A related issue that researchers must consider is whether to specify a response scale that includes a midpoint. Unfortunately, studies examining the impact of including scale midpoints on item reliability and validity have produced conflicting findings (see Krosnick & Fabrigar, 1997, in press). Thus, current empirical research does not provide a basis for a simple recommendation regarding the use of scale midpoints. However, a variety of conceptual issues should be considered in making such a decision (see Krosnick & Fabrigar, 1997, in press).

3. Although various item selection procedures are somewhat distinct, the performance of an item across different selection procedures is not unrelated. An

item performing well on one procedure often will tend to perform well on other procedures. For example, the pattern of results for an item-total correlation analysis will often suggest similar choices with respect to item selection as a factor analysis (Gorsuch, 1983), although a factor analysis does provide additional information.

4. Throughout our discussion of EFA, we assume that a researcher has conducted an EFA based on the common factor model with an oblique rotation. We do so because we believe this approach is the most appropriate type of EFA for the vast majority of research questions investigated by social psychologists (Fabrigar, Wegener, et al., 1999; Wegener & Fabrigar, 2000). When other types of EFA are used (or other types of analyses, such as principal components analysis), the information provided is somewhat different from what we describe here (see Gorsuch, 1983).

5. If a researcher were to specify a CFA model with the maximum number of items with multiple factor loadings in which the model is still identified, this would be mathematically identical to an EFA model with the same number of factors (see Fabrigar, Wegener, et al., 1999). In effect, the researcher would be conducting an EFA without rotation for simple structure. Such an approach would have no advantages over EFA and would be much more cumbersome to implement and interpret.

6. Equivalence reliability generally is defined as the extent to which two parallel measures of the same construct are correlated with one another. In many respects, equivalence reliability is an alternative type of internal consistency in which one compares two distinct sets of items rather than all possible split halves of a single set of items (as in Cronbach alpha). Alternatively, equivalence reliability can be conceptualized as a form of convergent validity. In traditional treatments of convergent validity (Campbell & Fiske, 1959), emphasis is placed on assessing the correlation between two maximally different methods of measurement. In contrast, most tests of equivalence examine the correlation between two measures that are quite similar in methodology.

7. One also encounters issues of intrarater reliability (e.g., consistency of ratings made on two occasions by the same rater) and interrater reliability (i.e., consistency across raters) when raters code open-ended responses by research participants (see Bakeman [2000] and King, Chapter 8, this volume, for detailed discussions of interrater agreement and reliability).

## REFERENCES

Abelson, R. P., Kinder, D. R., Peters, M. D., & Fiske, S. T. (1982). Affective and semantic components in political person perception. *Journal of Personality and Social Psychology, 42,* 619-630.

Aiken, L. R. (1997). *Psychological testing and assessment* (9th ed.). Boston: Allyn & Bacon.

Allen, M. J., & Yen, W. M. (1979). *Introduction to measurement theory.* Belmont, CA: Wadsworth.

Bakeman, R. (2000). Behavioral observation and coding. In H. T. Reis & C. M. Judd (Eds.), *Handbook of research methods in social and personality psychology* (pp. 138-159). New York: Cambridge University Press.

Bollen, K. A. (1989). *Structural equations with latent variables.* New York: Wiley.

Breckler, S. J. (1984). Empirical validation of affect, behavior, and cognition as distinct components of attitude. *Journal of Personality and Social Psychology, 47,* 1191-1205.

Browne, M. W. (1984). The decomposition of multitrait-multimethod matrices. *British Journal of Mathematical and Statistical Psychology, 37,* 1-21.

Budner, S. (1962). Intolerance of ambiguity as a personality variable. *Journal of Personality, 30,* 29-50.

Cacioppo, J. T., Crites, S. L., Jr., Gardner, W. L., & Berntson, G. G. (1994). Bioelectrical echoes from evaluative categorizations: I. A late positive brain potential that varies as a function of trait negativity and extremity. *Journal of Personality and Social Psychology, 67,* 115-125.

Cacioppo, J. T., Martzke, J. S., Petty, R. E., & Tassinary, L. G. (1988). Specific forms of facial EMG response index emotions during an interview: From Darwin to the continuous flow hypothesis of affect-laden information processing. *Journal of Personality and Social Psychology, 54,* 592-604.

Cacioppo, J. T., & Petty, R. E. (1979). Attitudes and cognitive response: An electrophysiological approach. *Journal of Personality and Social Psychology, 37,* 2181-2199.

Cacioppo. J. T., & Petty, R. E. (1982). The need for cognition. *Journal of Personality and Social Psychology, 42,* 116-131.

Campbell, D. T., & Fiske, D. W. (1959). Convergent and discriminant validation by the multitrait-multimethod matrix. *Psychological Bulletin, 56,* 81-105.

Campbell, D. T., & O'Connell, E. J. (1967). Method factors in multitrait-multimethod matrices: Multiplicative rather than additive? *Multivariate Behavioral Research, 2,* 409-426.

Chaiken, S., Liberman, A., & Eagly, A. H. (1989). Heuristic and systematic processing within and beyond the persuasion context. In J. S. Uleman & J. A. Bargh (Eds.), *Unintended thought* (pp. 212-252). New York: Guilford.

Converse, P. E. (1964). The nature of belief systems in the mass public. In D. E. Apter (Ed.), *Ideology and discontent* (pp. 206-261). New York: Free Press.

Crites, S. L., Jr., Fabrigar, L. R., & Petty, R. E. (1994). Measuring the affective and cognitive properties of attitudes: Conceptual and methodological issues. *Personality and Social Psychology Bulletin, 20,* 619-634.

Cronbach, L. J. (1951). Coefficient alpha and the internal structure of tests. *Psychometrika, 16,* 297-334.

Cronbach, L. J., & Meehl, P. E. (1955). Construct validity in psychological tests. *Psychological Bulletin, 52,* 281-302.

Cunningham, W. A., Preacher, K. J., & Banaji, M. R. (2001). Implicit attitude measures: Consistency, stability, and convergent validity. *Psychological Science, 12,* 163-170.

Davidson, A. R., & Jaccard, J. (1979). Variables that moderate the attitude-behavior relation: Results of a longitudinal survey. *Journal of Personality and Social Psychology, 37,* 1364-1376.

Doll, J., & Ajzen, I. (1992). Accessibility and stability of predictors in the theory of planned behavior. *Journal of Personality and Social Psychology, 63,* 754-765.

Eagly, A. H., Mladinic, A., & Otto, S. (1994). Cognitive and affective bases of attitudes toward social groups and social policies. *Journal of Experimental Social Psychology, 30,* 113-137.

Edwards, K. (1990). The interplay of affect and cognition in attitude formation and change. *Journal of Personality and Social Psychology, 59,* 202-216.

Embretson, S. E., & Reise, S. P. (2000). *Item response theory for psychologists.* Mahwah, NJ: Lawrence Erlbaum.

Fabrigar, L. R., & Petty, R. E. (1999). The role of the affective and cognitive bases of attitudes in susceptibility to affectively and cognitively based persuasion. *Personality and Social Psychology Bulletin, 25,* 363-381.

Fabrigar, L. R., Wegener, D. T., MacCallum, R. C., & Strahan, E. J. (1999). Evaluating the use of exploratory factor analysis in psychological research. *Psychological Methods, 4,* 272-299.

Fazio, R. H., Jackson, J. R., Dunton, B. C., & Williams, C. J. (1995). Variability in automatic activation as an unobtrusive measure of racial attitudes: A bona fide pipeline? *Journal of Personality and Social Psychology, 69,* 1013-1027.

Fazio, R. H., & Zanna, M. P. (1981). Direct experience and attitude-behavior consistency. In L. Berkowitz (Ed.), *Advances in experimental social psychology* (Vol. 14, pp. 161-202). New York: Academic Press.

Festinger, L., & Carlsmith, J. M. (1959). Cognitive consequences of forced compliance. *Journal of Abnormal and Social Psychology, 58,* 203-210.

Finch, J. F., & West, S. G. (1997). The investigation of personality structure: Statistical models. *Journal of Research in Personality, 31,* 439-485.

Floyd, F. J., & Widaman, K. F. (1995). Factor analysis in the development and refinement of clinical assessment instruments. *Psychological Assessment, 7,* 286-299.

Friedenberg, L. (1995). *Psychological testing: Design, analysis, and use.* Boston: Allyn & Bacon.

Gaito, J. (1980). Measurement scales and statistics: Resurgence of an old misconception. *Psychological Bulletin, 87,* 564-567.

Gorsuch, R. L. (1983). *Factor analysis* (2nd ed.). Hillsdale, NJ: Lawrence Erlbaum.

Greenwald, A. G., & Banaji, M. R. (1995). Implicit social cognition: Attitudes, self-esteem, and stereotypes. *Psychological Review, 102,* 4-27.

Greenwald, A. G., McGhee, D. E., & Schwartz, J. L. K. (1998). Measuring individual differences in implicit cognition: The implicit association test. *Journal of Personality and Social Psychology, 74,* 1464-1480.

Hammond, K. R. (1948). Measuring attitudes by error-choice: An indirect method. *Journal of Abnormal and Social Psychology, 43,* 38-48.

Himmelfarb, S. (1993). The measurement of attitudes. In A. H. Eagly & S. Chaiken, *The psychology of attitudes* (pp. 23-88). Fort Worth, TX: Harcourt Brace Jovanovich.

Izard, C. E. (1977). *Human emotions.* New York: Plenum.

Jackson, D. N. (1971). The dynamics of structured personality tests. *Psychological Review, 78,* 229-248.

Janada, L. H. (1998). *Psychological testing: Theory and applications.* Boston: Allyn & Bacon.

John, O. P., & Benet-Martinez, V. (2000). Measurement: Reliability, construct validation, and scale construction. In H. T. Reis & C. M. Judd (Eds.), *Handbook of research methods in social and personality psychology* (pp. 339-369). New York: Cambridge University Press.

Jöreskog, K. G. (1974). Analyzing psychological data by structural analysis of covariance matrices. In R. C. Atkinson, D. H. Krantz, R. D. Luce, & P. Suppes (Eds.), *Contemporary developments in mathematical psychology* (Vol. 2, pp. 1-56). San Francisco: W. H. Freeman.

Katz, D., & Stotland, E. (1959). A preliminary statement to a theory of attitude structure and change. In S. Koch (Ed.), *Psychology: A study of a science: Vol. 3. Formulations of the person and the social context* (pp. 423-475). New York: McGraw-Hill.

Kenny, D. A., & Kashy, D. A. (1992). Analysis of the multitrait-multimethod matrix by confirmatory factor analysis. *Psychological Bulletin, 112,* 165-172.

Kerr, N. L., Aronoff, J., & Messe, L. A. (2000). Methods of small group research. In H. T. Reis & C. M. Judd (Eds.), *Handbook of research methods in social and personality psychology* (pp. 160-189). New York: Cambridge University Press.

Kidder, L. H., & Campbell, D. T. (1970). The indirect testing of social attitudes. In G. F. Summers (Ed.), *Attitude measurement* (pp. 333-385). Chicago: Rand McNally.

Knowles, E. S. (1988). Item context effects on personality scales: Measuring changes the measure. *Journal of Personality and Social Psychology, 55,* 312-320.

Krosnick, J. A., & Fabrigar, L. R. (1997). Designing rating scales for effective measurement in surveys. In L. Lyberg, P. Biemer, M. Collins, E. De Leeuw, C. Dippo, N. Schwarz, & D. Trewin (Eds.), *Survey measurement and process quality* (pp. 141-164). New York: Wiley.

Krosnick, J. A., & Fabrigar, L. R. (in press). *Designing questionnaires to measure attitudes.* New York: Oxford University Press.

Likert, R. (1932). A technique for the measurement of attitudes. *Archives of Psychology, 140,* 44-53.

Loevinger, J. (1957). Objective tests as instruments of psychological theory. *Psychological Reports, 3,* 635-694.

Lord, F., & Novick, M. R. (1968). *Statistical theories of mental tests.* New York: Addison-Wesley.

Macrae, C. N., Bodenhausen, G. V., Milne, A. B., & Jetten, J. (1994). Out of mind but back in sight: Stereotypes on the rebound. *Journal of Personality and Social Psychology, 67,* 808-817.

Marsh, H. W., & Grayson, D. (1995). Latent variable models of multitrait-multi-method data. In R. H. Hoyle (Ed.), *Structural equation modeling: Concepts, issues, and applications* (pp. 177-198). Thousand Oaks, CA: Sage.

McKinley, R. L., & Mills, C. N. (1989). Item response theory: Advances in achievement and attitude measurement. In B. Thompson (Ed.), *Advances in social science methodology* (Vol. 1, pp. 71-135). Greenwich, CT: JAI.

Messick, S. (1989). Validity. In R. L. Linn (Ed.), *Educational measurement* (3rd ed., pp. 13-103). New York: Macmillan.

Millsap, R. E. (1992). Sufficient conditions for rotational uniqueness in the additive MTMM model. *British Journal of Mathematical and Statistical Psychology, 45,* 125-138.

Mueller, D. J. (1986). *Measuring social attitudes: A social handbook for researchers and practitioners.* New York: Teachers College Press.

Nisbett, R. E., & Wilson, T. D. (1977). Telling more than we can know: Verbal report on mental processes. *Psychological Review, 84,* 231-259.

Nosek, B. (2002). *Moderators of the relationship between implicit and explicit attitudes.* Unpublished doctoral dissertation, Yale University.

Osgood, C. E., Suci, G. J., & Tannenbaum, P. H. (1957). *The measurement of meaning.* Urbana: University of Illinois Press.

Ostrom, T. M. (1989). Interdependence of attitude theory and measurement. In A. R. Pratkanis, S. J. Breckler, & A. G. Greenwald (Eds.), *Attitude structure and function* (pp. 11-36). Hillsdale, NJ: Erlbaum.

Petty, R. E., & Cacioppo, J. T. (1986). *Communication and persuasion: Central and peripheral routes to persuasion.* New York: Springer-Verlag.

Petty, R. E., & Cacioppo, J. T. (1996). *Attitudes and persuasion: Classic and contemporary approaches.* Boulder, CO: Westview.

Petty, R. E., Haugtvedt, C. P., & Smith, S. M. (1995). Elaboration as a determinant of attitude strength. In R. E. Petty & J. A. Krosnick (Eds.), *Attitude strength: Antecedents and consequences* (pp. 93-130). Mahwah, NJ: Lawrence Erlbaum.

Remmers, H. H. (1963). Rating methods in research on teaching. In N. L. Gage (Ed.), *Handbook of research on teaching* (pp. 329-378). Chicago: Rand McNally.

Rosenthal, R., & Rosnow, R. L. (1991). *Essentials of behavioral research: Methods and data analysis* (2nd ed.). New York: McGraw-Hill.

Rotter, J. B. (1966). Generalized expectancies for internal versus external control of reinforcement. *Psychological Monographs, 80*(1, Whole No. 609).

Russell, J. A. (1980). A circumplex model of affect. *Journal of Personality and Social Psychology, 39,* 1161-1178.

Schmitt, N. (1996). Uses and abuses of coefficient alpha. *Psychological Assessment, 8,* 350-353.

Schuman, H., & Presser, S. (1981). *Questions and answers in attitude surveys: Experiments on question form, wording, and context.* San Diego: Academic Press.

Schwarz, N., & Hippler, H. J. (1991). Response alternatives: The impact of their choice and ordering. In P. Biemer, R. Groves, N. Mathiowetz, & S. Sudman (Eds.), *Measurement error in surveys* (pp. 41-56). Chichester, UK: Wiley.

Steinberg, L., & Thissen, D. (1995). Item response theory in personality research. In P. E. Shrout & S. T. Fiske (Eds.), *Personality research, methods, and theory: A festschrift honoring Donald W. Fiske* (pp. 161-181). Hillsdale, NJ: Lawrence Erlbaum.

Steyer, R., & Schmitt, M. J. (1990). The effects of aggregation across and within occasions on consistency, specificity, and reliability. *Methodika, 4,* 58-94.

Sudman, S., Bradburn, N. M., & Schwarz, N. (1996). *Thinking about answers: The application of cognitive processes to survey methodology.* San Francisco: Jossey-Bass.

Thurstone, L. L. (1928). Attitudes can be measured. *American Journal of Sociology, 33,* 529-554.

Thurstone, L. L., & Chave, E. J. (1929). *The measurement of attitude.* Chicago: University of Chicago Press.

Tisak, J., & Tisak, M. S. (2000). Permanency and ephemerality of psychological measures with application to organizational commitment. *Psychological Methods, 5,* 175-198.

Tittle, C. R., & Hill, R. J. (1967). Attitude measurement and prediction of behavior: An evaluation of conditions and measurement techniques. *Sociometry, 30,* 199-213.

Townsend, J. T., & Ashby, G. (1984). Measurement scale and statistics: The misconception misconceived. *Psychological Bulletin, 96,* 394-401.

Tucker, L. R., & Lewis, C. (1973). A reliability coefficient for maximum likelihood factor analysis. *Psychometrika, 38,* 1-10.

Visser, P. S., Fabrigar, L. R., Wegener, D. T., & Browne, M. W. (2003). *Analyzing social psychological multitrait-multimethod data.* Unpublished manuscript, University of Chicago.

Weary, G., & Edwards, J. A. (1994). Individual differences in causal uncertainty. *Journal of Personality and Social Psychology, 67,* 308-318.

Webster, D. M., & Kruglanski, A. W. (1994). Individual differences in need for cognitive closure. *Journal of Personality and Social Psychology, 67,* 1049-1062.

Wegener, D. T., Downing, J., Krosnick, J. A., & Petty, R. E. (1995). Measures and manipulations of strength-related properties of attitudes: Current practice and future directions. In R. E. Petty & J. A. Krosnick (Eds.), *Attitude strength: Antecedents and consequences* (pp. 455-487). Mahwah, NJ: Lawrence Erlbaum.

Wegener, D. T., & Fabrigar, L. R. (2000). Analysis and design for nonexperimental data: Addressing causal and noncausal hypotheses. In H. T. Reis & C. M. Judd (Eds.), *Handbook of research methods in social and personality psychology* (pp. 412-450). New York: Cambridge University Press.

Wegener, D. T., & Petty, R. E. (1998). The naive scientist revisited: Naive theories and social judgment. *Social Cognition, 16,* 1-7.

Widaman, K. F. (1985). Hierarchically nested covariance structure models for multitrait-multimethod data. *Applied Psychological Measurement, 9,* 1-26.

## CHAPTER 8

# Measures and Meanings

## The Use of Qualitative Data in Social and Personality Psychology

LAURA A. KING

*University of Missouri, Columbia*

Q ualitative data typically are defined as unstructured sources of information that do not lend themselves readily to quantification. Such data may emerge from interviews, written answers to questions, videotaped conversation, and other sources. Relative to more structured data, gathering these data typically involves a larger amount of time and effort on the part of participants and investigators alike. As a result, there is certainly a temptation to forgo the use of such data. There are times, however, when qualitative data are the only appropriate means to answer the scientist's questions. Although open-ended measures may be very attractive to those who are fascinated by the immediacy of human experience that such measures are more likely to convey, the onus of responsibility is on the researcher to demonstrate that all the work is warranted—that qualitative measures provide something beyond what might have been accomplished with more straightforward measures.

In approaching qualitative data, one must decide, from among a very rich array of

prospects, which are the most important for study. A useful distinction to be made is that between "top-down" and "bottom-up" approaches. In the top-down approach, the researcher comes to the data interested in examining a theoretically derived construct or hypothesis. Of course, it is hoped that any person conducting any empirical study has a theory that drives that particular investigation. However, in all research, qualitative or otherwise, the data sometimes present interesting new dilemmas. A bottom-up approach to qualitative data involves coming to the data themselves to see what's there. Although this sort of procedure may appear alarmingly post hoc, it is worthwhile to note that no researcher has unlimited foresight and that it is sometimes worthwhile to examine surprises (as is often the case in more straightforward quantitative investigations, to be sure).

Some areas of social science (and the humanities) regard its "unquantifiable" nature as essential to qualitative data. Sociologists and anthropologists may routinely come to their data and engage in a more intuitive or intellectual "data processing" in order to come to conclusions. Although such analyses remain subject to scientific rigor (Altheide & Johnson, 1994), concern for issues of reliability, sample size, generalizability, replicability, establishing causality, and control groups are not as pressing as they typically are in social psychology (Blaikie, 2000; Vidich & Lyman, 1994). These differences in emphases are understandable given the heightened interest of these researchers in more contextualized phenomena. Research in these areas is more likely to be characterized as reflecting a level of comfort with, and confidence in, more bottom-up approaches to analyses. Though top-down approaches are also used, even in these contexts, questions that are "second nature" to social psychologists (e.g., replicability of results) are rarely major concerns (Denzin, 1983; Guba & Lincoln, 1989; Phillips, 2000).

In contrast, purely qualitative inquiries are rare in personality and social psychology. Perhaps the use of psychobiography in personality psychology is an exception (see Elms, 1994; Runyan, 1982). In personality and social psychology, qualitative data typically reside alongside more structured data (e.g., questionnaires or laboratory manipulations). Although qualitative data may represent the centerpiece of a program of research, such data rarely are treated in purely qualitative ways. Nevertheless, it is worth noting how much qualitative data have become incorporated into research in personality and social psychology. Many procedures that have become essential parts of our methodological toolbox involve the problem of transforming unstructured free responses into quantifiable units. Researchers in social psychology have turned to personal narratives (Baumeister, Wotman, & Stillwell, 1993; Georgeson, Harris, Milich, & Young, 1999), diary entries, idiographic goals (e.g., Emmons & King, 1988), dyadic interactions (Berry & Miller, 2001), historical documents (Winter, 1992), poems (Stirman & Pennebaker, 2001),

scientific abstracts (Pennebaker & King, 1999), facial pictures, and videotapes (Bonanno et al., 2002; Dovidio, Kavakami, & Gaertner, 2002; Keltner & Bonanno, 1997) to examine important independent and dependent variables. However and importantly, in social psychological inquiries, qualitative data typically are conceived in terms of quantifiable research goals, and they are quickly transformed into quantitative data for analyses.

## QUALITATIVE DATA IN SOCIAL PSYCHOLOGY: AN EMPIRICAL EXAMPLE

A study by Stirman and Pennebaker (2001) provides an illustration of the contrast between typical uses of qualitative data in other fields and the approach used by social psychologists. These researchers were interested in examining the apparent tendency of poets to commit suicide. Previous research in this area was more typical of purely qualitative research (focusing on only on a single poet's work, examining a few poems from the individual's oeuvre, and using a single rater—usually the author of the research). No control groups were used (e.g., Hoyle, 1968; Lester, 1994). Stirman and Pennebaker (2001) adopted a more typical social psychological approach to this question, using qualitative data in a quantitative way. They content analyzed poems from three different life periods (early, mid, and late career) for each of a sample of 18 poets. A control group of nine nonsuicidal poets was matched with nine suicidal poets for age, nationality, and mood disorder (which is also, apparently, fairly common in poets). Stirman and Pennebaker hypothesized that suicidal poets would distinguish themselves from nonsuicidal poets by various aspects of the language used in their poems. Specifically, they predicted that suicidal poets would show tendencies toward self-absorption, preoccupation with death, and social detachment in their poems, compared to their nonsuicidal counterparts. Using a computerized word count system, these researchers found support for their hypotheses. First, suicidal poets were more likely than nonsuicidal poets to use first person references throughout their careers. These poets also showed a tendency toward using more death-related words. Even more striking, suicidal poets tended to increase in social detachment, as manifested in a decrease in the use of words such as "us," "we," and "our" as they approached the end of their lives. This investigation shows attention to the typical concerns of social psychologists in any study, but qualitative data clearly occupy center stage.

## ADVANTAGES OF ASKING OPEN-ENDED QUESTIONS

Although they present some obvious challenges, there are some clear advantages to asking one's open-ended research questions.

### Qualitative Data May Answer Many Questions at Once

Open-ended responses, like autobiographical stories or interview responses, allow us to examine a variety of psychological processes that may be involved in a particular experience, simultaneously and automatically. Processes such as dissociation, denial, and defensiveness can be seen to occur alongside other coping processes and may be particularly difficult to measure using more direct means. For example, in examining widows talking about the death of a spouse, Keltner and Bonanno (1997) looked not only at what the women said but also at facial expressions that occurred spontaneously and simultaneously with those verbalizations. In examining these data, Keltner and Bonanno coded for the occurrence of Duchenne (i.e., genuine or

authentic) smiling and laughter and found, surprisingly, that instances of such smiling even during a conversation about bereavement predicted better adjustment at a later time. Qualitative data allow us to examine questions not only of content but also of intensity, style, mannerism, and so on. We can examine not only what was said but *how* it was said. Qualitative data simply provide a richer, more varied pool of information.

### Qualitative Data Allow Us to Measure What Isn't Said or Can't Be Said

Considering variables such as dissociation, denial, and defensiveness, we can certainly posit that one of the defining features of these variables is that people don't know they are doing them. They are non-conscious. Qualitative measures have been especially useful in tapping variables that participants cannot or will not report on with accuracy. The problem of nonconscious psychological processes led to the development of projective techniques for use in measuring unconscious motives (Morgan & Murray, 1935). Of course, the use of projective techniques has been the subject of a great deal of debate over the years. Sidestepping that debate entirely, it remains clear that, at times, even in laboratory research, variables that the investigator would like to measure are not always easily tapped using straightforward manipulations or questionnaires. Even if they are aware of their motives or values, participants may be too embarrassed, ashamed, or concerned with the impression they are making to respond honestly to direct questions.

McClelland (1980; McClelland, Koestner, & Weinberger, 1989) drew the distinction between respondent and operant behaviors. Respondent behaviors are those that are performed self-consciously and that may involve a person's awareness that he or she is acting consistently with his or her own values. An example of a respondent behavior would be a response to a questionnaire item (e.g., "How positively do you generally feel about homosexuals?"). Operant behaviors are performed unself-consciously and spontaneously. When we are interested in operant behaviors, we may need to resort to qualitative data. An example of this sort of behavior is a person's spontaneous stylistic behavior in an interaction with a member of an out-group.

An example is provided by research by Dovidio and colleagues on the relation of racial prejudice measures to actual behavior by European Americans in interactions with African Americans. Dovidio et al. (2002) were interested in the implications of racial attitudes for behaviors during actual interaction with members of an out-group. In this study, the racial attitudes of European American participants were measured in two ways. First, participants completed explicit questionnaire measures of prejudice. Second, they completed an implicit attitudes test, using a reaction time measure that tested the ease with which participants associated positive and negative terms with black and white faces. Next, the participants interacted with white and black confederates while being videotaped. Participants also rated the level of friendliness that they believed they conveyed during the interaction. Measures of behavior during the interactions were gleaned via content analysis of the participants' verbal productions during the interaction (i.e., what they actually said) as well as their nonverbal behaviors (e.g., seating position, distance from confederate, etc.). Interestingly, the more respondent or explicit measure of prejudice related systematically to the participants' self-rated friendliness as well as to the positivity of participants' explicit verbal productions during the interaction. However, the more implicit attitudinal measure related systematically to participants' nonverbal behavior as well as to confederates' ratings of participant friendliness. Importantly, aspects of this dependent measure could not have

been measured using anything other than qualitative data. Without qualitative data, the conclusions of the investigation would have been quite different—that people's explicitly stated attitudes relate to their friendliness during interactions with others. The inclusion of qualitative data allowed for a more accurate depiction of the ways that implicit and explicit attitudes are conveyed in behavior, sometimes subtle behavior, toward another.

## Qualitative Data Give Us the Flavor of the Whole

In addition to allowing access to the unconscious and the unspoken, qualitative data allow for a sense of the coherence of human experience. Asking only highly structured questions constrains our capacity as researchers to fully tap into the human experience of the variables of interest. Although we can certainly gain enormously from purely quantitative investigations, at the same time those aspects of an individual that qualitative data are so useful for gleaning— issues of style, spontaneity, intensity, and the embeddedness of a phenomenon in the psychological life of the person—can be lost. It has often been said that humans make meaning by telling stories. Collecting accounts of personal experience is a way of collecting units of meaning.

My own research interests are in the area of personality, motivation, and meaning-making. I became particularly interested in how individuals experience changes in themselves during and after important life transitions or traumatic life events. Clearly, personality characteristics measured via questionnaires haven't been shown to reflect much change in personality over time, so looking for change or development through such questionnaires didn't seem like a promising approach. Using open-ended questions—about the stories of people's life experiences—clearly emerged as the ideal, if sometimes challenging, methodology.

Throughout this chapter, I will make use of examples from my work, especially from a study of parents of children with Down's syndrome (DS) (King, Scollon, Ramsey, & Williams, 2000). In that study, we were interested in examining how the stories that these parents told about the important life transition of discovering they would be rearing a child with DS would relate to aspects of their well-being and personality development. Participants in the study were 87 parents who provided sometimes quite compelling accounts of this life experience and completed measures of psychological well-being and personality development. Excerpts from their narratives demonstrate the kind of power that can be conveyed in qualitative data.

> The first 24 hours we were led to believe that our daughter was so bad off that we actually prayed to God to take her from us now versus later.

> A wave of feelings passed over me: shock, fear, and tremendous sadness and protectiveness toward my son.

> My heart felt as though it would break . . . Could our family face this sadness?

Although all three of these parents may have responded with high ratings to a questionnaire item asking if they had experienced distress upon learning of their children's diagnoses, even a 7 on a 7-point scale cannot convey the vividness of these narratives.

## Qualitative Data Are (Relatively) Timeless

Another advantage of open-ended responses is that we don't have to decide right away what we want to know from these data. Questionnaire data run the risk of becoming seriously outdated. Changes in the meanings of items and traits cause problems in revisiting a data set after many years. Qualitative data such as

written or transcribed protocols or videotaped interactions simply exist—they simply are. Even if the questions that drove their generation fade from interest, these productions can always be scored for the current research issue, whatever it is. Research by McAdams and colleagues on the intimacy motive provides an excellent example, using old stories and recoding them with a new system.

McAdams (1980) designed the intimacy motive scoring system to measure an individual's recurrent concern for warm interpersonal encounters for their own sake. This coding scheme answered a gap in the motivation literature on the human need for affiliation (which tended to emphasize more instrumental attempts to create and preserve existing interpersonal bonds). This coding scheme was developed at least two decades after most of the previously designed motivational coding systems. McAdams and Bryant (1987) were interested in examining how this (at the time) newly developed intimacy motive would relate to important life outcomes. Fortunately, longitudinal data had been collected on a group of more than 1,000 participants who had generated imaginative stories in response to pictures for studies on other motives. McAdams and Bryant again content analyzed these stories specifically for intimacy motive imagery. They found that intimacy motivation was related to positive life outcomes (heightened happiness and need gratification) for women and lack of strain and lack of uncertainty for men. This study demonstrates how qualitative data can be revisited with the changing interests of researchers. The data provide an enduring resource of information.

Historical documents also can provide rich sources of data for the social and personality psychologist interested in qualitative analyses. For instance, Winter (1992) examined the inauguration speeches of American presidents for motivational content. He found that various motive configurations were associated with particular historical events in one's presidency (e.g., high affiliative concern was associated with frequency of scandal; high power was associated with being viewed as a successful leader).

Another example of the multiple uses of one set of qualitative data is provided by a special section of the *Journal of Personality and Social Psychology* edited by Folkman (1997). All the articles in this special section used the same set of qualitative data, namely, interviews from a sample of bereaved gay men who had lost their longtime partners to AIDS. All the participants in this study had participated in a longitudinal study of adaptation to bereavement. All had been interviewed, and these transcribed interview protocols were given to four different research teams, each of whom analyzed them from its own perspective—engaging in a Rashomon-style exchange over the same data set. All the approaches demonstrated some important relations, all using different coding methods and schemes. Such a convergence would have been impossible without the incandescence that is part and parcel of qualitative data.

A caveat is appropriate at this point. The stories used by McAdams and Bryant were imaginative stories told in response to Thematic Apperception Test (TAT) (Morgan & Murray, 1935) pictures. As such, they may be somewhat decontextualized narratives, created "on the spot" in response to somewhat arbitrary stimuli. In addition, the interviews used in the bereavement project had all been collected within a few years of the coding that was conducted on those data. Although I have stated rather boldly that qualitative data simply "are," it is certainly important to consider the historical and cultural contexts of these data. Just as self-report traits may change in meaning, so might words used in the natural language of participants. In addition, responses to particular stems may not be appropriate for use in any investigation. When revisiting a qualitative data archive, it is important to consider the ramifications of the context of the initial data collection.

## METHODS OF QUALITATIVE RESEARCH

The use of qualitative data in a study has implications at nearly every stage of a research project. The special requirements of these data must be considered as decisions are made with regard to framing research questions, designing materials, recruiting participants, data coding and analyses, and finally interpretation and communication of results. In the next few sections, I will review some of the issues that should be considered in such an investigation.

### Participant Selection and Recruitment

Some investigations that use qualitative methods are certainly applicable to the "captive audience" of a university participant pool. For instance, diary methods, which require daily contact of some sort with the study, are more readily performed with individuals who are likely, by virtue of necessity, to be in close physical proximity to the site of the study. At some institutions, it is possible to collect qualitative data over the course of a semester as part of a class, centered around the daily study (Emmons & King, 1988). Although using such samples is enormously convenient, Web-based data collection might well allow researchers to begin to include less studied samples in diary and experience sampling studies.

Given the added time that typically is required for participants in the collection of qualitative data, some special consideration should be given to participant compensation. In work with nonstudent samples, monetary compensation often is a necessity. Furthermore, presenting a study to community adults may require differing recruitment techniques. In our work, we have used newspaper ads but also have found it useful to visit participant groups of interest wherever they might congregate (e.g., support group or informational meetings for parents of children with Down's syndrome; gay advocacy groups, gay bars, and bookstores for gay men and lesbians; support groups for divorced women). Often, it is important to inform participants that some of the questions they will be answering are open-ended. These questions likely will add to the time to complete the study because of lengthy interviews or the need for written responses. However, it is also worth noting that often it is within the open-ended questions that participants find the most engaging and interesting aspects of our work. Many times, I have received letters or notes from participants commenting on the value that answering these questions had for them. We typically try to present our work as focusing on finding out what participants already know—that we are simply trying to acquire an understanding of what their life experiences have shown them. We are asking participants to share important aspects of their lives with us; therefore, establishing a sense of trust and dispelling (potentially legitimate) concerns over psychologists' tendency to pathologize are crucial.

## Deciding What Questions to Ask and How to Ask Them

The type of methodology used to collect the data itself is obviously a key concern. Logistical issues such as time constraints and person-hours clearly play a role in these decisions. More important, concern for the match between how one has conceptualized a variable and how it might be measured ought to drive the design of study. Some variables may be better suited to an interview format in which an interviewer can prompt participants for more information when necessary. At other times, a researcher might be interested in the participants' own preexisting stories of

a life experience. In such cases, prodding may be inappropriate.

Qualitative data also may be collected through channels other than the verbal one. In this case, videotaping may be necessary. Videotaped interactions have proven to be a rich source of qualitative data. However, again, it is often necessary to assign individuals, couples, or groups a task to get them started, so that the activity of interest will actually find its way onto the videotape. If a variable is thought to be of particular relevance only during times of stress, it may be necessary to create a stressful atmosphere in order to gauge its importance (Campbell, Simpson, Kashy, & Rholes, 2001).

## Coding the Data

As I've already mentioned, in the process of social psychological inquiry, the movement from qualitative to quantitative approaches is extremely quick. Thus, having an idea of how one plans to treat the qualitative data will help in selecting the questions to ask and the types of responses that will be most worthwhile. If responses are to be quantified using a coding scheme, the question that emerges is, which one?

### Extant Coding Schemes

A variety of coding schemes have been developed for analyzing narrative and other qualitative data. Creating a new coding scheme for the purposes of content analysis is not terribly different from the rightfully maligned practice of proliferating self-report measures. It is certainly desirable to consult existing content-analytic schemes before embarking on the creation of a new system. Using an extant content-analytic scheme allows one to take advantage of a long history of trial and error by previous researchers. In addition, these schemes often have a body of literature behind them offering persuasive evidence of reliability and validity. Finally, many extant schemes have been published along with expertly scored practice materials that are invaluable in learning and eventually training teams of coders.

An impressive compilation of thematic coding systems was published in a volume edited by Smith (1992). This handbook is an excellent resource for researchers interested in learning and teaching a variety of coding schemes. Chapters include theoretical treatments, literature reviews, and coding manuals for implicit motives (e.g., achievement, power, affiliation, affiliative trust-mistrust, intimacy), attributional and cognitive orientations (e.g., personal causation, explanatory style, integrative complexity), and psychosocial orientations (e.g., psychological stances toward the environment, responsibility). Expertly scored practice materials are provided for every coding scheme. In my experience, graduate and undergraduate students alike can be trained to score narrative protocols reliably and efficiently using this handbook. The Smith volume, however, is hardly exhaustive. As with any study, a good rule of thumb is to check the literature prior to collecting data in order to explore preexisting coding strategies.

Coding systems for other types of data also are extant. For instance, the Facial Action Coding System (FACS) (Ekman & Friesen, 1978) codes for particular muscle movements in the face. This system provides a level analysis of facial movements especially as they are associated with particular emotional expressions. More global systems also have been developed that allow for a less fine-grained analysis of facial expressions. Social psychologists have developed methods of coding for body movements, attractiveness, deception, and other nonverbal behaviors. Although many systems allow one to learn a system independently, workshops that allow for training in various methods may also provide an important resource for acquiring the skills to use qualitative data effectively.

## Creating New Coding Schemes

Although there clearly is a wealth of existing coding schemes, there are times when a theoretically driven research question requires the development of a new coding scheme. For instance, in a study of the relations of private wishes to personality traits (King & Broyles, 1997), we collected three wishes from each of more than 400 undergraduates who had also completed trait measures of the big five personality factors (neuroticism, extraversion, openness to experience, agreeableness, and conscientiousness) (Costa & McCrae, 1988). The Five Factor Model (FFM) approach posits that traits have motivational properties so that they ought to be represented in motivational tendencies. Our study of private wishes sought to examine whether traits might be evident in the content of these flights of fancy. We developed a coding scheme specifically for content relevant to the FFM. To develop this system, we gave our coders a brief workshop on the FFM. We gave them sample items from the short questionnaire measure of the FFM to examine so that they would have a strong understanding of each of the five traits. Finally, the raters categorized each wish as relevant to one or more of the five traits. As predicted, the content of wishes related to personality traits. For instance, people high in neuroticism were more likely to wish to stop worrying. Those high in extraversion made more impulsive wishes (e.g., "an unlimited supply of beer"). Agreeable folks were more likely to make altruistic wishes and wishes for peace and harmony (e.g., "for the world to be a safer, friendlier place"). The highly conscientious were more likely to make wishes for achievement, and those high in openness to experience made nonconformist, highly intellectual wishes (e.g., "to do away with social conformity," "to be fluent in six languages"). Note that the construction of this coding scheme was helped immensely by the existence of extremely well-specified definitions of the traits in question.

In developing an ad hoc coding scheme, a variety of issues present themselves. How does one go about constructing a reliable coding scheme that is comprehensible to coders, that is likely to be represented in the data collected with adequate variance, and that taps into the construct of interest? One possibility is to consult the history of the construction of such schemes in personality psychology. Historically, personality psychologists interested in thematic content analysis have used criterion groups to create scoring systems for motives. In this literature, individuals who were known, a priori, to be high in a motive were asked to tell an imaginative story in response to a picture, and those stories were compared to stories told by individuals who were not assumed to be high on the motive in question. For instance, for the intimacy motive scoring system, McAdams (1980) compared stories told by sorority members who had just participated in a unity ceremony to those who had not, with the former expected to be higher in concern for warm human interaction. Although this kind of inductive strategy for coding schemes has been useful, it is not always possible to identify such a priori groups.

Alternatively, as was the case in our wishes study, given a variable that is well defined, a coding scheme can be developed. A detailed theory of how the construct might communicate itself via narrative or other free response will allow the researcher to easily nominate ways that the psychological process of interest might reveal itself in the data.

Certainly, in developing a coding system, it is tempting to code as much as possible. However, it is important to keep in mind what a human rater can and cannot accomplish with efficiency and accuracy. Some advice for the creation of coding schemes can be gained by examining some of the existing schemes that have been developed. First, these systems are marked by their clarity. Definitions must be straightforward and understandable, for both raters and eventual readers of a manuscript. It is desirable to avoid too much overlap in dimension content, to avoid both confusion for raters and lack of discriminant validity in analyses. Removing redundancy in rating categories is a good idea because it is not at all unlikely that coders will start to rate similar dimensions in a simultaneous and (perhaps) haphazard way (for instance, if raters code for "joy" and "happiness"). Try to anticipate clear areas of potential confusion: For instance, is a passage coded for "dialogue" if the person states "we were not talking"? Clearly specify when not to code for a particular dimension. Giving examples of "close but not quite" passages will help eventual coders make reliable distinctions. It is also best to keep the coding categories to a reasonable number. For example, McAdams's intimacy scoring system comprises 10 categories. Typically, coding can be thought of as test construction—a researcher may begin with far more items on a scale than ultimately will be included in the final, most reliable version. Categories may be winnowed down throughout the coding process. Obviously, one can code for a variety of dimensions and later create composites, but it is important to consider coder decay—the tendency for coders to become exhausted and overwhelmed.

Another consideration in developing a coding scheme is what level of measurement to employ. Some coding strategies (e.g., Smith, 1992) typically code for instances of an image, word, phrase, or theme. Such coding obviously is done on a categorical basis and then summed over the story. It is also possible to code specific protocols for "fitting" a particular type (e.g., is this a redemption pattern—in which events go from bad to better?) (McAdams, Reynolds, Lewis, Patten, & Bowman, 2001). In contrast, it is possible to code narratives or other data using Likert-type scales (for instance, "How emotionally positive is this story?" on a scale from 1 meaning *not at all* to 7 meaning *extremely much*). These issues are important to consider for a variety of reasons. First, it is worthwhile to consider that interval level data can always be transformed down a notch in levels of measurement—by converting the ratings to ordinal scales or to categories, if it is clear that raters are seeing the variables as categorical. Interval ratings may also be somewhat easier for raters to perform with confidence. At times, naïve raters may blanch at the idea that they are making all-or-nothing judgments. Clearly, the choice of measurement technique ought to be tied closely to a consideration of the theoretical definition of a construct: Is it all or nothing? Is it conceptualized as existing along a continuum?

Finally, consider that a coding scheme, though developed in response to a particular demand (one data set), may have a life of its own beyond the initial investigation. It is essential to present enough information in the write-up so that a reader could choose to replicate the study in his or her own lab. Given the need for brevity in manuscripts, making coding schemes available on the World Wide Web presents an outstanding option. Tips for training raters on the system as well as expertly scored practice materials also are invaluable additions to a Web site.

Our research on parents of children with DS provides an example of the construction of a theoretically derived coding scheme (King, Scollon, et al., 2000). In that study, we asked the participants to describe how they found out they would be parenting a child with DS. We were interested in examining stories of life transition, particularly, in order to examine whether these stories might show signs of the processes thought to underlie personality development. Block (1982) discussed Piaget's developmental process of accommodation as mechanisms of personality. Accommodation requires that one rethink one's essential beliefs about the self and the world—to create new structures through which to experience meaning. We thought that to the extent that

accommodation might be reflected in an individual's struggle to understand or find meaning in a major life event, it might manifest itself in the stories people told about those life experiences. Thus, based on Block's definition, we created a coding scheme that centered on those aspects of accommodation that might be found in the story of a life experience. Because this was a first investigation into content analyzing for accommodation, we included a broad range of potentially relevant variables, which were coded on scales from 1 (*not at all*) to 7 (*extremely much*). Initially, we started with nine dimensions, including "paradigmatic shift," "active vs. passive," "exploration," "traumatic," "gradual vs. sudden change," "closure," and "denial." Coding was completed by two raters who rated all the narratives, independently. These raters were blind to all other aspects of the data.

Because they were rather abstract, the accommodation coding dimensions were defined in great detail, as can be seen in Table 8.1. We completed a factor analysis of the coding and found that the dimensions tapped into two main issues: closure and accommodation. The three dimensions that held together as an accommodation factor are shown in Table 8.1. What follows is an excerpt from a participant's story, scoring high in accommodation.

> I cried some and experienced waves of "Unknown" embracing me. . . . I knew little about DS—it was an abstraction. Any handicap fell into the category of a childhood memory of seeing "waterheads," as I was told or remember, out on a shopping trip getting into a bus. My daughter was flesh and blood and a good nurser and that was the reality I remember dealing with. I thought very little about her future but I knew I would bow to no predictions. Irrational thoughts came to me at times but did not consume much thinking time: "I must have DS too, it just hasn't been discovered yet." Or "This child must be a consequence for wrong decisions in the past."

**Table 8.1** Content Categories for Accommodation Coding

| Category | Description |
| --- | --- |
| 1. Paradigmatic shift | This rating concerns the degree to which change entails a paradigmatic shift for the person. The new experience requires a revision of structures—an actual change in response to the environment and a qualitative change in how the person sees the world and him- or herself. The person has been forced to change, centrally and qualitatively, his or her views of the self and the world. |
| 2. Exploration | How much has the person searched and struggled with the change? This may include commenting on his or her own coping processes as well as talking about the process of making sense of the experience. |
| 3. Activity versus passivity | Is the narrator primarily a passive recipient of experience or primarily actively taking part in what is happening? |

The composite accommodation measure predicted personality development concurrently and 2 years later. Applying Block's conceptualization to the stories we collected represents a top-down approach to this analysis. The winnowing down of dimensions to the most central ones is also a common part of such investigations. We came to the narratives with a flexible scheme that was dictated by theory, along with an investigator's hunches about how a particular psychological process might manifest itself in story.

### Using Naïve Coders

When using qualitative data in social and personality psychology, in general, at least two independent raters are required for at least some of the ratings that are done, in order to allow for reliability estimates. Because of the logistical realities of academic research, these raters often are graduate or undergraduate research assistants. As such, they tend to be truly naive in their interactions with the research materials. Training these individuals to be proficient raters may be a unique challenge. The process ought to be conceived of as occurring in two stages, training and coding.

*The Training Phase.* Raters ought to be given sufficient time and material to engage in intense practice, with feedback, during the training phase. Although taking the time to train coders may seem like bit of a burden, this training phase can be a valuable time to edit the coding scheme, for instance, to identify early problems in reliability. Especially if it is necessary to create a new coding scheme, it is always recommended that raters be given a trial period with the scheme and that they be encouraged to report back their responses to the scheme after a brief amount of practice. We often ask coders to report the numbers they have assigned to various protocols. It is vital that they realize that disagreement is not a problem at this stage. Often, wide differences in initial coding help to identify problematic dimensions and can be useful in resolving ambiguities for all coders. Raters must be given an opportunity to discuss particularly difficult or complex categories with the other raters and the principal investigator. Repeated meetings and training sessions may be necessary. An appropriate metaphor is an immersion course in a second language. I encourage raters to mentally code everything they read, hear, or see for the relevant dimensions. In our study of parents of children with DS, undergraduate raters were given detailed descriptions of the coding dimensions. In addition, across several meetings, coders analyzed a variety of stories for these dimensions, including stories of life transition collected from other samples, such as divorced women. In this case, the emphasis was not on mastering an existing scheme but on ascertaining that all coders understood the "gist" of the instructions and could recognize potential aspects of accommodation when they saw it. Again, for these ratings, the emphasis was on consistency within each rater, rather than getting a "right answer."

For many existing schemes, there are plenty of available practice materials. In other cases, narratives that were used for other investigations can be useful practice materials. Finally, it may be necessary to find creative alternatives for practice materials. In my lab, where the qualitative data typically are narratives, raters have practiced on works of fiction, poetry, letters to the editor, and published soap opera summaries. Other practice materials for coding of nonverbal behavior may be TV clips, magazine photos, and films.

However one chooses to train coders, at some point they are ready to begin actual coding. With regard to ad hoc coding schemes, this may occur when the investigator has a sense that "everyone gets it." This was more or less how we completed training for the DS study. In other cases, there are actual tests that can be administered (for instance, for the coding manuals in Smith [1992]). In this case, after sufficient practice, raters can take the test to ensure that their ratings are mapping onto expert scoring (typically to within 96% of expert scoring).

*The Coding Phase.* Although communication among raters is invaluable during training, once training is complete, it is important that raters be told not to talk to each other about specific aspects of the coding once the "official" coding has begun. All raters must

be blind to the other raters' ratings as well as to the hypotheses of the study and other aspects of the participants that may be under investigation. One way to assure raters that consulting with each other to ensure high reliability is not necessary is to emphasize the importance of each rater being consistent within his or her own ratings. That is, raters should be encouraged to develop their own sense of what is "high" on a given dimension and to stick with that standard throughout the coding. Coders should keep their practice materials from the training phase, so that they can consult these when they are confused or unsure about their coding. In training raters to code for motive imagery, for instance, previous training materials that have been "corrected" by expert scoring can allow them to check their intuitions with previous materials.

Even with well-trained coders, differences of opinions do erupt in coding. In most cases, data for analyses are supplied by averaging over the ratings, so these differences are not crucial. However, if the study involves categorizing data, it may be desirable to obtain a "right answer" in the end. Typically, a consensus can be reached with some discussion, particularly with at least one expert coder in attendance. However, it is important that the ratings prior to discussion are retained for the calculation of reliability estimates.

*Naïve Coders and the Bottom-Up Approach.* Naïve coders may relate to the data in only top-down sorts of ways. They have been trained on a particular coding scheme and are likely, therefore, to attend to *just* those dimensions that the scheme presents as relevant. Yet, reading and thinking about the raw data certainly can lend itself to more bottom-up discoveries. How can the researcher remain open to such developments while using relatively naive coders? One solution, obviously, is to read all or most of the protocols oneself. With a large sample, this is not always feasible. Instead, the coders can serve as conduits of interesting information. In the initial stages of content analyses, our team of coders is invited to discuss with us any other interesting things they happen upon—to share particularly striking narratives with the group during the coding process. In our lab, coders meet to discuss coding progress one or two times a week. (Specific stories are not discussed, but dimensions are. In this way, raters can discuss general issues without revealing their codes to each other.) I typically ask coders to keep an eye out for what I might be missing and to jot down ideas as they read the narratives, in order to continue to get a sense of what is interesting about the stories.

An example of this process is provided, once again, by our study of parents of children with DS. This study was conducted specifically to explore the possibility that accommodation might be found in stories of life transition. However, another interesting aspect of these narratives presented itself as we embarked on our coding. In addition to coding for accommodation, three additional coders coded the emotional tone of the beginnings and endings of the stories. While conducting this coding, these coders noted a fascinating aspect of the stories these parents shared. For most of the protocols, the story began with a doctor's announcement of the child's diagnosis of DS, in the hospital, immediately or shortly after birth. Sometimes, however, the story began not with this announcement but rather at an earlier point in time. For instance, one mother wrote about a dream she had months prior to the child's birth. Another wrote about having a sinking suspicion during her pregnancy that the child she was carrying would have DS.

From a literary perspective, what we observed was clearly foreshadowing. In literature, it is clear that foreshadowing can be a compelling way to enhance the coherence of a narrative from one moment of the drama to the next. It has been suggested that constructing a coherent narrative about a traumatic life

event can play a helpful role in coping (Pennebaker & Seagal, 1999). Thus, there was reason to believe that the use of foreshadowing in stories might relate to positive psychological functioning. A coding scheme for foreshadowing was developed, and all the narratives were coded by all raters for the presence or absence of this narrative device.

Dramatic examples of foreshadowing did indeed emerge in a portion of these stories. For instance, one participant described how, at their baby shower, her husband opened a child care book at random and started reading loud. They both recoiled in horror as they realized he was reading about DS. Another mother began her story with a visit to an amusement park during her pregnancy. It happened that there were a number of children with DS at the park, and she took this as a sign that the child she was carrying would also have DS (King, Scollon, et al., 2000). Interestingly, in accord with our predictions, foreshadowing was associated with heightened well-being for these parents.

## Reliability and Validity

Because social and personality psychologists tend to treat qualitative data in a quantitative way, these data are expected to meet the same standards of reliability and validity as more structured measures. In asking about reliability, we want to know if a measure is relatively free of error of measurement—are the ratings consistent across raters? In asking about validity, we want to know that there is evidence that the measure used actually taps the construct under investigation.

### Reliability

Using qualitative data, the question of reliability typically is phrased in terms of the relationships among ratings done by different raters. In calculating reliabilities, the implications of decisions that have been made along the way in the investigation (e.g., What scale of measurement was used to code the data? How many raters were used? How much of the data did each rater actually rate?) come to the fore. My purpose in reviewing these issues here is to emphasize the implications of these decisions for reliability and to give practical suggestions for obtaining acceptable reliability estimates.

First, note the difference between coder agreement and coder reliability. Interrater agreement refers to the degree to which coders give the exact same rating to a narrative, videotape, or other item to be coded. Agreement typically is a concern when ratings have been done using nominal (or categorical) scales. The simplest and, perhaps, most easily understood measure of agreement is the percentage of agreement. It is important to note, of course, that some agreement among raters may occur by chance, so the percentage of agreement may, in fact, overestimate the actual level of agreement by judges that is due to their recognition of the variables of interest. A more sophisticated measure of agreement, one that is useful when categories are mutually exclusive, is Cohen's $\kappa$ (Cohen, 1960), which includes an estimate of the agreement that would be likely to occur by chance. In cases where the codes produced by raters are nominal but the categories are not mutually exclusive, other alternatives may be phi coefficients among ratings or, again, simple percentage agreements. In our study of parents of children with DS, we used phi coefficients (essentially correlations between dichotomous ratings) to express the strong degree of agreement among our judges for the ratings of foreshadowing (average phi = .91).

In contrast to agreement, reliability typically refers *not* to the exact agreement of ratings but rather to the extent to which ratings are proportional across judgments. Typically, in this case, ratings have been conducted on an interval scale (e.g., scales from 1 to 7 ratings) or a ratio scale (e.g., raters

have counted images and added these up within passages). Measuring reliability in this case means gauging the consistency across judges in their patterns of ratings. Imagine that three raters read the passage below (from the parents of children with DS) and coded it for emotional positivity, on a scale from 1 (*not at all*) to 7 (*extremely much*):

> It was long enough ago that the word was Mongoloid. I was alone and it was late at night when the doctor told me.... I laugh at this now because I was 33—I called my parents. I think I wanted them to fix things—they had been pretty good at that in the past.... Then I realized that I was mourning as if my child had died yet I still had a nice fat baby in the nursery. I rang for him to be brought to me expecting him to be a monster instead of the cute thing I saw in the delivery room. I tore all of his clothes off of him and just looked at him. He was beautiful. (King, 2001)

If the three raters rated this passage 4, 5, and 7, respectively, there are clearly disagreements in their assessments of the absolute level of the positivity of the passage. However, if, in the context of all the ratings these raters did, we find that this passage actually was rated relatively highly by all raters, the reliability will be high. For instance, if the rather curmudgeonly rater who gave this passage a 4 consistently rated very positive passages as 4's while our very positive rater consistently rewarded such passages with 7's, the ratings will be reliable. Again, reliability estimates are not concerned with the mean differences among raters but are ways of gauging their proportionality or rank order consistency.

The most obvious and convenient way to calculate reliability in this case is to simply calculate the correlations among the ratings and to report, perhaps, the average correlations among multiple raters, or the Cronbach's alpha for a composite rating. In the study of parents of children with DS, we used interrater correlations to justify the creation of composites for all the accommodation dimensions. It is worth noting that in this study, all the raters rated all the stories, and this decision allowed us the greatest freedom in calculating the reliability.

It is not always the case that the same raters will rate all materials. Sometimes, data may be collected over the course of a longer time period, and so raters are replaced. At other times, the data sets are so large that it is nearly impossible to have a pair or trio of raters rate all of them. Such situations require us to consider the role of rater variance in the reliability estimate. In this case, the intraclass correlation is preferred because it allows the researcher to decide exactly what the place of interrater variance ought to be vis-à-vis the reliability of an instrument. To appreciate this issue, it is helpful to imagine these data in a way that may not come intuitively to many researchers—that is, to think of each rater as a level of an independent variable in an experiment.

To understand the effects of the levels of the independent variable (i.e., the raters) on the dependent variable (i.e., the ratings), we must partition the variance in the ratings into variance attributable to rater, variance attributable to the object being rated (i.e., the person), and error variance. Thus, we can think of the ratings as dependent variables in a rater × person analysis of variance (ANOVA). Such an analysis, in actual practice, provides a clear sense of the role of rater variance in the ratings. Any output for an ANOVA will include the variance attributable to the independent variables (i.e., the mean square for rater) and that attributable to the person being rated (i.e., the mean square for person), as well as the leftover (unsystematic) error variance. Note that the variance due to person here represents the degree to which raters were sensitive to the changes in the dimensions of interest across protocols. The variance due to raters represents the characteristic idiosyncrasies of each rater.

First, let's consider the optimal case, in which all raters have rated all the protocols. In this situation, we would use the average among all raters as the actual score given to a protocol. Differences among the raters can be assumed to cancel out in the averaging of ratings, so rater variance should not be considered error. To estimate the reliability of the composite score, we could conduct a rater × person two-way ANOVA on the ratings. The output would provide the variances for raters, persons, and error. To calculate the Spearman-Brown correlation, these mean squares would be inserted into the formula as follows (Ebel, 1951; Tinsley & Weiss, 1975):

$$\frac{MS_{person} - MS_{error}}{MS_{person}}.$$

Note that $MS_{error}$ term above represents only random error. The variance partitioned off for raters is not included in the calculation at all.

However, in cases where not all coders have coded the entire data set, or if "doubling up" has occurred on only a subset of cases, the final ratings given to protocols are *not* composites of multiple ratings by the same raters. As a result, between-rater variance is rightfully treated as error. Although using a composite of judges' ratings allows us to use the reliability of the composite, in this case we really need the reliability of an average single judge's ratings. Here a simple one-way ANOVA (analyzing ratings by persons) provides the variances for the intraclass reliability estimate:

$$\frac{MS_{person} - MS_{error}}{(MS_{person} + MS_{error})(K - 1)}.$$

where K = the number of judges rating each person. (If K varies across individuals, the average number of judges can be calculated for inclusion in this formula; see Tinsley and Weiss [1975].) Note that in this equation, the $MS_{error}$ includes the between rater variance as error.

The bottom line is that if raters complete ratings on only a portion of the data, the reliability estimates should treat between-rater differences as error and the reliabilities will be lowered accordingly. Note that for all estimates of reliability, increasing the number of raters will increase the interrater reliability. However, the addition of raters has less and less impact on reliability as more raters are added. In terms of what are acceptable reliabilities, generally the same rules of thumb can be used as apply to questionnaire data—reliabilities below .60 are likely to raise eyebrows.

In sum, reliability estimates should be chosen with attention to the scale of measurement used, the number of coders, and the amount of overlap by coders. Some methods for computing reliability are fairly easy (for instance, computing percentage agreements, interrater correlations, or alpha reliability across composites for coders), whereas others can be more challenging logistically (for instance, computing mean square estimates for variance attributed to person × rater). As a rule, researchers probably select the reliability estimate that gives them the best result, but these must always be selected within the confines of the data themselves. Although many textbooks review the issues of reliability, I recommend an article by Tinsley and Weiss (1975). It has been extremely useful in obtaining reliability estimates given varying numbers of coders, levels of measurement, and research goals. The advice offered is straightforward and extremely helpful.

## Validity

The validity of an instrument concerns how much the measure actually taps what we want it to. Although reliability tells us about the consistency of a measure, it is possible to have very high reliability and very low validity. Because reliability refers to systematic variance, if all raters consistently make the same mistakes, reliability will be high, yet these highly reliable ratings will consistently miss the variable in question. Once again, decisions affecting the quality of an investigation from its inception clearly impinge on eventual validity: Was the coding scheme sufficiently clear? Were the raters appropriately trained? Was the proficiency of the raters well gauged? Although reliability clearly is a challenge, validity issues may present even greater difficulty, particularly for newer coding schemes.

Convergent validity can be difficult to gauge, particularly if a construct is understood to be strongly intertwined with its own measurement method. For many years, the TAT measures of motivation were held in low regard because they failed to show convergent validity with questionnaire measures of the same motives (see King, 1995, for a review). However, theoretical justifications for these null results provided a new way to think of these measures (McClelland et al., 1989). It is important to remember that the lack of relation between self-report and content-analytic measures may be substantively interesting and not necessarily indicative of invalidity of either type of measure. For instance, in the study by Dovidio and colleagues reviewed earlier, the spontaneous nonverbal behavior shown by white participants in the presence of a black confederate was not related to their verbalizations or to their self-reported attitudes, yet clearly this behavior has importance in its own right. Qualitative measures are used exactly because they tap into something that more structured measures cannot get to; thus, it should not be surprising when these measures fail to converge.

Seeking to establish criterion-related validity may be a more profitable approach to establishing the validity of qualitative methods.

This possibility is well illustrated in the classic distinction in the Type A Behavior Pattern literature. Research comparing the Type A Structured Interview (which relies on the coding of nonverbal behavior) with the Jenkins Activity survey (a reliable questionnaire) has demonstrated that, reliability differences not withstanding, the more qualitative measure does a superior job of predicting coronary heart disease (e.g., Matthews, 1988).

## ADDITIONAL CHALLENGES OF USING QUALITATIVE DATA IN SOCIAL PSYCHOLOGY

### Methodological Problems and Confounds

There are a variety of confounds that may be unique to the use of qualitative data. One problem in verbal reports is that of verbosity. Individuals who simply talk a lot more than others may score higher on measures based on free responses. Typically, researchers include the length of a protocol as a control variable in analyses or may convert scores to "images per 1,000 words" or some similar measure to account for differences in word usage. Other potential confounds in coding nonverbal behavior are the effect of attractiveness, smiling, and clothing on ratings. Typically, researchers strive to equalize these characteristics across rated targets, or code for these potential confounds in order to statistically control for them later.

### Losing the Trees for the Forest

Perhaps because social psychological research is more likely to (rapidly) quantify qualitative data, the risk of losing the whole in pursuit of numerical descriptions of the data is more pressing. Yet, one of the very strengths of qualitative data is their capacity to convey a sense of the whole. Overcoming

this problem is a challenge. Clearly, simply including excerpts of narratives is one way to attempt to preserve the integrity of the whole. However, this solution probably is profoundly unsatisfying for both the reader and the researcher. In addition, the press for brevity in journal articles may decrease the likelihood of even this level of inclusion (or to the relegation of these excerpts to rarely read appendices). What other alternatives exist? One possibility is to return to the single case to examine how individual narratives reflect and challenge group based results (see Allport [1961]; this advice certainly would also apply to purely quantitative work). My work on the relations between the content of implicit motives (measured via imaginative stories) and personal goals demonstrates how the examination of individual cases can enlighten even null results. In this case, no evidence emerged for the kinds of straightforward relations one might expect between implicit motives and goal content (e.g., individuals high on need for achievement did not have a high number of achievement-related personal goals) (King, 1995). An examination of a few single cases, however, demonstrated that these two types of motivation measures related within a given person in complex, sometimes idiosyncratic ways that could not be captured in group analyses. It is important that such an examination not be presented as an afterthought. Such analyses may inspire research on a broader sample. Another possibility would be to combine quantitative analyses with more purely qualitative analyses. Such a possibility may require interdisciplinary research that acknowledges and negotiates the varying biases and expertise associated with differing areas of social science. Finally, it might be worthwhile to consider alternative outlets for research that is more purely qualitative, keeping in mind that it is often a question of where and when, not *if*, a scientifically sound, provocative article will be published.

## Special Ethical Considerations

A final unusual problem in the use of qualitative data is special consideration for ethical treatment of the data. Narratives, interviews, and videotaped interactions or monologues may reveal more than the typical questionnaire about a particular research participant. Participants who are asked to share stories of their personal experiences must be assured that the data will be published only in group format. If a researcher would like to use excerpts from various participants to enliven his or her research report, he or she ought to ask for permission from these participants to do so. Typically, if individuals are to be videotaped, they should give their permission to be so taped. If telling participants beforehand about the taping might interfere with natural behavior, the participants may be taped surreptitiously but later should be informed of the taping and offered the chance to destroy the tape.

Finally, during coding, it is extremely important that coders treat the research protocols with the appropriate level of respect. In my lab, student raters are asked to sign a "contract" that reviews the appropriate treatment of qualitative data. Raters are not to talk about these data with anyone who is not in the lab. Raters must behave professionally while in the lab, in case research participants come by to drop off questionnaires or be interviewed. Furthermore, if a rater recognizes a particular participant from his or her research materials, the rater must stop working on those materials immediately and turn them over to the principal investigator for reassignment to another rater. It is important for raters to recognize that participants have shared important aspects of their lives with us. Without their candor and willingness to share, our work would be impossible. Their materials must be treated with the highest degree of respect.

## NEW APPROACHES TO QUANTIFYING QUALITATIVE DATA

Advances in technology have led to the development of a number of innovative computerized systems for analyzing qualitative data, including NUD*IST, nVivo, HyperRESEARCH, and ATLAS.ti. Each of these systems certainly warrants a chapter (or book) of its own, and fortunately, such chapters and volumes have been written (e.g., Fielding & Lee, 1991; Richards & Richards, 1994). Critiques also are available that compare and contrast the strengths and weaknesses of each of these (Huberman & Miles, 1994) and compare these systems to human ratings (Rosenberg, Schnurr, & Oxman, 1990). These systems provide ways for researchers to manage qualitative data. One issue is that these packages don't actually code for you; they simply allow you to make use of their various features for organizing data, tracking patterns that your exploration has uncovered. As such, these tools may be best suited to more modestly sized data sets and for use by expert coders (see Loxley, 2001). Although differing in their specific features, these packages essentially help a researcher taking a "bottom-up" approach to build a conceptual framework for a data set. Coming from a top-down approach, they allow a researcher to organize text features that are theoretically relevant in hypothesis testing.

Some packages allow for a simultaneous "macrolevel" accounting of the patterns emerging in the data. For instance, ATLAS.ti uses semantic categories to group codes into families. NUD*IST is an index-based approach that, in addition to performing code and retrieve functions, also provides nodes for an index system that functions parallel to the microlevel coding. This index system allows the research to track and also consider dynamic connections between the general constructs emerging in the content analyses.

Using these technologies is a truly interactive experience, and the potential for theory building appears very strong. Most of the packages are available in demonstration versions on the World Wide Web. As the creators of NUD*IST themselves have commented, this system "Offers many ways for a researcher never to finish a study" (Richards & Richards, 2001, p. 458).

Perhaps because The Linguistic Inquiry and Word Count (LIWC) (Pennebaker & Francis, 1996) was designed by a social psychologist, its reliability has been empirically addressed (Pennebaker & King, 1999) and it has been used on very large data sets successfully (e.g., Pennebaker, Mayne, & Francis, 1997). As LIWC processes text, every word in a protocol is matched against a catalog of words in the LIWC dictionaries. These dictionaries include a variety of topics of interest to social psychologists, including positive and negative emotion, self-references, social words, death-related words, and cognitive words (e.g., thinking, causation). The output is SPSS ready and includes the percentage of words that the person used that fit into each of the LIWC dictionaries. LIWC is enormously flexible. The various dictionaries can be combined in a variety of ways to tap into whatever construct interests the researcher. A weakness of a word count strategy is that words are necessarily decontextualized, so LIWC misses sarcasm, metaphor, and other aspects of language that are less than straightforward.

To use these programs, protocols must be transcribed into text files for the computer. Although this may be a small obstacle (we sometimes ask participants to type their stories onto a computer), it might also make research on archival texts that have not been transcribed laborious. Text analysis programs represent a potential boon to qualitative research, but it is important to bear in mind that not all research questions lend themselves to such a molecular level of analysis. The human reader may never be replaced entirely by computerized analyses.

Technology also has begun to show promising inroads in other areas in which qualitative data have required a great deal of time and effort to quantify. For instance, Cohn and colleagues (Cohn, Zlochower, Lien, Hua, & Kanade, 2000) have been developing facial feature matching software to code for emotional facial expression. These innovations may allow researchers to avail themselves of rich qualitative data sources without the effortful training and coding that such data typically have required. Of course, such innovations must be shown to have excellent convergent validity with manual coding in order to prove truly useful for researchers.

## CONCLUSION

Using qualitative approaches allows the researcher to tap into a well of rich information. When I first thought about what it meant to be a psychologist, this is what I thought I'd be doing: learning from people doing what they do—that is, making meaning out of their experiences. Qualitative data allow us to examine the natural behavior of human beings in its various forms. Decisions about what we study and how we study it have far-reaching implications for the eventual usefulness of such inquiries. Qualitative research in social and personality psychology involves a number of challenges, but in the end the best of this work can be seen to embody the best of the hard and the soft in our science. The key is to balance the desire to wring as much from the data as possible with maintaining the dignity of the whole, to not lose the "big picture" in the search of that which easily lends itself to quantification.

# REFERENCES

Allport, G. A. (1961). *Pattern and growth in personality*. New York: Holt.

Altheide, D. L., & Johnson, J. M. (1994). Criteria for assessing interpretive validity in qualitative research. In N. K. Denzin & Y. S. Lincoln (Eds.), *Handbook of qualitative research* (pp. 485-500). Thousand Oaks, CA: Sage.

Baumeister, R. F., Wotman, S. R., & Stillwell, A. M. (1993). Unrequited love: On heartbreak, anger, guilt, scriptlessness, and humiliation. *Journal of Personality and Social Psychology, 64*, 377-394.

Berry, D. S., & Miller, K. M. (2001). When boy meets girl: Attractiveness and the five-factor model in opposite sex interactions. *Journal of Research in Personality, 35*, 62-77.

Blaikie, N. (2000). *Designing social research: The logic of anticipation*. Malden, MA: Blackwell.

Block, J. (1982). Assimilation, accommodation, and the dynamics of personality development. *Child Development, 53*, 281-295.

Bonanno, G. A., Keltner, D., Noll, J. G., Putnam, F. W., Trickett, P. K., LeJeune, J., & Anderson, C. (2002). When the face reveals what words do not: Facial expressions of emotion, smiling, and the willingness to disclose sexual abuse. *Journal of Personality and Social Psychology, 83*, 94-110.

Campbell, L., Simpson, J. A., Kashy, D. A., & Rholes, W. S. (2001). Attachment orientations, dependence, and behavior in a stressful situation: An application of the actor-partner interdependence model. *Journal of Social & Personal Relationships, 18*, 821-843.

Cohen, J. (1960). A coefficient of agreement for nominal scales. *Educational and Psychological Measurement, 20*, 37-46.

Cohn, J. F., Zlochower, A., Lien, J., Hua, W., & Kanade, T. (2000). Automated face analysis. In C. Rovee-Collier & L. Lipsitt (Eds.), *Progress in infancy research* (Vol. 1, pp. 155-182). Mahwah, NJ: Lawrence Erlbaum.

Costa, P. T., & McCrae, R. R. (1988). From catalog to classification: Murray's needs and the five-factor model. *Journal of Personality and Social Psychology, 55*, 258-265.

Denzin, N. K. (1983). The art and politics of interpretation. In N. K. Denzin & Y. S. Lincoln (Eds.), *Handbook of qualitative research* (pp. 500-515). Thousand Oaks, CA: Sage.

Dovidio, J. F., Kawakami, K., & Gaertner, S. L. (2002). Implicit and explicit prejudice and interracial interaction. *Journal of Personality and Social Psychology, 82*, 62-68.

Ebel, R. L. (1951). Estimation of the reliability of ratings. *Psychometrika, 16*, 407-424.

Ekman, P., & Friesen, W. V. (1978). *Facial Action Coding System manual*. Palo Alto, CA: Consulting Psychologists Press.

Elms, A. C. (1994). *Uncovering lives: The uneasy alliance of biography and psychology*. New York: Oxford University Press.

Emmons, R. A., & King, L. A. (1988). Conflict among personal strivings: Immediate and long-term implications for psychological and physical well-being. *Journal of Personality and Social Psychology, 48*, 1040-1048.

Fielding, N. G., & Lee, R. M. (Eds.). (1991). *Using computers in qualitative research*. London: Sage.

Folkman, S. (1997). Introduction to the special section: Use of bereavement narratives to predict well-being in gay men whose partner died of AIDS—Four theoretical perspectives. *Journal of Personality and Social Psychology, 72*, 851-854.

Georgeson, J. C., Harris, M. J., Milich, R., & Young, J. (1999). "Just teasing . . .": Personality effects on perceptions and life narratives of childhood teasing. *Personality and Social Psychology Bulletin, 25*, 1254-1267.

Guba, E. G., & Lincoln, S. L. (1989). *Fourth generation evaluation*. Newbury Park, CA: Sage.

Hoyle, J. F. (1968). Sylvia Plath: A poetry of suicidal mania. *Literature of Psychology, 18*, 187-203.

Huberman, M. A., & Miles, M. B. (1994). Data management and analysis methods. In N. K. Denzin & Y. S. Lincoln (Eds.), *Handbook of qualitative research* (pp. 428-445). Thousand Oaks, CA: Sage.

Keltner, D., & Bonanno, G. (1997). A study of laughter and dissociation: Distinct correlates of laughter and smiling during bereavement. *Journal of Personality and Social Psychology, 73*, 687-702.

King, L. A. (1995). Wishes, motives, goals, and personal memories: Relations and correlates of measures of human motivation. *Journal of Personality, 63*, 985-1007.

King, L. A. (2001). The hard road to the good life: The happy, mature person. *Journal of Humanistic Psychology, 41*, 51-72.

King, L. A., & Broyles, S. (1997). Wishes, gender, personality, and well-being. *Journal of Personality, 65*, 50-75.

King, L. A., Scollon, C. K., Ramsey, C. M., & Williams, T. (2000). Stories of life transition: Happy endings, subjective well-being, and ego development in parents of children with Down Syndrome. *Journal of Research in Personality, 34*, 509-536.

Lester, T. (1994). Emotional self-repair and poetry. *Omega, 28*, 79-84.

Loxley, W. (2001). Drowning in words? Using NUD*IST to assist in the analysis of long interview transcripts from young injecting drug users. *Addiction Research and Theory, 9*, 557-573.

Matthews, K. (1988). CHD and Type A behavior: Update on and alternative to the Booth-Kewley and Friedman quantitative review. *Psychological Bulletin, 104*, 373-380.

McAdams, D. P. (1980). A thematic coding system for the intimacy motive. *Journal of Research in Personality, 14*, 413-432.

McAdams, D. P, & Bryant, F. B. (1987). Intimacy motivation and subjective mental health in a nationwide sample. *Journal of Personality, 55*, 395-413.

McAdams, D. P., Reynolds, J., Lewis, M., Patten, A. H., & Bowman, P. J. (2001). When bad things turn good and good things turn bad: Sequences of redemption and contamination in life narrative and their relation to psychosocial adaptation in midlife adults and in students. *Personality and Social Psychology Bulletin 27*, 474-485.

McClelland, D. C. (1980). Motive dispositions: The merits of operant and respondent measures. In L. Wheeler (Ed.), *Review of personality and social psychology* (Vol. 1, pp. 10-41). Beverly Hills, CA: Sage.

McClelland, D. C., Koestner, R., & Weinberger, J. (1989). How do self-attributed and implicit motives differ? *Psychological Review, 96*, 690-702.

Morgan, C. D., & Murray, H. A. (1935). A method for investigating fantasies. *Archives of Neurology and Psychiatry, 34*, 289-306.

Pennebaker, J. W., & Francis, M. E. (1996). Cognitive, emotional, and language processes in disclosure: Adjustment to college. *Cognition and Emotion, 10*, 601-626.

Pennebaker, J. W., & King, L. A. (1999). Linguistic styles: Language use as an individual difference. *Journal of Social Psychology, 77*, 1293-1312.

Pennebaker, J. W., Mayne, T. J., & Francis, M. E. (1997). Linguistic predictors of adaptive bereavement. *Journal of Personality and Social Psychology, 72*, 863-871.

Pennebaker, J. W., & Seagal, J. D. (1999). Forming a story: The health benefits of narrative. *Journal of Clinical Psychology, 55,* 1243-1254.

Phillips, D. C. (2000). *The expanded social scientists' bestiary: A guide to fabled threats and defenses of naturalistic social science.* Oxford, UK: Rowman and Littlefield.

Richards, T., & Richards, L. (1994). Using computers in qualitative research. In N. K. Denzin & Y. S. Lincoln (Eds.), *Handbook of qualitative research* (pp. 445-462). Thousand Oaks, CA: Sage.

Rosenberg, S. D., Schnurr, P. P., & Oxman, T. E. (1990). Content analysis: A comparison of manual and computerized systems. *Journal of Personality Assessment, 54,* 298-310.

Runyan, W. M. (1982). *Life histories and psychobiography: Explorations in theory and method.* New York: Oxford University Press.

Smith, C. (Ed.). (1992). *Motivation and personality: Handbook of thematic content analysis.* New York: Cambridge University Press.

Stirman, S. W., & Pennebaker, J. W. (2001). Word use in the poetry of suicidal and nonsuicidal poets. *Psychosomatic Medicine, 63,* 517-522.

Tinsley, H. E. A., & Weiss, D. J. (1975). Interrater reliability and agreement of subjective judgments. Journal *of Counseling Psychology, 22,* 358-376.

Vidich, A., & Lyman, S. (1994). Locating the field. In N. K. Denzin & Y. S. Lincoln (Eds.), *Handbook of qualitative research* (pp. 19-22). Thousand Oaks, CA: Sage.

Winter, D. G. (1992). Content analysis of archival materials, personal documents, and everyday verbal productions. In C. P. Smith (Ed.), *Motivation and personality: Handbook of thematic content analysis* (pp. 110-126). New York: Cambridge University Press.

## CHAPTER 9

# Implicit Methods in Social Psychology

JOHN F. KIHLSTROM

*University of California, Berkeley*

If social psychology were concerned merely with the impact of the social situation on individual behavior, social psychologists would have no interest in people's mental states. They would be concerned solely with measuring various features of the social environment and various aspects of people's behavior within that environment. But long before the cognitive revolution in psychology, social psychologists believed that social behavior was determined by the person's *mental representation* of the situation in which that behavior took place. The central role of mental states, in turn, explains why, almost from the beginning, social psychologists have relied on self-reports of attitudes, stereotypes and other beliefs, preferences, values, goals, and motives. Self-report questionnaires and other survey instruments have not been merely a convenient and inexpensive way of collecting information about people's behavior (although they have been that, too).

Rather, the questionnaire method has been central to social psychology because social psychologists have embraced the twin assumptions that people were aware of the attitudes, beliefs, and values that guided their behavior, and that they would be willing to reveal them if asked appropriately.

Of course, social psychologists were not stupid. They fully understood that some of the mental states in question were highly charged, and perhaps even embarrassing, and that people might not be willing to talk about them with strangers. Consider, for example, the lengths to which Alfred Kinsey and his associates went to get people to talk about their sex lives—as well as the difficulties encountered in today's climate of political correctness in getting people to talk frankly about their views with respect to gender, race, and ethnicity. Social psychologists also understood that the investigative situation itself was problematic. By virtue of demand characteristics

AUTHOR'S NOTE: Preparation of this chapter was supported by National Institute of Mental Health Grant MH-35856. I thank Jack Glaser, Tina Pantaleakos, and Carol Sansone for their comments.

(Kihlstrom, 2002; Orne, 1962; also see Haslam & McGarty, Chapter 11, this volume), experimenter bias (Rosenthal, 1963), evaluation apprehension (Rosenberg, 1965), reactance (Brehm, 1966), and a host of other factors, research designs might not possess the kind of external validity that would permit us to conclude that people actually thought or felt what they seemed to think and feel. Accordingly, social psychologists have exercised a great deal of ingenuity in getting around these problems, from unobtrusive or nonreactive behavioral measures (see Wegener & Fabrigar, Chapter 7, this volume) to psychophysiological recordings (see Cacioppo, Lorig, Nusbaum, & Berntson, Chapter 17, this volume).

Beginning in the 1980s, a new dimension was added to the problem of self-reports by the increasing recognition that people's experiences, thoughts, and actions could be influenced by percepts and memories of which they were unaware (Kihlstrom, 1984, 1987). If unconscious thoughts, feelings, and desires exist and can influence social behavior while remaining unconscious, then even the most sophisticated questionnaires and surveys will not succeed in tapping the mental states that underlie what we do when we interact with other people. This chapter surveys a number of methods recently introduced for assessing people's unconscious, or implicit, attitudes, beliefs, and other mental states relevant to social interaction (for alternative coverage of this material, see Fazio & Olson, 2003). Although there is some overlap between these "implicit" methods and those generally called "unobtrusive," there is an important conceptual distinction. Unobtrusive methods are used to assess attitudes, beliefs, and values of which people are aware, but that they may be unwilling to reveal to the investigator. By contrast, implicit methods are used to assess attitudes, beliefs, and values of which people are unaware. This creates additional methodological problems for the investigator.

## THE PSYCHODYNAMIC HERITAGE

Of course, the notion of unconscious determinants of behavior was not entirely new, given that it lies at the roots of Freud's psychoanalytic theory of the mind and behavior. According to Freud, conscious experience, thought, and action were determined by unconscious sexual and aggressive motives, as well as defense mechanisms unconsciously deployed against these primitive drives in order to reduce the anxiety caused by their conflict with the constraints of the real and social world. If Freud was right—and many personality and social psychologists working in the first half of the 20th century thought he was—then a variety of new techniques was needed to go beyond self-report to tap people's *un*conscious beliefs, feelings, and desires.

### Projective Tests

In Freud's own work, these unconscious motives were ostensibly discovered, and brought to the light of conscious awareness, by means of the clinical technique of free association. But very quickly a number of formal tests were developed for this purpose, beginning with Jung's adaptation of Freud's own technique of free associations to serve as a "complex indicator" (Jung, 1918/1969). Standardized versions of Jung's procedures, accompanied by rudimentary norms, were quickly developed (Kent & Rosanoff, 1910; Rapaport, Gill, & Schafer, 1968; Rapaport, Schafer, & Gill, 1944-1946); these in turn led to the development of word-association norms for purposes of research with normal individuals (e.g., Russell & Jenkins, 1954). A number of other techniques were soon added (Lindzey, 1959), including the Rorschach Inkblot Test, the Thematic Apperception Test (TAT) (see King, Chapter 8, this volume), and the Draw-a-Person Test. Even the Wechsler-Bellevue Intelligence Scale (WBIS), forerunner to the Wechsler Adult Intelligence Scale and perhaps the prototypical example of a performance-based test of cognitive ability, was co-opted for the purposes of projective personality assessment, both in the clinic (Rapaport, Gill, et al., 1968) and by the United States Central Intelligence Agency (Bem, 1983; Marks, 1979; Marks & Greenfield, 1984a, 1984b).

All of this work was predicated on the projective hypothesis (Frank, 1939a, 1948; Rapaport, 1942), in which the subject is given the opportunity "to reveal his way of organizing experience by giving him a field (objects, materials, experiences) with relatively little structure and cultural patterning, so that the personality can project upon that plastic field his way of seeing life, his meanings, significances, patterns, and especially his feelings" (Frank, 1939b, p. 403). Although the use of projective techniques does not necessarily mean that the affects, drives, and other mental states revealed by the test are unconscious, that is the general assumption behind their use. As Rapaport, Gill, et al. wrote:

> The use of projective tests assumes that the examiner is after something in the subject which the subject *does not know about* or is *unable to communicate*; otherwise the examiner would ask him about it directly. . . . By means of projective tests we discover tremendous aggressions in persons who appear meek, or great dependent needs in suspicious and manly-appearing [*sic*] persons who deny having any such inclinations. If taken seriously, these tests therefore refer to unconscious *motivation* of action and behavior, and necessitate a personality theory that assumes the existence of, and accounts for, these motivations. (Rapaport, Gill, et al., 1968, pp. 227-228)

Despite their continued popularity among many clinical psychologists, it is now generally understood that projective techniques are not satisfactory psychometric instruments (Lilienfeld, Wood, & Garb, 2001). Even in the few instances where projective techniques

proved to have some validity, there is no evidence that the scores in question actually represented a subject's *unconscious* mental state. Consider, for example, the recent literature promoting the TAT as a measure of implicit, or unconscious, motivation (McClelland, Koestner, & Weinberger, 1989). The low correlation between TAT and questionnaire measures of achievement motivation is often interpreted as a reflection of the independence of unconscious and conscious motivation, but it could simply mean that TAT measures lack convergent validity. Similarly, the fact that implicit and explicit measures of motivation predict different classes of behavior is often taken as evidence of a pattern of discriminant validity, but the same pattern of correlations could be interpreted as a result of method variance. If the TAT, Rorschach (Bornstein, 2001), and other projective methods are to acquire the status of "implicit" methods, more is needed than evidence for their reliability, validity, and utility. What is needed is convincing evidence that they tap *unconscious* mental states.

## The Subtle and the Obvious

Running parallel with the psychodynamic literature on projective techniques, some hint of the unconscious also can be found in the distinctions between *samples* and *signs*, and between *subtle* and *obvious* items, in the psychometric literature on objective tests of personality. Most personality and attitude questionnaires assume, at least tacitly, that the test items represent *samples* of the respondent's actual behavior—that is, that there is some degree of isomorphism between the person's performance on the test and what he or she thinks and does in the real world outside the testing situation. In such tests, face validity is very high. Other tests, however, assume no such isomorphism. From this point of view, test items are intrinsically interesting units of behavior that are *signs* of some underlying disposition. The original versions of the Minnesota Multiphasic Personality Inventory (MMPI) and its "normal" offspring, the California Psychological Inventory (CPI), were both constructed under the sign assumption. As a result, they contain many "subtle" scale items that lack face validity, even though they correlate with some empirical criterion (Goldberg & Slovic, 1967; Seeman, 1952). Ironically, then, the prototypical "objective" tests of personality make the same assumption as do the Rorschach and other projective techniques—that test responses are signs of underlying dispositions, not samples of behavior (Meehl, 1945).

The preference for empirically valid signs over face-valid samples reached its apex in Berg's *deviation hypothesis*, which held that even preferences for random drawings could be used as personality scale items, so long as people with different dispositions expressed different preferences (Berg, 1955). In fact, however, most empirically derived personality scales (including those of the MMPI and CPI) contain a mix of face-valid items that are obviously related to the substantive domain under consideration, and "subtle" items that do not appear to relate to the domain. Although an early analysis by Seeman found that subtle and obvious items were equally good predictors of criterion behavior (Seeman, 1952), later studies found that obvious MMPI items performed better than subtle items (Duff, 1965; Goldberg & Slovic, 1967). In addition, a study by Hase and Goldberg (1967) showed that questionnaires constructed by "rational" means, such that each scale item possessed face validity, performed better than questionnaires constructed by "empirical" means that resulted in a mix of obvious and subtle items (see also Ashton & Goldberg, 1973; Jackson, 1975).

Scales consisting entirely of subtle items have been advocated in some corners on the ground that subjects who approach personality questionnaires with a defensive attitude will not see through them, and thus will be tricked into self-disclosure. Similarly, at least in principle, subtle items might be useful with subjects who are appropriately motivated toward self-disclosure but are simply unaware of their traits and other mental characteristics. However, it appears that personality tests are disguised in this way at the expense of validity (Mischel, 1968, 1972). Of course, the reply to this weak evidence for the empirical validity of subtle questionnaire items might be the same as for the TAT: that subtle items, reflecting unconscious tendencies, should not be expected to correlate with obvious items that reflect conscious awareness, and that as such, subtle items might predict different criteria than do obvious items. However, there is no evidence for the discriminant validity of subtle versus obvious items. Nor—and this is the central point—is there any evidence that subtle items tap traits, attitudes, and the like of which the subject is unaware. The first lesson of 100 years of personality assessment is this: If you want to know what people can tell you, you should ask them.[1] If you want to know what people *cannot* tell you, unfortunately, subtle questionnaire items, like projective techniques, would appear to be risky choices for the assessment of unconscious mental states.

## THE PRIMING SOLUTION

If not projective tests, or inventories of subtle items, then *what?* One answer to this question is provided by research in implicit memory (Schacter, 1987). Neurological patients with bilateral lesions to the hippocampus and associated structures in the medial temporal lobe characteristically are unable to remember the events and experiences that have transpired since the onset of their brain damage. However, it is now known that this anterograde amnesia affects only conscious recollection. When patients are tested with techniques that do not require conscious recollection, they typically show that some traces of post-morbid experience have been encoded, remain in storage, and interact with ongoing experience, thought, and action—albeit outside conscious awareness. To take a familiar example, patients who have studied a list of words often show various *priming* effects, as on tests of word-stem and word-fragment completion, perceptual identification and lexical decision, and free association or category generation—even though they cannot recall or recognize the items they studied. Because the list items are not accessible to conscious recollection, priming evidently is an effect of *unconscious* memory. The dissociation between explicit and implicit memory also can be observed in neurologically intact subjects who are not particularly amnesic, as when explicit memory is affected by an experimental manipulation, such as level of processing, that has little or no effect on implicit memory.

These two examples, taken together, give us the definition of implicit memory as unconscious memory: In the amnesic patients, priming occurs in the *absence* of conscious recollection; in the normal subjects, priming occurs *independently* of conscious recollection. Note that the mere fact that a subject completes the stem *mar_____* with *market* rather than *marble* is not enough to qualify a behavior as an implicit or unconscious expression of memory. The word *market*, or at least some item plausibly related to it, has to have been on the study list—if not, there is no sense in talking about memory. But note, too, that the mere fact of priming is not sufficient to permit discussion of *unconscious* memory. Priming occurs in nonamnesic controls, and for deeply processed items as well. To qualify as unconscious, priming has to occur *in the absence of*, or *independently of*, conscious recollection.

The implicit-explicit distinction in memory can be extended to other domains as well, including perception (Kihlstrom, 1996;

Kihlstrom, Barnhardt, & Tataryn, 1992), thinking and problem solving (Dorfman, Shames, & Kihlstrom, 1996; Kihlstrom, Shames, & Dorfman, 1996), learning (Kihlstrom, 1996; Reber, 1967), emotion (Berridge & Winkielman, 2003; Kihlstrom, Mulvaney, Tobias, & Tobis, 2000); and motivation (Kihlstrom, Mulvaney, et al., 2000; McClelland et al., 1989). Along the same lines, it should be possible to use priming as a measure of the sorts of implicit, unconscious attitudes, beliefs, and values of interest to social psychologists. In a sense, deriving measures of individual beliefs, attitudes, feelings, values, and motives represents a revival of Jung's (1918/1969) use of response latencies on a word-association test as a "complex-indicator."

## The Importance of Matching Tasks

In all of this, it is critical that explicit and implicit expressions of memory be assessed with comparable tasks. Consider, for example, an experiment in which explicit memory is assessed with free recall but implicit memory is assessed with priming on stem completion. Such an experiment might well find that more target items are produced on the priming task than on the free recall task, but this would not be evidence of a dissociation between explicit and implicit memory. The reason is that stem completion is a variant on cued recall, in that the stem serves as a cue for recall of the whole word, and it is well known that cued recall typically is superior to free recall. The same consideration would apply to a comparison of free recall with priming on perceptual identification: Perceptual identification is a variant on recognition, in that the entire study item is represented on the memory test, and it is well known that recognition is superior to recall.

In psychometric terms, then, recognition is an "easier" test of memory than cued recall, which in turn is an "easier" test of memory than free recall. And in statistical terms, "dissociation" is just neuropsychological jargon for statistical interaction: Dissociations occur when one variable, such as population (e.g., amnesic vs. nonamnesic) or experimental manipulation (e.g., level of processing), interacts with another variable (e.g., explicit vs. implicit test) to affect performance. It is well known that spurious interactions can occur as artifacts of task difficulty (e.g., Chapman & Chapman, 1973, 2001). Accordingly, in any study of dissociations between explicit and implicit measures, it is important that the tasks be matched as closely as possible on relevant psychometric characteristics.

To clinch the case for a dissociation between explicit and implicit memory, we must show not just that implicit memory occurs in the absence of, or independently of, explicit memory. We must also show that the cues available to the subject remain constant across tasks. Thus, the appropriate explicit comparison for stem completion is stem-cued recall. In stem-cued recall, the subject is asked to fill in a stem with an item from a previously studied word list, thus requiring conscious recollection; in stem completion, the subject is asked to fill in the stem with any appropriate word, thus obviating conscious recollection. Similarly, the appropriate explicit comparison for perceptual identification is recognition. In recognition, the subject is presented with a copy of a previously studied word and asked whether it was on a previously studied word list; in perceptual identification, the subject is presented with the word and asked to identify what it is. In the best comparisons, different items are tested explicitly and implicitly, so that performance on one test does not contaminate performance on the other.

The importance of test matching is illustrated by a classic experiment on "repression" performed by Weinberger and his colleagues (Weinberger, Schwartz, & Davidson, 1979). In this experiment, the investigators were interested in a group of subjects, labeled *repressors*, who reported low levels of trait anxiety on the Taylor Manifest Anxiety Scale (MAS) but high levels of defensiveness on the Marlowe-Crowne Social Desirability Scale (SDS). In other words, they reported low levels of distress, but their high levels of social desirability suggested that they might be repressing distress that they were actually experiencing unconsciously. Other groups showing different patterns of MAS and SDS scores, such as nondefensive nonanxious (low MAS, low SDS) and nondefensive anxious (high MAS, low SDS) subjects, served as comparison subjects (for alternative classification schemes, see Mulvaney, Kihlstrom, Figueredo, & Schwartz, 1992; Weinberger & Schwartz, 1990). In the experiment, Weinberger et al. asked their subjects to read phrases with sexual and aggressive content. Despite their general denial of distress, "repressors" showed increased response latencies and elevated levels of physiological response during the task (see also Asendorf & Scherer, 1983). Weinberger et al. concluded that the "repressors" were repressing after all: Although they denied being in distress, they clearly were disturbed by what they were asked to read. Put another way, repressive style entails a dissociation between explicit and implicit expressions of anxiety (Kihlstrom, Mulvaney, et al., 2000)—at least in principle.

The Weinberger et al. (1979) study is very provocative and deserves its status as a minor classic in the experimental study of psychodynamics and defense, but it is not definitive evidence of unconscious emotion. Setting aside the question of whether repressors really were repressing anxiety or instead merely denying felt distress to the investigators, the study did not properly test for the dissociation between explicit and implicit emotion. For such a test to be valid, the cues presented to the subject would have to be the same for both explicit and implicit conditions. For example, subjects might have to rate their emotional response to each phrase in the explicit condition, and rate the difficulty of reading the phrase in the implicit condition. But in the Weinberger et al. experiment, the "explicit" measure was reports of generalized distress on the MAS, whereas the "implicit" measure was behavioral or physiological response to specific sexual and aggressive phrases. There was no assessment of explicit emotional response to the phrases, so in the final analysis we don't know whether the "repressors" were repressing anything at all. To validate the concept of repression, we need evidence of a dissociation between explicit and implicit measures of emotional response *to the same stimulus*. To validate the concept of "repressive style" as an individual-difference, we need evidence that this dissociation is greater in individuals identified as repressors, as opposed to nondefensive subjects who truly are high or low in anxiety.

## Priming as a Measure of Implicit Attitudes

Of course, the Weinberger et al. study of repression was performed before the criteria for explicit-implicit dissociations had been formulated, but the lesson holds. More recently, Banaji and Greenwald applied the explicit-implicit distinction to the central social psychological concept of attitude and other constructs, such as stereotypes and prejudice (Banaji & Greenwald, 1994; Blair, 2001; Brauer, Wasel, & Niedenthal, 2000; Greenwald & Banaji, 1995; Greenwald, Banaji, Rudman, et al., 2002; see also Wilson, Lindsey, & Schooler, 2000). Although social psychology traditionally has assumed that people are aware of their attitudes, these authors have suggested that people may possess positive and negative *implicit attitudes* about themselves and other people, attitudes that can affect ongoing social behavior outside of conscious awareness.

An early example of the use of priming to study implicit attitudes is research by Gaertner and McLaughlin on racial stereotypes (Gaertner & McLaughlin, 1983). In this

experiment, subjects were presented with pairs of letter strings and were asked to judge simply whether both were words. On some trials, the first word was *black* or *white*, and the second word was associated with the racial stereotypes of whites or blacks, such as *smart* or *lazy*. In such a situation, the first word can be considered as a prime for processing the second word. Note that the subject's task had nothing to do with social judgment. Nevertheless, white subjects responded more quickly when the stimulus paired a positive word such as *smart* with the prime *white* than when it was paired with the prime *black*; there was no difference with negative words such as *lazy*. Wittenbrink and colleagues, in a similar study, found that *white* primed lexical decisions concerning positive trait terms, whereas *black* primed lexical decisions concerning negative characteristics (Wittenbrink, Judd, & Park, 1997). Similarly, Blair and Banaji had subjects make lexical decisions about words such as *doctor* and *nurse* that were primed by male or female first names, such as *Jack* or *Jill* (Blair & Banaji, 1996). The general finding of their research was that response latencies were shorter when there was a congruence between the gender of the name and the gender-role connotations of the word, as in *Jack-doctor* vs. *Jill-doctor*. On the basis of results such as these, we might conclude that the lexical decision task reveals people's implicit, or unconscious, stereotypes concerning race and gender.

Another priming-based approach to implicit attitudes is represented by a series of studies by Banaji and her colleagues of the "false fame" effect documented by Jacoby (Jacoby, Kelley, Brown, & Jasechko, 1989; Jacoby, Woloshyn, & Kelley, 1989). Jacoby has interpreted this effect in terms of priming: Priming increases familiarity, which is incorrectly interpreted as evidence of fame. In their experiments, Banaji and Greenwald adapted Jacoby's procedure by dividing the study and test lists into equal numbers of male and female names (Banaji & Greenwald, 1995). They found that the false fame effect was greater for male than for female names, and a signal-detection analysis indicated that subjects adopted a lower criterion for judging male names as famous than they did for female names. Because the average subject was more likely to associate fame with males than with females, Greenwald and Banaji concluded that the paradigm of false fame provided evidence for "implicit gender stereotypes that associate male gender, more than female gender, with achievement" (Greenwald & Banaji, 1995, p. 16).

## Critique of Priming

By this point in time, a fairly large number of such studies have been published, too many to be reviewed comprehensively in this chapter (for comprehensive coverage, see Fazio & Olson, 2003). However, before we interpret such studies as providing evidence of unconscious racism and sexism on the part of subjects, a few questions need to be addressed. First, it is not entirely clear that the performance of subjects in these sorts of experiments is indicative of their personal attitudes, as opposed to the structure of the social environment. For example, perhaps doctors *really are* more likely to be named Jack and nurses more likely to be named Jill; and given the hegemony of the patriarchy, it may well be that an unfamiliar male is more famous (at least in some quarters) than an unfamiliar female. And although whites are no smarter than blacks, and blacks are no lazier than whites, it may be that the subjects' behavior was influenced by their knowledge of this common social stereotype, rather than their personal endorsement of it. This is especially a problem because the experimental task does not require subjects to make statements about themselves, but only to make judgments about language.

Moreover, many studies of implicit social cognition fail to test for differences between in-groups and out-groups, or other stakeholders with respect to the belief or attitude in question. A finding that whites, but not blacks, are more likely to associate whiteness with smartness, and that males, but not females, were more likely to associate maleness with fame, might well support the attribution of subjects' experimental behavior to their social attitudes rather than the structure of the society in which they live. Of course, it could also happen that blacks and women adopt prevailing social stereotypes concerning race and gender, but an in-group vs. out-group difference would at least provide some converging evidence that priming was a measure of individuals' actual social attitudes rather than something more generic, such as their abstract knowledge of stereotypes and prejudice found in their society.

More important in the present context, most ostensible studies of implicit social cognition either fail to make a comparison with an explicit measure of the same attitude or employ an explicit measure that is inadequate to the task. From the point of view of *implicit* social cognition, it is not interesting if subjects betray, by their performance in a priming task, attitudes, stereotypes, and prejudices that they are fully aware of harboring. Priming effects that are congruent with a subject's conscious beliefs and attitudes may well be interesting unobtrusive or nonreactive measures, but more is required to make the inference that people's unconscious attitudes, beliefs, and values actually are different from their conscious ones. In addition to the indirect assessment of implicit attitudes, beliefs, and values, there must be a comparative direct assessment of their explicit counterparts, and the correlation between explicit and implicit measures of the same attitude must be low—certainly nonsignificant, preferably zero.

Many studies simply fail to provide this sort of comparison, in which case they stand as little more than demonstrations that attitudes, beliefs, and values can be displayed in priming effects. When studies do provide this comparison, they often give contradictory results. For example, Gaertner and McLaughlin (1983) found that implicit racial stereotyping occurred regardless of subjects' scores on a questionnaire measure of racial prejudice, whereas Wittenbrink et al. (1997) found many positive correlations between explicit and implicit measures. As it happens, the Gaertner and McLaughlin (1983) and Wittenbrink et al. (1997) studies used different questionnaires to assess implicit racial prejudice, but perhaps the most important problem is that they used questionnaires at all. As noted earlier, the most compelling demonstrations of the dissociation between explicit and implicit memory are provided by studies in which the stimuli presented to the subjects are the same, but the task demands are different. In memory studies, the explicit task refers to a past event, whereas the implicit task does not. Following this example, future attempts to use priming tasks to demonstrate a dissociation between explicit and implicit attitudes, beliefs, and values should keep the stimuli presented to the subject constant, and vary whether the experimental task refers expressly to the subject's mental state.

A final problem is that although implicit attitudes, beliefs, and values should function as individual difference variables, they are not always treated as such. In the Gaertner and McLaughlin (1983) study, for example, priming scores were the dependent variables in an experiment in which individual differences in racial prejudice served as a blocking variable in an analysis of variance design, and there was no attempt to take account of individual differences in priming. In the Wittenbrink et al. (1997) study, by contrast, both explicit and implicit measures of prejudice were construed as individual-difference variables entered into a multivariate analysis. Historically, of course, social psychologists have been allergic to individual differences (Bowers, 1973; Cronbach, 1957), but it may also be that priming scores are not well suited to being treated as individual-difference measures. For example, their distributions are naturally skewed, sometimes highly so, and often characterized by substantial within-subject variability, requiring large numbers of trials to achieve satisfactory levels of reliability.

These considerations underscore the point that the study of implicit attitudes, beliefs, and values described in this chapter reverses the role of priming in experiments, from that of *dependent variable* to that of *independent variable*. That is to say, we wish to use priming not merely as a expression of attitudes, beliefs, and values that are already known from people's responses on paper-and-pencil questionnaires, but as an alternative measure of these attitudes, beliefs, and values that will predict people's behavior in a way that their self-reports will not. The two roles may work at cross-purposes. In experimental work, where the goal is to determine how minds work in general, the best dependent variables are those that show relatively little between-subjects variance. In individual-differences work, where the goal is to predict what different people will do in a particular situation, the best independent variables are those that show relatively wide dispersion across the population. To the extent that response latencies measure how minds work in general, rather than how particular individual minds work, they may simply not present enough variance to make them useful measures of individual differences.

## THE IMPLICIT ASSOCIATION TEST

Although priming studies of implicit social cognition remain popular, Greenwald and his colleagues recently have introduced another procedure, the Implicit Association Test (IAT), for the measurement of implicit attitudes, beliefs, and values (Greenwald, McGhee, & Schwartz, 1998).[2] Based on the general principle of stimulus-response compatibility (DeHouwer, 2001), the IAT requires subjects to make a series of dichotomous judgments about instances of various concepts, such as black and white American names (e.g., *Alonzo* or *Adam*, *Amanda* or *Aiesha*) and positive and negative words (e.g., *caress* or *abuse*, *freedom* or *crash*). These responses are made by pressing different keys on a keyboard or button box. When the two concept sets are combined, Greenwald and his colleagues found that response latencies are faster when associated concepts share a response key, compared to when they do not. Accordingly, in the example cited, the observation of faster latencies when a subject has to make the same response to white names and positive words, compared to white names and negative words, reveals an implicit association between white and positivity. By the same token, observation of faster latencies when a subject has to make the same response to black names and positive words, compared to black names and negative words, reveals an implicit association between black and positivity.

Using this procedure, Greenwald, McGhee, et al. (1998) showed that subjects implicitly associate flowers with pleasantness and insects with unpleasantness (Experiment 1); that Korean subjects implicitly associate Korean names with pleasantness and Japanese names with unpleasantness, and that Japanese subjects do the opposite (Experiment 2); and that white subjects implicitly associate white names with pleasantness and black names with unpleasantness. In the latter two experiments, the IAT proved to be more sensitive to individual differences in ethnic or racial prejudice (or, if you will, more discriminating) than explicit measures such as the feeling thermometer or the semantic differential (see also Greenwald & Farnham, 2000). In the Korean-Japanese study, the IAT correlated significantly with the feeling thermometer but not with the semantic differential. In the black-white study, which also included three standard questionnaire measures of racist beliefs, the correlations were uniformly non-significant. Taken together, these findings suggest not only that the IAT can measure

people's racial or ethnic prejudices, but also that it reveals prejudices of which the subjects themselves are unaware.

## The IAT as a Psychometric Device

Since its formal introduction in 1998, the IAT has become extremely popular as a method for measuring implicit attitudes, beliefs, and values in a number of domains. A search of the PsycINFO database (keyword: "IAT") identified at least eight studies using the IAT published in 1999 and 2000, and as many as 20 published in 2001 alone. Given the inevitable delays of the scholarly publication process, this record of adoption is quite remarkable. Of particular interest is a multi-method psychometric study comparing three implicit measures of racial prejudice, including a priming procedure and two versions of the IAT, in which all tests were completed in each of four testing sessions separated by two weeks (Cunningham, Preacher, & Banaji, 2001). Treating each individual trial as if it were an item on a test, the two versions of the IAT yielded acceptable if not outstanding estimates of internal consistency, perhaps reflecting the inherent instability of response latency measures noted earlier—as well as the fact that IAT measures of prejudice are calculated as difference scores. Raw test-retest correlations for the IAT were relatively low, but after correction for measurement error these rose considerably. And although the bivariate correlations among the implicit measures were quite low, first- and second-order confirmatory factor analyses revealed substantial convergence among them. Although these findings still must be confirmed in other domains, taken together they suggest that the IAT is a promising psychometric instrument for the evaluation of implicit social attitudes, beliefs, and values.

However, if utility (or efficiency) of measurement is considered as an important property of a psychometric device (Mischel, 1968), it is not clear that the IAT is superior to a standard priming procedure. In the Cunningham et al. (2001) study, the two versions of the IAT correlated .30 and .48, respectively, with the Modern Racism Scale, while the corresponding correlation for the priming procedure was only .26. By any reasonable standard, a priming procedure is easier to construct, administer, and interpret than the IAT. If a *low* correlation with explicit measures is a desirable characteristic of an implicit measure (and it must be desirable, if the implicit measure is to be truly implicit), then this status is achieved far more economically by a standard priming procedure than by the IAT. Of course, for any psychometric procedure there are always trade-offs between reliability and validity of measurement, on one hand, and utility, on the other. Investigators may be willing to sacrifice some utility in the service of increased reliability and validity. Further comparative studies probably are in order.

Of course, these psychometric analyses are purely internal. What about the relation with external factors? To establish their validity, all psychological tests, like the constructs they purport to measure, must relate in significant ways to reasonable external criteria (Cronbach & Meehl, 1955; Loevinger, 1957). One very interesting finding is that IAT measures of bias and prejudice toward an outgroup occur even following a minimal group manipulation (Ashburn-Nardo, Voils, & Monteith, 2001). In successive experiments, the IAT revealed prejudice by white American subjects against names ostensibly associated with *Surinam* (a real but unfamiliar country), *Marisat* (a nonexistent country), and members of artificial groups (*Quans* and *Xanthies*) created by random assignment. Such a finding strengthens the inference that the IAT really measures prejudice after all. Another supportive finding is that IAT measures of anti-black prejudice predict the quality of white subjects' actual behavioral interactions (e.g., body openness, eye contact, and friendly laughter) with black targets (McConnell & Leibold, 2001). Similarly, IAT measures of self-esteem predicted subjects' response to task failure,

such as buffering (Greenwald & Farnham, 2000). In fact, the implicit measure of self-esteem was somewhat more strongly predictive of buffering than the explicit measures employed. Finally, Greenwald, Banaji, Rudman, et al. (2002) have shown that the IAT gives more satisfactory results than explicit measures such as an attitude thermometer or standard questionnaires, when compared against the predictions of a variant on Heider's (1946) balance theory.

## Critique of the IAT

More studies of this sort are needed, especially in light of the fact that responses on the IAT, and perhaps measures of priming as well, are subject to the influence of a number of nuisance variables. For example, in their original paper, Greenwald, McGhee, et al. (1998) noted that response latencies are affected by differences in the familiarity of the stimuli to which subjects respond, as well as by differences in evaluation. More recently, Brendl, Markman, and Messner (2001) argued that IAT indices of anti-black attitudes could be obtained not only from subjects who actually held negative attitudes toward blacks but also from subjects who held neutral or positive attitudes toward blacks, so long as they were less favorable than their attitudes toward whites. Preferring white over black names is not necessarily evidence of racism: It may be no different from any other forced "choice" between two positively valued objects, such as favoring Stravinsky over Schoenberg or *tiramisu* over *zabaglione*. More important, Brendl et al. (2001) showed through computational modeling that "evidence" of prejudice on the IAT could emerge not only from differences in familiarity of the targets being evaluated, as Greenwald, McGhee, et al. (1998) had also suggested, but also from differences in task difficulty, which can induce subjects to shift their response criterion between the response-compatible and response-incompatible blocks of the IAT procedure. Differences in target familiarity can be controlled for, at least in principle; but because response-incompatible judgments are inherently more difficult than response-compatible ones, this problem will remain. Brendl et al. remind us that although prejudice (conscious or not) may well produce an effect on the IAT (or, indeed, on any measure involving response latencies), an effect on the IAT or similar measure may not indicate prejudice, for the simple reason that such an effect may have multiple causes, such as target familiarity or task difficulty, that have nothing to do with prejudice.

The question of whether the IAT actually assesses people's attitudes and beliefs raises the critical and thorny question of whether the attitudes and beliefs revealed by the IAT really are unconscious—that is, whether subjects' responses on the IAT can be predicted by measures of their corresponding explicit attitudes and beliefs. In this regard, the evidence remains mixed. In their original paper, Greenwald, McGhee, et al. (1998) reported that the average correlation between explicit and implicit measures of the same construct ($r = .25$) was lower than the average correlations among explicit measures ($r = .60$), but the implicit-explicit correlations were still numerically positive. Similar findings were obtained by Greenwald and Farnham (2000) in a comparison of explicit and implicit self-esteem. In the Cunningham et al. (2001) study, a first-order confirmatory factor analysis revealed significant relations between all three implicit measures of racism and an explicit measure, and in fact the two paths involving the IAT were stronger than the path involving the priming-based measure. In a second-order analysis, in which the three tests were considered to converge on a single latent variable, the association between implicit and explicit prejudice remained strong. Another study of racial attitudes found that the IAT was correlated significantly with an explicit questionnaire measure of racial prejudice (McConnell & Leibold, 2001). A recent

analysis of four data sets collected over the Internet yielded implicit-explicit correlations ranging from .174 to .775, and averaging approximately .43 (Greenwald, Nosek, & Banaji, 2002, Tables 2-6 and p. 20).

Like Greenwald, Cunningham et al. (2001) noted that the overall implicit-explicit relationship was weaker than the individual relations among the implicit-implicit relationships, but the fact remains that the implicit-explicit relationship was far from trivial in magnitude. In all these studies, explicit and implicit attitudes were dissociated in the weak sense of not being highly correlated (no correlation is perfect), but not in the strong sense of being entirely unrelated. In a sense, the question is whether the glass is half empty or half full, and it risks reviving one of the less savory aspects of the trait-situation debate that bedeviled the psychology of personality in the 1970s and early 1980s: Whose correlations are bigger? It should be understood, first, that the explicit measures used in these studies are various forms of questionnaires and self-ratings, and the IAT is first and foremost a behavioral measure of human performance. Correlations between these two classes of measures are notoriously (and, still, controversially) low. The explicit-implicit correlations obtained by Greenwald, McGhee, et al. (1998), for example, were well in line with the typical correlation between questionnaire measures of traits and attitudes, on one hand, and actual attitude-relevant behavior on the other (Sherman & Fazio, 1983). In a recent report on the psychometric characteristics of their instrument, Greenwald, Nosek, et al. (2002) clearly state that "superior IAT measures should yield higher values for these [implicit-explicit] correlations" (p. 5) and that "even the smallest positive implicit-explicit correlations appear to demand an interpretation in terms of construct overlap" (p. 20). Given that truly implicit measures of attitude and belief should be dissociated—that is, *un*correlated—with their explicit counterparts, it seems clear that Greenwald, Banaji, and their colleagues tend to view the IAT as an unobtrusive measure of subjects' attitudes, beliefs, and values, not as a measure of truly unconscious mental states.

In the final analysis, the issue of the implicit-explicit relationship can be settled only by employing measures of explicit attitudes, beliefs, and values that are comparable to our measures of their implicit counterparts—whether the implicit measures are provided by the IAT, priming, a psychophysiological measure, or something else. Only when sources of method variance are minimized, if not eliminated, can we hope to determine the true relation between explicit and implicit measures of social attitudes, beliefs, and values. It is not at all clear that the solution to this problem will be as straightforward for implicit attitudes, beliefs, and values as it was for implicit memories, but the ambiguity of the current situation calls out for some determined effort to resolve it.

## THE UNOBTRUSIVE, THE AUTOMATIC, THE IMPLICIT—AND THE PSYCHOLOGIST'S FALLACY

Based on the model of implicit memory, an increasing number of investigators are coming to take seriously the proposition that unconscious attitudes, beliefs, and values can influence people's social interactions. Of course, such an idea was central to psychoanalytic theory, but the connection to modern cognitive psychology frees the idea of unconscious influence from its Freudian death grip. Now, when social psychologists talk of the unconscious, they use the same concepts and methods as their cognitive colleagues—at least in principle. This line of inquiry is still in its infancy, or perhaps the toddler stage (though we can hope it will avoid the Terrible Twos and the White Food Stage), and it is extremely promising—not least because it links the interest in unconscious processes clearly present in cognitive psychology with the interest in

linking cognition to actual social behavior that is the core of social psychology.

Nevertheless, if genuine progress is to be made, investigators need to distinguish among three quite different topics: unobtrusive, nonreactive methods of measuring attitudes, beliefs, and values; the automatic generation of these mental states, whether conscious or unconscious; and truly implicit, unconscious, attitudes, beliefs, and values. The relations among these are somewhat complicated. Presumably, unobtrusive measures are used to reveal attitudes, beliefs, and values of which the person is consciously aware, but unwilling to disclose to others. Automatic processes may unconsciously activate attitudes, beliefs, and values, but these mental states themselves are not necessarily unconscious. Implicit attitudes, beliefs, and values may well affect a person's conscious experience, thought, or action, but these mental states are, by definition, not accessible to conscious awareness. If we are interested in the truly unconscious determinants of social behavior, we cannot be satisfied merely with the development of unobtrusive measures, or even with the demonstration that certain attitudes, beliefs, and values are generated automatically. We must also demonstrate that these mental states are unconscious, in the sense that they can be dissociated from, and are not predicted by, their explicit counterparts.

Herein lies the problem: What do we take as evidence for an unconscious mental state? Long ago, William James noted that the unconscious "is the sovereign means for believing what one likes in psychology, and of turning what might become a science into a tumbling-ground for whimsies (James, 1890/1980, p. 163). James also cautioned psychologists against the *psychologist's fallacy*, which he defined as "the confusion of his own standpoint with that of the mental fact about which he is making his report" (James, 1890/1980, p. 196). The psychologist's fallacy, in which we assume not only that every event has a psychological explanation, but also that *our* psychological explanation is the correct one, is hard enough to resist with respect to people's *conscious* mental states, as when we infer people's attitudes, beliefs, and values from their behavior. But it is particularly vicious with respect to people's *unconscious* mental states, when they are in no position to authoritatively correct our inferences. Psychoanalysts and some other insight-oriented psychotherapists have been doing this sort of thing to their patients for a hundred years (Freud, 1905/1953). In the current revival of interest in the psychological unconscious, it is important that we not perpetuate their errors (Kihlstrom, 1997).

The study of implicit memory and its cognate phenomena addresses this problem in a number of ways. First, the implicit expression of episodic memory, whether in the form of priming or some other effect, has to be related plausibly to some independently verifiable event in the subject's past personal experience. Second, the dissociation between implicit and explicit memory is documented by comparing subjects' performance on two closely matched tests, one that refers to, and requires, conscious recollection of a prior event and another one that does not. Something similar needs to happen in the study of implicit social cognition if implicit attitudes, beliefs, and values are to be considered truly unconscious. First, we need assurance that the effect under consideration, whether a priming effect or an implicit association or something else, really is an expression of the person's attitudes and beliefs, rather than an artifact of some stimulus property such as familiarity or some task property such as difficulty. Ordinarily, such evidence would be provided by a positive correlation between the effect and the person's responses to a questionnaire or some other measure. (e.g., Fazio, Sanbonmatsu, Powell, & Kardes, 1986), but that sort of evidence is not available when it comes to truly implicit attitudes, beliefs, and values, because by definition they should not correlate with their explicit counterparts. In fact, we want the correlations between explicit and implicit measures to be as close to zero as possible, and to be reassured that the low correlations are not procedural or statistical artifacts.

In such a situation, the validity of tests of implicit attitudes, beliefs, and values will rest on a package of both convergent and discriminant evidence (Cronbach & Meehl, 1955; Loevinger, 1957). On the discriminant side, it must be demonstrated that implicit attitudes, beliefs, and values are essentially uncorrelated with their explicit counterparts (see Cook & Groom, Chapter 2, this volume). Moreover, it is important that the explicit measures employed be comparable with the implicit measures under consideration. It is not enough to compare priming or implicit associations with questionnaire responses or thermometer settings. The explicit and implicit tests must be as closely comparable as possible, differing chiefly in whether they require subjects to reflect consciously on their attitudes, beliefs and values. On the convergent side, it must be demonstrated that implicit attitudes, beliefs, and values are associated with construct-relevant behaviors or experimental manipulations, just as their explicit counterparts are. Depending on theoretical considerations, it may well be that explicit and implicit attitudes, beliefs, and values are affected by different manipulations, correlate with different variables, and predict different behaviors. Or, it might be that implicit attitudes, beliefs, and values are more strongly related to some external variables than are their explicit counterparts. Whatever proves to be the case, it is important that these external relations should be construct-relevant, as defined by the investigator's theory of the construct under investigation. In this way, we can avoid the psychologist's fallacy and have a genuine science of the unconscious, not a tumbling ground for whimsies.

**NOTES**

1. The second lesson is that no amount of statistical finesse (Jackson, 1971) can substitute for a few intelligent people writing items based on clear definitions of the construct to be measured (Ashton & Goldberg, 1973; Hase & Goldberg, 1967; Jackson, 1975).

2. Extensive information on the IAT, including demonstrations, generic software for constructing experiments, and bibliographies of published and unpublished work, is available on the World Wide Web at the following URLs: https://implicit.harvard.edu/implicit/ and http://faculty.washington.edu/agg/iat_materials.htm. These Web sites also make reference to an "IAT Corp." which presumably was established to promote the IAT as a psychometric instrument for assessment of social beliefs and attitudes.

**REFERENCES**

Asendorf, J. B., & Scherer, K. R. (1983). The discrepant repressor: Differentiation between low anxiety, high anxiety, and repression of anxiety by autonomic fl-verbal patterns of behavior. *Journal of Personality and Social Psychology, 45,* 1334-1346.

Ashburn-Nardo, L., Voils, C. I., & Monteith, M. J. (2001). Implicit associations as the seeds of intergroup bias: How easily do they take root. *Journal of Personality and Social Psychology, 81*(5), 789-799.

Ashton, S. G., & Goldberg, L. R. (1973). In response to Jackson's challenge: The comparative validity of personality scales constructed by the external (empirical) strategy and scales developed intuitively by experts, novices, and laymen. *Journal of Research in Personality, 7*(1), 1-20.

Banaji, M. R., & Greenwald, A. G. (1994). Implicit stereotyping and unconscious prejudice. In M. P. Zanna & J. M. Olson (Eds.), *The psychology of prejudice: The Ontario Symposium* (Vol. 7, pp. 55-76). Hillsdale, NJ: Lawrence Erlbaum.

Banaji, M. R., & Greenwald, A. G. (1995). Implicit gender stereotyping in judgments of fame. *Journal of Personality and Social Psychology, 68,* 181-198.

Bem, D. J. (1983). Toward a response style theory of persons in situations. In R. A. Dienstbier & M. M. Page (Eds.), *Nebraska Symposium on Motivation 1982: Personality—current theory and research* (Vol. 30, pp. 201-231). Lincoln: University of Nebraska Press.

Berg, I. A. (1955). Response bias and personality: The deviation hypothesis. *Journal of Psychology, 40,* 61-72.

Berridge, K. C., & Winkielman, P. (2003). What is an unconscious emotion: The case for unconscious "liking." *Cognition and Emotion, 17,* 181-211.

Blair, I. V. (2001). Implicit stereotypes and prejudice. In G. Moskowitz (Ed.), *Cognitive social psychology: On the tenure and future of social cognition* (pp. 359-374). Mahwah, NJ: Lawrence Erlbaum.

Blair, I. V., & Banaji, M. R. (1996). Automatic and controlled processes in stereotype priming. *Journal of Personality and Social Psychology, 70,* 1142-1163.

Bornstein, R. F. (2001). Clinical utility of the Rorschach Inkblot Method: Reframing the debate. *Journal of Personality Assessment, 77*(1), 39-47.

Bowers, K. S. (1973). Situationism in psychology—Analysis and a critique. *Psychological Review, 80,* 307-336.

Brauer, M., Wasel, W., & Niedenthal, P. M. (2000). Implicit and explicit components of prejudice. *Review of General Psychology, 4,* 79-101.

Brehm, J. W. (1966). *A theory of psychological reactance.* New York: Academic Press.

Brendl, C. M., Markman, A. B., & Messner, C. (2001). How do indirect measures of evaluation work? Evaluating the inference of prejudice in the Implicit Association Test. *Journal of Personality and Social Psychology, 81*(5), 760-773.

Chapman, L. J., & Chapman, J. P. (1973). Problems in the measurement of cognitive deficits. *Psychological Bulletin, 79*(6), 380-385.

Chapman, L. J., & Chapman, J. P. (2001). Commentary on two articles concerning generalized and specific cognitive deficits. *Journal of Abnormal Psychology, 110*(1), 31-39.

Cronbach, L. J. (1957). The two disciplines of scientific psychology. *American Psychologist, 12,* 671-684.

Cronbach, L. J., & Meehl, P. E. (1955). Construct validity in psychological tests. *Psychological Bulletin, 52,* 281-302.

Cunningham, W. A., Preacher, K. J., & Banaji, M. (2001). Implicit attitude measures: Consistency, stability, and convergent validity. *Psychological Science, 12,* 163-170.

DeHouwer, J. (2001). A structural and process analysis of the Implicit Association Test. *Journal of Experimental Social Psychology, 37,* 443-451.

Dorfman, J., Shames, V. A., & Kihlstrom, J. F. (1996). Intuition, incubation, and insight: Implicit cognition in problem solving. In G. Underwood (Ed.), *Implicit cognition* (pp. 257-296). Oxford, UK: Oxford University Press.

Duff, F. L. (1965). Item subtlety in personality inventory scales. *Journal of Consulting Psychology, 29*(6), 565-570.

Fazio, R. H., & Olson, M. A. (2003). Implicit measures in social cognition research: Their meaning and use. *Annual Review of Psychology, 54,* 297-327.

Fazio, R. H., Sanbonmatsu, D. M., Powell, M. C., & Kardes, F. R. (1986). On the automatic activation of attitudes. *Journal of Personality and Social Psychology, 50,* 229-238.

Frank, L. K. (1939a). Projective methods for the study of personality. *Journal of Psychology, 8,* 389-413.

Frank, L. K. (1939b). Projective methods for the study of personality. *Transactions of the New York Academy of Sciences, 1,* 129-132.

Frank, L. K. (1948). *Projective methods.* Springfield, IL: C. C. Thomas.

Freud, S. (1953). *Fragment of an analysis of a case of hysteria* (Vol. 7). London: Hogarth Press and the Institute of Psycho-analysis. (Original work published 1905)

Gaertner, S. L., & McLaughlin, J. P. (1983). Racial stereotypes: Associations and ascriptions of positive and negative characteristics. *Social Psychology Quarterly, 46,* 23-30.

Goldberg, L. R., & Slovic, P. (1967). Importance of test item content: An analysis of a corollary of the deviation hypothesis. *Journal of Counseling Psychology, 14*(5), 462-472.

Greenwald, A. G., & Banaji, M. R. (1995). Implicit social cognition: Attitudes, self-esteem, and stereotypes. *Psychological Review, 102,* 4-27.

Greenwald, A. G., Banaji, M. R., Rudman, L. A., Farnham, S. D., Nosek, B. A., & Mellott, D. S. (2002). A unified theory of implicit attitudes, stereotypes, self-esteem, and self-concept. *Psychological Review, 109*(1), 3-25.

Greenwald, A. G., & Farnham, S. D. (2000). Using the Implicit Association Test to measure self-esteem and self-concept. *Journal of Personality and Social Psychology, 79*(6), 1022-1038.

Greenwald, A. G., McGhee, D. E., & Schwartz, J.L.K. (1998). Measuring individual differences in implicit cognition: The Implicit Association Test. *Journal of Personality and Social Psychology, 74,* 1464-1480.

Greenwald, A. G., Nosek, B. A., & Banaji, M. R. (2002). *Scoring procedures to improve implicit association test measures.* Unpublished manuscript, University of Washington. Retrieved from http://faculty.washington.edu/agg/iat_materials.htm

Hase, H. D., & Goldberg, L. R. (1967). Comparative validity of different strategies of constructing personality inventory scales. *Psychological Bulletin, 67*(4), 231-248.

Heider, F. (1946). Attitudes and cognitive organization. *Journal of Psychology, 21,* 107-112.

Jackson, D. N. (1971). The dynamics of structured personality tests: 1971. *Psychological Review, 78*(3), 229-248.

Jackson, D. N. (1975). The relative validity of scales prepared by naive item writers and those based on empirical methods of personality scale construction. *Educational and Psychological Measurement, 35,* 361-370.

Jacoby, L. L., Kelley, C., Brown, J., & Jasechko, J. (1989). Becoming famous overnight: Limits on the ability to avoid unconscious influences of the past. *Journal of Personality and Social Psychology, 56,* 326-338.

Jacoby, L. L., Woloshyn, V., & Kelley, C. (1989). Becoming famous without being recognized: Unconscious influences of memory produced by dividing attention. *Journal of Experimental Psychology: General, 118,* 115-125.

James, W. (1980). *Principles of psychology.* Cambridge, MA: Harvard University Press. (Original work published 1890)

Jung, C. G. (1969). *Studies in word-association.* New York: Russell & Russell. (Original work published 1918)

Kent, G. H., & Rosanoff, A. J. (1910). A study of association in insanity. *American Journal of Insanity, 67,* 37-96.

Kihlstrom, J. F. (1984). Conscious, subconscious, unconscious: A cognitive perspective. In K. S. Bowers & D. Meichenbaum (Eds.), *The unconscious reconsidered* (pp. 149-211). New York: Wiley.

Kihlstrom, J. F. (1987). The cognitive unconscious. *Science, 237*(4821), 1445-1452.

Kihlstrom, J. F. (1996). Perception without awareness of what is perceived, learning without awareness of what is learned. In M. Velmans (Ed.), *The science of consciousness: Psychological, neuropsychological, and clinical reviews* (pp. 23-46). London: Routledge.

Kihlstrom, J. F. (1997). Suffering from reminiscences: Exhumed memory, implicit memory, and the return of the repressed. In M. A. Conway (Ed.), *Recovered memories and false memories* (pp. 100-117). Oxford, UK: Oxford University Press.

Kihlstrom, J. F. (2002). Demand characteristics in the laboratory and the clinic: Conversations and collaborations with subjects and patients. *Prevention & Treatment* [Special issue honoring Martin T. Orne], *5.* Retrieved from http://journals.apa.org/prevention/volume5/pre0050036c.html

Kihlstrom, J. F., Barnhardt, T. M., & Tataryn, D. J. (1992). Implicit perception. In R. F. Bornstein & T. S. Pittman (Eds.), *Perception without awareness: Cognitive, clinical, and social perspectives* (pp. 17-54). New York: Guilford.

Kihlstrom, J. F., Mulvaney, S., Tobias, B. A., & Tobis, I. P. (2000). The emotional unconscious. In E. Eich, J. F. Kihlstrom, G. H. Bower, J. P. Forgas, & P. M. Niedenthal (Eds.), *Cognition and emotion* (pp. 30-86). New York: Oxford University Press.

Kihlstrom, J. F., Shames, V. A., & Dorfman, J. (1996). Intimations of memory and thought. In L. M. Reder (Ed.), *Implicit memory and metacognition* (pp. 1-23). Mahwah, NJ: Lawrence Erlbaum.

Lilienfeld, S. O., Wood, J. M., & Garb, H. N. (2001). The scientific status of projective techniques. *Psychological Science in the Public Interest, 1*(2), 27-66.

Lindzey, G. (1959). On the classification of projective techniques. *Psychological Bulletin, 56,* 158-168.

Loevinger, J. (1957). Objective tests as instruments of psychological theory. *Psychological Reports, 3,* 635-694.

Marks, J. D. (1979). *The search for the "Manchurian candidate": The CIA and mind control.* New York: Times Books.

Marks, J., & Greenfield, P. M. (1984a). The CIA inside the mind: Part 1. *Psychology News, 35,* 8-11.

Marks, J., & Greenfield, P. M. (1984b). How the CIA assesses weaknesses: The Gittinger Personality Assessment System. *Psychology News, 36,* 7, 10-12, 19.

McClelland, D. C., Koestner, R., & Weinberger, J. (1989). How do self-attributed and implicit motives differ? *Psychological Review, 96,* 690-702.

McConnell, A. R., & Leibold, J. M. (2001). Relations among the Implicit Association Test, discriminatory behavior, and explicit measures of racial attitudes. *Journal of Experimental Social Psychology, 37*(5), 435-442.

Meehl, P. E. (1945). The dynamics of "structured" personality tests. *Journal of Clinical Psychology, 1,* 296-303.

Mischel, W. (1968). *Personality and assessment.* New York: Wiley.

Mischel, W. (1972). Direct versus indirect personality assessment: Evidence and implications. *Journal of Consulting and Clinical Psychology, 38,* 319-324.

Mulvaney, S., Kihlstrom, J. F., Figueredo, A. J., & Schwartz, G. E. (1992). A continuous measure of repressive style. *EGAD Quarterly, 1,* 40-49.

Orne, M. T. (1962). On the social psychology of the psychological experiment: With particular reference to demand characteristics and their implications. *American Psychologist, 17,* 776-783.

Rapaport, D. (1942). Principles underlying projective techniques. In M. M. Gill (Ed.), *Collected papers of David Rapaport* (pp. 91-97). New York: Basic Books.

Rapaport, D., Schafer, R., & Gill, M. M. (1944-1946). *Diagnostic psychological testing.* New York: Josiah Macy Jr. Foundation.

Rapaport, D., Gill, M. M., & Schafer, R. (1968). *Diagnostic psychological testing* (Rev. ed.) (R. R. Holt, Ed.). New York: International Universities Press.

Reber, A. S. (1967). Implicit learning of artificial grammars. *Journal of Verbal Learning and Verbal Behavior, 6,* 855-863.

Rosenberg, M. J. (1965). When dissonance fails: On eliminating evaluation apprehension from attitude measurement. *Journal of Personality and Social Psychology, 1*(1), 28-42.

Rosenthal, R. (1963). On the social psychology of the psychological experiment: The experimenter's hypothesis as unintended determinant of experimental results. *American Scientist, 51,* 270-282.

Russell, W. A., & Jenkins, J. J. (1954). *The complete Minnesota norms for responses to 100 words from the Kent-Rosanoff Word Association Test* (Technical Report No. 11, Contract N8 ONR 66216, Office of Naval Research). Minneapolis: University of Minnesota.

Schacter, D. L. (1987). Implicit memory: History and current status. *Journal of Experimental Psychology: Learning, Memory, and Cognition, 13,* 501-518.

Seeman, W. (1952). "Subtlety" in structured personality tests. *Journal of Consulting Psychology, 16,* 278-283.

Sherman, S. J., & Fazio, R. H. (1983). Parallels between attitudes and traits as predictors of behavior. *Journal of Personality, 51,* 308-345.

Weinberger, D. A., & Schwartz, G. E. (1990). Distress and restraint as superordinate dimensions of adjustment: A typological perspective. *Journal of Personality, 58,* 381-417.

Weinberger, D. A., Schwartz, G. E., & Davidson, R. J. (1979). Low-anxious, high-anxious, and repressive coping styles: Psychometric patterns and behavioral and physiological responses to stress. *Journal of Abnormal Psychology, 88,* 369-380.

Wilson, T. D., Lindsey, S., & Schooler, T. Y. (2000). A model of dual attitudes. *Psychological Review, 107*(1), 101-126.

Wittenbrink, B., Judd, C. M., & Park, B. (1997). Evidence for racial prejudice at the implicit level and its relationship with questionnaire measures. *Journal of Personality and Social Psychology, 72,* 262-274.

CHAPTER 10

# Mediated and Moderated Effects in Social Psychological Research
## *Measurement, Design, and Analysis Issues*

RICK H. HOYLE AND JORGIANNE CIVEY ROBINSON

*University of Kentucky*

The most rudimentary research questions in social psychology concern the direct and unqualified association between two constructs. Classic examples are, Does behavior reflect attitudes? and Does similarity breed attraction? Although such questions represent a fundamental, perhaps essential, starting point for research on social behavior, they are but a starting point for constructing a detailed and informative account of it. In a theory-oriented discipline such as social psychology, we want to know how attitudes give rise to behavior and why similarity engenders attraction. Moreover, we want to know the situations in which, or the people for whom, these associations are strongest and weakest—that is, the conditions that qualify the association.

Questions of "how" and "why" concern mediators. *Mediators* are variables that represent constructs proposed to explain the association between two variables. In social psychology, mediators, sometimes termed intervening variables or mechanisms, usually reflect cognitive, affective, or motivational processes by which an independent variable influences a dependent variable. For instance, attitudes might influence behavior through an elaborate cognitive process that involves selective attention and biased processing of behavioral cues in the immediate environment (i.e., selective attention and biased processing *mediate* the attitude-behavior relation). Mediators enrich theoretical accounts of social phenomena by virtue of their focus on process.

Questions that address the conditions that qualify an association concern moderators. *Moderators* are variables that represent constructs proposed to magnify, attenuate, cancel, or reverse the association between two vari-

AUTHORS' NOTE: During the writing of this chapter, Rick Hoyle was supported by grants R01-DA12371 and R43-DA1123 from the National Institute on Drug Abuse and grant R01-MH01003 from the National Institute of Mental Health. Jorgianne Robinson was supported by a Wethington Fellowship from The Graduate School at the University of Kentucky.

ables. Statistical moderation can take many forms, but the defining feature of a moderated effect is that the association between the independent variable and the dependent variable differs in strength or form at different levels of the moderator. For example, attitudinal similarity might be more predictive of attraction for women than for men (i.e., gender *moderates* the similarity-attraction effect). Moderators define the limits of theoretical accounts of social phenomena through their focus on qualifying conditions.

The basic logic of research on mediated and moderated effects is straightforward, although there are complications and potential pitfalls to the implementation of either. In the simplest studies of mediation or moderation, a third variable is introduced into a research design that previously focused exclusively on the effect of an independent variable on a dependent variable. In the case of mediation, the third variable usually is reflective of a process (e.g., emotion regulation, deliberation) and believed to be associated with both the independent and dependent variables. In the case of moderation, the third variable usually captures some relatively fixed characteristic of the individuals or groups being studied (e.g., gender, group size), feature of the immediate situation (e.g., number of people present, presence or absence of a mirror), or secondary quality of the independent variable (e.g., attitude importance, domain of ego threat) and need not be associated with either the independent or dependent variable in order to moderate their association.

At the conceptual level, the evaluation of a mediated effect involves partitioning the effect of an independent variable on a dependent variable into two portions, the direct effect and the indirect effect. This evaluation assumes a documented or demonstrable effect of the independent variable on the dependent variable, and the question is whether any portion of this effect can be attributed to a particular intervening variable. The *direct effect* is that portion of the effect that is not transmitted through the intervening variable. In the three-variable case, the remaining portion of the effect is transmitted through the intervening variable as an *indirect effect*. Although the inferential outcome of a test of mediation often is cast in either-or terms, this need not be the case. It is possible that a particular mediator accounts for none of a documented direct effect, all of the effect, or some, but not all, of the direct effect. Because any particular intervening variable likely represents only one of several mechanisms by which an independent variable influences a dependent variable, the latter inferential outcome, *partial mediation*, is a more likely outcome than *full mediation*, if an inference favoring mediation is warranted.

The evaluation of a moderated effect, in conceptual terms, involves an evaluation of the effect (direct or indirect) of an independent variable on a dependent variable at different levels of a moderator variable. In contrast to evaluations of mediated effects, there is no assumption of a previously documented or demonstrable association between the independent and dependent variables. Indeed, one of the more appealing features of research that includes possible moderator variables is the prospect of finding an effect (albeit a qualified effect) of the independent variable on the dependent variable when no *main effect* (i.e., unqualified association) can be inferred. Traditionally in social psychology, moderated effects have been referred to as *interaction effects* and evaluated as a matter of course in research involving factorial designs, from which data typically are analyzed using analysis of variance. Increasingly, however, social psychological studies include at least one independent variable or moderator variable that is measured along a continuum rather than manipulated. The inclusion of such variables is a departure from a pure factorial design, and the resultant data are best analyzed using techniques that do not evaluate interaction effects as a matter of course (e.g., multiple regression). In such cases, researchers must manually construct *interaction terms* and evaluate them in strategically specified predictive equations. Inferences regarding moderation are complicated by the fact that there are many patterns by which the effect of an independent variable on a dependent variable can vary across levels of a moderator variable. These range from the crossover pattern, in which the independent variable has opposite effects on the dependent variable at the two levels or extremes of the moderator variable, to interactions in which the effect is discernibly stronger or weaker but does not change direction when moving from one extreme to the other along the scale of the moderator variable.

In the remainder of this chapter, we describe and illustrate, using a detailed example, basic strategies for designing studies of mediated and moderated effects in social psychology. These strategies address the three primary concerns of social psychological research: measurement, design, and analysis. In the measurement section, we outline a general approach to measurement that provides a strong foundation for testing hypotheses that involve mediation or moderation. With regard to design, we discuss strategies for gathering data that allow for inferences essential to definitive tests of mediation and moderation. Finally, we outline statistical approaches to testing for mediated and moderated effects. We conclude the chapter with a section on the various stumbling blocks to a full implementation of the strategies we present.

## MEASUREMENT ISSUES

One approach to empirical research in social psychology is to develop a list of variables relevant to a phenomenon of interest, find a single self-report measure of each, and, on one occasion, administer the set to as many participants as possible from the population of interest. There are numerous drawbacks to this *opportunistic approach* to empirical research. All variables are measured at the same time, at one point in time, and the same strategy is used to measure all variables, yielding a single score for each one. Although the opportunistic approach would appear to be maximally flexible, affording the researcher considerable latitude in how to analyze the data once they are gathered, the approach is severely limited because, with rare exceptions, the status any variable is assigned in a statistical hypothesis test is arbitrary.

Persuasive tests of mediated and moderated effects are possible only in studies that conceptualize and measure constructs with reference to their predetermined status in a theoretical account of the phenomenon or process of interest, a *reasoned approach* to empirical research. In such theoretical accounts, hypothetical constructs can be classified uniquely as causes, effects, mediators, or moderators, and the variables that represent them in empirical research can, in turn, be classified uniquely as independent, dependent, intervening, and moderator variables, respectively. Access to a rich and detailed theoretical account is essential to the development and testing of hypotheses regarding social behavior, particularly hypotheses that posit mediated and moderated effects.

### Practical Benefits of Theory

Because of Lewin's (1951) early influence, social psychologists have long been committed to building theoretical accounts of the phenomena and processes they study. The most complete, and therefore useful, accounts clearly specify the status of the constructs they comprise. The fundamental distinction is between cause and effect and their empirical counterparts, the independent and dependent variables. At the core of this distinction is the concept of causality (Mark & Reichardt, Chapter 12, this volume; West, Biesanz, & Kwok, Chapter 13, this volume). The fundamental criteria for establishing *causality* are that (a) the cause and effect are associated (i.e., causation implies correlation), (b) the cause precedes the effect in time, and (c) the cause-effect association persists after the cause has been isolated from potential confounding variables either through randomized experimentation or through statistical control. (See Pearl, 2000, for a detailed treatment that addresses both statistical and philosophical concerns and Salmon, 1997, for a purely philosophical treatment.) The first criterion is met through empirical means, although attempts to establish an association through empirical means might initially be motivated by a theoretical account that prescribes the association. The temporal relation between constructs is difficult to establish; however, a well-articulated theory makes use of logic and published findings to assert the temporal precedence of some constructs over others. Finally, firm causal inferences from a documented association between two constructs requires that the association remain after the putative cause has been isolated from other constructs. These potential alternative causes range from features of the typical operational definition of the putative cause (e.g., self-report bias, experimental artifacts) to constructs that are similar to or frequently co-occur with it. Thorough theoretical accounts prescribe processes that are specific to the posited causal constructs. Satisfaction of these criteria establishes an important asymmetry in the association between two constructs such that, with a reasonable degree of certainty, one can be designated the cause and the other the effect.

In addition to causes and effects, detailed theoretical accounts specify mediators and moderators. Among the constructs elaborated in theories, mediators typically are the most abstract, as they often are mentalistic or otherwise phenomenological in nature (Kimble, 1989). Mediators occupy a position of both cause and effect in models that include mediated effects. In a three-variable model, the intervening variable is a proximal *effect* of the independent variable (or its interaction with a moderator) and a proximal *cause* of the

dependent variable. Moderators typically are less abstract, often referring to fixed qualities of individuals or groups or salient features of situations. Although moderators may be specified in the initial statement of a theoretical account, they also may be added to the account on the basis of empirical findings that emerge from tests of the theory's basic tenets using different methods and samples. For this reason, moderators often signal an evolved theoretical account that has increased in specificity in order to more precisely account for manifestations of the phenomenon.

## Formally Designating the Status of Variables in a Model

An effective way of communicating statistical hypotheses regarding the status of and associations among a set of variables is the path diagram. A *path diagram* represents variables either as boxes or ellipses, and associations between variables as either straight, single-headed arrows or curved, double-headed arrows. Boxes indicate variables for which there are scores in the data matrix (e.g., scale scores, observer ratings); ellipses indicate latent variables, which are inferred from the commonality among subsets of observed variables but for which there are not scores in the data matrix (e.g., factors, components). Straight lines indicate directional associations (i.e., regression terms), and curved lines indicated nondirectional associations (i.e., correlation terms). Although path diagrams are a staple of structural equation modeling, when used for communicating the status of and associations among a set of variables, they neither convey nor imply a particular analysis strategy. In the section of this chapter on analysis issues, we outline multiple statistical approaches to evaluating the associations depicted in the path diagrams we present.

Figure 10.1 is a path diagram representation of a model that includes the four types of variables we have described, nonarbitrarily

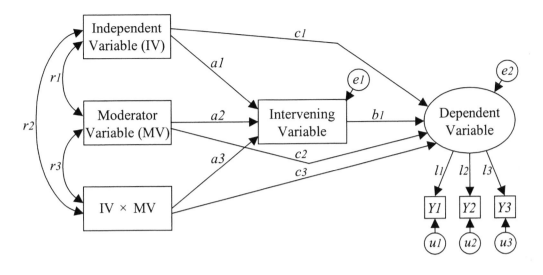

**Figure 10.1** Path Diagram Illustrating the Status of Four Types of Variables and the Associations Between Them in a Prototypic Model Grounded in Theory

arranged on the basis of reasoned conceptualization and measurement. At the core of the model is the basic association between an independent and a dependent variable. The independent variable is represented at the left of the diagram as a box, indicating that it is in the data set as a single (perhaps composite) score. The dependent variable is represented at the right of the diagram as an ellipse, indicating that it is not explicitly represented in the data set. The dependent variable in this case is a *latent variable* inferred from the commonality among three variables for which there are scores in the data set, $Y1$, $Y2$, and $Y3$. Notice that two arrows point to each of these variables. This indicates that variability in $Y1$, $Y2$, and $Y3$ has been partitioned into two sources—that portion each shares with the other two (i.e., the latent variable) and that portion unique to each one, designated $u1$, $u2$, and $u3$, respectively. The strength of the association between $Y1$, $Y2$, and $Y3$ and the latent variable they represent is captured in the factor loadings, $l1$, $l2$, and $l3$. In this hypothetical model, only the dependent variable was operationally defined in multiple ways and

modeled as a latent variable; however, as we demonstrate later in the chapter, the strongest model is one in which all variables are assessed using multiple operations. The association between the independent and dependent variables is expressed in $c1$, a regression coefficient. Variability in the dependent variable not explained by other variables in the model is captured by the residual, $e2$.

At the center of the path diagram in Figure 10.1 is a single box representing an observed intervening variable. Note that the inclusion of this intervening variable provides an alternative means by which the independent variable can influence the dependent variable. The combination of paths $a1$ and $b1$ represents the indirect effect of the independent variable on the dependent variable through the intervening variable. This indirect effect can be contrasted with the direct effect of the independent variable on the dependent variable via path $c1$.

A model that includes only the independent, dependent, and intervening variables connected by paths $a1$, $b1$, and $c1$ makes a "main effect" assumption regarding the independent-dependent variable association and its explanation by the intervening variable. In all likelihood, the magnitude of the *c1* path would vary across populations and situations. Indeed, it is possible that the linear effect of the independent variable on the dependent variable is apparent *only* for certain people or under certain conditions. Moderator variables capture such qualifying conditions, and one position a moderator variable might occupy in a model is illustrated by the remaining two variables in Figure 10.1. Note that statistical tests of moderator hypotheses require, in addition to the independent variable, two variables, one for which data were gathered directly, labeled "Moderator Variable" in the diagram, and one either implicit in the statistical analysis (e.g., interaction effects in analysis of variance) or created by the investigator, labeled "IV × MV" in the diagram. Although it is the latter that represents the moderated effect of the independent variable, the former must be included for statistical reasons (Cohen, Cohen, West, & Aiken, 2003; Evans, 1991). The moderated effect of the independent variable on the dependent variable, *c3*, or indirectly via *a3* and *b1*, is the effect of the interaction term, IV × MV, above and beyond the main effects of the independent variable (*c1*, *a1* $\rightarrow$ *b1*) and moderator variable (*c2*, *a2* $\rightarrow$ *b1*) on the dependent variable. In this model, the unqualified *and* qualified effects of the independent variable on the dependent variable are expressed both as direct effects and indirect effects through the intervening variable.

The only details in Figure 10.1 we have not covered are the curved arrows that connect the independent and moderator variables and their interaction term. These represent possible covariation between each pair of variables, and the coefficients *r1*, *r2*, and *r3*, index that covariation. Although the magnitude of these coefficients is not always evident to researchers testing moderated effects (e.g., when multiple regression analysis is used), knowledge of this information is important. Of particular concern are coefficients *r2* and *r3*, which can be

sufficiently large that statistical tests of the moderated effect are compromised (more will be said about this in the section of this chapter devoted to analysis issues). This collinearity problem is remedied rather simply by rescaling scores on the independent and moderator variables as deviations from their mean score, a strategy known as *centering*. An additional virtue of centering is that it facilitates interpretation of effects by establishing a zero point for variables in the model (Aiken & West, 1991). Both the *r1* coefficient and the *c2* path have significant implications for statistical tests of moderated effects as well, but we defer our discussion of these implications until the section of the chapter on analysis issues.

To summarize, the path diagram is a useful tool for communicating the status of variables in a data set and the form of the associations among those variables. Path diagrams distinguish between observed and latent variables and between directional and nondirectional associations. Our labeling allows for important distinctions between types of directional associations. Path coefficients we label "*a*" concern the association between independent and intervening variables. Those we label "*b*" concern the association between intervening and dependent variables. Coefficients we label "*c*" concern the association between independent and dependent variables. Path diagrams also distinguish between errors of measurement, which we label "*u*" (for "uniqueness"), and errors of prediction, which we label "*e*." These are the basic building blocks for describing and implementing tests of mediated and moderated effects and provide a foundation for identifying and discussing relevant measurement, design, and analysis issues in the remainder of the chapter.

### An Example

In one theoretical account of the association between attitudes and behavior, the association between an attitude toward an

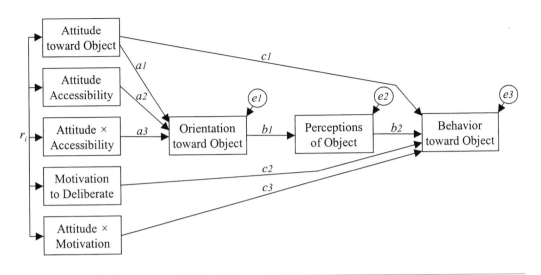

**Figure 10.2**   Path Diagram Depicting Moderated Influence of Attitude on Behavior Mediated Through Orientation Toward and Perceptions of the Attitude Object

NOTE: The 10 nondirectional associations, indicated as $r_i$, between the independent variable, moderator variables, and interaction terms are not shown.

object and behavior toward the object is moderated by two factors: attitude accessibility and motivation to deliberate about the object (Fazio, 1990). When attitude accessibility is high and motivation to deliberate is low, the association between attitude and behavior should be strong. Conversely, when the attitude is relatively inaccessible and the motivation to deliberate about the object is relatively high, the association between attitude and behavior toward an object should be weak. In other words, the influence of attitudes on behavior is qualified by accessibility of the relevant attitude and motivation to deliberate about the object of the attitude.

Research inspired by this model has focused on the mechanism by which highly accessible attitudes influence behavior. One such mechanism is the orientation of visual attention toward the object. That is, when an attitude is accessed, it functions to orient visual attention toward the object (Roskos-Ewoldsen & Fazio, 1992). Attention directed toward the object gives rise to perceptions of the object, which are proximal determinants of behavior toward

the object (Fazio & Williams, 1986). This attitude-to-behavior process model is shown as a path diagram in Figure 10.2.

In the path diagram, Attitude toward Object, as specified in the theoretical account, is an independent variable. Attitude Accessibility and Motivation to Deliberate are moderator variables, and their moderation of Attitude toward Object is expressed in the Attitude × Accessibility and Attitude × Motivation interaction terms. Orientation toward Object and Perceptions of Object are intervening variables that mediate the unqualified (i.e., direct) effect of attitude on behavior as well as the effect of attitude on behavior as qualified (i.e., moderated) by attitude accessibility. Behavior toward Object is, in this theoretical account, a dependent variable.

### Optimal Measurement

Researchers are tempted to take at face value the empirical associations between variables in a model such as the one depicted in Figure 10.2; however, these associations reflect more than just the strength and direction of associations in the context of the model. They also reflect the quality of the operational definitions—their reliability and validity as observable manifestations of the constructs prescribed by the theoretical account guiding the research. Although the reliability and validity of operational definitions is important in any social psychological study, the importance of these concerns is magnified in studies of mediated and moderated effects. As we illustrate in the section on analysis issues, fallible measures of intervening variables can lead to an inference of no mediation when the intervening variable partially or fully mediates the independent-dependent variable association, or only partial mediation when, in fact, the intervening variable fully accounts for the association. The fallibility of moderator variables is particularly worrisome because it compounds error in the operational definition of the independent variable. For these reasons, reliable and valid measures are essential in research on mediated and moderated effects.

Any variable could be measured in a variety of ways. Specific strategies range from the ubiquitous self-report method to emerging strategies such as physiological monitoring (Cacioppo, Tassinary, & Berntson, 2000) and implicit associations (e.g., Greenwald & Farnham, 2000). For instance, in the attitude-to-behavior process model, attitude accessibility typically is measured as the latency in responding to attitudinal statements or in pressing a computer key indicating *like* or *dislike* when presented an image or descriptor of the attitude object (e.g., Fazio, Powell, & Williams, 1989; Roskos-Ewoldsen & Fazio, 1992). Although attitude accessibility is virtually always indexed as response latencies, the stimulus to which research participants respond and the medium by which the stimulus is presented vary from one study to the next.

The goal of this measurement strategy is to capture variability in the theoretical construct,

attitude accessibility. It is well known, however, that any measurement strategy captures other sources of variability as well. These sources can range from nuisance constructs such as fleeting distractions or facility with language to problematic confounding constructs such as socioeconomic status or concern for appropriateness. Variability that is common to variables that were measured in the same way but represent different constructs is referred to as *method variance*. First highlighted by Campbell and Fiske (1959) in their demonstration of the insights provided by a matrix of correlations among several traits each measured using several methods (i.e., multitrait-multimethod matrix), method variance reflects not *what* a score represents but *how* it was obtained.

The critical concern when key constructs are measured using a single method is that the substantive and methodological sources that give rise to variability in scores generated by the measure are completely confounded. In such cases, extraneous method constructs are an alternative explanation for any observed associations. The method explanation is particularly compelling when all variables in a model are measured using the same method. The solution to this problem is rather straightforward: Either within each study or across studies within a research program, operationally define key constructs using different strategies. When constructs are operationally defined using multiple, different measurement strategies, it is possible to divorce construct-relevant from construct-irrelevant variance, thereby clarifying inferences from observed associations between variables.

As an example, assume that we measured attitude toward an object with multiple measures reflecting different measurement strategies. More specifically, imagine that we acquired data on five measures of attitude: peer report (*Y1*), teacher report (*Y2*), self-report feeling thermometer (*Y3*), self-report semantic differential (*Y4*), and self-report

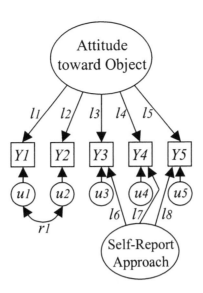

**Figure 10.3** Path Diagram Illustrating the Partitioning of Variability in Indicators of Attitude Toward an Object Into Common, Unique, and Method Components

Likert-type scale (*Y5*). We might model the theoretical construct represented by these measures, attitude toward object, as shown in Figure 10.3. The path diagram in Figure 10.3 reflects a *measurement model.* That is, the focus is within rather than between constructs. The model indicates that variability in each of our measures can be attributed to three sources: construct, method, and uniqueness. First, look above the boxes representing our five measures. Note that a single latent variable, Attitude toward Object, influences all five variables; the strength of this influence would be captured in the factor loadings, *l1* to *l5*. Now look below the five boxes. Note that each variable is influenced by its own uniqueness term. In many measurement models, these two components, commonality and uniqueness, would be all that is required to model the theoretical construct as represented by these measures. For illustrative purposes, the model depicts two additional features of measurement models. First, note that *u1* and *u2* are correlated. Recall that *Y1* and *Y2* are peer and teacher reports, respectively. The

correlation, *r1*, reflects the fact that these two measures share something in common that they do not share with the remaining measures; both represent a third-party perspective regarding the participant's attitude. (Because only two variables are involved, we model this commonality as a simple correlation rather than as a factor.) *Y3*, *Y4*, and *Y5* are affected by a second latent variable (technically, a subfactor), which reflects the fact that they share a common influence beyond the influence they share with *Y1* and *Y2*. Factor loadings *l6* to *l8* reflect the influence of this method factor on these variables and, when contrasted with *l3* to *l5*, provide information about the relative influence of construct and method on those measures.

Were this measurement model substituted for the Attitude toward Object box in Figure 10.2, associations involving the attitude construct would not be biased by measurement error in the variables representing that construct because variability unique to individual measures or subsets of the measures (i.e., parcels) would be divorced from variability common to all the measures. This is a powerful strategy for contending with measurement error that is particularly advantageous for tests of association involving mediators and moderators, for which the ill effects of measurement error are pronounced.

## DESIGN ISSUES

Although our focus now shifts to issues of design in studies of mediated and moderated effects, measurement remains a primary concern, for even if all constructs that are not manipulated are measured using several different strategies and measurement error extracted, the correct inference regarding the associations in a model is not always clear. The efficacy of a set of measures for testing mediated and moderated effects can vary dramatically depending on *when* the measures were administered relative to each other. The issue of timing is relevant for two key issues in such tests of reasoned models: causal priority and tests of mediated effects.

Before elaborating on these issues, we note three basic strategies for administering a set of measures relevant to questions involving mediation or moderation in quasi- and nonexperimental designs. The most rudimentary is sometimes referred to as the *one-shot strategy* and epitomizes the opportunistic approach to empirical research. In this strategy, all measures are administered at one sitting. A more sophisticated approach is the *sequential strategy*. In this strategy, the variables are assigned different statuses by the investigator, and the timing of measurement for each variable corresponds to its status in some model. For instance, if an investigator wants to test the hypothesis that attitude toward an object causes behavior toward the object and this causal influence is mediated by orientation toward the object, he or she might measure attitude at one point in time, orientation at a later point in time, and behavior at a later

point still. A third approach is the *replicative strategy*, in which *all* variables in the model are measured at two or more points in time.

### Asserting Causal Priority

Most theoretical accounts go beyond simply stating that two constructs are associated to posit that one causes the other. Tests of such propositions make serious demands on the design of the study. The opportunistic approach described at the beginning of the chapter is not adequate for tests of causal priority because, in the absence of explicit temporal ordering, the status of most variables generated by this one-shot strategy in a statistical model is arbitrary.

The sequential strategy offers some improvement in this regard; however, it is limited in an important way: Unless the putative cause is manipulated and participants are randomly assigned to levels of it, there is no means of differentiating directional and nondirectional associations between variables. This situation is illustrated in Figure 10.4. The simple path diagram in the top portion of the figure represents a sequential model in which attitude toward an object was measured at Time 1 and behavior toward the object at Time 2. The ambiguity in the meaning of a significant path, *c*, stems from the fact that attitude at Time 1 is not isolated from stable behavioral tendencies toward the object, and behavior at Time 2 is not isolated from stability in attitude toward the object. As such, it is not clear whether *c* is a true representation of the association between attitude and behavior, or whether it, to some unknown degree, reflects the stable association between attitude and behavior. Moreover, despite the fact that the sequential measurement strategy has introduced a temporal distinction between attitude and behavior toward the object, it is not possible to infer directionality. There is no statistical procedure for sorting out the various explanations

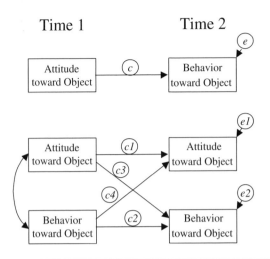

**Figure 10.4**   Path Diagrams Illustrating Two Strategies for Testing the Causal Influence of Attitude on Behavior: The Sequential Strategy (Top) and the Replicative Strategy (Bottom)

for an association, and the ambiguity persists even in the context of more complex models such as the one shown in Figure 10.2.

One solution to this inferential conundrum is illustrated in the path diagram in the bottom portion of Figure 10.4. Note that attitude and behavior toward the object are measured at both points in time, reflecting the replicative strategy. By including behavior at Time 1, it is possible to model the stability of behavior toward the object, reflected in $c2$, yielding a model in which the association of interest between attitude at Time 1 and behavior at Time 2, $c3$, is based only on variability in behavior unique to Time 2. The inclusion of attitude at Time 2 permits the modeling of stability in attitude toward the object, $c1$, as well as the possibility that the direction of influence runs from behavior to attitude, $c4$. In the absence of random assignment to levels of a manipulated variable, the replicative measurement of key constructs allows for persuasive tests of causal hypotheses by ruling out alternatives that undermine causal inferences using data generated by one-shot and sequential strategies.

## Timing and Tests of Mediation

Another issue relevant to when constructs are measured concerns the spacing between measurement occasions. For instance, referring back to Figure 10.4, we might ask whether the test of the critical association reflected in $c3$ is more persuasive if Time 1 and Time 2 are separated by 15 minutes, 3 days, or a month. There are no simple recommendations regarding the spacing between measurement occasions; however, it is important that the spacing be consistent with the framing of the measures. For instance, if, in a study conforming to the design illustrated at the bottom of Figure 10.4, the spacing between Time 1 and Time 2 were 1 week, it would not be reasonable to ask respondents to report on their behavior during the past 30 days (a frame often used in research on problem behaviors such as drug use).

A more subtle point concerns the spacing between the independent and intervening variables and the intervening and dependent variables in a model such as the ones depicted in Figures 10.1 and 10.2. The issues are easiest to describe in a model with a single intervening variable such as the model shown in Figure 10.1. Assuming the model corresponds to a theoretical account in which the intervening variable explains the association between the independent variable and the dependent variable, the paths of interest are $a1$, $b1$, and $c1$. If the effect of the independent variable on the dependent variable is fully mediated by the intervening variable, then paths $a1$ and $b1$ will be nonzero in magnitude and path $c1$ will, within sampling error, be zero. A key concern is too strong an association between the independent variable and the intervening variable, which would be reflected in a large value for $a1$. All else being equal, as $a1$ increases, $b1$ decreases. And as $b1$ decreases, $c1$, which we would like to equal zero, increases. Among other things, the magnitudes of $a1$ and $b1$ are affected by the spacing between the independent and intervening variables and the intervening and dependent variables, respectively. Given that our goal in testing for mediation is to find $c1 = 0$ (more on this later), and that $c1$ is diminished as $b1$ increases in strength and $b1$ is diminished as $a1$ increases in strength, it is advantageous to measure an intervening variable closer in time to the dependent variable than to the independent variable. In short, tests of mediated effects are maximally powerful when $b1$ is larger than $a1$.

## Experimental Designs

Although the dependent variable is measured or observed in all studies of mediated and moderated effects, independent, moderator, and intervening variables can, to considerable benefit, be manipulated and participants randomly assigned to levels of these variables in such studies. In social psychological studies designed to test moderated effects, it is not uncommon for both the independent variable and the moderator variable to be manipulated. The payoff of this approach is twofold. Both the independent and moderator variables are

unambiguously causally prior to the dependent variable, and, assuming random assignment to condition, there is no concern that the moderator variable could be caused by the independent variable, ruling out the possibility that it mediates rather than moderates the effect of the independent variable on the dependent variable.

Although moderated effects can be evaluated fully in a single experiment, such is not the case with mediated effects. Tests of mediated effects require an evaluation of the effect of the independent variable on the intervening variable and, if both are manipulated in a single experiment, there is, by definition, no effect of the independent variable on the intervening variable. Nonetheless, the question of causal priority is critical in tests of mediation, and the experimental design, when properly applied, is unmatched in its ability to answer this question. The use of experimental designs to evaluate mediated effects fully requires a series of experiments. The effect of the independent variable on the dependent variable is evaluated in an experiment in which the independent variable is manipulated and the dependent variable measured. The effect of the intervening variable on the dependent variable is evaluated in an experiment in which the intervening variable is manipulated and the dependent variable measured. (Conceivably, these two effects could be studied in a single experiment in which the independent and intervening variables are orthogonally manipulated.) The effect of the independent variable on the intervening variable is evaluated in a design in which the independent variable is manipulated and the intervening variable is measured. More typically, mediated effects are evaluated in individual experiments in which the independent variable is manipulated and the intervening and dependent variables measured. Although this approach has the desirable property that it allows a strong inference of causality regarding the effect of the independent variable on the dependent and intervening variables, it is no better than the one-shot non-experimental strategy for inferring a causal effect of the intervening variable on the dependent variable.

## ANALYSIS ISSUES

There are two major analytic approaches to testing mediated effects. Common to the two approaches is this basic question: Is some portion of the effect of an independent variable on a dependent variable attributable to an intervening variable? In the *serial approach* to addressing this question, the data are evaluated against a sequential list of criteria that must be met in order for this question to be answered affirmatively (Baron & Kenny, 1986).

1. The independent variable is associated with the dependent variable.

2. The independent variable is associated with the intervening variable.

3. The intervening variable is associated with the dependent variable, controlling for the independent variable. At this step, an additional evaluation is made regarding the magnitude of the association between the independent and dependent variables, controlling for the intervening variable. If the effect is, within sampling error, zero, then the correct inference is that the intervening variable fully explains the effect of the independent variable on the dependent variable. If, controlling for the intervening variable, the effect remains significantly different from zero, then the correct inference is partial mediation.

There are two primary statistical procedures for implementing the serial approach to testing mediated effects. If the independent variable is manipulated or measured on a nominal scale, thereby defining levels of a factor, the effect of the independent variable on the dependent and intervening variables typically is evaluated using analysis of variance.

(Note that the intervening variable is treated as a dependent variable at this stage of the analysis.) If these effects are statistically significant, then analysis of covariance is used to evaluate the effect of the intervening variable (which now is treated as a covariate) on the dependent variable, controlling for the independent variable. If the effect of the covariate is significant in this analysis, then there is statistical evidence of a mediated effect. If the effect of the independent variable also is significant, then the correct inference is partial mediation. If the effect of the independent variable is nonsignificant, then the findings warrant an inference of full mediation.

If the independent variable is operationally defined in such a way that it is not properly viewed as defining a factor typical of factorial designs, then all three steps can be evaluated more effectively using regression analysis. (Regression, of which analysis of variance and covariance are special cases, could be used for manipulated or nominally scaled independent variables as well.) In the three-variable case, Steps 1 and 2 require simple regression runs in which the dependent and intervening variables, in turn, are regressed on the independent variable. Assuming statistical support at Steps 1 and 2, Step 3 requires regressing the dependent variable simultaneously on the intervening and independent variables and evaluating first the coefficient for the intervening variable, then the coefficient for the independent variable. If the coefficient for the intervening variable is statistically significant, then there is evidence of a mediated effect. If the coefficient for the independent variable is nonsignificant, then there is evidence of full mediation. Otherwise, the correct inference is partial mediation.

An alternative strategy is the *integrated approach*, in which all relevant effects are evaluated within a single model. The model includes both the direct effect of the independent variable on the dependent variable and the indirect effect of the independent

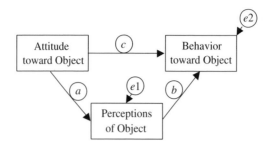

**Figure 10.5** Path Diagram Depicting a Model in Which the Attitude-Behavior Association Is Mediated by Perceptions of the Object

variable on the dependent variable through an intervening variable. The basic model for the three-variable case is shown in Figure 10.5. The coefficients in such models typically are estimated using maximum likelihood procedures (as opposed to ordinary least squares typical of regression) using structural equation modeling. The test of primary interest in these models is the indirect, or *ab*, effect. This test is available in most software packages for estimating structural equation models, although new tests that are not yet available in these packages promise greater power and precision (MacKinnon, Lockwood, Hoffman, West, & Sheets, 2002).

There are two approaches to evaluating moderated effects as well. In the *interaction approach*, the interaction effect is evaluated in the context of a single model that also includes the unqualified effects of the independent and moderator variables on the dependent variable. As with tests of mediation, when the independent variable and/or moderator variable are manipulated or measured on a nominal scale, the evaluation typically is accomplished with analysis of variance. As implemented in most statistical software packages, the interactions among all variables in factorial design are evaluated automatically. Multiple regression is preferable when either the independent or the moderator variable is operationally defined to define a continuum. Evaluation of interaction

effects in multiple regression models requires the creation of interaction terms after centering scores on the independent and moderator variables.

Alternatively, moderated effects can be evaluated using the *multigroup approach*. This approach is particularly attractive when the moderator variable is manipulated or nominally scaled and the independent variable is operationally defined in such a way that it could be modeled as a latent variable. In the multigroup approach, a single predictive equation is estimated separately for groups that vary on the moderator variable. Corresponding coefficients are statistically compared and, to the extent that they differ from one group to another, the grouping variable moderates the effect of that variable on the dependent variable. Most statistical software packages do not provide an option to compare coefficients when the equations are estimated for the groups using ordinary least squares regression; hence, hand calculation sometimes is required. When the equations are estimated as structural equation models, the tenability of between-groups equality constraints imposed on the relevant coefficients can be evaluated without hand calculation. If equality constraints on the coefficients representing the effect of the independent variable are not tenable across levels of the moderator variable, then there is statistical support for a moderated effect. If the model includes an intervening variable and indirect effect, this strategy can be used to test for *moderated mediation*, variability in the degree of mediation across the groups representing different levels of the moderator variable.

## Analysis Issues Specific to Mediation

In our discussion of considerations regarding when to measure, we highlighted the interdependence of effects involved in tests of mediation. The relevant effects are illustrated in Figure 10.5, which displays in path diagram form a simplified version of the attitude-to-behavior process model that has provided context for our discussion. The direct effect of attitude on behavior is represented by *c*, and the *a*/*b* combination captures the indirect effect of attitude on behavior through perceptions. If the theoretical account that inspired this model specifies that perceptions fully mediate the attitude-behavior association, then we would hope to find $c = 0$ in this model. As noted earlier, the *c* path is influenced by the strength of *b*, the influence of perceptions on behavior, and the strength of *b* is influenced by the strength of *a*, the influence of attitude on perceptions. As such, it is critical that we not underestimate *b* lest we overestimate *c* and infer partial or no mediation through perceptions.

We already noted that it is advantageous to position measurement of the intervening variable—perceptions, in our example—closer in time to the dependent variable than to the independent variable to avoid the situation in which *b* is diminished because so much variability in the intervening variable is accounted for by the independent variable (via path *a*) that little is left to explain variability in the outcome. Another means by which *b* can be underestimated and *c* overestimated involves measurement error. To illustrate this point, assume that we had population data on error-free measures, and we knew that $c = 0$, $a = .3$, and $b = .4$. Now assume that we have data

from a sample and our measure of perceptions of the object, the intervening variable, is not error free. We can show the ill effects of measurement error in the intervening variable by substituting hypothetical values in the following equation (Hoyle & Kenny, 1999):

$$c_{obs} = (1 - r_{zz})\, ab + c.$$

In this equation, $r_{zz}$ is an estimate of the reliability (e.g., coefficient alpha, test-retest *r*) of our measure of perceptions of the object. The resultant value, $c_{obs}$, is the value of *c* we would observe given certain values of *a* and *b* (.3 and .4, respectively, in this case) and certain levels of reliability of the measure of perceptions of the object. Recall that we know that $c = 0$ in the population, a value that indicates full mediation of the attitude-behavior association by perceptions of the object. If our measure of perceptions were perfectly reliable, indicated by a value of 1.0, we would expect to observe the population value of zero for $c_{obs}$ because $(1-1)\,(.3)(.4) + 0 = 0$. If $r_{zz} = .9$, then we would expect to observe $c = .012$. If $r_{zz} = .8$, a value more typical of measures in social psychological research, we would expect to observe $c = .024$. It is not uncommon for the reliability of measures in social psychological research to hover closer to .7. Were this the case, we would expect to observe $c = .036$ despite the fact that $c = 0$ in the population. With a relatively modest sample size, this coefficient would be significantly greater than zero, leading to the erroneous inference that perceptions do not fully mediate the attitude-behavior association. In practice, this error is more pronounced because, in the strongest cases of mediation, the value of *c* is trivial but greater than zero. For instance, if $c = .07$ in the population, a value that might be viewed as trivial, the estimate of *c* when $r_{zz} = .7$ will be .11, an effect size that cannot be ignored.

It is clear that error in measures of intervening variables poses significant problems for tests of mediated effects. As such, it is crucial that researchers deal with measurement error in such models. One approach is to select a measure with well-documented high reliability, at least .9. Such measures are not always available. An alternative is to model the intervening variable as a latent variable, as illustrated for attitude in Figure 10.3, thereby removing uniqueness from the variable before estimating associations between variables. Depending on the amount of information available on the intervening variable, it can be modeled in one of four ways. The best approach is to obtain multiple measures representing different measurement strategies. This approach has the additional benefit of allowing the removal of variability attributable to measurement strategy. Typically, investigators might have only one measure of a mediator, but the measure is a multi-item scale. When this is the case, the individual items can be treated as indicators of the latent variable, a strategy that provides no information about method variance but nonetheless segregates commonality across items from uniqueness associated with individual items or subsets of items. Sometimes the number of items in such scales is too large to effectively model a latent variable of which each item is an indicator (see Marsh & Hau, 1999). In such cases, a compromise solution is to sort items into four or more composites, referred to as *parcels*. Parcels may correspond to subscales, subsets of items that emerge from factor analysis, or arbitrary groupings of items. A final strategy for dealing with measurement error in an intervening variable concerns the situation in which there is only a single indicator. Assuming there exists enough prior research on the indicator to provide a good estimate of its reliability, the indicator can be modeled with a fixed error term equal to $(1 - r_{zz}) s^2$, where $r_{zz}$ is the reliability estimate and $s^2$ is the variance of scores on the indicator.

## Analysis Issues Specific to Moderation

Measurement error also is detrimental to statistical tests of moderation. Unlike in tests of mediation, in which the primary concern is measurement error in one variable (the intervening variable), in tests of moderation the concern involves two variables (the independent variable and the moderator variable). In the same way that the moderated effect is represented as a product of the independent and moderator variables, error in the variable that represents the moderated effect, the interaction term, is a product of the error in the independent variable and the moderator variable (Busemeyer & Jones, 1983). Specifically, the reliability of the interaction term can be computed as

$$\frac{r_{ii} r_{mm} + r_{im}^2}{1 + r_{im}^2},$$

where $r_{ii}$ and $r_{mm}$ are reliabilities of the independent and moderator variables, respectively, and $r_{im}$ is the correlation between the two. When the independent and moderator variables are uncorrelated, the reliability of the product term is the product of the two reliabilities. Thus, if we assume typical values of reliability, say .8, the reliability of the product term will vary between .64, when the independent and moderator variables are uncorrelated, and .7, when they are strongly correlated. This diminished reliability is especially problematic because the detection of moderated effects under typical research conditions is a challenge for reasons other than measurement error (McClelland & Judd, 1993).

As with tests of mediation, tests of moderation are strengthened when measurement error is extracted from variables prior to estimating associations. This extraction for independent and moderator variables can be accomplished using one of the strategies described earlier for modeling intervening variables; however, extracting measurement error from the interaction term is significantly more complicated. One approach to this problem would be the specification of a latent variable representing the interaction term. This specification is complicated by the fact that the loadings and uniqueness terms associated with this latent variable are nonlinear transformations of their counterparts in the latent variables for the independent and moderator variables (Kenny & Judd, 1984). Although this nonlinearity can be incorporated into the specification of the latent variable representing the term, if the number of indicators of the independent and moderator variables exceeds three, the specification becomes prohibitively complex.

One solution to this problem would be to limit the number of indicators of the independent and moderator variables to two or three, either by limiting the number of measures of each or, in the case of multi-item scales, creating item parcels. An alternative approach is to use the multigroup approach described earlier. For instance, we might divide a sample of 100 participants into two groups of 50 corresponding to those highest and lowest in attitude accessibility. We could then fit a model to data from the two groups, a model in which attitude toward the object is modeled as a latent variable and specified as a cause of behavior. Using equality constraints, we could compare the strength of the influence of attitude on behavior for high and low accessibility groups. If the strength of this association, reflected in the path coefficient, differs across groups, then we infer that accessibility moderates the attitude-behavior association. There are two drawbacks to this compromise strategy. First, we have taken a measure of accessibility that differentiates among respondents in terms of milliseconds and reduced it to a coarsely categorized variable with only two values. Second, although we have effectively modeled measurement error out of the attitude measures, we have not addressed the

issue of measurement error in the measure of attitude accessibility. The first drawback is not a concern if the moderator variable is categorical and can take on relatively few values (e.g., male vs. female, Hispanic vs. African American vs. White). The second drawback can be addressed by choosing or developing measures of the moderator variable that are highly reliable (i.e., $r_{mm} > .90$). In short, tests of moderation are significantly compromised by measurement error in the independent and moderator variables; hence, effective tests of moderated effects require careful attention to measurement error at both the measurement and analytic phases.

As with tests of mediated effects (but for different reasons), multicollinearity can pose a problem for tests of moderated effects. If raw scores on a single indicator of the independent variable and a single indicator of the moderator variable are multiplied to form the interaction term, the latter will be highly correlated with one or both of the original variables (Aiken & West, 1991). The magnitude of these correlations (e.g., $r2$ and $r3$ in Figure 10.1) can be substantial (> .80) and give rise to the problem typically associated with multicollinearity in prediction equations—inflated standard errors. Fortunately, there is a rather simple fix for this form of multicollinearity, which is an artifact of scaling rather than a substantively meaningful instance of correlation. If the distributions of the variables are normal, then subtracting scores on each variable from the mean on that variable (i.e., centering) prior to creating the interaction term will result in a zero correlation between the interaction term and the independent and moderator variables.

The magnitude of the correlation between the independent variable and the moderator variable (e.g., $r1$ in Figure 10.1) and the correlation between each and the dependent variable (e.g., reflected in $c1$ and $c2$ in Figure 10.1) influence the likelihood of detecting a significant moderated effect in the presence of measurement error. To illustrate this point, assume that we have measures of attitude and attitude accessibility that, when multiplied, yield an interaction term with reliability of .70. Moreover, assume that we wish to achieve statistical power of .80 for detecting a medium effect of Attitude × Accessibility on behavior. How large must our sample be? If attitude and attitude accessibility were not correlated with each other but were strongly correlated with behavior, then we would need a sample size exceeding 250 in order to realize statistical power of .80. If, on the other hand, attitude and attitude accessibility were moderately correlated with each other but neither was correlated with behavior, then we would need a sample of about 140 to achieve the same level of statistical power. The basic principle is that tests of moderated effects are most powerful when the independent and moderator variables are correlated with each other but unrelated to the dependent variable.

This rather simple principle gives rise to a number of important considerations. One concerns the associations between the independent and moderator variables, attitude and attitude accessibility in our example, and the dependent variable, behavior. If power is maximized when these effects are zero, under what conditions might we expect them to be zero? Focusing first on the independent variable, it is well known that when the effect of an independent variable on a dependent variable is moderated but the interaction effect is ignored, the independent and dependent variable would be related in a curvilinear fashion. In the case of a crossover interaction, in which the effect of the independent variable on the dependent variable reverses when moving from one extreme to the other of a moderator variable, the linear effect of the independent variable on the dependent variable, ignoring the moderated effect, will be near zero. As such, moderated effects that involve a change in the direction of the association between an independent and

dependent variable are, statistically speaking, easiest to detect.

Considerations regarding the association between moderator and dependent variables are somewhat more complex. As noted early in the chapter, the moderator hypothesis implies nothing about the association between the moderator and dependent variables. In fact, the differential status of the independent and moderator variables is easiest to defend when there is no reason to suspect that the moderator variable could cause the dependent variable (i.e., when the two are uncorrelated). To the extent that the moderator variable could be construed as a cause of the dependent variable, then it is better viewed as a second independent variable that operates synergistically with the other independent variable to produce variability in the dependent variable (Carver, 1989).

We have noted that both the reliability of the interaction term and the statistical power of the test of a moderated effect are greater when the independent and moderator variables are associated. If the independent and moderator variables are associated, a key concern is the nature of that association. It is important to establish that the independent variable is not causally associated with the moderator variable. To draw on our example, for attitude accessibility to qualify as a moderator of the attitude-behavior association, there must not be a causal association between attitude and attitude accessibility. If an association between attitude and attitude accessibility could be construed as causal, then it is possible that attitude accessibility is a mediator rather than a moderator of the attitude-behavior association. As with the question of whether a potential moderator variable might better be construed as an independent variable, the issue cannot be resolved statistically outside a research design that allows for a persuasive test of the directionality of an association.

# STUMBLING BLOCKS

A commitment to the principles outlined in this chapter cannot always be translated into a research study that gives evidence of that commitment. In this final section, we touch on four impediments to full implementation of the measurement, design, and analysis strategies we have proposed.

## Ambiguous Theory

The reasoned approach to measurement presupposes a reasonably detailed theoretical account of the phenomenon under investigation. The attitude-to-behavior process model we used to illustrate the approach is such an account. Unfortunately, such models are somewhat rare, leaving investigators to, at best, combine the opportunistic and reasoned approaches to measurement. This state of affairs is problematic, for the determination of how a variable figures into a social process rarely can be made on purely statistical grounds. If theory is not available and definitive statistical tests are not possible, then the placement of variables within a model is arbitrary and, therefore, inferences are, at best, suggestive of future research.

Theory can be ambiguous in a different way. It is possible, for example, that a theoretical account proposes a set of mediating mechanisms, but it is not clear what variables might stand in for the constructs in statistical tests of a model. The most useful theoretical accounts provide information not only about how constructs are associated with each other but also about how those constructs are associated with variables that might represent them (Edwards & Bagozzi, 2000). Less useful are theories that accord a prominent role to constructs that have no evident concrete manifestation.

## One-Shot Data

We have noted that a key consideration beyond how variables are measured is when

they are measured. Even when a theoretical account is very specific regarding the status of key constructs in a model of the process under investigation, the placement of variables representing these constructs in a statistical model is, with few exceptions, arbitrary when the variables all are measured at the same time. One exception is the randomized experiment, which clearly distinguishes the independent variable from all other variables in the model. It is important to acknowledge, however, that even in randomized experiments, the fact that potential intervening and moderator variables typically are measured at the same time is an issue. In non-experimental designs, the placement of the independent variable is a concern as well. We noted the considerable inferential power gained by adding a second measurement occasion, noting the importance of a replicative rather than sequential measurement strategy. Apart from a replicative measurement strategy, non-experimental data cannot be used to develop a definitive test of a model that includes mediated or moderated effects.

## Limited Sample Size

A concern when using statistical models that allow modeling of measurement error is sample size. This is because the maximum likelihood estimation characteristic of statistical approaches involving latent variables is a large-sample technique. Invariably, this concern leads to the question, How large is large enough? A growing literature suggests that "large" is not as substantial as once thought; however, it is equally clear that a sample that is large enough for tests of one model would be inadequate for tests of another. Under ideal circumstances—that is, normally distributed variables and an approximately correct model—maximum likelihood performs reasonably well with samples as small as 50 (although stability can be an issue; see Marsh & Hau, 1999). The ideal circumstances are rare in practice, and a more reasonable recommendation given typical circumstances would be samples of at least 200 (Hoyle & Kenny, 1999). When it is not possible to achieve a sample this large, then it is critical that all measures are highly reliable ($r_{xx} > .90$) in order to avoid the ill effects of measurement error.

### Limited Number of Indicators

A more general concern is the number of measures, or indicators, of key constructs available for most statistical tests. Since the 1950s, social psychologists have been aware of the virtues of multiple indicators for teasing apart variability attributable to the construct of interest and systematic error introduced by the method of measurement (Campbell & Fiske, 1959). Relatively recent advances in statistical software have brought techniques that can be used to model measurement error (e.g., structural equation modeling) into the mainstream. Yet, the inclusion of multiple measures and, better still, multiple operational definitions of key constructs in social psychological research remains the exception rather than the rule. As we have discussed in this chapter, if a construct serves as an intervening or moderator variable in a model, then the issue of error in the operational definition of the construct takes center stage. In the absence of multiple measures or multi-item scales whose subscales, individual items, or arbitrary groups of items (i.e., parcels) can serve as indicators, tests of mediated and moderated effects are significantly compromised.

## CONCLUSION

We have drawn a distinction between two approaches to measurement in social psychological research: the opportunistic approach, in which all variables are measured on one occasion using a single method, and the reasoned approach, in which variables are assigned different statuses in a model based on theory, and the strategy by which they are measured and treated in statistical analyses is governed by their status in the model. We focused most of our attention on intervening and moderator variables, demonstrating that these variables warrant particular scrutiny in light of their sensitivity to measurement error and complications that arise from assumptions regarding the temporal ordering of the variables. Substantive theory is central to the reasoned approach, and a recurring theme in the chapter is the fact that the absence of a detailed theoretical account introduces a measure of arbitrariness into measurement, design, and analysis. To overcome these obstacles to high-quality research, we urge investigators to (a) start with a well-developed theoretical account; (b) use this account to distinguish among independent, dependent, intervening, and moderator variables; (c) develop a measurement strategy that is sensitive to the differing status of variables in the model; and (d) operationally define each construct with multiple indicators, preferably representing different modes of measurement. In our view, a single study that meets these criteria stands to contribute more to our understanding of the phenomenon under investigation than several studies that take the opportunistic approach.

## REFERENCES

Aiken, L. S., & West, S. G. (1991). *Multiple regression: Testing and interpreting interactions.* Thousand Oaks, CA: Sage.

Baron, R. M., & Kenny, D. A. (1986). The moderator-mediator variable distinction in social psychological research: Conceptual, strategic, and statistical considerations. *Journal of Personality and Social Psychology, 51,* 1173-1182.

Busemeyer, J. R., & Jones, L. D. (1983). Analysis of multiplicative combination rules when the causal variables are measured with error. *Psychological Bulletin, 93,* 549-562.

Cacioppo, J. T., Tassinary, L. G., & Berntson, G. G. (Eds.). (2000). *Handbook of psychophysiology* (2nd ed.). New York: Cambridge University Press.

Campbell, D. T., & Fiske, D. W. (1959). Convergent and discriminant validation by the multitrait-multimethod matrix. *Psychological Bulletin, 56,* 81-105.

Carver, C. S. (1989). How should multifaceted personality constructs be tested? Issues illustrated by self-monitoring, attributional style, and hardiness. *Journal of Personality and Social Psychology, 56,* 577-585.

Cohen, J., Cohen, P., West, S. G., & Aiken, L. S. (2003). *Applied multiple regression/correlation analysis for the behavioral sciences* (3rd ed.). Mahwah, NJ: Lawrence Erlbaum.

Edwards, J. R., & Bagozzi, R. P. (2000). On the nature and direction of relationships between constructs and measures. *Psychological Methods, 3,* 155-174.

Evans, M. G. (1991). The problem of analyzing multiplicative composites: Ipnteractions revisited. *American Psychologist, 46,* 6-15.

Fazio, R. H. (1990). Multiple processes by which attitudes guide behavior: The MODE model as an integrative framework. In M. P. Zanna (Ed.), *Advances in experimental social psychology* (Vol. 23, pp. 75-109). New York: Academic Press.

Fazio, R. H., Powell, M. C., & Williams, C. J. (1989). The role of attitude accessibility in the attitude-to-behavior process. *Journal of Consumer Research, 16,* 280-288.

Fazio, R. H., & Williams, C. J. (1986). Attitude accessibility as a moderator of the attitude-perception and attitude-behavior relations: An investigation of the 1984 presidential election. *Journal of Personality and Social Psychology, 51,* 505-514.

Greenwald, A. G., & Farnham, S. D. (2000). Using the Implicit Association Test to measure self-esteem and self-concept. *Journal of Personality and Social Psychology, 79,* 1022-1038.

Hoyle, R. H., & Kenny, D. A. (1999). Sample size, reliability, and tests of statistical mediation. In R. H. Hoyle (Ed.), *Statistical strategies for small sample research* (pp. 195-222). Thousand Oaks, CA: Sage.

Kenny, D. A., & Judd, C. M. (1984). Estimating the nonlinear and interactive effects of latent variables. *Psychological Bulletin, 96,* 201-210.

Kimble, G. A. (1989). Psychology from the standpoint of a generalist. *American Psychologist, 44,* 491-499.

Lewin, K. (1951). *Field theory in social science: Selected theoretical papers* (D. Cartwright, Ed.). New York: Harper & Row.

MacKinnon, D. P., Lockwood, C. M., Hoffman, J. M., West, S. G., & Sheets, V. (2002). A comparison of methods to test mediation and other intervening variable effects. *Psychological Methods, 7,* 83-104.

Marsh, H. W., & Hau, K.-T. (1999). Confirmatory factor analysis: Strategies for small sample sizes. In R. H. Hoyle (Ed.), *Statistical strategies for small sample research* (pp. 251-284). Thousand Oaks, CA: Sage.

McClelland, G. H., & Judd, C. M. (1993). Statistical difficulties of detecting interactions and moderator effects. *Psychological Bulletin, 114,* 376-390.

Pearl, J. (2000). *Causality: Models, reasoning, and inference.* New York: Cambridge University Press.

Roskos-Ewoldsen, D. R., & Fazio, R. H. (1992). On the orienting value of attitudes: Attitude accessibility as a determinant of an object's attraction of visual attention. *Journal of Personality and Social Psychology, 63,* 198-211.

Salmon, W. C. (1997). *Causality and explanation.* New York: Oxford University Press.

# Part III

# DESIGN AND ANALYSIS

## Section C

### Research Designs: Deciding the Specific Approach for Testing the Research Question(s), Why, and How

## CHAPTER 11

# Experimental Design and Causality in Social Psychological Research

S. Alexander Haslam

*University of Exeter*

Craig McGarty

*The Australian National University*

## INTRODUCTION

In the quest to enhance understanding, scientific research can have many goals—to monitor, to describe, to predict, to explain. Each of these activities has a place in every scientific discipline, and this is no less true of social psychology. Indeed, because social psychology is part of our everyday experience, we each perform these activities routinely as we go about our daily lives. For example, if someone is hostile toward us, we are likely (a) to observe that person's future behavior carefully, (b) to tell our friends exactly what happened to us, (c) to try to anticipate when or whether that person will behave this way again, and (d) to try to find out exactly *why* the person was hostile. Was it something about us (our nationality, our gender)? Was it something about the hostile person (his or her personality, or low self-esteem)? Or was it something about the situation (previous personal grievances, current social conflicts)?

In social psychology, as in other branches of the discipline, all these activities are important, and each presents its own challenges. In this chapter, we focus on the activity that many researchers consider most fundamental to social psychological investigation and the one that presents the most profound difficulties—that of providing social psychological *explanation*. As we will see, there are a number of reasons why the task of explanation proves difficult; however, two factors are basic. The first is the

AUTHORS' NOTE: We would like to thank Lucy O'Sullivan, Andrew Livingstone, Jolanda Jetten, Stephen Monsell, Tom Postmes, and the editors for their comments on various drafts of this chapter.

ease (and regularity) with which explanation is confused with description. The second is the difficulty of establishing *causal relations* between two or more social elements: the thing or things to be explained (the *dependent variable[s]* or *DVs*) and the thing or things that provide the causal explanation (the *independent variable[s]* or *IVs*).

These problems constitute an important scientific and philosophical topic in their own right. For this reason, psychologists and social psychologists have had quite a bit to say about them, and we will discuss some of their insights in more detail later.

## Designing Controlled Experiments: The Aims and Structure of This Chapter

Although challenging, the task of making causal statements (and of detecting erroneous causal inferences) becomes easier when we realize that this rests upon an ability to conduct research in which the researcher has *control of the causal variable*. The principal way in which this is achieved is by conducting *appropriately designed experiments*. The business of designing and conducting such experiments is the focus of this chapter.

In simple terms, the chapter looks at the strategies researchers can employ to reduce the uncertainty with which causal statements can be made on the basis of experimental evidence. Along the way, it also identifies a number of design features that can undermine such confidence and introduce uncertainty into the process of explanation.

The chapter is organized into four main sections. The first looks at what we can hope to achieve when we conduct experiments and also identifies situations in which experiments are not appropriate. The second section discusses the key *components* of any experiment and the choices that need to be made in order to explore research questions as effectively as possible. The three components on which we

focus are (a) the IV(s), (b) the DV(s), and (c) the participant sample.

Although variables and participants represent the essential ingredients of any experiment, their quality alone does not guarantee that the experiment will be effective. As with a cake, they have to be assembled appropriately—usually on the basis of a tried and tested recipe. It is on this *assembly process* and some of the basic recipes for experimental design that we focus in the third section of the chapter. In particular, we examine features of design that can threaten *experimental validity* by compromising researchers' ability to interpret experimental results correctly and to draw appropriate inferences from them. The two forms of threat on which we focus are (a) those that compromise the interpretation of the relationship between manipulated and measured variables (*threats to internal validity*) and (b) those that compromise a researcher's ability to generalize experimental findings to other non-experimental settings (*threats to external validity*).

In the fourth section, we explore a range of issues surrounding the interpretation of results from experiments. We start by considering the implications of social psychological research on causal inference and then go on to discuss a number of specific methodological and theoretical issues that are the focus of current interest and debate. In particular, we discuss the logic and limitations of mediational and other forms of correlational analysis.

## WHY AND WHEN SHOULD WE DO EXPERIMENTS?

Imagine a research program in which a researcher is interested in understanding the social psychology of prejudice toward minority groups. This is an example that we develop throughout the chapter, so at the outset, it is worth thinking generally about the sorts of questions that are likely to motivate this researcher and to which he or she will be seeking answers. The researcher may be interested in understanding the rise of anti-Semitism in 1930s Germany, for example, or the reasons for the resurgence of antiminority sentiment in extremist political parties in contemporary Western democracies (e.g., Augoustinos & Reynolds, 2001).

As a starting point, the researcher may hypothesize that individuals display prejudice toward other groups because those individuals have a dysfunctional personality (perhaps they are authoritarians or petty tyrants; Adorno, Frenkel-Brunswik, Levinson, & Sanford, 1950; Altmeyer, 1988; Ashforth, 1994). In seeking to take this question further, the research must now decide what form of research to conduct. Among other things, this means deciding whether or not it is possible and appropriate to conduct experimental research.

### The Logic of Experiments

In simple terms, experiments are distinguished from other forms of research (e.g., surveys) by the fact that they involve attempts not only to measure variables but also to *manipulate* them. Where survey-based research into authoritarianism and prejudice might measure levels of authoritarianism and acts of prejudice in a given community, an experiment might involve attempts to manipulate authoritarianism and then to measure the impact of this manipulation on people's hostility toward others.

A recent example of research that is directly relevant to our research question is provided by the illusory correlation research of David Hamilton and his colleagues. This research was initiated by Hamilton and Gifford (1976) as part of an attempt to understand why it is that people often develop negative stereotypes of minority groups. In line with a social cognitive approach to such issues (e.g., see Fiske &

Taylor, 1984), these researchers' distinctiveness account argued that such stereotypes could develop because memory processes tend to overrepresent distinctive behaviors performed by distinctive groups.

To test this idea, Hamilton and Gifford (1976, Experiment 1) conducted a now-famous experiment in which participants were presented with 39 behavioral statements about different individuals who were identified as members of one of two groups, Group A and Group B. There were 26 statements about Group A, of which 18 were favorable and 8 unfavorable, and 13 about Group B, of which 9 were favorable and 4 unfavorable. Thus, numerically, Group B was a minority, but the ratio of favorable to unfavorable statements was the same for both groups. Despite this, on a range of measures, participants tended to represent Group B less favorably than Group A. In other words, it appeared that subjects formed an illusory correlation between minority group membership and negative behavior.

In controlled experiments, a manipulation takes place under conditions in which researchers have taken steps to ensure that the *only* difference between the groups of participants whose responses are compared is in the variable that has been manipulated. In Hamilton and Gifford's (1976) experiment, the only immediately obvious difference between Group A and Group B was in the number of statements about each, and thus there appeared to be strong grounds for concluding that it was Group B's minority status that led to it being judged more negatively than Group A.

The basic scientific logic of the social psychological experiment is that it attempts to reduce the range of possible explanations for some difference between experimental conditions to just two possibilities: (a) the effect of some combination of the experimental factors and (b) chance. As is well known, statistical logic never allows us to decide between these two alternatives, but it does allow us to estimate the degree to which chance or random variation is a plausible explanation. To the extent that we can confidently reject chance as an explanation for some difference, we can be more confident that our experimental manipulation has produced the effect. This allows us to define the perfect experiment as one in which we can confidently reject chance as an explanation of any effect (this is achieved through adequate statistical power) and in which, at the same time, we can rule out other interpretations or processes.

## Replication

However basic one's experimental design, perfection is rarely, if ever, achieved. This is why researchers view *replication* as such an important part of science. Replication is one way of reducing uncertainty about our results. If we can show the same effects under varying circumstances, then we can be more confident in rejecting chance as an explanation of our results and zero in on the experimental manipulation as the causal factor. Indeed, one reason why Hamilton and Gifford's research is so widely cited in social psychology textbooks is that the results have proved easy to replicate. As a result, the illusory correlation effect is widely regarded as both *reliable* and *robust*.

## Identifying Plausible Confounds

The other benefit we derive from programs of research is the ability to rule out some specific alternative explanations of our findings. However, there are several notes of caution here. In particular, it is wise to bear in mind that there is always an infinite number of alternative explanations for any given experimental effect. That is, it is always possible to assert that any IV that is remotely interesting enough to merit consideration in the social psychological literature is confounded with some other variable that appears relevant to the pattern of results that have been observed.

For example, in Hamilton and Gifford's (1976) original study, the size of the groups was confounded with the alphabetical superiority of the letters used to describe them (McGarty & de la Haye, 1997). It may be the case, then, that results did not reflect negative reactions to smaller groups, but instead negative reactions to groups called B rather than A. More subtly still, in all illusory correlation studies, the total number of statements about a group (A or B) is confounded with the number of positive statements about it. Thus, it could be argued that the illusory correlation effect reflects the fact that there are simply more positive statements about one group than about the other (Smith, 1991). Indeed, elaborating on such arguments, our own work has suggested that the illusory correlation effect partly reflects the fact that under conditions where participants are motivated to differentiate between the two groups (because the labeling implies that there is some difference between them) (Bless, Strack, & Schwarz, 1993), there are *real differences* in the amount of support for the conclusion that Group A is better than Group B rather than for the conclusion that B is better than A. That is, in the Hamilton and Gifford study, 22 pieces of information support the view that A is good and B is bad (the 18 positive statements about Group A and the 4 negative statements about Group B) but only 17 support the view that B is good and A is bad (the 9 positive statements about Group B and the 8 negative statements about Group A).

As a result of the ever-present danger of confounds, the universe of possible social psychological experiments is not meaningfully divided into studies that have confounds and those that do not, but into studies where a plausible claim for the existence of a confound has been made and those where no such claim has been made (as yet).[1] Although this sounds depressing, fortunately many possible confounds can be eliminated on the basis of past empirical research and *theory*. These help us to recognize when confounds that seem plausible are unlikely to be. Therefore, a sound theoretical knowledge of any research area is always necessary to rebut such claims and to winnow the full set of confounds down to a manageable and useful array.

In the case of the illusory correlation effect, does it make theoretical sense to argue that people have a preference for letter A over B? Should we conclude that this confound undermines the internal validity of the original experiment (i.e., our confidence that the effect has occurred for the reasons proposed by the researchers)? The answer depends on our choice of DV and the existence of plausible causal relationships between the proposed confound and that DV. For a confound to be taken seriously, there must be some plausible path between that confounding factor (either alone or in interaction with other factors manipulated in the experiment) and the DV. The only way to arbitrate claims of confounds is on the basis of theoretical knowledge of the relevant variables.

Accordingly, if the DV in a piece of illusory correlation research is *liking*, then familiarity with the literature on letter preference effects tells us that the confound is a plausible cause of the results. This is because research suggests that, other things being equal, people prefer groups labeled "A" to those labeled "B" (see McGarty & de la Haye, 1997). However, if the DV is *accurate recall*, then the confound is less likely to have caused the results, because (to our knowledge) there is no literature or theory that supports a link between alphabetical superiority and memory.

## Multiple Factors

Importantly, experiments provide us with the opportunity to consider the simultaneous effects of multiple factors. The primary question when we consider multiple factors is

whether there are statistical interactions between them. The existence of such interactions is important because the claims we can make about the relationship between IVs and DVs become much more complex when interactions are present (see Aiken & West, 1991, for a detailed treatment of this topic).

In practice, then, experiments often involve attempts to see whether particular *combinations* of IVs produce particular effects. Classic examples in persuasion research (see Petty, 1997) show that the relationship between message complexity and persuasion depends on factors such as the intelligence of the audience and the presence or absence of distractions. That is, people may be more convinced by complex messages, but only when they are sufficiently intelligent to process the message and there are no distractions present to inhibit message processing.

Experiments represent the best possible way to disentangle these sorts of questions in social psychology, as in other fields of inquiry. However, there are good reasons *not* to use experiments for answering some questions. What are these?

## When Not to Conduct Experiments

The two main reasons for not conducting experimental research are that it is (a) not feasible or (b) not ethical to conduct a true experiment. The former is most obviously relevant in cases where the causal variables cannot be varied over the time course of an experiment. If the key variable controlling some process is relatively stable, then it may be impossible to manipulate. For example, if authoritarianism is a relatively enduring and stable aspect of a person, then we may simply be unable to vary it. We might be able to manipulate an analog construct (e.g., concrete thinking) but still not be able to vary the key theoretical variable.

Similar limitations may apply for ethical reasons. It may be possible to vary some factors, but it may not be ethical or desirable to do so (see Kimmel, Chapter 3, this volume). The level of fear or anger that a person experiences in an experiment may be quite easy to vary, but we nevertheless might be reluctant to make our participants either afraid or angry.

Another bad reason for doing experiments arises from attempts to generalize results directly to other settings and situations. Experiments are well suited to testing theories, and it is these theories that we need to generalize, not the results of the experiment per se. A good example of this distinction is provided by the famous minimal group studies of Tajfel, Flament, Billig, and Bundy (1971). The studies found that people who were assigned to groups that had no prior meaning at all were willing to discriminate in favor of a member of their in-group over a member of an out-group, even though they did not know the people in question and had no opportunity to benefit from this behavior.

If one were to generalize directly from this finding to the world at large, one might conclude that people automatically favor their in-group over comparison out-groups. Indeed, researchers often use the minimal group findings to make exactly this claim (see Jost & Elsbach, 2001). However, this is not the theoretical point that social identity researchers were trying to make when they conducted the research, and neither is it a basic assumption of social identity theory (see McGarty, 2001; Turner, 1999). To generalize directly from experimental findings rather than from theory is to be guilty of *naive empiricism* (see below), and although it is tempting to do this, it can lead to serious misunderstanding.

The final bad reason for doing experiments hinges on a naive ideological commitment to the experimental method. As we have been at pains to point out elsewhere (Haslam & McGarty, 1998, in press), being a good researcher is not about *whether* you do experiments but about *when* you do them. Experiments help us to answer many important questions about a given topic, but they can

never answer them all. Accordingly, they need to be seen as just one tool in the researcher's arsenal, and they need to be used prudently rather than impulsively, often in conjunction with other methods. For example, if one wanted to fully understand prejudice toward minorities in contemporary society, it would be foolish simply to conduct experiments—these would almost certainly need to be complemented with the other research strategies that are discussed in other chapters of this volume (e.g., surveys, quasi-experiments, and case studies; Mark & Reichardt, Chapter 12, this volume; West, Biesanz, & Kwok, Chapter 13, this volume). Indeed, it is worth adding that it would also be foolish to confine one's thinking to issues of psychology (Reicher, 2001).

## EXPERIMENTAL COMPONENTS

### Independent Variables (IVs)

As noted above, the defining features of experiments are (a) that they attempt to manipulate one or more variables, not just to measure them, and (b) that the various levels of manipulated variables represent the only difference between groups whose responses are compared. Where the responses of two or more different groups are compared, the best way to achieve this is through *random assignment* of participants to experimental conditions in which they are exposed to different levels of the variable in question.

#### Randomization

A full explanation of the reasons for randomly assigning participants to conditions appeals to a knowledge of statistical principles that were first elaborated by Fisher (e.g., 1926). The short explanation is that the procedure ensures that experiments don't *build in differences* between groups—either on potentially significant dimensions (e.g., in terms of sex, age, intelligence, or personality) or on seemingly trivial ones (eye color, hair length, weight). Accordingly, randomization involves *strictly unsystematic* assignment of participants to conditions (for example, based on the toss of a coin).

An example can illustrate why it is important to recognize that even the most trivial systematic difference can undermine a researcher's ability to make an appropriate causal inference. Imagine that we conducted a study to examine the impact of discrimination on collective self-esteem in which we had two conditions: one where people were given the opportunity to discriminate (the experimental condition) and one where they were not (the control condition) (see Oakes & Turner, 1980). We might place people into different conditions on the basis of their position on a roll, putting people whose names are high in the alphabet in the control condition and those with names low in the alphabet in the experimental condition. This violation of the principle of random assignment may seem relatively inconsequential, and we may have good reasons for doing it (e.g., to minimize administrative confusion). Nonetheless, the procedure may inadvertently build ethnic differences into the two groups, so that people from one geographical region (perhaps where names starting with Y and Z are common) are in the experimental condition and people from another region in the control condition. In this case, any difference subsequently observed in the self-esteem of participants in the two conditions might therefore be due to differences in ethnicity rather than differences in physical reinforcement.

The primary strength of the experimental method is thus that, *providing participants are randomly assigned to conditions*, researchers can be sure that effects observed on the DV are due to one of two things: their manipulation of the IV or chance. In this way, it gives researchers *experimental control* both over what they investigate and over the causal interpretation of their findings.

## Theoretical Relevance

It follows from the above that all experiments must contain at least one manipulated variable—an IV. On the basis of a theory or hypothesis, this variable is predicted to have a causal effect on at least one measured outcome variable—a DV. The goals in selecting an IV for an experiment are quite straightforward: they are (a) to identify a variable that *can* be manipulated and (b) to ensure that this variable corresponds as closely as possible to the theoretical variable in which the researcher is interested. However, satisfying these objectives can be quite difficult—partly because there is often an inherent tension between them.

To explain these points, let us develop an example in which a researcher is interested in the social psychological underpinnings of discrimination (e.g., Hogg & Sunderland, 1991; Hunter, Platow, Bell, Kypri, & Lewis, 1997; Long & Spears, 1997; Oakes & Turner, 1980). Social identity theorists (after Tajfel and Turner [1979]) have argued that, in particular social contexts (e.g., where groups are perceived to be in conflict and the relations between them are unstable), a desire to increase group-based self-esteem can increase people's willingness to engage in acts of discrimination (e.g., as found in the minimal group studies discussed above; Tajfel, Flament, et al. [1971]).

Among other things, this theory suggests that if group relations are unstable and people are given an opportunity to discriminate against an out-group, their collective self-esteem (CSE) will increase. However, self-esteem is not expected to increase if they are not given this opportunity. Alternatively, the theory has been interpreted as suggesting that if people have low collective self-esteem, they will be motivated to discriminate, but if they have high self-esteem they will not (Hogg & Abrams, 1990; Hogg & Sunderland, 1991; see Turner, 1999, for an extended discussion of these inferences and their limitations).

If we were to design an experiment to test the second of the above theoretical propositions, it would need to manipulate people's self-esteem in order to see whether this has any effect on discrimination. As often occurs in social and other psychological research, an immediate problem that arises here is that it is impossible to manipulate something like self-esteem *directly*. We cannot open up a person's head and switch the self-esteem synapse (if there were such a thing) from "off" to "on." Similarly, we cannot directly manipulate a whole host of social psychological variables such as mood, self-efficacy, and personality. Indeed, as we noted above, even if we could, it often would be ethically unacceptable to do so (see Kimmel, Chapter 3, this volume; Ni Bhrolcháin, 2001).

The problem here relates to general issues of research validity and psychological measurement. It arises from the fact that social psychological research generally is concerned with making statements about theoretical variables—usually mental states or processes—that are not directly observable. This means that researchers often have to manipulate theoretical variables *indirectly*, by using IVs that they believe will have a specific impact on a given mental process or state. In other words, they have to make decisions about how to *operationalize* the IV. Often this requires not only extensive reading in a given area but also extensive *piloting*. In piloting, researchers conduct small-scale studies to examine the impact of multiple plausible manipulations and select the one that appears most suitable.

Piloting may lead researchers to conclude that in a given study, the best way to manipulate someone's mood is for the researcher to play happy or sad music to that person. Similarly, it may lead the researcher to manipulate collective self-esteem by telling some research participants that their group has performed poorly on a test and other participants that their group has performed well.

## Manipulation Checks

Having performed indirect manipulations of this sort, it often is necessary for researchers to show that those manipulations have had the desired effect on the relevant theoretical variable. Researchers typically achieve this by employing a *manipulation check* (indeed, many editors of social psychology journals require these to be conducted as a matter of principle before accepting research for publication). A manipulation check is a DV, but unlike other DVs, it checks that the manipulation of an IV has had an effect on a theoretically relevant *causal* variable. For this reason, obtaining an effect on this type of measure is not an end it itself but rather a way of ensuring that an experiment actually has been conducted (i.e., that the IV has been effectively manipulated).

So, after making people listen either to a dirge or a dance-track, a researcher may ask them how they feel in order to check that the people who listened to the dance-track were in a better mood. Likewise, having attempted to manipulate participants' collective self-esteem by giving false feedback about their group's test performance, the researcher could ask them to complete a series of self-esteem measures (e.g., Crocker & Luhtanen, 1990). If participants who were given positive feedback tend to have higher scores on relevant scales, then this suggests that the manipulation has been successful and that they have "gotten to first-base."

Researchers usually are keen to obtain very big effects on manipulation checks. If they do not, they generally will seek to strengthen the manipulation of the IV. This might involve increasing its duration or intensity, reinforcing it with additional manipulations, or simply using a different (superior) manipulation. Such steps often are necessary because for experiments to have the best chance of succeeding (i.e., for the IV to have an effect on the DV), the researcher needs to *ensure that the manipulation of the IV is as strong as possible.* Indeed, if there were a first rule of experimentation, this might be it.

### Between- and Within-Subjects Designs

In most of the above examples, we have referred to *between-subjects designs* in which one group of participants is exposed to one level of a given IV and another group is exposed to another level (e.g., where the study contains two experimental groups or an experimental group and a control group).

However, the manipulation of IVs does not have to involve different groups of participants. It is also possible (and common) to conduct experiments using within-subjects designs in which the *same* participants are exposed to different levels of the IV (see West, Biesanz, & Kwok, Chapter 13, this volume). As we have seen, this approach typically is adopted in illusory correlation research where the same participants make judgments of both large and small stimulus groups.

Several factors contribute to a researcher's decision to manipulate an IV within or between subjects. Two of the main advantages of within-subjects manipulations are (a) that they dramatically reduce the number of participants needed in any given experiment and (b) that they remove all the differences between the participants in different conditions that are produced by chance as a result of the random assignment of different participants to different conditions.

However, despite their apparent elegance, within-subjects procedures also have drawbacks. In particular, as we will see below, they potentially introduce some quite serious threats to internal validity.

### Dependent Variables (DVs)

Of course, the main "prize" in any experiment is not to obtain effects on manipulation checks but to obtain them on other DVs. In a

discrimination experiment, the researchers will not be satisfied with the knowledge that they have changed people's collective self-esteem; instead, they want to know whether this change in self-esteem has had any effect on discrimination. To do this, the experiment obviously has to include DVs—in this case, measures of discrimination—on which such effects might emerge.

As with IVs, any DV that is selected needs to be relevant to the theoretical argument that the researcher is examining. For example, in a study seeking to test social identity theory's assertion that intergroup discrimination can increase self-esteem, it is important that the DV is a measure of *collective* (i.e., group-based) self-esteem (e.g., as measured by agreement with the statement "I feel good about my group") (Crocker & Luhtanen, 1990) rather than *personal* self-esteem (e.g., as measured by agreement with the statement "I feel that I have a number of good qualities") (Rosenberg, 1965). This is because the theory makes it clear that when people are acting as group members, their actions will affect their sense of self defined at a collective rather than a personal level (i.e., in terms of social identity rather than personal identity) (Turner, 1999, p. 24).

### Scale Construction

Although many experiments incorporate only one or two DVs, it is common for scores on these variables to be composites of responses on *multiple* measures (see Wegener & Fabrigar, Chapter 7, this volume). By taking *multiple measures* of the same theoretical construct (e.g., self-esteem, prejudice), researchers can be more confident in their characterization of participants with respect to that construct. For example, if you wanted to find out whether potential employees were reliable, it is likely that you would want to examine a number of aspects of their behavior: Do they turn up to work on time? Are they often absent for no reason? Do they meet deadlines?

As part of this process, researchers again often conduct pilot studies in order to ensure that responses on multiple measures can be organized to form *coherent and reliable scales* and/or *subscales*. For example, in developing a measure of work reliability, a researcher may find that arrival and departure time measure "time-keeping," while an ability to remember appointments and meet deadlines measure "dependability." Accordingly, in their research, they may measure reliability using two subscales, one quantifying time-keeping, the other dependability.

Scale coherence usually is established in two phases. The first checks that responses on individual items are correlated, typically performed by conducting an exploratory factor analysis to verify the existence of a unitary dimension. This is then followed by computation of a reliability coefficient such as Cronbach's alpha. If these checks prove successful, responses on individual items are then aggregated to create a single scale (see Wegener & Fabrigar, Chapter 7, this volume for more details about scale construction). In this way, Rosenberg's (1965) scale comprises 10 items that are combined to form a single measure of personal self-esteem, and Crocker and Luhtanen's (1990) instrument comprises four 4-item subscales, each intended to measure slightly different components of collective self-esteem (referred to as private, public, membership, and identity).

### The Relevance-Sensitivity Trade-Off

As with IVs, the operationalization of DVs can involve a trade-off between theoretical relevance and practical considerations. In the choice of DVs, there is sometimes a conflict between what experimenters would *like to measure* and what they *can measure*. This conflict contributes to a *relevance-sensitivity trade-off* (Haslam & McGarty, 1998), which reflects the fact that when a DV is highly relevant to a given issue, it often tends to be less sensitive to changes in the IV.

As an example, consider a team of researchers that is interested in studying the effect of group interaction on prejudice (e.g., Haslam & Wilson, 2000). To understand why racially motivated attacks are more likely to be committed by groups rather than by individuals, the researchers might hypothesize that interaction among members of groups that are prejudiced has the effect of polarizing and consensualizing their prejudice (see Haslam, Turner, Oakes, McGarty, & Reynolds, 1998; Moscovici & Zavalloni, 1969). In this way, interaction is expected to strengthen the prejudice of already-prejudiced groups and the agreement among its members. To test this hypothesis, researchers might conduct a study in which they manipulate the IV (interaction) by asking people to perform a given task on their own or in a group of like-minded other people.

The most dramatic demonstration would then show that people in groups are much more likely than individuals to display extreme forms of prejudice toward out-group members—for example, by subjecting them to racial abuse and perhaps even physical violence. Again, we can see that there are serious ethical problems with this research. But even if these didn't exist, it would be unlikely that any experimental manipulation of the IV (interaction) would ever be strong enough to bring about sizable change in the DV (number of racial attacks) unless the study was going to include an awful lot of very intense interaction. So the DV isn't sensitive enough to detect the IV's impact. Indeed, were even a small effect to emerge on the dependent measure, this would be very impressive indeed (Prentice & Miller, 1992).

To deal with this problem, the researchers would have to design a study with a much more sensitive DV. They could see whether putting prejudiced people into a group and making them interact makes them more likely to endorse racist statements or to express racist attitudes. Even here, though, the scales may have to examine relatively subtle rather than more blatant forms of racism (i.e., "modern racism" rather than "old-fashioned racism") (McConahay, Hardee, & Batts, 1981; for a discussion, see Walker, 2001). But although the DV might now be sensitive enough to detect changes in the IV, its link to the theoretical variable of interest is less direct and much more open to question. Clearly, people may argue that there is only a weak relationship between prejudicial attitudes and prejudicial behavior (e.g., Fishbein, 1997; LaPiere, 1934). In this case, it could be argued that the researchers have simply replaced one research question with another.

The way in which researchers usually seek to deal with the tension between relevance and sensitivity in their choice of DVs is to select variables on which they *can* obtain effects (i.e., variables that are sensitive enough) and seek to ensure that these are as relevant as possible. However, in some cases this strategy opens their work up to a charge of *nonrelevance*— and these charges are commonly made against experimentalists researching in all areas of psychology. The charge is particularly likely to be seen as justified if researchers frame their work in terms of variables that they never actually investigate. In the above example, the researchers might make claims about the importance of their work for helping reduce racial attacks (and obtain research funding on this basis) but never actually establish the link between their DV and this phenomenon.

Just how big a problem this lack of relevance is for experimental research has been a matter of debate for some time (dating back to the so-called "crisis in social psychology" in the 1970s) (e.g., see Israel & Tajfel, 1972; McGarty & Haslam, 1997). Nevertheless, most researchers would agree that it is important to try to establish the relevance of an experiment's dependent measures to any phenomenon in which they are interested.

The main strategy for establishing this link is to back up experimental research that produces effects on a given DV with additional research demonstrating a causal (not just a correlational) relationship between that variable and one of greater relevance. In the prejudice example, having found that interaction affects prejudicial attitudes, researchers could then conduct additional experiments to address the question of whether prejudicial attitudes affect prejudicial acts. Indeed, ideally they (or someone else) would have established the link between attitudes and behavior *before* they conducted the experiment into the effects of interaction on attitudes. However, it remains the case that such links are often taken for granted rather than established systematically.

## The Experimental Sample

As well as deciding what they are going to manipulate and measure in an experiment, researchers must decide who the participants will be (see also Miller, Chapter 5, this volume; Shoda, Chapter 6, this volume). In many cases, the choice of a sample is unproblematic. For example, if researchers are interested in looking at the impact of organizational performance on managers' ratings of a person's leadership, they will almost certainly want to conduct their research on managers (e.g., Meindl, 1993). Similarly, if researchers are investigating the impact of a given teaching method on schoolchildren's attitudes toward members of various ethnic groups, then they will want to include schoolchildren in their study (e.g., Aronson, Blaney, Stephin, Sikes, & Snapp, 1978).

But what if researchers are interested in examining normal psychological processes in the general ("normal") population? Who should they study then? If research practice is a guide, the most common answer to this question is "students." Indeed, investigations indicate that in about 80% of published research articles, the participants in social psychology experiments are first-year undergraduates (e.g., West, Newsom, & Fenaughty, 1992). In these cases, the choice of participants seems to have been pretty straightforward.

However, it seems appropriate to interrogate experimentalists' reliance on first-year students—if only to answer the concerns that those (and other) students themselves often voice about the apparent limitations of this strategy (Chow, 1995). "How," they ask, "can one hope to make general statements about psychological processes among members of society at large on the basis of studies which focus on a class of people that represents only a small subset of that society—and one that, demographically, is not particularly representative of the whole (tending to be wealthier, more educated, more motivated, etc.)?" This question (and the criticism it implies) appears more compelling when students learn that the researcher in question is interested in such things as attitudes, prejudice, group dynamics, and personality. The questions are asked even more forcefully once one observes that student populations usually are studied in the laboratory rather than in the situations they encounter in their everyday lives (Vissers, Heyne, Peters, & Guerts, 2001; see Cook & Groom, Chapter 2, this volume). How can laboratory-based studies of people who are generally intelligent, healthy, assertive, and tolerant tell us anything about the psychological makeup of the general population, whose actions take place in a world of politics, poverty, oppression, struggle, and intolerance?

Many non-experimental social psychologists ask this same question, and go on to argue that the conclusions inferred from most experimental samples are necessarily flawed. Many experimentalists also would argue that research should not be based *solely* on student samples. Most would

encourage a researcher to conduct experiments using other specialized samples wherever possible (e.g., Tajfel & Fraser, 1978). Unfortunately, though, samples of certain types of participants (e.g., CEOs, members of racist organizations) are often hard to find and often unwilling to participate in research. Moreover, even if they consent to participate, there may be particular problems associated with studying them (e.g., ethical and practical).

More important, though, experimentalists generally argue that it *is* possible to gain significant insights into human nature on the basis of samples and situations that are not representative of the breadth of human society and experience (e.g., Chow, 1995; Mook, 1980; Turner, 1981). The arguments marshaled to support this point are quite complex, but they rest on two main points: representativeness and the importance of theory (see also Miller, Chapter 5, this volume; Shoda, Chapter 6, this volume).

### Representativeness

The first argument indefence of experimental practice relates to the concept of a *representative sample*. A core point here is that to be able to apply research findings to a particular population (e.g., most "normal" people), experimental samples and situations do not have to be representative of that population in *every* respect. Instead, the experimental sample only has to be representative of that population on *theoretically relevant* dimensions.

If a researcher theorizes that group interaction affects decision making by leading to polarization (Moscovici & Zavalloni, 1969), this means that the sample has to be representative of the population to which the research will be generalized only on dimensions that relate to group membership, group interaction, and group decisions. For example, the participants need to be able to be placed in groups, they need to be able to interact, and they need to be able to make decisions.

### The Importance of Theory

A second point that is absolutely critical here, though, is that researchers *must have a theoretical framework* (normally but not always called *a theory*) in order to make judgments about what is (and what is not) a relevant dimension of the experimental sample and situation. Note too that this also applies even if the sample is directly relevant to the issue being studied. For example, in a study of children's moral reasoning, researchers need to ensure that the children in their sample are representative of the population to which they wish to apply their research, not just in terms of age but also on dimensions of intelligence and maturity. If researchers do not attempt to ensure that their experimental subpopulation is representative in this way and they attempt to generalize any empirical findings they obtain straight to the social world at large, then, as we noted above, they are guilty of naive empiricism.

For example, if researchers conduct a study with some students and find that they become more left-wing after holding a group discussion about politics, they may be tempted to suggest that group discussion will make everybody more left-wing. However, this strategy is dangerous largely because it is merely a form of *induction*—a very weak (though quite common) form of scientific reasoning. This important point is illustrated schematically in Figure 11.1.

Theory offers the scientific solution to this problem because it allows experiments to test theoretical ideas using any sample and in any situation where theoretically relevant variables can be manipulated. In the above example, we could test the theory that group discussion makes attitudes more risky by exposing *any sample* to group discussion and measuring their responses on measures of risk *as defined by the subpopulation from which the sample is drawn* (which may be different for parents and for juvenile delinquents, for example). We could then see if these attitudes were more extreme after discussion than they were before it. We would then generalize our research to the larger world not on the basis of the experimental data itself (which would almost certainly vary across samples, situations, and cultures) (Sohn, 1992), but *on the basis of the theory* that it supports. At a later date, researchers could conduct further research that either corroborated or challenged that theory. Indeed, this is exactly what happened in the study of group decision making in which researchers initially thought that discussion made all decisions more risky (Stoner, 1961) but went on to find that it had the effect of making them more polarized (i.e., more risky if they were initially risky, more cautious if they were initially cautious) (McGarty, Turner, Hogg, Davidson, & Wetherell, 1992; Moscovici & Zavalloni, 1969).

### Using Specialized Samples

As we have seen, researchers often want to conduct experiments using specialized samples that are particularly relevant to the phenomena they are investigating. One reason for doing so is that it may be difficult to manipulate a given variable using a nonspecialized sample. In this case, the researcher may resort to quasi-experimental methodology in which participants are not randomly assigned to conditions but are assigned on the basis of their preexisting membership of a particular group (see Mark & Reichardt, Chapter 12, this volume).

This strategy creates problems when seeking to establish causality, however, because participants in different experimental conditions are likely to differ on more than just the

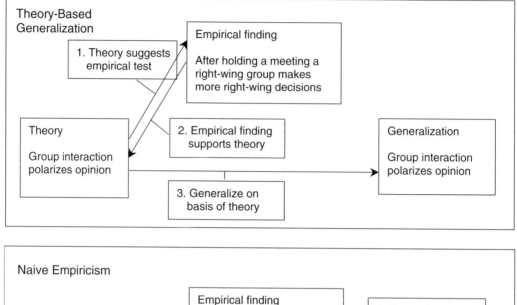

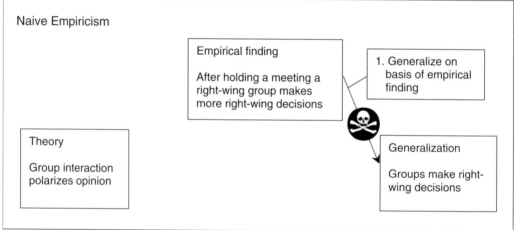

**Figure 11.1**   The Distinction Between Theory-Based Generalization and Naive Empiricism

IV of interest. One way of addressing these problems is by *matching*. Matching involves ensuring that different experimental groups do not differ appreciably on dimensions that could be implicated in any effects obtained on the DV (i.e., theoretically relevant variables).

Matching is very common in research where it is almost impossible (as well as unethical) to manipulate theoretically relevant variables. Such variables include social, educational, and cultural background;

personality, and prejudice level. Matching basically involves researchers systematically assigning participants to groups on the basis of differences in the variable of interest (e.g., personality, prejudice level) but seeking to ensure that they do not differ systematically on other key variables (e.g., age, sex, or socioeconomic background). Matching also can be used to establish relevant *baselines* against which performance can be appraised. For example, in a study to investigate work-related stress, a researcher may seek to obtain controls matched on variables such as age, sex, and years of education, in order to gauge the *relative* stress of a particular person or group in a given social setting (e.g., shift workers) (Meers, Maassen, & Verhaagen, 1994). This procedure allows the researcher to eliminate the variables on which the participants are matched as potential causes of any differences in stress.

Although it sounds promising, matching is never as effective as randomization in removing differences between groups. This is partly because matching is very difficult to do successfully, especially if the researcher is attempting to match participants on more than one or two variables.

## EXPERIMENTAL ASSEMBLY

### Threats to Internal Validity

The previous two sections have outlined the purpose and ingredients of experiments. Equally important are questions relating to the way experiments are put together and conducted—not least because it is very easy to construct bad experiments or to conduct experiments badly. In particular, a number of features of design can compromise an experiment's internal validity, leading researchers to interpret the effects they obtain incorrectly.

### Dealing With Confounds

As we noted above, internal validity is compromised when researchers think that their research findings show one thing but they in fact show something else. In the case of experiments, this problem arises from the fact that although particular findings allow researchers to know *whether* there is something to explain, they do not always allow researchers to know what the explanation is. This is because it is much easier to ascertain *that* an IV has had an effect than it is to ascertain *why* it has had an effect.

Problems in establishing an experiment's internal validity often occur when experimenters don't really manipulate what they think they're manipulating but actually manipulate something else. Earlier we mentioned the example of Hamilton and Gifford's (1976) illusory correlation research, in which the researchers thought they were manipulating distinctiveness but in fact can be seen to have manipulated alphabetical superiority, the number of positive statements about the groups, or the amount of support for differentiating hypotheses about the groups.

Where alternative explanations of experimental outcomes like this are identified, it is usually because the experiment involves an *unintended* manipulation of an extraneous variable—in other words, a confounding. As we noted above, this is very common (indeed, in a sense, unavoidable) in experimental research, and many disagreements between researchers are based on differing views about the existence of confounds and about what exactly experimenters have manipulated in their experiments. Often, as we have seen, these disagreements are quite nuanced and hinge on subtle re-interpretation of the status of an IV.

### Uncertainty Management

The general way in which issues of interpretation are played out is through a process of *uncertainty management* (Haslam & McGarty, 2001, in press). In the first phase of this process, a particular experimental result is established with a degree of certainty and a particular interpretation is widely endorsed (e.g., in textbooks). Subsequently, though, other researchers increase uncertainty by calling the received interpretation into question. The field may then progress through attempts to resolve the uncertainty that has arisen. This cycle is one that has been played out in relation to most major topics in social psychology, and it is fair to say that most social psychologists establish their professional credentials by contributing to one or more of these three phases of uncertainty management.

This typically is done in one of two ways. The first is simply to conduct an additional study in which alternative interpretations are competitively tested—typically through independent manipulation of multiple relevant variables. This is how researchers (e.g., Berndsen, Spears, van der Pligt, & McGarty, 1999; Haslam, McGarty, & Brown, 1996; McGarty & de la Haye, 1997) have addressed alternative interpretations of the findings of Hamilton and Gifford's (1976) illusory correlation research that we discussed earlier.

Another way of dealing with this problem is to ensure *in advance* that experiments include manipulation checks. As we noted above, these can help establish whether indirect manipulations of IVs have had the desired effect. Furthermore, if data from manipulation checks are available, modern regression techniques allow researchers to conduct *path analyses* to test whether the effect of an experimental manipulation can be ascribed to the putative IV (see Baron & Kenny, 1986; Hoyle & Robinson, Chapter 10, this volume, for more details).

## Ruling Out Alternative Hypotheses: Dealing With Specific Threats to Internal Validity

Beyond this general point about problems of interpretation, Campbell and Stanley (1963) made a major contribution to the analysis of internal validity by cataloging specific ways in which it could be threatened. In the remainder of this section, we will briefly discuss each of these in turn, as well as the main ways to deal with them.

### Maturation Effects

One of the main causes of interpretational problems in experiments is the passage of time. This is a serious problem in experiments that have within-subjects designs in which participants are required to make a number of responses. Here the basic principle of experimental design—namely, that researchers need to take steps to ensure that the *only* difference between groups of participants whose responses are compared is in the variable that has been manipulated—is compromised by the fact that between the two observations, other things *apart from the manipulation* will have occurred. Here both the participants and their circumstances will have changed—and these changes, *not the treatment*, may be responsible for the change between the two observations (the pretest and the posttest).

Any such temporal changes are generally referred to as instances of *maturation effects*. Two forms of maturation effect are particularly important: *practice effects* and *fatigue effects*. Both relate to the fact that by the time they complete a particular DV, participants already have had some experience of completing it before.

### History Effects

Time also exerts indirect effects on participants because it is associated with changes occurring in the world that they inhabit. Between any two observations, participants may be affected by any number of things going on in the world—change in the weather, the economy, the political climate, and so on. Any such changes that take place over the course of a study are referred to as *history effects*.

Maturation effects and history effects threaten internal validity because they can lead to *systematic differences between observations* at different phases of a study. This is one reason why participants exposed to different levels of a within-subjects variable are not perfectly matched.

### Experiment Effects

Other factors relating to the *experimental situation itself* may mean that participants are systematically different at different phases of an experiment. First, when participants are observed or asked to respond for a second time (i.e., in a posttest), their responses may be affected by their awareness of having responded previously (in a pretest). Problems like this are known as *testing effects*. Testing effects are actually one aspect of the more general issue of experimental *reactivity*. This refers to the fact that the process of *making observations can change observations*. If reactivity affects participants' responses in experiments, it can cause serious problems of interpretation.

We will discuss two specific sources of reactivity—experimenter bias and demand characteristics—in more detail below. This is because, unlike the other threats to internal validity considered in this section, these problems call for special forms of experimental control (e.g., using deception) that are similar to those used to deal with threats to external validity. For this reason, even though they represents threats to both internal and external validity, we will deal with these problems in our discussion of threats to external validity.

One basic form in which reactivity commonly manifests itself is through *order effects*. These arise if the responses to treatments change depending on the order in which the treatments occur. Other features of the experiment may also change between any two observations, and these *instrumentation effects* undermine validity in much the same way. Instrumentation refers to *any* feature of the experiment related to the collection of data—for example, whom it is collected by, where it is collected, and the methods used for collection.

### Sample Effects

A final set of threats to internal validity relate to strategies for selecting participant samples and the effects of those strategies. The first of these are *selection effects*, and along lines suggested above, these arise when participants are assigned to different levels of an IV on the basis of some specific criteria (e.g., their age or their score on a particular test). As we have noted several times already, the basic problem posed by selection effects is that because participants are not randomly assigned to conditions, any change in the DV may be due to things *associated with* the IV rather than the IV itself.

A more subtle problem arises when an IV is manipulated within subjects and participants are selected because of their extremity (or peculiarity) on the variable of interest. The problem here is that due to *regression to the mean*, one is unlikely to observe such extremity again (for a further treatment of this issue, see Mark & Reichardt, Chapter 12, this volume).

A final threat posed by sampling strategies is the problem of participant *mortality effects*. In the time between any two observations, *particular* participants may withdraw from a study. Where this occurs, it may be the characteristics of the withdrawing participants that are responsible for any effects rather than the experimental manipulation. This is a particular problem in experiments that are conducted "online" (see Birnbaum, Chapter 16, this volume).

The basic problem posed by all these threats to internal validity is the same—that is, they produce systematic differences between experimental observations beyond those caused by manipulation of the IV. As we have seen, these effects are often subtle and, indeed, quite intriguing. Faced with a list of potential experimental problems, you may also wonder why researchers ever go to the trouble of trying to conduct valid experiments.

### Experimental Control

The good news is that despite the subtlety of many of the above problems, all can be addressed (often quite easily) by appropriate experimental design. Indeed, the basic principle used to eliminate threats to validity is one that we have talked about at length: *experimental control*. As we have pointed out, the main way of achieving experimental control is through a combination of randomization and/or matching. For example, an effective way of dealing with order effects, practice effects, and fatigue effects is either (a) to randomize the order in which participants complete dependent measures, (b) to make participants in both an experimental and a control group complete all dependent measures in the same order, or (c) to systematically vary the order in which items are presented, through *counterbalancing*.

These points about experimental control can be demonstrated by describing one of the main forms of what Campbell and Stanley (1963) call a *true experimental design*. This design deals effectively with all the above threats (see also Mark & Reichardt, Chapter 12, this volume). It involves supplementing a basic *pretest-treatment-posttest* design with an additional *pretest-posttest* control. This control condition uses different participants but a pretest and posttest that are *identical in every respect* (e.g., including the same measurement procedures and the same experimenters).

If participants are randomly assigned to these two conditions, we can compare the results obtained at the posttest in the experimental condition with those obtained at the posttest in the control condition. Here a significant difference *must* result from the

manipulation of the IV rather than from any of the threats to internal validity described above.

As an example, consider researchers who are interested in establishing the ability of a particular social contact program to reduce prejudice. To do this, they could randomly assign participants to experimental and control conditions and start by measuring the prejudice of each group of participants (due to random assignment, there should be no substantial difference between them). They could then make people in the experimental group take part in the social contact program but leave the control group alone (this constitutes the manipulation of the IV). Later, they could measure the prejudice levels of both groups again. If the posttest shows that prejudice is much lower in the experimental group than in the control group (and there had been no difference between the groups before), then the researchers can correctly attribute this difference to the positive effects of the program. Similarly, if prejudice is now clearly greater in the experimental group than in the control group, they would have to conclude that this form of social contact is having a harmful effect.

### Threats to External Validity

In the previous section, we discussed how the addition of a between-subjects manipulation to a within-subjects experiment resulted in an almost perfect basic experimental design. There is only one real problem with this strategy, and this is that the effects of testing across the two observations (the pretest and posttest) may *interact* with the experimental manipulation, so that participants who are exposed to a particular level of a treatment react to the first phase of testing differently from those who are exposed to another level (e.g., in a control condition where they receive no treatment). This reactivity does not undermine the experiment's internal validity—because the effect is still due to the experimental manipulation—but it creates interpretative problems nevertheless. This is because the results of the study may generalize only to situations where people have been given the pretest. In other words, the pretest-posttest design can compromise *external validity*.

For example, in our study looking at the impact of social contact on prejudice, it may be the case that after participants have participated in a contact program, they reinterpret the meaning of the items in prejudice scales, so that they display less prejudice when responding on those scales at the posttest. The results of this research would thus tell us only about the effectiveness of contact as a means of changing the interpretation of prejudice scales; they would not necessarily tell us anything about the effectiveness of contact as a means of reducing prejudice.

To address the problem, a simple modification to the above design involves eliminating the first observation, so that there is no pretest for the experimental treatment to react with. Indeed, this design is the basic building block of most experimental research—largely because it is simple, neat, and effective.

However, experimental pretests are not the only things that threaten an experiment's external validity. Earlier, we made the point that in order to generalize from an experimental sample to another population, the sample must be representative of the population on theoretically relevant dimensions. A related question concerns the process by which researchers seek to generalize from experimental *situations* to situations beyond the experiment.

This is another complex issue and one on which a multitude of opinions exists. Broadly speaking, debate centers on a number of features of experimental design that are seen to have the potential to compromise external validity. These include (a) the *reactivity* of participants both to features of experimental design (as discussed above) and to the experimenter's hypothesis and (b) the *artificiality* of experimental settings (Chow, 1995).

### Reactivity

Research by Rosenthal (e.g., 1966) suggested that even if an experiment is believed to be testing a hypothesis in an evenhanded way, researchers may lead participants to behave in the way that they want. For example, this might occur because participants are sensitive to the experimenter's power (Spears & Smith, 2001) and respond to cues in the experiment that implicitly tell them what is expected of them. A question like "Do you *really* want to do that?" may lead participants to assume that the correct answer is "No" and to respond accordingly. These cues are known as the experiment's *demand characteristics* (Orne, 1962), and they can be thought of as *norms* that participants conform to (or, on occasion, reject) (Barber & Silver, 1968) because they appear to be guides to behavior in the situation they confront.

Behavior in the form of *experimenter bias* can have a similar effect. This refers to any behavior by the researcher that prevents a fair test of the experimental hypothesis. The experimenter may react more positively to responses that are to his or her liking (for example, by nodding or smiling). Less subtly, the researcher may "prod" participants so that they behave in the desired way in order to support the experimental hypothesis. Obviously, such *cheating* compromises the worth of any research, and the problems it creates will never be remedied by improvements to experimental design. In contrast, the issue of *unintentional* experimenter bias often can be attended to quite easily—for example, by using an experimenter who is *blind* to the condition in which participants are placed.

Because participants' awareness of an experiment's hypothesis can jeopardize both external and internal validity, social psychologists often go to considerable trouble to conceal the purpose of any experiment they conduct. This can be done by means of *deception*—either misinforming participants about the purpose of an experiment or using *concealment* to avoid telling them the whole truth. This may involve presenting participants with a plausible (but misleading) *cover story* that informs them that an experiment is about one thing when really it is about another.

For the straightforward reason that these procedures involve a failure to be entirely truthful, their use raises obvious ethical issues. Moreover, because the procedures are a common feature of experiments in social psychology, researchers in the field have a particular need to address these issues. In practical terms, it means that social psychological experiments are far more likely to require systematic *debriefing* of participants than those in other fields—to explain the nature of, and reasons for, deception or concealment (see Kimmel, Chapter 3, this volume).

### Artificiality

The biggest threat to external validity concerns the ability of researchers to generalize on the basis of experiments that study psychology in controlled laboratory situations (Chow, 1995). When researchers conduct experiments, they try to manipulate theoretically relevant variables while holding all others constant. But does this emphasis on control deprive those variables of their meaning and richness (Gergen, 1997; Leaf, 1993)?

The arguments that experimentalists use to defend their practices are similar to those that we presented in discussing the logic of representative sampling. Most researchers agree that experiments simplify the situations that confront people in their daily lives. Indeed, the experimental control that produces this simplicity gives experimental research its explanatory power (Dawes, 1996; Mook, 1980). But we argue that whether or not, in any given case, this practice constitutes *over*simplification is an empirical and theoretical issue. In other words, it is something that can be established only by considering each case on its merits and doing additional research if necessary.

In this chapter, we have typically described simple experiments involving only one IV, but in fact, as suggested above, few experiments examine variables in isolation. They usually explore complex interactions between *multiple psychological and situational* features. If a theory or explanatory principle is challenged by the findings that such research produces, researchers can reject or modify that theory or principle accordingly. This should lead to a better theory, on the basis of which it is more appropriate to generalize.

## INFERRING CAUSAL RELATIONSHIPS FROM EXPERIMENTAL RESEARCH

### Lessons From the Social Psychology of Causal Inference

Research in social psychology often involves the assumption that, as they go about their daily lives, people act like intuitive or naive scientists (e.g., Kelley, 1967). In contrast, our present focus is on providing guidance for *actual* scientists. As it happens, though, some of the mistakes that can be made in drawing causal inference from research are precisely those that confront decision makers and reasoners in everyday life. It is therefore possible to "mine" the psychological literature on causal inference to identify problems that people run into as practicing researchers.

## Detecting Covariation

In both cognitive and social psychology, the primary focus in the literature on inference has been on the detection of covariation (Cheng, 1997; Kelley, 1967; van Overwalle, 1998; see McGarty, 1999, for a review). This is because one thing cannot be the cause of another unless it covaries with it. Indeed, although correlation does not imply causation, causation does imply reasonably strong correlations (except in the case of statistical suppression; see below). This simple idea lies at the heart of path analysis, structural equation modeling, statistical mediation, and the use of latent variables in factor analysis, and we can use this same idea in considering the role of cause in social psychological experiments. Just as an inability to detect covariation accurately will have some consequence for our understanding of events in our everyday lives, so the inability to detect covariation accurately in research undermines scientific understanding.

It is possible for research to qualify this link between causation and correlation in three important ways. First, a cause must occur before its consequences—the assumption of *causal order*. One of the attractions of the experimental method is that it can allow us to guarantee the order of our variables: Manipulated IVs are never caused by DVs (although this is not to say that the measurement of our DVs never changes the meaning that our experimental manipulations have for our participants).

Second, we must be able to identify the presence of the covarying factors. We cannot plausibly claim that two variables covary unless we can identify precisely if and when each of the variables occurs. Indeed, this is why experiments use manipulation checks—to tell us that a putative causal variable is present. We must also be able to distinguish each variable from other variables. This is why we have spent so much space addressing issues of extraneous variables, confounds, and interaction effects.

The third qualification is that we need to be sure that the causal relationship actually holds. As we have already seen, we can quantify our confidence through the use of appropriate statistics and reduce uncertainty about relationships by replicating our experimental procedures.

## Beyond Covariation

We noted that the primary focus of research on causal inference is on covariation detection, *but is it enough to say that factors covary?* Precisely because correlation does not imply causation, a mere statement about covariation is unlikely to provide a wholly satisfactory explanation. Ahn, Kalish, Medin, and Gelman (1995) have shown this in the causal inference literature. When people are offered explanations that fail to go beyond covariation, they usually are left dissatisfied. Ahn et al.'s participants considered simple interpersonal events of the form "Harry hit Jack" and were then given the opportunity to request further information. They generally requested information of the form "Is Harry aggressive?" or "Does Harry dislike Jack?" rather than covariational information of the form "Does Harry hit other people?" or "Has Harry hit Jack before?"

This suggests that people want explanations that go beyond covariation and that point to underlying factors or processes. The producers and consumers of social psychological and other research have the same preference for genuine explanation rather than mere description. Moreover, the charge that the demonstration of some relationship is "merely descriptive" (or redescriptive) is one that can apply equally well to experimental and other methods. When we show the effect of an IV on a DV, we may be confident that the former has had an effect but still be left wondering about the process that produced the effect. We can know *what* happened but not *how* and *why*.

As an example of the difficulty of disentangling explanation and description, we can return to our earlier study in which a researcher observes a relationship between personality and prejudice and goes on to hypothesize that individuals display prejudice toward members of other groups because those individuals have a dysfunctional personality. In this case, to demonstrate that their personality *led* those individuals to be prejudiced is no easy thing. In particular, it *cannot* be established merely by demonstrating *that* they were prejudiced and *that* their personality is of a certain type. Indeed, it could not even be demonstrated by showing that *all* people with a certain personality are prejudiced and that *all* people with a different personality are unprejudiced (i.e., that personality type is completely correlated with hostility). In this example, our data may reflect a plethora of other causal relations, including ones in which the causal sequence is *reversed* (e.g., the possibility that prejudiced people develop particular personalities) or those in which an association is produced by a *third factor* or *tertiam quid* (e.g., the possibility that personality and prejudice are both products of cultural background or social norms).

## Mediational Analysis

The desire to answer "why" questions rather than only "what" questions partly explains why theory plays such an important role in science. It also explains why the idea of statistical *mediation*, a set of methods for identifying causal mechanisms, enjoys such popularity in the field. The topic is covered elsewhere in this handbook (see Hoyle & Robinson, Chapter 10, this volume), but it is important to make a number of basic points here.

### The Logic of Mediation

The idea that causation implies correlation lies at the center of efforts to demonstrate mediation. Essentially, if some third variable—the *mediator, mediating variable*, or *MV*—captures the mechanism that links an IV to a DV, there should be some overlap between this MV and the IV in the prediction of the DV. For this reason, when the MV is entered into a regression equation, there should be a reduction in the strength of the relationship between the IV and DV as well as evidence of a clear relationship between the MV and the DV (Baron & Kenny, 1986).

Experiments in social psychological now commonly examine mediational relationships by entering some hypothetical measure of the mechanism into a regression equation. As testament to this, Baron and Kenny's (1986) article on mediation has been cited more than 3,000 times in the last 10 years, and a high proportion of these citations are in social psychology.

### Problems of Interpretation

Although the conditions specified by Baron and Kenny (1986) are consistent with the existence of mediation, there are a number of problems associated with attempts to interpret the results of mediational analysis. First, the conditions are also consistent with a range of conditions where mediation does not hold. If the IV, MV, and DV are all affected by some fourth variable, then relationships that are spuriously consistent with mediation may be demonstrated. This possibility normally can be discounted by experimental manipulation of the IV, so we will not discuss it further here. However, if the MV is merely a good measure of the IV (akin to a manipulation check), rather than a measure of a process created by the IV, then there is a good chance that something that *looks like* mediation (but is actually *pseudo-mediation*) will be demonstrated.

More alarmingly, there are conditions under which mediation should hold but the conditions specified by Baron and Kenny (1986) will not reveal it. In particular, if some other variable suppresses the relationship between the IV and MV, then there will be no evidence of mediation unless this other variable is measured in the study and entered into the regression equation. Imagine, for example, that low self-esteem (IV) is hypothesized to create frustration (MV), which in turn creates aggression (DV). If participants vary greatly on some variable that acts as a suppressor variable in that context (e.g., power or emotional expressivity), then any relation between the variables may be masked in that setting. For example, differences in power might mask the relationship between the IV and DV, and differences in emotional expressivity may mask relationships that involve the MV.

These observations suggest that mediational techniques can be useful tools with which to augment one's analysis of designed experiments. However, contrary to popular opinion, they are not an elixir, capable of magically revealing latent process variables. They do not allow definitive statements about causal relationships, and—to their credit—the experts who have popularized these methods have never claimed otherwise (for cautionary notes, see also Sigall & Mills, 1998).

## CONCLUSION

Elaborating on the arguments in previous sections, we conclude this chapter by reflecting on the question of whether or not the primary achievement of the experiment—the ability to make causal statements on the basis of control—is its ultimate downfall. Is it the case, as critics sometimes argue, that an obsession with control of IVs turns social

reality into science fiction? Are laboratory experiments distorted caricatures of the external world that can offer only pallid and trivial understanding of the rich phenomena they seek to investigate?

In responding to such questions, it is worth noting that there is little or no research to suggest that psychological processes and the impact of psychological states necessarily differ between experiments and the so-called real world. This is for the simple reason that experimental settings—even those of the laboratory—are still a part of that real world. Effects produced in experiments therefore can be reproduced in the real world, and real world phenomena can be reproduced in experiments. As Turner (1981) put it, there is no Great Wall of China between the two.

Indeed, it is possible to turn arguments about the irrelevance of psychological experiments on their head. In most sciences, experiments are used to create ideal circumstances that would not otherwise occur in real life. In psychology too, experiments are useful *precisely because* they control for the influence of extraneous variables that cloud the analysis of everyday behavior.

Looked at in this way, where there is a problem with generalizing from experimental research to the real world, it will often arise not from the fact that the research is invalid but from the fact that it is *irrelevant*. One of the main problems with experimental research is thus that researchers may be led to examine the impact of particular variables *because they can*, rather than because they *should*. For example, although social psychology is frequently defined as the science of social interaction, the proportion of social psychological studies that actually involve social interaction has declined dramatically over the last 30 years (from about 60% of articles in the *Journal of Personality and Social Psychology* in 1968 to around 20% in 1998) (Haslam & McGarty, 2001; see also Haslam & Reicher, 2002).

Presumably, this is because studies that involve social interaction are harder to conduct, to analyze, and to publish (e.g., see Gonzalez & Griffin, Chapter 14, this volume). But if topics are studied only because they are easy to investigate or because their findings are easy to publish, it will often be the research *questions* that are at fault and not the *conclusions*.

Along these lines, in a recent review of the use of the experimental method in 100 years of social psychological research, we followed Tajfel (1972) in concluding that:

> It is not the case that experiments per se are bad or good, trivial or non-trivial. As with any other method, the quality and utility of

experiments is always constrained by the quality and utility of the ideas and theories they test. A trivial idea makes for a trivial experiment. But experiments can test powerful ideas and they can also be tools of revolutionary science. The more willing we are to put them to this use the more likely it is that we will rediscover and share in a science that is dynamic and challenging. (Haslam & McGarty, 2001, p. 18)

To the extent that social psychology falls short of its scientific goals, it is therefore not our experimental tools we should blame. By the same token, these tools should not, on their own, be seen as sufficient for our discipline's progress.

## NOTE

1. Note that Sigall and Mills (1998) contested this claim and argued that there are many examples of experimental findings for which there is no plausible alternative explanation. They provide one example—research by Zajonc (1968)—where there appears to be no alternative explanation for the effects of the conceptual variable (number of exposures to stimuli) on the DV (preference for the stimuli). We would point out, however, that the conceptual variable here actually is familiarity, not number of exposures, and it is easy to craft alternative explanations for this "mere exposure" effect. For example, one could claim that the number of exposures reduces the surprise value of the stimulus set rather than familiarity with any single stimulus.

## REFERENCES

Adorno, T. W., Frenkel-Brunswik, E., Levinson, D. J., & Sanford, R. N. (1950) *The authoritarian personality*. New York: Harper.

Ahn, W. K., Kalish, C. W., Medin, D. L, & Gelman, S. A. (1995). The role of covariation versus mechanism information in causal attribution. *Cognition, 54,* 299-352.

Aiken, L. S., & West, S. G. (1991). *Multiple regression: Testing and interpreting interactions*. Newbury Park, CA: Sage.

Altmeyer, B. (1988). *Enemies of freedom: Understanding right-wing authoritarianism*. San Francisco: Jossey-Bass.

Aronson, E., Blaney, N., Stephin, C., Sikes, J., & Snapp, M. (1978). *The jigsaw classroom*. Beverly Hills, CA: Sage.

Ashforth, B. E. (1994). Petty tyranny organizations. *Human Relations, 47,* 755-778.

Augoustinos, M., & Reynolds, K. (Eds.). (2001). *Understanding prejudice, racism and social conflict*. London: Sage.

Barber, T. X., & Silver, M. J. (1968). Fact, fiction, and the experimenter bias effect. *Psychological Bulletin, 70,* 1-29.

Baron, R. M., & Kenny, D. A. (1986). The moderator-mediator variable distinction in social psychological research: Conceptual, strategic, and statistical considerations. *Journal of Personality and Social Psychology, 51,* 602-619.

Berndsen, M., Spears, R., van der Pligt, J., & McGarty, C. (1999). Determinants of intergroup differentiation in the illusory correlation task. *British Journal of Social Psychology, 90,* 201-220.

Bless, H., Strack, F., & Schwarz, N. (1993). The informative functions of research procedures: Bias and the logic of conversation. *European Journal of Social Psychology, 23,* 149-166.

Campbell, D. T., & Stanley, J. C. (1963). *Experimental and quasi-experimental designs for research.* Chicago: Rand McNally.

Cheng, P. W. (1997). From covariation to causation: A causal power theory. *Psychological Review, 104,* 367-405.

Chow, S. L. (1995). In defence of experimental data: Data in a relativistic milieu. *New Ideas in Psychology, 13,* 259-279.

Crocker, J., & Luhtanen, R. (1990). Collective self-esteem and ingroup bias. *Journal of Personality and Social Psychology, 58,* 60-67.

Dawes, R. M. (1996). The purpose of experiments: Ecological validity versus comparing hypotheses. *Behavioural and Brain Sciences, 19,* 20.

Fishbein, M. (1997). Predicting, understanding and changing socially relevant behaviours. In C. McGarty & S. A. Haslam (Eds.), *The message of social psychology: Perspectives on mind in society* (pp. 77-91). Oxford, UK: Blackwell.

Fisher, R. A. (1926). *The design of experiments* (1st ed.). London: Oliver and Boyd.

Fiske, S. T., & Taylor, S. E. (1984). *Social cognition.* Reading, MA: Addison-Wesley.

Gergen, K. J. (1997). Social psychology as social construction: The emerging vision. In C. McGarty & S. A. Haslam (Eds.), *The message of social psychology: Perspectives on mind in society* (pp. 113-128). Oxford, UK: Blackwell.

Hamilton, D. L., & Gifford, R. K. (1976). Illusory correlation in intergroup perception: A cognitive basis of stereotypic judgments. *Journal of Experimental Social Psychology, 12,* 392-407.

Haslam, S. A., & McGarty, C. (1998). *Doing psychology: An introduction to research methodology and statistics.* London: Sage.

Haslam, S. A., & McGarty, C. (2001). A hundred years of certitude? Social psychology, the experimental method and the management of scientific uncertainty. *British Journal of Social Psychology, 40,* 1-21.

Haslam, S. A., & McGarty, C. (in press). *Doing research in psychology: Understanding methods and statistics.* London: Sage.

Haslam, S. A., McGarty, C., & Brown, P. (1996). The search for differentiated meaning is a precursor to illusory correlation. *Personality and Social Psychology Bulletin, 22,* 611-619.

Haslam, S. A., & Reicher, S. (2002). *A user's guide to "The Experiment"— Exploring the psychology of groups and power: Manual to accompany the BBC video.* London: BBC Worldwide.

Haslam, S. A., Turner, J. C., Oakes, P. J., McGarty, C., & Reynolds, K. J. (1998). The group as a basis for emergent stereotype consensus. *European Review of Social Psychology, 9,* 203-239.

Haslam, S. A., & Wilson, A. (2000). Is prejudice really personal? The contribution of a group's shared stereotypes to intergroup prejudice. *British Journal of Social Psychology, 39,* 45-63.

Hogg, M. A., & Abrams, D. (1990). Social motivation, self-esteem and social identity. In D. Abrams & M. A. Hogg (Eds.), *Social identity theory: Constructive and critical advances* (pp. 28-47). London: Harvester Wheatsheaf.

Hogg, M. A., & Sunderland, J. (1991). Self-esteem and intergroup discrimination in the minimal group paradigm. *British Journal of Social Psychology, 30,* 51-62.

Hunter, J. A., Platow, M. J., Bell, L. M., Kypri, K., & Lewis, C. A. (1997). Intergroup bias and self-evaluation: Domain-specific self-esteem, threats to identity and dimensional importance. *British Journal of Social Psychology, 36,* 405-426.

Israel, J., & Tajfel, H. (Eds.). (1972). *The context of social psychology: A critical assessment.* London: Academic Press.

Jost, J. T., & Elsbach, K. D. (2001). How status and power differences erode personal and social identities at work: A system justification critique of organizational applications of social identity theory. In M. A. Hogg & D. J. Terry (Eds.), *Social identity processes in organizational contexts* (pp. 181-196). Philadelphia: Psychology Press.

Kelley, H. H. (1967). Attribution theory in social psychology. In D. Levine (Ed.), *Nebraska Symposium on Motivation* (Vol. 15, pp. 192-238). Lincoln: University of Nebraska Press.

LaPiere, R. T. (1934). Attitudes vs. actions. *Social Forces, 13,* 230-237.

Leaf, R. C. (1993). Control, volition and the experimental method. *New Ideas in Psychology, 11,* 3-33.

Long, K., & Spears, R. (1997). The self-esteem hypothesis revisited: Differentiation and the disaffected. In R. Spears, P. J. Oakes, N. Ellemers, & S. A. Haslam (Eds.), *The social psychology of stereotyping and group life* (pp. 296-317). Oxford, UK: Blackwell.

McConahay, J. B., Hardee, B. B., & Batts, V. (1981). Has racism declined in America? It depends on who is asking and what is being asked. *Journal of Conflict Resolution, 25,* 563-579.

McGarty, C. (1999). *The categorization process in social psychology.* London: Sage.

McGarty, C. (2001). Social identity theory does not maintain that identification produces bias and self-categorization theory does not maintain that salience is identification. *British Journal of Social Psychology, 40,* 173-176.

McGarty, C., & de la Haye, A. (1997). Stereotype formation: Beyond illusory correlation. In R. Spears, P. J. Oakes, N. Ellemers, & S. A. Haslam (Eds.), *The social psychology of stereotyping and group life* (pp. 145-170). Oxford, UK: Blackwell.

McGarty, C., & Haslam, S. A. (Eds.). (1997). *The message of social psychology: Perspectives on mind in society.* Oxford, UK: Blackwell.

McGarty, C., Turner, J. C., Hogg, M. A., Davidson, B., & Wetherell, M. S. (1992). Group polarization as conformity to the most prototypical group member. *British Journal of Social Psychology, 31,* 1-20.

Meers, A., Maassen, A., & Verhaagen, P. (1994). Subjective health after six months and after four years of shift work. *Ergonomics, 21,* 857-859.

Meindl, J. R. (1993). Reinventing leadership: A radical, social psychological approach. In J. K. Murnigham (Ed.), *Social psychology in organizations: Advances in theory and research* (pp. 89-118). Englewood Cliffs, NJ: Prentice Hall.

Mook, D. G. (1980). In defense of external invalidity. *American Psychologist, 38,* 379-388.

Moscovici, S., & Zavalloni, M. (1969). The group as a polarizer of attitudes. *Journal of Personality and Social Psychology, 12,* 125-135.

Ni Bhrolchain, M. (2001). "Divorce effects" and causality in the social sciences. *European Sociological Review, 17,* 33-57.

Oakes, P. J., & Turner, J. C. (1980). Social categorization and intergroup behaviour: Does minimal intergroup discrimination make social identity more positive? *European Journal of Social Psychology, 10,* 295-301.

Orne, M. (1962). On the social psychology of the psychological experiment with particular reference to demand characteristics and their implications. *American Psychologist, 17,* 776-783.

Petty, R. (1997). The evolution of theory and research in social psychology: From single to multiple effect and process models of persuasion In C. McGarty & S. A. Haslam (Eds.), *The message of social psychology: Perspectives on mind in society* (pp. 268-290). Oxford, UK: Blackwell.

Prentice, D. A., & Miller, D. T. (1992). When small effects are impressive. *Psychological Bulletin, 112,* 160-164.

Reicher, S. D. (2001). Studying psychology studying racism. In M. Augoustinos & K. Reynolds (Eds.), *Social psychological approaches to prejudice and racism* (pp. 273-298). London: Sage.

Rosenberg, M. (1965). *Society and the adolescent self-image.* Princeton, NJ: Princeton University Press.

Rosenthal, R. (1966). *Experimenter effects in behavioral research.* New York: Appleton-Century-Crofts.

Sigall, H., & Mills, J. (1998). Measures of independent variables are useful in social psychology experiments but are they necessary? *Personality and Social Psychology Review, 2,* 218-226.

Smith, E. R. (1991). Illusory correlation in a simulated exemplar-based memory. *Journal of Experimental Social Psychology, 27,* 107-123.

Sohn, D. (1992). Knowledge in psychological science: That of process or population? *Journal of Psychology, 126,* 5-16.

Spears, R., & Smith, H. J. (2001). Experiments as politics. *Political Psychology, 22,* 309-330.

Stoner, J.A.F. (1961). *A comparison of individual and group dimensions involving risk.* Unpublished mater's thesis, School of Industrial Management, Massachusetts Institute of Technology.

Tajfel, H. (1972). Experiments in a vacuum. In J. Israel & H. Tajfel (Eds.), *The context of social psychology: A critical assessment* (pp. 69-119). London: Academic Press.

Tajfel, H., Flament, C., Billig, M. G., & Bundy, R. F. (1971). Social categorization and intergroup behaviour. *European Journal of Social Psychology, 1,* 149-177.

Tajfel, H., & Fraser, C. (1978). Social psychology as social science. In H. Tajfel & C. Fraser (Eds.), *Introducing social psychology: An analysis of individual reaction and response* (pp. 21-53). Harmondsworth, UK: Penguin.

Tajfel, H., & Turner, J. C. (1979). An integrative theory of intergroup conflict. In W. G. Austin & S. Worchel (Eds.), *The social psychology of intergroup relations* (pp. 33-47). Monterey, CA: Brooks/Cole.

Turner, J. C. (1981). Some considerations in generalizing experimental social psychology. In G. M. Stephenson & J. H. Davis (Eds.), *Progress in applied social psychology* (Vol. 1, pp. 3-34). Chichester, UK: Wiley.

Turner, J. C. (1999). Some current themes in research on social identity and self-categorization theories. In N. Ellemers, R. Spears, & B. Doosje (Eds.), *Social identity: Context, commitment, content* (pp. 6-34). Oxford, UK: Blackwell.

van Overwalle, F. (1998). Causal explanation as constraint satisfaction: A critique and a feedforward alternative. *Journal of Personality and Social Psychology, 74,* 312-328.

Vissers, G., Heyne, G., Peters, V., & Guerts, J. (2001). The validity of laboratory research in social and behavioral science. *Quality and Quantity, 35,* 129-145.

Walker, I. (2001). The changing nature of racism: From "old" to "new." In M. Augoustinos & K. Reynolds (Eds.), *Social psychological approaches to prejudice and racism* (pp. 24-42). London: Sage.

West, S. G., Newsom, J. T., & Fenaughty, A. M. (1992). Publication trends in the *Journal of Personality and Social Psychology*: Stability and change in topics, methods, and theories across two decades. *Personality and Social Psychology Bulletin, 18,* 473-484.

Zajonc, R. B. (1968). Attitudinal effects of mere exposure. *Journal of Personality and Social Psychology, 9*(Monograph Suppl. 2, Pt. 2).

## CHAPTER 12

# Quasi-Experimental and Correlational Designs
## Methods for the Real World When Random Assignment Isn't Feasible

MELVIN M. MARK

*The Pennsylvania State University*

CHARLES S. REICHARDT

*University of Denver*

Is hindsight, as the expression would have us believe, really 20/20? How much do "rose-colored glasses" impair one's vision? Can there be "power to the people" when individuals in a community band together to act collectively?

For causal questions such as these, randomized experiments are perhaps the most widely used, and best, kind of research design. In the classic randomized experiment, individuals are randomly assigned to one of two (or more) conditions (see Haslam & McGarty, Chapter 11, this volume). For example, imagine a social psychologist with the hypothesis that positive mood works like "rose-colored glasses" to prevent people from seeing the unflattering characteristics of a generally likable person. To test this hypothesis, a researcher might randomly assign participants to receive either a positive or a negative mood induction, and then compare the participants' ratings of a fictitious target person presented on video. The primary advantage of randomized experiments is that they support credible causal conclusions more reliably than do other research designs.

Nonetheless, researchers would be at a relative disadvantage if they did not have other design options in their methodological toolkits. Alternative designs are useful for at least four reasons. First, randomized experiments are not always feasible. For instance, it is probably not practical to study the effects of community activist groups with a randomized experiment. Second, for at least some research questions, even if random assignment is feasible, it may be possible only in special circumstances; yet, it may be important to see what happens in circumstances where random assignment is infeasible. For example, researchers can manipulate mood using a randomized experiment in the laboratory, but researchers might want to know if similar findings occur in everyday settings, with natural mood inductions, without the trappings of an artificial research laboratory. Third, ethical considerations may preclude random assignment. For example, ethics might prohibit random assignment to a treatment condition that imposes an emotionally forceful negative event to assess its effects on hindsight. Fourth, the questions that interest social psychologists are not always causal in nature. For example, questions about personality characteristics can be either causal or correlational.

In this chapter, we describe alternative research designs that can circumvent the limitations of randomized experiments. We do so by illustrating how we have used these designs to address the questions listed at the start of the chapter. Our presentation focuses primarily on quasi-experimental designs, but we also consider correlational designs.

## QUASI-EXPERIMENTAL DESIGNS: AN OVERVIEW

The development of the theory, methods, and nomenclature of quasi-experimentation owes much to the work of Donald T. Campbell and his associates (Campbell & Stanley, 1966; Cook & Campbell, 1979; Shadish, Cook, & Campbell, 2002). "Quasi" is Latin and means "as if," "like," or "an approximation." Thus, a quasi-experiment is an approximation of an experiment, a "near experiment." Like randomized experiments, quasi-experiments are used to estimate the effects of one or more treatments on one or more outcome variables. The difference is that quasi-experiments don't have random assignment to treatment conditions. In quasi-experimental designs, the prospective causal variable typically is called the "treatment" or "intervention," and the potential effect is often called the "outcome."

## A Counterfactual Conception of Causality

Quasi-experiments are intended to probe causal relations. Thus, to understand them, it is useful to understand what is meant by causality. The literature on causality is complex and vast. Fortunately, even a general appreciation of this literature can enhance understanding of the theory and practice of quasi-experimentation (also see West, Biesanz, & Kwok, Chapter 13, this volume).

Probably the most common conception of causality in the social sciences is based on the counterfactual definition of a causal effect. According to the counterfactual definition, the effect of a treatment—as compared to an alternative treatment or a no-treatment control—is the difference between (a) the outcome that occurred after the treatment was administered, to one or more participants in a given context; and (b) the outcome that *would have occurred* if, instead, an alternative treatment or no treatment had been administered to the same participants in the same context. As an example, take the question of whether positive mood acts like "rose-colored glasses" and keeps people from seeing a target's negative attributes. In part, addressing this causal question would require us to observe a set of participants who, after a positive mood induction, are asked to rate the target person. Counterfactually, what we would really like to do would be to observe the very same participants, exposed to the alternative treatment (a neutral or negative mood induction), but at the same time and in the same context as we observed them in the positive mood condition. Such a difference is called the ideal comparison.

Although it defines what is meant by a treatment effect, the ideal comparison cannot be attained in practice. The ideal comparison is impossible because it requires implementing two mutually exclusive treatments on the same people at the same time. The research designs we use can only approximate the ideal but unattainable comparison. Sometimes the comparison a research design uses is a good approximation to the ideal comparison. Other times it is not. The validity of the results of a study depends on how good an approximation the research design is to the ideal but impossible counterfactual comparison.

The counterfactual definition of the effect of a cause is central to thinking about causality. Two additional considerations also are important. One is the acknowledgment that there are real mechanisms that underlie cause-and-effect relationships. That is, processes exist that mediate the relationship between treatment and outcome variables. Contemporary concern about underlying mechanisms is reflected in the growing attention to structural equation modeling and other techniques that can be used to test the contribution of hypothesized mediators (see Hoyle & Robinson, Chapter 10, this volume). A second important consideration is the recognition that causal relationships are contingent. That is, the effect of a treatment can vary substantially, depending upon such factors as the characteristics of the person who receives the treatment and the nature of the settings in which the treatment is implemented (House, 2001). Increased appreciation of the often complex, contingent nature of causal relations is reflected in increased attention in research to moderators, that is, to variables that modify the strength and perhaps the direction of an effect. It is also reflected in the growing interest in meta-analysis (Wood & Christensen, Chapter 15, this volume), which allows investigators both to look for moderators that vary across studies and to search for relatively robust effects that hold across the persons and settings in individual studies. Although mediators, moderators, and meta-analysis are important, these topics receive little attention in the present chapter. Instead, our focus is on the comparisons used in various quasi-experimental and correlational designs, and on the extent to which such comparisons are good approximations to the ideal but unattainable counterfactual comparison—or, in other words, on the extent to which the designs are strong or weak with respect to internal validity (Reichardt & Mark, 1998; Shadish et al., 2002).

## From the Concept of Causality to Kinds of Comparisons

As the idea of "counterfactual" implies, the process of drawing a causal inference is inherently comparative. Thinking counterfactually, one would like to compare the outcome that occurred following a treatment with the outcome that *would have occurred* if the treatment had not been implemented (or an alternative treatment had been implemented). Of course, in the absence of time travel, one cannot obtain this counterfactual comparison on the same people in the same setting at the same time. Something else has to differ. For example, one can compare different people, some exposed to the treatment and some not, at the same time.

Although other forms of comparison are possible (Mark, 1986; Reichardt, 2000), the most common quasi-experimental designs involve comparisons either *across times* or *across different groups of individuals*. In the following sections, we describe each of these types of quasi-experimental designs and illustrate them with studies we have conducted.

## COMPARISONS ACROSS TIME

*Can there be "power to the people" when individuals in a community band together to act collectively?* Steiner and Mark (1985) were interested in whether and to what extent community-based activist groups are effective. Rather than attempt to simulate an activist group in the laboratory, Steiner and Mark examined a community action group that protested a bank's announced plan to increase the mortgage interest rates for a subset of its customers. In addition to a variety of other actions, the community action group organized a "mass withdrawal," encouraging people to stop doing business with the bank. This provided an opportunity to address a question rarely studied in the literature on community organizations: How effective are such groups' actions?

## The One-Group, Pretest-Posttest Design

Let us imagine that Steiner and Mark compared (a) the average monthly passbook savings account holdings at the bank during the month before the mass withdrawal with (b) the average holdings in the month after. Such a comparison is called a one-group, pretest-posttest design. This design can be represented schematically as

$$O \; X \; O$$

where X represents the treatment, O represents the outcome variable (or "an observation"), and time passes from left to right (e.g., the first observation—that is, the pretest—takes place before the treatment is implemented). If Steiner and Mark had used this design, they would have found a decline in the balance of savings accounts, with this total declining roughly 10% from the month before the group's action to the month after. How confident could Steiner and Mark have been that this drop was due to the actions of the community action group?

A number of "threats to internal validity" make it difficult to conclude that the activities of the community group caused the decline in the bank's holdings. *Internal validity* refers to the extent to which accurate

conclusions can be drawn about whether and to what degree the treatment-as-manipulated makes a difference in the outcome-as measured (Shadish et al., 2002). *Threats* to internal validity refer to categories of factors that can lead to inaccurate conclusions about this causal relationship. One important threat to internal validity, *history*, refers to the possibility that specific events, other than the treatment, occurred between the pretest and the posttest and caused a change in the outcome of interest. For example, if the community's major employer had laid off its workers at the same time as the community action group staged its mass withdrawal, the decline in the bank's savings account holdings could have been the result of the layoff rather than the community group's actions.

Other validity threats also could have posed problems if Steiner and Mark had used the one-group, pretest-posttest design. *Maturation* refers to the possibility that naturally occurring processes that arise over time within participants, could affect the outcome variable. In a long study, maturation includes changes associated with growing older, such as getting smarter or having fewer behavior problems. In shorter studies, maturation can refer to changes such as becoming more tired or getting hungrier. In some cases, maturation includes long-term trends in a community or other population. In the context of the study of community action groups, maturation includes the possibility that there was a relatively steady, long-term decline in total savings at the bank, perhaps due to a long-term decline in people's saving patterns. Another threat to internal validity, sometimes described as a special case of maturation, is *seasonality*. This refers to the possibility that change in an outcome variable is the result of regular seasonal patterns. For example, savings can fluctuate from month to month because of gift buying during winter holidays or because of vacation spending during the summer. *Regression toward the mean* is also a potential threat to validity; it refers to the possibility that change in the outcome variable occurs because the pretest level was unusually high or low and the outcome variable simply returned to a more "normal" level at the posttest.

Three other validity threats apply in general to the one-group, pretest-posttest design, but do not seem plausible in the simplified pretest-posttest version of the Steiner and Mark study. *Testing* refers to the possibility that the very act of measurement at the pretest causes a change in the outcome variable at the posttest. For example, in a one-group, pretest-posttest study of the effects of an SAT preparation course, testing would be a problem if students scored higher on the posttest simply because the pretest familiarized them with the test format. *Instrumentation* refers to the possibility that a change in the measuring instrument is responsible for an apparent effect. Instrumentation effects can arise from changes in the definition of an outcome variable or in the measurement procedures. *Attrition* occurs when participants drop out of the study. This change in the sample can bias the estimate of the treatment effect.

Although the one-group, pretest-posttest design is often easy to implement in practice, it is also commonly subject to one or more of the preceding threats to internal validity. Out of the long list of validity threats that can plague this design—history, maturation, seasonality, regression toward the mean, testing, instrumentation, and attrition—one or more often is sufficiently plausible that confident conclusions about the effect of the treatment cannot be drawn. In the one-group, pretest-posttest design, the pretest stands in for the ideal counterfactual (i.e., what would have happened if the treatment had not occurred), but, for a variety of reasons—summarized in the long list of internal validity threats above—the pretest often does not provide a good approximation to the desired counterfactual outcome. Accordingly, Steiner and

Mark chose not to use this simple design. However, in special circumstances the context in which the design is implemented may make the various threats to validity implausible (see, e.g., Eckert, 2000), or supplementary information, apart from the research design, may render the validity threats implausible and thus allow confident conclusions. We return to such possibilities in a later section. In general, however, the one-group, pretest-posttest design seldom is adequate for testing hypotheses in social psychology. But more complex designs involving comparisons across times can sometimes suffice. Such designs are described next.

### Interrupted Time-Series Designs

Instead of the one-group pretest-posttest design, Steiner and Mark (1985) used the simple interrupted time-series (ITS) design in their study of the effectiveness of the community action group. ITS designs extend the one-group, pretest-posttest design, which uses a single pretest and a single posttest observation, by adding observations both before and after the treatment. Using the same notation as earlier, the simple ITS design can be symbolized as

$$O\ O\ O\ O\ O\ O\ X\ O\ O\ O\ O\ O\ O.$$

Figure 12.1 presents a subset of the data from Steiner and Mark. The community action group called for the mass withdrawal campaign to begin in July, 1999, which is labeled Month 35 and denoted by a vertical line in the figure. The trend in savings balances before the campaign is upward, as indicated by the regression line drawn through the pretreatment observations. The trend in savings balances after the campaign started is relatively flat, and there is a sharp drop right at Month 35. These shifts in the regression lines suggest that the mass withdrawal campaign was effective in reducing savings

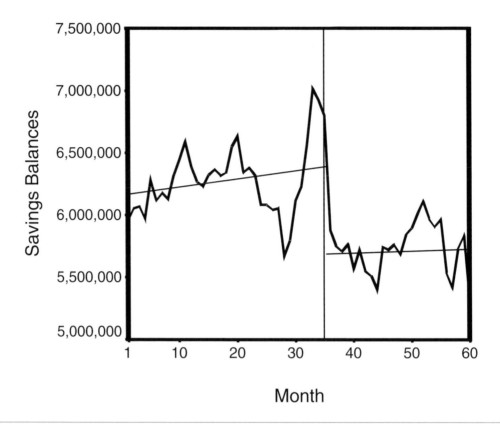

Figure 12.1

balances, both immediately and increasingly over time.

The ITS design helps rule out several of the validity threats that plague the one-group, pretest-posttest design. For example, maturation often is a plausible threat in the one-group, pretest-posttest design. In the ITS design, in contrast, the effect of maturation (e.g., a general upward or downward trend in the observations) can be identified and taken into account. Maturation usually should be evident as an ongoing upward or downward trend, and a treatment effect appears as a rise or fall *relative to* the maturational trend. Similarly, regression toward the mean is often plausible in the one-group, pretest-posttest design but can be assessed (and, therefore, ruled out) in an ITS design;

an abnormally high or low observation shortly before the treatment will appear deviant relative to the other pretest observations. The threat of testing also is generally controlled for in the ITS design. With repeated observations prior to the treatment, it is usually implausible that a sizable testing effect would coincide with the intervention.

On the other hand, the simple ITS design does not rule out all threats to internal validity. For example, history is often plausible. In fact, history effects are as likely in the simple ITS design as in the one-group, pretest-posttest design, *if* the time interval between observations is the same. However, time-series designs often have shorter intervals between observations, making history effects less likely. Instrumentation also can threaten the simple

ITS design. In some cases, the introduction of a treatment is associated with a change in the way observations are defined or recorded. This is common, for example, in ITS studies of the impact of legal changes, where a law that changes the punishment for a crime also changes the definition of the crime (e.g., Marsh, 1985). The threats of history and instrumentation sometimes can be addressed by careful analysis of the historical record and record-keeping procedures, respectively. For example, Steiner and Mark (1985) consulted bank officials to assess whether there had been changes in record keeping at the time of the community group's actions. Similarly, they looked for general changes in the local economy and asked bank officials and community members about historical events that might have caused a downturn in savings. They found no evidence of such changes. Rather than relying solely on such detective work, researchers often attempt to control history by using a more complex ITS design, most often by adding a control group.

*Interrupted Time-Series
Designs With a Control Group*

One way to address threats to the validity of the simple ITS design is to add time-series observations from a group of respondents who were not exposed to the treatment. Schematically, the design appears as

$$\frac{O\ O\ O\ O\ O\ O\ X\ O\ O\ O\ O\ O\ O}{O\ O\ O\ O\ O\ O\ \ \ O\ O\ O\ O\ O\ O}.$$

The top line represents time-series data from a group of participants who were exposed to the treatment, and the bottom line represents time-series data from a comparison group that did not receive the treatment. The dashed line is used to show that these two groups are nonequivalent (i.e., not created by random assignment). For example, Steiner and Mark (1985) could have examined savings

account data over time from a bank in a nearby community that was not subject to the community action group's activities. In general, adding a control group to the simple ITS design helps to control for history threats. For example, if an overall decline in the economy had been responsible for the drop in savings that Steiner and Mark observed, a similar effect should have occurred in the savings account holdings at a bank in a nearby community. In this case, however, there would have been a problem using a control time series from a nearby bank if people moved their savings from the targeted bank to the neighboring bank. (We return to the idea of a control group in the more general discussion of between-group designs below.)

Comparisons other than a control group can be added to the simple ITS design, to try to reduce the plausibility of problems of history and instrumentation. One design option is known in the time-series literature as the ITS with removed treatment design. For instance, if the community action group in the Steiner and Mark example had called off its actions and encouraged people to return their savings to the bank in question, the researchers could have assessed whether bank holdings went back up. History and instrumentation usually cannot explain such occurrences as both a decrease in savings account balances at the start of the mass withdrawal campaign and a subsequent increase after the campaign ends, so they become less plausible as threats to validity. In another complex design, the ITS with nonequivalent dependent measures design, two different outcome variables are measured in time-series form. One outcome measure is expected to be influenced by the treatment, while the other is not; but both should be affected by the same validity threats. If the first outcome changes and the second does not, threats to validity (which should have the same effects in the two time series) become less plausible. For example, if the community action group had targeted savings accounts but not checking accounts, Steiner and Mark could have used checking account data as a nonequivalent dependent variable.

### Analysis of Interrupted Time-Series Designs

The statistical analysis of ITS designs is more complicated than the analysis of traditional experimental designs. The primary difficulty with time-series observations is that data points adjacent in time are more likely to be similar than data points more distant in time. This phenomenon, called autocorrelation, can lead to erroneous conclusions from traditional hypothesis tests and confidence intervals. Several strategies can be used to deal with autocorrelation. For longer time series, perhaps the most common approach involves the use of autoregressive integrated moving average (ARIMA) models. In essence, the ARIMA approach calls for an empirical determination of the nature of the autocorrelation, which allows statistical procedures to adjust for the problems that autocorrelation introduces. Additional methods of analysis are available for shorter time series (see, e.g., Mark, Reichardt, & Sanna, 2000).

## COMPARISONS ACROSS GROUPS

*Is hindsight 20/20?* Hindsight bias refers to the tendency for people, once the outcome of any event is known, to overestimate how predictable the outcome was in foresight. In other words, hindsight bias leads people to believe that they "knew all along" that things would turn out as they did. Although hindsight bias has been demonstrated in a wide range of circumstances, Mark and Mellor (1991) speculated that self-serving biases should reduce or eliminate the hindsight bias under certain conditions. In particular, when people directly experience a negative outcome

for which they feel responsible (or feel responsible for not preparing for), they may conclude that it was not foreseeable. If the negative outcome were so darned foreseeable, why wouldn't they have avoided it or at least prepared for it?!

The one-group, pretest-posttest design and the simple ITS design wouldn't be very useful in addressing Mark and Mellor's question. In those designs, the effect of the treatment is estimated by comparing the same individuals at different points in time, specifically by comparing their standing on the outcome variable before the treatment with their standing on the outcome variable after the treatment. Mark and Mellor's research question called instead for comparing different groups of individuals who were subjected to different treatments. That is, they needed to compare hindsight judgments from people who were negatively affected by an event and hindsight judgments from people who were not negatively affected.

### The Regression-Discontinuity Design

Although the randomized experiment often is the best design for comparing groups of individuals who receive different treatments, there are ethical concerns with randomly assigning people to a truly negative and self-relevant treatment—the kind of treatment presumably most likely to eliminate hindsight bias. Fortunately, reflecting the opportunism that often characterizes good quasi-experimental research, Mark and Mellor found a natural event that allowed them to use a relatively strong alternative: the quasi-experimental, between-groups design known as the regression-discontinuity design.

The regression-discontinuity design uses a very different approach to assignment to treatment conditions from the randomized experiment. The regression-discontinuity design requires that participants be measured, prior to the treatment, on a special form of pretest that we call the quantitative assignment variable, or QAV (Reichardt & Mark, 1998). The QAV is used to assign participants to conditions based on a specified cutoff value. Those who score above the cutoff value are assigned to one condition, and those who score below the cutoff are assigned to the other condition. Participants are subsequently measured on the outcome variable, and the treatment effect is estimated as a discontinuity in the QAV-outcome relationship at the cutoff.

Mark and Mellor (1991) used the regression-discontinuity design to examine whether hindsight bias is attenuated among those who experience a severely negative and self-relevant event. They addressed this question in the context of a company that laid off a large number of workers. Whether or not a worker was laid off depended on the number of years he or she had been with the company, that is, on seniority. In other words, seniority served as the QAV: Workers could be arrayed based on the number of years of seniority, and there was a cutoff, specifically at 19 years, with individuals below the cutoff assigned to the layoff group and people above the cutoff assigned to what Mark and Mellor called the "survivor group"; that is, they were able to continue working. The cutoff in this case was chosen by the company, based on how many workers had to be laid off. The value of the regression-discontinuity design is that there is no reason to believe a priori that the cutoff would be related in any way to workers' judgments about the foreseeability of the layoff, unless being laid off affected these judgments.

Six weeks after the layoff, Mark and Mellor surveyed laid-off workers and survivors and asked them how predictable they thought the layoff was in advance. Figure 12.2 shows the results. Data from those who were laid off are plotted on the left side of the figure, and data from those who were not laid off are plotted on the right side. As the regression lines fit through the data in each

half of the figure reveal, hindsight bias (i.e., the stated predictability of the layoff) decreased in both groups as seniority increased. More importantly, there is a dramatic discontinuity in hindsight bias exactly at the cutoff (19 years of seniority). If the layoff had no effect on hindsight bias, the two regression lines should connect as one straight line. The downward shift in the regression line for the laid-off workers, compared to the regression line for the survivors, is evidence that the layoff caused a reduction in hindsight bias. The design's name, "regression-discontinuity," comes from the fact that the treatment effect is estimated by a discontinuity between the two regression lines.

A graphical representation of regression-discontinuity findings, such as Figure 12.2, highlights the source of the design's inferential strength. In general, no plausible threats to validity exist that are likely to produce a discontinuity precisely at the cutoff between the treatment conditions. However, the estimate of the treatment effect can be biased if the relationship between the QAV and the outcome variable is curvilinear but a linear relationship is fit to the data. To address this problem, curvilinearity in the data should be modeled in the analysis. In short, statistical analysis of the regression-discontinuity design typically involves predicting the outcome variable in a series of regression analyses, where the predictors are the QAV (transformed by subtracting the cutoff value, so that the treatment effect is estimated at the cutoff point), a dummy code representing condition (e.g., laid off versus survivors), and a term representing the interaction of condition and the QAV. Note that the condition variable estimates the difference between conditions that exists over and above the relationship between the QAV and the outcome. In addition, polynomials of the transformed QAV and interaction are included; if they are not significant, they are dropped out. Estimation of the polynomials serves to test

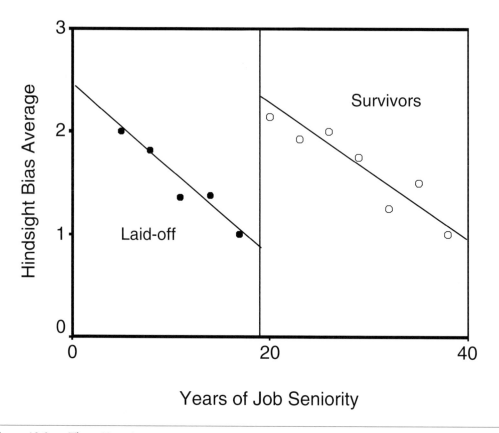

**Figure 12.2**    Three-Year Averages

for the possibility of a nonlinear relationship that could otherwise masquerade as a treatment effect. In addition, researchers who use the regression-discontinuity design should be aware that the design has substantially less power than a randomized experiment (Cappelleri, Darlington, & Trochim, 1994).

The regression-discontinuity design is among the strongest quasi-experimental designs. At its best, the design comes close to the randomized experiment in terms of allowing confident causal inferences, and it can be feasible in circumstances in which practical or ethical considerations rule out random assignment. In particular, random assignment may be unacceptable for treatments designed for those most in need (e.g., compensatory education programs) or most meritorious (e.g., promotions). If an acceptable measure of need or merit could be developed, it could serve as the QAV for the regression-discontinuity design. However, in practice, the regression-discontinuity design has rarely been used (Shadish et al., 2002; Trochim, 1984). Still, a researcher who has the regression-discontinuity design in his or her toolkit may be sensitized to look for those circumstances that fit the requirements of the design. For example, large organizations' major personnel functions, such as promotions and hiring, may meet the requirements of the regression-discontinuity design. If so, this could offer opportunities to study a variety of social psychological phenomena, including affect, coping, expectations, and hindsight, using a relatively strong quasi-experimental design in a real world setting and with a relatively powerful treatment (Mellor & Mark, 1998).

## Nonequivalent Group Designs

*How much do "rose-colored glasses" impair vision?* Drawing on previous research on the effects of mood (e.g., Schwarz & Clore, 1983), Sinclair, Mark, and Clore (1994) hypothesized (in part) that, relative to people in a bad mood, people in a good mood would attend less to the strength of the arguments in a persuasive message (and thus be more persuaded by a weak argument). Imagine that, to test this hypothesis, a researcher approaches students on a college campus on days with either notably pleasant or notably unpleasant weather. Based on the results of Schwarz and Clore (1983), the researcher presumes (and verifies with a manipulation check) that people are in a more positive mood on days with pleasant weather. The student participants are asked to listen to a brief and weakly argued message advocating comprehensive exams as a requirement for graduation. Assume that, as predicted, the participants approached on pleasant days are more persuaded by the message than participants on the unpleasant days (as would be expected, if people in a good mood are relatively inattentive to the strength of an argument).

This design is a posttest-only nonequivalent group design, shown schematically as

$$\frac{\text{X O}}{\text{O}} \ .$$

In this design, one group of participants is exposed to the treatment, while another is not (or, alternatively, is exposed to a different treatment condition). Both groups are then measured on the outcome variable. The design is a quasi-experiment because the participants are not randomly assigned to the treatment conditions. As a result, the participants in the treatment conditions are likely to be nonequivalent—hence, the name for the design.

Although this elementary quasi-experiment often is easy to implement, it usually does not provide credible conclusions. Instead, the internal validity threat of initial selection differences looms large. In the preceding example, different kinds of people may tend to be out and about on pleasant days, as opposed to unpleasant days. For example, perhaps only highly dedicated students tend to be on campus on days with bad weather (making their way to class), while less motivated students spent time hanging around campus only on nice days. In short, the two groups could differ in any of a large number of ways, and these initial differences, rather than participants' mood, could account for observed differences on the outcome variable.

A pretest measure is often added to the posttest-only nonequivalent group design to assess the size of initial selection differences and thereby to try to take account of their effects. The resulting, pretest-posttest nonequivalent group design can be depicted schematically as

$$\frac{\text{O X O}}{\text{O} \quad \text{O}} \ .$$

It would likely be difficult for the researcher in the preceding example to obtain a pretest measure, which would be an assessment of students' reactions to weak arguments on an earlier day with "neutral" weather. However, the pretest-posttest nonequivalent group design is common in many research areas. For example, it is widely used in studies of educational and clinical interventions (Lipsey & Wilson, 1993). Social psychologists can find this design used in applied research areas, addressing questions such as the degree to which educational interventions can reduce either prejudice (Signorella, Frieze, & Hershey, 1996) or susceptibility to heuristics and biases (Lehman, Lempert, & Nisbett, 1988).

In some instances, the pretest-posttest nonequivalent groups design may provide sufficient evidence to allow a tentative conclusion about the effects of a treatment variable. In general, however, the validity threats that can plague this design deserve serious consideration. Although the pretest offers some possibility of accounting for initial selection differences, in general there will always be at least some remaining uncertainty as to whether selection has been adequately controlled for. In addition to initial selection differences, the pretest-posttest nonequivalent groups design is subject to a set of validity threats such as "selection by history" and "selection by instrumentation," among others. *Selection by history*, for example, refers to the possibility that the two groups are subject to different historical forces. If so, even if the groups start out close together on the outcome variable at the pretest, they might end up further apart at the posttest simply because of differential history effects, even in the absence of any treatment effect. *Selection by instrumentation* refers to the possibility that the two conditions experience different instrumentation problems. For instance, this might happen if one observer is collecting data for the treatment condition and another observer for the control (e.g., because they are at different sites), and one observer's standards change over time but the other's don't.

### Analysis of the Pretest-Posttest Nonequivalent Group Design

A variety of statistical procedures are frequently used to estimate treatment effects in nonequivalent group designs. The task is the same in each case: to take account of the biasing effects of initial selection differences (Reichardt, 1979). The problem is that no analytic procedure is guaranteed to adjust properly for the effects of selection differences. As a result, a common recommendation is to conduct multiple analyses (that make varying assumptions about the nature of selection differences), in search of convergent results to add

confidence to the conclusions. Nonetheless, there will always be some remaining uncertainty as to whether selection has been adequately controlled for.

The simplest analytic approach is to estimate the treatment effect as the difference between the treatment groups in the mean change from pretest to posttest scores. Called either a change-score or gain-score analysis, this requires that operationally identical measures be used at the pretest and posttest. The change-score analysis assumes that the mean change in each of the treatment groups would be the same in the absence of a treatment effect. Although this assumption is reasonable under some circumstances, it can be seriously incorrect when the two groups are maturing at different rates. Even if the groups start out close together on the pretest, they can end up farther apart at the posttest simply because of differential maturation rates, even in the absence of a treatment effect. This validity threat is called selection by maturation.

Analysis of covariance (ANCOVA) is another common analytic approach. To control for the effects of selection differences, ANCOVA estimates the effect of the treatment by comparing individuals who are matched statistically on their pretest scores. The problem is that the treatment groups may have initial selection differences on variables besides the pretest, in which case the results from ANCOVA will remain biased. The solution is to include in the statistical model all the variables that affect the posttest and on which there are initial selection differences. But this raises a new problem: knowing which variables need to be included, and measuring them. Another problem with ANCOVA is that measurement error in the pretest, or in any other covariate, will bias the estimate of the treatment effect. The effects of such measurement error can be removed by using latent variable models such as in structural equation modeling (see Hoyle & Robinson, Chapter 10, this volume), though such analyses require multiple measures of each covariate.

Selection modeling is another analytic approach for estimating treatment effects in nonequivalent group designs. In essence, selection modeling fits two equations to the data. One equation models the process by which individuals were selected into treatment conditions. The second equation is a causal model of the posttest scores and includes the results from the first equation. Selection modeling is more complex statistically than the other approaches noted above. Discussions of these and related analysis strategies are provided in Winship and Morgan (1999), Reichardt and Mark (2001), and Shadish et al. (2002).

### The Pretest-Posttest Nonequivalent Group Design With Separate Pretest and Posttest Samples

In some quasi-experimental designs, the data from the pretest and posttest come from independent samples. Schematically, the design is

$$
\begin{array}{c|c}
O & X\ O \\
\hline
O & O
\end{array}.
$$

where the vertical line indicates that the pretest measure is collected on a different sample than the posttest measure. For example, Forgas and Moylan (1987) tested the effects of mood on political and other judgments by approaching people outside a movie theater showing either a comedy or a serious drama. People were asked questions either before they went in to see the movie or after. Different sets of respondents were questioned before and after the movie because the pretest measure of mood could have alerted the respondents to the types of changes that were expected. Note that although using different samples of respondents for the pretest

and posttest assessments solves some problems, it can cause others, such as introducing differences between the pretest and posttest samples. For example, people might be in more of a hurry or be more distracted on their way into a movie than on their way out, or people might refuse to participate at one time more than at the other.

### Complex Nonequivalent Group Designs

The credibility of nonequivalent group designs often can be improved by making the designs more complex. For example, Sinclair et al. (1994) used the inferentially weak posttest-only nonequivalent group design to assess the effects of mood on the persuasiveness of arguments, but they greatly enhanced the interpretability of the results by embedding the design within a more elaborate set of comparisons.

As described earlier, previous research had shown that, relative to respondents in a positive mood, those in a negative mood are more likely to attend to the content of persuasive messages. As a result, research has shown, those in a negative mood show a much larger difference, in terms of persuasion, between a weak argument and a strong argument. Sinclair et al. were interested in whether these effects of mood on persuasion resulted from affect-as-information (Schwarz & Clore, 1983), which posits that negative mood serves as a cue that the environment is dangerous, risky, or threatening, and therefore calls for careful attention. Conversely, the affect-as-information hypothesis proposes, positive mood serves as a cue that the environment is nonthreatening, a condition that elicits less detailed and careful processing.

Sinclair et al. tested this hypothesis using (in part) the posttest-only nonequivalent group design that was described previously. That is, they approached undergraduates on either notably pleasant or notably unpleasant

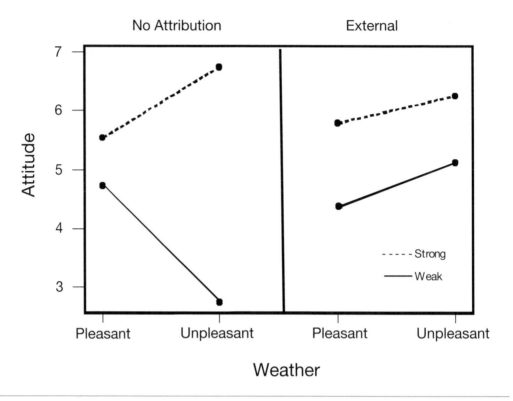

**Figure 12.3**

days and asked them to listen to a message advocating the implementation of comprehensive final exams. In addition, Sinclair et al. randomly assigned participants to hear a message with either weak or strong arguments. The left-hand side of Figure 12.3 presents the results—for the part of the design described so far. As shown in the left portion of Figure 12.3, relative to people who were approached on a pleasant day, those approached on an unpleasant day were substantially more persuaded by the strong message and substantially less persuaded by the weak message. That is, participants on an unpleasant day were more sensitive to and more strongly affected by the manipulation of the strength of the argument.

The pattern of results in the left-hand portion of Figure 12.3 is considerably more

persuasive than the earlier, stripped-down version used to illustrate the posttest-only nonequivalent group design (which corresponds to the findings for the weak argument conditions only). Comparing responses to both strong and weak messages rules out, for example, the possibility that people are simply more negative generally in their evaluations on unpleasant days. The underlying logic is akin to that of the nonequivalent dependent measure, discussed previously in the context of interrupted time-series designs.

Sinclair et al. added even more comparisons by manipulating another variable. They randomly assigned participants to either make or not make an external attribution regarding the weather. Participants in the external attribution condition were told that weather could affect moods and were asked to rate the weather so the researchers could control for any "mood-weather effects that could affect other responses." The no-attribution participants were not given this explanation before they listened to either the weak or strong message. The attribution manipulation was included because previous research by Schwarz and Clore (1983) had shown that affect-as-information effects do not occur when people are led to make an external attribution for their mood. As shown in the right-hand panel of Figure 12.3, weather and argument strength did not interact for the participants who made an external attribution.

The complete pattern of results from Sinclair et al., as summarized in Figure 12.3, provides a far more compelling case than would a stripped-down version of the study using only the posttest-only nonequivalent group design. Not only do the multiple comparisons and complex pattern of findings increase confidence that one has observed a cause-and-effect relationship, but the pattern of results also helps clarify the psychological processes underlying that relationship. In the case of Sinclair et al., the very different pattern of effects for the external and no-attribution conditions supports the hypothesis that affect-as-information is the underlying process.

## Summary

In the preceding sections, we have reviewed a range of quasi-experimental designs, from those that typically are weak inferentially, such as the one-group, pretest-posttest design, to more rigorous designs that allow relatively confident causal inference, such as the regression-discontinuity and interrupted time-series designs. We have also considered complex designs that combine experimental and quasi-experimental design features. As illustrated by the Sinclair et al. (1994) example, such hybrid designs often can provide credible evidence of cause-and-effect relations while also providing evidence

about underlying psychological processes. That a complex pattern of predictions and findings can both enhance the credibility and expand the scope of causal inferences is one of the most important principles of research design in general and quasi-experimentation in particular (Campbell, 1966; Mark, 1990; Reichardt, 2000; Trochim, 1985).

## CORRELATIONAL DESIGNS

Unlike quasi-experiments, correlational designs are not always used to assess causality. Correlational studies have long been used to examine the factorial structure of intelligence and personality, for example, with no causal conclusion intended. However, because this chapter focuses on assessing causality, our concern here is solely with the use of correlational designs to draw inferences about cause and effect.

Correlational designs used to probe causality are like quasi-experiments in that individuals are not randomly assigned to treatment conditions. It is a bit more difficult to be clear about how correlational designs are *un*like quasi-experiments, because there does not appear to be a clear, universally agreed upon distinction. One seemingly common approach is to say that, unlike in quasi-experiments, in correlational designs there either is not a treatment or the design does not allow confidence that one variable is the treatment and the other the outcome. In other words, correlational designs lack the standard features of quasi-experimental design, such as pretests (Shadish et al., 2002). Or we could focus on the way the cause is measured: In correlational designs, the cause typically is a continuously scaled variable, whereas in quasi-experiments the cause typically is a discretely scaled variable (where "discrete" means categorical, with relatively few categories). For instance, in the Sinclair et al. (1994) study of the effect of mood, weather—the indicator of mood—was scaled into two discrete categories, pleasant or unpleasant. Thus, the design was characterized as a quasi-experiment. In contrast, weather could have been measured in a more continuous manner, perhaps leading the study to be characterized as correlational. If the causal variable is measured continuously, the analysis of data from correlational designs typically is conceptualized in terms of correlations, rather than in terms of the mean differences that are the typical focus in the analysis of quasi-experiments.

### Threats to the Validity of Correlational Designs

Correlational designs are conceptually similar to simpler nonequivalent group quasi-experiments. As with nonequivalent group designs, selection differences are the most prominent threats to validity in correlational designs. For example, as noted in the previous example of a study of the effects of mood on persuasion, students who tend to be on campus on pleasant days may differ from those on campus on unpleasant days, and these differences can bias the estimate of the treatment effect. The threat to validity of selection differences applies at least as much in correlational designs as in nonequivalent group designs. In the literature on correlational designs, however, selection differences typically are labeled the problem of omitted third variables.

Another notable disadvantage of correlational designs involves their handling of time lags. A prototypical feature of quasi-experimental designs is that the treatment is implemented before the outcome is measured. In fact, a time sequence between the cause and the effect is embodied in the usual schematic depictions of quasi-experiments, where the X representing the treatment comes to the left of—that is, earlier in time than—the O representing the outcome variable. In contrast, correlational designs often are

implemented without a time lag between the putative cause and effect. For example, in a correlational study of the effects of stress on physical health, a single questionnaire might be used to ask respondents about their current levels of both stress and physical health.

Such a design is called cross-sectional and introduces two critical difficulties. First, cross-sectional correlational designs are subject to the validity threat of "ambiguous temporal precedence" (Shadish et al., 2002). That is, the purported cause might instead be the effect. For example, in studying the effects of stress on physical health, a researcher might unwittingly be assessing the effects of physical health on stress. Second, the size of a treatment effect is likely to vary with the interval between treatment implementation and outcome measurement (Gollob & Reichardt, 1987, 1991; Reichardt, 2002). For example, the effect of stress on physical health presumably varies depending on whether the time lag between a stressor and the measure of physical health is a day, a week, a month, a year, or a decade. When stress and physical health are assessed concurrently, it is not clear which time lag the results apply to, if any.

To avoid ambiguities about time lags, the measures of the cause and effect in a correlational design must be tied to specific, distinct times. If data are collected at the same time, one way to insert a time lag between, say, stress and physical health is to have respondents report their current degree of physical health and their level of stress as it was at a prior time. The problem is that retrospective reports are notoriously inaccurate in ways that can bias the results (e.g., Schwarz & Oyserman, 2001). For example, those in poor health may simply be more likely to recall negative stressors than those in good health. In general, longitudinal designs are better at inserting a reliable time lag between cause and effect, and it is encouraging to note that longitudinal designs appear to be increasing in frequency.

## The Analysis of Data From Correlational Designs

A third variable is a variable that is correlated with the cause and influences the outcome variable. For example, the variable of financial resources is likely to be a third variable in a correlational analysis of the effects of stress on physical health, because financial resources are likely to be related to stress and to have an effect on physical health. As previously noted, omitting third variables can bias the analysis of data from correlational designs in the same way that selection differences can introduce bias in quasi-experiments.

Structural equation modeling (SEM) is the most widely used method to control for the effects of third variables in correlational designs (Hoyle & Robinson, Chapter 10, this volume). To control for the effects of third variables, they must be measured and included in the structural equation model. In the typical correlational design, potential third variables are rampant, and it is exceptionally difficult to be confident that they have all been measured and included in the analysis. As a result, it is usually not possible to be confident that the effect of the cause of interest has been estimated without bias, perhaps severe bias. Moreover, even if all third variables are identified, they can at best be measured only fallibly. Measurement error in a third variable biases the treatment effect estimate. To deal with bias that results from measurement error, latent variables are used in the structural equation model. Latent variable models require multiple measures of each third variable and, in essence, use factor analysis to separate the underlying construct of interest from measurement error and other irrelevancies. If the correct factor model has been specified, SEM removes the bias resulting from measurement error by controlling for the underlying construct rather than for the fallible measures. However, the more serious problem of omitted third variables remains.

As with quasi-experiments, the best way to reduce causal ambiguity in correlational analyses is with design elaborations. Especially likely to be useful are hybrid designs that include nonequivalent dependent measures and the addition of discrete comparison groups in which the treatment is expected to have different effects. Adding waves of data over time is also recommended because, among other advantages, multiple waves of data enable researchers to use latent growth curve models with time-varying covariates (e.g., Muthen, 1991), allowing comparisons to be drawn across times as well as across people, which is another useful design-and-analysis elaboration.

## BEYOND INDIVIDUAL STUDIES: RESEARCH PROGRAMS, LINES OF RESEARCH, AND RESEARCH SYNTHESES

One of the common shortcomings of methodological treatises is that they often focus only on individual studies, seemingly implying that individual studies are the prime or only unit of scientific progress. To the contrary, most researchers realize that although individual studies are the building blocks, real progress in science usually comes from converging evidence across multiple studies. Thus, our discussion of quasi-experimental and correlational methods should be viewed in this broader context of the field.

Our sense is that, in social psychology, it is rare for a causal question to be addressed only with quasi-experimental or correlational methods. Instead, quasi-experimental and correlational methods are likely to be used in conjunction with experimental methods, either in a single investigator's research program or across investigators in a research area. In some cases, quasi-experimental or correlational methods serve as the forerunners of experimental methods. For instance, correlational or quasi-experimental findings may foster the development of hypotheses grounded in real world observations. In other cases, experimental studies come first but leave open questions of construct and external validity (Cook & Campbell, 1979; Shadish et al., 2002). Construct validity is concerned with the conceptual interpretation of the treatment and outcome variables, that is, with the accuracy of labeling, in abstract, conceptual terms, the specific, concrete research operations that constitute the treatment and the outcome. External validity refers to the accuracy of inferences about the degree to which a finding about a causal relationship can be generalized to persons, settings, and times other than those observed in a specific study. Questions about construct and external validity in experimental research are sometimes best addressed in real world settings that may not readily allow random assignment to conditions. Iteration between experimental methods, on one hand, and quasi-experimental or correlational methods, on the other, will often enhance construct and external validity. Such iteration has in fact taken place in several of the examples presented in this chapter.

As described in the section on the regression-discontinuity design, Mark and Mellor (1991) took advantage of a company's work layoff to examine whether a highly self-relevant, negative outcome reduces the magnitude of hindsight bias. Mark and Mellor were drawn to the layoff as a research site in part because it allowed them to examine hindsight in the context of an event that was extremely important for the respondents. This, they believed, would allow them to examine the impact of self-protective mechanisms that had not been addressed adequately in the large experimental literature on hindsight bias, which in general had relied on judgments about relatively trivial events. In addition, because the workers were laid off based on seniority, Mark and Mellor were able to use a strong quasi-experimental design, that

is, the regression-discontinuity design. Nevertheless, the retrospective and quasi-experimental nature of the study left some ambiguity about whether the findings were the result of self-protective motives, as hypothesized. For example, it is possible (even if unlikely) that the results were instead due to differences in pre-layoff exposure to information that coincided with the cutoff. A randomized experiment could further reduce uncertainty about the causal relationship.

In fact, Louie and her colleagues (Louie, 1999; Louie, Curren, & Harich, 2000) and Mark, Reiter, Eyssell, Cohen, and Mellor (in press) have replicated Mark and Mellor's (1991) quasi-experimental study with controlled experiments, also adding comparisons that clarify the causal process. For example, Louie (1999) replicated the finding that there is no hindsight bias among those who experience a negative self-relevant outcome. Louie also examined the attributions that people made, and the pattern of attributions was consistent with the operation of self-serving processes. In general, measurement of potential process variables will be easier in a lab experiment, such as those carried out by Louie and her colleagues, than in a quasi-experiment in a field setting. Louie (1999) also showed that a manipulation intended to constrain self-serving biases eliminated hindsight bias among those who experienced a positive self-relevant outcome. These experimental replications, with their use of procedures to clarify underlying causal processes, are important both for increasing confidence that the effect Mark and Mellor (1991) observed was causal and for demonstrating that it was the result of self-serving biases.

In similar fashion, the Sinclair et al. (1994) study, which used a quasi-experimental manipulation of mood, was conducted in the context of an ongoing line of research, to which many investigators have contributed, on the effects of mood and the processes that underlie mood effects. In many studies, mood has been experimentally manipulated, using a variety of procedures such as exposing people to film clips, asking them to recall happy or sad memories, having them listen to different styles of music, having them work in a pleasant or unpleasant room, or giving them positive or negative feedback. Sinclair and his colleagues could easily have used such a procedure to randomly assign people to mood conditions. However, several considerations led them to use a hybrid (quasi-experimental and experimental) design. First, most research on the effects of transitory mood states used some form of experimental mood induction, and researchers should attempt to add "multiplism" on those aspects of research that are most homogenous (Cook, 1985). Second, also for reasons of multiplism, there are benefits to having at least some studies in a line of research take place outside laboratory settings. In part, the benefit is that nonlaboratory settings tend to avoid, or at least reduce, the possibility that findings are due to artifacts such as demand characteristics. In addition, a naturalistic manipulation of mood enhances construct validity, by helping to ensure that the mood effects in the literature can be obtained with everyday determinants of mood, and not just as a result of the particular kind (or intensity) of mood induction used in the laboratory. Third, because of the experimental parts of the hybrid design, Sinclair and his colleagues were optimistic that interpretable results would arise even if the mood manipulation were quasi-experimental. Fourth, Schwarz and Clore (1983) had shown that weather could serve effectively as a naturalistic mood induction.

In short, we do not intend this chapter to serve as an unabashed advocacy of the use of quasi-experimental and correlational methods in social psychology. Such methods, if used judiciously, bring advantages relative to the traditional experimental methods that appear to predominate in mainstream social psychology. Quasi-experiments sometimes can be used in settings or with populations where randomized experiments are either infeasible or impractical. They also can allow social psychologists to investigate the effects of interventions that are both more intense and more unobtrusive than would be possible in randomized experiments. We believe, however, that quasi-experiments are best seen as a potential complement to, rather than a substitute for, experimental methods.

## CONCLUSIONS

In closing, we offer a few overall conclusions.

### *Design Matters*

Both correlational and the weaker quasi-experimental designs will in general be susceptible to threats to internal validity that preclude confident causal inference. But even weak designs may be valuable for hypothesis generation and when causal inference is not a key research goal. And stronger quasi-experimental designs, such as the regression-discontinuity and interrupted time-series designs, often can provide credible causal conclusions.

### *But Design Is Not Everything*

As illustrated by Steiner and Mark's (1985) consultation with bank officials and others about changes in record keeping and sources of history effects, supplementary information can help in assessing the plausibility of threats to validity. In addition, just because a threat is generally plausible for a given design does not mean that it will always be plausible for that design. For example, maturation might not be a plausible explanation for changes in attitudes during a 10-minute experiment. Often, existing evidence and common sense can be helpful in assessing whether a threat to validity is plausible.

## The Pattern of Observed Effects Also Matters

In the absence of random assignment, causal inference often can be enhanced by adding comparisons that produce a complex pattern of results, thereby making alternative explanations less plausible. This is the case for the Sinclair et al. (1994) study, where it is difficult to imagine a threat to internal validity that could explain the predicted pattern. As an added benefit, predicting and observing a complex pattern will often help clarify the mediating process, which also adds confidence to inferences about cause and effect.

## Recognizing and Reporting Threats to Validity Matters Too

The credibility of causal inference depends on both the research design and the analysis of data. In some circumstances, a weak design can yield credible results, and in some circumstances, the implementation of a strong design can be severely compromised. But in all cases, causal inference is fallible. Research reports should explicitly acknowledge the plausible threats to validity that are present and critically discuss how well these threats have been taken into account.

## Finally, Social Psychologists Should Not Be One-Trick Ponies

The randomized experiment is a wonderful method, generally considered—for good reason—the gold standard in causal research. At the same time, all methods have limitations. Quasi-experimental methods, especially stronger quasi-experimental designs, can bring important contributions to "critical multiplism" (Cook, 1985), especially when considered in the context of programs of research that also include experimental methods.

## REFERENCES

Campbell, D. T. (1966). Pattern matching as an essential in distal knowing. In K. R. Hammond (Ed.), *The psychology of Egon Brunswik* (pp. 81-106). New York: Holt, Rinehart & Winston.

Campbell, D. T., & Stanley, J. C. (1966). *Experimental and quasi-experimental designs for research*. Skokie, IL: Rand McNally.

Cappelleri, J. C., Darlington, R. B., & Trochim, W. M. K. (1994). Power analysis of cutoff-based randomized clinical trials. *Evaluation Review, 18,* 141-152.

Cook, T. D. (1985). Postpositivist critical multiplism. In R. L. Shotland & M. M. Mark (Eds.), *Social science and social policy* (pp. 21-62). Beverly Hills, CA: Sage.

Cook, T. D., & Campbell, D. T. (1979). *Quasi-experimentation: Design and analysis issues for field settings*. Skokie, IL: Rand McNally.

Eckert, W. A. (2000). Situational enhancement of design validity: The case of training evaluation at the World Bank Institute. *American Journal of Evaluation, 21,* 185-193.

Forgas, J. P., & Moylan, S. (1987). After the movies: The effects of transient mood states on social judgments. *Personality and Social Psychology Bulletin, 13,* 478-489.

Gollob, H. F., & Reichardt, C. S. (1987). Taking account of time lags in causal models. *Child Development* [Special section on structural equation modeling], *58,* 80-92.

Gollob, H. F., & Reichardt, C. S. (1991). Interpreting and estimating indirect effects assuming time lags really matter. In L. M. Collins & J. L. Horn (Eds.), *Best methods for the analysis of change: Recent advances, unanswered questions, future directions* (pp. 243-259). Washington, DC: American Psychological Association.

House, E. R. (2001). Unfinished business: Causes and values. *American Journal of Evaluation, 22*(3), 309-315.

Lehman, D. R., Lempert, R. O., & Nisbett, R. E. (1988). The effects of graduate training on reasoning: Formal discipline and thinking about everyday-life events. *American Psychologist, 43*, 431-442.

Lipsey, M. W., & Wilson, D. B. (1993). The efficacy of psychological, educational, and behavioral treatment: Confirmation from meta-analysis. *American Psychologist, 48*, 1181-1209.

Louie, T. A. (1999). Decision makers' hindsight bias after receiving favorable and unfavorable feedback. *Journal of Applied Psychology, 84*, 29-41.

Louie, T. A., Curren, M. T., & Harich, K. R. (2000). "I knew we would win": Hindsight bias for favorable and unfavorable team decision outcomes. *Journal of Applied Psychology, 85*, 264-272.

Mark, M. M. (1986). Validity typologies and the logic and practice of quasi-experimentation. In W. M. K. Trochim (Ed.), *Advances in quasi-experimental design and analysis* (pp. 47-66). San Francisco: Jossey-Bass.

Mark, M. M. (1990). From program theory to tests of program theory. In L. Bickman (Ed.), *New directions for program evaluation: Program theory in program evaluation* (pp. 37-51). San Francisco: Jossey-Bass.

Mark, M. M., & Mellor, S. (1991). The effect of the self-relevance of an event on hindsight bias: The foreseeability of a layoff. *Journal of Applied Psychology, 76*, 569-577.

Mark, M. M., Reichardt, C. S., & Sanna, L. J. (2000). Time series designs and analyses. In H. E. A. Tinsley & S. R. Brown (Eds.), *Handbook of applied multivariate statistics and mathematical modeling* (pp. 353-389). New York: Academic Press.

Mark, M. M., Reiter, R., Eyssell, K. M., Cohen, L., & Mellor, S. (in press). "I couldn't have seen it coming": The impact of negative self-relevant outcomes on retrospections about foreseeability. *Memory*.

Marsh, J. C. (1985). Obstacles and opportunities in the use of research on rape legislation. In R. L. Shotland & M. M. Mark (Eds.), *Social science and social policy* (pp. 295-310). Beverly Hills, CA: Sage.

Mellor, S., & Mark, M. M. (1998). A quasi-experimental design for studies on the impact of administrative decisions: Applications and extensions of the regression-discontinuity design. *Organizational Research Methods, 1*, 315-333.

Muthen, B. (1991). Analysis of longitudinal data using latent variable models with varying parameters. In L. M. Collins & J. L. Horn (Eds.), *Best methods for the analysis of change: Recent advances, unanswered questions, future directions* (pp. 1-17). Washington, DC: American Psychological Association.

Reichardt, C. S. (1979). The statistical analysis of data from nonequivalent group designs. In T. D. Cook & D. T. Campbell, *Quasi-experimentation: Design and analysis issues for field settings* (pp. 147-205). Skokie, IL: Rand McNally.

Reichardt, C. S. (2000). A typology of strategies for ruling out threats to validity. In L. Bickman (Ed.), *Research design: Donald Campbell's legacy* (Vol. 2, pp. 89-115). Thousand Oaks, CA: Sage.

Reichardt, C. S. (2002). The priority of just-identified, recursive models. *Psychological Methods, 7*, 307-315.

Reichardt, C. S., & Mark, M. M. (1998). Quasi-experimentation. In L. Bickman & D. Rog (Eds.), *Handbook of applied social research* (pp. 193-228). Newbury Park, CA: Sage.

Reichardt, C. S., & Mark, M. M. (2001). Nonequivalent group designs. In N. Smelser & P. Baltes (Eds.), *International encyclopedia of the social and behavioral sciences* (pp. 10655-10660). Oxford, UK: Elsevier.

Schwarz, N., & Clore, G. L. (1983). Mood, misattribution, and judgments of well-being: Informative and directive functions of affective states. *Journal of Personality and Social Psychology, 45,* 513-523.

Schwarz, N., & Oyserman, D. (2001). Asking questions about behavior: Cognition, communication and questionnaire construction. *American Journal of Evaluation, 22,* 127-160.

Shadish, W. R., Cook, T. D., & Campbell, D. T. (2002). *Experimental and quasi-experimental designs for generalized causal inference.* Boston: Houghton Mifflin.

Signorella, M. L., Frieze, I. H., & Hershey, S. W. (1996). Single-sex versus mixed-sex classes and gender schemata in children and adolescents: A longitudinal comparison. *Psychology of Women Quarterly, 20,* 599-607.

Sinclair, R. L., Mark, M. M., & Clore, G. L. (1994). Mood-related persuasion depends on (mis)attributions. *Social Cognition, 12,* 309-326.

Steiner, D., & Mark, M. M. (1985). The impact of a community action group: An illustration of the potential of time series analysis for the study of community groups. *American Journal of Community Psychology, 13,* 13-30.

Trochim, W. M. K. (1984). *Research design for program evaluation: The regression-discontinuity approach.* Newbury Park, CA: Sage.

Trochim, W. M. K. (1985). Pattern matching, validity, and conceptualization in program evaluation. *Evaluation Review, 9,* 575-604.

Winship, C., & Morgan, S. L. (1999). The estimation of causal effects from observational data. *Annual Review of Sociology, 25,* 659-707.

## CHAPTER 13

# Within-Subject and Longitudinal Experiments
## Design and Analysis Issues

STEPHEN G. WEST

*Arizona State University*

JEREMY C. BIESANZ

*University of Wisconsin–Madison*

OI-MAN KWOK

*Arizona State University*

In this chapter, we consider within-subject and longitudinal (repeated measure) experimental designs and their use in answering both traditional and emerging questions in social psychology. In the within-subject design, each participant receives two or more treatments. Following each treatment, the outcome variable is assessed. Such designs are particularly useful in research contexts in social psychology in which the outcome measure is expensive to collect (e.g., MRI measures of cortical activity), there are very large individual differences on the outcome variable and a subtle effect that requires a high power test is sought, or a special population of limited size is of focal interest (e.g., decision making by accountants or physicians). Within-subject designs assume that each treatment has only a short-term effect, so that treatments delivered later in the experiment are not affected by earlier treatments. In contrast, in the longitudinal experimental

AUTHORS' NOTE: We thank Leona Aiken, Patrick Curran, and the editors for their comments on an earlier version of this chapter. Correspondence should be directed to Stephen G. West, Psychology Department, Arizona State University, Tempe, AZ 85287-1104 or via e-mail to sgwest@asu.edu.

design, each participant is given a single treatment and then measured on the outcome variable at multiple time points. Here the focus is on the longer-term changes in the treatment effect and the processes related to the development of an outcome over time.

Although important examples of within-subject designs have been published in such diverse areas of social psychology as expectancy effects, person perception, and attitude change, such designs traditionally have not been commonly used in social psychology. A decade ago, Keren (1993) observed that different substantive areas of psychology varied greatly in their utilization of between- versus within-subject designs. Areas such as psychophysics and perception strongly emphasized within-subject designs, whereas areas such as personality and social psychology strongly emphasized between-subject designs. We surveyed the two sections of the 2000 and 2001 volumes of the *Journal of Personality and Social Psychology* (*JPSP*; 303 articles) and the *Journal of Experimental Social Psychology* (*JESP*; 80 articles) for studies involving within-subject designs. Consistent with Keren's observation, we were able to locate very few studies (< 2%) in which a central theoretical variable of interest was manipulated within subjects. Some additional studies included within-subject design features, but these typically were controls for incidental factors such as order of presentation of multiple exemplars of stimuli or multiple dependent variables. Although social psychology's emphasis on between-subject designs is often appropriate, within-subject designs offer advantages in some research areas.

Major advances have occurred in longitudinal research that permit improved studies of change over time. Personality and social psychologists have primarily used traditional approaches and are just beginning to make limited use of exciting new design and analysis techniques in this area. In the 303 articles published in the 2000 and 2001 volumes of *JPSP*, we identified 25 (8%) studies that included a pretest and posttest, another 32 (11%) using three or more measurement waves, and another 5 (2%) using both a pretest and two or more subsequent waves of measurement. Of note, the majority (68%) of the 37 total studies involving multiple measurement waves were reported in the "Personality Processes and Individual Differences" section. In comparison to earlier findings by West, Newsom, and Fenaughty (1992), these findings seem to indicate that a small but increased interest in longitudinal studies is occurring, primarily among personality researchers and some basic social psychologists conducting non-experimental research. Few social psychologists are taking advantage of the power of longitudinal experiments with repeated measurements to study processes over time.[1]

Because of space constraints, our focus in this chapter will be limited to experimental contexts with quantitative outcome variables in either basic laboratory or applied settings, conditions that characterize most social psychological research (West, Newsom, et al., 1992). A companion piece (Biesanz, West, & Kwok, in press) considers approaches to longitudinal research in naturalistic settings that more often typify personality research.

## PERSPECTIVES ON CAUSAL INFERENCE

The increased prominence of time in within-subject and longitudinal designs raises both new issues and new opportunities. To aid our understanding, it will be helpful to draw on the perspectives of Donald Rubin (e.g., Holland, 1986; Rubin, 1978) and Donald Campbell (e.g., Campbell & Stanley, 1966; Shadish, Cook, & Campbell, 2002) and their colleagues on causal inference (see also Mark & Reichardt, Chapter 12, this volume). Our presentation begins with the simple case in which there are two treatment conditions, a treatment condition T and a control condition C. The outcome variable is measured following the treatment. For example, in classic research on aggression, T might be a frustration (e.g., the individual participant $i$ is prevented from solving a problem by a confederate), C might be no frustration ($i$ is allowed to solve the problem), and the outcome variable $Y$ is a measure of aggression, such as the intensity of electric shocks ostensibly delivered to the confederate. Keep in mind that both the T and C conditions may have potential positive or negative effects on the outcome. For example, placebo conditions often lead to effects on outcome variables in well-controlled pharmaceutical experiments.

Rubin's causal model (see Holland, 1986) begins with a consideration of the *ideal* case under which a causal effect could be observed. Suppose we have a single participant $i$ who will receive the treatment. The *causal effect* is defined as the difference between the participant's outcome, $Y_T$ in the treatment condition and the participant's outcome, $Y_C$, in the control condition conducted under identical circumstances. In symbols, the causal effect is $Y_T - Y_C$. Now, in practice, this ideal case can never be achieved because "identical circumstances" can never be achieved. For example, in our experiment on aggression, achieving identical circumstances would require that the researcher give the treatment (the frustrating experience) to participant $i$ at the beginning of the experiment and then measure the participant's level of aggression at the end of the experiment, following which the researcher would return the participant to the identical moment at the beginning of the experiment and now give the same participant $i$ the control condition (no frustration) and then measure the participant's level of aggression at the end of the experiment. Despite the impossibility of its ever being achieved, the ideal case serves as a useful reference point from which to consider three design elements that we introduce below.

## THREE DESIGN ELEMENTS

### Basic Within-Subject Design

Both the treatment and control conditions may be given to the participant. As one example, participant $i$ would initially be exposed to treatment condition T and the outcome would be measured. Following this, the participant $i$ would be exposed to control condition C and the outcome would be measured. This within-subject design gives us the causal effect as $Y_T - Y_C$ provided that two strong assumptions are met. The first assumption, *temporal stability*, means that the effect of the treatment cannot depend on time—the magnitude of the treatment effect must be identical regardless of when the T and C conditions are delivered. Campbell and Stanley (1966) provided a practical list of common threats to this assumption; the list is presented in Table 13.1 (section A). The second assumption, *causal transience*, means that the effects of each treatment do not persist over time. Otherwise stated, the effect of each treatment (e.g., the frustration) is expected to be only temporary, with the participant's level on the outcome of interest as well as levels of other motivational, emotional, and cognitive states and physiological states returning to the baseline levels prior to the introduction of the second treatment.

### Unit Homogeneity

Alternatively, researchers can assume that the participants (experimental units) are identical. The causal effect is now $Y_{T(1)} - Y_{C(2)}$, where the number in parentheses indicates the participant (unit) that receives each treatment condition. This approach is often viable in experiments in engineering; however, in

**Table 13.1**   Some Threats to Internal Validity in Within-Subject and Longitudinal Designs

A. Threats associated with temporal stability (after Campbell & Stanley, 1966)

1. *History.* Specific events may occur between measurements that affect the outcome. Attitudes toward raising tuition may change following a tuition increase proposal by college regents.

2. *Maturation.* Within-participant processes unrelated to the treatment may affect the outcome. Children's cognitive abilities increase as they age, and students' mood states are more positive on weekends.

3. *Testing.* Scores on subsequent measures may be affected by prior measurement. Reporting depressed mood on a first measurement may increase the likelihood of reporting depressed mood on the next measurement.

4. *Instrumentation.* Changes in the capabilities of the measuring instrument may occur across measurements. Aggressive acts at age 4 (e.g., biting) are different from aggressive acts at age 16 (e.g., fighting with weapons). Measures may have ceiling or floor effects such that change cannot be detected.

5. *Statistical Regression.* Participants selected on the basis of the extreme high or low scores at Time 1 may score closer to the mean at Time 2 even in the absence of treatment. A group of students selected because they have 1 day of illness Year 1 will have on average more than 1 day of illness Year 2.

B. Violations of the stable unit treatment value assumption (SUTVA) (after Cook & Campbell, 1979; West, Biesanz, & Pitts, 2000)

6. *Atypical Reactions of Participants.* Participants aware of the nature of other experimental conditions may change their response on the outcome variable as a result of this knowledge. Patients in medical research sometimes have given up when they learned or inferred that they were assigned to the control group.

7. *Treatment Diffusion or Compensatory Treatment by Treatment Providers.* In applied research, control group participants may receive treatment from another source (e.g., medication from black market) or treatment staff may provide compensatory services (e.g., extra nursing care).

---

research with humans, it is rare that participants can be assumed to be identical. Even monozygotic (identical) twins may differ in their life experiences, attitudes, relationship status, current mood state, and so on.

### Randomization

The key feature of randomization is that assignment to treatment conditions is generated by a random process such as flipping a coin, so that each participant has an identical chance of being assigned to the T or C group. The important result of this process is that at the beginning of the experiment, prior to the receipt of any treatment, the mean scores of the participants in the T and C groups will be approximately equal on all possible background variables, whether measured or unmeasured. Consequently, following treatment, the difference between the mean of the treatment group and the mean of the control group on the outcome of interest, $M_T - M_C$, will be an unbiased estimate of the magnitude of the causal effect.

Randomization shifts the focus from comparisons involving a single participant to comparisons involving a sample of participants.[2] We can no longer make causal statements about any individual participant. We can only compare the *average* outcome for the participants receiving the treatment with the average outcome for the participants receiving the control condition. Second, the causal effect is now an unbiased *estimate* of the true causal effect. In any particular replication of the experiment, this estimate is likely to be too high or too low. The researcher can know only that the estimate of the causal effect would on average be correct in the hypothetical case of the same experiment being exactly replicated a very large number of times. Third, randomization does not provide assurance that participants are equated at the beginning of the experiment, even on average, if some participants are not present for the measurement of the outcome variable. Participant loss (attrition) from the experiment potentially can seriously undermine the strength of the causal inferences.

In research with human participants, the researcher must also assume that neither the randomization process nor the participant's (or others') awareness of other participants' treatment conditions affect the outcome. This assumption is known as the stable unit treatment value assumption, or SUTVA. In the typical 1-hour social psychological experiment conducted by trained researchers with individual participants who do not leave the laboratory, current evidence suggests that SUTVA does not appear to be a major problem. However, in basic and applied experiments that take place across days, weeks, or years, the possibility that subjects in different treatment conditions affect each other becomes far more likely. Table 13.1, section B, presents some illustrations (see also West, Biesanz, et al., 2000).

## WITHIN-SUBJECT EXPERIMENTS

Within-subject experiments in practice typically combine the design elements of randomization with within-subject design or unit homogeneity. This combination helps minimize the possibility of potential violations of the assumptions of temporal stability and causal transience. As a means of illustrating the ideas in this section, we will use an example patterned after an experiment by Kaplan, Reckers, West, and Boyd (1988).

This more applied example with four treatment levels allows presentation of the full range of approaches to controlling for order effects. These approaches cannot be distinguished with only two treatments.

Professional tax accountants were presented with a series of descriptions of tax cases and were asked about the likelihood that they would take a "shady" but not illegal deduction for each case. Likelihood was measured on a scale from 0% to 100%. In two cases, there was a high probability that taking the deduction would lead to a government audit, whereas in the other two cases this probability was low (audit probability). In two cases, the taxpayer preferred to take audit risks, whereas in the other two cases the taxpayer preferred to avoid government audits (risk preference). Thus, the design was a 2 (Audit Probability) × 2 (Risk Preference) factorial: T1 = audit low, risk low; T2 = audit low; risk high; T3 = audit high, risk low; T4 = audit high, risk high.

## Approaches to Controlling for Order of Treatment Conditions

### Random Ordering

One approach to controlling for order effects is to generate several different random orders of the four treatment conditions. Participants are then randomly assigned to one of the orders. With four treatment conditions, there are 4! (4 factorial) or 24 different unique orders in which the treatments might be presented. Ideally, the use of all possible orders with multiple replications of each order both balances potential artifactual effects and provides some ability to test for order effects. Normally in practice, however, the researcher can implement only a small random subset of the possible orders. For example, using a table of random numbers, we generated the following four orders of treatment conditions.

|  | Measurement Occasion (Trial) | | | |
|---|---|---|---|---|
|  | 1 | 2 | 3 | 4 |
| Order 1 | T4 | T1 | T2 | T3 |
| Order 2 | T3 | T1 | T2 | T4 |
| Order 3 | T3 | T2 | T4 | T1 |
| Order 4 | T1 | T2 | T3 | T4 |

If the magnitude of the causal effect changes over time (violation of temporal stability), then the estimate of the causal effect may be biased because not all the treatment conditions appear equally on each trial—the design is not balanced. For example, T3 appears twice on Trial 1 and never on Trial 2. Consequently, unless participants can be randomly assigned to all possible random orders, this approach does not necessarily eliminate bias in any particular experiment.

### Counterbalancing

Counterbalancing is a very simple approach to achieving a more balanced design. In counterbalancing, one random order of presentation of the treatments is generated, and then a second reversed order of presentation is then created, as illustrated below.

|  | Measurement Occasion (Trial) | | | |
|---|---|---|---|---|
|  | 1 | 2 | 3 | 4 |
| Order 1 | T4 | T1 | T2 | T3 |
| Order 2 | T3 | T2 | T1 | T4 |

In some contexts, counterbalancing may be a sufficient method of controlling for temporal changes in the magnitude of the causal effect. On the other hand, counterbalancing does not lead to a fully balanced design in which each treatment condition appears on each trial. For example, if there were a large increase in the magnitude of the causal effect from Trial 1 to Trial 2 (e.g., a "warm-up" effect), this effect would be present for treatments on the second trial (T1 and T2—low audit), but not for treatments on the first trial (T3 and T4—high audit) and would lead to a possible bias in the estimate of the causal effect.

### Latin Square Designs

When it can be implemented, the Latin square design often will be the optimal approach. In Latin square designs, each treatment condition appears once on each trial across orders (rows) and once in each order across trials (columns). For our tax deduction example with four treatments, one possible Latin square is shown below.

|  | Measurement Occasion (Trial) | | | |
|---|---|---|---|---|
|  | 1 | 2 | 3 | 4 |
| Order 1 | T4 | T2 | T1 | T3 |
| Order 2 | T3 | T1 | T2 | T4 |
| Order 3 | T2 | T3 | T4 | T1 |
| Order 4 | T1 | T4 | T3 | T2 |

This balance of treatment conditions means that most forms of violation of the temporal stability and causal transience assumptions will have minimal effects on the estimate of the causal effect. For example, if there is a "practice effect" such that any treatment will have a larger effect on Trial 2 than Trial 1, then this effect is constant across the four treatment conditions and the estimate of the causal effect of treatment will not be biased. On the other hand, if there is a differential practice effect such that only T1 produces a larger effect on Trial 2 than on Trial 1, the estimate of the causal effect will be biased. Latin square designs provide an excellent method of addressing temporal stability but cannot rule out all forms of violations of causal transience. If it is believed that the effect of a treatment may carry over to the following trial, the researcher should extend the time between trials or introduce intervening activities between trials.

**Table 13.2**    Analysis of Variance Source Table for Latin Square Design

| Source | df | MS | F | p |
|---|---|---|---|---|
| Between subjects | 19 | | | |
| Order | 3 | 6.50 | 1.43 | ns |
| Error between | 16 | 4.45 | | |
| Within subjects | 60 | | | |
| Treatment | 3 | 8.53 | | |
| Audit Probability | 1 | 12.00 | 10.17 | .0025 |
| Risk | 1 | 4.54 | 3.85 | .06 |
| Audit × Risk | 1 | 9.05 | 7.67 | .008 |
| Trials | 3 | 1.02 | 0.86 | ns |
| Latin Square residual | 6 | 0.39 | 0.33 | ns |
| Error within | 48 | 1.18 | | |

NOTE: The overall treatment effect has 3 degrees of freedom (*df*) and is partitioned into an audit probability main effect, a risk main effect, and an Audit Probability × Risk interaction, with 1 *df* each. The rows containing these effects are offset.

Latin square designs also permit researchers to perform partial tests of the assumptions. To illustrate, we simulated a data set for our tax deduction example in which five participants (total $n = 20$) were randomly assigned to each of the four orders of presentation in the Latin square above. The results of the illustrative analysis are presented in Table 13.2.

The substantive effects of interest are the audit probability main effect, the risk main effect, and the Audit Probability × Risk interaction. The statistically significant Audit Probability × Risk interaction suggests that the taxpayer's risk preference and the risk of audit combine to determine the likelihood of taking a shady tax deduction. In the present illustration, the interaction is a synergistic one, such that the combination of a low probability of being audited and a taxpayer willing to take an audit risk produces a substantially higher likelihood of taking the shady deduction ($M_{T1} = 64$, $M_{T2} = 39$, $M_{T3} = 35$, $M_{T4} = 39$).

In addition to the substantive effects of interest, checks on the assumptions of the design are provided. The nonsignificant trials effect indicates that the likelihood of taking the deduction does not change over trials. The between-subjects order effect and the Latin

square residual effect provide two separate *partial* tests of violations of the assumptions of temporal stability and causal transience. The between-subjects order effect also reflects any failure of randomization to precisely equate the subjects in the four groups that receive different orders of the treatment conditions. As a within-subjects effect, the test of the Latin square residual or (AB) (see Winer, Brown, & Michels, 1991, pp. 703-704) will nearly always provide a far more stringent test of the assumptions of temporal stability and causal transience. The nonsignificant effects indicate that violations of the assumptions were not detected in our illustration. Cochran and Cox (1957) and Winer et al. (1991) provide more complete presentations.

## Randomized Matched Designs (Predictor Sort Designs)

Thus far, we have assumed that the same participant receives each treatment condition. Another way of constructing a "within-subject" design is to use the design element of unit homogeneity. In the approach using randomized matched designs (also known as predictor sort designs), pairs, triples, or quadruples of participants who have similar characteristics are identified and matched. The matching may be performed on the basis of a single pretest variable, or it may be performed using a composite of several variables. Randomization then takes place within each matched set. To illustrate, let us return to our example. Suppose that accountants' fiscal conservatism has a strong association with their propensity to recommend shady deductions. From a large pool of potential participants, we can identify several sets of four participants (blocks) who have similar scores on a pretest measure of fiscal conservatism and then randomly assign the participants within each block to one of the four treatment conditions. To illustrate, the four participants with the highest scores on fiscal conservatism are identified as block 1, the next four highest are identified as block 2, and so on. Within each block, a participant is randomly assigned to each of the four treatment conditions. In the statistical analysis, each block of participants is treated *as if* it were a single participant measured under each of the four treatment conditions, but because different participants receive each treatment, this design rules out potential threats of temporal stability and causal transience. To the extent that the participants within each block are closely matched and matching variable(s) are strongly related to the outcome variable, this design will approach the statistical power of an actual within-subject design. In some cases, the gain in statistical power can be substantial. Student (1931) showed that an early randomized experiment on 10,000 children comparing their gains in height and weight from consumption of pasteurized versus raw milk would have achieved the same statistical power if 50 matched pairs of identical twins had been randomly assigned to treatment conditions instead.

## Moderator Effects

The designs we have considered so far assume that the magnitude of the treatment effect will be *constant* for all participants. In other cases, researchers may hypothesize that the magnitude of the treatment effect will vary depending on the participant's level on a background variable—a *moderator* effect or Treatment × Background Variable interaction (see also Hoyle & Robinson, Chapter 10, this volume). Background variables may include continuous variables such as personality traits (e.g., neuroticism), attitudes, or aptitudes (e.g., IQ), or categorical variables such as gender or attachment style. In moderator analyses in within-subject designs, a strong (usually reasonable) assumption is made that the participant's level on the background variable does not change during the experiment.

Consider a simple two-condition within-subjects design in which each participant is asked to evaluate an equally qualified in-group and out-group member on the outcome variable of suitability for employment. The researcher has also collected a continuous measure of each participant's level of prejudice prior to the experiment. The experimenter hypothesizes that there will be no relationship between level of prejudice and the evaluation for the in-group member, but that the out-group member will receive an increasingly negative evaluation as the participant's level of prejudice increases. With only two within-subject treatment conditions (in-versus out-group), the treatment effect and the Treatment × Background Variable interaction effect can be tested using a simple difference score method[3] (Judd, Kenny, & McClelland, 2001). The difference between the outcomes for each participant in the in-group and out-group conditions, $D = Y_{IN} - Y_{OUT}$, is first computed. Then, the continuous measure of prejudice, $X$, must be centered (i.e., put in deviation form, $X_C = X - M_X$, where $X_C$ is the centered variable, $X$ is the original measure of prejudice, and $M_X$ is the mean of the sample on the measure of prejudice). Finally, the difference score is regressed on the centered prejudice score, $X_C$, using the regression equation $\hat{D} = b_0 + b_1 X_C$. In this equation, the test of $b_1$ is equivalent to the test of the Prejudice × In-group versus Out-group interaction, and the test of $b_0$ corresponds to the in-group versus out-group effect, so long as prejudice is centered. With more complex designs (e.g., more than two treatment groups), moderator effects are most easily tested within the framework of the general linear model (Maxwell & Delaney, 2003). These models can be extended to designs with more than one background variable and more than two levels of within-subjects treatment conditions.

## Mediation

Mediation occurs when a treatment causes changes in a mediating variable (immediate outcome), which, in turn, causes changes in the outcome variable, $T \rightarrow M \rightarrow O$. For example, frustration may be hypothesized to lead to specific areas of cortical activation (measured by MRI), which, in turn, lead to aggression. Baron and Kenny (1986) developed a framework for testing mediation in between-subject designs, which we will utilize here. The Baron and Kenny framework recently was extended by Judd et al. (2001) to within-subject designs. We consider only designs in which there are two treatment groups (see also Hoyle & Robinson, Chapter 10, this volume).

In the Judd et al. framework, three conditions are needed in a within-subject design to show that the data are consistent with a mediational model. First, the treatment must produce changes in the outcome variable, $T \rightarrow O$. Second, the treatment must produce changes in the mediator, $T \rightarrow M$. These first two conditions can be tested directly using a repeated measures *t* test or ANOVA. Finally, the mediator must be shown to account for a significant portion of the relationship between the treatment and the outcome. The final condition can be tested by creating two

sets of difference scores for each participant: $D_M = M_1 - M_2$ for the difference between the scores on the mediator and $D_O = O_1 - O_2$ for the difference between the scores on the outcome variable in the two treatment groups. The difference in the outcomes is then regressed on the difference in the mediators, $\hat{D}_O = b_0 + b_1 D_M$. The test of $b_1$ represents the test of the final condition for mediation. In addition, if $b_0$ does not differ from 0, then the results are consistent with a model in which the entire treatment effect operates through the mediating variable.

Tests of mediation involve strong assumptions (Holland, 1988; MacKinnon, Lockwood, Hoffman, West, & Sheets, 2002). The assumptions of temporal stability and causal transience must be met. The mediator must be measured without error and be causally prior to the outcome. The relationship between the mediator and outcome must be linear; the variances of the outcome variable in the two treatment groups must be equal in the population. Methods for testing mediation with more than two treatment groups, models involving both mediation and moderation, and methods for when the assumptions of the basic model are violated are described by Judd et al. (2001).

## Summary and Conclusions

Within-subject experimental designs provide a relatively strong basis for estimating the causal effects of treatments. The primary issues that must be addressed are the assumptions of temporal stability and causal transience. We presented several strategies that reduce, but do not fully eliminate, threats to internal validity. Consequently, if researchers base the selection of a research design solely on the criterion of internal validity, then simple randomized between-subjects experiments conducted in the laboratory often will be the method of choice.

Earlier, we noted that within-subject designs are rarely reported in two of the leading journals in social psychology. We also observed that they are common in some areas of psychology, such as perception and psychophysics (Keren, 1993). How can we account for this?

First, many social psychological manipulations, particularly when employed in contexts using minor or more substantial deception, make it very difficult or impossible to return participants to their original baseline state. Even under more favorable conditions in which the stronger within-subject designs (e.g., Latin square designs; randomized matched designs) yield internal validity comparable to between-subjects laboratory experiments, the within-subject designs require more careful thought on the part of the researcher to identify potential threats and to incorporate design features that help rule out those specific threats.

Second, social psychological researchers have not historically placed a high priority on designs that achieve high levels of statistical power (see Rossi, 1990). The easy availability of large numbers of our favorite research participants, college undergraduates, at many large universities may reduce the *perceived* need for designs that maximize statistical power.

Third, much of the careful thinking about within-subject designs was originally undertaken by experimental psychologists such as Benton Underwood and psychological statisticians such as Ben Winer in the 1960s. The insights of this earlier era have been crowded out of the curriculum in psychology and are not being transmitted to new generations of researchers (see Aiken, West, Sechrest, & Reno, 1990).

There are some developing counter forces that may presage a reinvigoration of the within-subject design. One of the chief advantages of the within-subject design is its efficiency in achieving adequate statistical power with the minimum number of participants. The number of participants needed to achieve a desired level of statistical power (e.g., .80) in a within-subjects design with two treatment groups and a correlation of .5 between-subjects' responses in the two treatment conditions is only 25% of the number needed in the corresponding between-subjects design (Venter & Maxwell, 1999). Some emerging research areas are likely to place a high priority on this advantage. As noted earlier, researchers who investigate questions requiring specialized populations and researchers for whom data collection is very expensive will benefit greatly from the use of within-subject designs. In addition, when multiple replications of each treatment condition are possible within subject, the causal effect may once again be estimated separately for each participant rather than for the entire sample (see Anderson, 1982). Given the increasing realization that statistical models that assume a constant treatment effect across different individuals may often be unrealistic, the fact that such designs permit tests of this assumption should increase their use. Our hope is that researchers will rediscover the careful thinking of a distinguished previous generation of researchers concerning the advantages and disadvantages of within-subject designs.

## LONGITUDINAL EXPERIMENTS

In the basic two-group between-subjects randomized experiment depicted in Figure 13.1 (section A), the researcher randomly assigns participants to the treatment or control group. Following the delivery of the treatment, the researcher collects the outcome variable from each participant. Longitudinal experiments extend this basic design by assessing the outcome variable on more than one measurement occasion. As we will illustrate later, the repeated measurements provide a far greater ability to examine the temporal course of the effects of social psychological manipulations.

A. Randomized posttest only

|  | | Posttest |
|---|---|---|
| Treatment | | $M_1$ |
| Control | | $M_1$ |

B. Randomized pretest-posttest design

| *Pretest* | | *Posttest* |
|---|---|---|
| $M_1$ | Treatment | $M_2$ |
| $M_1$ | Control | $M_2$ |

C. Solomon four-group design

| *Pretest* | | *Posttest* |
|---|---|---|
| $M_1$ | Treatment | $M_2$ |
| $M_1$ | Control | $M_2$ |
| | Treatment | $M_1$ |
| | Control | $M_1$ |

D. Longitudinal experiment (Four Waves)

| | *Measurement Wave (Trial)* | | | |
|---|---|---|---|---|
| | 1 | 2 | 3 | 4 |
| Treatment | $M_1$ | $M_2$ | $M_3$ | $M_4$ |
| Control | $M_1$ | $M_2$ | $M_3$ | $M_4$ |

**Figure 13.1** Some Randomized Experimental Designs

NOTE: All participants are randomly assigned to treatment groups. The same outcome measurement is collected at each measurement wave. Measurement wave is indicated by a subscript (1, 2, 3, 4).

Given that randomization has occurred successfully, the two major threats to the inference of the causal effect are attrition and violations of SUTVA.

## Threats to Causal Inference

### Attrition

Attrition, or loss of participants from measurement, can occur for a variety of reasons, particularly when the experiment is extended in time and when participants leave the laboratory. In some basic and many applied experiments in social psychology, participants are measured daily, once a week, once a month, once a year, or on a less regular basis. In these longitudinal designs with multiple measurement occasions, participant attrition becomes an important threat to the validity of the causal inferences. Of particular concern is differential attrition from the treatment and control groups. Even if the rate of attrition is identical in the T and C groups, there may still be reason for concern. For example, in an educational experiment testing a new curriculum, if the least intelligent students drop out of the T group and the most intelligent students drop out of the C group, any results showing higher standardized test scores in the treatment relative to the control group would be highly suspect.

The best solution to problems of attrition is to prevent it from occurring. This strategy requires careful planning during the development of the experimental protocol. A considerable craft knowledge of techniques for keeping participants involved in longitudinal research has developed over the past few decades (see Ribisl et al., 1996). These methods require that experimental staff have multiple ways of locating participants, send participants reminders, and have plans for alternative data collection procedures if a participant does not show up or moves to another location. Of importance, participants in the control group should receive just as much attention as those in the treatment group. Multiyear longitudinal experiments using these retention procedures often have been able to limit attrition to less than 5% of the original sample.

In cases in which attrition cannot be prevented, statistical analyses may be conducted to probe the effects of attrition and adjust for the effects of attrition. If pretest measures can be collected on all participants, these measures provide critical information about the nature of the participants who do not complete posttest measurement (attriters). Prediction of attrition status (1 = completer; 0 = attriter) from (a) the pretest score, (b) the treatment condition, and (c) the interaction of pretest and treatment in a logistic regression analysis helps researchers understand the nature of the attrition problem (West & Sagarin, 2000). A main effect of the pretest score indicates that the researcher should be very cautious in generalizing the results of the experiment to the full population from which the participants were sampled, whereas an interaction between the pretest and the treatment indicates that the nature of the participants who dropped out differed in the T and C conditions. This latter finding indicates a potentially serious threat to causal inference. When attrition does occur, the application of analyses based on modern missing data theory (Schafer & Graham, 2002) can adjust treatment effects for the effects of any variables measured at

pretest. Outcome data collected during early measurement periods following treatment can provide useful information to adjust estimates of treatment effects during later measurement periods, after attrition has occurred. In addition, West and Sagarin (2000) described methods of estimating upper and lower bounds to treatment effects given the possibility that attrition may be associated with important, but unmeasured, variables.

### SUTVA

Of most concern in longitudinal experiments in social psychology is the second part of SUTVA, the possibility that participants communicate about experimental procedures, potentially contaminating the estimates of the causal effects. Traditionally, social psychologists have followed the procedure of swearing participants to secrecy, although the effectiveness of these procedures in experiments over extended time periods has not been examined carefully. The use of subtle treatments of which the participant may not be fully aware and procedures that minimize information about the existence of other treatment conditions also may be helpful in many cases. When treatments are not subtle, most effective will be procedures that geographically and/or temporally separate participants.

## Some Longitudinal Experimental Designs

In our presentation below, we consider several traditional and new designs and analytic approaches for longitudinal experimental designs.

### Pre-Post Randomized Experiment

The pre-post randomized experiment depicted in Figure 13.1 (section B) adds to the basic randomized design the feature of a pretest on the outcome variable. Thus, this design combines the design features of randomization and within-subject design. This design has long been used in some areas of social psychology (e.g., attitude change). The chief advantage of the pre-post design is that, given a fixed number of participants, the statistical power typically is higher than in the posttest-only design. To the extent that there is a relationship between the pretest and the posttest (e.g., in an attitude change experiment, more positive attitudes at pretest are associated with more positive attitudes at posttest), the ability to detect true treatment effects will be increased. For example, to detect a standardized effect size $d = .50$, where $d$ is the difference in standard deviations between the treatment and control groups (which Cohen, 1988, describes as a moderate effect size), the researcher will need 126 participants (63 T, 63 C) to be able to reject the null hypothesis 80% of the time. However, if there is a .60 correlation between the pretest and the posttest, this number falls to 82 (36% reduction). Statistical procedures decrease the magnitude of the error variance by removing the portion that is accounted for by the subjects' pretest scores. When the relationship between the pretest and posttest is linear and the strength of this relationship does not differ in the treatment and control conditions, then analysis of covariance provides the proper adjustment. In other cases, more complex statistical models are required (see Huitema, 1980; Little, An, Johanns, & Giordani, 2000; Maxwell & Delaney, 2003).

A second key advantage of the pre-post randomized experiment is often overlooked (Shadish et al., 2002). As we noted earlier, if pretest measures can be collected on all participants, these measures provide critical information that can be used to study the effects of attrition and to provide improved estimates of the causal effect both by using modern missing data techniques and by statistically equating groups on observed pretest differences.

### Solomon Four-Group Design

One potential criticism of the pre-post randomized experiment is that generalization of the causal effect may be limited to contexts in which a pretest measurement is taken. For example, the pretest measurement may sensitize the participants to the subsequent treatment, making it more effective. Or, repeated testing may alter the participant's response (see Table 13.1, section A). To address such criticisms, researchers can employ the Solomon four-group design illustrated in Figure 13.1 (section C), which represents a combination of the simple posttest-only randomized experiment and the pretest-posttest randomized experiment. Subjects are randomly assigned to one of the four groups, and the magnitude of the treatment effect in the posttest-only versus pretest-posttest measurement conditions can be compared. In cases in which the estimates of the causal effect in the two measurement conditions differ, researchers must decide whether the posttest-only or the pretest-posttest measurement condition best represents the context to which they wish to generalize. Typically, the posttest-only estimate will be chosen. In cases in which they do not differ, the estimates of the causal effects from the two measurement conditions can be combined using meta-analytic procedures suggested by Braver and Braver (1988) or through missing data techniques (Schafer & Graham, 2002).

### Multiwave Longitudinal Experiment

In multiwave longitudinal experiments, participants are randomly assigned to treatment conditions and then measured on the outcome variable at several time points following treatment (see Figure 13.1, section D). Longitudinal designs and analy-

**Table 13.3**    Univariate Analysis of Variance of Disliking Ratings

| Source | df | MS | F | p |
|---|---|---|---|---|
| Treatment (in-group vs. out-group) | 1 | 37,206 | 43.2 | <.0001 |
| Error between | 76 | 861 | | |
| Trials | 3 | 760 | 7.0 | .0002 |
| Treatment × Trials | 3 | 450 | 4.2 | .0068 |
| Error within | 228 | 108 | | |

ses have been an especially active area of methodological activity over the past decade (e.g., Collins & Sayer, 2001; Singer & Willett, 2003), and some of the newer approaches are beginning to be used in some areas of personality research (Biesanz et al., in press). Our presentation considers both traditional and emerging designs and analyses that are applicable in social psychology. To illustrate these analyses, we will use a single hypothetical example loosely based[4] on the data of Ryan and Bogart (2001). Imagine that each participant ($n = 78$) plays a laboratory game each week for 4 weeks with a confederate who acts in a generally cooperative manner. Prior to the initial game, participants are randomly assigned to one of two descriptions of the confederate: The confederate is a member of a disliked out-group ($T_1$) or an in-group ($T_2$). The participant's *disliking* for the partner (confederate) is rated each week for 4 weeks on a measure of disliking on which +100 represents *dislike very much*, 0 is neutral, and –100 represents *like very much*. The use of fewer than four measurement waves may sharply limit the analysis options and make it more difficult to separate measurement error from true change (Singer & Willett, 2003).

## Analysis Approaches: Traditional and Modern

We consider in this section a variety of statistical approaches to the analysis of longitudinal experiments involving continuous outcome measures.[5] As a baseline corresponding to the standard current practice in social psychology, we considered only the data collected on the first measurement wave following treatment (randomized posttest-only design; see Figure 13.1, section A). This analysis showed a significant causal effect of treatment: $M_{T1} = +26.19$, $M_{T2} = -4.42$; $F(1, 76) = 55.24$, $p < .001$. Thus, this analysis shows that there is an immediate in-group vs. out-group effect but does not inform us about the longer-term effects of the manipulation.

## Univariate Analysis of Variance

One of the classic methods of analyzing data from a longitudinal experiment is to use a mixed, between-within univariate analysis of variance (ANOVA). In this approach, treatment condition is the between-subjects factor and trials (measurement occasion) is the within-subjects factor. Applying this method to the full four waves of the present data set, we obtain the following results (rounded for ease of presentation).

Table 13.3 presents the results of the ANOVA and Figure 13.2 presents the means, where ◆ represents the out-group mean and ▲ represents the in-group mean for each trial. Most important these results indicate that the magnitude of the in-group vs. out-group effect varies across trials—there is a In-group vs. Out-group × Trials interaction. These results indicate that the difference in disliking for the in-group relative

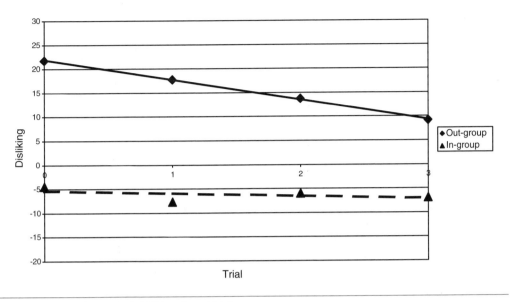

**Figure 13.2** Change in Disliking Over Trials

NOTE: ◆ represents the out-group mean for each trial, and ▲ represents the in-group mean for each trial. The solid line and the dashed line are the best-fitting straight lines for each group.

to the out-group varies as a function of trial. However, an important caveat must be placed on this finding: The basic between-within ANOVA makes the strong assumptions that (a) the variance of the dependent variable (disliking) is identical between the in-group and out-group treatment conditions and across trials and (b) the correlation between the residuals on each pair of trials is the same between the in-group and out-group conditions and over time. This assumption is known as sphericity,[6] and it is commonly violated with real data sets. Indeed, with the present data, Mauchly's test of sphericity rejected this assumption ($p$ = .02). Violations of this assumption can seriously compromise the interpretation of the results, as the Type I error rate ($\alpha$) may be either too low or more typically too high in value, sometimes substantially so (e.g., true $\alpha$ may be as high as .15 instead of nominal $\alpha$ = .05), depending on the structure of the data. Three potential approaches may be taken to this problem.

*Three Possible Improvements to the Univariate Analysis of Variance Approach*

*Correction of* p *Values.* The first approach attempts to correct the reported $p$ values through an adjustment of the degrees of freedom of the $F$ test of the within-subject effects in the univariate ANOVA so that the Type I error rate will be correct. The Geisser-Greenhouse (GG) adjustment tends to be slightly conservative in small samples (the reported $p$ value tends to be lower than the true level of $\alpha$). The Huynh-Feldt (HF) adjustment tends to be slightly liberal. In the present case, the $p$ values for the trials' main effect are GG $p$ = .0003 and HF $p$ = .0002; for the Treatment × Trials interaction they are GG $p$ = .0092 and HF $p$ = .0080.

*Multivariate Approach.* The second approach uses a multivariate analysis of

**Table 13.4** Repeated Measures Multivariate Analysis of Variance of Disliking Ratings

| Source | Numerator df | Denominator df | F | p |
|---|---|---|---|---|
| Between | | | | |
| Treatment | 1 | 76 | 43.2 | <.0001 |
| Within | | | | |
| Trials | 3 | 74 | 6.2 | .0008 |
| Treatment × Trials | 3 | 74 | 3.0 | .0371 |

variance (MANOVA) approach. In the MANOVA procedure with four trials, a set (equal to the number of trials minus 1; here 4 − 1 = 3) of contrasts with one degree of freedom are formed to represent the information about the differences between the means contained in the trials variable. A key feature of the MANOVA procedure is that the degree of relationship between the residuals associated with each pair of these contrasts is estimated, so that there is no necessity to assume sphericity. Thus, the MANOVA approach makes less restrictive assumptions and should be more generally applicable. The between-subjects treatment effect in this analysis will be identical to that of the univariate approach, but the within-subject effects will, in general, differ.

Returning to our example data set, the MANOVA approach produces the results shown in Table 13.4. Once again, the same pattern of results is obtained, although the p value for the MANOVA approach, particularly for the In-group vs. Out-group × Trials interaction, is substantially reduced.

If the assumptions of the traditional univariate ANOVA approach are met, it will be more powerful than the MANOVA approach. However, the extent to which the assumptions are met is difficult to discern because tests of sphericity can easily fail to detect violations of this assumption. Consequently, the MANOVA approach generally will be preferred because it provides better control over the Type I error rate, although this control may sometimes come at a cost of decreased statistical power. Algina

and Keselman (1997) presented a full discussion of the trade-offs among the approaches. These trade-offs depend on several features of the data structure, including the number of trials, the value of $\varepsilon$, and the sample size.

*Contrast Approach.* The third approach is closely related to the MANOVA approach but makes the questions addressed by the analysis more precise. Instead of performing an omnibus test of all possible forms of the effect of trials and the Treatment × Trials interaction, the researchers define a set of orthogonal contrasts that reflect precisely the pattern of results that they hypothesize. This strategy bypasses the sphericity assumption because the *df* in the numerator = 1, and it also has the advantage of being a more informative and more powerful test of the hypothesized effects of interest (Abelson & Prentice, 1997; Maxwell & Delaney, 2003).

Suppose we had originally hypothesized that the treatment would lead to a linear decrease in disliking over trials in the treatment condition, but that there would be no change in the disliking over trials in the control condition. One way this linear pattern can be represented is as a one-degree of freedom contrast in which Trial 1 is given a weight of −3, Trial 2 a weight of −1, Trial 3 a weight of +1, and Trial 4 a weight of + 3 (i.e., −3, −1, + 1, + 3). The other two degrees of freedom associated with the trials effect can be represented as two other orthogonal one degree of freedom contrasts, a quadratic

**Table 13.5**   Linear Contrast Analysis of Repeated Measures Disliking Ratings

| Source | df | MS | F | p |
|--------|----|----|----|----|
| Between | | | | |
| Treatment | 1 | 76 | 43.2 | <.0001 |
| Within | | | | |
| Trials (linear) | 1 | 2,202 | 15.1 | .0002 |
| Treatment × Trials (linear) | 1 | 1,264 | 8.7 | .0043 |
| Error (linear) | 76 | 146 | | |
| Trials (residual) | 2 | 39 | 0.4 | ns |
| Treatment × Trials (residual) | 2 | 43 | 0.5 | ns |
| Error (residual) | 152 | 89 | | |

effect $(-1 +1 +1 -1)$ and a cubic effect $(-1\ 3\ -3 +1)$. In the present example, when we test this linear trend, we find the results shown in Table 13.5

In the present example, the 1 *df* linear effect of Treatment × Trials linear contrast is significant, accounting for approximately $(8.7/(3.0 \times 3) = 97\%$ of the 3 *df* omnibus interaction effect. The straight lines in Figure 13.2 represent the linear effect over trials within each treatment condition. Given that the hypothesis is true, this test is both more precise and more powerful. To aid in our interpretation of the results, we can also form a confidence interval (CI) that provides an indication of the estimate of the slope within each treatment group. If we rescale the results so that there is a 1 unit difference between the weights $(-1.5, -0.5, +0.5, +1.5)$, then the slope in each group represents the change in the outcome variable corresponding to a 1-unit change in trials—a directly interpretable value. For the out-group, the 95% CI ranges from $-2.282$ to $-1.895$, indicating a drop of about 2 points on the disliking measure on each subsequent trial. For the in-group, the 95% CI on the linear slope is $-1.661$ to $1.085$, which overlaps 0, indicating no change in disliking is occurring over time.

Abelson and Prentice (1997) reminded us that only the hypothesized contrast should be significant if our hypothesis is true. For example, in the present example there could

have been a general downward trend in disliking in the in-group condition that reaches a minimum, following which disliking increases. To help rule out the possibility that some other nonlinear pattern may produce a better account for the data, an omnibus test of the residual effects associated with the other possible contrasts (here, $3 - 1 = 2$) should be performed. In the present case, both the residual trials effect, $F(2, 152) = 0.4$, ns, and the residual Treatment × Trials interaction, $F(2, 152) = 0.5$, ns, failed to approach statistical significance, providing support for the hypothesized linear effects. To provide the most stringent test of the hypothesized linear contrasts, the test of the residual contrast effects should be as powerful as possible, perhaps even using $\alpha = .20$. If either of the residual contrast effects is statistically significant, the hypothesized linear model is not adequate to account for the data.

*Growth Models*

In the past decade, growth models (also known as multilevel models, hierarchical linear models, and random coefficient models) have been proposed as a method of analyzing longitudinal data. Growth models have been represented within two different statistical traditions. The first comes from the work on hierarchical linear models[7] (e.g., Raudenbush & Bryk, 2002), which can be seen as an extension of the ANOVA

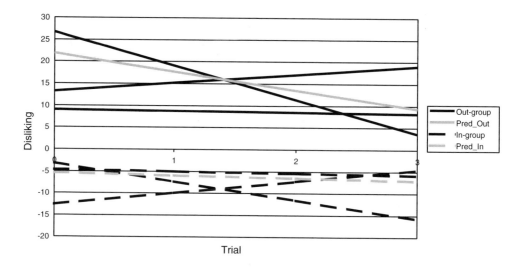

**Figure 13.3**    Disliking Across Trials (Individual Trend)

NOTE: The dark solid lines represent the best-fitting straight lines for three sample participants in the out-group. The dark dashed lines represent the best-fitting straight lines for three sample participants in the in-group. The gray solid and dashed lines represent the best-fitting straight lines for the entire out-group ($n = 39$) and in-group ($n = 39$) conditions, respectively.

approach we have been discussing. The second comes from structural equation modeling (e.g., Collins & Sayer, 2001), another distinctly different statistical tradition. Although each tradition provides important advantages and disadvantages in thinking about problems, many (but currently not all) of the analyses that can be performed within one tradition also can be performed within the other (Mehta & West, 2000). We focus on the hierarchical linear model tradition here because it more closely parallels ANOVA.

Conceptually, multilevel models have two levels. In our current example, in the Level 1 analysis we would calculate a regression line, $\hat{Y}_{ti} = \beta_{0i} + \beta_{1i}\,\text{Trials}_{ti}$, for each of the participants. $\beta_{0i}$ is the intercept for participant $i$, the value when $Trials = 0$. $\beta_{1i}$ is the slope of the regression line for participant $i$. In Figure 13.3, we present these regression lines for three participants in the treatment group and three participants in the control group. Given that we probably would like to estimate the causal effect immediately after the

delivery of the treatment (i.e., immediate treatment effect), we would rescale Trials to have values of 0, 1, 2, and 3 (i.e., rescaled Trials = Original Trials −1). As another alternative (not shown here), we could estimate the treatment effect at the end of the experiment (Original Trial 4) by rescaling Trials = Original Trials −4. This series of Level 1 analyses would yield an estimate of the regression intercept and slope for each participant (78 intercepts, 78 slopes). We would then take each of these estimates as the outcome variables in our Level 2 analyses. Treatment condition would be used to estimate the intercepts and the slopes obtained in the Level 1 analyses. Following the standard notation in this area, the equations predicting the intercept and the slope for participant $i$ are

$$\hat{\beta}_{0i} = \gamma_{00} + \gamma_{01}\,\text{Treatment}_i$$

$$\hat{\beta}_{1i} = \gamma_{10} + \gamma_{11}\,\text{Treatment}_i.$$

In these equations, $\hat{\beta}_{0i}$ is the predicted intercept and $\hat{\beta}_{1i}$ is the predicted slope for participant $i$. In the Level 2 equation for the intercept, $\gamma_{00}$ is the mean of all the individual intercepts, and $\gamma_{01}$ is the causal effect of the treatment condition on the intercepts. In the Level 2 equation for the slope, $\gamma_{10}$ is the mean of all the slopes, and $\gamma_{11}$ is the effect of treatment condition on the slopes. In practice, Levels 1 and 2 are estimated simultaneously, which both yields more precise estimates of the important parameters of the model and allows for great flexibility in the structure of the data (as we will see below).

Multilevel longitudinal models produce two types of results. First are Wald tests[8] ($z$ tests) of the effects of the coefficients ($\gamma$'s) in the Level 2 equations for the slope and intercept. In the present example, we find

| Term | Coefficient | SE | df | $z$ | $p$ |
|------|------------|-----|-----|------|-------|
| $\gamma_{00}$ | 8.2 | 1.8 | 76 | 4.6 | $<.0001$ |
| $\gamma_{01}$ | 13.6 | 1.8 | 76 | 7.6 | $<.0001$ |
| $\gamma_{10}$ | $-2.4$ | 0.6 | 232 | $-3.9$ | $.0001$ |
| $\gamma_{11}$ | $-1.8$ | 0.6 | 232 | $-2.9$ | $.0036.$ |

For the Level 2 equation predicting the intercepts, $\gamma_{00} = 8.2$ indicates that the mean intercept of the in-group and out-group conditions was 8.2 on the initial measurement just after treatment (Trial 0) given that treatment was effect coded $T = +1$ and $C = -1$. Coefficient $\gamma_{01} = 13.6$ is the difference between the mean intercept and the intercepts in the out-group vs. in-group conditions ($T_1 = 8.2 + 13.6 = 21.8$; $T_2 = 8.2 - (+13.6) = -5.4$). For the Level 2 equation predicting the slopes, $\gamma_{10} = -2.4$ is the mean slope and $\gamma_{11} = 1.8$ is the effect of treatment on the slopes (slope for out-group condition is $-2.4 - 1.8 = -4.2$; slope for the in-group is $-.2.4 - (-1.8) = -0.6$). In terms of the ANOVA contrast analysis, the test of $\gamma_{11}$ is the analog to the test of the Out-group vs. In-group × Trials (linear) interaction.

However, the hierarchical linear model analysis adds a second layer of tests that can provide useful information about individual variability around the mean values. In our example, these effects (known as random effects) are $\tau_{00}$ (variance of the intercepts), $\tau_{11}$ (variance of the slopes), and $\tau_{01}$ (covariance of the slopes and intercepts of the participants) and are presented below.

| Effect | Estimate | SE | $z$ | $p$ |
|--------|----------|-----|------|------|
| $\tau_{00}$ | 190.0 | 41.4 | 4.6 | .0001 |
| $\tau_{11}$ | 11.7 | 5.1 | 2.3 | .0115 |
| $\tau_{01}$ | $-7.7$ | 11.0 | $-0.7$ | ns |

The significance of $\tau_{00}$ and $\tau_{11}$ indicates that there are reliable individual differences in the effect of the treatment on disliking on rescaled trial 0 ($\tau_{00}$) and on the rate of linear decline across trials ($\tau_{11}$). The covariance between the slope and the intercept ($\tau_{01}$) describes the relationship between the magnitude of the person's initial standing within his or her treatment group and his or her slope. In the present case, this term was not statistically significant, so there does not appear to be a relationship (correlation = $-.16$, ns). A negative value of this term would indicate that individuals with larger intercepts tend to have relatively more negative slopes, whereas a positive value would indicate that individuals with larger intercepts tend to have relatively more positive slopes. As noted above, standard ANOVA models assume a constant treatment effect for all individuals, an assumption that clearly is violated in the present example. The significant treatment effect (T vs. C) explains some (49%) of the variance in the intercepts, but there is still significant unexplained variance in the intercepts after the treatment is accounted for. Similarly, the significant treatment effect explains some (20%) of the variance in the slopes. That significant variance in the intercepts and slopes remains unexplained indicates that there are potential background variables (e.g., pretest attitude, gender) that may account for this variability. These background variables can be added to the Level 2 equations predicting the individual intercepts and slopes, for example, $\hat{\beta}_{0i} = \gamma_{00} + \gamma_{01}$ Treatment$_i + \gamma_{02}$ Gender$_i$ for the intercepts. Thus, considerations of potential moderator effects come directly out of this approach.

So far in our consideration of multilevel models, we have accounted for differences between participants, but we have ignored other potential problems with the error structure that were manifested earlier as a violation of the sphericity assumption. The family of multilevel models offers a wide range of options for modeling the error structure; the range of these options increases as the number of trials increase. Multilevel and closely related mixed linear models can accommodate most forms of problems that arise in the error structure that can potentially undermine the statistical tests of treatment effects.

### Extensions

Growth models can be extended in a number of ways. A few of these extensions are briefly outlined below.

1. *Time-Varying Covariates.* Variables that change over time (e.g., mood) can be included as predictors in the Level 1 equation, $\hat{Y}_{ti} = \beta_{0i} + \beta_{1i}$Trials$_{ti} + \beta_{2i}$Mood$_{ti}$.

2. *Nonlinear Growth.* Models in which growth is nonlinear can be included in a variety of ways. If the growth is expected to reach a maximum value and then decrease (or to reach a minimum value and then increase), then a quadratic term may be added to the Level 1 equation, as

$$\hat{Y}_{ti} = \beta_{0i} + \beta_{1i}\text{Trials}_{ti} + \beta_{2i}(\text{Trials}_{ti})^2.$$

Alternatively, if growth is expected to increase toward a maximum possible value

or to decrease toward a minimum possible value (as in some learning experiments), models that represent growth to an asymptote can be utilized (Cudeck, 1996). Finally, if a second-stage process that changes the growth trajectory is expected to come into play at some point following treatment, piecewise models can be used to model the two phases of the treatment effect (Cudeck & Klebe, 2002). The causal effect of the treatment can be estimated for any feature of the growth model that is of interest.

3. *Time-Varying Measurement and Missing Data.* Even in experiments in which measurement is planned to take place at fixed intervals (e.g., every 3 months), the participants are not always assessed at the planned time because of scheduling or other problems. For example, Participant 1 may be assessed at months 2, 7, 9, and 11, whereas Participant 2 may be assessed at months 4, 6, 8, and 12 of the study. Growth models can include the precise time of assessment as a variable and properly model these effects. In addition, if there are missing observations (e.g., Participant 1 is assessed at months 2 and 7, misses month 9, and is reassessed at month 11), the participant's data can still often be included in the analysis without biasing the results.[9]

4. *More Complicated Models.* Structural equation approaches to growth permit the estimation of a variety of more complicated models that address new questions. These include such questions as whether the slope in one series (e.g., cognitive development) is related to the slope in another series (e.g., social development) and whether the slope of an earlier set of measurements (e.g., gains in reading in elementary school) relates to the slope of a later set of measurements (e.g., aggression in middle school).

### Mediation

Growth models present advantages and challenges for the study of mediation. Given that the treatment produces changes in the mediator and in the outcome, the temporal ordering of the multiple waves of measurement can make it possible to clearly establish that the effect of the treatment on the mediator precedes the effect of the treatment on the outcome. Although several forms of mediation can be tested within the multilevel framework, they are easier to conceptualize in terms of path diagrams from the structural equation modeling tradition.

Figure 13.4 shows three path models illustrating some issues in mediation. Figure 13.4(A) shows an autoregressive model in which there is no growth. Causal arrows go from M1 to O2, M2 to O3, and M3 to O4. These paths represent the effect of the mediator on the outcome one measurement period later. If these paths are significant, the data provide evidence for the conditions of relationship and temporal precedence consistent with the causal ordering $M \rightarrow O$ that is necessary for inferring mediation. In contrast, Figure 13.4(B), in which growth in the mediator causes growth in the outcome, represents a more difficult form of mediation to demonstrate. Figure 13.4(C) represents an alternative hypothesis in which growth in the mediator and growth in the outcome represent two parallel growth processes, both of which are caused by the treatment. Conclusively distinguishing empirically between the models represented by Figures 13.4(B) and 13.4(C) can be difficult. Strong interpretations of mediation require temporal precedence.

## SUMMARY AND CONCLUSIONS

The randomized longitudinal experiment with multiple measurement waves opens up a number of interesting questions for social psychological research. These questions can be related to the magnitude of the treatment effect as time passes, potential moderators of both the initial effect of treatment and the longer-term pattern of change, and a variety of forms of questions related to the issue of longitudinal processes and mediation. Among the newer approaches are models that permit tests of hypotheses in which the treatment leads to different processes that may affect the outcome in strikingly different ways at different points in time. Our brief overview of these models is by no means complete: More in-depth discussions of a fuller range of possible models can be found in Collins and Sayer (2001) and Singer and Willett (2003).

Beyond the wider range of questions that may be addressed, longitudinal experiments offer other advantages. We have seen that even the simple pretest-posttest randomized experiment can lead to substantial increases in statistical power, and this advantage can be further increased by growth modeling. Growth models also do not assume the treatment leads to the identical causal effect for all participants. Thus, they lead naturally into studies of how personality factors may moderate the effects of social psychological treatments. Furthermore, growth models accommodate a variety of error structures, permitting more accurate tests of hypotheses when the assumptions of the basic ANOVA model are violated.

We believe that longitudinal experimental methods are likely to become increasingly important in social psychology over the next decade. Social psychologists historically have focused on demonstrating the existence of theoretically predicted effects. Once an effect was produced, it typically was simply assumed to persist over time, without empirical evidence in support of that assumption. Social psychologists appear to be becoming increasingly interested in mediation over time, the relationship between processes, and dynamical systems. Given these developments, designs and analyses that can capture these phenomena will be increasingly sought after. The longitudinal

Measurement Wave

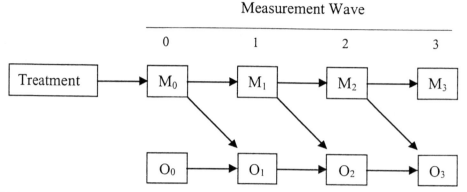

(A) An autoregressive mediational model.

(B) Mediation involving relationships between slopes.

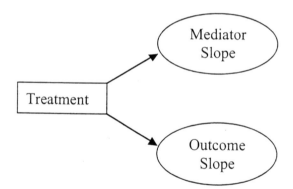

(C) Treatment as a common cause of mediator and outcome slopes.

**Figure 13.4**   Some Issues in Mediation: Illustrations of Two Types of Mediational and One
Common Cause Model

designs and analyses introduced in this chapter hold great promise of serving as useful models for understanding both linear and nonlinear relationships over time.

## FINAL CONCLUSION

The present chapter has provided an introduction to within-subject designs and longitudinal experiments and their analysis given continuous measures of the outcome variable. Both sets of designs have considerable ability to yield accurate estimates of causal effects. The within-subject experimental design must meet the assumptions of temporal stability and causal transience. Thus, the use of within-subject designs requires that researchers carefully think through the primary threats to validity in their own research area and then add design features that address these threats. Within-subject designs greatly reduce the sample size required to reach the desired level of statistical power, and they are particularly valuable when there are large individual differences in the outcome measures.

Longitudinal experiments also can increase the power of statistical tests. They also allow researchers to study change in the magnitude of the causal effect over time, to gain a greater understanding of individual differences in treatment effects, and to explore the relationships between processes over time. These designs require careful attention to the threats to validity outlined in Table 13.1, section A. The increased complexity of the hypotheses also requires that researchers carefully think through the specification of their models and the scaling of independent variables in their statistical models. Given care in their implementation, these designs are valuable additions to social psychologists' methodological armamentarium that can greatly strengthen researchers' ability to understand linear and nonlinear processes over time.

---

# NOTES

1. Although we have not done a formal study, journals reporting more applied research such as the *American Journal of Community Psychology*, *Health Psychology*, and the *Journal of Consulting and Clinical Psychology* have reported a number of longitudinal experiments.

2. Given random selection from a population, randomization permits strong inferences about the magnitude of the average causal effect in the population. However, random selection is rarely achieved in social psychological research, so other nonstatistical rationales must be developed for generalization of causal effects (see West, Biesanz, & Pitts, 2000).

3. Some psychologists may be concerned about the use of difference scores because Cronbach and Furby (1970) recommended against their use. Willett (1988) provided an extensive discussion of the conditions under which change scores are and are not appropriate. Even Cronbach and Furby did not object to the use of difference scores in randomized experiments.

4. Carey Ryan generously made the data from a remarkable study (Ryan & Bogart, 2001) of change in stereotype accuracy available to us. Ryan and Bogart's is one of the few multiwave studies involving two groups published in the social psychological literature, but it does not involve randomization to treatment conditions. For purposes of illustration, we have used only portions of the *actual* data as the basis for our hypothetical experiment. Readers should note that we have significantly altered the description of the variables to prevent readers from becoming confused about the Ryan and Bogart results, and we use a 50% random sample of their data to create a between-subjects design. Thus, the results reported in this section are purely illustrative and do *not* have implications for the interpretation of Ryan and Bogart's original findings.

5. In the analyses presented below, the comparison of $p$ values across analyses provides an indication of the power of each statistical test; however, such interpretations must be made *very cautiously* because they presume that all assumptions are met in the population, so that the actual Type I error rate is .05. With an actual data set, the extent to which the assumptions are met will not be fully known. A $p$ value may also be larger because a statistical test makes more realistic assumptions for the data in the population.

6. Technically, the assumption described is actually compound symmetry, which is closely related to sphericity in the present design. A formal definition of the sphericity condition requires matrix algebra. Standard tests (e.g., Mauchly's test) may not be sufficiently powerful to detect appreciable violations of the sphericity assumption and may perform poorly when the errors have a non-normal distribution within conditions.

7. Closely related to multilevel models are mixed models, which reduce the set of multilevel equations to one single-level equation. Differences between mixed and hierarchical linear models arise because some more complex error structures potentially available in the mixed model form cannot be easily re-expressed in the multilevel form.

8. Wald tests are presented here because they are easy to describe and interpret; however, they are only approximate. Model comparison procedures described in Raudenbush and Bryk (2002) permit exact tests of hypotheses.

9. Technically, growth curve models yield proper estimates of growth parameters when data are missing at random (MAR). MAR means that the reason the data are missing is unrelated to the subject's level on the dependent variable. For example, if *Y* is a measure of substance use and some participants miss assessments when their substance use is high, growth curve models would not provide proper estimates (see Schafer & Graham, 2002).

## REFERENCES

Abelson, R. P., & Prentice, D. A. (1997). Contrast tests of interaction hypotheses. *Psychological Methods, 2,* 315-328.

Aiken, L. S., West, S. G., Sechrest, L., & Reno, R. R. (1990). Graduate training in statistics, methodology, and measurement in psychology: A survey of Ph.D. programs in North America. *American Psychologist, 45,* 721-734.

Algina, J., & Keselman, H. J. (1997). Detecting repeated measures effects with univariate and multivariate statistics. *Psychological Methods, 2,* 208-218.

Anderson, N. H. (1982). *Methods of information integration theory.* New York: Academic Press.

Baron, R. M., & Kenny, D. A. (1986). The moderator-mediator distinction in social psychological research: Conceptual, strategic, and statistical considerations. *Journal of Personality and Social Psychology, 51,* 1173-1182.

Biesanz, J. C., West, S. G., & Kwok, O.-M. (in press). Personality over time: Methodological approaches to the study of short-term and long-term development and change. *Journal of Personality.*

Braver, M. W., & Braver, S. L. (1988). Statistical treatment of the Solomon four-group design: A meta-analytic approach. *Psychological Bulletin, 104,* 150-154.

Campbell, D. T., & Stanley, J. C. (1966). *Experimental and quasi-experimental designs for research.* Boston: Houghton Mifflin.

Cochran, W. G., & Cox, G. M. (1957). *Experimental designs* (2nd ed.). New York: Wiley.

Cohen, J. (1988). *Statistical power analysis for the behavioral sciences* (2nd ed.). Mahwah, NJ: Lawrence Erlbaum.

Collins, L. M., & Sayer, A. G. (2001). *New methods for the analysis of change.* Washington, DC: American Psychological Association.

Cronbach, L. J., & Furby, L. (1970). How we should measure "change": Or should we? *Psychological Bulletin, 74,* 68-80.

Cudeck, R. (1996). Mixed-effects models in the study of individual differences with repeated measures data. *Multivariate Behavioral Research, 31,* 371-403.

Cudeck, R., & Klebe, J. J. (2002). Multiphase mixed-effects models for repeated measures data. *Psychological Methods, 7,* 41-63.

Holland, P. W. (1986). Statistics and causal inference [with discussion]. *Journal of the American Statistical Association, 81,* 945-970.

Holland, P. W. (1988). Causal inference, path analysis, and recursive structural equation models [with discussion]. In C. Clogg (Ed.), *Sociological methodology 1988* (pp. 449-493). Washington, DC: American Sociological Association.

Huitema, B. E. (1980). *The analysis of covariance and alternatives.* New York: Wiley.

Judd, C. M., Kenny, D. A., & McClelland, G. H. (2001). Estimating and testing mediation and moderation in within-subject designs. *Psychological Methods, 6,* 115-134.

Kaplan, S. E., Reckers, P.M.J., West, S. G., & Boyd, J. H. (1988). An examination of tax reporting recommendations of professional tax preparers. *Journal of Economic Psychology, 9,* 427-443.

Keren, G. (1993). Between- or within-subjects designs: A methodological dilemma. In G. Keren & C. Lewis (Eds.), *A handbook for data analysis in the behavioral sciences: Methodological issues* (pp. 257-272). Hillsdale, NJ: Lawrence Erlbaum.

Little, R. J., An, H., Johanns, J., & Giordani, B. (2000). A comparison of subset selection and analysis of covariance for the adjustment of confounders. *Psychological Methods, 6,* 115-134.

MacKinnon, D. P., Lockwood, C. M., Hoffman, J. M., West, S. G., & Sheets, V. (2002). A comparison of methods to test the significance of the mediation and intervening variable effects. *Psychological Methods, 7,* 83-104.

Maxwell, S. E., & Delaney, H. D. (2003). *Designing experiments and analyzing data: A model comparison perspective* (2nd ed.). Mahwah, NJ: Lawrence Erlbaum.

Mehta, P., & West, S. G. (2000). Putting the individual back in individual growth curves. *Psychological Methods, 5,* 23-43.

Raudenbush, S. W., & Bryk, A. S. (2002). *Hierarchical linear models: Applications and data analysis methods.* Thousand Oaks, CA: Sage.

Ribisl, K. M., Watlon, M. A., Mowbray, C. T., Luke, D. A., Davidson, W. A., & Bootsmiller, B. J. (1996). Minimizing participant attrition in panel studies through the use of effective retention and tracking strategies: Review and recommendations. *Evaluation and Program Planning, 19,* 1-25.

Rossi, J. S. (1990). Statistical power of psychological research: What have we gained in 20 years? *Journal of Consulting and Clinical Psychology, 58,* 646-656.

Rubin, D. B. (1978). Bayesian inference for causal effects. *Annals of Statistics, 6,* 34-58.

Ryan, C. S., & Bogart, L. M. (2001). Longitudinal changes in the accuracy of new group members' in-group and out-group stereotypes. *Journal of Experimental Social Psychology, 37,* 118-133.

Schafer, J. L., & Graham, J. W. (2002). Missing data: Our view of the state of the art. *Psychological Methods, 7,* 147-177.

Shadish, W. R., Cook, T. D., & Campbell, D. T. (2002). *Experimental and quasi-experimental design for generalized causal inference.* Boston: Houghton Mifflin.

Singer, J. D., & Willett, J. B. (2003). *Applied longitudinal data analysis: Modeling change and event occurrence.* New York: Oxford University Press.

Student [W. S. Gosset]. (1931). The Lanarkshire milk experiment. *Biometrika, 23,* 398-406.

Venter, A., & Maxwell, S. E. (1999). Maximizing power in randomized designs when *N* is small. In R. H. Hoyle (Ed.), *Statistical strategies for small sample research* (pp. 31-58). Thousand Oaks, CA: Sage.

West, S. G., Biesanz, J. C., & Pitts, S. C. (2000). Causal inference and generalization in field settings: Experimental and quasi-experimental designs. In H. T. Reis & C. M. Judd (Eds.), *Handbook of research methods in social and personality psychology* (pp. 40-84). New York: Cambridge University Press.

West, S. G., Newsom, J. T., & Fenaughty, A. M. (1992). Publication trends in *JPSP*: Stability and change in the topics, methods, and theories across two decades. *Personality and Social Psychology Bulletin, 18,* 473-484.

West, S. G., & Sagarin, B. J. (2000). Participant selection and loss in randomized experiments. *Research design: Donald Campbell's legacy* (Vol. 2, pp. 117-154). Thousand Oaks, CA: Sage.

Willett, J. B. (1988). Questions and answers in the measurement of change. *Review of Research in Education, 15,* 345-422.

Winer, B. J., Brown, D. R., & Michels, K. M. (1991). *Statistical principles in experimental design* (3rd ed.). New York: McGraw-Hill.

## CHAPTER 14

# Measuring Individuals in a Social Environment

## Conceptualizing Dyadic and Group Interaction

RICHARD GONZALEZ

*University of Michigan*

DALE GRIFFIN

*Stanford University*

Currently, a controversy is dividing physicists: Do the basic laws of nature operate only at the level of elementary particles (the reductionist position) or also (and differently) at higher levels of matter? If proponents of the former position are correct, then a complete explanation of physics can be achieved by studying the most basic particles in isolation. A similar controversy has long divided researchers in personality and social psychology: Do the basic laws of behavior operate only at the level of the individual person or also (and differently) at higher levels of social interaction? Are dyads and groups somehow more than the sum of their individual constituents? Do they have a level of existence that cannot be defined in individualistic terms? Can we

understand human psychology by studying one human at a time?

Let us be candid about what this chapter will accomplish: We do not offer answers to the thorny questions we posed above. Instead, we offer some methodological pointers for thinking about dyadic and group data in ways that help clarify what these questions mean. We explore, through several graphical examples, the interpretational complexities that are part and parcel of any dyadic or group design. Our approach has both a negative agenda—to point out common pitfalls of dyadic analysis—and a positive agenda—to explore the conceptual benefits of marrying theory and methodology in the study of dyads and groups. In particular, we encourage researchers to "think outside the box" when analyzing dyadic data—where the box represents the confines of standard data analytic methods and is defined by the classic assumption of "independent" data points.

There is no doubt that traditional analytic methods encourage a reductionist or individualistic perspective, which has a long and honored tradition in social psychology. Social psychology, at least in the American tradition, has been defined as the study of the individual in a social context. Even though the most common, pervasive, and powerful social contexts are those made up of other people, it is no accident that most of the great demonstrations of the "power of the situation" feature an active individual facing an impassive and inflexible social group. Whether it is the unyielding and unanimously mistaken majority of Asch's conformity studies, the magisterial and unshakable experimenter of Milgram's compliance studies, the forbidding and frightening scientist of Schachter's fear and affiliation studies, or the unconcerned and distracted onlookers of Darley and Latane's bystander intervention studies, the social context—that is, the other people—is constrained to uniformity to provide a controlled experience for the "real" participants in the studies.

There are good reasons for the individualistic approach of classic experiments on the influence of "social" context. The experimental method itself, the manipulation and control of factors that allows the experimenter to draw the cherished causal inference, brings with it some basic ground rules: Individuals within conditions should be treated exactly alike to eliminate confounding and to reduce within-cell error variance. The standard between-subjects analysis of variance, which goes hand in hand with the simple factorial experimental design so beloved by classic social psychologists, requires that each data point has "independent and identically distributed errors" (known as the IID assumption). Each participant in a study is explicitly required to be independent of every other participant except for the common effect of the manipulation. Thus, the very issue of how people combine, interact, and affect each other is stripped away from the classic experimental design in social psychology.

The decision to remove actual group interaction from the standard toolkit of social psychologists was a deliberate and considered one. It marked the end of the ascendancy of the "group dynamics" approach developed by Lewin and his students and colleagues. This change in emphasis and design reflected both statistical and theoretical influences. Group dynamics researchers who had studied actual groups—their interactions and changes over time—became frustrated with the amount of effort required to gain one additional data point, because the independence assumption meant that responses from all members of a group were aggregated or collapsed into a single value (usually the group mean). Furthermore, the main outcome variables of interest shifted from qualities of the group (e.g., group cohesion, norms, intergroup communication, group performance) to qualities of individuals (e.g., anxiety, attitude change, attribution, individual performance). Theories that once focused on the forces that held groups together or led to their disintegration were now adapted to focus on the forces that led to consistency between attitudes and behavior, or between expression and emotion.

One of the social psychologists who influenced this transition was Harold Kelley. He is well known for his contributions to attribution theory, a defining approach to individual social cognition. He also codeveloped an influential and important theory of social interaction called Interdependence Theory. One of the reasons that attribution theory has sparked much more empirical research than interdependence theory is that the study of interdependence cannot be done within the confines of the statistical independence assumption. (A second reason is that some types of interdependence, such as that which might develop in an intimate romantic relationship, are difficult to study within the confines of the 30-minute laboratory experiment.) Remarkably, it is only within the last 10 years that a sizable number of social psychologists have returned to looking at groups as molecules, as entities that are more than a collection of individual atoms. The good news is that this is happening at all. The bad news is that the same statistical limitations that shackled the original group dynamics movement, in particular the statistical independence assumption, are still limiting the conceptualization, design, and analysis of dyads and groups.

In this chapter, we discuss techniques that will help social psychologists move beyond the statistical independence assumption in dyadic and group research designs. We first discuss the common error of creating independence within an intrinsically non-independent data set. Then we consider three analytic models for "breaking apart" individual and group levels of analysis while preserving the basic structure of non-independence. Throughout, the lesson is that an analytic or statistical strategy should reflect theoretical assumptions about the mechanism or model of non-independence. There is no single way to analyze data from dyads or groups. As is always the case, the "right way" to analyze one's data depends on the research question one is asking. The main lesson we hope to convey to the reader is that the researcher must first be mindful of the type of research question being asked because the nature of the research question leads one to different analytic approaches.

## NON-INDEPENDENCE AND INTERDEPENDENCE

The independence assumption generally comes in the form of a linear model such as $Y_{ij} = \mu + \alpha_i + \varepsilon_{ij}$ where $Y_{ij}$ is the jth dependent variable in the ith condition. This is the standard model for a one-way analysis of variance. The variable $Y$ is what is observed. In an experiment, the $\alpha_i$ reflects the shared effect of the manipulation on every member of a given cell or condition. The term $\mu$ is the grand mean of the dependent variable, which is a scaling constant that applies to all observations in the study. The $\varepsilon_{ij}$ reflects the set of unique influences on an individual that are unshared with the other members in that cell or condition. This "unshared" effect is at the heart of the independence assumption because it is assumed that each of the errors $\varepsilon_{ij}$ is independent from the others.

To appreciate how a violation of independence might occur, consider a somewhat contrived example. If three members of one condition are surveyed on a sunny day whereas all others are surveyed on a rainy day (weather is unrelated to the experimental manipulation), a possibility of "shared error" is created that would violate the independence assumption. The violation of independence would make the statistical model written above inappropriate because the resulting $p$ value would be incorrect. This is because the three individuals might respond similarly to each other due to their shared sunny environment (even though they experienced it at different times), and not simply because of their shared experimental condition. This violation of independence can be modeled as a correlation between the error terms, so that the error terms would now have a systematic component caused by a shared influence as well as a random unique component. (See Kenny and Judd [1986] for a complete treatment of the effects of a violation of the independence assumption.)

In a non-experimental observational study, the $Y$ represents the observed variable, the $\mu$ reflects the grand mean of the observed variable, the $\alpha_i$ reflects the shared effect of some fixed value of the predictor variable (say, an individual's rating of political conservatism) on the observed variable, and the $\varepsilon_{ij}$ again reflects the set of unique unshared influences on an individual. For example, some respondents might be sampled during the summer and others during the winter, and people's expressed attitudes might vary across the seasons even though their true level of political conservatism does not. Such shared errors violate the traditional regression model just as much as they violate the traditional analysis of variance model closely associated with experiments. As with the case of experiments, such violations of independence could be modeled by allowing for correlated errors.

Non-independence is simply a statistical issue that invokes no assumptions about the cause of the relationship: Are sets of scores correlated beyond the shared effect of being in the same experimental condition or having the same fixed quantity of an explanatory variable? That is, are there subsets of similar scores within an experimental condition or within a level of a predictor variable? The correlation may come about because of third variables (such as the weather or time of year) or from social interaction (perhaps the development of shared norms) or "contagion" between the participants (in the extreme, a "group mind" as postulated by Le Bon, 1897/2001). Typically, in experiments or surveys, non-independence is a nuisance, and we correct for it by adding a new factor or predictor variable to account for shared effects of weather or season or gender of the interviewer; this in effect shifts the shared effect from error (where it is a problem) to the fixed structural model, where it belongs (at least in traditional designs). A violation of independence can seriously influence the conclusions from a statistical test in that the $p$ value can be seriously distorted (Kenny & Judd, 1986).

In dyadic and group designs, the "non-independence in the errors" is due to group membership. Two members of the same couple or group are correlated by virtue of the experience of being in the same group. Group membership will create correlated errors in much the same way that we discussed above. However, there is a major difference in connotation that we want to highlight. Usually, the violation of independence is a nuisance that the investigator wants to correct or avoid. However, in the case of dyads and groups, the violation of independence may be the very phenomenon the social psychologist is trying to assess: Are the scores of people within the same dyad or group similar to each other—that is, does the group display a shared culture or outlook or even a personality? To convey this subtle difference, we use the term *interdependence* (rather than non-independence, or violation of independence) to refer to correlated error due to social interaction. The underlying statistical model, however, is the same. The key difference in how we handle interdependence as compared to non-independence is that we will use the nature of the correlated error to test hypotheses specific to the underlying social dynamics (rather than try to "correct" for the correlated error, as is usually done in the case of non-independence).

To be explicit, we again write the linear model and show how it describes interdependence. In symbols, we have $Y_{ij} = \mu + \alpha_i + \varepsilon_{ij}$, where $\mu$ reflects the grand mean of the dependent variable and $\alpha_i$ represents the effect of a manipulated variable such as exposing couples to one of two experimental treatments (or the different values of a predictor variable). In much the same way that subjects measured on sunny days versus rainy days can lead to correlated error, group membership can lead to correlated errors $\varepsilon_{ij}$ for individuals in the same group. Thus, the group can be conceptualized as a confounding variable. Data from two individuals who are married might be related to each other because the two individuals are married, in addition to being related to each other because the two individuals were exposed to the same experimental treatment (or have similar values on a predictor variable). However, if we are interested in the psychology of social interaction, we do not necessarily want to discard completely (i.e., partial out or correct for) the correlated error structure. As we show below, interesting insight about underlying process can be gleaned by modeling the correlation between the errors. That is, the interdependence of the error terms can tell us quite a bit about the social psychology of interaction among dyad and group members.

## THE INTRACLASS CORRELATION

The magnitude of the interdependence present in a variable is indexed by the intraclass correlation (ICC, often denoted $r_{xx}$). As we will soon see, the ICC is the basic building block of dyadic and group designs. The ICC, which comes in many forms and has several uses (Shrout & Fleiss, 1979), indexes the similarity of scores on the variable in terms of the proportion of shared variance within clusters to the overall variation across all scores. The ICC can be viewed as an index of agreement within or across judges, a building block of Cronbach's alpha indexing the reliability of a multi-item scale, or a measure of effect size for ANOVA models (Haggard, 1958).

In the case of dyadic and group designs, the ICC has a specific meaning because it assesses the degree of agreement within group members. For example, if husbands and wives rate their feeling of security in their relationship (that is, the husband and the wife each rate their own level of security), the data come naturally in pairs due to marriage. This pairing, or clustering, could produce a correlation within the cluster that may differ from the correlation between two individuals who are not married. The ICC provides an index of this correlation. The standard independence assumption is that all observations are independent from each other. The ICC provides a measure of agreement within couple

members, so it provides a natural measure of interdependence. The ICC would be a relevant measure if a researcher was interested in testing whether there was agreement between the husband and the wife on their ratings of security in the relationship.

We now consider some special cases of the ICC. If each wife provides a rating that is equal to her husband's, but the ratings differ between couples, then the ICC will be 1 because couples are maximally similar (i.e., all the variance is between couples). If ratings vary within couples just as much as they vary between couples, then the ICC will equal 0 because there is no evidence of similarity or dissimilarity within couples. If ratings vary more within couples than they do between couples, the ICC will be negative, indicating that individuals within groups are more dissimilar than expected by chance. Notice the analogy to the traditional $F$ test used in the ANOVA model: When variance is primarily between conditions, the $F$ ratio is larger than 1; when variance is primarily within conditions, the $F$ ratio is smaller than 1. The development of the ANOVA model by R. A. Fisher at the beginning of the 20th century was in fact a modification of the basic intraclass correlation then in use (Haggard, 1958). The ANOVA approach can be restated in terms of the ICC, but because of its traditional association with experimental methods (particularly factorial experimental methods), the ANOVA approach has become almost synonymous with the independence assumption. Repeated measures, or within-subject, ANOVAs allow a restricted pattern of correlated errors across people or across time, and multivariate (M)ANOVAs allow unrestricted correlations across outcome variables. Thus, specific generalizations of the independence condition are in common use (e.g., a paired $t$ test allows correlated error across the two observations from the same person). The task of the social psychologist studying interdependence is to make use of such generalizations in order to answer specific psychological questions (e.g., what is the level of husband/wife agreement?).

The ICC can be used to index non-independence or interdependence across a wide range of applications, from diary studies in which individuals are measured a number of times (time is embedded within individuals, and an individual's scores may be similar across those times) to educational studies in which students within classes share a common environment (students are nested within schools, and the students within a school may be similar) to studies of close relationships in which individuals mutually influence each other. In each of these designs and many others, the presence of non-independence or interdependence provides a challenge and an opportunity. The challenge is to deal with the level-of-analysis problem (e.g., individuals versus classes versus schools), both statistically and conceptually. The opportunity is to go beyond merely acknowledging the degree of non-independence and unpack the meaning of the shared effects. For example, interdependence means that interacting individuals influence each other's outcomes. If a researcher is examining the impact of social interaction, then the degree of interdependence might be the central measure of interest and should be modeled directly rather than treated as a statistical nuisance that needs to be corrected. Such theoretical presumptions guide the way that data must be structured and analyzed.

Throughout the rest of this chapter, we focus on examples of one particular class of designs, observational studies of dyadic inter-action, and systematically develop models for conceptualizing different types of dyadic processes. Our modest goal is to end the hegemony of the independence assumption and its atomic perspective and to celebrate the return of the molecular model to social psychology. We hope to provide an intuitive understanding of diverse dyadic models by graphical demonstrations. All the conceptual principles that are presented apply to experimental designs as well, but we expect that the most common application will be to observational designs. We describe three prototypical designs for modeling dyad-level data: the latent dyadic model, the actor-partner model, and the slopes-as-outcomes (HLM) model. Although each model is built upon a common building block (the intraclass correlation), each solves the levels-of-analysis or multilevel problem in a different way, with very different implications for theory building and theory testing.

The latent dyadic model places the main causal forces giving rise to shared behavior or attitudes at the level of latent or underlying dyadic effects. An example of a research question that can be tackled by the latent dyadic model is "What is the dyadic-level correlation between a couple's rating of security in the relationship and a couple's level of intimacy?" The actor-partner model places the main causal forces giving rise to individual behavior as acting between individuals. An example of a research question that can be addressed by the actor-partner model is "Which is a stronger predictor of the husband's rating of intimacy—his rating of security or his wife's rating of security?" These two models require the same type of data to be collected: Ratings on each variable are collected from each member of the couple. The slopes-as-outcome model emphasizes causal forces acting between levels, and for dyads this model requires a more complicated data collection where data from each member of the couple are collected over multiple times (as in a diary study). An example of a research question that can be tackled by the slopes-as-outcome model is "Does the level of security as rated by the couple members moderate how conflict in the relationship today predicts an individual's feeling of intimacy with the partner on the next day?" Note how these three models are not simply different statistical frameworks that are available for the data analyst; they imply different underlying causal structures and thus permit different conclusions to be made from one's data. (Note, however, that the plausibility of these conclusions depends on the plausibility of the assumed causal structure.)

Before we turn to our three focal models, we mention a hybrid model that combines a classic experimental approach with actual social interaction. Kenny's Social Relations Model (Kenny & La Voie, 1984) brings the logic of factorial composition to interpersonal interaction by systematically pairing different interaction partners (a "round robin design") and measuring the outcome. This approach, which can be seen as a rare marriage of social and personality psychology, is not reviewed below because it solves the non-independence problem by design (the experimenter's control over the sequence of interaction partners) rather than by analysis, per se. In fact, in a full round robin or factorial design, the experimenter can reduce the ICC to zero. Our interest in this chapter is in focusing on the special case where group membership comes "as is" (e.g., a husband and a wife, and one generally cannot pair each husband with all wives!).

The application to experiments involving dyadic interaction is similar to the observational case. Indeed, if husband and wives are brought into the lab and placed into experimental conditions, the analytical options remain the same as with observational studies. An experimental setting may introduce new types of designs (such as a female confederate who interacts with all participants in the study), and these design changes do have implications for data analysis. For instance, even though the experiment might involve dyadic interaction between the confederate and each participant, the confederate usually does not provide data (usually only the participant in the dyad is the subject of the study and provides data). In such cases interdependence, while it may be occurring between the confederate and the research participant, would not be present in the data. Once again, the devil is

in the details, and different experimental designs may call for variations in how to handle dyadic or group interdependence.

## GRAPHICAL REPRESENTATION OF THE INTRACLASS CORRELATION

The intraclass correlation is one of the oldest, as well as one of the most versatile, statistics. The original computation method for the intraclass correlation proposed by Karl Pearson (1901) was quite intuitive. He focused on the similarity of all possible pairwise combinations of the members from within the same group. Imagine that the researcher is studying roommates who live in three-bedroom apartments, so there are three individuals living in each apartment. Each roommate provides a rating of satisfaction with the living situation. The following comparisons are possible for each score: Roommate 1 is compared to Roommate 2, Roommate 1 is compared to Roommate 3, and Roommate 2 is compared to Roommate 3. Originally, this pairwise intraclass correlation was computed using a special way of coding data, which we describe below. Although other methods of computation have been developed, the method we present is identical to the maximum likelihood estimate of the ICC seen in hierarchical linear modeling programs (when groups have equal size). This equivalence is nice because the relatively simple pairwise approach helps illustrate the more complicated maximum likelihood estimate that is generated from statistics packages, which may not be easy to understand.

Consider a simple example of five male homosexual couples where each member of the couple provides a rating of his own level of intimacy in the relationship. Let's say that the scores on this dependent variable were (1, 2), (3, 4), (4, 4), (5, 4), and (2, 3). The two members of a given couple are denoted within a set of parentheses. We could enter

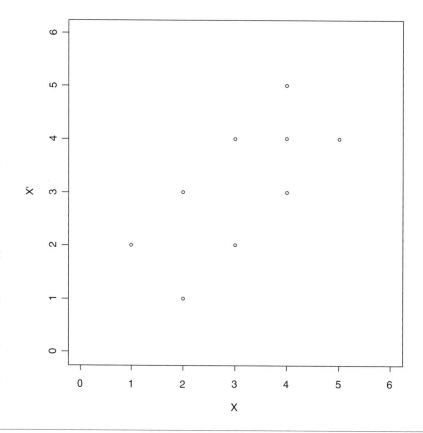

**Figure 14.1**     Graphical Illustration of the Pairwise Coding Using Data for Five Homosexual Couples on a Single Dependent Variable

these 10 data points in one long column—1, 2, 3, 4, 4, 4, 5, 4, 2, 3—along with an associated column of codes that tell us of which dyad the individual was a member. The pairwise approach involves re-entering the same data but in a different order, an order that switches the two individuals within the same dyad. So, for these data the second column would be 2, 1, 4, 3, 4, 4, 4, 5, 3, and 2. To understand how this coding works, it is helpful to plot these data, calling the first column $X$ and the second column of reordered data $X'$ (see Figure 14.1).

This plot appears to show a positive correlation between the two columns, but actually it shows more. If we connect the two points of the same dyad with a line segment, we see some structure around the identity line. It is

this very structure that is the violation of the independence assumption and provides information about the degree of interdependence. These data are not randomly scattered on the plane; instead, points are joined as pairs according to dyadic structure—group membership defines an association between pairs of points. Figure 14.2 shows the same points displayed with the additional structure.

Figure 14.2 shows that the two members of each dyad tended to agree, and as the data show, the members in four of the five couples differed by one point on this scale. Thus, pairs within dyads tend to be similar, but there is quite a bit of variation across dyads, as indicated by the line segments intersecting the identity line at different places. Perfect agreement corresponds to a point on the

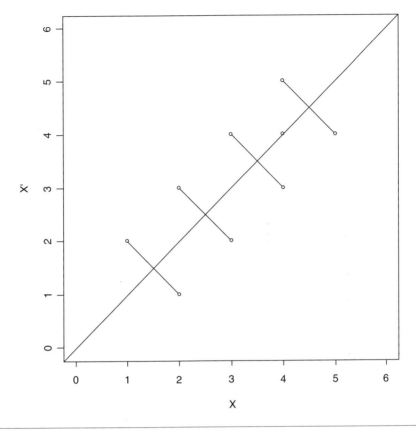

**Figure 14.2**   The Data From Figure 14.1, With Line Segments Connecting Points for Members of the Same Couple

identity line, as seen in the couple that had the score (4, 4). It turns out that the traditional Pearson correlation between these two variables (i.e., variables that have been "pairwise" or double coded) provides the pairwise ICC, which is the maximum likelihood estimator. In this example, the intraclass correlation is relatively high at 0.706, suggesting a high level of within-dyad agreement.

A different example shows what the plot would look like when there is little similarity within dyads. Consider the data (1, 5), (2, 5), (3, 1), (4, 1), and (5, 3). Again, string these data into one long column, $X$, create a second column that contains the recoded pairwise data $X'$, examine the plot, and compute the Pearson correlation between the two columns $X$ and $X'$. As one would expect with

these data, Figure 14.3 reveals relatively little agreement within dyads; instead, there is a type of dissimilarity such that when one member of the couple scored relatively high (i.e., above the mean), the other member scored relatively low, indicating some sort of complementarity within the couple. Indeed, the plot shows that the pairs of points are not close to the identity line (which would have signified agreement); the Pearson correlation between $X$ and $X'$ is $-0.615$.

These plotted examples used data for which dyad members are indistinguishable, or exchangeable, in the sense that we have no theoretical reason to distinguish one person from another. Other examples of exchangeable dyads are same-sex twins, members of a work group, and members of a jury (except

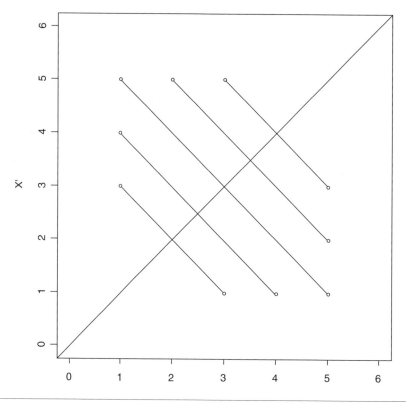

**Figure 14.3** A Second Example of the Pairwise Coding Illustrating Little Within-Couple Agreement

for possibly the foreperson). A reader may think of ways of making the individuals distinguishable, such as coding the older same-sex twin, or the seniority of each member of the work group, or the chair each juror took at the deliberation table. Although each of these additional variables provides a means in principle for distinguishing the members of a group, our use of the term "exchangeable" refers more to the underlying theoretical variable of interest.

A more familiar type of dyad is where members are distinguishable by some theoretically meaningful variable; examples include heterosexual couples where sex is the distinguishing variable, a landlord/tenant pair, and a medical team of a doctor and an aide. Distinguishable dyads have the key characteristic that it is appropriate to place data from all members of one "type" under

one column in the data file and members of the other type in a second column, and compute a regular Pearson correlation. In exchangeable dyads, this is not possible because it is not clear "who should be in Column 1 and who should be in Column 2." The pairwise ICC in the distinguishable case provides different information from the regular Pearson coefficient because the ICC indexes absolute rather than relative similarity. The computation involves a slight modification to the procedure used in the exchangeable case. Rather than taking the Pearson correlation between $X$ and $X'$ as in the exchangeable case to compute the pairwise ICC, one computes a partial correlation between $X$ and $X'$ controlling for the distinguishing variable (e.g., including a single dummy code for gender). (See Gonzalez and Griffin [1999] for details.)

The data coding for the pairwise approach can be extended to groups of larger size, but it becomes somewhat tedious because the coding must include all possible pairs of group members. For example, if Amos, Bram, and Carl (A, B, C) make up a triad, column $X$ would need six rows to do the pairwise coding: using first letters of their names, we would enter data from A, A, B, B, C, C. In column $X'$ we place the pairwise coding where each partner is listed adjacent to each member (but excluding self pairings). Thus, column $X'$ would be B, C, A, C, A, B, which lines up against column $X$ to include all possible pairwise codes; in this case and any time there are equal numbers within each group, the Pearson correlation of columns $X$ and $X'$ provides the maximum likelihood estimator of the ICC (the same estimate of the ICC that would result from a hierarchical linear modeling program using maximum likelihood). Elsewhere we discuss simple computational formulae for the pairwise ICC in groups and explain the difference between the pairwise ICC and the ANOVA-based ICC (Gonzalez & Griffin, 2001). Throughout the remainder of this chapter, we focus on dyads because our goal is to convey the basic ideas. Although the basic ideas scale naturally from dyads to larger groups, readers interested in groups larger than dyads should consult our other papers for specific details (e.g., Gonzalez & Griffin, 2001).

## INDIVIDUAL AND GROUP EFFECTS: ONE IS NOT ENOUGH

We now move to the case of two variables, say level of intimacy and degree of commitment to the relationship. Research questions in social psychological research usually involve multiple variables, so we need to extend the measure of interdependence presented above to handle more than one dependent variable. We present an example to show why it is useful, even necessary, to consider effects both at the level of the individual and at the level of the group. That is, we can ask whether two variables are related at the dyadic level and also whether the same two variables are related at the individual level. Does a couple's joint level of commitment correlate with the couple's joint intimacy rating? Does the wife's rating of commitment correlate with her intimacy rating, and does that correlation differ from the husband's correlation between the same two variables? Asking research questions at multiple levels (dyadic and individual) creates opportunities for new theory testing. We now illustrate this distinction with some examples.

Let's make up a simple example with five homosexual couples (i.e., five exchangeable dyads). The scores for the five dyads on level of intimacy are as before, with the example showing high agreement: (1, 2), (3, 4), (4, 4), (5, 4), and (2, 3). The scores for degree of commitment also show high agreement (pairwise ICC = .834): (5, 5), (2, 1), (3, 3), (3, 2), and (4, 5). Let's call these two variables $X$ and $Y$, respectively, and we will also create the pairwise coded version of these variables $X'$ and $Y'$. The two pairwise plots for level of intimacy and degree of commitment are presented in Figure 14.4. Next to each line segment depicting a dyad, we place a number corresponding to which dyad it is; for example, on intimacy the point (3, 3) corresponds to Dyad 3 in our hypothetical data set.

Although both plots show a relatively high level of dyad-agreement (positive correlation within variables—meaning the lines perpendicular to the identity line are relatively "short" compared to the variation along the identity line), it is instructive to compare the dyad numbers listed in the intimacy plot with the dyad numbers listed in the commitment plot. At a higher level of analysis, there appears to be a negative correlation between the placement of these dyad numbers across variables: When both dyad members are low

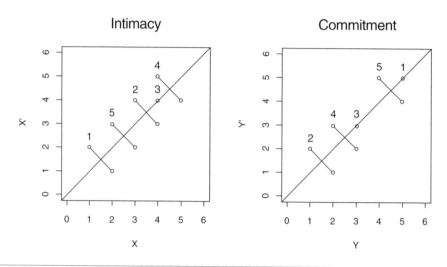

**Figure 14.4** Pairwise Plot for Two Dependent Variables With Dyad Number Next to Each Line Segment

on intimacy, such as Dyad 1, both dyad members tend to be high on commitment.

How can we capture this dyad-level relationship between joint standing on one variable and joint standing on a second variable? We need what is called the dyad-level correlation, which is obtained in two steps: calculating the cross-partner, cross-variable correlation and then correcting this correlation by the degree of within-dyad similarity on each variable. The cross-partner, cross-variable correlation can be visualized using a variation of the pairwise ICC plot where we place each *individual's* intimacy score on one axis and the *partner's* commitment score on the other axis, as shown in Figure 14.5. In other words, it is a cross-variable pairwise intraclass correlation.

The Pearson correlation between an individual's intimacy and the partner's commitment is –.656, which captures in a raw-score sense the negative relationship between the relative ordering of dyads on the intimacy pairwise ICC and the commitment pairwise ICC plots we showed earlier. The negative correlation can be seen by looking at the

10 points in the plot (ignoring the line segments connecting dyad members). These 10 points show a negative correlation between an individual's intimacy and the partner's commitment. To see the negative correlation, note that the scatterplot of points moves from the northwest corner to the southeast corner of the scatterplot. The line segments provide further information because they identify the pairs of points that belong to the same dyad—again giving a visual measure of the within-dyad similarity on each variable.

The key conclusions from this plot are (a) that when individual-level relations are stripped out of the data (by examining across-partner relations) there is a strong negative correlation, and (b) the dyads appear to be similar on both intimacy and commitment.

These two conclusions are jointly modeled in the dyad-level correlation that captures the relation between the two variables at the level of dyadic latent variables. To move to the latent or true-score level, the correlation between X and Y' is adjusted by a denominator that is made up of the product of the ICCs of each; this dyad-level correlation

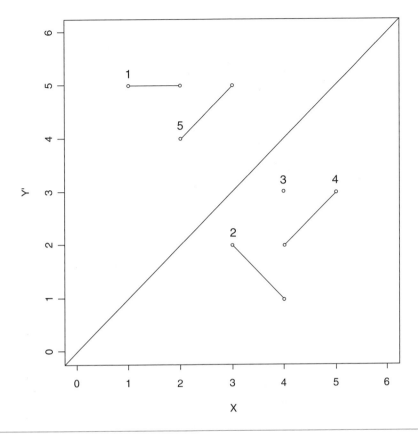

**Figure 14.5** Pairwise Plot of Variable *X* Against Variable *Y*′

measures whether the type of dyadic similarity on one variable—for example, when both members of a given couple are high—relates to the type of dyadic similarity on the other—for example, when both members are low (see Griffin & Gonzalez, 1995, and Gonzalez & Griffin, 2002, for details). Such a latent variable correlation also can be interpreted as the correlation between the "true" dyad-level scores on each variable—scores that have been purged of the unique individual-level effect of each dyad member.

This is one possible solution to the levels-of-analysis problem: Shared variance within a dyad is treated as a dyadic effect and related to create a dyadic-level correlation or regression; unshared variance is treated as an individual effect and related to create an individual-level correlation or regression (as we describe below). Note, however, that such a model is first and foremost a theoretical choice that implies that there is some underlying and unobserved group-level construct (dyadic personality? shared environment? group mind?) that gives rise to the observed similarity. This is an important point because it shows how the choice of one's statistical model reflects one's underlying theoretical model. Practically, this theoretical choice translates into a requirement that the ICC for each variable must be high, or at least marginally significant (Kenny & La Voie, 1985), which signals the presence of shared within-group variance.

This formulation extends the simple case of the ICC on one variable to cases with two or more dependent variables. There are four key correlations in the two variable case: the ICC for variable $X$, the ICC for variable $Y$, the dyad-level correlation described above, and an individual-level (within-dyad) correlation. To make a connection with the simple ICC on one dependent variable that we presented earlier, we now consider two linear equations, one for each variable, and show how to depict the four relevant correlations.

$$X_{ij} = \mu_x + \alpha_i + \varepsilon_{ij}$$
$$\Updownarrow_{r_d} \quad \Updownarrow_{r_i}$$
$$Y_{ij} = \mu_y + \alpha_i + \varepsilon_{ij}$$

The first equation yields the ICC for variable $X$, and the second equation the ICC for variable $Y$, as we saw before in the single-variable case. The $\alpha_i$s are random-effect terms that index dyad membership, and the $\mu$s reflect the grand means of each of the two variables. The additions in the two-variable case are the two vertical arrows that connect terms across the two equations. The arrow labeled $r_d$ depicts the dyad-level correlation, which is a correlation between the group level effects $\alpha_i$; the arrow labeled $r_i$ depicts the individual-level correlation, which is a correlation between the $\varepsilon$s. An intuition for the two correlations is that each represents a "unique" relation controlling for the other. In other words, the dyad-level correlation controls for the individual effect, and the individual-level correlation controls for the dyad-level effect (see Kenny & La Voie, 1985). For details of how to estimate this model using the pairwise approach, see Griffin and Gonzalez (1995). In the distinguishable case, this latent variable model can be implemented using standard structural equation modeling (SEM) programs (Gonzalez & Griffin, 1999).

Although this is not a standard HLM model (discussed below), even with exchangeable dyads the model can be instantiated in HLM as a special case of multivariate outcomes, where both variables $X$ and $Y$ are treated as outcome variables. For details on how to implement this model in the context of an HLM program, see Gonzalez and Griffin (2002). Under maximum likelihood estimation and when all the groups have the same number of members, the parameters estimated in HLM are identical to the parameters estimated with the pairwise approach (e.g., Griffin & Gonzalez, 1995). The individual-level correlation is also identical to the "average within-dyad" partial correlation one would estimate if dyad was entered as a grouping or dummy code (i.e., controlling for the variability of group means), a procedure that can be implemented easily in multiple regression (Cohen & Cohen, 1983). However, a complete analysis of one's dyadic data should do more than examine the individual-level variance. As we have been arguing in this chapter, there is useful psychological information in the group-level variances and covariances. The latent variable model permits a decomposition of individual- and group-level effects so that both types of effects may be examined simultaneously.

## The Use of Dyad Means as Indicators of Shared Variance

The reader may ask, "Why not use the dyad mean as an index of 'dyad-level score' and then correlate the dyad means? What is the value added in running this complicated latent variable model? Is it not the case that if we compute the dyad means for intimacy and the dyad means for commitment, and then correlate the two sets of means, that we can get an estimate of the group level correlation?" Indeed, in the hypothetical example presented earlier, we observed a value of −.80

as the correlation between the two sets of group means, which at least in terms of sign is consistent with the information from the graphical representation we presented.

However, there is a major problem with using dyad means as a measure of dyadic effect because the mean aggregates across both individual-level and dyad-level processes. The correlation between dyad means consists of multiple components, and some of these components do not reflect dyad-level processes. It is possible that the correlation between the dyad means could be negative even when the actual dyad-level correlation is positive. Indeed, there are many possible ways in which the correlation of dyad means can be misleading (see Griffin & Gonzalez, 1995). Thus, a correlation between dyad means cannot be interpreted meaningfully in the context of this model except as an "aggregate," or combination, of both dyadic and individual effects.

The plots presented above show why it is inappropriate to discard one of the dyad members, which is a common simplifying strategy among some data analysts who study dyads. There is information in the degree of similarity or shared variance within a dyad that is conceptually meaningful. To discard such information is to ignore potentially interesting findings about social behavior. Most important, examining individuals "outside the group context" provides little information about what part of the apparently "individual" behavior is shared and what is unique.

## INFLUENCE AND INTERACTION: A MODEL OF INTERDEPENDENCE

The latent variable model of dyadic influence implies that dyadic influence flows from a shared dyadic construct to each individual's behavior. However, the same data can be analyzed under the assumptions that the influence flows from individual to individual (without latent variable constructs), and that an individual's outcome is created by his or her own qualities (the "actor effect") plus the qualities of the partner (the "partner effect"). (See Figure 14.6 for a graphical depiction.) Although the parameters of the "actor-partner" model are in fact algebraic transformations of those given by the latent variable model, the focus and interpretation of the parameters are quite different, with the actor-partner model fitting Kelley's interdependence model where all forces are between individuals. In the actor-partner model, there is no underlying dyadic effect giving rise to observed similarity; similarity on X is simply unexplained (i.e., correlated predictor variables), whereas similarity on Y is generated by the actor and partner predictor variables plus correlated (unexplained) residuals. Note that the actor-partner model does not directly model group processes in terms of relationship parameters that are related to similarity (as does the latent variable model presented earlier). Instead, the actor-partner model merely "corrects" for the fact that individuals are nested within dyads or groups, and it models relationship parameters in terms of regression coefficients that can be interpreted in terms of an actor's influence on the self and the partner's influence on the self.

How should one choose between the actor-partner model or the latent variable model? Because the two models are transformations of each other (i.e., identical goodness-of-fit estimates, and the parameters of one model can be mapped one-to-one to parameters in the other model when certain equality constraints are placed on parameters), the choice is not a statistical one. Rather, the choice should be based on what the investigator wants to highlight in the data. If the investigator wishes to highlight how similarity within group on one variable correlates or predicts similarity within group on another variable,

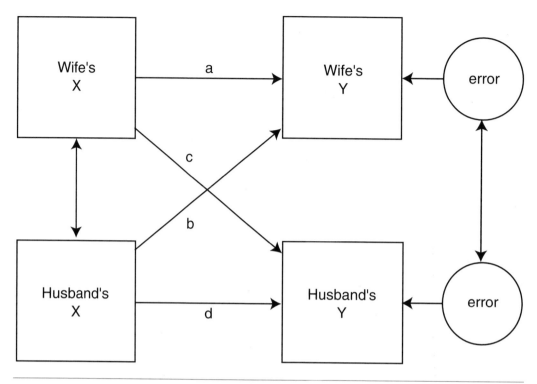

**Figure 14.6** The Actor-Partner Model

then the latent variable model would be appropriate. If the investigator wishes to highlight how predictors measured on the self and other relate to outcomes for the self and other, then the actor-partner model would be appropriate because it corrects for interdependence.

When the members of couples or dyads are distinguishable (e.g., mixed-sex romantic couples), it is straightforward to estimate the models implied by the actor-partner model using structural equation modeling (Gonzalez & Griffin, 1999). One benefit of using a structural equations modeling approach is that the software allows for straightforward testing of equality constraints (e.g., one can test whether the wife's influence on the husband is different from the husband's influence on the wife). However, when the members are exchangeable, standard

methods are inappropriate, and even hierarchical linear modeling programs take some coaxing to fit the model (Campbell & Kashy, 2002). In the exchangeable case, the pairwise coding approach we introduced above provides appropriate maximum likelihood estimates of the actor, partner, and interaction parameters when the pairwise columns are analyzed with standard multiple regression programs. However, special standard errors must be used to test the parameters because of the presence of interdependence (Gonzalez & Griffin, 2001). In particular, the special standard errors adjust for the non-independence on both $X$ and $Y$; when the intraclass correlations on $X$ and $Y$ are 0, then the tests automatically simplify to usual standard errors for the regression model.

Thibaut and Kelly (1959) presented a specific theoretical model of interdependence involving three components: how an actor influences his or her own behavior, how the partner influences the actor's behavior, and how the actions of the pair as a joint entity influence the actor's behavior. This theoretical framework can be translated into a more general actor-partner model that includes an interaction term as well as the two main effects (one for actor and one for partner). This more general actor-partner model presents a point of departure from the latent variable model because, with the inclusion of the interaction term, the two models are no longer statistically indistinguishable. The details of this more general model still need to be developed, with statistical testing procedures requiring proof and simulation. Kenny (1996) provided some initial proposals on how to operationalize the interaction term. These advances provide an interesting example of how developments in statistical theory are being motivated by particular theoretical problems in social psychology.

## HIERARCHICAL LINEAR MODELING: SAME OLD STORY OR A NEW PERSPECTIVE?

Most readers will be aware that there is a new "toolbox" for thinking about nested or multilevel data that has been developed in educational studies. Research on classroom performance led to emergence of a new standard approach, used when individuals are nested within dyads, or pupils are nested within classrooms, or workers are nested within organizations. These new programs (including HLM for Hierarchical Linear Models and MLNwin for Multi-Level models) automatically adjust in their own way for the levels of analysis displayed in the

plots we presented above. The standard hierarchical linear models invoke theoretical assumptions about how to divide up and use within-group shared variance. The key assumption is that interdependence within groups, or individuals across time, can be captured in a within-unit regression model described by an intercept (representing the elevation of the set of outcomes points) and a set of slopes (representing the relation between predictors and the outcomes). These within-unit intercepts and slopes are then described in terms of a "fixed" component that is common to all units and a "random" component that consists of the variability among the units. A significant random component of a slope or intercept means that there is meaningful systematic variation between the units on that parameter. When significant "random" variation exists among the within-unit parameter values, the analyst searches for "cross-level interactions": higher-level factors (e.g., the average SES of the school) that predict variations in the within-unit parameter of interest (e.g., the relation between incoming GPA and graduation test scores).

Consider a multilevel analysis carried out by Murray, Bellavia, Rose, and Griffin (2003) examining how individuals (nested in married couples) responded to daily conflicts with their partners. The authors hypothesized that conflicts on a given day could give rise to individuals feeling more or less intimate with their partners the next day, and the direction and magnitude of this cross-day relationship would be moderated by the individual's level of felt security in the relationship. Each individual within each couple filled out a set of daily diaries for 21 days. Clearly, a number of different sources of non-independence exist in these data. First, there are multiple observations across time from each individual (generally, we will treat this within-individual level as "Level 1" and

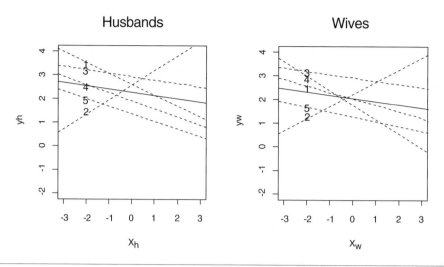

**Figure 14.7**    Graphical Depiction of the Slopes-as-Outcomes Model

model the slopes and intercepts from this level in terms of predictors from higher levels, e.g., from the individual or couple level). Second, at each point there are observations from matched husbands and wives that may or may not correspond or be similar. Third, the slopes and intercepts that are computed within each individual at Level 1 may be similar within couples. In a typical slopes-as-outcomes model with dyadic data, the first and third types of non-independence are modeled and the second is not.

To illustrate the slopes-as-outcomes approach, data from five dyads are plotted in Figure 14.7. Each dotted line represents a best-fitting line for the 20 daily points where today's feeling of intimacy is predicted by the amount of conflict experienced yesterday. The X variable (amount of conflict yesterday) has been centered so that the 0 point corresponds to the mean level for that individual. In such a transformed model, the Level 1 or within-individual across-time intercept reflects how intimate one partner feels the day after an average amount of conflict. The

Level 1 slope reflects reactivity: how much one's level of intimacy today depends on the amount of conflict experienced yesterday. The solid line refers to the best-fitting line (defined by slope and intercept) across all individuals—this is the fixed effect. There is a small but nonsignificant negative slope between conflict and intimacy for men and women. The average level of intimacy, the elevation of the fixed line, is virtually identical for men and women. The focus of the slopes-as-outcomes model, however, is on the variability of the individual lines around the fixed line.

Consider the partners from Marriage 2 (the number next to each regression line refers to couple number). In this small subsample of men and women, they are the only ones who show a positive slope between yesterday's conflict and today's feelings of intimacy. This illustrates both the covariation between partners (essentially the ICC between partner's Level 1 coefficients) and the as-yet-unexplained variability of the slopes and intercepts. This variability is then explained in terms of higher-level factors (e.g., individual- or couple-level factors) that cause some individuals or couples to be more reactive than others, or for some to react positively and others to react negatively. In accord with Murray et al.'s (2003) hypothesis, individuals with high levels of felt security responded to higher levels of conflict than average by drawing closer to their partners, whereas those with low levels of felt security responded to higher than average conflict days by drawing away from their partners.

In this model, romantic partners are treated as parallel multivariate measures so that interdependence is modeled (i.e., accounted for in the model) but is not the focus. The focus, instead, is on explaining or predicting the Level 1 slopes and intercepts by higher-level factors. However, the Level 1 slopes can include across-partner (within-level) interdependence directly at Level 1, for example, by examining whether a man's report of conflict on a given day predicted his wife's report of conflict. Both the multivariate outcome model and the cross-partner analysis just described are limited to cases where the dyad members are distinguishable. It is a challenge to extend the same models to the exchangeable case.

Despite the power and elegance of the "slopes-as-outcomes" model, it is designed to answer one particular kind of question: What group-level factors predict the elevation and slope of within-group relations? As such, it does a fine job of identifying the individual effect in context. However, this standard multilevel model does not deal with all the research questions stated above. Instead, it focuses primarily on how the pattern of relations at Level 1 depends on the values of the higher-level units. Also, the multilevel framework can get very complicated when one allows for non-independence due to time, interdependence within a variable (the

ICC), and interdependence across multiple dependent variables (such as in the latent dyadic model). Specific implementation of HLM models are beyond the scope of this chapter. We refer the reader to book-length treatments such as Raudenbush and Byrk (2002) and Snijders and Boskers (1999), where details such as centering of variables, definition of latent variables, and various implementation details are described. For a discussion of centering in HLM models, see Hoffman and Gavin (1998).

## MORALS

In most chapters such as this, a major goal is to highlight a hot new analytic technique available to the researcher. As such, one would expect us to showcase HLM as the new kid on the scene and expect us to convince readers to use it in their analyses. However, our approach has been to present HLM as a statistical framework that provides a direct way to estimate parameters of interest under a particular model, the slopes-as-outcomes model. We did not offer HLM as the "correct" way to analyze one's data. We hope that the reader has extracted some lessons from this chapter beyond the simple awareness of how to use the hottest new technique currently available. Our goals were (a) to show that there are deeper ways of thinking about the degree of interdependence among interacting individuals and (b) to provide some intuitions about how to think about violations of independence, why it might present a problem for standard statistical tests, and why interdependence provides an opportunity for researchers interested in studying interacting individuals. The violation of independence suggests that interacting individuals are not "isolated." As such, interdependence is a signal that the very phenomenon researchers are seeking—people influencing each other—is present in one's data.

We presented three different theoretical models. Each of these models provides a different way to think about one's data and highlights different features. The latent variable model places similarity at the forefront; it models similarity directly within dyads both within a variable and across multiple variables. It answers individual-level questions such as "What is the correlation between an individual's rating of commitment and the same individual's rating of intimacy?" as well as group-level questions such as "Are couples in which both individuals are high on commitment also the couples in which both individuals are high on intimacy?" The actor-partner model places interpersonal influence at the forefront; it models interdependence across variables and corrects for interdependence within variables. It answers questions such as "Which variable is a better predictor of her intimacy rating: his commitment to the relationship or her commitment rating?" The slopes-as-outcomes model places individual processes at the forefront; it models these processes (often over time) as a function of other variables (which can be variables from the individual actor or the partner, or can be a unit variable such as number of children). It answers questions such as "Does the level of commitment each partner feels moderate how today's intimacy in the relationship predicts tomorrow's level of intimacy?"

Which model is correct? Which model should I use on my data? Unfortunately, these are not questions that can be answered with simulation or mathematical reasoning. It turns out that all the models presented here (as well as others presented by Kenny, 1996) are in some sense correct. In fact, some statistical programs can be used to estimate all three models. For example, an HLM program can be used to estimate the latent

variable model (Gonzalez & Griffin, 2002; Griffin & Gonzalez, 1995). But special tricks are needed because the latent variable model is in a sense "multivariate" and HLM programs are designed primarily for univariate regressions (that is, the slopes-as-outcomes framework needs to be "tweaked" to estimate the parameters of the latent variable model). Another example is that an SEM program, which is used to estimate the latent variable model (with dyad and individuals as latent variables), also can be used to estimate the regression-based actor-partner model (Gonzalez & Griffin, 2001).

Our point is that the particular statistical program one uses is not the real issue, because with a little bit of work it is possible to make a program estimate the necessary parameters. One should not use HLM merely because it is what other researchers in one's area are using. We encourage researchers to ask themselves the critical question, "Which model is most appropriate for the information I want to extract from my data?" The answer to this question determines how to proceed with specific analytic techniques. The different models we presented have (superficially) different ways of handling the non-independence that results from group membership. Which method is right for you depends mostly on the theoretical question you want to answer.

This answer may not be satisfying to people who want to know which technique to use to analyze a data set in front of them. But we believe that without knowing the underlying theoretical framework that motivated the research question, it would be inappropriate to make a blanket recommendation. Instead, we offered the pairwise approach as a tutorial method to illustrate several issues surrounding interdependence and offered three conceptual frameworks against which various psychological research questions can be modeled. As David Kenny has said, interdependence is the "very stuff" of relationships. Once one understands how to measure interdependence, then there is an immediate realization that the way to handle interdependence depends on the underlying model one has in mind. A general statistical framework that can be guided by theory and mold itself to the specific needs of a researcher is the best analytic tool that anyone could wish for.

## REFERENCES

Campbell, L., & Kashy, D. A. (2002). Estimating actor, partner, and interaction effects for dyadic data using PROC MIXED and HLM: A guided tour. *Personal Relationships, 9,* 327-342.

Cohen, J., & Cohen, P. (1983). *Applied multiple regression/correlation analysis for the behavioral sciences* (2nd ed.). Hillsdale, NJ: Lawrence Erlbaum.

Gonzalez, R., & Griffin, D. (1999). The correlational analysis of dyad-level data in the distinguishable case. *Personal Relationships, 6,* 449-469.

Gonzalez, R., & Griffin, D. (2001). A statistical framework for modeling homogeneity and interdependence in groups. In G. Fletcher & M. Clark (Eds.), *Blackwell handbook of social psychology: Vol 2. Interpersonal processes* (pp. 505-534). Malden, MA: Blackwell.

Gonzalez, R., & Griffin, D. (2002). Modeling the personality of dyads and groups. *Journal of Personality, 70,* 901-924.

Griffin, D., & Gonzalez, R. (1995). The correlational analysis of dyad-level data: Models for the exchangeable case. *Psychological Bulletin, 118,* 430-439.

Haggard, E. A. (1958). *Intraclass correlation and the analysis of variance.* New York: Dryden Press.

Hoffman, D. A., & Gavin, M. B. (1998). Centering decisions in hierarchical linear models: Theoretical and methodological implications for organizational science. *Journal of Management, 23,* 623-641.

Kenny, D. A. (1996). Models of non-independence in dyadic research. *Journal of Social and Personal Relationships, 13,* 279-294.

Kenny, D. A., & Judd, C. M. (1986). Consequences of violating the independence assumption in the analysis of variance. *Psychological Bulletin, 99,* 422-431.

Kenny, D. A., & La Voie, L. (1984). The social relations model. In L. Berkowitz (Ed.), *Advances in experimental social psychology* (Vol. 18, pp. 142-182). Orlando, FL: Academic Press.

Kenny, D. A., & La Voie, L. (1985). Separating individual and group effects. *Journal of Personality and Social Psychology, 48,* 339-348.

Le Bon, G. (2001). *The crowd: A study of the popular mind.* New York: Dover Publications. (Original work published 1897)

Murray, S. L., Bellavia, G., Rose, P., & Griffin, D. (2003). Once hurt, twice hurtful: How perceived regard regulates daily marital interaction. *Journal of Personality and Social Psychology, 84*(1), 126-147.

Pearson, K. (1901). Mathematical contributions to the theory of evolution IX. On the principle of homotyposis and its relation to heredity, to the variability of the individual, and to that of the race. *Philosophical Transactions of the Royal Society of London: Series A, 197,* 285-379.

Raudenbush, S., & Byrk, A. (2002). *Hierarchical linear models: Applications and data analysis methods* (2nd ed.). Thousand Oaks, CA: Sage.

Shrout, P. E., & Fleiss, J. L. (1979). Intraclass correlations: Uses in assessing rater reliability. *Psychological Bulletin, 86,* 420-428.

Snijders, T., & Bosker, R. (1999). *Multilevel analysis: An introduction to basic and advanced multilevel modeling.* Thousand Oaks, CA: Sage.

Thibaut, J. W., & Kelley, H. H. (1959). *The social psychology of groups.* New York: Wiley.

## CHAPTER 15

# Quantitative Research Synthesis

## Examining Study Outcomes
## Over Samples, Settings, and Time

WENDY WOOD

*Texas A&M University*


P. NIELS CHRISTENSEN

*San Diego State University*

Research synthesis is a technique for reviewing research literatures that provides quantitative estimates of the size and pattern of results across studies. In many ways, this technique is analogous to other scientific research methods. Research synthesists generate hypotheses about a phenomenon, collect data, analyze the data with meta-analytic statistical techniques, and draw conclusions. A unique feature of research synthesis is that the study, and not the individual participant, is the primary unit of analysis. The set of studies evaluated in a synthesis likely represents the efforts of multiple researchers who tested different samples of participants using a variety of operations of variables in varying experimental contexts at a variety of points in time. Thus, syntheses can provide estimates of effects across studies, measures, research contexts, and time periods. This chapter describes the process of conducting a research synthesis.

Research synthesis is a quantitative alternative to narrative reviews (e.g., term papers), which provide qualitative summaries of research findings. A hallmark of research synthesis is the use of systematic decision rules and procedures (Lipsey & Wilson, 2001). Narrative reviews can be conducted systematically but often are not

AUTHORS' NOTE: Preparation of this chapter was supported by a grant from the National Institute of Mental Health (1R01MH619000-01). The authors thank Alice H. Eagly, Blair Johnson, and Jeanne Twenge for their thoughtful comments on an earlier draft of the chapter.

(see Bushman & Wells, 2001; Cooper & Rosenthal, 1980). Following a systematic process does not ensure that everyone agrees with the conclusions, but it does make each step of a synthesis explicit and available to others' scrutiny. This use of systematic procedures to identify, code, and analyze study findings becomes increasingly important with greater numbers and greater complexity of the studies included in the review. For example, the classic Smith and Glass (1977) synthesis of psychotherapy outcomes included more than 300 studies—an accomplishment that would have been difficult with narrative reviewing techniques.

Another benefit of quantitative reviews is the use of effect size estimates. Effect sizes represent the direction and magnitude of an effect apart from its statistical significance. Narrative reviews often base conclusions on the statistical significance of individual study findings in the reviewed literature. This can be misleading, especially when the reviewed studies used small sample sizes that may not have provided sufficient power to detect effects. Then reviews can wrongly conclude that an effect is not present when in fact it is (Schmidt, 1996). In addition, when exact effect sizes are estimated for each study, the overall variability can be calculated across the study effects. Low variability might indicate that the reviewed studies converge on a common conclusion, whereas high variability might indicate that study findings are influenced by factors that vary across studies (e.g., attributes of the research participants). In general, understanding the variability in a phenomenon can be just as important as understanding its overall size.

In this chapter, we draw on our own experiences in conducting research syntheses to develop general introductory guidelines for how to conduct such reviews. First, we give examples from two of our own syntheses that illustrate the various purposes for conducting reviews. Then we describe the procedures involved in conducting a research synthesis, emphasize the key decisions at each stage of the process, and consider some of the potential pitfalls associated with quantitative reviewing. We conclude with a discussion of how to interpret synthesis results.

## USES FOR QUANTITATIVE RESEARCH SYNTHESIS

### Evaluating Existing Theories

The question of whether media violence affects aggression might have an obvious answer to anyone who has spent a Saturday morning watching cartoons with young viewers. However, both scientists and the general public have debated the existence of media violence effects. A large body of empirical research has tested this effect, and a number of literature reviews have compiled the research findings. Although some early reviews failed to detect much of a relationship (e.g., Freedman, 1988; McGuire, 1986), most subsequent reviews concluded that media violence increases aggression (e.g., Felson, 1996; Geen, 1998; Heath, Bresolin, & Rinaldi, 1989; Paik & Comstock, 1994).

Given the practical and theoretical importance of media violence effects, these conclusions deserve critical scrutiny. In general, a research synthesis is only as good as the studies on which it is based. If the primary studies being reviewed are poorly constructed or share a common flaw, then the review conclusions may suffer from a "garbage-in, garbage-out" problem (Cook & Leviton, 1980; Sharpe, 1997). With respect to media violence, many studies have used correlational designs. Syntheses of such studies, like the individual research reports, cannot demonstrate a causal effect of media violence on viewer aggression. In addition, media violence effects as studied in the laboratory may differ from the real world settings in which people usually watch and react to violent programs. Thus, the external validity of many laboratory experiments—and syntheses of these experimental findings—may not be appropriate for drawing conclusions about media exposure and aggression in everyday life.

To provide a targeted answer to the question of whether media violence has a causal impact on aggressive responses in everyday contexts, we (Christensen & Wood, in press; Wood, Wong, & Chachere, 1991) conducted a synthesis of 24 experiments. The studies in our review ensured the validity of causal inferences by randomly assigning participants to be exposed to violent or nonviolent media. Furthermore, participants' aggressive responses following media exposure were assessed during naturally occurring social interaction with peers or strangers. By limiting the synthesis to reports that satisfied these constraints, we were able to draw conclusions about the causal effect of media violence in everyday situations. The results indicated that exposure to media violence does increase aggression: Approximately 20% more participants assigned to the media violence conditions displayed greater than average aggression, when compared with the participants assigned to control conditions.

The central question addressed in research syntheses on media violence also was the focal question in most of the primary research reviewed. This synergy between syntheses and primary research emerges when topics of current interest to the field generate considerable primary research, and this interest, along with the available data base, then enables quantitative research reviews. Although aggregated findings often can be anticipated from the findings of the individual studies in a review, some reviews have yielded surprising results. For example, in a synthesis concerned with domestic violence, Archer (2000) challenged the common notion that such physical aggression is perpetrated primarily by men. Although men were found to engage in more intense aggression against their partners than did women—and thus men inflicted greater physical harm—women were found to engage in more frequent acts of aggression against their partners than did men (although see Frieze, 2000; O'Leary, 2000). Follow-up syntheses are also useful when primary research has yielded an inconsistent pattern of effects. By identifying key moderators of an effect, a synthesis can potentially explain the inconsistency. For example, a number of syntheses have addressed the elusive phenomenon of mental telepathy, and the most recent review obtained reliable evidence of telepathy primarily in research that followed a standard paradigm (Bem, Palmer, & Broughton, 2001; see also Bem & Honorton, 1994; Milton & Wiseman, 1999).

## Testing Novel Hypotheses

Meta-analytic syntheses in social psychology sometimes test hypotheses that were not the focus of the primary reports and can be addressed only when findings are aggregated across studies. Synthesists can examine whether an effect depends on the features of the studies that vary in the reviewed literature. For example, some of the research syntheses on sex differences have evaluated primary studies that included only one sex, allowing the synthesist to compare findings from male-only studies with those from female-only ones (see Eagly & Wood, 1991). Also, syntheses have effectively evaluated changes in social phenomena over time by examining whether study findings depend on the year when data were collected or a report was published (see Twenge, 2002).

To illustrate how research syntheses test new hypotheses not addressed in primary research, we describe Ouellette and Wood's (1998) synthesis of the effects of intentions on behavior. These researchers were interested in the fact that people intend to act in certain ways, such as to adopt a healthy lifestyle, but these intentions don't always translate into actions. There is even a holiday based on this phenomenon, the New Year's resolution. For a few days or weeks in January, most people can stick to resolutions such as exercising or eating healthy foods, but then most revert back to their old behavior patterns.

Why is it so difficult for people to make changes in many of the behaviors they perform every day? One explanation is that behavior is guided by multiple systems, only some of which are conscious and involve explicit intentions. When behavior is well practiced, so that it becomes habitual, it can be cued automatically by features of the environment with minimal awareness. Ouellette and Wood (1998) hypothesized that habits can explain why people do not always act on their conscious intentions. Over time, when explicit intentions such as New Year's resolutions conflict with automatic habitual responses, the habits often will win out.

Meta-analytic techniques were ideal to test this hypothesis. Even though no primary studies had examined the different systems guiding behavior, a broad literature exists on behavior prediction. Ouellette and Wood divided 64 prediction studies into groups based on whether they investigated a behavior that was likely to be guided by habits or by intentions. Behaviors such as drinking coffee and wearing seatbelts are ones for which people can establish habits because they have sufficient opportunity to perform the behavior in stable contexts. For these behaviors, the synthesis revealed that people followed their established routines and their behavior was not influenced strongly by their stated intentions. In contrast, it is difficult to establish habits for behaviors such as getting a flu shot or donating blood, which occur only once or a few times a year. For these behaviors, the synthesis revealed that people were highly likely to carry out their intentions. In general, then, the synthesis provided evidence for a new hypothesis that was not tested by the individual studies in the review but that could be evaluated when the studies were aggregated.

## PROCEDURES IN CONDUCTING A RESEARCH SYNTHESIS

### Determining if You Have Enough Studies

A research synthesis requires the existence of a number of primary studies that are relevant to the research hypothesis. The question of how many studies are needed is a question of the power of statistical tests. That is, does the synthesis have sufficient power to detect the overall effect and the variability in effect estimates? Although research syntheses are often reputed to have high statistical power, this is not always the case (Hedges & Pigott, 2001). A statistical rule of thumb is that larger numbers of studies are required when the effect of interest is small and highly variable and when the reviewed studies are underpowered (see Cohen, 1988, 1992). From a statistical perspective, only two studies would be needed to detect an effect typical of the size found in social psychology (Hedges & Pigott, 2001).[1] However, almost 30 studies would be required for sufficient power to detect a medium degree of variability in the effect estimates (Hedges & Pigott, 2001). From a practical standpoint, the required number of studies is jointly determined by the constraints of power and the meaningfulness of the results once synthesized.

A typical assumption in meta-analysis is that the studies to be aggregated are replications of each other. However, this is rarely true in practice. Researchers often build on each other's work by varying aspects of an earlier research design to determine boundary conditions or to examine the variety of processes that generate an effect. For this reason, research literatures typically include numbers of studies that vary in their specific features or operations but test a common theoretical or conceptual idea. Critics of the technique have argued that aggregating across studies with diverse operations and participant samples is tantamount to combining "apples and oranges" (Cook & Leviton, 1980; Sharpe, 1997). As we explain below, meta-analytic statistical techniques that estimate the extent of variability across study findings provide a way to assess whether it is reasonable to aggregate across a given set of studies and to treat them as tests of a common hypothesis.

## Defining the Problem, Variables, and Sample

The first step in a synthesis is developing a clear research question. Typically, a synthesis evaluates evidence for the relation between two variables, and this relation often involves the influence of an independent variable on a dependent variable. To frame the research question appropriately, reviewers will need to evaluate the history of the research problem in the literature.

Theoretical explanations for the effect can help to identify the appropriate ways to define the variables of interest and the sample of studies to be included in the review. Because individual studies can differ widely in the operations they use to measure and manipulate variables, synthesists have to develop their own definitions of variables that can be applied systematically to the reviewed studies. These definitions need not include all available operations of constructs in the literature. For example, Ouellette and Wood (1998) restricted their definition of habits to frequency of past behavior and did not include potentially less reliable measures, such as people's reports of whether they performed a behavior out of habit.

The research question directing the synthesis also determines how the sample of studies is defined and how the boundary conditions is defined and how the boundary conditions are set for including and excluding research. In our experience, the decision about what studies to include is fluid and often changes as the review progresses. It is not uncommon for reviewers to modify the research question, the definition of variables, and the boundary conditions for the sample as they discover the full range of variables and designs that have been used to test the research hypothesis.

To generate an optimal sample definition, synthesists need detailed knowledge of the research question and the relevant literature. When samples are defined too broadly, they include heterogeneous sets of studies that tap diverse psychological processes. Such a high level of variability can obscure the effect of interest. For example, if Christensen and Wood (in press) had included studies of exposure to print media in addition to video, the less vivid written presentation might have reduced media effects or limited them only to participants who attended to and comprehended the printed material. Of course, if a reviewer were interested in comparing media effects across modality, it would be appropriate to include print and video presentations in the sample of studies and to conduct analyses to compare them.

The opposite problem occurs when samples are defined too narrowly. In that case, reviews may generate a limited conclusion that does not make a significant contribution beyond the individual studies themselves. One example of a narrow sample definition occurs when researchers aggregate findings across multiple studies within a single research report. Single-report syntheses provide estimates of an effect size in a particular experimental context. Because the cumulative sample size across studies is larger than that of individual studies, these syntheses provide greater power for tests of statistical significance. However, the conclusions of such a synthesis are limited to the specific research participants, stimuli, and setting of the initial studies.

Sample definitions sometimes specify that only high-quality studies are eligible to be included. However, including studies with lower methodological quality is not likely to bias the review's conclusion if each study has its own unique flaws and the overall effect aggregates across the individual study biases. Another reason to include studies regardless of quality is that scientists differ in their evaluations of quality, and decisions about what methodologies to include and exclude may be hard to defend. Yet, restrictive methodological criteria have the advantage of yielding results from the most credible studies. In our example at the beginning of this chapter, Christensen and Wood (in press) focused on studies with high internal and external validity in order to provide clear evidence of the causal direction of the media effect and its size in everyday social interaction. Selecting studies for certain criteria also makes sense when systematic study biases can be identified in the sample. For example, if small-sample studies get published primarily when their effects are statistically significant, then including such studies will likely inflate the overall estimate of effect size (Johnson, Carey, & Muellerleile, 1997; Kraemer, Gardner, Brooks, & Yesavage, 1998). Although there is no all-purpose solution to the problem of study quality, we recommend adopting lenient selection criteria for methodologies while coding each study for a wide range of methodological and procedural features. This allows researchers to evaluate the potential impact of the various methodological variations.

## Locating Relevant Studies

The standard goal of a research synthesis is to describe either the universe of studies that has examined a particular relation or an unbiased sample of this universe. For this reason, it is important to include all relevant research in the study sample. When a research literature is very large, one solution is to randomly select a subset of studies to evaluate.

Given the goal of describing the universe of studies, both published and unpublished studies are eligible for inclusion. Including unpublished studies is especially important when there is reason to expect publication bias, especially the tendency for studies with small samples to be published only when their effects achieve statistical significance. Publication bias might seem less of a concern when the relation tested in the meta-analysis was not examined in the original studies, as occurred with Ouellette and Wood's (1998) finding that behavioral intentions are weak predictors when habits exist to direct actions. But even then, we strongly advise including unpublished research to ensure that the sample of studies in the review validly represents the sample of studies conducted on the issue.

A variety of strategies can be used to locate relevant studies. Because each search strategy is likely to provide some unique information, reviewers should use all the strategies available. The most common technique for locating studies is to conduct a search of computerized databases (e.g., PsycInfo, WorldCat). These can be used to identify articles that mentioned certain terms in their titles or abstracts (e.g., the variables of interest in the review) and articles that were classified in the database as being relevant to general index terms. Unpublished studies often can be located through searches of Dissertation Abstracts or ERIC (Educational Resources Information Center). Another strategy is the descendancy approach, in which reviewers identify an important early article and then search a database for subsequent articles that cited the initial work. The result of these computerized database searches typically is a list of titles and abstracts, which needs to be evaluated further for eligibility for the review. Typically, reviewers will need to locate and read the actual articles to determine whether they meet the study inclusion criteria.

Another standard strategy is to use the ancestry approach, searching the reference lists of reviews and articles. Additional articles also can be identified through hand searches of relevant journals. Sometimes reviewers also use an "invisible college" strategy and contact active researchers in an area and others who might have relevant research that is unpublished or in the process of being published. In general, the process of locating studies in research synthesis bears some similarity to the procedures of sampling respondents in survey methodologies; like participant sampling, it is important that study identification proceed systematically. Synthesists should document the search strategies that they used, along with the key terms used to search computerized databases. When these are reported in sufficient detail, other researchers can replicate the search process.

## Forming the Meta-Analytic Database

To form the meta-analytic data set, coders read through eligible studies to extract the relevant information and record it on a standard coding form. The database is compiled from these forms. It consists of codes of the potentially important study attributes along with effect sizes, or quantitative estimates of each study's findings.

### Coding Study Features

What information should be coded from each study? In general, synthesists code features of the studies, such as their methodology, along with the theoretically identified conditions that might reduce or strengthen the effect.

Because study methodology can affect study findings, codes should be formed to reflect features of each study's methods. For example, Christensen and Wood (in press) coded whether the media violence studies in their sample were conducted in laboratory settings or in everyday contexts (e.g., schools, playgrounds). Laboratory studies generally reported larger effects of exposure to media violence, presumably because they provided greater control over extraneous variables and less random variation. Other aspects of study methodology that often are evaluated in meta-analyses include the reliability of the measures (e.g., the number of items for each measure); aspects of the procedure and design, including indicators of treatment strength (e.g., length of film, extremity of violence depicted); and attributes of the research participants, such as sex and age (see review by Wilson & Lipsey, 2001).

A variety of additional study attributes could influence study findings, including the year the study was completed, the nationality of the research participants, and the identity of the study authors. For example, a number of syntheses have reported that the original researchers who identify a phenomenon tend to obtain stronger evidence of the predicted effect than subsequent or unrelated researchers (e.g., Johnson & Eagly, 1989; Wood, Lundgren, Ouellette, Busceme, & Blackstone, 1994). These effects of researcher identity could reflect a variety of factors, including the original researchers' superior understanding of the phenomenon as well as the tendency for subsequent research efforts to examine the boundary conditions for an effect by identifying when it appears and when it does not.

The moderating factors that theoretically are expected to affect the size of the relation of interest are another important source of coded variables. For example, Ouellette and Wood (1998) evaluated the relation between people's intentions and behavior by coding whether the studied behaviors were ones for which habits were likely to operate. In addition, synthesists sometimes derive codes from sources other than the original articles. For example, Costa, Terracciano, and McCrae's (2001) meta-analysis of cross-cultural sex differences in personality included codes representing the status of women compared with men for each culture studied in the reviewed research. They were then able to evaluate whether personality sex differences varied with men's and women's status in societies. In Eagly and Steffen's (1986) synthesis on sex differences in aggression, undergraduate students rated the reviewed studies for how much harm the students would expect to experience in each experimental setting. The researchers then predicted the sex differences in aggression from male and female students' perceptions of harm. Thus, syntheses can test a variety of theories using coded variables from the studies themselves and from external sources.

Study codes typically are recorded on standard forms (see Stock, 1994, for an example of a coding form). Because it is important that coding be done accurately, multiple coders should individually complete the coding forms, and their responses should be compared. Wide disagreement among coders suggests that variables need to be more clearly defined and that the coding procedure needs to be implemented again. The agreement or interrater reliability between coders will need to be calculated (e.g., Cohen's kappa) and reported along with the synthesis results (see Orwin, 1994, for reliability statistics).

### Selecting Computer Programs to Calculate and Analyze Effect Sizes

The goal of effect size calculations is to convert the outcome information provided by each study into a common metric. This allows synthesists to aggregate and compare the outcomes of independent studies that may have used different research designs and operations of variables. This chapter does not address the technical details of the statistical computations involved in meta-analysis. A number of statistical computing packages have been developed that can perform the two central meta-analytic computations: first calculating effect size estimates and then analyzing the estimates generated (e.g., Borenstein & Rothstein's, 1999, *Comprehensive Meta-Analysis*; Johnson's, 1993, *DSTAT 1.10*; Lipsey & Wilson's, 2001, *MS Excel* Effect Size Computation Program and *SPSS* Macros for Meta-Analysis; Shadish, Robinson, & Lu's, 1999, *ES*; Wang & Bushman's, 1999, *SAS* Macros for Meta-Analysis). As we explain in the section on analysis techniques, the unique properties of meta-analytic data make it inappropriate to use standard statistical packages.

Each of the available programs has specific strengths and weaknesses. For example, *DSTAT* and *ES* provide highly comprehensive facilities to calculate effect sizes from complex experimental designs. *Comprehensive Meta-Analysis*, the *SPSS Macros*, and the *SAS Macros* provide a useful range of analytic procedures once effect sizes have been calculated. Yet, to use any of these programs effectively, analysts need to understand how to select the data from a research report, design a meta-analytic database, and select an analysis strategy. The present chapter provides a guide for making these decisions.

### Calculating Effect Sizes

A number of statistics can be used to represent the size of an effect. Regardless of the particular statistic, the effect size is given a positive or negative sign to indicate the direction of the relation between the two variables of interest. The signs are applied so that studies with opposite outcomes have opposing signs. The sign is given in a way that ensures readers' easy interpretation. A positive sign often is used to signify a relation in the predicted direction, and a negative sign is used to signify an unexpected outcome. However, this strategy does not always convey a clear meaning. In some cases, such as when inverse relations are predicted, interpretation would be clearer if expected outcomes had a negative sign.

One commonly used effect size is the standardized mean difference, which represents the size of the relation of interest in terms of standard deviation units. It is calculated as

$$g = \frac{M_E - M_C}{SD_{pooled}},$$

where $M_E$ is the sample mean in the experimental group, $M_C$ is the sample mean in the control group, and $SD$ is the pooled standard deviation for the groups. Because this formula overestimates population effect sizes, especially when they are based on small samples, the estimate typically is corrected for this bias, $d = J(m)g$, where $d$ is an unbiased estimator of the population effect size and $J(m)$ is the correction,

$$J(m) = 1 - \frac{3}{4m - 1},$$

where $m$ is the degrees of freedom, or $n_E + n_C - 2$. Researchers often label the uncorrected effect size estimate as $g$ and the corrected estimate as $d$.

The standardized mean difference is commonly used as the effect size metric when the majority of reviewed studies report comparisons between two groups, such as an experimental group and a control group. Thus, this effect size often has been used in syntheses of experimental research in social psychology. Unfortunately, the statistic $d$ rarely can be taken directly from the research reports, and it typically needs to be calculated by the analyst.

To calculate $d$ for a between-subjects experimental design, the study's means, standard deviations, and sample sizes can be inserted into the formulas above. The estimate

of the pooled standard deviation, $SD$, represents the square root of the pooled variances of the two groups and is the same variance estimate as that used to calculate an $F$ or $t$ test difference between two groups. The formula is computed as

$$SD = \frac{\sqrt{(n_E - 1)\,SD_E^2 + (n_C - 1)\,SD_C^2}}{n_E + n_C - 2},$$

where $n_E$ and $n_C$ are the number of observations in the experimental and control groups, respectively, and $SD_E$ and $SD_C$ are the standard deviations for the experimental and control groups, respectively. When the groups to be compared are from a within-subjects design, the correct variance estimate is the standard deviation of the differences between paired observations. Also, when the standard deviation for the overall sample is given, it needs to be converted to the pooled within-cell standard deviation. This is accomplished by removing from the overall estimate the variance that is due to the difference between the experimental and control conditions being compared (Hedges & Olkin, 1985).

It is also possible to calculate effect sizes from the probability values associated with statistical tests. The $p$ value of the comparison of interest, the sample size, and the direction of the effects (i.e., whether the experimental or control condition obtained the higher score) can be entered into most meta-analytic computer programs to yield an effect size estimate. Yet, probabilities often do not allow for exact estimates. They may be presented as levels (e.g., $p < .05$, $p < .01$), or a study report might simply note that a finding is statistically significant and thus imply that $p < .05$. In this case, the most reasonable assumption is that $p$ is equal to the specified level. Obviously, this yields only an approximate estimate of the true effect size, and alternate information should be used when available.

Most meta-analytic computer programs also can calculate effect sizes from chi-square tests of association or from proportions of study participants in experimental groups that meet a criterion value on some measure (e.g., the percentage of media viewers who engaged in aggressive acts). However, if chi-square values have more than one degree of freedom, they cannot be converted directly into effect sizes. Instead, the frequency tables need to be converted into comparisons between two groups, perhaps by aggregating across the data that are presented.

Another frequently used effect size estimate is the correlation coefficient, $r$. It is also corrected for overestimation bias that occurs especially with small samples,

$$G_r = r + \frac{r(1 - r^2)}{2(n - 3)},$$

where $G_r$ is the approximation of the population effect size and $n$ is the sample size. Because the sampling distribution of the correlation coefficient does not follow a normal curve, it is conventional to use Fisher's $r$-to-$Z$ transform and to perform meta-analytic calculations on the $Z$ values. Correlation coefficients typically are used in syntheses if most of the reviewed studies report relations between two continuous variables. But because $r$ can be transformed easily into $d$ and vice versa, the choice of an effect size metric for meta-analysis is somewhat arbitrary. A simple rule of thumb that holds for small and moderate-sized effects is that $r$ values are numerically about half (or slightly more than half) the size of $d$ values, so that $r = .20$ corresponds to $d = 0.40$. In general, the convention is to use the metric that most closely represents the way the majority of study findings were originally reported.

An advantage to using the correlation coefficient as an index of effect size is that this statistic often can be extracted directly from study reports. However, $r$ statistics are not all interchangeable, and relations reported in the form of a point-biserial $r$ will need to be converted to a product-moment $r$ (see Rosenthal, 1991). In addition, when regression models are reported, standardized beta weights can be interpreted as correlation coefficients only when the model has a single predictor. In regressions that include multiple predictors, the regression weight for the variable of interest is adjusted for the other predictors. Thus, the results of regressions with multiple predictors cannot be used to represent the simple relation between the two variables of interest (although see Becker & Schram, 1994, for more complex solutions).

In general, calculating effect sizes involves many complex decisions. To ensure reliability, we recommend that two people independently complete these calculations and compare their results.

## PROBLEMS (AND SOLUTIONS) WHEN CALCULATING EFFECT SIZES

### Independence of Observations

Single studies often report multiple outcomes that could be included in the data set. For example, a study might report media effects on both verbal and physical aggression. Including multiple outcomes from a single study violates the assumption of most meta-analytic techniques that each outcome is independent of the others. One solution is to generate a single effect size estimate for each study, perhaps by computing an average or some other measure of central tendency (see Gleser & Olkin, 1994). Another example of multiple outcomes occurs when studies provide more than one form of results that could be used to calculate an effect size. For example, a study might provide means and standard deviations along with a *t* value. When both sources yield similar information, analysts can compute effect size estimates from both and take their average. When the estimates are highly discrepant, the analyst could select the one that appears most valid or could exclude the study from the review because the findings are too ambiguous.

Although independence of effects is a goal in forming the meta-analytic database, it is not always possible. For example, a synthesist might not be interested solely in the overall effect of exposure to media violence but also in whether the effect varies with sex of viewer. One strategy is to conduct the analysis in stages with two data sets. The primary data set would evaluate media effects across all study participants by calculating a single effect size for each study. In this data set, all effects would be independent. Then, in a second stage to test for sex effects, a subset of studies could be selected that reported the findings separately for the sexes. For this subset, each study would yield an effect size for males and an effect size for females, and analyses could then compare the sexes. Although the data in this second stage are not independent and run the risk of biasing meta-analytic test statistics (see Gleser & Olkin, 1994), they provide information about the moderating variable of interest.

## Complex Primary Study Designs

Calculation of effect size estimates is not straightforward in studies with experimental designs that varied factors in addition to the relation of interest. The effect sizes in these studies need to be comparable to those in the other studies in the review. First, select the appropriate experimental condition(s) to compare to the control condition(s). Because experiments may have multiple experimental conditions and multiple controls, the experimental versus control comparison selected in each study should afford clear inferences about the treatment of interest. For example, a study of viewer aggression might have included experimental conditions in which participants were angered before exposure and other conditions in which they were not. The experimental condition(s) to use in the effect size calculations depend on the control condition(s) in the study. When control participants were not angered, the no-anger treatment is the appropriate treatment comparison. When controls were angered, then the anger-plus-media condition is appropriate to detect media exposure effects. Of course, a study code would need to be added to the synthesis to indicate whether participants for a particular study were angered; then analyses can be conducted to compare the media effect in studies in which participants were angered versus those in which they were not.

Another concern is how to represent the error term when computing effect sizes from analysis of variance designs that varied multiple factors. When the irrelevant factors in a design are individual difference variables (e.g., measures of viewers' dispositional level of aggressiveness), a one-way experimental design can be approximated to compare the two groups of interest by recalculating the error terms of the analysis of variance to include the irrelevant factors. The composite error term can then be used in the effect size calculations (see Johnson & Eagly, 2000; Morris & DeShon, 1997). However, when other factors in the design represent powerful experimental manipulations that ordinarily do not coexist with the relation of interest, they may not be appropriate to include in the error term. The general rule for error terms is that all effect sizes in the review should be based on the same sources of variability.

These complex issues indicate how important it is that reviewers understand a study's experimental design before estimating the size of its effects. A useful strategy for reviewers, suggested by Johnson and Eagly (2000), is to generate a packet of descriptions of the sources of variance in common experimental designs in the reviewed literature (for summaries of designs, see Maxwell & Delaney, 1999; Myers & Well, 1991). A number of articles provide additional advice on the statistical issues to consider when aggregating data from different types of experimental designs (e.g., Dunlap, Cortina, Vaslow, & Burke, 1996; Morris & DeShon, 1997, 2002).

### Corrections for Effect Size Bias

We noted that the effect size statistics calculated from individual studies are often corrected because they are biased estimators of the population effect size. A variety of other corrections are available to adjust individual effect sizes for bias, artifact, or error. Some of the most elaborate adjustments have been proposed by Hunter and Schmidt (1994). They recommend adjusting for unreliability of measurement, artificial dichotomization of a continuous variable, imperfect construct validity, and range restriction. The goal of these corrections is to generate an idealized estimate of the magnitude of the true population effect size. Thus, the corrections are useful to demonstrate how large the true relation would be if it were not contaminated by these artifacts. The corrections are not appropriate to generate an estimate of the relation that was obtained in practice in a given research literature. Unfortunately, such adjustments typically are not an option in analyses of social psychological research because the original studies usually do not provide the information necessary to calculate adjustments.

### Strategies for Nonreported Results

A number of studies may not have reported sufficient statistical information to calculate effect sizes for the relation of interest. Several strategies exist to handle the resulting problem of missing data.

Sometimes reviewers fill in or impute values for missing effects. For example, an effect size of 0.00 could be entered when studies report that findings are not statistically significant. However, this procedure may be highly inaccurate—even large effects may not be significant when a study's sample size is small. It is also possible to replace missing effect sizes with a mean or some other estimated value (see Pigott, 1994). An alternate strategy, using a "vote-counting procedure," is possible when studies do not provide sufficient information to calculate an exact effect size but they do report the direction of the effect (Bushman, 1994; Bushman & Wang, 1996). This procedure calculates effect sizes from a tally of how many studies obtained a result in a given direction or how many studies obtained a statistically significant result. Regardless of the specific strategy used to address missing data, analysts should conduct "sensitivity" analyses to compare the findings from only the studies that generated an exact effect size with the findings from analyses that also include imputed values or analyses that are based on direction of effect.

## ANALYZING META-ANALYTIC DATA

The first step in analyzing meta-analytic data is to develop an understanding of the attributes of the data set. A visual display of the findings can be helpful. Some meta-analytic computer programs provide these automatically in forest plots and other displays. Stem and leaf plots are useful to convey the "big picture" from review findings. For example, Christensen (2003) used this technique to display the effect size findings from his synthesis of research relating people's self-esteem to their identification with various social groups (see Table 15.1). Each number

**Table 15.1**    Distribution of Effect Sizes (rs) on a Stem and Leaf Plot from Christensen (2003)

| Stem | Leaf |
|------|------|
| +.7  | 0 |
| +.6  | |
| +.5  | 23 |
| +.4  | 00447789 |
| +.3  | 01111222245567 |
| +.2  | 00000000112233334455777789999 |
| +.1  | 00001112222445556667777789999 |
| +.0  | 12333344444555666778999 |
| −.0  | 974332 |
| −.1  | 74 |
| −.2  | 90 |
| −.3  | 7 |

SOURCE: Adapted from Christensen (2003).

NOTE: Each correlation is composed of one stem and one leaf. The numbers on the left side are the stems or the first numeral in the correlation. The numbers on the right side are the leaves or the second numeral in the correlation. Each numeral on the right side is one leaf and indicates a unique correlation. Positive numbers suggest that higher levels of social identification are associated with higher levels of self-esteem.

on the right of the vertical bar signifies a study finding. The graph is read from left to right, with the number on the left of the bar representing the first numeral of the effect size and the number on the right representing the second numeral. Thus, this plot indicates that most study findings cluster around $r = .10$ and .20; people have higher self-esteem when they identify more strongly with political, religious, school, and racial and ethnic groups.

The shape of the distribution of effects in the plot can reveal much about the sample of studies (Greenhouse & Iyengar, 1994; Light, Singer, & Willett, 1994). Note that the overall pattern in Table 15.1 generally follows a normal distribution. If small effect sizes did not appear in the distribution—in particular, if no small effects were obtained from studies with small sample sizes—then this could indicate that the selection of studies is biased

to represent statistically significant findings. Such a bias could emerge if statistically significant results were more likely to be published. Of course, when reviewers have adequately sampled sources of unpublished data and included unpublished findings in the data set, publication pressures are less likely to distort the results of the review.

Displaying the distribution of effect sizes also can be informative about outlying, extreme effects that are unrepresentative of the sample of studies and may even be spurious. Such extreme values require close scrutiny because they have a disproportionate influence on the means, variances, and other statistics. With careful inspection, reviewers may be able to identify how studies with deviant findings differ from the rest of the sample. Some meta-analysts advocate removing the most extreme outliers or adjusting them to more moderate values prior to conducting additional analyses (Hedges & Olkin, 1985; see Johnson, 1993, for a computer application).

Special statistical procedures and computer programs are required to analyze meta-analytic data. Effect sizes differ from data points in primary research because each effect is associated with its own unique variance. In addition, meta-analytic statistical analyses provide useful information that is not generated by conventional statistics with primary data. That is, meta-analytic techniques provide estimates of the consistency or homogeneity of effect sizes across studies.

*Step 1: Choosing a Model*

Synthesists have a choice about whether to use fixed-effects or random-effects procedures in the analysis. Although many published meta-analyses have assumed fixed-effects models, and these are computationally simpler than random-effects models, new computing programs are available that offer both procedures (e.g., Borenstein & Rothstein, 1999;

Lipsey & Wilson's, 2001, adaptation of *SPSS*; Wang & Bushman, 1999).[2]

From the perspective of statistical inference, the choice of model is similar to the choice of whether to use fixed-effects or random-effects models in analysis of variance. Fixed-effects models are appropriate if meta-analysts wish to make inferences about the effect-size parameters in the reviewed studies or about an identical set (Hedges & Vevea, 1998). In these models, the study effects estimate the population effect with the only error being from the random sampling of participants within the studies. Random-effects models allow inferences that generalize beyond the specific set of reviewed studies to a broader population. These models are appropriate when random differences are likely to exist between studies, and these differences include more than just participant-level sampling error (e.g., random variations in experimental procedures and settings).

From a practical standpoint, a review's conclusions can be affected by the decision to use a fixed- or random-effects model. Fixed-effects models usually have greater power to detect effects and yield smaller confidence intervals, whereas random-effects models tend to be more conservative. However, neither model appears especially robust when its assumptions are violated (Field, 2001; Overton, 1998). Thus, it is important to select the appropriate model for the data and the research question. In general, we recommend conducting sensitivity analyses, which involve calculating both models and comparing their results (Lipsey & Wilson, 2001).

### Step 2: Estimating Means and Variability

An initial step in meta-analysis is to aggregate effect sizes across studies to determine the overall strength of the relation between variables. To illustrate the specific procedures involved in aggregating and analyzing

effects, we will present a simple fixed-effects analysis on a standardized mean difference statistic (Hedges & Olkin, 1985).

Study outcomes are combined by averaging the $d$ values across the number of studies, $k$. Each study outcome, $d_i$, is weighted by the reciprocal of its variance, and a mean weighted effect size, $d.$, is computed as a weighted average of the individual studies' effect sizes. Typically, this is calculated as

$$ d. = \frac{\sum_{i=1}^{k} w_i\, d_i}{\sum_{i=1}^{k} w_i}, $$

where the weights for each study outcome, $w_i$, are defined as

$$ w_i = \frac{1}{v_i} = \frac{2\,(n_{iE} + n_{iC})\, n_{iE}\, n_{iC}}{2\,(n_{iE} + n_{iC})^2 + n_{iE}\, n_{iC}\, d_i^2}, $$

in which $v_i$ is equal to the variance of the effect size estimate. This weighting procedure gives greater influence to the studies with more reliably estimated outcomes, which in general are those with the larger sample sizes. Similar weighting procedures are used when aggregating correlation effect size estimates (Hedges & Olkin, 1985; Rosenthal, 1991).

To help interpret the effect size, a confidence interval can be computed around the mean:

$$ d. \pm 1.96 \sqrt{\text{variance}}, $$

where 1.96 is the unit-normal value for a 95% confidence interval and the variance is defined as the reciprocal of the sum of the weights (as defined in the equation for weights given above). If the confidence interval includes zero, then it can be concluded that the relation of interest is not statistically significant.

Meta-analytic statistics also provide an estimate of the homogeneity or consistency of effect sizes. The test statistic, $Q$, evaluates the hypothesis that the effect sizes are consistent (Hedges & Olkin, 1985). This statistic is calculated as

$$Q = \sum_{i=1}^{k} w_i (d_i - d)^2,$$

$Q$ has an approximate $\chi^2$ distribution with $k - 1$ degrees of freedom. A significant $Q$ rejects the null hypothesis that the study outcomes differ only by unsystematic sampling error. If the $Q$ statistic is not significant, it is likely that the study outcomes all represent a common population parameter. However, nonsignificant tests also could be due to statistical power that is inadequate to detect variability when the number of effects is small or when they come from studies with small samples. Thus, a large but nonsignificant $Q$ statistic can suggest variability in study outcomes (Johnson & Turco, 1992).

## Step 3: Investigating Possible Moderators

A large or significant $Q$ statistic suggests that the variability in effect sizes is more than just sampling error. Researchers may believe that this variability is systematic and that the relation of interest increases or decreases systematically with a third, moderating variable. For example, the relation between media violence and viewer aggression might be stronger in countries like the United States, in which a history of high exposure to media violence could make people more accepting of violence, than in countries with less exposure.

To evaluate moderating effects, synthesists can use an analog to analysis of variance in order to examine moderators that are assessed categorically (e.g., nationality of study participants) or an analog to multiple regression to examine moderators assessed on a continuous scale (e.g., year of publication, mean age of study participants). Categorical models divide studies into groups based on the moderator of interest and evaluate whether differences between groups can account for the variability in study outcomes apparent in the significant $Q$ statistic. Continuous models use regression procedures to estimate whether some third, continuous variable is associated with the size of the relation between the two variables of interest. Both of these approaches yield a test of the systematic variance associated with each moderator (i.e., $Q_B$ in categorical models, a test based on the regression coefficient in continuous models) and a test of the remaining, unexplained variability ($Q_W$ in categorical models, $Q_E$ in continuous models; see Hedges & Olkin, 1985). Significant remaining variability in moderator analyses violates the fixed-effects assumption that only random participant-level variability will remain after accounting for moderators. In this case, it is probably appropriate to use random-effects models that include a term to represent the random variability associated with studies. A relatively straightforward adaptation of such an approach is a mixed-effects model, which first accounts for the systematic effects of moderators through fixed-effects analyses and then uses random-effects procedures to estimate the remaining unmeasured random effect and the participant-level sampling error (Shadish & Haddock, 1994).

Although research syntheses is ideally suited to testing moderating relations, it generally is less effective at testing for mediators, or the extent to which one factor affects another factor through some intervening process (see Hoyle & Robinson, Chapter 10, this volume, for a discussion of mediating and moderating relations). When the studies in a research literature did not assess a common mediating process, it is not possible to evaluate mediation at an aggregate level. However, studies sometimes vary moderators that provide insight into mediating processes (see Shadish, 1996, for strategies to test meta-analytic mediation).

### Step 4: Reporting Findings

To have maximal impact, research syntheses need to provide clear and coherent answers to research questions that are compelling to a broad audience. It can be challenging for synthesists to present findings in a simple, clear fashion after they have conducted complex data analyses involving myriad study details. Yet, some of the most useful information about a research literature is simply descriptive, such as graphs displaying study outcomes and tables systematically describing study attributes. Also useful are tables reporting central tendencies of the aggregated effects and estimates of their variability, including (a) unweighted mean effect sizes, (b) weighted mean effect sizes and variability estimates for fixed- and random-effects models, (c) confidence intervals, and (d) sample sizes (see Rosenthal, 1995). In general, reports of findings should be organized to provide clear answers to the questions that initially motivated the synthesis.

## DRAWING CONCLUSIONS FROM META-ANALYSES

### Interpreting Effect Size Statistics

In science as in life, size matters. Large effects are sometimes thought to be important ones. However, variability of the effects also matters. A mean effect that is based on highly variable study outcomes may not converge on the truth as much as obscure it. When variability is marked, understanding of the factors that moderate the size of an effect will likely be more meaningful than interpreting the size of the effect.

A much-respected statistician, Jacob Cohen (1992), provided informal guidelines to interpret the size of effects. He believed that small effects, $d$s < 0.20 or $r$s < .10, are typical of findings in personality, social, and clinical psychology. He termed large effects, $d$s > 0.80 or $r$s > .50, more typical of sociology, economics, and experimental and physiological psychology; these fields apparently investigate potent variables or use methods with strong experimental control. This observation makes the important point that the size of an effect is dependent on both the impact of treatment variables and the amount of experimental control. Finally, Cohen described medium-sized effects, $d$s = 0.50 or $r$s = .25, as being of sufficient magnitude that they are likely to be apparent to a careful observer in daily life. Although these guidelines are widely cited, Cohen cautioned that they represent subjective assessments that should be used only in the absence of a better basis for interpretation.

One common way of interpreting effect magnitude is to calculate effect size in the form of a squared correlation coefficient. The $r^2$ statistic is interpreted as the percentage of variability that is explained by an effect of a given magnitude. Thus, an effect size of $d = 0.40$ or $r = .20$ accounts for about 4% of the variance. However, it may not be appropriate to apply this method to interpret an aggregated correlation across a sample of studies. When some of the studies reported a positive relation and others a negative relation, the aggregated effect will necessarily underestimate the extent to which the two variables are related.

Empirical evidence of the effect sizes typical of social psychology was provided by Richard, Bond, and Stokes-Zoota (2001, in press) in their review of 322 meta-analyses conducted on social psychological topics. Aggregating across the 474 effect sizes provided by the reviews, the mean effect size in social psychology proved to be $r = .21$. The largest magnitude effects emerged from group discussion, in that hearing others' arguments caused group members to shift their attitudes to be more extreme ($r = .75$, $k = 12$), and from assessments of the reliability of measures, in that measures tend to consistently yield similar scores ($r = .75$, $k = 154$).

Even if social psychologists can typically expect to obtain small-to-medium-sized effects, this does not mean that social psychological phenomena are inconsequential. Small effects can be impressive. For example, an effect that is small for any one observation can magnify over time as effects cumulate. Abelson (1985) made this point in the context of baseball, by demonstrating that a batter's skill has only a small impact on what happens at any single time at bat: Even for the best batters, the typical outcome is to make an out. However, batters' skill has important effects on team performance when cumulated across a game and a season. Similarly, small discriminatory biases against female employees may have little impact on any one salary or promotion decision, but across a whole career of such decisions, women may end up with substantially lower salaries and lower status positions than men (Martell, Lane, & Emrich, 1996). Small effects also can be meaningful when aggregated across large numbers of people. For example, Bushman and Anderson (2001) noted that if media violence increased aggressiveness in only 1% of viewers, the substantial numbers of viewers in the United States means that large numbers of people would be incited to act more aggressively.

Another approach to interpreting effect size values is to convert them into a more intuitively meaningful metric. For example, Rosenthal and Rubin's (1983) binomial effect size display translates correlation of effect sizes into an indicator of "success rate" in an experimental versus a control group. Success rate is meant to be defined broadly and in a given synthesis might represent, for example, the incidence of viewer aggressiveness. To understand this approach, imagine that a "success threshold" is set at the median of the distribution of scores on a dependent variable for both treatment and control groups. Then the groups are separated, and the proportion in each group is calculated that is above the overall success threshold. Interestingly, the success differential between the two groups is always equal to the correlation effect size between the two groups. Thus, if a correlation is $r = .2$ between an outcome measure (e.g., aggressive behavior) and whether people were in an experimental group (e.g., watched a violent video) or control group (watched a nonviolent video), then the experimental group's "success" rate of acting aggressively will be 20% higher than the control group's. This demonstration of treatment impact illustrates the importance of effects that might otherwise be interpreted as relatively small.

Finally, another way to interpret the magnitude of effects is to compare them with effect sizes in similar domains. For example, Bushman and Anderson (2001) provided a framework for readers to understand the practical value of media violence effects by noting that they are larger than the relation between (a) condom use and sexually transmitted HIV, (b) passive smoking at work and lung cancer, (c) exposure to lead and IQ scores in children, (d) calcium intake and bone mass, and (e) homework and academic achievement. These contexts provide a framework to better understand the impact of exposure to media violence.

## The Impact of Syntheses Findings and the Future of Research Syntheses

Although research syntheses are sometimes treated as simply summaries of past research, they also are likely to spark additional investigation in several ways (Eagly & Wood, 1994). For example, a synthesis that provides a summary evaluation of existing knowledge can be an initial step in generating novel hypotheses about the mechanisms through which the effect emerges and the boundary conditions for the effect. Syntheses also spur additional investigation by identifying new phenomena that can be evaluated only across studies (e.g., effects of year of publication).

Another reason for additional investigation is to validate synthesis conclusions when the findings of the synthesis are correlational. Findings are correlational when the original studies used correlational designs or when the synthesis used study-level variables (e.g., year of study publication) as moderators of the effect of interest. Using study-level variables as moderators can be highly informative but, like all correlational strategies, raises questions about how to interpret the results. For example, to demonstrate that people act on their intentions primarily when habits have not developed, Ouellette and Wood (1998) divided studies into groups reflecting whether habits would be likely to develop with the behaviors investigated in the studies. Give that the studies in each group may have varied on a number of dimensions from those in other groups, it is not clear how to interpret any between-group differences. Thus, the researchers conducted an additional primary study to demonstrate that intention effects emerge primarily in the absence of habit. Because of the importance of the primary research findings to interpreting the synthesis results, Ouellette and Wood reported the two studies in a single article. In this way, the validity of synthesis conclusions can be enhanced through pairing with the results of other research methods with complementary strengths.

In general, the future of research synthesis as a methodological technique is ensured by the sheer amount of research data being produced each year. As the amount of information increases, so does the need for systematic procedures to distill this information. Advances in information technology are likely to further facilitate use of research syntheses, including the development of electronic depositories to store and codify research findings (e.g., the Cochrane Collaboration's, 2002, medical research archive). Given the power of the technique and the availability of new computer technologies to support it, research syntheses is likely to remain a popular tool for summarizing existing findings and testing novel hypotheses.

## NOTES

1. This calculation is based on a mean effect size of $r = .21$ and a median study sample size of $n = 127$. These estimates were obtained from 322 syntheses in social psychology, which yielded 474 effect sizes (Richard, Bond, & Stokes-Zooka, 2001, in press; also Charles Bond, personal communication, November, 2002). Note further that the analysis assumes a fixed-effects model, which is described in the section "Analyzing Meta-Analytic Data."

2. Lipsey and Wilson (2001) have made their computer programs available on the Internet. Copies of the program to calculate effect sizes (using Microsoft's Excel spreadsheet program) and the program to analyze effect sizes (using SPSS/Win Version 6.1) can be downloaded at the following URL address: http://mason.gmu.edu/~dwilsonb/home.html

# REFERENCES

Abelson, R. P. (1985). A variance explanation paradox: When a little is a lot. *Psychological Bulletin, 97,* 129-133.

Archer, J. (2000). Sex differences in aggression between heterosexual partners: A meta-analytic review. *Psychological Bulletin, 126,* 651-680.

Becker, B. J., & Schram, C. M. (1994). Examining explanatory models through research synthesis. In H. Cooper & L. V. Hedges (Eds.), *The handbook of research synthesis* (pp. 357-381). New York: Russell Sage.

Bem, D. J., & Honorton, C. (1994). Does psi exist? Replicable evidence for an anomalous process of information transfer. *Psychological Bulletin, 115,* 4-18.

Bem, D. J., Palmer, J., & Broughton, R. S. (2001). Updating the ganzfeld database: A victim of its own success? *Journal of Parapsychology, 65,* 207-218.

Borenstein, M., & Rothstein, H. (1999). *Comprehensive meta-analysis: A computer program for research synthesis.* Englewood Cliffs, NJ: Biostat.

Bushman, B. J. (1994). Vote-counting procedures in meta-analysis. In H. Cooper & L. V. Hedges (Eds.), *The handbook of research synthesis* (pp. 193-213). New York: Russell Sage.

Bushman, B. J., & Anderson, C. A. (2001). Media violence and the American public: Scientific facts versus media misinformation. *American Psychologist, 56,* 477-489.

Bushman, B. J., & Wang, M. C. (1996). A procedure for combining sample standardized mean differences and vote counts to estimate the population standardized mean difference in fixed effects models. *Psychological Methods, 1,* 66-80.

Bushman, B. J., & Wells, G. L. (2001). Narrative impressions of literature: The availability bias and the corrective properties of meta-analytic approaches. *Personality and Social Psychology Bulletin, 27,* 1123-1130.

Christensen, P. N. (2003). *Motivational connections between the group and the self: A review with meta-analytic support for the relationship between social identification and self-esteem.* Unpublished manuscript, San Diego State University, San Diego, CA.

Christensen, P. N., & Wood, W. (in press). Effects of media violence on viewers' aggression in unconstrained social interaction: An updated meta-analysis. In R. Preiss, B. Gayle, N. Burrell, M. Allen, & J. Bryant (Eds.), *Mass media effects research: Advances through meta-analysis.* Hillsdale, NJ: Lawrence Erlbaum.

Cochrane Collaboration (2002). Retrieved December 11, 2002, from http://www.update-software.com/collaboration/

Cohen, J. (1988). *Statistical power analysis for the behavioral sciences* (2nd ed.). Hillsdale, NJ: Lawrence Erlbaum.

Cohen, J. (1992). A power primer. *Psychological Bulletin, 112,* 155-159.

Cook, T. D., & Leviton, L. C. (1980). Reviewing the literature: A comparison of traditional methods with meta-analysis. *Journal of Personality, 48,* 449-472.

Cooper, H., & Rosenthal, R. (1980). Statistical versus traditional procedures for summarizing research findings. *Psychological Bulletin, 87,* 442-449.

Costa, P. T., Terracciano, A., & McCrae, R. R. (2001). Gender differences in personality traits across cultures: Robust and surprising findings. *Journal of Personality and Social Psychology, 81,* 322-331.

Dunlap, W. P., Cortina, J. M., Vaslow, J. B., & Burke, M. J. (1996). Meta-analysis of experiments with matched groups or repeated measures designs. *Psychological Methods, 1,* 170-177.

Eagly, A. H., & Steffen, V. J. (1986). Gender and aggressive behavior: A meta-analytic review of the social psychological literature. *Psychological Bulletin, 100,* 309-330.

Eagly, A. H., & Wood, W. (1991). Explaining sex differences in social behavior: A meta-analytic perspective. *Personality and Social Psychology Bulletin, 17,* 306-315.

Eagly, A. H., & Wood, W. (1994). Using research syntheses to plan future research. In H. Cooper & L. V. Hedges (Eds.), *The handbook of research synthesis* (pp. 485-500). New York: Russell Sage.

Felson, R. B. (1996). Mass media effects on violent behavior. *Annual Review of Sociology, 22,* 103-128.

Field, A. P. (2001). Meta-analysis of correlation coefficients: A Monte Carlo comparison of fixed- and random-effects models. *Psychological Methods, 6,* 161-180.

Freedman, J. L. (1988). Television violence and aggression: What the evidence shows. In S. Oskamp (Ed.), *Applied social psychology annual: Television as a social issue* (Vol. 8, pp. 144-162). Newbury Park, CA: Sage.

Frieze, I. H. (2000). Violence in close relationships–development of a research area: Comment on Archer. *Psychological Bulletin, 126,* 681-684.

Geen, R. G. (1998). Aggression and antisocial behavior. In D. T. Gilbert, S. T. Fiske, & G. Lindzey (Eds.), *The handbook of social psychology* (4th ed., Vol. 2, pp. 317-356). Boston: McGraw-Hill.

Gleser, L. J., & Olkin, I. (1994). Stochastically dependent effect sizes. In H. Cooper & L. V. Hedges (Eds.), *The handbook of research synthesis* (pp. 339-355). New York: Russell Sage.

Greenhouse, J. B., & Iyengar, S. (1994). Sensitivity analysis and diagnostics. In H. Cooper & L. V. Hedges (Eds.), *The handbook of research synthesis* (pp. 383-398). New York: Russell Sage.

Heath, L., Bresolin, L. B., & Rinaldi, R. C. (1989). Effects of media violence on children. *Archives of General Psychiatry, 46,* 376-379.

Hedges, L. V., & Olkin, I. (1985). *Statistical methods for meta-analysis.* Orlando, FL: Academic Press.

Hedges, L. V., & Pigott, T. D. (2001). The power of statistical tests in meta-analysis. *Psychological Methods, 6,* 203-217.

Hedges, L. V., & Vevea, J. L. (1998). Fixed- and random-effects models in meta-analysis. *Psychological Methods, 3,* 486-504.

Hunter, J. E., & Schmidt, F. L. (1994). Correcting for sources of artificial variation across studies. In H. Cooper & L. V. Hedges (Eds.), *The handbook of research synthesis* (pp. 323-336). New York: Russell Sage.

Johnson, B. T. (1993). *DSTAT 1.10: Software for the meta-analytic review of research literatures.* Hillsdale, NJ: Lawrence Erlbaum.

Johnson, B. T., Carey, M. P., & Muellerleile, P. A. (1997, February 5). Large trials versus meta-analysis of smaller trials. *Journal of the American Medical Association, 277,* p. 377.

Johnson, B. T., & Eagly, A. H. (1989). Effects of involvement on persuasion: A meta-analysis. *Psychological Bulletin, 104,* 290-314.

Johnson, B. T., & Eagly, A. H. (2000). Quantitative synthesis of social psychological research. In H. T. Reis & C. M. Judd (Eds.), *Handbook of research methods in social and personality psychology* (pp. 496-528). Cambridge, UK: Cambridge University Press.

Johnson, B. T., & Turco, R. M. (1992). The value of goodness-of-fit indices in meta-analysis: A comment on Hall and Rosenthal. *Communication Monographs, 59,* 388-396.

Kraemer, H. C., Gardner, C., Brooks, J. O., III, & Yesavage, J. A. (1998). Advantages of excluding underpowered studies in meta-analysis: Inclusionist versus exclusionist viewpoints. *Psychological Methods, 3,* 23-31.

Light, R. J., Singer, J. D., & Willett, J. B. (1994). The visual presentation and interpretation of meta-analysis. In H. Cooper & L. V. Hedges (Eds.), *The handbook of research synthesis* (pp. 439-453). New York: Russell Sage.

Lipsey, M. W., & Wilson, D. B. (1993). The efficacy of psychological, educational, and behavioral treatment: Confirmation from meta-analysis. *American Psychologist, 48,* 1181-1209.

Lipsey, M. W., & Wilson, D. B. (2001). *Practical meta-analysis. Applied social research methods series* (Vol. 49). Thousand Oaks, CA: Sage.

Martell, R. F., Lane, D. M., & Emrich, C. (1996). Male-female differences: A computer simulation. *American Psychologist, 51,* 157-158.

Maxwell, S. E., & Delaney, H. D. (1999). *Designing experiments and analyzing data: A model comparison perspective.* Mahwah, NJ: Lawrence Erlbaum.

McGuire, W. J. (1986). The myth of massive media impact: Savagings and salvagings. In G. Comstock (Ed.), *Public communication and behavior* (Vol. 1, pp. 173-257). San Diego: Academic Press.

Milton, J., & Wiseman, R. (1999). Does psi exist? Lack of replication of an anomalous process of information transfer. *Psychological Bulletin, 125,* 387-391.

Morris, S. B., & DeShon, R. P. (1997). Correcting effect sizes computed from factorial ANOVA for use in meta-analysis. *Psychological Methods, 2,* 192-199.

Morris, S. B., & DeShon, R. P. (2002). Combining effect size estimates in meta-analysis with repeated measures and independent-groups designs. *Psychological Methods, 7,* 105-125.

Myers, J. L., & Well, A. D. (1991). *Research design and statistical analysis.* New York: HarperCollins.

O'Leary, K. D. (2000). Are women really more aggressive than men in intimate relationships? Comment on Archer (2000). *Psychological Bulletin, 126,* 685-689.

Orwin, R. G. (1994). Evaluating coding decisions. In H. Cooper & L. V. Hedges (Eds.), *The handbook of research synthesis* (pp. 139-162). New York: Russell Sage.

Ouellette, J. A., & Wood, W. (1998). Habit and intention in everyday life: The multiple processes by which past behavior predicts future behavior. *Psychological Bulletin, 124,* 54-74.

Overton, R. C. (1998). A comparison of fixed effects and mixed (random effects) models for meta-analysis tests. *Psychological Methods, 3,* 354-379.

Paik, H., & Comstock, G. (1994). The effects of television violence on antisocial behavior: A meta-analysis. *Communication Research, 21,* 516-546.

Pigott, T. D. (1994). Methods for handling missing data in research synthesis. In H. Cooper & L. V. Hedges (Eds.), *The handbook of research synthesis* (pp. 163-176). New York: Russell Sage.

Richard, F. D., Bond, C. F., Jr., & Stokes-Zoota, J. J. (2001). That's completely obvious . . . and important: Lay judgments of social psychological findings. *Personality and Social Psychology Bulletin, 27,* 497-505.

Richard, F. D., Bond, C. F., Jr., & Stokes-Zoota, J. J. (in press). One hundred years of social psychology quantitatively described. *Review of General Psychology.*

Rosenthal, R. (1991). *Meta-analytic procedures for social research: Applied social research methods series* (Vol. 6). Thousand Oaks, CA: Sage.

Rosenthal, R. (1995). Writing meta-analytic reviews. *Psychological Bulletin, 118,* 183-192.

Rosenthal, R., & Rubin, D. B. (1983). A simple, general purpose display of magnitude of experimental effect. *Journal of Educational Psychology, 74,* 166-169.

Schmidt, F. L. (1996). Statistical significance testing and cumulative knowledge in psychology: Implications for training of researchers. *Psychological Methods, 1,* 115-129.

Shadish, W. R. (1996). Meta-analysis and the exploration of causal mediating processes: A primer of examples, methods, and issues. *Psychological Methods, 1,* 47-65.

Shadish, W. R., & Haddock, C. K. (1994). Combining estimates of effect size. In H. Cooper & L. V. Hedges (Eds.), *The handbook of research synthesis* (pp. 261-281). New York: Russell Sage.

Shadish, W. R., Robinson, L., & Lu, C. (1999). *ES: Effect size calculator.* St. Paul, MN: Assessment Systems Corp.

Sharpe, D. (1997). Of apples and oranges, file drawers and garbage: Why validity issues in meta-analysis will not go away. *Clinical Psychology Review, 17,* 881-901.

Smith, M. L., & Glass, G. V. (1977). Meta-analysis of psychotherapy outcomes. *American Psychologist, 32,* 752-760.

Stock, W. A. (1994). Systematic coding for research synthesis. In H. Cooper & L. V. Hedges (Eds.), The handbook of research synthesis (pp. 125-138). New York: Russell Sage.

Twenge, J. M. (2002). Birth cohort, social change, and personality: The interplay of dysphoria and individualism in the 20th century. In D. Cervone & W. Mischel (Eds.), *Advances in personality science* (pp. 196-218). New York: Guilford.

Wang, M. C., & Bushman, B. J. (1999). *Integrating results through meta-analytic review using SAS software.* Cary, NC: SAS Institute.

Wilson, D. B., & Lipsey, M. W. (2001). The role of method in treatment effectiveness research: Evidence from meta-analysis. *Psychological Methods, 6,* 413-429.

Wood, W., Lundgren, S., Ouellette, J. A., Busceme, S., & Blackstone, T. (1994). Minority influence: A meta-analytic review of social influence processes. *Psychological Bulletin, 115,* 323-345.

Wood, W., Wong, F. Y., & Chachere, J. G. (1991). Effects of media violence on viewers' aggression in unconstrained social interaction. *Psychological Bulletin, 109,* 371-383.

# Part IV

## Emerging Interdisciplinary Approaches: The Integration of Social Psychology and Other Disciplines

## CHAPTER 16

# Methodological and Ethical Issues in Conducting Social Psychology Research via the Internet

MICHAEL H. BIRNBAUM

*California State University, Fullerton*

When I set out to recruit highly educated people with specialized training in decision making, I anticipated that it would be a difficult project. The reason I wanted to study this group was that I had been obtaining some very startling results in decision-making experiments with undergraduates (Birnbaum & Navarrete, 1998; Birnbaum, Patton, & Lott, 1999). Undergraduates were systematically violating stochastic dominance, a principle that was considered both rational and descriptive, according to cumulative prospect theory and rank dependent expected utility theory, the most widely accepted theories of decision making at the time (Luce & Fishburn, 1991; Quiggin, 1993; Tversky & Kahneman, 1992). These theories were recognized in the 2002 Nobel Prize in Economics shared by

Daniel Kahneman, so these systematic violations required substantial changes in thinking about decision making.

The results were not totally unexpected, for they had been predicted by my configural weight models of decision making (Birnbaum, 1997). Nevertheless, I anticipated the challenge that my results might apply only to people who lack the education required to understand the task. I wanted to see if the results I obtained with undergraduates would hold up with people highly trained in decision making, who do not want to be caught behaving badly with respect to rational principles.

From my previous experiences in research with special populations, I was aware of the difficulties of such research. In previous work, my students and I had printed and mailed materials to targeted participants

AUTHOR'S NOTE: This research was supported by grants from the National Science Foundation to California State University, Fullerton, SBR-9410572, SES 99-86436, and BCS-0129453.

(Birnbaum & Hynan, 1986; Birnbaum & Stegner, 1981). Each packet contained a self-addressed and stamped envelope as well as the printed materials and cover letter. We then sent, by mail, reminders with duplicate packets containing additional postage out and back. As packets were returned, we coded and entered data, and then verified the data. All in all, the process was slow, labor-intensive, expensive, and difficult.

I had become aware of the (then) new method for collecting data via the Web (HTML forms), and I decided to try that approach, which I thought might be more efficient than previous methods. I knew that my targeted population (university professors in decision making) could be reached by e-mail and would be interested in the project. I thought that they might be willing to click a link to visit the study and that it would be convenient for them to do online. I was optimistic, but I was unprepared for how successful the method would prove.

Within 2 days of announcing the study, I had more than 150 data records ready to analyze, most from people in my targeted group. A few days later, I was receiving data from graduate students of these professors, then from undergraduates working in the same labs, followed by data from people all over the world at all hours of the day and night. Before the study ended, I had data from more than 1,200 people in 44 nations (Birnbaum, 1999b). Although the results did show that the rate of violation of stochastic dominance varied with gender and education, even the most highly educated participants had substantial rates of violation, and the same conclusions regarding psychological processes were implied by each stratum of the sample. That research led to a series of new studies via the Web, to test new hypotheses and conjectures regarding processes of decision making (Birnbaum, 2000a, 2001b; Birnbaum & Martin, in press).

My success with the method encouraged me to study how others were using the Web in

their research, and to explore systematically the applicability of Web research to a variety of research questions (Birnbaum, 1999b, 2000b, 2000c, 2001a, 2002; Birnbaum & Wakcher, 2002). The purpose of this chapter is to review some of the conclusions I have reached regarding methodological and ethical issues in this new approach to psychological research.

The American Psychological Society page of "Psychological Research on the Net," maintained by John Krantz, is a good source for review of Web experiments and surveys (http://psych.hanover.edu/research/exponnet.html). In 1998, this site listed 35 studies; by 1999, the figure had grown to 65; as of December 9, 2002, there were 144 listings, including 43 in social psychology. Although not all Web studies are listed in this site, these figures serve to illustrate that use of the method is still expanding rapidly.

The Internet is a new medium of communication, and as such it may create new types of social relationships, communication styles, and social behaviors. Social psychology may contribute to understanding characteristics and dynamics of Internet use. There are now several reviews of the psychology of the Internet, a topic that will not be treated in this chapter (see Joinson, 2002; McKenna & Bargh, 2000; Wallace, 2001). Instead, this chapter reviews the critical methodological and ethical issues in this new approach to psychological research.

## MINIMUM REQUIREMENTS FOR ONLINE EXPERIMENTING

The most elementary type of Internet study was the e-mail survey, in which investigators sent text to a list of recipients and requested that participants fill in their answers and send responses by return email. This type of research saved paper and mailing costs; however, it did not allow easy coding and construction of data files, it did not allow the possibility of anonymous participation, and it could not work for those without e-mail. It also annoyed people by clogging their e-mail folder with unsolicited (hence suspicious) material.

Since 1995, a superior technique, HyperText Markup Language (HTML) forms, has become available. This method uses the World Wide Web (WWW) rather than the e-mail system. HTML forms allow one to post a Web page of HTML, which automatically codes the data and sends them to a CGI (Common Gateway Interface) script, which saves the data to the server. This method avoids clogging up mailboxes with long surveys, does not require e-mail, and can automatically produce a coded data file ready to analyze.

Anything that can be done with paper and pencil and fixed media (graphics, photographs, sound, or video) can be done in straight HTML. For such research, all one needs are a Web site to host the file, a way to recruit participants to that URL, and a way to save the data.

To get started with the technique, it is possible to use one of my programs, (e.g., SurveyWiz or FactorWiz), which are available from the following URL: http://psych.fullerton.edu/mbirnbaum/programs/

These free programs allow a person to create a Web page that controls a simple survey or factorial study without really knowing HTML (Birnbaum, 2000c). Readers are welcome to use these programs to create practice studies, and even to collect pilot data with nonsensitive content. The default CGI included saves the data to my server, from which you can download your data.

To go beyond the minimal requirements—for example, to learn how to install server software on your lab's computer (Schmidt, Hoffman, & MacDonald, 1997), add dynamic functionality (present content that depends on the participant's behavior), or

measure response times (Birnbaum, 2000b, 2001a; McGraw, Tew, & Williams, 2000b)—see the resources at the following URLs: http://ati.fullerton.edu and http://psych.fullerton.edu/mbirnbaum/www/links.htm

## POTENTIAL ADVANTAGES OF RESEARCH VIA THE WWW

Some of the advantages of the new methods are that one can now recruit participants from the entire world and test them remotely. One can test people without requiring them to reveal their identities or to be tested in the presence of others. Studies can be run without the need for large laboratories, without expensive dedicated equipment, and without limitations of time and place. Online studies run around the clock anywhere that a computer is connected to the WWW. Studies can be run by means of the (now) familiar browser interface, and participants can respond by (now) familiar methods of pointing and clicking or filling in text fields.

Once the programming is perfected, data are automatically coded and saved by a server, sparing the experimenter (and his or her assistants) from much tedious labor. Scientific communication is facilitated by the fact that other scientists can examine and replicate one's experiments precisely. The greatest advantages probably are the convenience and ease with which special samples can be recruited, the low cost and ease of testing large numbers of participants, and the ability to do in weeks what used to take months or years to accomplish.

On the other hand, these new methods have limitations. For example, it is not yet possible to deliver stimuli that can be touched, smelled, or tasted. One cannot deliver drugs or shocks, nor can one yet measure Galvanic Skin Response, PET scans, or heart rates. It is not really possible to control or manipulate the physical presence of other people. One can offer real or simulated people at the other end of a network, but such manipulations may be quite different from the effects of real personal presence (Wallace, 2001).

When conducting research via the Web, certain issues of sampling, control, and precision must be considered. Are people recruited via the Web more or less "typical" than those recruited by other means? How do we know if their answers are honest and accurate? How do we know what the precise conditions were when the person was being tested? Are there special ethical considerations in testing via the Web?

Some of these issues were addressed in "early" works by Batinic (1997), Birnbaum (1999a, 1999b), Buchanan and Smith (1999), Pettit (1999), Piper (1998), Reips (1997), Schmidt (1997a, 1997b), Schmidt, Hoffman, et al. (1997), Smith and Leigh (1997), Stern and Faber (1997), and Welch and Krantz (1996). Over the last few years, there has been a great expansion in the use of the WWW in data collection, and much has been learned or worked out. Summaries of more recent work are available in a number of recent books and reviews (Birnbaum, 2000b, 2001a; Janetzco, Meyer, & Hildebrand, 2002; Reips, 2001a, 2001b, 2002). This chapter will summarize and contribute to this growing body of work.

## EXAMPLES OF RECRUITING AND TESTING PARTICIPANTS VIA THE INTERNET

It is useful to distinguish the use of the WWW to recruit participants from its use to test participants. The cases of four hypothetical researchers will help to illustrate these distinctions. One investigator might recruit participants via the Internet and then send them printed or other test materials by mail, whereas another might recruit participants from the local "subject pool" and test them via the Internet. A third investigator might

both recruit and test via the Web, and a fourth might use the WWW to recruit criterion groups in order to investigate individual differences.

In the first example, consider the situation of an experimenter who wants to study the sense of smell among people with a very rare condition. It is not yet possible to deliver odors via the WWW, so this researcher plans to use the WWW strictly for recruitment of people with the rare condition. Organizations of people with rare conditions often maintain Web sites, electronic newsletters, bulletin boards, and other means of communication. Such organizations might be asked to contact people around the world with the targeted, rare condition. If an organization considers research to be relevant and valuable to the concerns of its members, the officers of the organization may offer a great deal of help in recruiting its members. Once recruited, participants might be brought to a lab for testing, visited by teams traveling in the field, or mailed test kits that the participants would administer themselves or take to their local medical labs.

The researcher who plans to recruit people with special rare conditions can be contrasted with the case of a professor who plans to test large numbers of undergraduates by means of questionnaires. Perhaps this experimenter previously collected such data by paper-and-pencil questionnaires administered to participants in the lab. Questionnaires were typed, printed, and presented to participants by paid research assistants, who supervised testing sessions. Data were coded by hand, typed into the computer, and verified.

In this second example, the professor plans to continue testing participants from the university's "subject pool." However, instead of scheduling testing at particular times and places, this researcher would like to allow participation from home, dorm room, or wherever students have Web access. The advantages of the new procedure are largely convenience to both experimenter and participants, along with cost savings for paper, dedicated space, and assistants for in-lab testing, data coding, and data entry. This hypothetical professor might even conduct an experiment, randomly assigning undergraduates to either lab or Web, to ascertain if these methods make a difference.

In the third example, which describes my initial interest in the method, the experimenter plans to compare data from undergraduates tested in the lab against special populations, who could be recruited and tested via the Web. This experimenter establishes two Web pages, one of which collects data from those tested in the lab. The second Web page contains the same content but receives data from people tested via the WWW. The purpose of this research would be to ascertain whether results observed with college students are also obtained in other groups of people who can be reached via the Web (Birnbaum, 1999b, 2000a, 2001a, 2001b; Krantz & Dalal, 2000).

In the fourth example, a researcher compares criterion groups, in order to calibrate a test of individual differences or to examine if a certain result interacts with individual differences (Buchanan, 2000). Separate Web sites are established that contain the same materials, but people are recruited to these URLs by methods intended to reach members of distinct criterion groups (Schillewaert, Langerak, & Duhamel, 1998). One variation of this type of research is cross-cultural research, in which people who participate from different countries are compared (Pagani & Lombardi, 2000).

## Recruitment Method and Sample Characteristics

Although the method of recruitment and the method of testing in either Web or lab are independent issues, most of the early Web studies recruited their participants from the Web and recruited their lab samples from use the university's "subject pool" of students. Therefore, many of the early studies compared two ways of recruiting and testing participants.

Because the "subject pool" is finite, at some universities there is competition for the limited number of subject-hours available for research. In addition, the lab method usually is more costly and time-consuming *per subject* compared to Web studies, where there is no additional cost once the study is on the WWW. For these reasons, Web studies usually have much larger numbers of participants than do lab studies.

Participation in psychological research is considered an important experience for students of psychology. Web studies allow students to be able to participate in psychological studies even if they attend universities that do little research or if they engage in "distance" learning (taking courses via TV or the Web).

Table 16.1 lists a number of characteristics that have been examined in comparisons of participants recruited from subject pools and via search engines, e-mail announcements, and links on the Web. I will compare "subject pool" against Web recruitment, with arguments why or where one method might have an advantage over the other.

### Demographics

College students who elect to take psychology courses are not a random sample of the population. Almost all have graduated high school, and virtually none have college degrees. At many universities, the majority of this pool is female. At my university, more than two thirds are female, most are between 18 and 20 years of age, and none of them has graduated college. Within a given university, despite efforts to encourage diversity, the student body is often homogeneous in age, race, religion, and social class. Although many students work, most lower-division students are supported by their parents, and the

**Table 16.1**     Characteristics of Web-Recruited Samples and College Student "Subject Pool"
Participants

| | Recruitment Method | |
|---|---|---|
| *Characteristic* | *Subject Pool* | *Web* |
| Sample sizes | Small | Larger |
| Cross-cultural studies | Difficult | Easier |
| Recruitment of rare populations | Difficult | Easier |
| Sample demographics | Homogeneous | Heterogeneous |
| Age | 18-22 | 18-80 |
| Nationality/culture | Relatively homogeneous | Heterogeneous |
| Education | 12-14 years | 8-20 years |
| Occupation | Students, part-time work | Various, more full-time |
| Religion | Often homogeneous | More varied |
| Race | Depends on university | More varied |
| Self-selection | Psychology students | Unknown factors; depends on recruitment method |
| Gender | Mostly female | More equal, depending on recruitment method |

positions they hold typically are low-paying, part-time jobs.

Those who choose to take psychology are not a random sample of college students; at my university, they are less likely to be majors in engineering, chemistry, mathematics, or other "hard" subjects than to be undeclared or majoring in "soft" subjects. This is a very specialized group of people.

There are three arguments in favor of sticking with the "subject pool." The first is that this pool is familiar to most psychologists, so most reviewers would not be suspicious of a study for that reason. When one uses a sample that is similar to those used by others, one hopes that different investigators at similar universities will find similar results. Second, it is often assumed that processes studied are characteristic of all people, not just students. Third, the university student pool consists of a homogeneous group. Because the student body *lacks* diversity, one expects that the variability of the data resulting from individual differences on these characteristics will be

small. This homogeneity should afford greater power compared with studies with equal-sized samples that are more diverse.

## Web Participants Do Not Represent a Population

When one recruits from the Web, the method of recruitment will affect the nature of the sample obtained. Even with methods intended to target certain groups, one cannot control completely the nature of the sample obtained via the Web. For example, other Webmasters may place Web links to a study that attract people who are different from the ones the experimenter wanted to recruit. A study designed to assess alcohol use in the general population, for example, might be affected by links to the study posted in self-help groups for alcoholics. Or links might be posted in an upscale wine tasting club, which might recruit a very different sample. There are techniques for checking what link on the Web led each participant to the site, so one can study how the people got there (Schmidt, 1997a), but at the end of the day one must concede that the people recruited are not a random sample of any particular population.

I think it would be a mistake to treat samples recruited from the Web as if they represented some stable population of "Web users." First, the populations of those who have *access* to the Web and those who *use* the Web are (both) rapidly changing. Those with access could potentially get on the Web; however, the population of people who use the Web at any given time is a nonrandom sample of those with access. Second, those who receive the invitation to participate are not a random sample of all Web users. Third, those who agree to complete a study are not a random sample of those who see the invitation. Fourth, there usually is no real control of who will receive the invitation, once it has been placed in a public file on the Web.

Researchers who have compared data from the Web against data from students have reported that participants recruited via the Web are on average older, better educated, more likely male (though females may still be in the majority), and more likely employed in full-time jobs. Layered over these average differences, most studies also reported that the variance, or diversity, of the samples is much greater on the Web on all characteristics than one usually finds in the subject pool. Thus, although one finds that the average years of education of a Web sample is greater than the average number for college sophomores, one also finds adults via the Web who have no high school diploma, which one does not find in college samples.

## Effect of Diversity on Power and Generality

The theoretical problem of diversity is that it may produce greater error variance and therefore reduce power compared to a study in which participants are homogeneous.

However, in practice, the greater diversity in Web samples may actually be a benefit for three reasons.

First, demographic characteristics rarely have shown large correlations with many dependent variables, so diversity of demographics does not necessarily generate much added error variance. Second, sample sizes in Web studies usually outweigh any added variance resulting from heterogeneity, so it is usually the Web studies that have greater power (Musch & Reips, 2000; Krantz & Dalal, 2000). Third, with very large samples, one can partition the data on various characteristics and conduct meaningful analyses within each stratum of the sample (Birnbaum, 1999b, 2001a). When similar results are found with males and females, with young and old, with rich and poor, with experts and novices, and with participants of many nations, the confidence that the findings will generalize to other groups is increased.

In the case that systematically different results are obtained in different strata, these can be documented and an explanation sought. If results do correlate with measures of individual differences, these can be better studied in samples with greater variance. Web samples are likely better for studying such correlations precisely because they do have greater variation. For example, if a person wanted to study the correlates of education, a "subject pool" sample would not have enough variance on education to make the study worthwhile, whereas a Web-recruited sample would have great variance on this variable.

Cases in which demographic characteristics have been shown to correlate with the dependent variable include surveys intended to predict the proportion who will vote Republican or Democratic in the next election. Here the interest is not in examining correlations but in forecasting the election. Neither surveys of college students nor large convenience samples obtained from volunteers via the WWW would likely yield accurate predictions of the vote (Dillman & Bowker, 2001). It remains to be seen how well one might do by statistically "correcting" Web data based on a theory of the demographic correlates. For example, if results depend on gender and education, one might try to weight cases so that the Web sample had the same gender and education profile as those who vote. It remains to be seen how well one might do with this approach.

The failure of the famous 1936 *Literary Digest* Poll, which incorrectly predicted that Alf Landon would defeat Franklin D. Roosevelt for president, is a classic example of how a self-selected sample (even with very large sample size) can yield erroneous results (Huff, 1954). Bailey, Foote, and Throckmorton (2000) reviewed this topic in the area of sex surveys. In addition to sampling issues, these authors also discussed the conjecture that people might be less biased when answering a questionnaire via the Internet than they would when responding in person.

Some survey researchers use the Web to collect data from what they believe is a *representative* sample, even if it is not random. These researchers establish a sample with proportions of various characteristics (gender, age, education) that match those in the general population, much like the Nielsen Families for TV ratings, and then return to this group again and again for different research questions. See the URL http://www.nielsenmedia.com/whatratingsmean/

Baron and Siepmann (2000) described a variation of this approach, in which a fixed list (of 600 selected volunteers) is used in study after study. A similar approach has been adopted by several commercial polling organizations that have established fixed samples that they consider to be representative. They sell polling services in their fixed sample for a price.

No method yet devised uses true random sampling. Random digit dialing, which is still popular among survey researchers, has two serious drawbacks: First, some people have

more phone numbers than others, so the method is biased to obtain relatively more of such people. Second, not everyone telephoned agrees to participate. I am so annoyed by calls at home, day and night, from salespeople who pretend to be conducting surveys that I no longer accept such calls. Even though the dialing may be random, therefore, the sample is not.

Because no survey method in actual use employs true random sampling, most of these arguments about sampling methods are "armchair" disputes that remain unresolved by empirical evidence. Because experiments in psychology do not employ random sampling of either participants or situations, the basis for generalization from experiments must be based on proper substantive theory, rather than on the statistical theory of random sampling.

## EXPERIMENTAL CONTROL, MEASUREMENT, AND OBSERVATION

Table 16.2 lists a number of characteristics of experiments that may differ between lab and Web studies. Some of these distinctions are advantages or disadvantages of one method or another. The issues that seem most important are experimental control of conditions, precision of stimulus presentation, observation of behavior, and the accuracy of measurement.

### Two Procedures for Holding an Exam

To understand the issue of control, consider the case of a professor who plans to give an exam intended to measure what students learned in a course. The exam is to be held with closed books and closed notes, and each student is to take the exam in a fixed period of time, without the use of

**Table 16.2**    Comparisons of Typical Lab and WWW Experiments

| Comparison | Research Method | |
| --- | --- | --- |
| | *Lab* | *Web* |
| Control of conditions, ease of observation | Good control | Less control; observation not possible |
| Measurement of behavior | Precise | Sometimes imprecise; pilot tests, lab vs. Web |
| Control of stimuli | Precise | Imprecise |
| Dropouts | A serious problem | A worse problem |
| Experimenter bias | Can be serious | Can be standardized |
| Motivation | Complete an assignment | Help out; interest; incentives |
| Multiple submission | Not considered | Not considered a problem |

computers, calculators, or help from others. The professor might give the exam in a classroom with a proctor present to make sure that these rules are followed, or the professor might give the exam via the Internet.

Via the Internet, one could ask the students if they used a computer or got help from others, for example, but one cannot be sure what the students actually did (or even who was taking the exam) with the same degree of certainty as is possible in the classroom. This example should make clear the lack of control in studies done via the WWW.

## Precision of Manipulations and Measurements

In the lab, one can control the settings on a monitor, control the sound level on speakers or headphones, and control the noise level in the room. Via the Web, each user has a different monitor, different settings, different speakers or earphones, and a different background of noise and distraction.

In addition to better control of conditions, the lab also typically allows more precise measurement of the dependent variables as well as affording actual observation of the participant.

The measurement devices in the lab include apparatus not currently available via the Web (e.g., EEG, fMRI, eye-trackers). In addition, measurement of dependent variables such as response times via the WWW face a variety of problems resulting from the different conditions experienced by different participants. The participant via the WWW, after all, may be watching TV, may have other programs running, may decide to do some other task on the computer in the middle of the session, or may be engaged in conversation with a roommate. Such sources of uncertainty concerning conditions can introduce both random and systematic error components compared to the situation in the lab. Krantz (2001) reviewed additional ways in which the presentation of stimuli via the WWW lacks the control and precision available in the lab. Schmidt (2001) has reviewed the accuracy of animation procedures.

At the user's (i.e., participant's) end, there may be different types of computers, monitors, sound cards (including no sound), systems, and browsers. It is important to check that the Web experiment works with the major systems (e.g., Windows, Mac, Linux) and different browsers for those systems (Netscape Navigator, Internet Explorer, etc.).

Different browsers may render the same page with different appearances, even on the same computer and system. Suppose the appearance (such as, for example, the spacing of a numerically coded series of radio buttons) is important and is displayed differently by different browsers (Dillman & Bowker, 2001). If so, it may be necessary to restrict which browsers participants can use, or at least keep track of data that are sent by different browsers.

## The Need for Pilot Work in the Lab

Because the ability to observe the participant is limited in WWW research, one should do pilot testing of each Web experiment in the lab before launching it into cyberspace. As part of the pilot-testing phase, one should observe people as they work through the online materials and interview them afterward to make sure that they understood the task from the instructions in the Web page.

Pilot testing is part of the normal research process in the lab, but it is even more important in Web research because of the difficulty of communicating with participants. Pilot testing is important to ensure that instructions are clear and that the experiment works properly. In lab research, the participant can ask questions and receive clarifications. If many people ask the same question, the lab assistant will become aware of the problem. In Web research, the experimenter needs to anticipate questions or problems that participants may have and to include instructions or other methods for dealing with them.

I teach courses in which students learn how to conduct their research via the Web. By watching participants in the lab working on my students' studies, I noticed that some participants click choices before viewing the information needed to make their decisions. Based on such observations, I advise my students to place response buttons *below* the material to be read rather than above it, so

that the participant at least has to scroll past the relevant material before responding. It is interesting to rethink paper-and-pencil studies, for which the same problem may have existed but may have gone undetected.

A student of mine wanted to determine the percentage of undergraduates who use illegal drugs. I recommended a variation of the random response method (Musch, Broeder, & Klauer, 2001), in order to protect participant anonymity. In the method I suggested, the participant was instructed to privately toss two coins before answering each question. If both coins fell "heads," the participant was to respond "yes" to the question; if both were "tails," the participant was to respond "no." When the coins were mixed (one heads and one tails), the participant was to respond with the truth. This procedure allows the experimenter to calculate the proportions in the population, without knowing for any given participant whether the answer was produced by chance or truth.

For example, one item asked, "Have you used marijuana in the last 24 hours?" From the overall percentages, the experimenter should subtract 25% "yes" from the "yes" percentage (those who got two heads) and multiply the difference by 2 (because only half of the data are based on truth). For example, if the results showed that overall 30% said "yes," then $30\% - 25\% = 5\%$ (among the 50% of those who had mixed coins and who responded truthfully by saying "yes"); so, 5% times $2 = 10\%$, the estimated percentage who actually used marijuana during the last 24 hours, assuming that the method works.

The elegance of this method is that no one (besides the participant) can ever know from the answers whether or not that person did or did not use marijuana, even if the participant's data were by identified by name! However, the method does require that participants follow instructions.

I observed 15 pilot participants who completed my student's questionnaire in the laboratory. I noticed that only one participant took out any coins during the session. Indeed, that one person asked, "It says here we are supposed to toss coins; does that mean we should toss coins?" Had this study simply been launched into cyberspace without pilot testing, we might never have realized that most people were not following instructions.

I suggested that my student add instructions emphasizing the importance of following the procedure with the coins and that she add two questions to the end of the questionnaire: "Did you actually toss the coins as you were instructed?" and "If not, why not?" About half of the participants responded that they had *not* followed instructions, giving various reasons, including "lazy," "I had nothing to hide," and "I don't mind telling the truth." Still, even among those who *said* they had followed instructions, one can worry that either by confusion or dissimulation, these students still had not followed instructions. And those who say they followed instructions are certainly not a random sample of all participants.

Clearly, in the lab, one could at least verify that each student has coins, tosses the coins for each question, and gives at least the superficial appearance of following instructions. In the lab, it might be possible to obtain blind urine samples against which the results of the questionnaire method could be compared. Questions about the procedure would be easy for the participant to ask and easy for the experimenter to answer. Via the Web, we can instruct the participant and we can ask the participant if he or she followed instructions, but we cannot really know what the conditions were with the same confidence we have when we can observe and interact with the participant.

## The Need for Testing of HTML and Programming

One should also conduct tests of Web materials to make sure that all data coding

and recording are functioning properly. When teaching students about Web research, I find that students are eager to upload their materials to the Web before they have really tested them. It is important to conduct a series of tests to make sure that each radio button functions correctly and that each possible response is coded into the correct value in the data file (see Birnbaum, 2001a, Chapters 11, 12, and 21).

My students tell me that their work has been checked, yet when I check it, I detect many errors that my students have not discovered on their own. It is possible to waste the time of many people by putting unchecked work on the Web. In my opinion, such waste of people's time is unethical; it is a kind of vandalism of scientific resources and a breach of trust with the participant. The participants give us their time and effort in the expectation that we will do good research. They do not intend that their efforts will be wasted. Errors will happen because people are human; knowing this, we have a responsibility to check thoroughly to ensure that the materials work properly before launching a study.

## Testing in Both Lab and Web

A number of studies have compared data collected via the WWW with data collected in the laboratory. Indeed, once an experiment has been placed online, it is quite easy to collect data in the laboratory, where the experimenters can better control and observe the conditions in which the participants completed their tasks. The generalization from such research is that despite some differences in results, Web and lab research reach much the same conclusions (Batinic, Reips, & Bosnjak, 2002; Birnbaum, 1999b, 2000a, 2000b, 2001a, 2002; Birnbaum & Wakcher, 2002; Krantz, Ballard, & Scher, 1997; Krantz & Dalal, 2000; McGraw, Tew, & Williams, 2000a, 2000b). Indeed, in cognitive psychology, it is assumed that if one programs the experiments correctly, Web and lab results should reach the same conclusions (Francis, Neath, & Surprenant, 2000; McGraw et al., 2000a).

However, one should not expect Web and lab data to agree exactly, for a number of reasons. First, the typical Web and lab studies differ from each other in many ways, and each of these variables might make some difference. Some of the differences are as follow.

Web versus lab studies often compare groups of participants who differ in demographic characteristics. If demographic characteristics affect the results, the comparison of data will reflect these differences (e.g., Birnbaum, 1999b, 2000a).

WWW participants may differ in motivation (Birnbaum, 2001a; Reips, 2000). The typical college student usually participates as one option toward fulfilling an assignment in a lower-division psychology course. Students learn about research from their participation. Because at least one person is present, the student may feel some pressure to continue participation, even though the instructions say that quitting is at any time permitted. Participants from the Web, however, often search out the study on their own. They participate out of interest in the subject matter, or out of desire to contribute to scientific progress. Reips (2000) argued that because of the self-selection and ease of withdrawing from an online study, the typical Web participant is more motivated than the typical lab participant.

Analyses show that Web data can be of higher quality than lab data. For this reason, some consider Web studies to have an advantage over lab studies (Baron & Siepmann, 2000; Birnbaum, 1999b; Reips, 2000). On the other hand, one might not be able to generalize from the behavior of those who are internally motivated to people who are less motivated.

When we compare Web and lab studies, there are often a number of other confounded

variables of procedure that might cause significantly different results. Lab studies may use different procedures for displaying the stimuli and obtaining responses. Lab research may involve paper-and-pencil tasks, whereas WWW research uses a computer interface. Lab studies usually have at least one person present (the lab assistant), and perhaps many other people (e.g., other participants). Lab research might use dedicated equipment, specialized computer methods, or manipulations, whereas WWW research typically uses the participant's self-selected WWW browser as the interface. Doron Sonsino (personal communication, 2002) is currently working on pure tests with random assignment of participants to conditions to examine the "pure" effect of the set of Web versus lab manipulations.

## Dropouts and Between-Subjects Designs

Missing data, produced by participants who quit a study, can ruin an otherwise good experiment. During World War II, the Allies examined bullet holes in every bomber that landed in the United Kingdom after a bombing raid. A probability distribution was constructed, showing the distribution of bullet holes in these aircraft. The decision was made to add armor to those places where there were *fewest* bullet holes.

At first, the decision may seem in error, perhaps misguided by the gambler's fallacy. To understand why the decision was correct, however, think of the missing data. The dropouts in this research are the key to understanding the analysis. Even though dropouts were usually less than 7%, the dropouts are the whole story. The missing data, of course, were the aircraft that were shot down. The research was not intended to determine where bullets hit aircraft, but rather to determine where bullet holes are in planes that *return*. Here, the correct decision was made to put extra armor around the pilot's seat and to strengthen the tail because few planes with damage there made it home. This correct decision was reached by having a theory of the missing data.

Between-subjects designs are tricky enough to interpret without having to worry about dropouts. For example, Birnbaum (1999a) showed that in a between-subjects design, with random assignment, the number 9 is rated significantly "bigger" than the number 221. It is important to emphasize that it was a between-subjects design, so no subject judged both numbers. It can be misleading to compare data between subjects without a clear theory of the response scale. In this case, I used my knowledge of range-frequency theory (Parducci, 1995) to devise an experiment that would show a silly result. My purpose was to make people worry about all those other between-subjects studies that used the same method to draw other dubious conclusions.

In a between-subjects design, missing data can easily lead to wrong conclusions. Even when the dropout rate is the same in both experimental and control groups, and even when the dependent variable is objective, missing data can cause the observed effect (in a true experiment with random assignment to conditions) to show the opposite conclusion of the truth.

Birnbaum and Mellers (1989) illustrated one such case in which, even if a treatment is harmful, a plausible theory shows how one can obtain equal dropouts and the harmful treatment appears beneficial in the data. All that is needed is that the correlation between dropping out and the dependent variable be mediated by some underlying construct. For example, suppose an SAT review course is harmful to all who take it; for example, suppose all students lose 10 points by taking the review. This treatment will still look beneficial if the course includes giving each student a sample SAT exam. Suppose those who do well on the sample exam go on to take the

SAT and those who do poorly on the practice test drop out. Even with equal dropout rates, the harmful SAT review will look beneficial because those who do complete the SAT will do better in the treatment group than will the control group.

In Web studies, people find it easy to drop out (Reips, 2000, 2001a, 2001b, 2002). In within-subjects designs, the problem of attrition affects only external validity: Can the results be generalized from those who finish to the sort of people who dropped out?

For between-subjects designs, however, attrition affects internal validity. When there are dropouts in between-subjects designs, it is not possible to infer the true direction of the main effect from the observed effect. Think of the bullet holes case: Dropouts were less than 7%, yet the true effect is opposite the observed effect, because to protect people from bullets, places with the *fewest* bullet holes should get the most armor.

Because of the threat to internal validity of missing data, this topic has received some attention in the growing literature of Web experimentation (Birnbaum, 2000b, 2001a; Frick, Bächtiger, & Reips, 2001; Reips, 2002; Reips & Bosnjak, 2001; Tuten, Urban, & Bosnjak, 2002). An idea showing some promise is the use of the "high threshold" method to reduce dropouts (Reips, 2000, 2002). The idea is to introduce manipulations that are likely to cause dropouts early in the experimental sessions, *before* the random assignment to conditions. For example, ask people for their names and addresses first, then present them with a page that loads slowly, then randomly assign those who are left to the experimental conditions.

### Experimenter Bias

A potential advantage of Web research is the elimination of the research assistant. Besides the cost of paying assistants, assistants can bias the results. When assistants understand the purpose of the study, they might do things that bias the results in the direction expected. There are many ways that a person can reinforce behaviors and interfere with objectivity, once that person knows the research hypothesis (Rosenthal, 1976, 1991).

A famous case of experimenter bias is that of Gregor Mendel, the monk who published an obscure article on a genetic model of plant hybrids that became a classic years after it was published. After his paper was rediscovered, statisticians noticed that Mendel's data fit his theory *too* well. I do not think that Mendel intentionally faked his data, but he probably did see reasons why certain batches that deviated from the average were "spoiled" and should not be counted (see http://www.unb.ca/psychology/likely/evolution/mendel.htm). He might also have helped his theory along when he coded his data, counting medium-sized plants as either "tall" or "short," depending on the running count, to help support his theory.

Such little biases as verbal and nonverbal communication, flexible procedures, data coding, or data entry would be a big problem in certain areas of research, such as ESP or the evaluation of benefits of "talk" psychotherapies, where motivation is great to find positive effects, even if the effects are small. The potential advantage of Web experimentation is that the entry and coding of data are done by the participant and computer, and no experimenter is present to possibly bias the subject or the data entry in a way that is not documented in the materials that control the study.

## Multiple Submissions

One of the first questions any Web researcher is asked is "How do you know that someone has not sent thousands of copies of the same data to you?" This concern has been discussed in many papers (Birnbaum, 2001a; Reips, 2000; Schmidt, 1997a, 2000), and the consensus of Web experimenters is that multiple submission of data has not been a serious problem (Musch & Reips, 2000).

When sample sizes are small, as they are in lab research, then if a student (perhaps motivated to get another hour of credit) participated in an experiment twice, then the number of degrees of freedom for the error term is not really what the experimenter thinks it is. For example, if there were a dozen students in a lab study, and if one of them participated twice, then there were really only 11 independent sources of error in the study. The consequence is that the statistical tests need to be corrected for the multiple participation by one person. (See Gonzalez & Griffin, Chapter 14, this volume.)

On the WWW, the sample sizes typically are so large that a statistical correction would be minuscule, unless someone participated a very large number of times. Several methods have been proposed to deal with this potential problem.

The first method to avoid multiple submission is to analyze why people might participate more than once and then take steps to remove those motivations. Perhaps the experiment is interesting and people don't know they should participate only once. In that case, one can instruct participants that they should participate only once.

If the experiment is really enjoyable (e.g., a video game), perhaps people will repeat the task for fun. In that case, one could provide an automatic link to a second Web site where those who have finished the experiment proper could visit and continue to play with the materials as much as they like, without sending data to the real experiment.

If a monetary payment is to be given to each participant, there might be a motive to be paid again and again. Instructions might specify that each person can be paid only once. If the experiment offers a chance at a prize, there might be a motive to participate more than once to give oneself more chances. Again, instructions could specify that if a person participates more than once, only one chance at the prize is given, or even that a person who submits multiple entries will be excluded from any chance at a prize.

A second approach is to allow multiple participation but ask people how many times they have previously completed the study. The experimenter would then analyze the data of those who have not previously participated separately from those who already have. This method also allows one to analyze how experience in the task affects the results.

A third method is to detect and delete multiple submissions. One technique is to examine the Internet Protocol (IP) address of the computer that sent the data and delete records submitted from the same IP. (One can easily sort by IP or use statistical software to construct a frequency distribution of IP.) The IP does not uniquely identify a participant because most of the large Internet service providers now use dynamic IP addresses and assign their clients one of their IPs as they become available. However, if one person sends multiple copies during one session on the computer, the data would show up as records from the same IP. (Of course, when data are collected in a lab, one expects the same IP to show up again and again because that same lab computer is used repeatedly.)

A fourth method that is widely used is to request identifying information from participants. For example, in an experiment that offers payments or cash prizes, participants are willing to supply identifying information (e.g., their names and addresses) that would be used to mail payments or prizes. Other examples of identifying information are the last four digits of a student's nine-digit ID, e-mail address, a portion (e.g., last four digits) of the participant's Social Security Number, or a password assigned to each person in a specified list of participants.

A fifth method is to check for identical data records. If a study has a large number of items, it is very unlikely that two records will have exactly the same responses.

In my experience, multiple submissions are infrequent and usually occur within a very brief period of time. In most cases, the participant has apparently pushed the *Submit* button to send the data, read the thank you message or debriefing, and used the *Back* button on the browser to go back to the study. Then, after visiting the study again, and perhaps completing the questionnaire, changing a response, or adding a comment, the participant pushes the *Submit* button again, which sends another set of data. If the responses change between submissions, the researcher should have a clear policy of what to do in such cases. In my decision-making research, I want each person's last, best, most considered decision. It is not uncommon to see two records that arrive within 2 minutes in which the first copy was incomplete and the second copy is the same except that it has responses for previously omitted items. Therefore, I always take only the last submission and delete any earlier ones from the same person. There might be other studies where one would take only the first set of data and delete any later ones sent after the person has read the debriefing.

If this type of multiple submission is considered a problem, it is possible to discourage it by an HTML or JavaScript routine that causes the *Back* button not to return to the study's page. Cookies, in this case data stored on the participant's computer indicating that the study has already been completed, could also be used for such a purpose. Other methods, using server-side programming, also are available (Schmidt, 2000); these can keep track of a participant and refuse to accept multiple submissions.

I performed a careful analysis of 1,000 successive data records in decision making (Birnbaum, 2001b), where there were chances at cash prizes and one can easily imagine a motive for multiple entries. Instructions stated that only one entry per person was allowed. I found 5% were blank or incomplete (i.e., they had fewer than 15 of the 20 items completed) and 2% contained repeated e-mail addresses. In only one case did two submissions come from the same e-mail address more than minutes apart. These came from one woman who participated exactly twice, about a month apart, and who interestingly agreed on 19 of her 20 decisions. Less than 1% of remaining data (excluding incomplete records and duplicate e-mail addresses) contained duplicate IP addresses. In those cases, other identifiers indicated that these were from different people who were assigned the same IPs, rather than from the same person submitting twice. Reips (2000) found similar results, in an analysis done in the days of mostly fixed IP addresses.

## ETHICAL ISSUES IN WEB AND LAB

The institutional review of research should work in much the same way for an online study as for an in-lab study. Research that places people at more risk than the risks of everyday life should be reviewed to ensure that adequate safeguards are provided to the participants. The purpose of the review is to determine that the potential benefits of the research outweigh any risks to participants, and to ensure that participants will have been clearly warned of any potential dangers and clearly accepted them. A comparison of ethical issues as related to lab and Web is presented in Table 16.3.

### Risks of Psychological Experiments

For the most part, psychology experiments are not dangerous. Undoubtedly, it is less dangerous to participate in the typical 1-hour experiment in psychology than to drive 1 hour in traffic, spend 1 hour in a hospital, serve 1 hour in the armed forces, work 1 hour in a mine or factory, serve 1 hour on a jury,

or shop 1 hour at the mall. As safe as psychology experiments are, those done via the Internet must be even safer than lab research because they can remove the greatest dangers of psychology experiments in the lab.

The most dangerous aspect of most psychology experiments is the trip to the experiment. Travel, of course, is a danger of everyday life and is not really part of the experiment; however, this danger should not be underestimated. Every year, tens of thousands are killed in the United States, and millions are injured, in traffic accidents. For example, in 2001, the Department of Transportation reported 42,116 fatalities in the United States and more than 3 million injuries (see http://www.dot.gov/affairs/nhtsa5502.htm).

How many people are killed and injured each year in psychology experiments? I am not aware of a single such case in the last 10 years, nor am I aware of a single case in the 10 years preceding the Institutional Review Board (IRB) system of review. I suspect that if this number were large, professionals in the IRB industry would have made us all aware of them.

The second most dangerous aspect of psychology experiments is the fact that labs often are in university buildings. Such buildings are known to be more dangerous than most residences. For example, many buildings of public universities in California were not designed to satisfy building codes because the state of California previously exempted itself from its own building codes in order to save money.

An earthquake occurred at 4:31 a.m. on January 17, 1994, in Northridge, California (see http: //www.eqe.com/publications/northridge/executiv.htm). Several structures of the California State University at Northridge failed, including a fairly new building that collapsed (see http://www.eqe.com/publications/northridge/commerci.htm). Had the earthquake happened during the day, there undoubtedly

**Table 16.3**     Ethical Considerations of Lab and Web Research

| Ethical Issue | Experimental Setting | |
|---|---|---|
| | Lab | Web |
| Risk of death, injury, or illness | Trip to lab; unsafe public buildings; contagious disease | No trip to lab; can be done from typically safer locations |
| Participant wants to quit | Human presence may induce compliance | No human present; easy to quit |
| "Stealing" of ideas | Review of submitted papers and grant applications | Greater exposure at earlier date |
| Deception | Small numbers—concern is damage to people | Large numbers—risk to science and all society |
| Debriefing | Can (almost) guarantee | Cannot guarantee; free to leave before debriefing |
| Privacy and confidentiality | Data on paper, presence of other people, burglars, data in proximity to participants | Insecure transmission (e.g., e-mail); hackers, burglars, increased distance |

would have been many deaths resulting from these failures (see http://geohazards.cr.usgs.gov/northridge/). Some of those killed might have been participants in psychology experiments.

Certainly, the risks of such dangers as traffic accidents, earthquakes, communicable diseases, and terrorist attacks are not dangers caused by psychology experiments. They are part of everyday life. However, private dwellings usually are safer from these dangers than are public buildings, so by allowing people to serve in experiments from home, Web studies must be considered less risky than lab studies.

### Ease of Dropping Out From Online Research

Online experiments should be more acceptable to IRBs than lab experiments for another reason. It has been demonstrated that if an experimenter simply tells a person to do something, most people will "follow orders," even if the instruction is to give a potentially lethal shock to another person (Milgram,

1974). Therefore, even though participants are free to leave a lab study, the presence of other people may cause people to continue who might otherwise prefer to quit. However, Web studies do not usually have other people present, so people tested via the WWW find it easy to drop out at any time, and many do.

Although most psychological research is innocuous and therefore legally exempt from review, most psychological research is reviewed anyway, either by a campus-level IRB or by a departmental IRB. It is interesting that nations that do not conduct prior review of psychology experiments seem to have no more deaths, injuries, property damage, or hurt feelings in their psychology studies than we have in the United States, where there is extensive review. Mueller and Furedy (2001) have questioned if the IRB system in the United States is doing more harm than good. The time and resources spent on the review process seems an expense that is unjustified by its meager benefits. We need a system that quickly recognizes research that is exempt and identifies it as such, in order to save valuable scientific resources. For more on IRB review, see Kimmel (Chapter 3, this volume).

## Ethical Issues Peculiar to the WWW

In addition to the usual ethical issues concerning the safety of participants, there are ethical considerations in Web research connected with the impact of one's actions on science and other scientists. Everyone knows a researcher who holds a grudge because he or she thinks that another person has "stolen" an idea revealed in a manuscript or grant application during the review process. Very few people see manuscripts submitted to journals or granting agencies, certainly fewer than would have access to a study posted on the Web. Furthermore, a Web study shows what a person is working on well ahead of the time that a manuscript would be under review. There undoubtedly will be cases in which one researcher will accuse another of stealing ideas from his or her Web site without giving proper credit.

There is a tradition of "sharing" on the Web; people put information and resources on the Web as a gift to the world. However, Web pages should be considered published, and one should acknowledge credit to Web sites in the same way that one cites journal articles that have contributed to one's academic work.

Similarly, one should not interfere with another scientist's research. "Hacking" into another person's online research would be illegal as well as improper, but even without hacking, a person can do many things that could adversely affect another's research program. We should proscribe interference of any kind with another's research, even if the person who takes the action claims to act out of good motives.

## Deception on the WWW

Deception concerning inducements to participate would be a serious breach of ethics

that not only would annoy participants but would affect others' research as well. For example, if a researcher promised to pay each participant $200 for 4 hours and then failed to pay the promised remuneration, such fraud not only would be illegal but also would give a bad name to all psychological research.

Similarly, promising to keep sensitive data confidential and then revealing such personal information in the newspaper would be the kind of behavior we expect from a reporter in a nation with freedom of the press. Although we expect such behavior from a reporter, and we protect it, we do not expect it from a scientist. Scientists should keep their word, even when they act as reporters.

Other deceptions, such as were once popular in social psychology, pose another tricky ethical issue for Web-based research. If Web researchers were to use deception, it is likely that such deceptions would become the source of Internet "flames," public messages expressing anger and disapproval. The deception thus would become ineffective, but worse, people would soon come to doubt anything said by a psychologist. Such cases could easily give psychological research on the Web a bad reputation. The potential harm of deception to science (and therefore to society as a whole) probably is greater than the potential harm of such deception to participants, who would be more likely annoyed than harmed.

Deception in the lab may be discovered and research might be compromised at a single institution for a limited time among a limited number of people. However, deception on the Web could easily create a long-lasting bad reputation for all of psychology among millions of people. One of the problems of deceptive research is that the deception does not work—especially on the Web, it would be easy to expose and publicize to a vast number of people. If scientists want truthful data from participants, it seems a poor idea to have a dishonest reputation.

Probably the best rule for psychological experiments on the WWW is that false information should not be presented via the Web.

I do not consider it to be deception for an experimenter to describe an experiment in general layman's terms without identifying the theoretical purpose or the independent variables of a study. The rule against false information does not require that a person give complete information. For example, it is not necessary to inform subjects in a between-subjects design that they have received Condition A rather than Condition B.

## Privacy and Confidentiality

For most Web-based research, the research is not sensitive, participants are not identified, and participation imposes fewer risks than those of "everyday life." In such cases, IRBs should treat the studies as exempt from review.

In other cases, however, data might be slightly sensitive and partially identifiable. In such cases, identifiers used to detect multiple submissions (e.g., IP addresses) can be cleaned from data files once they have been used to accomplish their purpose.

As is the case with sex surveys conducted via personal interview or questionnaire, it usually is not necessary to keep personal data or to keep identifiers associated with their data. However, there may be such cases, for example, when behavioral data are to be analyzed with medical or educational data for the same people. In such cases, security of the data may require that data be sent or stored in encrypted form. Such data should be stored on a server that is well protected both from burglars who might steal the computer (and its hard drive) and from hackers who might try to steal the electronic information. If necessary, such research might rely on the https protocol, such as that used by online shopping services to send and receive credit card numbers, names, and addresses.

As we know from the break-in of Daniel Ellsberg's psychiatrist's office, politicians and government officials at times seek information to discredit their "rivals" or political "enemies." For this reason, it is useful to take adequate measures to ensure that information is stored in such a way that if the records fell into the wrong hands, they would be of no use to those who stole them. Personal identifiers, if any, should be removed from data files as soon as is practical.

A review of Web researchers (Musch & Reips, 2000) found that "hackers" had not yet been a serious problem in online research. Most of the early studies, however, dealt with tasks that were not sensitive or personal—nothing of interest to hackers. However, imagine the security problems of a Web site that contained records of bribes to public officials, or lists of their sexual partners. Such a site would be of great interest to members of the tabloid press and political opponents. Indeed, the U.S. Congress set a bad example in the Clinton-Lewinsky affair by posting to the Web testimony in a grand jury hearing that had not been cross-examined, even though such information is sealed by law. In most psychology research, with simple precautions, it is probably more likely that information would be abused by an employee (e.g., an assistant) on the project than by a "hacker" or burglar.

The same precautions should be taken to protect sensitive, personal data in both lab and Web. Don't leave your key to the lab around, and don't leave or give out your passwords. Avoid storing names, addresses, or other personal information (complete Social Security Numbers) in identifiable form. It may help to store data on a different server from the one used to host the Web site. Data files should be stored in folders to which only legitimate researchers have password access. The server that stores the data should be in a locked room, protected by strong doors and locks, whose exact location is not public.

In most cases, such precautions are not needed. Browsers automatically warn a person when a Web form is being sent unencrypted, with a message to the effect that "the data are being sent by e-mail and can be viewed by third parties while in transit. Are you sure you want to send them?" Only when a person clicks a second time, assuming the person has not turned this warning off, will the data be sent. A person makes an informed decision to send such data, just as a person accepts lack of privacy when using e-mail. The lack of security of e-mail is a risk most people accept in their daily lives. Participants should be made aware of this risk but not bludgeoned with it.

I don't believe it is necessary to insult or demean participants with excessively lengthy warnings of implausible but imaginable harms in informed consent procedures. Such documents have become so wordy and legalistic that some people agree or refuse without reading. The purpose of such lengthy documents seems to me (and to our participants) to be designed to protect the researcher and the institution rather than the participant and society.

### Good Manners on the Web

There are certain rules of etiquette on the WWW, known as "Netiquette." Although these, like everything else on the WWW, are in flux, there are some that you should adopt to avoid getting in trouble with vast numbers of people.

1. Avoid sending unsolicited e-mails to vast numbers of people unless it is reasonable to expect that the vast majority *want* to receive your e-mail. If you send such "spam," you will spend more time responding to the "flames" (angry messages) than you will spend analyzing your data. If you want to recruit in a special population, ask an organization to vouch for you. Ask leaders of the organization to send the message describing your study and why it would be of benefit to the members of the list to participate.

2. Do not send attachments of any kind in any e-mail addressed to people who don't expect an attachment from you. Attachments can carry viruses, and they clog up mailboxes with junk that could have been better posted to the Web. If you promised to provide the results of your study to your participants, you should post your paper on the Web and just send your participants the URL, not the whole paper. If the document is put on the WWW as HTML, the recipient can safely click to view it. If your computer crashed after you opened an attachment from someone, wouldn't you suspect that attachment to be the cause of your misery? If you send attachments to lots of people, odds are that someone will hold you responsible.

3. Do not use any method of recruiting that resembles a "chain letter."

4. Do not send blanket e-mails with readable lists of recipients. How would you feel if you got an e-mail asking you to participate in a study of pedophiles, and you saw your name and address listed among a group of registered sex offenders?

5. If you must send e-mails, keep them short, to the point, and devoid of any fancy formatting, pictures, graphics, or other material that belongs on the Web. Spare your recipient the delays of reading long messages, and give them the choice of visiting your materials.

## CONCLUDING COMMENTS

Because of the advantages of Web-based studies, I believe use of such methods will continue to increase exponentially for the next decade. I anticipate a period in which each area of social psychology will evaluate Web methods to decide whether they are suitable to that area's paradigm. In some areas of research, such as social judgment and decision making,

I think that the method will be adopted rapidly and soon taken for granted. As computers and software improve, investigators will find it easier to create, post, and advertise their studies on the WWW. Eventually, investigators will regard Web-based research as they now regard using a computer rather than a calculator for statistics, or using a computer rather than a typewriter to prepare a manuscript.

## REFERENCES

Bailey, R. D., Foote, W. E., & Throckmorton, B. (2000). Human sexual behavior: A comparison of college and Internet surveys. In M. H. Birnbaum (Ed.), *Psychological experiments on the Internet* (pp. 141-168). San Diego: Academic Press.

Baron, J., & Siepmann, M. (2000). Techniques for creating and using Web questionnaires in research and teaching. In M. H. Birnbaum (Ed.), *Psychological experiments on the Internet* (pp. 235-265). San Diego: Academic Press.

Batinic, B. (Ed.). (1997). *Internet für Psychologen*. Göttingen, Germany: Hogrefe.

Batinic, B., Reips, U.-D., & Bosnjak, M. (Eds.). (2002). *Online social sciences*. Seattle: Hogrefe & Huber.

Birnbaum, M. H. (1997). Violations of monotonicity in judgment and decision making. In A. A. J. Marley (Ed.), *Choice, decision, and measurement: Essays in honor of R. Duncan Luce* (pp. 73-100). Mahwah, NJ: Lawrence Erlbaum.

Birnbaum, M. H. (1999a). How to show that 9 > 221: Collect judgments in a between-subjects design. *Psychological Methods, 4*(3), 243-249.

Birnbaum, M. H. (1999b). Testing critical properties of decision making on the Internet. *Psychological Science, 10*, 399-407.

Birnbaum, M. H. (2000a). Decision making in the lab and on the Web. In M. H. Birnbaum (Ed.), *Psychological experiments on the Internet* (pp. 3-34). San Diego: Academic Press.

Birnbaum, M. H. (Ed.). (2000b). *Psychological experiments on the Internet*. San Diego: Academic Press.

Birnbaum, M. H. (2000c). SurveyWiz and FactorWiz: JavaScript Web pages that make HTML forms for research on the Internet. *Behavior Research Methods, Instruments, & Computers, 32*, 339-346.

Birnbaum, M. H. (2001a). *Introduction to behavioral research on the Internet*. Upper Saddle River, NJ: Prentice Hall.

Birnbaum, M. H. (2001b). A Web-based program of research on decision making. In U.-D. Reips & M. Bosnjak (Eds.), *Dimensions of Internet science* (pp. 23-55). Lengerich, Germany: Pabst Science Publishers.

Birnbaum, M. H. (2002). Wahrscheinlichkeitslernen. In D. Janetzko, M. Hildebrand, & H. A. Meyer (Eds.), *Das Experimental-psychologische Praktikum im Labor und WWW* (pp. 141-151). Göttingen, Germany: Hogrefe.

Birnbaum, M. H., & Hynan, L. G. (1986). Judgments of salary bias and test bias from statistical evidence. *Organizational Behavior and Human Decision Processes, 37*, 266-278.

Birnbaum, M. H., & Martin, T. (in press). Generalization across people, procedures, and predictions: Violations of stochastic dominance and coalescing. In S. L. Schneider & J. Shanteau (Eds.), *Emerging perspectives on decision research*. New York: Cambridge University Press.

Birnbaum, M. H., & Mellers, B. A. (1989). Mediated models for the analysis of confounded variables and self-selected samples. *Journal of Educational Statistics, 14*, 146-158.

Birnbaum, M. H., & Navarrete, J. B. (1998). Testing descriptive utility theories: Violations of stochastic dominance and cumulative independence. *Journal of Risk and Uncertainty, 17*, 49-78.

Birnbaum, M. H., Patton, J. N., & Lott, M. K. (1999). Evidence against rank-dependent utility theories: Violations of cumulative independence, interval independence, stochastic dominance, and transitivity. *Organizational Behavior and Human Decision Processes, 77*, 44-83.

Birnbaum, M. H., & Stegner, S. E. (1981). Measuring the importance of cues in judgment for individuals: Subjective theories of IQ as a function of heredity and environment. *Journal of Experimental Social Psychology, 17*, 159-182.

Birnbaum, M. H., & Wakcher, S. V. (2002). Web-based experiments controlled by JavaScript: An example from probability learning. *Behavior Research Methods, Instruments, & Computers, 34*, 189-199.

Buchanan, T. (2000). Potential of the Internet for personality research. In M. H. Birnbaum (Ed.), *Psychological experiments on the Internet* (pp. 121-140). San Diego: Academic Press.

Buchanan, T., & Smith, J. L. (1999). Using the Internet for psychological research: Personality testing on the World-Wide Web. *British Journal of Psychology, 90*, 125-144.

Dillman, D. A., & Bowker, D. K. (2001). The Web questionnaire challenge to survey methodologists. In U.-D. Reips & M. Bosnjak (Eds.), *Dimensions of Internet science* (pp. 159-178). Lengerich, Germany: Pabst Science Publishers.

Francis, G., Neath, I., & Surprenant, A. M. (2000). The cognitive psychology online laboratory. In M. H. Birnbaum (Ed.), *Psychological experiments on the Internet* (pp. 267-283). San Diego: Academic Press.

Frick, A., Bächtiger, M. T., & Reips, U.-D. (2001). Financial incentives, personal information, and drop-outs in online studies. In U.-D. Reips & M. Bosnjak (Eds.), *Dimensions of Internet science* (pp. 209-219). Lengerich: Pabst Science Publishers.

Huff, D. (1954). *How to lie with statistics.* New York: Norton.

Janetzko, D., Meyer, H. A., & Hildebrand, M. (Eds.). (2002). *Das Experimental-psychologische Praktikum im Labor und WWW* [A practical course on psychological experimenting in the laboratory and WWW]. Göttingen, Germany: Hogrefe.

Joinson, A. (2002). *Understanding the psychology of Internet behaviour: Virtual worlds, real lives.* Basingstoke, Hampshire, UK: Palgrave Macmillan.

Krantz, J. H. (2001). Stimulus delivery on the Web: What can be presented when calibration isn't possible? In U.-D. Reips & M. Bosnjak (Eds.), *Dimensions of Internet Science* (pp. 113-130). Lengerich, Germany: Pabst Science Publishers.

Krantz, J. H., Ballard, J., & Scher, J. (1997). Comparing the results of laboratory and World-Wide Web samples on the determinants of female attractiveness. *Behavior Research Methods, Instruments, & Computers, 29*, 264-269.

Krantz, J. H., & Dalal, R. (2000). Validity of Web-based psychological research. In M. H. Birnbaum (Ed.), *Psychological experiments on the Internet* (pp. 35-60). San Diego: Academic Press.

Luce, R. D., & Fishburn, P. C. (1991). Rank- and sign-dependent linear utility models for finite first order gambles. *Journal of Risk and Uncertainty, 4*, 29-59.

McGraw, K. O., Tew, M. D., & Williams, J. E. (2000a). The integrity of Web-based experiments: Can you trust the data? *Psychological Science, 11*, 502-506.

McGraw, K. O., Tew, M. D., & Williams, J. E. (2000b). PsychExps: An on-line psychology laboratory. In M. H. Birnbaum (Ed.), *Psychological experiments on the Internet* (pp. 219-233). San Diego: Academic Press.

McKenna, K.Y.A., & Bargh, J. A. (2000). Plan 9 from cyberspace: The implications of the Internet for personality and social psychology. *Personality and Social Psychology Review, 4*(1), 57-75.

Milgram, S. (1974). *Obedience to authority.* New York: Harper & Row.

Mueller, J., & Furedy, J. J. (2001). The IRB review system: How do we know it works? *American Psychological Society Observer, 14.* Retrieved March 23, 2003, from http://www.psychologicalscience.org/observer/0901/irb_reviewing. html

Musch, J., Broeder, A., & Klauer, K. C. (2001). Improving survey research on the World-Wide Web using the randomized response technique. In U.-D. Reips & M. Bosnjak (Eds.), *Dimensions of Internet science* (pp. 179-192). Lengerich, Germany: Pabst Science Publishers.

Musch, J., & Reips, U.-D. (2000). A brief history of Web experimenting. In M. H. Birnbaum (Ed.), *Psychological experiments on the Internet* (pp. 61-87). San Diego: Academic Press.

Pagani, D., & Lombardi, L. (2000). An intercultural examination of facial features communicating surprise. In M. H. Birnbaum (Ed.), *Psychological experiments on the Internet* (pp. 169-194). San Diego: Academic Press.

Parducci, A. (1995). *Happiness, pleasure, and judgment.* Mahwah, NJ: Lawrence Erlbaum.

Pettit, F. A. (1999). Exploring the use of the World Wide Web as a psychology data collection tool. *Computers in Human Behavior, 15*, 67-71.

Piper, A. I. (1998). Conducting social science laboratory experiments on the World Wide Web. *Library & Information Science Research, 20*, 5-21.

Quiggin, J. (1993). *Generalized expected utility theory: The rank-dependent model.* Boston: Kluwer.

Reips, U.-D. (1997). Das psychologische Experimentieren im Internet. In B. Batinic (Eds.), *Internet für Psychologen* (pp. 245-265). Göttingen, Germany: Hogrefe.

Reips, U.-D. (2000). The Web experiment method: Advantages, disadvantages, and solutions. In M. H. Birnbaum (Ed.), *Psychological experiments on the Internet* (pp. 89-117). San Diego: Academic Press.

Reips, U.-D. (2001a). Merging field and institution: Running a Web laboratory. In U.-D. Reips & M. Bosnjak (Eds.), *Dimensions of Internet science* (pp. 1-22). Lengerich, Germany: Pabst Science Publishers.

Reips, U.-D. (2001b). The Web experimental psychology lab: Five years of data collection on the Internet. *Behavior Research Methods, Instruments, & Computers, 33*, 201-211.

Reips, U.-D. (2002). Standards for Internet experimenting. *Experimental Psychology, 49*(4), 243-256.

Reips, U.-D., & Bosnjak, M. (2001). *Dimensions of Internet science.* Lengerich, Germany: Pabst Science Publishers.

Rosenthal, R. (1976). *Experimenter effects in behavioral research: Enlarged edition.* New York: Irvington.

Rosenthal, R. (1991). Teacher expectancy effects: A brief update 25 years after the Pygmalion experiment. *Journal of Research in Education, 1*, 3-12.

Schillewaert, N., Langerak, F., & Duhamel, T. (1998). Non-probability sampling for WWW surveys: A comparison of methods. *Journal of the Market Research Society, 40*(4), 307-322.

Schmidt, W. C. (1997a). World-Wide Web survey research: Benefits, potential problems, and solutions. *Behavioral Research Methods, Instruments, & Computers, 29*, 274-279.

Schmidt, W. C. (1997b). World-Wide Web survey research made easy with WWW Survey Assistant. *Behavior Research Methods, Instruments, & Computers, 29*, 303-304.

Schmidt, W. C. (2000). The server-side of psychology Web experiments. In M. H. Birnbaum (Ed.), *Psychological Experiments on the Internet* (pp. 285-310). San Diego: Academic Press.

Schmidt, W. C. (2001). Presentation accuracy of Web animation methods. *Behavior Research Methods, Instruments & Computers, 33,* 187-200.

Schmidt, W. C., Hoffman, R., & MacDonald, J. (1997). Operate your own World-Wide Web server. *Behavior Research Methods, Instruments, & Computers, 29,* 189-193.

Smith, M. A., & Leigh, B. (1997). Virtual subjects: Using the Internet as an alternative source of subjects and research environment. *Behavior Research Methods, Instruments, & Computers, 29,* 496-505.

Stern, S. E., & Faber, J. E. (1997). The lost e-mail method: Milgram's lost-letter technique in the age of the Internet. *Behavior Research Methods, Instruments, & Computers, 29,* 260-263.

Tuten, T. L., Urban, D. J., & Bosnjak, M. (2002). Internet surveys and data quality: A review. In B. Batinic, U.-D. Reips, & M. Bosnjak (Eds.), *Online social sciences* (pp. 7-26). Seattle: Hogrefe & Huber.

Tversky, A., & Kahneman, D. (1992). Advances in prospect theory: Cumulative representation of uncertainty. *Journal of Risk and Uncertainty, 5,* 297-323.

Wallace, P. M. (2001). *The psychology of the Internet.* Cambridge, UK: Cambridge University Press.

Welch, N., & Krantz, J. H. (1996). The World-Wide Web as a medium for psychoacoustical demonstrations and experiments: Experience and results. *Behavior Research Methods, Instruments, & Computers, 28,* 192-196.

## CHAPTER 17

# Social Neuroscience
## Bridging Social and Biological Systems

JOHN T. CACIOPPO
*University of Chicago*

TYLER S. LORIG
*Washington and Lee University*

HOWARD C. NUSBAUM
*University of Chicago*

GARY G. BERNTSON
*The Ohio State University*

## SOCIAL NEUROSCIENCE AND LINKS TO BIOLOGICAL SYSTEMS

Social psychology is the scientific study of social behavior, with an emphasis on understanding the individual in a social context. Accordingly, social psychologists study a delightfully diverse range of topics ranging from intrapersonal processes shaped by or in response to others such as the self, attitudes, emotions, social identity, normative beliefs, social perception, social cognition, and interpersonal attraction; to interpersonal processes such as persuasion and social influence, verbal and nonverbal communication, interpersonal relationships, altruism, and aggression; to group processes such as social facilitation, cooperation and competition,

AUTHORS' NOTE: Preparation of this chapter was supported by National Science Foundation Grant No. BCS-0086314. Correspondence should be addressed to John T. Cacioppo, Department of Psychology, University of Chicago, 5848 S. University Avenue, Chicago, IL 60637, Caccioppo@uchicago.edu.

equity, leadership, outgroup biases, group decision making, and organizational behavior. The methodological approaches taken by social psychologists historically, however, have been quite limited. The dominant methodology has been verbal reports, an approach that placed an emphasis on clever experimental design and inductive inference (Campbell & Stanley, 1963; Reis & Judd, 2000). With the advent of social cognition several decades ago, chronometric measures, masking, and priming techniques were added to the methodological armamentarium, and more important, this approach brought with it a conceptual framework for asking questions about the representation of and information processing components underlying social psychological phenomena.

Over the past decade, yet another conceptual approach and family of measures has been added to the repertoire, an approach that falls under the heading of social neuroscience (Berntson & Cacioppo, 2000; Cacioppo, 2002; Cacioppo & Berntson, 1992; Cacioppo, Berntson, Adolphs, et al., 2002; Ochsner & Lieberman, 2001). Biological and social psychology began as allied areas, but the vacuous application of overly simplistic biological causes (e.g., instincts) to explain social behavior led, by the middle of the 20th century, to a deep schism and enduring suspicion (Berntson & Cacioppo, 2000; Cacioppo, Berntson, Sheridan, & McClintock, 2000). Biopsychology began to emphasize neural substrates and production mechanisms for behavior, largely rejecting or ignoring mentalist and functionalist theories, whereas social psychology emphasized multivariate systems, situational influences, and applications (see Allport, 1947). These differences resulted in very different subject samples, research traditions, and technical demands, leaving what some regard as an impassable abyss between social and biological approaches (Scott, 1991).

Although autonomic and electromyographic measures have appeared in the social psychological literature (see reviews by Cacioppo & Petty, 1981, 1983; Shapiro & Crider, 1969), they generally were used either as interchangeable indices of arousal or as a way of validating self-report measures (Cacioppo, Berntson, & Crites, 1996). About half a century ago, for instance, Rankin and Campbell (1955) measured the electrodermal response of Caucasian participants to a Caucasian or African American experimenter as an index of arousal and thus, in this context, racial prejudice. Autonomic assessments of arousal in normal states is based on a theory in which autonomic activity ranges in a unitary fashion from low to high levels. This theory of autonomic organization and function has been disconfirmed (Berntson, Cacioppo, & Quigley, 1991). On the other hand, when autonomic measures validated simpler social psychological measurements, the more difficult and costly autonomic assessments could be discarded in favor of the simpler, less expensive verbal assessments (Cacioppo, Petty, & Tassinary, 1989). Although somatovisceral measures occasionally were identified that provided information not easily available using self-reports (e.g., Cacioppo, Martzke, Petty, & Tassinary, 1988; Cacioppo & Petty, 1981; Tomaka, Blascovich, Kelsey, & Leitten, 1993), outdated concepts of arousal remained the dominant biological concept in social psychology, as is evident from a perusal of the subject indexes of either of the last two editions of the *Handbook of Social Psychology.*

The past decade has seen a rapprochement between biological and social levels of analysis, however, in part because localized brain regions have been associated with social psychological constructs or processes (e.g., Adolphs, 1999; Cacioppo & Berntson, 1992; Cacioppo, Berntson, Adolphs, et al., 2002; Klein & Kihlstrom, 1998; Ochsner & Lieberman, 2001; Sarter, Berntson, & Cacioppo, 1996). In decades past, studies of the neurophysiological structures and functions associated with psychological events were limited primarily to animal models, post mortem examinations, and observations of the occasional unfortunate individual who suffered trauma to or disorders of the brain. Developments in electrophysiological recording, brain imaging, and neurochemical techniques within the neurosciences have increasingly made it possible to investigate the role of neural structures and processes in normal and disordered thought in humans. Contemporary studies of racial prejudice, for instance, have utilized facial electromyography (Vanman, 2001), event-related brain potentials (Ito & Cacioppo, 2000), and functional magnetic resonance imaging (fMRI) (Phelps et al., 2000) to investigate specific, implicit cognitive and affective processing stages. Moreover, advances in ambulatory recording and its combination with experience sampling methodologies have removed the tether of the laboratory to permit in vivo investigations of biology and social behavior (Hawkley, Burleson, Berntson, & Cacioppo, in press; Shiffman & Stone, 1998).

How might an investigator decide whether to incorporate a biological level of analysis? Contemporary work has demonstrated that theory and methods in the neurosciences can constrain and inspire social psychological hypotheses, foster experimental tests of otherwise indistinguishable theoretical explanations, and increase the comprehensiveness and relevance of social psychological theories (Cacioppo & Berntson, 1992; Cacioppo, Berntson, Adolphs, et al., 2002; Ochsner & Lieberman, 2001). Several principles from social neuroscience further suggest that understanding social behavior requires the joint consideration of social, cognitive, and biological levels of analysis in an integrated fashion. The principle of *multiple determinism*, for instance, specifies that a target event at one level of organization, but especially at molar or abstract (e.g., social) levels of organization, can have multiple antecedents within or across

levels of organization (Anderson, 1998; Cacioppo & Berntson, 1992). On the biological level, for instance, we have identified the contribution of individual differences in cardiac sympathetic reactivity, while on the social level, we have noted the important role of exposure to interpersonal stressors in daily life (Cacioppo, Berntson, Malarkey, et al., 1998; Kiecolt-Glaser, Glaser, Cacioppo, & Malarkey, 1998). Both operate, and our understanding of immunity and health is incomplete if either a biological or a social perspective is excluded.

A corollary to this principle, termed the *corollary of proximity*, is that the mapping between elements across levels of organization becomes more complex (e.g., many-to-many) as the number of intervening levels of organization increases (Cacioppo & Berntson, 1992). An important implication of this corollary is that the likelihood of complex and potentially obscure mappings increases as one skips levels of organizations. Cognitive neuroscience, therefore, is an important companion to social neuroscience because it helps bridge intervening levels of organization.

The principle of *nonadditive determinism* specifies that properties of the whole are not always readily predictable from the properties of the parts (Cacioppo & Berntson, 1992). Consider an illustrative study by Haber and Barchas (1983), who investigated the effects of amphetamine on primate behavior. The behavior of nonhuman primates was examined following the administration of amphetamine or placebo. No clear pattern emerged between the drug and placebo conditions until each primate's position in the social hierarchy was considered. When this social factor was taken into account, amphetamine was found to increase dominant behavior in primates high in the social hierarchy and to increase submissive behavior in primates low in the social hierarchy. The importance of this study derives from its demonstration of how the effects of physiological changes on social behavior can appear unreliable until the analysis is extended across levels of organization. A strictly physiological (or social) analysis, regardless of the sophistication of the measurement technology, may not have revealed the orderly relationship that existed.

Finally, the principle of *reciprocal determinism* specifies that there can be mutual influences between microscopic (e.g., biological) and macroscopic (e.g., social) factors in determining behavior (Cacioppo & Berntson, 1992). For example, not only has the level of testosterone in nonhuman male primates been shown to promote sexual behavior, but the availability of receptive females also influences the level of testosterone in nonhuman primates (Bernstein, Gordon, & Rose, 1983; Rose, Gordon, & Bernstein, 1972). The mechanisms underlying mind and behavior, therefore, may not be fully explicable by a biological or a social approach alone, but rather a multilevel integrative analysis may be required.

Incorporating biological levels of analysis in social psychological research can be achieved in a variety of ways. Because of space limitations, we focus here on using measures of physiological events to draw psychological inferences. We begin with a brief discussion of the subtractive method, a commonly used analytical framework, and we extend this approach to a more general framework.[1] These initial discussions are necessarily abstract. We therefore spend the remainder of the chapter discussing more concretely some of the newest and potentially most informative measurement approaches found in social psychology, brain imaging. This is not to diminish the importance of other approaches. Psychophysiological assessments have been successful in helping to illuminate social psychological processes and likely will prove important to use in combination with brain imaging (e.g., Cacioppo & Petty, 1986; Gardner, Gabriel, & Diekman, in press).

Suffice it to say here that the notion that autonomic and hormonal measures reflect emotional processes and that somatic or brain measures reflect cognitive processes is clearly antiquated and can be rejected. Interested readers may wish to consult the most recent edition of the *Handbook of Psychophysiology* (Cacioppo, Tassinary, & Berntson, 2000) for additional details on autonomic, electromyographic, electrophysiological, endocrinological, immunological, and various brain imaging and lesion approaches.

## Inferring the Psychological Significance of Physiological Signals

A general analytic framework that has aided the design and interpretation of studies in the area is the subtractive method that has been adapted from studies of mental chronometry (see Cacioppo & Petty, 1986). Donders (1868/1969), a Dutch physiologist, proposed that the duration of different stages of mental processing could be determined by subtracting means of simpler tasks that were matched structurally to subsequences of more complex tasks. At the simplest level, experimental design begins with an experimental and a control condition. The experimental condition represents the presence of some factor, and the control condition represents the absence of this factor. The experimental factor might be selected because it is theoretically believed to depend on $n$ information processing stages, and the construction of the control condition is guided to incorporate $n - 1$ information processing stages. This kind of analysis assumes, and depends mathematically on the assumption, that the information processing stages are arranged in strictly serial order, with each stage running to completion prior to the initiation of the next.

Nevertheless, the principle underlying the extension of the subtractive design to include physiological (e.g., functional magnetic resonance imaging) measures is twofold:

(a) physiological differences between experimental conditions thought to represent $n$ and $n - 1$ processing stages supports the theoretical differentiation of these stages and (b) the nature of the physiological differentiation of experimental conditions (e.g., the physiological signature of a processing stage) may further support a particular psychological characterization of that information processing stage. According to the subtractive method, the systematic application of the procedure of stage deletion (across conditions of an experimental design) makes it possible to deduce the physiological signature of each of the constituent stages underlying some psychological or behavioral response. For instance, if the experimental task ($n + 1$ stages) is characterized by greater activation of Broca's area than the control task, this is consistent with both the theoretical conception of the experimental and control tasks differing in one (or more) processing stage(s) and the differential processing stage(s) relating to language production.

If using reaction time measures, the psychological significance of timing differences comes primarily from the putative differences between experimental conditions. With biological measures, the psychological significance of specific physiological differences (e.g., activation of Broca's area) comes both from the theoretical differences between experimental conditions *and* from the prior scientific literature on the psychological significance of the observed physiological difference. The convergence of these two sources of information makes social neuroscience methods potentially quite powerful even though they tend to be more complicated and nuanced.

It is important to note a critical difference in the properties of the kinds of measures used for response time experiments and for physiological measurements. If we assume that a process takes a certain period of time because it is composed of a series of steps

that each takes a measurable time and wherein each must be completed before the next is begun, the decomposition of the total time into the time for each step seems relatively transparent. Note, however, that the conditions under which this kind of analysis fails are precisely those that hold in imaging experiments (see Townsend & Ashby, 1983).

When a particular hypothesized stage of information processing is thought to be responsible for the differential impact of two different conditions on behavior, analyses of concomitant physiological activity can be informative, in one of two ways. If the patterns of physiological activity resulting from the isolation of presumably identical stages are dissimilar, the similarity of the stages is challenged even though there may be similarities between the subsequent behavioral outcomes (see Cacioppo & Tassinary, 1990). If, on the other hand, similar patterns of physiological activity result from the isolation of stages that are hypothesized to be identical, convergent evidence is obtained that the same fundamental stage is operative. Note that the greater the extant evidence linking the observed physiological event/profile to a specific psychological operation, the greater the value of the convergent evidence. These data do not provide evidence for a strong inference that the stages are the same (Platt, 1964), but instead such a result raises a hypothesis that can be tested empirically in a subsequent study (Cacioppo & Tassinary, 1990).

Additional issues should be considered when using a subtractive framework to investigate elementary stages of psychological processes, whether using reaction time or physiological (brain) measures. The subtractive method contains the implicit assumption that a stage can be inserted or deleted without changing the nature of the other constituent stages. But this method has long been criticized for ignoring the possibility that manipulating a factor to insert or delete a processing stage might introduce a completely different processing structure (e.g., Townsend & Ashby, 1983). Using multiple operationalizations to insert or delete a stage may be helpful, but this still does not ensure strong inference. In addition, to construct the set of comparison tasks using the subtractive method, one must already have a clearly articulated hypothesis about the sequence of events that transpires between stimulus and overt response. This assumption renders the subtractive method particularly useful in testing an existing theory about the stages constituting a psychological process and in determining whether a given stage is among the set constituting two separate processes (Cacioppo, Berntson, Lorig, et al., in press). Note, however, that confirmatory evidence still can be questioned by the assertion that the addition or deletion of a particular stage results in an essentially different set of stages or substages, just as is the case with self-report or reaction time measures. If a large corpus of animal and human research links a psychological event to a processing operation, however, the plausibility of the alternative interpretation is greatly diminished.

Whenever a physiological response (or profile) found previously to vary as a function of a psychological processing stage or state is observed, yet another hypothesis is raised—namely, that the same processing stage or state has been detected. A person might be thought to be anxious because he or she shows physiological activation, inattentive because he or she shows diminished activation, happy because he or she shows an attenuated startle response, deceptive because he or she shows activation of the anterior cingulate, and so on. However, one cannot logically conclude that a processing stage or state definitely has been detected simply because a physiological response found previously to vary as a function of a psychological processing stage or state has been observed. (The logical flaw in this form of inference is termed affirmation of the consequent.) We therefore

next turn to a general framework for thinking about relationships between psychological concepts and physiological events, and we discuss the rules of evidence for and the limitations to inference in each (see, also, Cacioppo & Tassinary, 1990; Cacioppo, Tassinary, et al., 2000).

## The Psychological and Physiological Domains

A useful way to construe the potential relationships between psychological events and physiological events is to consider these two groups of events as representing independent sets (domains), where a set is defined as a collection of elements that together are considered a whole (Cacioppo & Tassinary, 1990). Psychological events, by which we mean conceptual variables representing functional aspects of embodied processes, are conceived as constituting one set, which we shall call Set $\Psi$. Physiological (e.g., brain, autonomic, endocrinological) events, by which we mean empirical physical variables, are conceived as constituting another, which we shall call Set $\Phi$. All elements in the set of psychological events are assumed to have some physiological referent—that is, the mind is viewed as having a physical substrate. This framework allows the specification of five general relations that might be said to relate the elements within the domain of psychological events, $\Psi$, and elements within the domain of physiological events, $\Phi$. These are as follow:

- A one-to-one relation, such that an element in the psychological set is associated with one and only one element in the physiological set, and vice versa.
- A one-to-many relation, meaning that an element in the psychological domain is associated with a subset of elements in the physiological domain.
- A many-to-one relation, meaning that two or more psychological elements are associated with the same physiological element.

- A many-to-many relation, meaning two or more psychological elements are associated with the same (or an overlapping) subset of elements in the physiological domain.
- A null relation, meaning there is no association between an element in the psychological domain and that in the physiological domain.

Of these possible relations, only the first and third allow a formal specification of psychological elements as a function of physiological elements (Cacioppo & Tassinary, 1990). The grounds for theoretical interpretations, therefore, can be strengthened if either (a) a way can be found to specify the relationship between the elements within $\Psi$ and $\Phi$ in terms of one-to-one or, at worst, in terms of many-to-one relationships; or (b) hypothetico-deductive logic is employed in the brain imaging studies (Cacioppo, Tassinary, et al., 2000; see Cook & Groom, Chapter 2, this volume).

Consider that when differences in brain images or physiological events ($\Phi$) are found in contrasts to tasks that are thought to differ only in one or more cognitive functions ($\Psi$), the data are often interpreted prematurely as showing that brain structure (or event) $\Phi$ is associated with cognitive function ($\Psi$). These data are also treated as revealing much the same information that would have been obtained had brain structure (or event) $\Phi$ been stimulated or ablated and a consequent change in cognitive function $\Psi$ been observed. This form of interpretation reflects the explicit assumption that there is a fundamental localizability of specific cognitive operations, as well as the implicit assumption that there is an isomorphism between $\Phi$ and $\Psi$ (Sarter, Berntson, et al., 1996). Interpreting studies of the form $P(\Phi/\Psi)$ (i.e., fMRI studies) as equivalent to studies of the form $P(\Psi/\Phi)$ is misleading unless one is dealing with 1:1 relationships.[2] This is a premise that needs to be tested rather than treated as an assumption, however. To demonstrate this, we examine in some detail a brain imaging measure that has particular potential for (but has sometimes been embraced uncritically in) social psychology—fMRI.

## Functional Magnetic Resonance Imaging (fMRI)

Magnetic resonance imaging (MRI) has revolutionized medical care and brain research because this technique can harmlessly provide detailed three-dimensional images of human anatomy. fMRI, a variation on MRI that provides images of dynamic processes, has great promise for adding to our understanding of the neural foundation of social cognition and behavior and is one of the most rapidly growing techniques in psychology. Among the potential advantages of fMRI techniques over earlier approaches for investigating brain-behavior relationships are (a) its noninvasive nature, making it possible to investigate social processes in normal humans; (b) improved spatial resolution over noninvasive electrophysiological measures, permitting more precise localization of specific anatomical regions involved in specific cognitive and affective operations or deficits and improved temporal resolution over PET imaging (seconds rather than minutes); (c) an improved signal-to-noise ratio, yielding more sensitive measurements; and (d) its relative safety compared to brain imaging techniques that require the introduction of radioactive agents into the body (Lang et al., 1998). Functional imaging studies like fMRI, however, accounted for less than 5% of the studies reported at the Society for Neuroscience meetings (Lorig, 2000). This fact is often surprising to those scientists looking to add this technique to their repertoire. Although there are many reasons that neuroscientists have preferred animal models and the manipulation of physiological events, the difficulty of drawing strong inferences from fMRI data is among the most important (Cacioppo, 2003).

Consider a very simple fMRI study concerning the perception of guilt in which subjects read a paragraph describing a mock crime. Subjects are told that one of the photographs they are about to see is of the perpetrator of the crime and their job is to select the perpetrator from a group of suspects. Each photograph is shown for a period of 2 seconds, and six different photographs are shown following each of 10 mock crime descriptions. Subjects indicate their suspected perpetrator after all six photographs are displayed in a trial. Brain images of the response to the suspected perpetrator are compared with brain images of the responses to the other suspects and show significant differences in several brain areas. Let us say that the amygdala and anterior cingulate show increased activity when viewing the suspected perpetrator (ignoring the constant activity in the visual system and fusiform face area).

In many ways, this study is as simple as an fMRI experiment can be. The stimuli are uncomplicated faces, and the reading of the mock crime takes place before the actual scan so there are no differential eye movements about which to be concerned. Because the response follows scanning, there is no overt motor behavior to influence the scan. Finally, because this is hypothetical, we will say that the activated areas are consistent in all the subjects and unambiguously statistically significant (see Davidson, Putnam, & Larson, 2000). Now, what has been learned from this study?

The conclusion that some might offer from this study is that guilt is indexed by amygdala and anterior cingulate activation. Given that the dependent measure is an fMRI response, such a conclusion would not be accurate, partly for interpretive reasons outlined above and partly for reasons that are more specific to fMRI studies. A detailed discussion of fMRI signal acquisition and analysis is beyond the scope of this chapter. Readers who wish an introduction to these topics might consult Bandettini, Birn, and Donahue (2000); Cacioppo, Berntson, Lorig, et al. (in press); Jezzard, Matthews, and Smith (2001); and Toga and Mazziotta (1996). The typical measurements obtained in fMRI and some of the strengths and weaknesses of these measures are discussed only briefly here.

## The BOLD Response

To begin our scrutiny of this experiment, first consider what is meant by "brain activity." The measurements provided by fMRI are not of neuronal activity per se. Instead, fMRI provides a measure of blood oxygenation related to glucose utilization (blood oxygen level dependent, or BOLD). Specifically, the increase in local blood flow (and hence oxygen delivery) exceeds cerebral blood volume changes. Because of the slight increase in local oxygen extraction, blood near a region of local activity will have a higher concentration of oxygenated hemoglobin than blood in locally inactive areas (Kutas & Federmeier, 1998). These differences can be detected using fMRI because as hemoglobin becomes deoxygenated, it becomes more paramagnetic than the surrounding tissue, thereby creating an inhomogeneous environment. The basis for fMRI is the fact that certain nuclei (e.g., hydrogen) have an intrinsic magnetic moment. When placed in a magnetic field, these nuclei behave like small magnets, and a small percentage of them align with the field. When a second field oscillating at the right frequency is introduced transiently, these nuclei are perturbed and their magnetic moments precess (rotate) around the direction of the stable (large) field. This rotation creates a signal that can be detected.

The moments of the nuclei become realigned with the larger field because of local inhomogeneities in the magnetic field, and the BOLD signal decays (Kutas & Federmeier, 1998). The rate at which the signal decays depends upon physical and physiological factors. For example, the signal decays more quickly in the presence of deoxyhemoglobin than oxygenated hemoglobin, so fMRI can detect the increased local levels of oxygenated hemoglobin that result from functionally induced increases in neuronal activity. The signal changes are quite small—0.5% –5.0% at 1.5 Tesla—but techniques have been developed to produce adequate signal-to-noise ratios to produce consistent findings.

Two common fMRI techniques for studying the time course of signal intensity changes in the brain are echo planar imaging (EPI) and spiral K-space imaging (Noll, Cohen, Meyer, & Schneider, 1995), which can generate a complete two-dimensional image in as little as 40 milliseconds following a single excitation of the spin system (Jezzard & Song, 1996). It is, however, sensitive to a number of artifacts. Temporal resolution of the fMRI initially was limited by the need to block experimental conditions in order to increase signal-to-noise ratios and find task-relevant brain activity. This limitation has been lessened by the demonstrated feasibility of selective averaging techniques (Buckner et al., 1996) and more recently by more sophisticated deconvolution methods for linearly modeling and analytically separating different hemodynamic responses that overlap in time across different experimental trials. This makes it possible to have rapidly occurring events activating proximal cortical areas and, with appropriate design constraints, model and separately detect the different BOLD responses.[3] Currently, the temporal resolution of the fMRI is thought to be limited by the fact that the hemodynamic response typically takes roughly 2–4 seconds to reach a peak following the operation(s) of interest and then another 6–12 seconds to decline, thereby following the actual synaptic activity by seconds. The BOLD response may not track mental activity sensitively on a millisecond by millisecond basis. However, when highly similar task demands are combined within a narrow temporal window, hemodynamic responses may modulate

more quickly around a higher base level within the affected cortical regions. In other words, if there is already a substantial BOLD response within a particular area, task modulation around that higher level may occur more quickly than a full BOLD response from baseline resting state. In this circumstance, then, the temporal resolution of the fMRI may begin to approach the Nyquist limit set by the scanning sample rate (or TR), which can be less than a second or two for whole brain scans or even approaching a few hundreds of milliseconds for a few slices if a priori hypotheses are more precise about the brain regions of interest.[4] If higher temporal resolution is required, fMRI studies can be complemented by event-related brain potential (ERP) studies. Furthermore, in principle, ERP data, although poorer in spatial resolution, provide signals that, through cross correlation with the hemodynamic measurements, may improve the ability to detect task-relevant brain activity with higher spatial resolution. The addition of metabolic as well as electrophysiological brain imaging methods to the armamentarium of social psychology makes it possible for investigators to conduct pioneering research on the human brain in areas where exploration previously was quite limited.

Roland (1993) has argued that tissue vascularization is proportionate to the number of synapses in the cortical volume of tissue rather than the number of cell bodies. As a result, hemodynamic responses should be more reflective of synaptic activity. Indeed, EEG, local field potentials, multiple unit activity, and laser Doppler flow measurement all show relatively good agreement with fMRI (see Heeger & Rees, 2002, for a review), providing evidence that increases in the BOLD response are associated with neural activity. These findings make it reasonable to regard BOLD as a proxy for neural activity, but one should not lose sight of the fact that fMRI detects hemodynamic rather than neural responses. Dissociations between neural responses and changes in the BOLD response can occur, however. For instance, some brain regions perfuse at different rates, which will affect relative comparisons within tasks in the same brain. This would make the associated change in BOLD activity small even though neural activity might be great, and therefore lead to a Type I error. The converse also can be true. Some areas may show a 100% increase in BOLD response while others show only a 10% increase in a specific task. The immense signal in the first area will certainly make the small increase less noticeable but not necessarily less important. The same logical argument also can be made about electrophysiological signals. It is also possible that a particular active neural area in the brain may recruit a BOLD response that overlaps less active neural areas, essentially "smearing" the locus of the activity.

Furthermore, it is important to realize that differences in experimental conditions may simply modulate distributed cortical networks differently rather than producing new areas of activity (Passingham, Stephan, & Kötter, 2002). For this reason, localization of fMRI and active neural regions is critically dependent on analytic approaches. This observation, which fits with the discussions above concerning the importance of analytical frameworks, is evident in studies of sensorimotor cortex, where functioning is well known and precise (Puce, 1995). It is tempting to apply these same methods to brain areas of greater interest to social psychologists, such as the limbic lobe, temporal regions, or frontal cortices. Hemodynamic and neurophysiological differences between these areas and the sensorimotor cortex (e.g., there is no "topological mapping" equivalent to those found in sensorimotor cortices) suggest that a cautious approach is needed (Cacioppo, Berntson, Lorig, et al., in press).

These caveats are by no means reasons to abandon or even lessen the enthusiasm for fMRI. Researchers new to this field and to neurobiology in general often presume that most of the technical questions about an imaging technique have been answered and that, given the right experimental design, they will soon learn how the brain accomplishes some task. In fact, they may. The right experimental design can go a long way toward reducing technical limitations in the instrumentation or data reduction. The cautionary note to be learned here is that the fMRI physicists, computer support staff, and neurologists staffing the fMRI center will not have definitive answers to a number of basic questions because many of the answers are not yet known (e.g., see note 3). Similarly, there is a tendency among physicists and radiologists to view the hemodynamic response function (the theoretical basis for detecting a task-relevant brain response) as relatively physiologically fixed and invariant rather than task dependent and psychologically modulated. Variations attributable to gender, age, and other individual difference factors can be substantial and may alter processes in ways that can mask theoretical principles (see Kosslyn et al., 2002). The fMRI is still developing as a technique, and a number of newly established journals report the substantial progress being made in the technical domain of this field. Consider the lessons of EEG research. New and important innovations to that technique have been made each year since its first use in humans more than 80 years ago. Similarly, new fMRI pulse sequences, such as those used to achieve faster scan rates, diffusion tensor imaging, and new analytic methods such as post hoc binning of events and structural equation modeling are being reported monthly. Skepticism and an alert mind are essential, as is establishing substantive collaborations with knowledgeable neuroscientists (e.g., psychobiologists, behavioral neurologists, neuroanatomists) who have experience in the brain-behavior literature and brain imaging methodologies (see Sarter et al., 1996).

## Task Demands

The social psychologist interested in fMRI is likely to have experts in MR physics and analysis available, but the social psychologist is likely to be the expert designing and adjusting the details of the behavioral task. Creating a useful and valid task for fMRI, or any other physiological measure, can be a challenge—at least as great as in any other social psychological investigation. For instance, because the scan takes place over several seconds, every thought, distraction, breath, odor, sound, or other stimulus encountered by the subject become a part of the scan. Consider this process analogous to taking a family photograph with a long time exposure. It would be ideal to have your subjects still for the several seconds needed to get the exposure. The smiles you hope to capture would be merged with the puzzled looks, breathing, gestures, and all the other movements captured while the lens aperture is open. Like your photographic subjects, who constantly move, neurons are constantly "doing things." Thoughts are fleeting; attention waxes and wanes. Brains do not remain cognitively or emotionally still during a scan, and this will lead to a "time exposure" of the relationship between the task of interest and the brain's response. Raichle and colleagues (e.g., Gusnard & Raichle, 2001; Raichle et al., 2001) have shown that the resting brain during baselines is *not* in a passive state but rather involves its own set of mental operations that must be understood to make sense of subtracted images involving baselines. The use of event-related designs and random or counterbalanced orders attenuates but does not eliminate some of these sources of variance.

Returning to the example of an fMRI study, the purpose of the hypothetical study was to examine the perception of guilt. Subjects read a mock crime scenario and viewed pictures. After a set of pictures was examined, participants told the experimenter which member of the set was most likely to be the perpetrator. Individual fMRI scans were sorted and perpetrators were averaged, as were nonperpetrators. The two averages were then compared. Although such a procedure will produce a difference mapping of brain activation, what process or set of processes is depicted where in this mapping may be difficult to discern. Consider the participant viewing photos and choosing one of them. Would this participant be more likely to internally verbalize quietly (e.g., "That's the one") when the photo of who the participant thought was the perpetrator was presented? Would the person make a "mental note" that it was picture number 2 or 3, then repeat the number until the end of the set? Would the person actually inhibit verbal responses to the perpetrator photo until it was time to reply to the experimenter? Would the participant show greater attention to that photo? Is the photo chosen novel in some way or systematically different from the others in a covert way? Are there conditioned emotional responses to some of the photos? Would participants use racial bias to select or purposively not select some photos? Would their eye movements be the same in response to the perpetrator's photo as to the others? Would participants think about other things after they made their choice or after they dismissed the other photos as nonperpetrators? For instance, if they rapidly dismissed a photo as a nonperpetrator, what would they think about during the rest of the 2 second scan as they waited for the next photo? The effects raised by these questions could produce systematic differences in brain activity between the perpetrator and nonperpetrator groups even though they have nothing to do with guilt. In fact, subjects are likely to do all these things, and all have direct effects on brain activity imaged with fMRI. Many of these effects are obvious. Eye movement differences should show up in frontal eye field areas and other motor and attentional areas. Broca's area could increase in activity if there is internal verbalization, and other frontal and parietal areas should be more active if participants are more attentive to the perpetrator photos or are holding information in working memory.

One of the most difficult and far-reaching problems is what happens during the viewing of nonperpetrator photos. If participants did rapidly dismiss some of the photos as nonperpetrators and had time to think or were simply bored, then the entire experiment is at risk. This is because fMRI relies either directly or indirectly on the comparison of images. In our experiment, it would have appeared quite reasonable to mathematically subtract the two sets of averaged data. Thus, any induced activity in the "control" task would have appeared as a reduction in activity in the "experimental" condition, and even if there were no direct subtraction, the nonperpetrator photos would have served as a baseline condition providing an implicit subtraction.

This example makes clear the fact that one cannot simply transplant a typical social psychological experiment (or any other type) into an fMRI setting. Not even event-related brain potential experiments can be translated directly into the magnet, although these tend to share more common features. Such an investigation may be useful, however, if it leads to specific hypotheses that are then tested in more focused research. That is, an investigator can consider the various alternative interpretations from a pilot study and draw from related research (e.g., animal research, brain lesion studies, other brain imaging investigations) to develop specific hypotheses about what processes may be manifesting in what regions of differential activation. Once a focused theoretical hypothesis has been articulated, more precisely designed comparison conditions can be developed to contrast it with alternative hypotheses. Investigators should be explicit, however, when conducting research for purposes of using regions of brain activation to generate hypotheses about possible mechanisms rather than testing competing hypotheses about underlying mechanisms.

The connotation of a "brain center" also warrants careful consideration. Parallel distributed processing theory and its descendants (see O'Brien & Opie, 1999, for a review) have almost completely supplanted the notion of brain centers. Applying this cognitive theory to the brain (Gazzaniga, 1989; Small, 1994), "processes" or "computations" underlying complex psychological functions are processed by multiple, spatially and temporally distributed brain areas. The fact that these networks of cells need blood means that the fMRI can be a wonderful tool for delineating the networks of neural resources that contribute to social interactions. Assigning a particular function, social or not, to the active voxels (volume elements) in an fMRI can be misleading, however. The active area is a part of a network and doesn't "hold" the function even if it is the only active area in a scan (other areas may also contribute but may not be seen because of small changes or susceptibility artifacts). It is much easier to answer the question, How does the brain muster its resources to accomplish some task? than to infer the reverse, What does this or that bit of tissue do?

*Tissue and Psychology*

The enigma of how brain cells accomplish psychological function can be partly explained by current research on language perception. Since the 1800s, neurologists and psychologists (e.g., Geschwind, 1965) have believed that perception of speech is associated with activity in the area of the brain called Wernicke's Area. However, as Bogen and Bogen (1976) pointed out, even Wernicke identified different cortical areas for this function, and over time, descriptions of Wernicke's area have spanned the left posterior superior temporal gyrus, the inferior parietal lobule, and even parts of the medial temporal gyrus, with almost no agreement between texts. Neurologists know that damage to areas within these regions can lead to a disruption in speech processing called receptive aphasia (Pincus & Tucker, 1985). EEG, ERP, PET, and fMRI studies all show the left and right posterior, superior temporal cortex of the brain to be active during speech perception (see Blumstein, 1997, for a review). This is one of the most consistent findings in all of cognitive neuroscience, and with findings regarding the role of Broca's area, it has led to the common notion of the left hemisphere being the "center" for language. Why should speech perception be so closely associated with left superior temporal gyrus? What do these networks really do? Recent research (Belin et al., 1998) has suggested that these cells, because of their structure and connections to other cells, parse highly overlapping temporal sequences of postsynaptic potentials. Thus, words with rapid formant structures produce greater overlap in the synaptic transmissions originating in the cochlea and are passed to successive levels of the auditory system, ultimately being decoded in the superior temporal cortex. Hopfield and Brody (2001) recently created an artificial neural network that works on the same principle and is capable of learning words.

This hypothesis suggests that although these cells do contribute to psychological function, their actual function is much simpler and, in some senses, is divorced from any psychological dimensions. Theorists using fMRI should take care that they are making inferences about groups of cells. The labels commonly used for these groups of cells make it tempting to diagram them as smaller versions of the "black box" that we've finally opened. Their labels do not diminish the fact that they are only collections of cells in close proximity. Rather than asking where the brain centers are for guilt, loyalty, and negative moods, one might instead ask what simple features of these complex psychological functions are

being processed by specific networks of neural systems.

## Electrophysiological Measures of Brain Activity

Although fMRI is one of the fastest growing measures of brain activity, more traditional and more widely used measures include the electroencephalograph (EEG) and event-related brain potentials (ERP). The EEG is a recording of minute electrical changes that occur on the scalp, and ERPs are the same signals but collected in a different paradigm and extracted and analyzed using an analytical approach that has become popular in fMRI studies as well. These measures do not provide redundant information but rather reflect complementary aspects of brain function. EEG and ERPs, for instance, provide greater temporal resolution than fMRI, whereas fMRI provides greater spatial resolution.

EEG is sometimes also known as spontaneous EEG, "ongoing EEG," or occasionally "qEEG" to indicate it has been quantified by automatic algorithm. EEG typically is recorded from the scalp through electrodes attached to the skin with electrode paste. There are usually many different electrodes, and modern systems go up to 256 active electrode sites. The paradigms for studying EEG are usually quite simple and involve recording activity for a relatively long time, such as trials of 20–40 seconds. Modern equipment and data processing techniques make recordings relatively insensitive to noise provided that the electrodes are in good contact with the scalp (low impedance), so that electromagnetically shielded chambers, while desirable, are not necessary for these recordings.

Because of the long data collection epochs, analysis usually is concerned with describing the amplitude of the traditional frequencies (alpha, beta, theta, etc.) (see Dorfman & Cacioppo, 1990). There are a variety of ways to reduce the massive amount of data produced from recording EEG. The most common is the use of spectral analysis based on Fourier transform. The result of this analysis is an estimate of the power (roughly the squared amplitude) of all the frequencies making up the EEG. Of the resulting frequency information, alpha (8–12 Hz) is clearly the most often used in psychological experiments, and the alpha power is found by integrating the data within the 8–12Hz bands. Alpha has a long history in psychology (Gevins & Shaffer, 1980) and has been thought to be associated (inversely) with cortical activation in the underlying region. As discussed earlier, the notion of cortical arousal supposes that the cortex is more or less active rather than producing different types of activity, each with a different effect. An excellent example of the notion of the inhomogeneity of brain activity is provided by the relatively recent research on the gamma band. Gamma is a very high frequency (30–50 Hz) found to be associated with becoming aware of stimuli or contingencies (Llinas & Ribary, 2001) and has been suggested to be responsible for "binding" perceptual features of stimuli together. It can occur with or without alpha but is more common when alpha is not present because subjects usually are attending to external stimulation. Phenomena such as gamma may be of interest to social psychologists; however, gamma activity, like fMRI responses, is best treated as an outcome rather than an invariant (Cacioppo & Tassinary, 1990). Thus, it is not sufficient to ask whether gamma is produced during attitude formation or disconfirmation of long-held beliefs or appears when a subject perceives an important social cue. Instead, such measures are best adopted either as part of a program of research to develop markers of specific psychological operations, or to test competing theoretical hypotheses that differ in their predictions about the activation of a specific brain region.

ERPs are recorded using the same equipment as EEG and represent a derived signal based on the EEG. The difference is that a series of events is presented to the subject and the time these events occur is indicated in the recorded data. Usually after the experiment, the EEG data are segmented into trials based on the event times. Because many events of a particular experimental condition are presented, the resulting time series can be averaged to produce the average voltage over time. This averaging is conducted for the other experimental conditions and the resulting average waveforms statistically compared. The advantage of this approach is that "random" activity or noise in each trial is averaged to zero. This approach treats any non-event locked brain response as noise. Although research using this assumption has led to great insights, new findings indicate that the pattern of "noise" may help in further understanding evoked responses (Makeig et al., 2002).

The events that are used in ERP experiments are multifarious. Images, sounds, tactile stimuli, subject responses, odors, and flavors all have been used to evoke brain responses in ERP paradigms. It is also quite possible and fruitful to mix stimuli, essentially using priming or attentional manipulations overlaid on the "main" ERP task. Because ERPs are well studied and relatively consistent, certain peaks and troughs in the averaged waveforms have been associated with cognitive operations. The P300 portion of the ERP is perhaps the most widely studied and is sensitive to a variety of manipulations, including stimulus relevance and frequency (for reviews, see Ford, 1999, and Polich & Kok, 1995).

We have used event-related brain potentials in variations of the oddball paradigm to study evaluative processes, with a small positive (P1) component emerging within 140 milliseconds over the corresponding sensory cortex (e.g., occipital region for visual stimuli) (Smith, Cacioppo, Larsen, & Chartrand, 2003) and a functionally and stochastically separate late positive potential (LPP) emerging several hundred milliseconds later and peaking approximately 600 milliseconds after stimulus onset over the associative cortex (centroparietal regions) (Cacioppo, Crites, Berntson, & Coles, 1993).

The P1 component is sensitive to negative stimuli and to affectively congruent stimuli (Smith et al., 2003). Two sources of evidence have led to the hypothesis that a neural circuit involving the superior colliculus, posterior pulvinar nucleus, and amygdala underlies the P1 negativity bias (Smith et al., 2003). First, patients with striate cortex lesions show preserved abilities to localize and discriminate visual stimuli that are not consciously perceived (blindsight). Second, neuroimaging studies have revealed correlations between amygdala, superior colliculus, and pulvinar cerebral blood flow in masked ("unseen") emotional conditions (e.g., Morris, Öhman, & Dolan, 1998). Thus, although the striate cortex visual pathway affords high resolution visual processing, the superior colliculus and pulvinar pathway affords relatively fast but low-resolution visual processing that can guide (motivate) attention without intention or awareness (LeDoux, 2000). Such an affective asymmetry serves to guide attentional and cognitive resources to potential threats in the environment even before they can be recognized (Smith et al., 2003).

The later ERP component, the LPP, is sensitive to subtler variations in stimuli ranging from foods (Cacioppo, Crites, Berntson, et al., 1993) and evocative pictures (Ito, Larsen, Smith, & Cacioppo, 1998) to personality traits (Cacioppo, Crites, Gardner, & Berntson, 1994; Crites, Cacioppo, Gardner, & Berntson, 1995) and racial categories (Ito & Cacioppo, 2000). The evaluative processes marked by LPP also can occur spontaneously (Ito & Cacioppo, 2000), uncoupled from verbal report (Crites, Cacioppo, Gardner, et al., 1995), however. In an illustrative study, Ito and Cacioppo (2000) assessed the implicit and explicit categorization of stimuli along evaluative (pleasant, unpleasant) and nonevaluative (people, no people) dimensions. Participants were exposed to stimuli that simultaneously varied along both dimensions, but half the participants were instructed to count the number of pictures that depicted people (or the absence of people) (nonevaluative categorization task) and half were instructed to count the number of pictures that depicted pleasant (or unpleasant) scenes (evaluative categorization task). As in prior research, the LPP was sensitive to participants' explicit categorization task. For instance, the LPP was larger in the evaluative task when a pleasant picture was presented within a series of unpleasant rather than pleasant pictures and when an unpleasant picture was presented within a series of pleasant rather than unpleasant pictures, and the LPP was larger in the evaluative task when an unpleasant picture was presented within a series of pleasant pictures than when a pleasant picture was presented within a series of unpleasant pictures (i.e., the negativity bias) (see Cacioppo, Gardner, & Berntson, 1999; Peeters & Czapinski, 1990; Taylor, 1991).

Importantly, the LPP also revealed implicit categorization along the non-task-relevant dimension, and the explicit task of categorizing stimuli along a non-evaluative dimension neither diminished nor delayed the LPP to variations in the *evaluative* dimension. In addition, clear evidence was found for an implicit negativity bias in which rare aversive stimuli spontaneously received greater processing than rare appetitive stimuli. As would be expected at low levels of hedonic activation, the negativity bias and implicit categorization effects have not been observed when using mildly evocative experimental stimuli such as words ("pleasant," "unpleasant") (Cacioppo, Crites, & Gardner, 1996; Crites & Cacioppo, 1996) rather than more evocative emotional pictures (e.g., Ito & Cacioppo, 2000; Ito, Larsen, et al., 1998). Together, these data suggest that early stages of evaluative processing occur automatically.

When ERPs are collected from electrodes that cover the entire scalp, it is possible to create a voltage "map" of the amplitude of electrical activity on the head at a particular time point of interest. This may be thought of analogously to a color-coded temperature map, and such maps are known as scalp topography maps. When viewing a scalp topography map, one is tempted to infer the source of the brain potential to the cortical area underneath the map location with the greatest amplitude.

Brain potentials recorded at the scalp are the result of sheets of neurons that simultaneously receive input from other cells. These inputs are excitatory and inhibitory postsynaptic potentials (EPSPs and IPSPs, respectively). The summations of these potentials are the most likely source for scalp recorded activity (see Nunez, 2000, for a review). If the sheets of neurons were radially arranged with respect to the skull (as they are in rat brains), it would be possible to infer with some accuracy that the area below a high voltage source was receiving input. Because human brains are highly convoluted, the cells that are active during an ERP may lie in a fissure and be oriented in a tangential plane. This will lead to a large displacement of the area of high voltage. For instance, a group of cells in primary auditory cortex (Heschel's gyrus) embedded in the superior temporal fissure would product their greatest amplitude at the top of the head. This is because, although the cells producing the activity are radially oriented to the surface of the brain, the brain in this fissure is folded in such a way that the cells "point" to the top of the head.

Recently, a variety of mathematical models have been applied to ERP data sets with good results. BESA (Scherg & Berg, 1991) and LORETA (Pascual-Marqui, Michel, & Lehmann, 1994) are two mathematically different approaches for placing ERP voltage sources (dipoles) into a three-dimensional map of the brain. Both appear quite promising for estimating the source of scalp recorded brain electrical activity. Hypotheses about the temporal features, however, remain the strength of EEG and ERP methods, whereas hypotheses about the spatial locus (not the kinetics) of cognitive or social operations remain the strength of fMRI methods.

## SUMMARY

Theory and methods in social neuroscience can draw upon evidence from the neurosciences to constrain and inspire social psychological hypotheses, foster experimental tests of otherwise indistinguishable theoretical explanations, and increase the comprehensiveness and relevance of social psychological theories. Our discussion of the principles of multiple determinism, nonadditive determinism, and reciprocal determinism illustrates that theory and methods from social neuroscience have the potential to extend investigations of underlying biological and psychological processes beyond the vistas accessible by self-report or chronometric measures alone. It is interesting in light of these principles that LeDoux (2000), in a recent *Annual Review of Neurosciences,* relatedly observed:

> It is widely recognized that most cognitive processes occur unconsciously, with only the end products reaching awareness, and then only sometimes. Emotion researchers, though, did not make this conceptual leap. They remained focused on subjective emotional experience. . . . The main lesson to be learned . . . is that emotion researchers need to figure out how to escape from the shackles of subjectivity if emotion research is to thrive. (p. 156)

A premise underlying this chapter is that LeDoux's observation applies not only to emotion but also to social representations, processes, and behavior more generally.

Some might argue, perhaps particularly after considering the complexities of experimental design, data acquisition, statistical analysis, and interpretation discussed in this chapter, that mappings between brain and social processes, representations, and behavior are not worth the effort. The fact that caution and expertise are needed because a particular methodology is complex is no reason to discount the method, however. After all, the same might be said about advanced statistical methods, yet no serious social psychologist would accept such an excuse for using inappropriate but simple statistical methods for addressing a question.

Novices may not know which measures or brain systems are most relevant to consider when addressing a theoretical question in social psychology, and there are no simple recipes that novices can use to cook up a study to address whatever social psychological question they may wish to ask. Indeed, our discussion of fMRI in this chapter was designed to show that social neuroscience methods place just as much if not more of a premium on carefully conceived hypotheses and experimental designs, valid and reliable operationalizations of independent and dependent variables, appropriate attention to individual differences and moderator variables involving contextual factors, and sophisticated selection and implementation of multivariate statistical techniques as any other method in social psychology.[5] On the other hand, with social psychologists moving beyond a sole reliance on verbal or chronometric methods, evidence is mounting against simple (e.g., singular, unidimensional, additive), serial processing models of complex social behaviors. Many of the principles and methods from the neurosciences are uniquely suited to foster these theoretical developments.

As in any new and complex perspective, incorporating neuroscientific theory and methods calls for diligent study of the relevant literatures, complemented by study and consultation with experts in these fields. There are now several texts that interested readers might consult (e.g., Cacioppo, Tassinary, et al., 2000; Gazzaniga, 2000; Jezzard, Matthews, et al., 2001), but ideally new students and investigators would also form collaborations with behavioral, cognitive, and social neuroscientists who share theoretical interests. Transdisciplinary training and research teams of this sort have particular potential to make major contributions to both the social sciences and the neurosciences. We look forward to these advances in the years to come.

## NOTES

1. All human behavior, at some level, is biological, but this is not to say that biological reductionism yields a simple, singular, or satisfactory explanation for complex behaviors, or that molecular forms of representation provide the only or best level of analysis for understanding human behavior. Molar constructs such as those developed by the social sciences provide a means of understanding highly complex activity without needing to specify each individual action of the simplest components, thereby providing an efficient means of describing the behavior of a complex system.

2. Research in which psychological or behavioral factors serve as the independent (or blocking) variables and physiological structures or events serve as the dependent variable can be conceptualized as investigating the $P(\Phi/\Psi)$. Research in which physiological structures or events serve as the independent (or blocking) variables and psychological or behavioral factors serve as the dependent

variable, in contrast, can be conceptualized as investigating the $P(\Psi/\Phi)$. These conditional probabilities are equal only when the relationship between is $\Psi$ and $\Phi$ is 1:1 (Cacioppo & Tassinary, 1990). Accordingly, approaches such as stimulation and ablation studies provide complementary rather than redundant information to studies in which physiological (e.g., fMRI) measures serve as dependent measures. This is because stimulation and ablation studies bear on the relationship $P(\Psi/\Phi)$, whereas studies in which physiological variables serve as dependent measures provide information about $P(\Phi/\Psi)$.

3. The use of deconvolution methods for analyzing event-related fMRI designs requires truly random intertrial intervals with a mean duration sufficient to model the hemodynamic responses of interest. The longer the putative hemodynamic response one wishes to model using deconvolution, the longer the mean intertrial interval should be.

4. Limiting analyses to regions of interest (ROIs) provides more focused tests of specific hypotheses. Including analyses of areas outside the ROI, however, provides discriminative evidence for the hypothesized region of activation and ensures that the area within the ROI is not active simply because of the decisions (e.g., thresholds) made by an investigator when reducing and analyzing the data.

5. We have emphasized how one might think about neurobiological and social processes and discussed some of the issues surrounding the acquisition and interpretation of data from fMRI. Equally important and complex are the issues involving data reduction and analysis in this field. Discussion of these issues is beyond the scope of this chapter, but the text by Jezzard, Matthews, et al. (2001) provides an excellent introduction to these issues.

## REFERENCES

Adolphs, R. (1999). Social cognition and the human brain. *Trends in Cognitive Sciences, 3,* 469-479.

Allport, G. W. (1947). Scientific models and human morals. *Psychological Review, 54,* 182-192.

Anderson, N. B. (1998). Levels of analysis in health science. A framework for integrating sociobehavioral and biomedical research. *Annals of the New York Academy of Science, 840,* 563-576.

Bandettini, P. A., Birn, R. M., & Donahue, K. M. (2000). Functional MRI: Background, methodology, limits, and implementation. In J. T. Cacioppo, L. G. Tassinary, & G. G. Berntson (Eds.), *The handbook of psychophysiology* (pp. 978-1014). New York: Cambridge University Press.

Belin, P., Zilbovicius, M., Crozier, S., Thivard, L., Fontaine, A., Masure, M. C., et al. (1998). Lateralization of speech and auditory temporal processing. *Journal of Cognitive Neuroscience, 10*(4), 536-540.

Bernstein, I. S., Gordon, T. P., & Rose, R. M. (1983). The interaction of hormones, behavior, and social context in nonhuman primates. In B. B. Svare (Ed.), *Hormones and aggressive behavior* (pp. 535-561). New York: Plenum.

Berntson, G. G., & Cacioppo, J. T. (2000). Psychobiology and social psychology: Past, present, and future. *Personality and Social Psychology Review, 4,* 3-15.

Berntson, G. G., Cacioppo, J. T., & Quigley, K. S. (1991). Autonomic determinism: The modes of autonomic control, the doctrine of autonomic space, and the laws of autonomic constraint. *Psychological Review, 98,* 459-487.

Blumstein, S. (1997). A perspective on the neurobiology of language. *Brain and Language. 60*(3), 335-346.

Bogen, J. E., & Bogen, G. M. (1976). Wernicke's region—where is it? *Annals of the New York Academy of Sciences, 280,* 834-843.

Buckner, R. L., Bandettini, P. A., O'Craven, K. M., Savoy, R. L., Petersen, S. E., Raichle, M. E., & Rosen, B. R. (1996). Detection of cortical activation during averaged single trials of a cognitive task using functional magnetic resonance imaging. *Proceedings of the National Academy of Science, 93*(25), 14878-14883.

Cacioppo, J. T. (2002). Social neuroscience: Understanding the pieces fosters understanding the whole and vice versa. *American Psychologist, 57,* 819-830.

Cacioppo, J. T., & Berntson, G. G. (1992). Social psychological contributions to the decade of the brain: Doctrine of multilevel analysis. *American Psychologist, 47,* 1019-1028.

Cacioppo, J. T., & Berntson, G. G. (2002). Social neuroscience. In J. T. Cacioppo, G. G. Berntson, R. Adolphs, C. S. Carter, R. J. Davidson, M. K. McClintock, B. S. McEwen, M. J. Meaney, D. L. Schacter, E. M. Sternberg, S. S. Suomi, & S. E. Taylor (Eds.), *Foundations in social neuroscience* (pp. 3-10). Cambridge: MIT Press.

Cacioppo, J. T., Berntson, G. G., Adolphs, R., Carter, C. S., Davidson, R. J., McClintock, M. K., McEwen, B. S., Meaney, M. J., Schacter, D. L., Sternberg, E. M., Suomi, S. S., & Taylor, S. E. (Eds.). (2002). *Foundations in social neuroscience.* Cambridge: MIT Press.

Cacioppo, J. T., Berntson, G. G., & Crites, S. L., Jr. (1996). Social neuroscience: Principles of psychophysiological arousal and response. In E. T. Higgins & A. W. Kruglanski (Eds.), *Social psychology: Handbook of basic principles* (pp. 72-101). New York: Guilford.

Cacioppo, J. T., Berntson, G. G., Lorig, T. S., Norris, C. J., Rickett, E., & Nusbaum, H. (in press). Just because you're imaging the brain doesn't mean you can stop using your head: A primer and set of first principles. *Journal of Personality and Social Psychology.*

Cacioppo, J. T., Berntson, G. G., Malarkey, W. B., Kiecolt-Glaser, J. K., Sheridan, J. F., Poehlmann, K. M., et al. (1998). Autonomic, neuroendocrine, and immune responses to psychological stress: The reactivity hypothesis. *Annals of the New York Academy of Sciences, 840,* 664-673.

Cacioppo, J. T., Berntson, G. G., Sheridan, J. F., & McClintock, M. K. (2000). Multilevel integrative analyses of human behavior: Social neuroscience and the complementing nature of social and biological approaches. *Psychological Bulletin, 126*(6), 829-843.

Cacioppo, J. T., Crites, S. L., Jr., Berntson, G. G., & Coles, M.G.H. (1993). If attitudes affect how stimuli are processed, should they not affect the event-related brain potential? *Psychological Science, 4,* 108-112.

Cacioppo, J. T., Crites, S. L., Jr., Gardner, W. L., & Berntson, G. G. (1994). Bioelectrical echoes from evaluative categorizations: I. A late positive brain potential that varies as a function of trait negativity and extremity. *Journal of Personality and Social Psychology, 67,* 115-125.

Cacioppo, J. T., Gardner, W. L., & Berntson, G. G. (1999). The affect system has parallel and integrative processing components: Form follows function. *Journal of Personality and Social Psychology, 76*(5), 839-855.

Cacioppo, J. T., Martzke, J. S., Petty, R. E., & Tassinary, L. G. (1988). Specific forms of facial EMG response index emotions during an interview: From Darwin to the continuous flow hypothesis of affect-laden information processing. *Journal of Personality and Social Psychology, 54,* 592-604.

Cacioppo, J. T., & Petty, R. E. (1981). Electromyograms as measures of extent and affectivity of information processing. *American Psychologist, 36,* 441-456.

Cacioppo, J. T., & Petty, R. E. (1983). *Social psychophysiology: A sourcebook.* New York: Guilford.

Cacioppo, J. T., & Petty, R. E. (1986). Social processes. In M. G. H. Coles, E. Donchin, & S. Porges (Eds.), *Psychophysiology: Systems, processes, and applications* (pp. 646-679). New York: Guilford.

Cacioppo, J. T., Petty, R. E., & Tassinary, L. G. (1989). Social psychophysiology: A new look. *Advances in Experimental Social Psychology, 22,* 39-91.

Cacioppo, J. T., & Tassinary, L. G. (1990). Inferring psychological significance from physiological signals. *American Psychology, 45*(1), 16-28.

Cacioppo, J. T., Tassinary, L. G., & Berntson, G. G. (Eds.). (2000). *Handbook of psychophysiology* (2nd ed.). Cambridge, UK: Cambridge University Press.

Campbell, D. T., & Stanley, J. C. (1963). *Experimental and quasi-experimental designs for research.* Chicago: Rand McNally.

Crites, S. L., Jr., & Cacioppo, J. T. (1996). Electrocortical differentiation of evaluative and nonevaluative categorizations. *Psychological Science, 7,* 318-321.

Crites, S. L., Jr., Cacioppo, J. T., Gardner, W. L., & Berntson, G. G. (1995). Bioelectrical echoes from evaluative categorization: II. A late positive brain potential that varies as a function of attitude registration rather than attitude report. *Journal of Personality and Social Psychology, 68,* 997-1013.

Davidson, R. J., Putnam, K. M., & Larson, C. L. (2000). Dysfunction in the neural circuitry of emotion regulation—A possible prelude to violence. *Science, 289,* 591-594.

Donders, F. C. (1969). On the speed of mental processes. *Acta Psychologia, 30,* 412-431. (Original work published 1868)

Dorfman, D. D., & Cacioppo, J. T. (1990). Waveform moment analysis: Topographical analysis of nonrhythmic waveforms. In J. T. Cacioppo & L. G. Tassinary (Eds.), *Principles of psychophysiology: Physical, social, and inferential elements* (pp. 661-707). New York: Cambridge University Press.

Ford, J. M. (1999). Schizophrenia: The broken P300 and beyond. *Psychophysiology, 36*(6), 667-682.

Gardner, W. L., Gabriel, S., & Diekman, A. B. (in press). Interpersonal processes. In J. T. Cacioppo, L. G. Tassinary, & G. G. Berntson (Eds.), *Handbook of psychophysiology.* New York: Cambridge University Press.

Gazzaniga, M. S. (1989). Organization of the human brain. *Science, 245,* 947-952.

Gazzaniga, M. S. (2000). *The new cognitive neurosciences* (2nd ed.). Cambridge: MIT Press.

Geschwind, N. (1965). The organization of language and the brain. *Science, 170,* 634-640.

Gevins, A. S., & Shaffer, R. E. (1980). A critical review of electroencephalographic (EEG) correlates of higher cortical functions. *CRC Critical Reviews in Bioengineering, 4*(2),113-164.

Gusnard, D. A., & Raichle, M. E. (2001). Searching for a baseline: Functional imaging and the resting human brain. *Nature Reviews: Neuroscience, 2,* 685-694.

Haber, S. N., & Barchas, P. R. (1983). The regulatory effect of social rank on behavior after amphetamine administration. In P. R. Barchas (Ed.), *Social hierarchies: Essays toward a sociophysiological perspective* (pp. 119-132). Westport, CT: Greenwood.

Hawkley, L. C., Burleson, M. H., Berntson, G. G., & Cacioppo, J. T. (in press). Loneliness in everyday life: Cardiovascular activity, psychosocial context, and health behaviors. *Journal of Personality and Social Psychology.*

Heeger, D. J., & Rees, D. (2002). What does fMRI tell us about neuronal activity? *Nature Reviews: Neuroscience, 3*(2), 142-151.

Hopfield, J. J., & Brody, C. D. (2001). What is a moment? Transient synchrony as a collective mechanism for spatiotemporal integration. *Proceedings of the National Academy of Science, 98,* 1282-1287.

Ito, T. A., & Cacioppo, J. T. (2000). Electrophysiological evidence of implicit and explicit categorization processes. *Journal of Experimental Social Psychology, 36,* 660-676.

Ito, T. A., Larsen, J. T., Smith, N. K., & Cacioppo, J. T. (1998). Negative information weighs more heavily on the brain: The negativity bias in evaluative categorizations. *Journal of Personality and Social Psychology, 75,* 887-900.

Jezzard, P., Matthews, P. M., & Smith, S. M. (2001). *Functional MRI.* Oxford, UK: Oxford University Press.

Jezzard, P., & Song, A. W. (1996). Technical foundations and pitfalls of clinical fMRI. *Neuroimage, 4*(3, Pt. 3), S63-S75.

Kiecolt-Glaser, J. K., Glaser, R., Cacioppo, J. T., & Malarkey, W. B. (1998). Marital stress: Immunologic, neuroendocrine, and autonomic correlates. *Annals of the New York Academy of Sciences, 840,* 656-663.

Klein, S. B., & Kihlstrom, J. F. (1998). On bridging the gap between social-personality psychology and neuropsychology. *Personality and Social Psychology Review, 2,* 228-242.

Kosslyn, S. M., Cacioppo, J. T., Davidson, R. J., Hugdahl, K., Lovallo, W. R., Spiegel, D., et al. (2002). Bridging psychology and biology: The analysis of individuals in groups. *American Psychologist, 57,* 341-351.

Kutas, M., & Federmeier, K. D. (1998). Minding the body. *Psychophysiology, 35*(2), 135-150.

Lang, P. J., Bradley, M. M., Fitzsimmons, J. R., Cuthbert, B. N., Scott, J. D., Moulder, B., et al. (1998). Emotional arousal and activation of the visual cortex: An fMRI analysis. *Psychophysiology, 35*(2), 199-210.

LeDoux, J. E. (2000). Emotion circuits in the brain. *Annual Review of Neuroscience, 23,* 155-184.

Llinas, R., & Ribary, U. (2001). Consciousness and the brain. The thalamocortical dialogue in health and disease. *Annals of the New York Academy of Sciences, 929,* 166-175.

Lorig, T. S. (2000, October). *Spheres of influence: Psychophysiology's place in a universe of neuroscience.* Paper presented to the meeting of the Society for Psychophysiological Research, Denver.

Makeig, S., Westerfield, W., Enghoff, S., Jung, T.-P., Townsend, J., Courchesne, E., et al. (2002). Dynamic brain sources of visual evoked responses. *Science, 295,* 690-694.

Morris, J. S., Öhman, A., & Dolan, R. J. (1998). Conscious and unconscious emotional learning in the human amygdala. *Nature, 393,* 467-470.

Noll, D. C., Cohen, J. D., Meyer, C. H., & Schneider, W. (1995). Spiral K-space MR imaging of cortical activation. *Journal of Magnetic Resonance Imaging, 5*(1), 49-56.

Nunez, P. (2000). Toward a quantitative description of large-scale neocortical dynamic function and EEG. *Behavioral Brain Science, 23*(3), 371-398.

O'Brien, G., & Opie, J. (1999). A connectionist theory of phenomenal experience. *Behavioral Brain Science, 22*(1), 127-148.

Ochsner, K. N., & Lieberman, M. D. (2001). The emergence of social cognitive neuroscience. *American Psychologist, 56*(9), 717-734.

Pascual-Marqui, R. D., Michel, C. M., & Lehmann, D. (1994). Low resolution electromagnetic tomography: A new method for localizing electrical activity in the brain. *International Journal of Psychophysiolology, 18*(1), 49-65.

Passingham, R. E., Stephan, K. E., & Kötter, R. (2002). The anatomical basis of functional localization in the cortex. *Nature Reviews: Neuroscience, 3,* 1-11.

Peeters, G., & Czapinski, J. (1990). Positive-negative asymmetry in evaluations: The distinction between affective and informational negativity effects. In W. Stroebe & M. Hewstone (Eds.), *European Review of Social Psychology* (Vol. 1, pp. 33-60). New York: Wiley.

Phelps, E. A., O'Connor, K. J., Cunningham, W. A., Funayama, E. S., Gatenby, J. C., Gore, J. C., et al. (2000). Performance on indirect measures of race evaluation predicts amygdale activation. *Journal of Cognitive Neuroscience, 12,* 729-738.

Pincus, J. H., & Tucker, G. J. (1985). *Behavioral neurology* (3rd ed.). Oxford, UK: Oxford University Press.

Platt, J. (1964). Strong inference, *Science, 146,* 347-353.

Polich, J., & Kok, A. (1995). Cognitive and biological determinants of P300: An integrative review. *Biological Psychology, 41*(2), 103-146.

Puce, A. (1995). Comparative assessment of sensorimotor function using functional magnetic resonance imaging and electrophysiological methods. *Journal of Clinical Neurophysiol*ogy, *12*(5), 450-459.

Raichle, M. E., MacLeod, A. M., Snyder, A. Z., Powers, W. J., Gusnard, D. A., & Shulman, G. L. (2001). A default mode of brain function. *Proceedings of the National Academy of Sciences, 98,* 676-682.

Rankin, R. E., & Campbell, D. T. (1955). Galvanic skin response to Negro and white experimenters. *Journal of Abnormal and Social Psychology, 51,* 30-33.

Reis, H. T., & Judd, C. M. (2000). *Handbook of research methods in social and personality psychology.* New York: Cambridge University Press.

Roland, P. (1993). *Brain activation.* New York: Wiley-Liss.

Rose, R. M., Gordon, T. P., & Bernstein, I. S. (1972). Plasma testosterone levels in the male rhesus: Influences of sexual and social stimuli. *Science, 178,* 643-645.

Sarter, M., Berntson, G. G., & Cacioppo, J. T. (1996). Brain imaging and cognitive neuroscience: Toward strong inference in attributing function to structure. *American Psychologist, 51*(1), 13-21.

Scherg, M., & Berg, P. (1991). Use of prior knowledge in brain electromagnetic source analysis. *Brain Topography, 4*(2), 143-150.

Scott, T. R. (1991). A personal view of the future of psychology departments. *American Psychologist, 46,* 975-976.

Shapiro, D., & Crider, A. (1969). Psychophysiological approaches in social psychology. In G. Lindzey & E. Aronson (Eds.), *Handbook of social psychology* (2nd ed., Vol. 3, pp. 1-49). Reading, MA: Addison-Wesley.

Shiffman, S., & Stone, A. A. (1998). Introduction to the special section: Ecological momentary assessment in health psychology. *Health Psychology, 17,* 3-5.

Small, S. J. (1994). Connectionist networks and language disorders. *Journal of Communication Disorders, 27*(4), 305-323.

Smith, N. K., Cacioppo, J. T., Larsen, J. T., & Chartrand, T. L. (2003). May I have your attention please: Electrocortical responses to positive and negative stimuli. *Neuropsychologia, 41,* 171-183.

Taylor, S. E. (1991). Asymmetrical effects of positive and negative events: The mobilization-minimization hypothesis. *Psychological Bulletin, 110,* 67-85.

Toga, A. W., & Mazziotta, J. C. (1996). *Brain mapping: The methods.* San Diego: Academic Press.

Tomaka, J., Blascovich, J., Kelsey, R. M., & Leitten, C. L. (1993). Subjective, physiological, and behavioral effects of threat and challenge appraisal. *Journal of Personality and Social Psychology, 65,* 248-260.

Townsend, J. T., & Ashby, F. G. (1983). *Stochastic modeling of elementary psychological processes.* Cambridge, UK: Cambridge University Press.

Vanman, E. J. (2001). Saying one thing and doing another: Predicting behavior using psychophysiologic markers of attitudes [Abstract]. *Psychophysiology, 38*(Suppl. 1), S14.

## CHAPTER 18

# Supplementing the Snapshots With Video Footage

## Taking a Developmental Approach to Understanding Social Psychological Phenomena

Eva M. Pomerantz

*University of Illinois, Urbana–Champaign*

Diane N. Ruble

*New York University*

Niall Bolger

*New York University*

T he methods of social psychology function much like a camera: They enable investigators to take snapshots of social phenomena, such as aggression, attraction, motivation, and prejudice. An investigator may zero in on a phenomenon, getting a close-up of the mechanisms involved. A wide-angle lens may be used in an effort to view the phenomenon in relation to other phenomena. The phenomenon may be photographed in a variety of situations. Over the course of time, an album of the phenomenon may be compiled; however, this is simply a collection of snapshots. Although there may be diversity in the pictures, each captures only a single instant in time. These snapshots are

AUTHORS' NOTE: We are grateful to the editors for their thoughtful feedback on this chapter. Work on this chapter was supported by NSF #BCS-9809292 and NIMH and ORWH #R01 MH57505 grants to Eva M. Pomerantz, NIMH #R01 MH37215 grant to Diane N. Ruble, and NIMH #R01 MH60366 grant to Niall Bolger. Correspondence regarding this manuscript may be addressed to Eva M. Pomerantz at Department of Psychology, University of Illinois, 603 E. Daniel St., Champaign, IL 61820 or at pomerntz@uiuc.edu.

not informative about the beginnings of the phenomenon or how it unfolds over time. What is needed are methods that function like a video camera. These are the methods of developmental psychology, through which people are followed over time as they make their way through life.

Our focus in this chapter is on how social psychologists may use these methods to acquire a richer understanding of the phenomena they study. We first discuss what it means to take a developmental approach; we then move to the issue of why one would want to take such an approach, with particular emphasis on why we have been motivated to do so in our own work. Subsequently, we discuss how to take a developmental approach, highlighting some of the benefits. We end with a discussion of work integrating developmental and social psychological approaches.

## WHAT DOES IT MEAN TO USE THE VIDEO CAMERA?

For many social psychologists, taking a developmental approach simply means studying phenomena in children that already have been studied in adults, to ensure that the principles governing adults' behavior also govern children's behavior (see Flavell & Ross, 1981). Although this can be an important benefit of taking a developmental approach (see Pomerantz & Newman, 2000), it does not reflect the essence of such an approach. In fact, it is just like taking a snapshot. At the heart of a developmental approach is a concern with how phenomena unfold over the life course. This involves two central sets of questions. Questions of *normative development* focus on issues related to the changes that people characteristically experience over the life course: How do people typically change as they progress through life? And what processes underlie the changes people normally experience as they move from one

developmental phase to the next? What moderates the changes people typically experience? Questions about the *development of individual differences* revolve around the issue of the process by which people come to differ from one another: What factors shape people as they progress through life? And how is it that these factors exert their influence? What moderates the impact of the factors that shape people? Thus, using the video camera means capturing how people typically change as they progress through life, while also focusing on the antecedents and consequences of individual differences over time.

## WHY USE THE VIDEO CAMERA?

Although we all enjoy looking at snapshots, they often leave us yearning to know more. We are left wondering about the life to which the moments captured in the snapshots belong. Snapshots, like social psychology, are captivating, but also like social psychology, they do not tell the whole story. Social psychology is especially accomplished at dissecting phenomena—pinpointing causal factors, identifying underlying processes, and understanding variations due to the environment as well as to the person. However, this scrutiny takes place at one point in time. The focus of social psychology is almost always on proximal influences, as if people exist only in the moment. Little attention is paid to factors that are distal in time. Indeed, in much of social psychological theory and research, the origins of phenomena are situated only in the recent past (for some exceptions, see Cross & Madson, 1997; Higgins, 1991). Of course, evolutionary and historical perspectives reach quite far back (e.g., Buss & Kenrick, 1998; Cohen, 2001). Yet, while doing so, they often neglect development across the life course.

Leaving out the history of people's development leads to an incomplete story, particularly in light of the impressive effects of early conditions and experiences that have been documented over the life course (e.g., Caspi, 2000; Sroufe, 2002). Social psychologists, however, rarely appear to be concerned with how a phenomenon unfolds over time. Nor is much attention given to the question of the process by which a phenomenon originates—that is, with how people become the way they are. As a number of investigators have argued (e.g., Higgins & Wells, 1986; Pomerantz & Newman, 2000; Ruble & Goodnow, 1998), elucidating the development of social psychological phenomena can provide important knowledge about such phenomena. Similar to Miller's (1999) argument regarding understanding culture, understanding development can provide insight into both the diversity and the regularity underlying social psychological phenomena. Moreover, the developmental approach provides useful methodological tools that often go unused by social psychologists.

In our own work, we have taken a developmental approach to understanding a number of social psychological phenomena, including gender beliefs (e.g., Alfieri, Ruble, & Higgins, 1996; Szkrybalo & Ruble, 1999), person perception (e.g., Alvarez, Ruble, & Bolger, 2001; Newman & Ruble, 1992), self-evaluation (e.g., Pomerantz & Ruble, 1997; Pomerantz & Saxon, 2001), social comparison (e.g., Frey & Ruble, 1985; Pomerantz, Ruble, Frey, & Greulich, 1995), social support (e.g., Bolger & Eckenrode, 1991; Bolger, Zuckerman, & Kessler, 2000), and the transition to parenthood (e.g., Hackel & Ruble, 1992; Ruble, Brooks-Gunn, et al., 1990). Throughout this chapter, we will touch on how the developmental approach has guided our work in these areas, with particular attention to the methods we have used. Our major emphasis, however, will be on our work concerning the effects of controlling environments on psychological functioning.

The effects of controlling environments have received much attention among social psychologists over the last several decades (for a review, see Deci, Koestner, & Ryan, 1999). In our work in this area, we drew from Deci and Ryan's impressive body of theory and research (for reviews, see Deci & Ryan, 1985, 1987), which initially led us to the conclusion that controlling environments are detrimental for people's psychological functioning. These investigators, along with a number of others (e.g., Harackiewicz, 1979; Lepper & Greene, 1975), have studied how controlling environments affect people, using the method of creating such environments in the laboratory. The major conclusion of this work is that controlling environments have negative effects on people (for a review, see Deci, Koestner, et al., 1999). Thus, we were quite surprised when we turned to research in developmental psychology to understand the effects on children of their parents' exertion of control over them. Although much of the research in this area is consistent with that in social psychology showing that controlling environments are detrimental to psychological functioning, much of it also shows that some forms of control used by parents with children are beneficial for children (for a review, see Pomerantz & Ruble, 1998a).

This discrepancy took us aback. After much thought, however, it led us to develop a novel hypothesis: Control, at least in certain forms, has both negative and positive qualities (e.g., Pomerantz & Ruble, 1998a, 1998b). We speculated that, on one hand, consistent with Deci and Ryan's work, as well as that of some developmental psychologists studying the effects of parents' use of control on children (e.g., Barber, 1996; Schaefer, 1965), control has negative qualities in that it intrudes on people's individuation and communicates to them that they are incompetent. Yet, based on a rather large body of findings from developmental psychology (e.g., Barber, 1996; Baumrind, 1967), we speculated that, on the other hand, control has positive qualities in that it provides guidance in meeting valued standards and conveys support.

For several reasons, we believed it was important to take a developmental approach to the issue of whether control has both positive and negative qualities. First, our knowledge of children's social-cognitive development suggested to us that sensitivity to the negative and positive qualities of control may change as children progress through elementary school and become more aware of issues related to competence in general. Second, we were interested in how this sensitivity shapes psychological functioning over time, with a particular emphasis on how it moderates the effects of controlling environments. Third, taking a developmental approach had some important methodological benefits. Most notably, it allowed us to take advantage of the ongoing intimate relationship between parents and children—a context in which we thought both the negative and positive qualities of control would be particularly salient, given that meeting valued standards and providing support are such important issues in these relationships.

## HOW TO USE THE VIDEO CAMERA

Using the video camera is quite different from taking snapshots. Developmental psychology uses designs that allow people to be followed as they progress through life; often, however, this is only simulated. Moreover, a diverse set of methods is used in developmental psychology. Although they are used on occasion in social psychology, they are used more commonly in developmental psychology. Operating the video camera often demands significantly more resources than taking snapshots. It is frequently the case that research conducted in developmental psychology not only costs more but also requires greater planning than that conducted in social psychology.

We hope this chapter provides an introduction to the issues involved in conducting developmental research, but we also recommend consulting developmental colleagues as well as additional sources (e.g., Friedman & Wachs, 1999; Funder, Parke, Tomlinson-Keasy, & Widman, 1993) in preparing to conduct developmental research. In discussing how to use the video camera, we focus on three major developmental designs. We then turn to a number of issues that are of special consideration when conducting developmental research, then finish with some of the benefits provided by developmental methods.

## Developmental Designs

One of the key issues in conducting developmental research is that of how to examine people as they make their way through life. There are three major designs used in studying development: the cross-sectional design, the longitudinal design, and the cross-sequential design (for more detail on longitudinal designs, see West, Biesanz, & Kwok, Chapter 13, this volume). Like the designs of social psychology, these designs all have important strengths and weaknesses. Together, they can provide important video footage on development over the life course. As we will highlight below, the choice of design depends on the question being asked as well as the available resources.

### The Cross-Sectional Design

In the cross-sectional design, people at varying phases of development are studied at one point in time. This design can be thought of as simulating development over time. As a shortcut to studying people as they progress through life, the cross-sectional design demands the fewest resources. As a consequence, the design is ideal for an initial test of an idea.

In one of our first steps toward investigating the issue of whether control has both negative and positive qualities, we employed the cross-sectional design. Our key hypothesis was that most children view parents' use of control in a negative as well as a positive light. However, we expected that the types of negative qualities children see in parents' use of control change over the course of children's development. We focused on the elementary school years because as children make their way through these years, they increasingly view ability as something that cannot easily change over time or across situations (for a review, see Rholes, Newman, & Ruble, 1990). Because viewing ability as something that cannot change easily is accompanied by a heightened concern with information about competence (Pomerantz & Saxon, 2001), it is possible that such a view of ability increases children's attention to competence-related information, particularly that which is threatening. This may cause the incompetence message of parents' use of control to be salient to children.

We examined whether there were developmental differences in children's views of parents' use of control with a cross-sectional design in which we interviewed children in second grade through fifth grades (Pomerantz & Eaton, 2000). We chose to study children in these grades because significant change appears to occur in children's understanding of ability beginning in grade (for a review, see Rholes et al., 1990), allowing us to capture subsequent changes in children's views of parents' use of control. Regardless of their grade in school, children were unanimous in saying that parents used control to promote children's well being. However, children also saw a darker side to parents' use of control. Children said that it made them feel that their autonomy was being suppressed. Consistent with our expectations, as children progressed through elementary school, they said that parents' use of control caused them to feel incompetent because it indicated that parents thought children were unable to be successful on their own. This view

of parents' use of control was associated with low self-esteem when children saw parents as using control frequently with them.

The cross-sectional design can be informative because it can document differences as a function of developmental phase. In our study, the data suggested that children's views of parents' use of control change over the course of development, so that children come to focus on what parents' use of control means in terms of their competence. However, because the cross-sectional design does not follow the same children over time, it has some significant weaknesses that can make conclusions about development tentative at best. First, because participants of different ages come from different cohorts (i.e., a group of people all born in the same year), it is not always clear if the observed "developmental" effects are due to development per se. It is possible instead that the effects could be driven by a difference between cohorts unrelated to development. Second, cross-sectional analyses cannot provide information about the shape of a developmental function. For instance, it is not informative in regard to whether change is continuous or steplike. Third, in a cross-sectional design, it is difficult to investigate the processes underlying developmental change. Such a design allows only for the examination of concurrent associations. Indeed, the cross-sectional design is much like those used in social psychology in that it provides snapshots of people at a single instance in time, with the exception that people are at different developmental phases. Thus, if it takes time for development to occur, the processes underlying development may go undetected. Fourth, and relatedly, the development of individual differences cannot be studied at only one point in time. As a consequence, it would not be possible in our study to examine why some children come to view parents' use of control as indicating that they are incompetent, whereas other children may not.

*The Longitudinal Design*

The use of the video camera approach is truly evident in the longitudinal design. Such a design is an optimal choice for examining the development of individual differences because a group of people is studied repeatedly over time, with responses examined as a function of time of assessment. The time period can vary from minutes, to days, to weeks or months, to years, to decades. For a discussion of the issue of timing between assessments, see the section on micro-analytic and macro-analytic strategies below.

Although the analysis of data from longitudinal designs can be complex, it is also an area where fundamental advances have been made. In the past two decades, techniques such as structural equation models (Bollen, 1989), multilevel models (Raudenbush & Bryk, 2002; Snijders & Bosker, 1999), and latent growth models (Molenaar, 1994; Nesselroade, McArdle, Aggen, & Meyers, 2002) have begun to supplant the traditional repeated measures ANOVA and multiple regression approaches as a way of analyzing developmental change. With these new techniques, it is possible to remove measurement error in models of change, manage missing data problems, handle categorical and continuous variables, and examine intervening processes through longitudinal systems of equations. The learning curve can be steep for these new techniques, but investigators with well-formulated developmental questions can reap great benefits from them. For a more detailed account of the analysis of longitudinal designs, see West et al. (Chapter 13, this volume).

Because longitudinal designs are ideal for answering questions about the development of individual differences, we have used such designs in our work aimed at understanding how controlling environments shape people. A key hypothesis of ours has been that, in addition to the normative developmental changes, there are individual differences in how control is viewed. Prior theory and research suggested to us that people's self-evaluative biases are important in determining whether the negative or positive qualities of control are salient to them. People possessing a negative self-evaluative bias may be sensitive to the negative qualities of control because of their tendency to interpret others' behavior as indicating that they lack competence (see Phillips, 1984). In contrast, people possessing a positive self-evaluative bias may be sensitive to the positive qualities of control because of their tendency to view the world through "rose-colored glasses." To investigate this possibility, we used a two-wave longitudinal design in which elementary school children were followed over a 6-month period (Pomerantz, 2001). Children's self-evaluative biases moderated the effects of parents' use of control on children's depression over time: Among children whose parents used control frequently, children with a negative bias became more depressed over time, whereas children with a positive bias became less depressed.

A major strength of the longitudinal design is that it allows for the examination of relations over time, with the provision that concurrent associations can be ruled out by adjusting for earlier variation. This is particularly useful in investigating the development of individual differences. Unfortunately, the longitudinal design has some major problems when documenting normative development. First, what are assumed to be effects of development actually may be effects of repeated testing. Second, there could also be problems resulting from environmental changes between assessment points, such as new messages in the popular press about the effects of parental involvement in children's lives. Third, a particular problem for studies spanning decades is that many people may drop out of the study, leaving a small, select sample, which may limit generalizability.

## The Cross-Sequential Design

To address the shortcomings of the cross-sectional and longitudinal designs, the cross-sequential design (Schaie, 1965, 1986) was developed. In this design, people at different phases of development are studied over time, thereby combining the best features of cross-sectional and longitudinal designs. Given that it requires significant resources, the cross-sequential design should be used in answering questions of normative development only after a cross-sectional design has yielded supportive evidence. The cross-sequential design not only can rule out alternative explanations for the differences among different phases of development but also allows for the examination of the processes underlying normative change over time. In addition, the cross-sequential design is an excellent choice for examining questions related to the development of individual differences. However, a simple longitudinal design, requiring fewer resources, would suffice if the individual differences are not expected to develop differently at different phases of life. Data analytic strategies for cross-sequential designs draw on the same pool of techniques used in longitudinal data analysis (see the earlier section on longitudinal designs).

Although we have not used such a design in our work on the effects of controlling environments, we have used it in other areas of our work. In our research on social comparison, for example, we used a cross-sequential design to understand how children's social comparison changes as they progress through elementary school (Pomerantz, Ruble, et al., 1995). In past work using a cross-sectional design, we had observed that younger elementary school children made fewer inquiries about their peers' progress than did their older counterparts (Frey & Ruble, 1985). Although we had several reasons for using the cross-sequential design, a major one was to ensure that this effect was indeed a developmental one. We observed the social comparison of children initially in kindergarten, first grade, and second grade once a year over the course of 3 years. The cohort of children beginning the study in kindergarten was followed until the children were in second grade, the cohort of children beginning the study in first grade was followed until the children were in third grade, and the cohort of children beginning the study in second grade was followed until the children were in fourth grade. During the first year of the study, a group of children in fifth grade was also included to identify the developmental trajectory. In line with our cross-sectional research on social comparison (Frey & Ruble, 1985), we found that as children progressed through school, they increasingly compared their work to that of their peers by asking their peers about their work.

The cross-sequential design has many benefits. First, less time is necessary than in a traditional single-cohort longitudinal design to cover a larger age range. In the example, five years of development (kindergarten through fourth grade) are covered in a matter of 3 years, not including the additional fifth graders. Thus, there should be less attrition, leading the sample to be less select and the results more generalizable. Second, the cross-sequential design allows the investigator to ensure that effects of age are not due to differences unrelated to development. In this design, different cohorts are tested when they are at the same age, with the time of assessment varying. Thus, in our study, children initially in kindergarten were tested when they were in second grade during the third year of assessment, children initially in first grade were also tested when they were in second grade but during the second year of assessment, and children initially in second grade were tested at this age during the first year of assessment. The responses of the three cohorts when children are at the same age can be compared statistically (for an example, see Pomerantz, Ruble, et al., 1995). Such a comparison can rule out cohort effects as well as time of assessment effects. Third, there is provision for replication within the study. The cross-sectional age differences observed during the first year of the study should parallel the age changes observed in cohorts over time. Thus, in the example, the cohort beginning the study in kindergarten should change in ways already seen in cross-sectional age differences at the start of the study. Fourth, the cross-sequential design provides the opportunity to examine underlying mechanisms over time. In the Pomerantz and colleagues study, for instance, we examined how children's views of inquiring about their peers' progress were related to their actual inquiries. The cross-sequential design also provides the opportunity to see if these mechanisms differ as a function of children's developmental phase (for an example, see Altermatt, Pomerantz, Ruble, Frey, & Greulich, 2002).

## *Operationalizing Developmental Phase*

Now that we have presented the three major developmental designs, we turn to the question of how to operationalize developmental phase. This is a crucial issue whose answer varies with the questions being asked and the part of life being studied. Developmental phases usually are determined on the basis of conceptually meaningful criteria. As may be evident by now, in our work on elementary school children, we have usually operationalized developmental phase as children's grade in school. This is in line with the bulk of research conducted on children during the elementary school years. Grade is used as a proxy of development phase at this time because both children's cognitive abilities and their social environments are assumed to vary as function of their year in school (see Higgins & Parsons, 1983). In work on infants, developmental phase is often operationalized in months of age because of the rapid cognitive and social developments that occur at this stage of life

(e.g., Schaffer & Emerson, 1964). After young adulthood, developmental phases span a longer period of time, such as a decade, because change often is assumed to take place at a slower rate (e.g., Roberts, Helson, & Klohnen, 2002).

Taking a developmental approach, however, does not always mean linking developmental phase to age. Developmental phases may have to do with major life events that typically are experienced as people progress through the life course but that are not necessarily related to age. It is important to note that developmental phase is not synonymous with age—or grade, for that matter. For example, much attention has been focused on transitions, which although often linked to age, are not always (for a review, see Ruble & Seidman, 1996). If it is the event rather than age that investigators believe defines a developmental phase, this should be taken into account in the design. In our work on the development of gender stereotype flexibility, we have tried to disentangle the effect of the transition from elementary school to junior high school from the effect of age (Alfieri et al., 1996). The key hypothesis guiding this research was that when children make the transition from junior high school to high school, for a variety of reasons they become more flexible about what females and males can and cannot do. We recruited two school districts: One made the transition at 7th grade, and the other made it at 8th grade. We then followed these children over two waves of data collection a year apart. Regardless of the age at which children made the transition, the transition was associated with an increase in gender stereotype flexibility among children.

Because a key aspect of the developmental approach is the investigation of change as people progress though life, the phase of life chosen to be studied needs to be one at which developmental change actually occurs. For example, in terms of normative development, if changes in relationships are of interest, then times such as the beginning of life, the birth of a sibling, entry into school, the transitions to adolescence and adulthood, entrance into a new career, marital transitions, and the death of a loved one may be the most fruitful to study because relationships may be undergoing the most change during these times. When studying the development of individual differences, it is important that there is change in the difference of interest during the developmental phase being studied. If not, then it will be difficult to detect the influence of the antecedent. The development of individual differences in adjustment to stress, for instance, needs to be studied in the context of a stressor. In this vein, Bolger, Zuckerman, and colleagues (2000) focused on the role of help giving in adjustment to stress in the face of an upcoming law exam. Moreover, a period in which the expected antecedents of the difference of interest are most likely to be influential is critical. One instance of this is that children's theories of ability may not be likely to influence children before children have developed the cognitive skills to understand the relation between ability, effort, and performance (e.g., Pomerantz & Ruble, 1997).

## Micro-Analytic and Macro-Analytic Strategies

When conducting developmental research, it is important to give consideration not only to defining developmental phase but also, when research is being conducted over time, to the timing between assessments. Developmental change can occur over extremely short periods of time as well as relatively long periods. Thus, although much developmental research relies on what might be thought of as macro-analytic designs, in that how people change over months, years, or even decades is examined, increasingly research has relied on micro-analytic designs in which change is examined as it occurs over seconds, minutes, hours, or days. For example, in our research on parents' use of

control, we postulated that children who lack competence would be particularly vulnerable to the negative qualities of control, with such effects occurring over the immediate course of children's interactions with their parents (Ng, Kenney-Benson, & Pomerantz, 2002). We coded mothers' use of control with their children and their children's persistence every 2 minutes during a 14-minute interaction. We then examined the extent to which mothers' use of control during a 2-minute segment was associated with a lack of persistence among children in the following 2-minute segment. In line with our expectations, when mothers exerted control over their children, low-achieving, but not high-achieving, children's persistence went down over the course of the interaction. Such a decrease was not evident when mothers did not use control.

Using micro-analytic designs is important because they can provide information about the processes underlying long-term changes (see Siegler & Crowley, 1991). We have found it particularly beneficial to combine micro-analytic and macro-analytic designs. For one, change over the long term is often an accumulation of short-term changes. In our work on parents' use of control, we have found that parents' controlling practices predict children's achievement over the course of a year, with parallel effects of parents' practices on children's performance from day to day (Ng et al., 2002; Pomerantz & Eaton, 2001). In addition, micro-analytic designs can provide important information about how change actually occurs. Sequential analyses of behavioral interactions are a particularly useful analytic tool to examine developmental processes in work involving naturalistic interactions because they can provide a window into natural cause-and-effect processes (for data analytic procedures, see Bakeman & Gottman, 1997). In our work on the factors that shape how children evaluate themselves, for instance, somewhat to our surprise we found that children asked by their peers about their progress frequently experience an increase over a year in their perceptions of competence (Altermatt et al., 2002). When we followed up this finding with sequential analyses examining children's discourse around peer progress inquiries, we found that when children were asked about their progress, the questioning more often than not provided them with the opportunity to state how well they were doing. Siegler and Crowley (1991) stressed that micro-analytic designs are useful because they can offer a dense number of observations in the course of change that cannot be provided by macro-analytic designs. As a consequence, micro-analytic designs can be used to study five dimensions of development: the path, rate, breadth, source, and variability (Siegler & Svetina, 2002).

In many cases, the timing between assessments may not be essential, in that the causal construct may be influencing the person constantly. In such cases, the choice of a micro-analytic or macro-analytic design is inconsequential. Similarly, the timing between assessments within either a micro-analytic or macro-analytic design is of little importance. However, quite often the timing between assessments is critical and needs attention. Thus, such choices may carry great weight. It may be that for some phenomena, development takes place over a matter of a few days and is then replaced by a new period of development. For example, studying the development of children's understanding of the constancy of gender, Szkrybalo and Ruble (1999) found that in preschool (but not in kindergarten and first grade), children showed a dramatic increase in their understanding after the first interview of the study. Szkrybalo and Ruble speculated that children at this age may be "ready" to process information about gender and that the interview may have led them to seek out additional information, which may have produced a rapid change in their understanding. Indeed, one father reported that his 3-year-old son was obsessed with gender after

the interview. In other cases, it may take time for the effects of development to take place. In such cases, there may be a lagged effect where no relation exists concurrently or even a year later but is evident 2 years later. For example, Pomerantz, Ruble, and colleagues (1995) found that as children progressed through elementary school, they increasingly understood the usefulness for evaluating their own progress of asking their peers about their progress. However, it took 2 years for this knowledge to translate into actually making peer progress inquiries, presumably because implementing such behavior is complicated: A peer of an equivalent ability-level must be asked in a manner that is not too intrusive.

## Identifying the Processes Underlying Developmental Change

Although documenting change that occurs as people progress through the life course is an important endeavor, it is only the first step in taking a developmental approach. The next step is identifying the processes underlying developmental change. Investigators concerned with development almost always have some theory about what underlies the developmental change in which they are interested. As noted earlier, in our research on children's views of parents' use of control, we expected there to be developmental differences in such views because of changes in children's understanding of ability as stable. As we hope is evident at this point, hypotheses about underlying processes are important in terms of both choosing how to operationalize developmental phase and deciding upon the time frame to be used. However, key to the developmental approach is identifying the processes underlying developmental change. One approach to this is using micro-analytic designs in conjunction with macro-analytic designs (see the earlier section on micro-analytic and macro-analytic strategies).

However, there are also other approaches that will be familiar to social psychologists.

One emerges from the mediational analytic approach (see Kenny, Kashy, & Bolger, 1998). Here, the hypothesized underlying process is examined, with particular attention to whether the process also shows developmental change and if it accounts for the change documented. In our research on children's conceptions of parental control, we took this approach by examining not only such conceptions but also children's understanding of ability. In a somewhat different vein, in our research on the development of person perception, we used mediational analysis to test the idea that different processes underlie the judgments of older and younger children (Alvarez et al., 2001). Prior research indicated that both younger and older children make trait-consistent behavioral predictions (e.g., Dozier, 1991). We showed, however, that only for older children did trait information actually underlie such predictions.

Another useful approach to understanding developmental processes that is also common in social psychology is that in which a mechanism hypothesized to be responsible for a developmental change is examined through experimental manipulation. Differences between developmental phases should be evident when the mechanism is present but not when it is absent. An excellent example of this may be found in a study conducted by Fung, Carstensen, and Lutz (1999). These investigators proposed that the decline in social contact in later life is driven, in part, by people's preferences for emotionally meaningful social partners, with such preferences due to the perception that time is limited. To examine this idea, both younger and older participants' perspectives on time were manipulated. The tendency for older people to prefer familiar social partners disappeared when an expansive future was imagined. When a hypothetical constraint was put on time, both younger and older people had a bias for familiar partners.

A less direct but very useful approach to detecting the mechanisms underlying developmental change is to examine whether developmental change exists in contexts differing in the mechanisms. Fung and colleagues took such an approach in their research on developmental change in social contact. These investigators postulated that the handover of Hong Kong to China could be construed as a sociopolitical time constraint, with the feeling that time was limited intensifying as the handover neared. One year prior to the handover, only older adults preferred familiar social contacts. However, 2 months prior, such a preference was evident for both younger and older adults. The age difference returned after the handover.

## Other Considerations in Conducting Developmental Research

As is probably evident by now, operating the video camera—that is, conducting developmental research—is quite different from taking snapshots—that is, conducting social psychological research. Consequently, a number of methodological issues need to be considered when conducting research in developmental psychology that are rarely of concern when doing so in social psychology. We focus on two such issues: recruitment of participants and procedural equivalence.

### Recruitment

The recruitment of participants is always of great import in conducting developmental research. A key question in this regard is simply how to recruit participants for developmental research, given that they are not available in an Introductory Psychology course. When working with school-aged children, recruitment generally is achieved by contacting schools with a brief proposal of the specific aims, methods, and benefits of the research. Once permission is obtained, it is most often the case that active consent procedures, or what some at the National Institutes of Health now label as "opt in" procedures, are employed in which letters describing the study are sent home to parents, who are then asked to reply as to whether their children may can participate. This procedure requires considerable effort on the part of investigators to ensure a representative sample. For instance, teachers may need to be offered incentives to encourage participation. This procedure often results in a well-functioning sample of children (e.g., Weinberger, Tublin, Ford, & Feldman, 1990), given that parents who take little interest in their children's lives are unlikely to read or reply to letters sent home.

Depending on the research questions, the methods to be used, the participating school district, and the university's review board, passive consent procedures—or what some at the National Institutes of Health prefer to call "opt out" procedures—sometimes may be used. Here, letters are sent home to parents, and parents are told that unless they respond, their children will participate in the research. Such procedures yield a more representative sample. As a consequence, they may be desirable when investigators have questions about children related to their socioeconomic status, cultural background, or family functioning. In addition, some methods may require passive consent procedures. For example, investigators concerned with peer acceptance and rejection often use sociometric methods (i.e., peer ratings); the validity of such methods depends on a large proportion of the population taking part in the research. However, it is unethical to use passive consent procedures in research involving circumstances that put children even at minimal risk, such as circumstances in which children are exposed to failure. Of course, passive consent procedures must be approved by the participating school district as well as the university's review board. Although schools often prefer passive consent procedures because of their administrative ease, many university review boards do not allow them, with some considering passive consent procedures to involve a waiver of informed consent. Boards that do allow passive consent procedures require substantial justification for their use. It must be clear that the question guiding the research cannot be answered without such procedures and that children are not at even minimal risk. Moreover, considerable care must be taken to ensure that parents do indeed receive notification of the research (e.g., multiple mailings) and are given ample time to respond with ease (e.g., allowing collect calls).

Recruitment to bring children into the laboratory may be done through schools as well, but newspapers, religious organizations, and other sources are also useful. Unless reimbursement for participation is offered, such recruitment may yield a select sample. In the case of recruiting on the other end of the life span, recruitment often is accomplished by visiting homes for senior citizens, bingo halls, or other places frequented by seniors. Another strategy is randomly choosing names from the phone book, which has the added benefit of providing a group of young and old participants for whom similar sampling procedures have been used. Indeed, a key issue in recruiting both young and old participants is to ensure equivalence across the different developmental phases (for a similar issue in cross-cultural research, see Miller, Chapter 5, this volume). When looking at children in different grades, children from different school districts should be distributed equally across grades. Such equivalence may be difficult at the other end of the life span when recruitment of older adults is done from such sources as senior citizen homes and recruitment of younger adults is done from Introductory Psychology courses.

### Procedural Equivalence

Another key consideration is whether there is equivalence across the different developmental phases to be studied in the procedures to be used. Such equivalence involves several key issues (for a similar issue in cross-cultural research, see Miller, Chapter 5, this volume). There may be key differences between the different developmental phases to be studied that may lead the same measures or manipulations to be perceived differently. At the most basic level, there may be differences in the capabilities of the participants at the different developmental phases. Investigators studying children must remember that young children have limited cognitive and language abilities that can reduce their understanding of questions; moreover, they have restricted attention spans. A similar consideration of the capabilities of participants is necessary when work is done on the other end of the life span, when cognitive resources, eyesight, mobility, and reaction times may have deteriorated to a point that they may affect older participants' ability to respond to certain types of questions. Measures and manipulations need to take limitations such as these into account while also remaining interesting and relevant to people at other developmental phases. Observational techniques are used frequently in studying children because they avoid many of the problems of questionnaires.

There are a number of other dimensions on which people at different developmental phases may differ. For example, focusing on children, Higgins and Parsons (1983) suggested that at each developmental phase, there are, among other things, new roles, new norms, and new goals. Children's perceptions of themselves and others also change as they progress through school (Rholes et al., 1990). Later in the life span, among other changes, there are changes in people's experience of time (e.g., Carstensen, Isaacowitz, & Charles, 1999), social contacts (e.g., Antonucci, Akiyama, & Merline, 2001), susceptibility to influence attempts (e.g., Pasupathi, 1999; Visser & Krosnick, 1998), and emotional experience (e.g., Carstensen, Pasupathi, Mayr, & Nesselroade, 2000). These differences may lead to differences in how people in different developmental phases interpret and react to measures and manipulations, which may cause problems for the interpretation of developmental changes. Hence, it is essential when conducting developmental research to be aware of the differences between different developmental phases. (For a review see Arnett, 2000; Eisenberg, 1998; Lachman, 2001.)

## Methodological Benefits of Conducting Developmental Research

Now that we have discussed some of the major issues in conducting developmental research, we turn to the advantages of doing so. Taking a developmental approach often means forsaking the experimental methods that are central to social psychology. However, this approach can have a number of methodological benefits. Pomerantz and Newman (2000) argued that studies in developmental psychology can provide external validity for results yielded by studies in social psychology. As Sears (1986) pointed out, research in social psychology generally has been carried out on college students, who are in a unique phase of life (see also Arnett, 2000). When patterns documented on college students are also found in children or in older adults, this suggests that the patterns exist in other phases of life as well. Relatedly, when an effect found in college students is replicated on children or older adults, evidence for the robustness of the effect is provided. This may be particularly useful for small effects. Prentice and Miller (1992) have argued that one way to establish the importance of small effects is to show that although they do not account for much variance in a given study, they are robust across heterogeneous conditions. Given the variety of differences (e.g., cognitive resources, life tasks, self-control) among children, young adults, and adults in other phases of the life course, replication on people at a variety of stages of development is particularly likely to indicate the robustness of an effect originally observed in young adults.

Developmental psychology can also offer social psychology some new techniques for conducting research (see Pomerantz & Newman, 2000). The characteristics of children or older adults may provide conditions that are hard to find in college students. For example, a good deal of research suggests that anxiety and depressive symptoms are not as highly correlated among children as among adults (for a review, see Alloy, Kelly, Mineka, & Clements, 1990). Investigators concerned with the distinct predictors of the two types of symptoms may find their task quite difficult among adults, for whom anxiety and depressive symptoms are often almost entirely overlapping. In addition, by studying children, investigators may sometimes be able to get around participants' concerns with social desirability, as children may be less concerned with impression formation in some areas, at least before entering adolescence. For example, adults generally are quite hesitant to provide negative feedback to other people or publicly compare themselves to others (Tesser & Rosen, 1975). In contrast, children, particularly those in the early years of elementary school, are less inhibited about doing so (e.g., Altermatt et al., 2002).

Social psychology relies heavily on laboratory methods. Such methods have the singular benefit that they can determine if a hypothesized causal process *can* occur. However, such methods cannot determine if such a process *actually* occurs in the real world. For example, there is now a large body of work documenting social-cognitive biases in the laboratory (for a review, see Kunda, 1999). However, these studies say little about how such biases work in the real world (see Jussim, 1993). Work by Jussim (for a review, see Jussim, 1991) on the self-fulfilling prophecy indicates that the social-cognitive biases documented in the laboratory are not as prevalent in the real world as in the laboratory. Most notably, such biases appear to account for only a small

proportion of the variance in teachers' perceptions of their students. For the most part, teachers' perceptions are accurate.

Developmental psychology has developed a number of strategies for studying people outside the laboratory. Many everyday interaction contexts provide excellent opportunities for observing ongoing day-to-day interaction with a variety of people. School or other community settings provide excellent sites for studying a number of phenomena. For example, although many social psychologists have studied social comparison in the laboratory by manipulating a variety of factors and then often forcing comparisons to be made (for a review, see Wood, 1989), developmental psychologists have studied social comparison as it naturally occurs in the classroom (e.g., Frey & Ruble, 1985). This trend has been followed recently by the study of adults' daily social comparisons (e.g., Wheeler & Miyake, 1992). Developmental investigators concerned with peer relations have also gone outside the classroom to the playground to observe naturally occurring interactions there (for a review, see Hart, 1993). However, the school is not the only site to observe ongoing day-to-day interaction. Studying parent-child interactions allows one to investigate phenomena in the context of an important, close, ongoing relationship that cannot be simulated in the laboratory. Sibling relationships can also provide such a context. Both types of relationships are ideal for studying, among other things, interpersonal interactions, social emotions, control, and power.

## BUT YOU CAN'T JUST USE ONLY THE VIDEO CAMERA

With the invention of the video camera, people did not stop taking snapshots. Along similar lines, we do not mean to suggest that taking videos should replace taking snapshots. In fact, using only the video camera would leave an incomplete picture of any phenomenon. Just as social psychology needs developmental psychology, developmental psychology needs social psychology. Most important, the experimental method is key to fully demonstrating causal relations; developmental psychologists have much to learn from the expertise of their social psychologist colleagues in creating believable and representative experimental manipulations to test hypotheses about causal processes suggested by correlational research. Also, by documenting so thoroughly the effects of situations, social psychology serves as an important resource in determining which environments may influence development and how. Indeed, much of the research on parenting has drawn from work in social psychology manipulating the situation. Continuing the metaphor, we might suggest that social psychology uses the snapshot to provide a high-resolution image of the situation, whereas developmental psychology's video camera does not provide high resolution "stills" of a particular situation but rather allows one to view cross-situational dynamics.

It is imperative that those taking the snapshots and those taking the videos consult with one another, so that the two focus on similar phenomena. Only through such dialogue can holistic understanding be cultivated. There are four key ways in which social and developmental psychology may be integrated to such an end. Notably, several investigators already have made progress along these lines. First, as Pomerantz and Newman (2000) have suggested, findings from developmental psychology may be used in model building in social psychology. One example of this is that developmental differences in a phenomenon that parallel situational differences may be indicative of the processes underlying the effects of situations (see Higgins & Wells, 1986; Pomerantz & Newman, 2000). In this vein, Stangor and Ruble (1989) used findings from their developmental research to develop hypotheses about people's differential recall for consistent versus inconsistent information

in the context of person perception. In a review of the literature on the effects of gender schemas on memory, these investigators (Ruble & Stangor, 1986) found that gender-consistent information (e.g., a boy playing football) is better remembered than gender-inconsistent information (e.g., a boy playing with dolls), except among young children (preschoolers), whose gender schemas are not fully developed. These children found it easier to remember inconsistent information. Thus informed by developmental work, Stangor and Ruble (1989) conducted an experimental study with college students and showed that incongruent information enjoys an encoding and recall advantage when people are in the early stages of forming an expectancy, a contention that received further support in a meta-analysis (Stangor & McMillan, 1992).

A second way in which developmental and social psychology may be integrated is by attempts to incorporate work by social psychologists into models of development. Recent work on the development of judgment and decision making in children provides an excellent example of this. As Jacobs and Klaczynski (2002) pointed out, developmental psychology generally has characterized children as becoming increasingly logical and efficient in their judgment and decision making as a result of advances in their reasoning abilities that occur as they progress through childhood and into adolescence. This characterization might be surprising to social psychologists well aware of the large body of research showing that although adults often make accurate decisions, they are also quite prone to biases, often relying on heuristics in judgment and decision making (for a review, see Dawes, 1998). Jacobs and Klaczynski (2002) have called for models of the development of judgment and decision making to take this into account.

Accordingly, several developmental investigators have begun to move away from paradigms that look at judgment and decision making that is based on reasoning abilities, instead using paradigms from social psychology that have been used to identify bias and reliance on heuristics. These investigators have found that although young children make some of the same mistakes as adults, these mistakes often increase as children progress through childhood and into adolescence (e.g., Davidson, 1995; Jacobs & Potenza, 1991). The recent work borrowing from social psychology suggests that the development of decision making cannot be viewed as a unidirectional progression in which advances in reasoning abilities enhance judgment and decision making. Jacobs and Klaczynski (2002) argued that instead, changes in knowledge, such as stereotypes, and the motivation to preserve social beliefs, such as religious beliefs, may foster mistakes in certain forms of judgment. Drawing from social psychology's reliance on dual system models (for a review, see Chaiken & Trope, 1999), these investigators emphasized that models of the development of judgment and decision making need to incorporate an experiential system and an analytic system. Taking a snapshot approach allowed for the identification of two systems existing early in children's development that may have distinct trajectories over time.

Third, an important integration of developmental and social psychology is understanding the consequences for development of phenomena identified in social psychology. An elegant example of this is provided by work on the deterioration of memory among the elderly. Drawing from the rich research in social psychology on the effects of stereotypes, Levy (1996) proposed that negative stereotypes about aging contribute to memory loss in old age. To test this idea, Levy activated positive stereotypes about aging in older adults without their awareness, which improved their performance on memory tests. Activating negative stereotypes had a negative effect. Levy and Langer (1994) found similar effects in cultures (i.e., the Chinese hearing and the

American deaf) where exposure to and acceptance of negative stereotypes about aging were assumed to be low. Thus, drawing from social psychological work, Levy showed that stereotypes play a large role not only for the way that young adults think and act but also for the course of the development of memory in old age.

Fourth, we have argued that whereas social psychology is concerned largely with influences in the immediate context, developmental psychology is concerned with understanding how prior life history shapes people over time. Integrating social and developmental concerns involves using methods that capture both temporal dynamics—as a video recording would—and situational detail—as a snapshot would. The increasing body of work using daily diary methods represents such an integrative approach (for a review, see Bolger, Davis, & Rafaelli, 2003). Bolger and colleagues, (e.g., Bolger, 1990; Bolger & Eckenrode, 1991; Bolger, Zuckerman, et al., 2000; Thompson & Bolger, 1999). For example, have used diary methods to study how prior personality and social relationships affect the daily course of adjustment to major anticipated challenging events such as the medical school admission test and the bar examination. Although such events are not usually thought of as developmental milestones, they are nonetheless career-determining challenges for those who aspire to become physicians or lawyers. Obtaining many assessments of daily experiences and coping efforts in the weeks surrounding these events yields an account of the course, timing, and sequencing of adjustment processes that traditional longitudinal designs cannot provide.

## CONCLUSION

It is our hope that while continuing to take snapshots, social psychologists will also use the video camera to understand how the phenomena they study unfold over time. Although taking a developmental approach may prove to be a challenge to the investigator who has not had experience with developmental methods, such an approach is essential to a complete understanding of social psychological phenomena. Moreover, taking up the video camera has the potential to enhance the research conducted by developmental psychologists by bringing attention to the theoretical and methodological innovations of social psychology that are relevant to understanding how people journey across the life span.

## REFERENCES

Alfieri, T., Ruble, D. N., & Higgins, E. T. (1996). Gender stereotypes during adolescence: Developmental changes and the transition to junior high school. *Developmental Psychology, 32,* 1129-1137.

Alloy, L. B., Kelly, K. A., Mineka, S., & Clements, C. M. (1990). Comorbidity of anxiety and depressive disorders: A helplessness-hopelessness perspective. In J. D. Maser & C. R. Cloninger (Eds.), *Comorbidity of mood and anxiety disorders* (pp. 499-543). Washington, DC: American Psychiatric Association Press.

Altermatt, E. R., Pomerantz, E. M., Ruble, D. N., Frey, K. S., & Greulich, F. (2002). The role of peer discourse in the development of self-evaluation. *Developmental Psychology, 38,* 903-917.

Alvarez, J. M., Ruble, D. N., & Bolger, N. (2001). Trait understanding or evaluative reasoning? An analysis of children's behavioral predictions. *Child Development, 72,* 1409-1425.

Antonucci, T. C., Akiyama, H., & Merline, A. (2001). Dynamics of social relationships in midlife. In M. E. Lachman (Ed.), *Handbook of midlife development* (Wiley series on adulthood and aging) (pp. 571-598). New York: Wiley.

Arnett, J. J. (2000). Emerging adulthood: A theory of development from the late teens through the twenties. *American Psychologist, 55,* 469-480.

Bakeman, R., & Gottman, J. M. (1997). *An introduction to sequential analysis.* New York: Cambridge University Press.

Barber, B. K. (1996). Parental psychological control: Revisiting a neglected construct. *Child Development, 67,* 3296-3319.

Baumrind, D. (1967). Child care practices anteceding three patterns of preschool behavior. *Genetic Psychology Monographs, 75,* 43-88.

Bolger, N. (1990). Coping as a personality process: A prospective study. *Journal of Personality and Social Psychology, 59,* 525-537.

Bolger, N., Davis, A., & Rafaelli, E. (2003). Diary methods. *Annual Review of Psychology, 54,* 597-616.

Bolger, N., & Eckenrode, J. (1991). Social relationships, personality, and anxiety during a major stressful event. *Journal of Personality and Social Psychology, 61,* 440-449.

Bolger, N., Zuckerman, A., & Kessler, R. C. (2000). Invisible support and adjustment to stress. *Journal of Personality and Social Psychology, 79,* 953-961.

Bollen, K. A. (1989). *Structural equations with latent variables.* New York: Wiley.

Buss, D. M., & Kenrick, D. T. (1998). Evolutionary social psychology. In D. T. Gilbert & S. T. Fiske (Eds.), *The handbook of social psychology* (4th ed., Vol. 2, pp. 982-1026). New York: McGraw-Hill.

Carstensen, L. L., Isaacowitz, D. M., & Charles, S. T. (1999). Taking time seriously. *American Psychologist, 54,* 165-181.

Carstensen, L. L., Pasupathi, M., Mayr, U., & Nesselroade, J. R. (2000). Emotional experience in everyday life across the adult life span. *Journal of Personality and Social Psychology, 79,* 644-655.

Caspi, A. (2000). The child is father of the man: Personality continuities from childhood to adulthood. *Journal of Personality and Social Psychology, 78,* 158-172.

Chaiken, S., & Trope, Y. (Eds.). (1999). *Dual-process theories in social psychology.* New York: Guilford.

Cohen, D. (2001). Cultural variation: Considerations and implications. *Psychological Bulletin, 127,* 451-471.

Cross, S. E., & Madson, L. (1997). Models of the self: Self-construals and gender. *Psychological Bulletin, 122,* 5-37.

Davidson, D. (1995). The representativeness heuristic and conjunction fallacy effect in children's decision making. *Merrill-Palmer Quarterly, 41,* 328-246.

Dawes, R. M. (1998). Behavioral decision making and judgment. In D. T. Gilbert & S. T. Fiske (Eds.), *The handbook of social psychology* (Vol. 1, pp. 497-548). New York: McGraw-Hill.

Deci, E. L., Koestner, R., & Ryan, R. M. (1999). A meta-analytic review of experiments examining the effects of extrinsic rewards on intrinsic motivation. *Psychological Bulletin, 125,* 627-668.

Deci, E. L., & Ryan, R. M. (1985). *Intrinsic motivation and self-determination in human behavior.* New York: Plenum.

Deci, E. L., & Ryan, R. M. (1987). The support of autonomy and the control of behavior. *Journal of Personality and Social Psychology, 53,* 1024-1037.

Dozier, M. (1991). Functional measurement assessment of young children's ability to predict future behavior. *Child Development, 62,* 1091-1099.

Eisenberg, N. (Ed.). (1998). *Handbook of child development: Vol. 3. Social, emotional, and personality development.* New York: Wiley.

Flavell, J. H., & Ross, L. (1981). Concluding remarks. In J. H. Flavell & L. Ross (Eds.), *Social-cognitive development* (pp. 306-316). New York: Cambridge University Press.

Frey, K. S., & Ruble, D. N. (1985). What children say when the teacher is not around: Conflicting goals in social comparison and performance assessment in the classroom. *Journal of Personality and Social Psychology, 48,* 550-562.

Friedman, S. L., & Wachs, T. D. (Eds.). (1999). *Measuring environment across the life span: Emerging methods and concepts.* Washington, DC: American Psychological Association.

Funder, D. C., Parke, R. D., Tomlinson-Keasy, C., & Widman, K. (Eds.). (1993). *Studying lives through time: Personality and development.* Washington, DC: American Psychological Association.

Fung, H. H., Carstensen, L. L., & Lutz, A. M. (1999). Influence of time on social preferences: Implications for life-span development. *Psychology and Aging, 14*(4), 595-604.

Hackel, L. S., & Ruble, D. N. (1992). Changes in the marital relationship after the first baby is born: Predicting the impact of expectancy disconfirmation. *Journal of Personality and Social Psychology, 62,* 944-957.

Harackiewicz, J., M. (1979). The effects of reward contingency and performance feedback on intrinsic motivation. *Journal of Personality and Social Psychology, 37,* 1352-1363.

Hart, C. H. (1993). *Children on playgrounds: Research perspectives and applications.* Albany: State University of New York Press.

Higgins, E. T. (1991). Development of self-regulatory and self-evaluative processes: Costs, benefits, and trade-offs. In M. R. Gunnar & L. A. Sroufe (Eds.),

*Self-processes and development: Twenty-third Minnesota symposium on child psychology* (pp. 125-165). Minneapolis: University of Minnesota Press.

Higgins, E. T., & Parsons, J. E. (1983). Social cognition and the social life of the child: Stages as subcultures. In E. T. Higgins, D. N. Ruble, & W. W. Hartup (Eds.), *Social cognition and social development* (pp. 15-62). New York: Cambridge University Press.

Higgins, E. T., & Wells, R. (1986). Social construct availability and accessibility as a function of social life phase: Emphasizing the "how" versus the "can" of social cognition. *Social Cognition, 4*, 201-226.

Jacobs, J. E., & Klaczynski, P. A. (2002). The development of judgment and decision making during childhood and adolescence. *Current Directions in Psychological Science, 11*, 145-149.

Jacobs, J. E., & Potenza, M. T. (1991). The use of judgment heuristics to make social and object decisions: A developmental perspective. *Child Development, 62*, 166-178.

Jussim, L. (1991). Social perception and social reality: A reflection-construction model. *Psychological Review, 98*, 54-73.

Jussim, L. (1993). Accuracy in interpersonal expectancies: A reflection-construction analysis of current and classic research. *Journal of Personality, 61*, 637-668.

Kenny, D. A., Kashy, D. A., & Bolger, N. (1998). Data analysis in social psychology. In D. T. Gilbert, S. T. Fiske, & G. Lindzey (Eds.), *Handbook of social psychology* (4th ed., Vol. 1, pp. 233-265). Boston: McGraw-Hill.

Kunda, Z. (1999). *Social cognition: Making sense of people.* Cambridge: The MIT Press.

Lachman, M. E. (Ed.). (2001). *Handbook of midlife development.* New York: Wiley.

Lepper, M. R., & Greene, D. (1975). Turning play into work: Effects of adult surveillance and extrinsic rewards on children's intrinsic motivation. *Journal of Personality and Social Psychology, 31*, 479-486.

Levy, B. (1996). Improving memory in old age through implicit self-stereotyping. *Journal of Personality and Social Psychology, 71*, 1092-1107.

Levy, B., & Langer, E. (1994). Aging free from negative stereotypes: Successful memory in China and among the deaf. *Journal of Personality and Social Psychology, 66*, 989-997.

Miller, J. (1999). Cultural psychology: Implications for basic psychological theory. *Psychological Science, 10*, 85-91.

Molenaar, P.C.M. (1994). Dynamic latent variable models in developmental psychology. In A. von Eye & C. C. Clogg (Eds.), *Latent variables analysis: Applications for developmental research* (pp. 155-180). Newbury Park, CA: Sage.

Nesselroade, J. R., McArdle, J. J., Aggen, S. H., & Meyers, J. M. (2002). Dynamic factor analysis models for representing process in multivariate time-series. In D. S. Moskowitz & S. L. Hershberger (Eds.), *Modeling intraindividual variability with repeated measures data: Methods and applications* (pp. 235-265). Mahwah, NJ: Lawrence Erlbaum.

Newman, L. S., & Ruble, D. N. (1992). Do young children use the discounting principle? *Journal of Experimental Social Psychology, 28*, 572-593.

Ng, F. F., Kenney-Benson, G. A., & Pomerantz, E. M. (2002). *Children's initial achievement moderates the effects of mothers' use of control and autonomy support.* Unpublished manuscript, University of Illinois, Urbana-Champaign.

Pasupathi, M. (1999). Age differences in response to conformity pressure for emotional and nonemotional material. *Psychology and Aging, 14*, 170-174.

Phillips, D. (1984). The illusion of incompetence among academically competent children. *Child Development, 55*, 2000-2016.

Pomerantz, E. M. (2001). Parent × Child socialization: Implications for the development of depressive symptoms. *Journal of Family Psychology, 15*, 510-525.

Pomerantz, E. M., & Eaton, M. M. (2000). Developmental differences in children's conceptions of parental control: "They love me, but they make me feel incompetent." *Merrill-Palmer Quarterly, 46*, 140-167.

Pomerantz, E. M., & Eaton, M. M. (2001). Maternal intrusive support in the academic context: Transactional socialization processes. *Developmental Psychology, 37*, 174-186.

Pomerantz, E. M., & Newman, L. S. (2000). Looking in on the children: Using developmental psychology as a tool for hypothesis testing and model building in social psychology. *Personality and Social Psychology Review, 4*, 300-316.

Pomerantz, E. M., & Ruble, D. N. (1997). Distinguishing multiple dimensions of conceptions of ability: Implications for self-evaluation. *Child Development, 68*, 1165-1180.

Pomerantz, E. M., & Ruble, D. N. (1998a). The multidimensional nature of control: Implications for the development of sex differences in self-evaluation. In J. Heckhausen & C. S. Dweck (Eds.), *Motivation and self-regulation across the life-span* (pp. 159-184). New York: Cambridge University Press.

Pomerantz, E. M., & Ruble, D. N. (1998b). The role of maternal control in the development of sex differences in child self-evaluative factors. *Child Development, 69*, 458-478.

Pomerantz, E. M., Ruble, D. N., Frey, K. S., & Greulich, F. (1995). Meeting goals and confronting conflict: Children's changing perceptions of social comparison. *Child Development, 66*, 723-738.

Pomerantz, E. M., & Saxon, J. S. (2001). Conceptions of ability as stable and self-evaluative processes: A longitudinal examination. *Child Development, 72*, 152-173.

Prentice, D. A., & Miller, D. T. (1992). When small effects are impressive. *Psychological Bulletin, 112*, 160-164.

Raudenbush, S. W., & Bryk, A. S. (2002). *Hierarchical linear models: Applications and data analysis methods* (2nd ed.). Thousand Oaks, CA: Sage.

Rholes, W. S., Newman, L. S., & Ruble, D. N. (1990). Understanding self and others: Developmental and motivational aspects of perceiving people in terms of invariant dispositions. In E. T. Higgins & R. M. Sorrentino (Eds.), *Handbook of motivation and cognition* (Vol. 2, pp. 369-407). New York: Guilford.

Roberts, B. W., Helson, R., & Klohnen, E. C. (2002). Personality development and growth in women across 30 years: Three perspectives. *Journal of Personality, 70*, 79-102.

Ruble, D. N., Brooks-Gunn, J., Fleming, A. S., Fitzmaurice, G., Stangor, C., & Deutsch, F. M. (1990). Transition to motherhood and the self: measurement, stability, and change. *Journal of Personality and Social Psychology, 58*, 450-463.

Ruble, D. N., & Goodnow, J. J. (1998). Social development. In D. T. Gilbert, S. T. Fiske, & G. Lindzey (Eds.), *The handbook of social psychology* (4th ed., Vol. 2, pp. 741-787). Boston: McGraw-Hill.

Ruble, D. N., & Seidman, E. (1996). Social transitions: Windows into social psychological processes. In E. T. Higgins & A. W. Kruglanski (Eds.), *Social psychology: Handbook of basic principles* (pp. 830-856). New York: Guilford.

Ruble, D. N., & Stangor, C. (1986). Stalking the elusive schema: Insights from developmental and social-psychological analyses of gender schemas. *Social Cognition, 4*, 227-261.

Schaefer, E. S. (1965). Children's reports of parental behavior: An inventory. *Child Development, 36,* 413-424.

Schaffer, H. R., & Emerson, P. E. (1964). The development of social attachments in infancy. *Monographs of the Society for Research on Child Development, 29*(2, Serial No. 94).

Schaie, K. W. (1965). A general model for the study of developmental problems. *Psychological Bulletin, 64,* 91-107.

Schaie, K. W. (1986). Beyond calendar definitions of age, time, and cohort: The general developmental model revisited. *Developmental Review, 6,* 252-277.

Sears, D. O. (1986). College sophomores in the laboratory: Influences of a narrow data base on social psychology's view of human nature. *Journal of Personality and Social Psychology, 51,* 515-530.

Siegler, R. S., & Crowley, K. (1991). The microgenetic method: A direct means for studying cognitive development. *American Psychologist, 46,* 606-620.

Siegler, R. S., & Svetina, M. (2002). A microgenetic/cross-sectional study of matrix completion: Comparing short-term and long-term change. *Child Development, 73,* 793-809.

Snijders, T.A.B., & Bosker, R. J. (1999). *Multilevel analysis: An introduction to basic and advanced multilevel modeling.* Thousand Oaks, CA: Sage.

Sroufe, L. A. (2002). From infant attachment to promotion of adolescent autonomy: Prospective, longitudinal data on the role of parents in development. In J. G. Borkowski & S. L. Ramey (Eds.), *Parenting and the child's world: Influences on academic, intellectual, and social-emotional development* (pp. 187-202). Mahwah, NJ: Lawrence Erlbaum.

Stangor, C., & McMillan, D. (1992). Memory for expectancy-congruent and expectancy-incongruent information: A review of the social and social developmental literatures. *Psychological Bulletin, 111,* 42-61.

Stangor, C., & Ruble, D. N. (1989). Strength of expectancies and memory for social information: What we remember depends on how much we know. *Journal of Experimental Social Psychology, 25,* 18-35.

Szkrybalo, J., & Ruble, D. N. (1999). "God made me a girl": Sex-category constancy judgments and explanations revisited. *Developmental Psychology, 35,* 392-402.

Tesser, A., & Rosen, S. (1975). The reluctance to transmit bad news. In L. Berkowitz (Ed.), *Advances in Experimental Social Psychology* (Vol. 8, pp. 193-232). New York: Academic Press.

Thompson, A., & Bolger, N. (1999). Emotional transmission in couples under stress. *Journal of Marriage and the Family, 61,* 38-48.

Visser, P. S., & Krosnick, J. A. (1998). Development of attitude strength over the life cycle: Surge and decline. *Journal of Personality and Social Psychology, 75,* 1389-1410.

Weinberger, D., Tublin, S., Ford, M., & Feldman, S. (1990). Preadolescents' social-emotional adjustment and selective attrition in family research. *Child Development, 61,* 1374-1386.

Wheeler, L., & Miyake, K. (1992). Social comparison in everyday life. *Journal of Personality and Social Psychology, 62,* 760-773.

Wood, J. V. (1989). Theory and research concerning social comparisons of personal attributes. *Psychological Bulletin, 106,* 231-248.

# Part V

## The Application of Social Psychology and Its Methods to Other Domains

## CHAPTER 19

# Program Evaluation, Action Research, and Social Psychology

## A Powerful Blend for Addressing Applied Problems

GEOFFREY MARUYAMA

*University of Minnesota*

*The greatest handicap of applied psychology has been the fact that, without proper theoretical help, it had to follow the costly, inefficient, and limited method of trial and error. Many psychologists working today in an applied field are keenly aware of the need for close cooperation between theoretical and applied psychology. This can be accomplished in psychology, as it has been accomplished in physics, if the theorist does not look toward applied problems with highbrow aversion or with a fear of social problems, and if the applied researcher realizes that there is nothing as practical as a good theory.*

—Kurt Lewin (1951, p. 169)

More than half a century after they were written, Lewin's words still capture essential issues of applied research, namely the role of theory in applied work and who should be engaged in it. Lewin's (1951) view is clear; for him, applied work should be an endeavor of researchers with good theoretical grounding, who have an interest in applied (social) problems, and who strive to blend theory and application. Tying to the title of this chapter, according to Lewin, social psychologists should be doing research and evaluation that address applied problems, which they do through the application of their

AUTHOR'S NOTE: I would like to acknowledge the cooperation I have received both from the staff at the Saint Paul Public Schools and from the Saint Paul Public Housing Agency. Support for work on students living in public housing was provided by the Family Housing Fund. Helpful comments were provided by Katherine Seiden and by the three editors of this handbook. All views expressed are the author's and do not necessarily reflect views of the University of Minnesota or the Saint Paul Public Schools.

theory and methods to those applied problems. Yet Lewin's view about the importance of theory stands in contrast to some others, who argue that much applied work should be focused on what works in local settings; for them, testing theories and searching for generalizable principles is an unnecessary distraction that takes away from the primary goal, that of finding out what works.

The primary battleground for disagreements about the role of theory is a field known as *program evaluation*. Program evaluation provides approaches for examining the effectiveness of programs and interventions. Lewin's applied research clearly fits under the umbrella of program evaluation. His best-known example is work he did during World War II that helped evaluate the effectiveness of efforts to reshape consumer eating patterns so diets would stay healthy even though there was limited availability of the meat sources that they most commonly ate. In addition to its evaluation function, that work advanced attitude theories in social psychology. In other words, Lewin managed to address social issues, evaluate the effectiveness of programs, and still inform theory. Although particularly nice in its ability to speak to practical and theoretical issues, his work is just one of many approaches to program evaluation.

## WHAT IS PROGRAM EVALUATION?

*Webster's Seventh New Collegiate Dictionary* provides the following definitions of "evaluate": (a) to determine or fix the value of and (b) to examine and judge. These definitions of evaluation are interesting, for a program evaluation purpose, namely, to judge is contained within them. Definitions of program evaluation link even more strongly to goals and purposes of evaluation. Patton (1986) defined program evaluation as "the systematic collection of information about the activities, characteristics, and outcomes of programs for use by specific people to reduce uncertainties, improve effectiveness, and make decisions with regard to what those programs are doing and affecting" (p. 14). Wilde and Sockey (1995) defined it as "The process of systematically aggregating and synthesizing various types and forms of data for the purpose of showing the value of a particular program" (p. 3). Scriven (1973) argued that evaluation has a single goal, namely, to determine the worth or merit of whatever is being evaluated.

In summary, social science definitions of evaluation show a high degree of consistency around issues of determining effectiveness and value. They are vague about the role of theory and avoid making it a specific part of evaluation (for a contrasting view, see Chen & Rossi, 1999). Researchers' definitions are highly consistent with the dictionary definitions of evaluate, suggesting that the general public should readily understand what program evaluation is and why it is useful.

Thinking of program evaluation as a tool for documenting the worth or value of a program links nicely with a current zeitgeist about *accountability*. Accountability reflects general interest by the public, funders, and program supporters in knowing whether or not resources are being invested wisely and if programs are working, in effect using available information (data) as documentation. Viewed from a social psychological perspective, the emphasis on accountability reflects movement of the public from being "naïve psychologists" (Heider, 1958) who "test" their theories in imprecise and aperiodic ways, to being more scientific and regular in using available data to test the accuracy of their expectations about how programs work. Successful accountability systems depend on frequent and effective program evaluation.

Accountability can be used to illustrate the scope of activities and fields in which evaluation is important, and where opportunities for program evaluation exist. For example, for more than a decade businesses have been interested in terms such as "total quality management" and "continuous quality improvement." A central part of quality improvement is making "data-driven decisions," recognizing programs that work, improving others that are not working well, and eliminating programs that cannot be improved enough to make them effective. Similarly, in the world of nonprofit social service agencies, organizations such as the United Way are asking agencies that receive funds to demonstrate that the money they are receiving is making a difference. Agencies able to construct effective evaluations of their programs not only can respond to their funders but also can make their programs better. In medical fields, finding effective treatments for medical problems and sharing them with practitioners has much in common with the accountability movements. The experimental approaches reflected in clinical trials are complemented by applied research looking at relations of many behaviors and attitudes with health and health risk factors, and of different types of programs with health behaviors. Regular reports in the media describe new correlates of health and risk that have been identified on the basis of evaluations that compare individuals choosing some intervention, practice, or drug regimen with others not using that approach. More recently, preK-12 schools have been added to the accountability mix, as policy makers have argued that schools should be able to demonstrate that they are successfully educating students. Federal education money has been directed toward "programs that work," namely, those that have been supported by independent research. For academics, accountability is making its way slowly to higher education, for there are increased expectations on the parts of students and funders that higher education can show that it is working effectively.

In sum, program evaluation encompasses a broad range of topic areas from business to social services to health care to education. As can be inferred from the issues just described, program evaluation is field based, occurring in natural settings rather than in laboratories. It is done collaboratively with practitioners, in their environments. It involves the process of designing investigations of how well different programs are working. Those investigations attempt to be as unobtrusive as possible. Investigations may be experimental, quasi-experimental (e.g., Mark & Reichardt, Chapter 12, this volume), or non-experimental, and involve qualitative (e.g., King, Chapter 8, this volume) as well as quantitative methods. Conducting an evaluation typically involves a series of steps, including identifying the central issues of the program that is to be evaluated, planning and implementing a design with components that assess program success, collecting and analyzing data, and then using findings to judge success of the program and to identify ongoing issues to examine. In summary, the general process of conceptualizing issues, operationalizing variables, collecting and analyzing data, and interpreting the data parallels a research orientation that is foundational to social psychology. In contrast, the problem focus, the lack of control, imperfect comparison groups, and working collaboratively with practitioners distinguish program evaluation from traditional research in social psychology. As a result, even though social psychologists have most of the research and technical skills needed for evaluation, they are likely to lack experience in the messy and less predictable world of evaluation.

## FRAMEWORK FOR THE CHAPTER

This chapter frames issues of program evaluation and then illustrates how evaluation methods work through application of the methods to a social issue. This section provides an overview of the issues, examines the way program evaluation blends social problems with social psychology, and describes how social issues lend themselves to program evaluation. Then reasons why many social psychologists are not well prepared to conduct program evaluations are presented. The following section compares different evaluation approaches and then focuses on a Lewinian approach to evaluation. The next section provides illustrations in the social issue area described, and the final section discusses limitations of various evaluation methods.

The social issue used for illustration is how to provide educational opportunity for all students. My initial introduction to the issue as a researcher occurred when I became a research assistant on an applied research/program evaluation study of school desegregation in California. As I began to look at the topic, I found that discussions of issues tied to equal opportunities can be traced back to the Common School movement championed by people like John Dewey and Horace Mann. The social science roots, however, go back only about 60 years, to research that was used to help shape the 1954 U.S. Supreme Court *Brown v. Board of Education* (1954) landmark decision. That decision examined how to provide comparable educational opportunities for all students so that they might be able to succeed based on their merits rather than the color of their skin. In it, the Court decided that segregation was not the avenue for equal opportunity and ordered that schools be desegregated "with all deliberate speed."

The Supreme Court decision marked the first time that social science information was used by the Supreme Court to influence public policy (e.g., Benjamin & Crouse, 2002). The Social Science Statement (1952) was not program evaluation; nevertheless, it pulled together social science information about psychological messages and processes that result from school segregation, in effect providing a conceptual framework including processes

and outcomes that could be employed in evaluating the success of school desegregation interventions as well as directing the Court toward a particular decision. The impact of the social science statement was apparent, for its arguments that segregation would affect the hearts and minds of children in a way unlikely ever to be undone appeared in Court statements supporting the decision (see, e.g., Gerard & Miller, 1975; Maruyama, 1984).

Eventually, the Court decision led to societal change and desegregation of schools. At that time, an important policy question was "Do desegregated schools provide equal educational opportunity for all students, or at least better opportunities than segregated schools?" Unfortunately, it is difficult to answer questions about interventions like desegregation, for determining whether or not a school is desegregated depends in part on the community racial composition. One can imagine a broad array of different types of schools with very different student compositions that are called desegregated, and a similarly wide range of schools that can be called segregated. A school called desegregated based on its racial composition might be called segregated if it were located in a community with a much different overall racial composition. Issues tied to school desegregation illustrate more general principles about evaluations of social programs: (a) it is difficult to speak about effectiveness of broad structural variables, for specific features within those structures are likely to account for most of the variability in outcomes; (b) evaluations need to carefully select the "control" or comparison information that is used to judge success of any particular intervention site, and (c) variability across sites within interventions, although in some ways problematic, also offers opportunities, for the range of different conditions provides a way to identify features of the setting and of the treatments that are likely to make a difference, and point to practices and approaches that are effective.

In contrast to typical research designs, it should be clear that program evaluations carry with them ambiguity and complexity. They force researchers to make decisions that they would likely not choose if they were conducting experimental research or working in a carefully controlled setting. Program evaluators in some instances seem as much detective as researcher, for the evidence requires considerable patching together of information and examination of an array of competing explanations.

Judged only in terms of educational outcomes, a broad answer then and now to the "Does desegregation provide equal opportunity?" question has to be "No," for there are major gaps between white students and students of color in educational achievement and educational attainment. But the specific question is not about equal educational outcomes, but about equal opportunities. So, overlaid upon the issue of trying to make sense of broad structural variables like desegregation, a major challenge for an evaluation of desegregation is to document whether or not students are provided with comparable opportunities, and how opportunities are related to outcomes. The analysis of opportunities includes a focus on the processes that are occurring, as judged by examination of a range of social psychological issues like the presence of biases, prejudice, and discrimination in the setting; attitudes held by individuals in the settings, their roots, and their consequences; the nature of the interactions that occur; and individual factors like motivation and self-concept. In other words, even though the issues are applied and practical, the variables are social psychological. Interestingly, they are psychological even to Supreme Court justices! The majority opinion of the Court held that unequal facilities and negative psychological messages that were part of segregation told students of color that society cared less about them and their educational accomplishments than it did about affluent white students.

The preceding discussion suggests that social psychological processes often provide central and critical ways of evaluating the success of programs. In addition, the research methods of social psychologists provide effective approaches for program evaluation. Nevertheless, there are several reasons why many social psychologists finish graduate school without much understanding about either what program evaluation is or how it can be used to address problems and advance theory (see, e.g., Maruyama, 1997). The first is that the universities typically organize based on disciplines and departments rather than problems, which deemphasizes the importance of skills that are focused on problems rather than disciplinary theories. Second, as has been mentioned, applied work is less predictable in terms of time and outcomes. It takes time to build relations with practitioners who work in applied settings, and many of the factors affecting the evaluation and how well it works are outside the control of the researcher. In the words of Schon (1995), applied work is work in the swamp rather than on the high ground, messy, slow, and potentially bad for getting tenure. Third, the findings from program evaluations may have greater practical than conceptual importance, which makes them more difficult to publish. Fourth, if social psychology graduate students are exposed to evaluation, it is likely as one of a variety of methodological tools used for applied research, and one that they might not have occasion to use, particularly if their research is done primarily on campus. Finally, to some, evaluation has been viewed as useful primarily in specific situations where theory might be subordinate to social problems, which may seem not particularly desirable in graduate programs with a strong emphasis on theory and theoretical contributions.

In sum, there are a number of reasons why program evaluation has not been an integral part of training in social psychology. The remainder of this chapter is intended to provide social psychologists who would like to improve their knowledge a brief introduction to the field. It first looks broadly at the program evaluation field, then focuses on action research, and finally provides illustrations of action research approaches to evaluation.

## THE PROGRAM EVALUATION FIELD

Even though program evaluation work may draw heavily from social psychology and other social sciences, as the corpus of work on evaluation approaches/methods has expanded, it has developed as its own field of study. Program evaluation's roots date back to people like Lewin (1948) and Tyler (1935), yet its development as a field has occurred primarily within the past 40 years (see, e.g., Shadish, Cook, & Leviton, 1991). Although there are social psychologists in the Donald Campbell and Thomas Cook tradition who provide a social psychological orientation to program evaluation, the substantial majority of evaluation researchers are not social psychologists. As a consequence, many evaluators do not possess the balance of conceptual and methodological skills that are parts of training in social psychology (see also Chen & Rossi, 1999). Rather, their training has been focused on methods and techniques that are needed to do effective evaluation as well as to interact successfully with and inform practitioners.

Most approaches to evaluation expect researchers to be "experts in theory." Its development as a practice-driven field (e.g., Shadish et al., 1991), however, has resulted in many evaluators being specialists who bring with them an array of evaluation perspectives, methods, and tools, and yet their background in theories beyond evaluation is limited. Such evaluators tend to focus on evaluation tools that uncover information about program success rather than on substantive theories. If, in contrast, a goal is to understand the conceptual underpinnings of programs, evaluators must be committed to discovering and examining hidden and overlooked substantive theories. They cannot count on getting that information from practitioners, who possess practical understanding of what works but who may not be clear about the theoretical bases of their practices.

Although substantive theories seem like they logically would be a part of evaluation, there are very different views about the role of theory. First, as argued above, evaluators holding a social psychological orientation have argued that because program designs are created using substantive theory and reflect theories, theory needs to be a fundamental part of evaluation (e.g., Shadish et al., 1991). In contrast, other evaluation theorists have argued that, for evaluation, theory is irrelevant. From their perspective, even though both research and evaluation share in the goal of production of knowledge, research and evaluation are far from synonymous, and some avoid using the term "evaluation research" (e.g., Worthen & Sanders, 1987). Worthen and Sanders (1987) note that, for research, generalizability of findings is important. Contrarily, they argue that in many evaluations, program-specific knowledge is what is desired and that researchers' grounding in traditional disciplines leads them to waste time worrying about issues like generalizability when they should be focused on whether or not the program being evaluated is working, and how it can be improved. Because programs differ from setting to setting, they argue that it is more important to know whether or not and how well programs work rather than why they work the way they do. Still other competing views argue that researchers should primarily empower practitioners to become evaluators of their programs and to take responsibility for ongoing evaluation. From those perspectives, researchers need to be much less intrusive with their skills and particularly with their theories (see, e.g., Worthen & Sanders, 1987). In summary, the range of perspectives explains why some evaluators ignore the conceptual underpinnings of programs they are evaluating.

It is difficult to argue against views that practitioners should learn to understand and to do program evaluation, or that what programs benefit from most is knowing specific things about their particular setting. Nevertheless, the failure to investigate issues like generalizability of findings and transportability of programs seems to limit the knowledge that can be created. In an experimenting society, viewing programs as replications across time and settings can develop effective practices more quickly and allow researchers to synthesize information in the same way that meta-analysis has integrated research literatures (e.g., Cooper, 1989). Patterns of findings will not all be correctly interpreted, but, overall, the process will lead to knowledge. Articulating underlying conceptual principles enriches understanding of programs and provides opportunities for applied settings to extend as well as to limit theories.

In contrast to the differing ways evaluators think about their roles, most perspectives on program evaluation seem to agree that practitioners are "experts in practice" and bring with them valuable knowledge about both underpinnings of programs and details of how they have been implemented. Working with practitioners to collect information on underlying programs is critical in getting to their roots, what makes them work, and what about them is generalizable and transferable. Not all evaluators, however, believe it is their role to collect that information, which leads to differences in how evaluators go about creating partnerships with practitioners.

Rather than trying to describe the range of approaches to program evaluation and consequences of different approaches, this chapter looks at program evaluation as it has developed from roots in field theory and action research (e.g., Lewin, 1951). Ironically, however, even the idea of action research has come to mean different things to different people. For one group, action research describes what in the evaluation literature has been called participatory action research, namely, work designed to promote active involvement of the program participants and staff in every stage of the research process (e.g., Chataway, 1997). Although there is much to be said for such work, for it creates an experimenting society that could have the capacity to continually self-evaluate, that perspective is not so clearly rooted in the work of Lewin. This chapter presents a perspective that ties back directly to Lewin, then provides examples of how that orientation can be applied to evaluate programs in education.

## ACTION RESEARCH AND PROGRAM EVALUATION

As is evident in the quotation at the beginning of this chapter, Lewin believed that theory should play an important role in applied research and in program evaluation. To him, many of the best theorists should be interested in tackling applied problems, and applied researchers need to keep their ties to theory. The vehicle for blending theory and practice is action research, which weaves together practical issues with theory and research. Action research is well suited for program evaluation and in many ways defines an ideal blend of theory/practice and collaboration. Falling short of that ideal should not necessarily deter researchers from engaging in evaluation, for many good evaluations have come from work that fails to meet one or more of the conditions Lewin described.

Unfortunately, Lewin died before he had fully articulated his thinking about action research and how it blends research and social issues, which left that task to his colleagues and students. As articulated by Chein, Cook, and Harding (1948), action research "is a field which developed to satisfy the needs of the socio-political individual who recognizes that, in science, he can find the most reliable guide to effective action, and the needs of the scientist who wants his labors to be of maximal social utility as well as of theoretical significance" (pp. 43-44). Chein et al.

(1948) recognized that not all scientists cared about whether or not their work could have significance beyond the theoretical, and they focused on those who cared, arguing that individuals with political interests should not separate those interests from their scientific methods.

Action research demands much more than just caring about social issues. It requires commitment to collaboration and involvement in identifying the interests and needs of the community, which is part of what links it to program evaluation. Insofar as action research should address important problems, even if it were to be developed independently of ongoing evaluation efforts, it ultimately should converge with them in its focus. Illustrating again by drawing from Chein et al. (1948), "The relations of the action researcher to the community and to society at large do not, however, begin at the point where he has made his discovery. These relations begin with the very definition of his research problems" (p. 44).

A third Lewinian principle evident in action research and important for program evaluation is that behaviors need to be examined in their natural setting. Lewin (e.g., 1948) spoke about "the behavior in the situation," testing problems in the settings in which they develop. Reflecting strong roots in traditional experimental methods, he further argued for conducting comparative research that examines the conditions and effects of various forms or variants of social action, creating natural experiments or quasi-experiments. Because the researchers are the ones who possess or acquire knowledge about conceptual bases of behavior to go along with their methodological skills, Lewin expected them often to become the best judges of and guides to effective action. But, to the extent that they work collaboratively with and recognize practitioners as experts about the local conditions and likely impacts of particular approaches on those local conditions, the relationship necessarily builds upon a foundation of ongoing respect and joint contributions.

Finally, Lewin (1946) argued that for action research to be effective, it needs to include a long-term commitment manifested in a series of steps and cycles. The steps constituting a cycle are shared across most evaluation approaches. They are problem identification, planning and implementing the components or action steps of an intervention, interpreting the findings, and then using those findings to redefine the problem (see also Bargal, Gold, & Lewin, 1992). Consistent with developing a long-term relationship, the steps are repeated in one or more additional cycles. As an aside, as a way of ensuring that implementation issues are understood, Stake (1967) recommends specificity in identifying what should be examined. He compares observed or actual patterns with intended or perceived patterns before (antecedents), during (transactions), and after (outcomes) implementation of an intervention. In other words, he includes in any evaluation a focus not only on what people think is happening (intended) in a setting but also on what really is happening (actual), and he looks at the setting before the intervention begins, during the implementation of a treatment, and after the intervention is fully implemented.

To date, very few social scientists have developed a long-term partnership with practitioners, worked with them to identify problems to address, constructed programs that would address problems, used the results to redesign the program, and then continued the partnership to examine how the revised program works (e.g., Campbell, 1969). In part, this may be because the knowledge acquired in later iterations is likely to have less theoretical importance (i.e., they are viewed as at least partial replication). It also is likely that researchers typically seek out applied settings with a particular study in mind and that their purpose is satisfied once the study is complete. Although I have been doing applied research tied to educational settings for almost 30 years, only recently have I spent enough time working continuously with practitioners on a set of problems that I feel that my work could be used to illustrate action research.

One of the likely changes occurring during the 21st century will be increased occurrences of long-term, collaborative relationships between researchers and practitioners. Society increasingly has been demanding that universities do more to address enduring social problems in long-term, substantive, and collaborative ways (e.g., Boyer, 1990; Maruyama, 1997), which makes it likely that many new partnerships will be created. As a part of those changes, more researchers will be likely to need and use skills in program evaluation methods.

## ACTION RESEARCH APPLIED TO ISSUES OF EDUCATIONAL OPPORTUNITY

My experience with action research has roots that go back a long way, to the first times that I tried to collaborate with schools to conduct field-based research. Although I vaguely recognized that my research needed to have relevance and value to the practitioners, I was carried by a naivete that because the work addressed an important social issue and might be important to the educational setting, schools would want to work with me—not exactly an action research approach! Through collaboration with more senior colleagues who provided technical assistance to schools, I managed to conduct some of the studies that I had designed. Over time, I became more sensitive to a quid pro quo, namely, that in good applied research, participants and researchers both benefit. Because practitioners often need evaluations of their programs for reasons like satisfying accountability concerns, many evaluations have benefits that are both conceptual and practical. An important point here is that if a researcher wants to begin doing applied work but has not built relationships, it is wise initially to work through and with colleagues who have built relationships, and to learn how

to address practitioner needs as well as the researcher's own needs.

Once I became director of an applied research center that worked with schools, I found myself on advisory committees and working more directly with schools on issues of importance to them. I got to know problems that grew out of the community, which moved me closer to the ideal starting point of action research. Eventually, I had an opportunity to spend half of my time for a year directing the Research, Evaluation, and Assessment department of an urban school district. That year became 4 years and the time provided chances to assess the effectiveness of programs offering opportunities to students and, consequently, action research experiences that I describe in this chapter.

Although I carried specific conceptual interests into my collaborative work, the major benefit stemming from my interests was that I became involved in schools and gained a much better understanding of practical nuances of design of applied research. Things I probably should have known but that were made clear through experience included the following:

- In educational settings, students are not captive audiences waiting for researchers.
- Class time is valued, so to give it up for research, there need to be benefits to participants.
- To expect students to fill out surveys outside class probably is unduly optimistic.
- Because of transportation issues, getting students to stay after school is unlikely.
- Long instruments are undesirable because students lose interest and because the instruments take up valuable class time.
- Assessments need to be written at the level of the participants, which eliminates many good measures from consideration.

Given the preceding examples, it is no surprise that through experience, evaluation researchers become more pragmatic and attuned to issues of practitioners and settings in which they work.

More important than specifics of work was a different perspective on what is important. Through increased involvement and changing roles, it became clear that the practical issues of greatest importance were not primarily those tied to group relations but ones that helped educators understand what affects the educational outcomes of different types of students. Specifically, in urban school districts today there are large numbers of students at risk of educational failure. How those students interact with other students is viewed as less important than increasing their achievement levels. That is, although being able to interact effectively with others is important, unless students develop skills needed to contribute to the workforce, their interaction skills don't do them much good. In effect, the practical problems of low achievement and group differences in achievement led educators to be most interested in questions like "What are the effects of changing structures of schools, including things like the time of day that classes start; the length of classes, the school day, and the school year; the size of the school and of the classes?," "Which programs work, and for whom?," "How well are schools and teachers doing in educating their students?," "Which groups of students are most needy, or ones whose needs are not being met?" and "How do we identify students for participation in enrichment programs?" All the preceding questions are ones that colleagues and I addressed as we worked our way through a tangle of issues of educational opportunity. The next section provides illustrations that address some of these questions while also giving examples of different types of evaluation.

## "Traditional" Evaluations of School Structures

Structure issues provide good examples of quasi-experimental designs. In some cases, structural changes are driven by practical as much as conceptual concerns, which may make it difficult to identify underlying frameworks. We examined a number of issues, including when school started each day and how long classes were. A study of the effects of switching to 90-minute classes in high school (e.g., Maruyama, 1996) is used to illustrate evaluation efforts. The primary arguments focused on psychological issues, namely, reducing the frenzy that characterizes many high schools, reducing violence that can occur in high schools between class periods, and personalizing large schools. Longer class periods can help because students have fewer classes and fewer peers to get to know, and teachers teach fewer students at any point in time so should get to know their students better. Comparisons of schools with differing class lengths and numbers of classes, along with analyses following schools across changes in schedules, revealed that having longer classes improved climate and engagement but didn't seem to change overall achievement levels. The schools in the research did not have large numbers of students of color, so relations between schedule and outcomes of students from different groups was not examined.

The project reflects traditional program evaluation, using a quasi-experimental design. Analyses are those that compare group means, and they can include multilevel analyses like hierarchical linear modeling or structural equation modeling of processes. Complications were tied to determining appropriate comparison groups in quasi-experimental designs (Should schools be their own comparisons across time, or should similar schools be contrasted?). As well as traditional outcome measures, schools administered to students and teachers attitude surveys designed specifically to address conceptual and practical issues of the intervention. Because respondents were kept anonymous, individual change could not be assessed. Inferences were drawn from aggregate data. Sample sizes were large. The impacts of structure, although highly significant, were relatively modest. Although the conceptual implications are somewhat limited, this type of evaluation provides researchers with an opportunity to get engaged and establish that they are willing to share their skills and be good collaborators.

## Policy-Relevant Evaluation: Modeling Impacts of School Accountability

A different type of evaluation attempts to anticipate likely consequences of implementing a change in policy or practice by using historical information to model likely consequences of proposed policy alternatives. The particular issue used for illustration focuses on state and federal regulations being developed that would hold schools accountable for the achievements of their students. As a result, it addresses issues that are highly political. In principle, accountability is designed to help disadvantaged students by ensuring that they are receiving educational opportunities comparable to those received by other students. Therefore, accountability seems to get right to the heart of educational opportunity issues. Unfortunately, ratings have many consequences besides identifying opportunity levels. First, because the public is likely to judge effectiveness of schools based upon their ratings, schools that do relatively poorly may be stigmatized. Second, one group promoting accountability was a group interested in showing shortcomings of public schools so it could advocate for vouchers and include private schools in choice programs. Third, some potential measures show substantial group differences that disadvantage groups such as students of color. If such measures are selected, there are questions about whether or not student ability is being measured adequately and about building in a bias against schools educating large numbers and

proportions of students of color. Fourth, judgments about students' performance on accountability measures might or might not take into account preexisting differences. Ignoring preexisting differences loses important information about changes (rates of growth) in achievement; it seems unfair to give schools credit or blame for the levels of achievement of the students they receive.

Colleagues and I modeled the consequences of different potential accountability systems. We used existing data, employing regression models to examine the consequences of different assumptions. We focused on using an array of predictor measures in an accountability system and on developing models that value growth (change) in achievement while also setting minimum standards that all students are expected to attain. We showed how different the consequences were of competing assumptions and how some models inevitably resulted in schools that educate disadvantaged students being identified as underperforming. The work helped inform policy makers and prevented imposition of a system that would (a) punish schools educating students who come to school lacking adequate preparation to succeed and (b) increase the stigma facing students of color. Nevertheless, to date no system has been adopted.

## Longitudinal Evaluation Designs and Collaborative Work: Understanding Relations of Poverty With Achievement

One of the consistent findings when examining demographic variables was that the best predictor of student achievement was poverty level, even though at the student level the typical measure has only three categories (not eligible for free or reduced-price lunch, eligible for reduced-price lunch, and eligible for free lunch). It was an even stronger predictor at the school level (percentage of students eligible for free or reduced-price lunch) and stronger yet as a predictor at the census tract level (median income of family or household, percentage of population living below the poverty level). The primary goal of this work, requiring collaboration across agencies, was to use a look across time to understand better how individual poverty was related to housing and neighborhood variables, so interventions could be designed to improve student outcomes. The work would not have been possible unless relationships already had been developed among the parties involved so there was a basis of trust underlying the collaboration. Throughout the process, we worked with an advisory committee including practitioners from the agencies involved.

This work was a collaboration among the schools, the public housing agency, and the researchers. It provided evaluation data for the public housing agency on relations of living in public housing with student achievements, helped schools see how effectively they had been educating students whose families lived in public housing, and gave the researchers a rich, unique data set. Developing the relationships, gaining access to the data, and securing funding took well more than a year (Just imagine if this were your dissertation!). Then file merging and data cleaning took another 6 months. Although analyses were multilevel and included many variables, predictions were straightforward. Affordable public housing reduces mobility, keeping students longer in the same school where teachers and staff get to know them, which should improve their educational outcomes. On the other hand, however, students in public housing tend to live in neighborhoods where the poverty rates are higher and may carry a stigma because they live in public housing, both of which could lower their achievement.

The evaluation looked at mobility across schools and home locations, focusing on the 8,000 students whose families lived in housing that is subsidized by the public housing agency. Students whose families lived in various types of public housing were compared with other disadvantaged students on stability/mobility as well as educational outcomes. Of particular interest were students whose families did not move and who stayed in the same school for a number of years. The evaluation examined how factors such as poverty, residential and school mobility, family background, neighborhood, school, and living in subsidized housing collectively affected student achievement. Analyses looked across several years at various student outcome measures (achievement test scores, attendance, graduation rates) to find trends. Achievement levels were found to be improving over time, but achievement levels of disadvantaged students still were low.

Findings from this work illustrate the importance of longitudinal data. When colleagues and I compared cohorts at a single point in time, it appeared that students were doing worse and worse as they got older. In contrast, when we followed students across their elementary school years, the pattern that emerged was one of slow growth. In other words, adopting a superior (growth) methodology produced findings contrary to those found when trying to examine housing and mobility factors within a single time period.

## METHODOLOGICAL TOOLS AND THEIR USES

One of the ironies of program evaluation is that it simultaneously demands sophisticated analyses and easy-to-understand results. Analysis methods for conceptual questions tend to be multivariate and often multilevel, reflecting the sophistication of the questions and complexity of the designs and the samples. In educational settings, for example, researchers often have students nested within classes and schools, and have unequal distributions of demographic variables, which can lead to improper interpretation of results unless appropriate controls are imposed. But policy makers typically don't understand complex analyses, may be suspicious of findings that emerge only when statistical controls are imposed, and want findings that are clear, understandable, and have direct implications for policy and practice. Analysis methods for policy makers and practitioners need to be simple, straightforward, and accessible. When trying to meet the standards of dual audiences, investigators need to be able conduct both types of analyses and hope for consistency. If results differ, then the evaluator again becomes investigator, trying to determine which findings are more plausible. Insofar as the complex analyses, if done properly, are likely to yield more accurate conclusions, the challenge most often is to find simple analyses whose results parallel those of the complex ones.

One option when having to present findings to policy makers is to complement the quantitative analyses with qualitative ones (focus groups, interviews) that provide rich information from a subset of the population. Most substantial evaluations today specifically include both quantitative data and qualitative data so they have multiple sources of support for and illustrations of inferences that they draw. Anecdotes that summarize the quantitative results are ideal, for they transmit the findings in understandable ways.

Finally, policy makers want clear guidance, whereas data often provide at best fuzzy suggestions. In such instances, researchers are likely to be uncomfortable, for no one wants to promote programs that don't work or end programs that are successful. In such circumstances it also is difficult to keep one's ideology out of the recommendations. The best solution I can offer is to be clear about results that are definitive so that they stand in contrast to ones where the data are more equivocal. One possible way is to present levels of confidence about the impact and meaning of particular findings.

## LIMITATIONS OF ACTION RESEARCH MODELS FOR PROGRAM EVALUATION

The greatest limitation of using action models is the large amount of time that needs to be committed to building relationships and addressing needs of different partners in the evaluation activities. Even then, in many situations, ideal conditions cannot be met. A second limitation is that parts of the work will sometimes be of lesser interest to researchers and may not be publishable. Third, practitioners who don't care about replicating the program elsewhere may not see value in articulating and testing a conceptual model. Fourth, the approach requires giving up the control of the laboratory and dealing with messiness that characterizes "real world" research.

## CLOSING NOTE

I currently am evaluating a magnet school program that has as its goals reducing isolation of students of color and increasing intergroup contact. Perhaps, then, I have come full circle, building relations with practitioners, collaboratively addressing important and timely problems, analyzing data to examine the effectiveness of programs, reconceptualizing programs to improve them, and starting over again. Sometimes the process goes back to the program just evaluated; other times, it moves to another program. Through collaboration, I learned a lot about contextual variables of the setting, and I now hold a perspective far different from the one I held when I began my work in schools. Through experience, I became an action researcher, and I hope I am seen by practitioners as a colleague, if perhaps one with somewhat esoteric interests. I look forward to seeing where action research will take me in the future and hope that many readers will attempt to take parallel paths as they address important practical issues.

## REFERENCES

Bargal, D., Gold, M., & Lewin, M. (1992). Introduction: The heritage of Kurt Lewin. *Journal of Social Issues, 48*(2), 3-13.

Benjamin, L. T., & Crouse, E. M. (2002). The American Psychological Association's response to *Brown v. Board of Education*: The case of Kenneth B. Clark. *American Psychologist, 57,* 38-50.

Boyer, E. (1990). *Scholarship reconsidered: Priorities of the professorate.* Princeton, NJ: The Carnegie Foundation for the Advancement of Teaching.

Brown v. Board of Education, 347 U.S. 483 (1954).

Campbell, D. T. (1969). Reforms as experiments. *American Psychologist, 24,* 409-429.

Chataway, C. J. (1997). An examination of the constraints on mutual inquiry in a participatory action research project. *Journal of Social Issues, 53*(4), 747-765.

Chein, I., Cook, S. W., & Harding, J. (1948). The field of action research. *American Psychologist, 3,* 43-50.

Chen, H.-T., & Rossi, P. H. (1999). *Theory-driven evaluation.* Thousand Oaks, CA: Sage.

Cooper, H. (1989). *Integrating research: A guide for literature reviews.* Newbury Park, CA: Sage.

Gerard, H. B., & Miller, N. (1975). *School desegregation: Outcomes for children.* New York: Plenum.

Heider, F. (1958). *The psychology of interpersonal relations.* New York: Wiley.

Lewin, K. (1946). Action research and minority problems. *Journal of Social Issues, 10,* 34-46.

Lewin, K. (1948). *Resolving social conflicts.* New York: Harper.

Lewin, K. (1951). *Field theory in social science: Collected theoretical papers* (D. Cartwright, Ed.). New York: Harper & Brothers.

Maruyama, G. (1983). Understanding the process of educational achievement. In L. Bickman (Ed.), *Applied social psychology annual* (Vol. 4, pp. 165-197).

Maruyama, G. (1996). Application and transformation of action research in educational research and practice. *Systems Practice, 9*(1), 85-101.

Maruyama, G. (1997). Academics and action in research universities of the 21st century. *Journal of Public Management and Social Policy, 3*(1), 20-28.

Patton, M. Q. (1986). *Utilization focused evaluation.* Beverly Hills, CA: Sage.

Schon, D. A. (1995, November/December). Knowing-in-action: The new scholarship requires a new epistemology. *Change,* pp. 27-34.

Scriven, M. (1973). The methodology of evaluation. In B. R. Worthen & J. R. Sanders (Eds.), *Educational evaluation: Theory and practice* (pp. 60-106). Belmont, CA: Wadsworth.

Shadish, W. R., Cook, T. D., & Leviton, L. C. (1991). *Foundations of program evaluation: Theories of practice.* Newbury Park, CA: Sage.

Social Science Statement. (1952). *The effects of segregation and the consequences of desegregation: A social science statement.* Appendix to Appellants' Briefs, Supreme Court of the United States.

Stake, R. E. (1967). The countenance of educational evaluation. *Teacher's College Record, 68,* 523-540.

Tyler, R. (1935). Evaluation: A challenge to progressive education. *Educational Research Bulletin, 14,* 9-16.

Wilde, J., & Sockey, S. (1995). *Evaluation handbook.* Albuquerque, NM: Evaluation Assistance Center-Western Region, New Mexico Highlands University. Retrieved from www.ncbe.gwu.edu/miscpubs/eacwest/evalhbl.htm

Worthen, B. R., & Sanders, J. R. (1987). *Educational evaluation: Alternative approaches and practical guidelines.* New York: Longman.

## CHAPTER 20

# Methodological Challenges and Scientific Rewards for Social Psychologists Conducting Health Behavior Research

PETER SALOVEY

*Yale University*

WAYNE T. STEWARD

*University of California, San Francisco*

Understanding the motivators of health-relevant behaviors offers an exciting opportunity for applying social psychological theory and findings. Research on attitudes, persuasion, social influence, and, generally, the interaction of person and situational variables in human motivation can guide public health officials in the design and implementation of interventions that have a significant impact on health and well-being. The success of these programs then provides a feedback mechanism to social psychologists evaluating the generalizability and utility of their work.

In this chapter, we focus most of our attention on the challenges of connecting social psychological theory and research to important health outcomes in ecologically complex settings. We choose this path not with the intention of making the study of health behaviors seem difficult: The value and rewards of conducting research on what can be life or death matters should be self-evident. However, social psychologists trained in traditional

AUTHORS' NOTE: The research reported in this chapter on the framing of health messages was supported by grants to Peter Salovey from the American Cancer Society (RPG-93–028–05-PBP), the National Cancer Institute (R01-CA68427), the National Institute of Mental Health (P01-MH/DA56826), the National Institute on Drug Abuse (P50-DA13334), and the Donaghue Women's Health Investigator Program at Yale University. Wayne T. Steward coauthored this chapter while at Yale University.

laboratory methods may encounter unexpected hurdles when confronting the challenges of health behavior research. We hope that this chapter provides ideas for helping social psychologists to overcome these obstacles. Some of the challenges—such as the ethical issues that arise in field-based health research—do not easily lend themselves to simple remedies. For these issues, we hope to provide readers with a sense of what to expect, so that they can make informed decisions about whether they wish to pursue this kind of research.

The chapter details three major challenges to the successful application of social psychological theory and research to health behavior. The first challenge is that social psychologists may find that they must serve two masters. The fields of social psychology and public health have somewhat different philosophies of science and practice. This tension is evidenced at every stage of research, from the initial motivation to conduct a study to the publication strategies concerning the final product. Second, social psychologists are faced with the specific challenges associated with actually testing a relevant, empirical question in this domain. They likely must make trade-offs between the superior control of laboratory-based studies and the greater external validity of field experimentation. Finally, aspiring social-health psychologists must consider a range of ethical issues that play out differently in field research—especially when vulnerable populations are involved—as compared with laboratory work. They must select carefully an appropriate control group and must always be mindful that their first responsibility is to the well-being of the participants. Each of these challenges is explored in the sections that follow. We also provide a brief discussion of professional development to guide young social psychologists in ways to obtain training in health behavior research.

## A BRIEF INTRODUCTION TO RESEARCH IN THE HEALTH, EMOTION, AND BEHAVIOR (HEB) LABORATORY

Throughout this chapter, we provide examples of actual research studies to elucidate methodological points and to provide the reader with a feel for the kind of work already being conducted in the field of social-health psychology. However, we sample most heavily from our own research program; the experience in moving from laboratory to field in order to complete these studies is instructive with respect to the goals of the present chapter. Therefore, we provide a brief introduction to the theoretical underpinnings and purpose of our work on the framing of health messages.

In many of our field experiments, we seek to promote health behaviors relevant to cancer or HIV/AIDS by presenting people with messages that are *framed* to discuss either the gains (benefits) of engaging in a behavior or the losses (costs) of not engaging in the behavior. All messages present similar information; however, in a *gain-framed* message, the emphasis is on the positive outcomes that result from engaging in a particular health behavior (e.g., "If you use sunscreen with SPF 15 or higher, you increase your chances of keeping your skin healthy and your life long"). In contrast, a *loss-framed* message emphasizes the negative outcomes that result from not engaging in the behavior (e.g., "If you don't use sunscreen with SPF 15 or higher, you increase your chances of damaging your skin and of bringing on an early death").

Although the information in the messages is similar, gain- and loss-framed messages may not be equally persuasive. According to prospect theory, people are willing to consider risky options when considering the potential losses or negative consequences of that choice but tend to avoid risks when considering the potential gains or benefits (Kahneman &

Tversky, 1979; Tversky & Kahneman, 1981). Focusing on losses motivates people to engage in behaviors with risky, or uncertain, outcomes. Focusing on gains motivates people to engage in behaviors with definite, or certain, outcomes.

Health behaviors can be classified according to the degree of uncertainty or psychological risk that typically is associated with them (Rothman & Salovey, 1997). Many people view behaviors that detect illness or abnormalities, such as mammography screening, as psychologically risky, or having an uncertain outcome, because there is some chance that illness may be discovered. Consistent with predictions deriving from prospect theory, individuals usually are more motivated to perform detection behaviors when they are exposed to loss-framed messages rather than to gain-framed messages (Banks et al., 1995; Meyerowitz & Chaiken, 1987; Schneider, Salovey, Apanovitch, et al., 2001). In contrast, prevention behaviors, such as using sunscreen while at the beach, are often thought to have a certain or definite outcome: These behaviors reduce one's chances of developing an illness. People usually are more motivated to perform prevention behaviors if they are exposed to gain-framed messages than if they are exposed to loss-framed messages (Detweiler, Bedell, Salovey, Pronin, & Rothman, 1999; Schneider, Salovey, Pallonen, et al., 2001).

This basic interaction between message framing and the perceived uncertainty of the various health behaviors is at the heart of this research and appears to be quite robust (Rothman, Martino, Bedell, Detweiler, & Salovey, 1999), and multiple experiments have addressed different aspects of this issue. We believe that these findings generalize over location (laboratory versus field), type of disease (fictitious versus real), and targeted populations (young adult college students versus diverse community-based samples).

# CHALLENGE #1:
# SERVING TWO MASTERS

Social psychology has a long tradition of moving between research focused on developing theories that are tested in laboratory settings and research focused on exploring generalizations to more ecologically interesting contexts, through which one tests the usefulness of theories in addressing real world problems. These two traditions have often created a split between what is loosely termed *basic* research and *applied* research (which is sometimes then mapped onto laboratory versus field, respectively). However, these categories may represent a false dichotomy, in that basic processes can be explored in the service of addressing a practical problem (e.g., understanding memory bias in the recall of threatening health-risk information). The National Institute of Mental Health has suggested that the term *translational research* might describe better the typical activities of social-health psychologists (National Advisory Mental Health Council, 2000). For example, Fishbein and his colleagues examined the relationships among attitudes, norms, intentions to perform a behavior, and actual behavior by studying the promotion of condom use (Albarracín, Johnson, Fishbein, & Muellerleile, 2001; Fishbein et al., 1995). The research both contributed to an understanding of how attitudes and norms influence behavior, a question of interest to basic science, and provided ideas for designing effective public health campaigns, a topic of interest to health educators. (For similar links between basic and applied research in other contexts, see chapters in this volume by Maruyama [Chapter 19]; Thompson, Kern, and Loyd [Chapter 21], and Harackiewicz and Barron [Chapter 22].)

Understanding the interplay between so-called basic and applied research is not a new issue for social psychology. One of the founders of our field, Kurt Lewin, advocated for what he termed *action research* (Lewin, 1946). Lewin viewed the acquisition of new knowledge as inseparable from using it to address social problems and encouraging social change. Most important, Lewin argued that there was a feedback loop between application and basic theory building such that attempts to put the theory into practice (followed by the evaluation of such efforts) would provide evidence for the validity of the theory and suggest ways in which the theory might need to be changed (Sadava, 1997). This idea was developed further by Chris Argyris in his *action science* approach to social and organizational psychology (Argyris, Putnam, & McLain, 1985). In this tradition, research subjects are viewed as clients to be helped, and theories are tested through interventions designed to change the behavior of these clients. For Argyris, the key to theory testing is intervention research.

In health psychology, the interplay between theory and application is evidenced by three different research strategies (described by Taylor, 1984; see also Salovey, Rothman, & Rodin, 1998). First, a study may test the application of general theory. In this situation, an investigator uses a psychological theory that might have been designed for another domain (or with no particular domain of application in mind at all) and attempts to apply it specifically to a health context. Our research represents application of general theory. We use prospect theory as the starting point for making predictions about whether gain- or loss-framed messages are more effective in encouraging various health behaviors. Whereas we have used the theory to promote different behaviors such as mammography, the use of sunscreen at the beach, and HIV testing, it also is applied in very different situations, such as casino gambling and international conflict. In fact, one of the original delineations of prospect theory was published in an economics journal (Kahneman & Tversky, 1979).

Second, psychologists may develop grounded theories to address specific health problems and then use the theories to guide future studies. These kinds of theories are termed *grounded* because they were developed (or *grounded*) in the domain in which they are being applied. For example, the transtheoretical model of behavior change (Prochaska, DiClemente, & Norcross, 1992) was created to understand the challenges faced as individuals attempt to change a health-damaging behavior or adopt a precautionary behavior. The first applications were focused on reducing the use of health-damaging substances such as nicotine. The transtheoretical model proposes five stages that a person passes through in the process of adopting a new behavior: *precontemplation* (a person is not considering adopting the behavior in the near future), *contemplation* (a person is considering adopting the behavior in the near future), *preparation* (a person is preparing to adopt the behavior in the very near future), *action* (a person is in the process of adopting the behavior), and *maintenance* (a person has adopted the new behavior and is now working to ensure that old behaviors are not resumed). The psychological mechanisms accounting for behavior change are thought to be different for individuals in these different stages of change. As such, different kinds of interventions might be targeted for these individuals, depending on the stage (see also Weinstein, Rothman, & Sutton, 1998).

Another grounded theory is the AIDS risk reduction model (ARRM) (Catania, Kegeles, & Coates, 1990), which postulates a set of psychological processes accounting for the modification of behaviors that transmit HIV. According to the ARRM, individuals must label a behavior as problematic and commit to making a behavior change before they start taking steps to enact the change. The ARRM effectively guides investigators in designing HIV prevention programs. Instead of indiscriminately promoting condom use or needle exchange in a particular community, investigators must first ensure that the relevant population is aware that particular behaviors are risky. For example, college students do not always realize that there are risks associated with their sexual behavior. Many students engage in serial monogamy; that is, they have only one sexual partner at any one time, and so label themselves as monogamous, but frequently change partners (Thompson, Anderson, Freedman, & Swan, 1996). Thus, they often do not attend to information targeted toward people with multiple partners.

Finally, psychologists may develop research to address a particular problem, without using theory as a guide. In problem-focused research, a scientist simply looks to see if a particular intervention can significantly influence behaviors relevant to a given concern. Any hypotheses guiding the study do not necessarily derive from more general predictions about human behavior; they may be specific only to the problem at hand. For example, Lerman and her colleagues (1996) examined women's interest in being tested for the breast-ovarian cancer susceptibility (BRCA1) gene. In their study, they measured a number of different variables (e.g., knowledge about genetic testing; sociodemographics) and explored whether they were associated with a decision to be tested for the BRCA1 gene. The purpose of the study was descriptive and exploratory: to gain a better understanding of those factors associated with decisions to be tested for BRCA1.

Social psychologists working in the health behavior field may find that these various research strategies are not equally appealing across all potential audiences. The various academic disciplines place differing emphasis on theory versus problem solving, although the importance of both is always acknowledged. Given the traditions of the fields, social psychologists tend to prefer research that is guided by theory, whereas public health professionals tend to be more problem driven. These different motivations, in turn, affect the approach one must use in designing a study. In general- or grounded-theory-driven research, questions of mechanism are paramount. Investigators explore why a particular set of

social psychological factors leads to certain health behaviors, and they are also interested in the conditions under which these associations are observed most strongly. As such, this kind of research often involves an exploration of variables that mediate or moderate relations between social psychological antecedents and health behavior outcomes. In contrast, public health professionals often prefer studies with a clear set of findings that can be communicated easily to practitioners. They are trying to develop interventions that can be distributed to the community at large, and interactions (moderators) are difficult to communicate and mechanism (mediators) may not be all that relevant. Therefore, clearly interpretable main effects are often more highly desired in investigations focused on public health problems.

These differences are also reflected in standards for publication. Because social psychology journals value theoretically motivated research and are especially interested in articles describing underlying mechanisms accounting for the scope conditions impinging on some phenomenon, articles in the most prestigious social psychological journals often report multiple studies and tend to be rather lengthy. In contrast, many journals read by public health researchers value shorter manuscript that efficiently identify a problem and present (usually) a single study with clear implications for practice. Preparing manuscripts for these two kinds of publications requires very different mindsets and may tap different writing talents.

Although the approaches favored by social psychology and public health may seem at odds, the standards of the two fields actually are quite complementary. As Lewin, Argyris, and others remind us, theory building and problem solving are inextricably linked. Given the important—literally life-saving—nature of many public health problems, we are reminded that the nuances of mechanism and moderation may need to give way to the necessity of application. Similarly, the consensually held values of social psychology remind public health professionals that the generalization of findings and recommendations in one health domain to another one is more likely to be appropriate when guided by an underlying theory that makes specific predictions about the conditions under which the predictors of health behavior or health behavior change are most likely to be observed.

We try to keep both perspectives in mind in our own work, which uses social psychological theory to guide, primarily, field-based experiments, focused on "real" health behaviors in ecologically complex settings (the mission statement of the Health, Emotion, and Behavior Laboratory is *Translating Psychological Science into Action*). We usually choose between social psychology and public health (or health communication) journals, depending on the emphasis on theory and mechanism versus immediate applicability of the findings. For example, in one set of experiments, we tested the predictions of prospect theory by first describing a mouth rinse as either detecting or preventing plaque buildup, and then promoting its use with gain- or loss-framed messages (Rothman, Martino, et al., 1999). Loss-framed messages were more effective at convincing people to try mouth rinse that detected plaque, whereas gain-framed messages were better at promoting a rinse that prevented plaque. This finding was replicated using a fictitious disease because we wanted to control for participants' prior knowledge about the health domain. In this set of studies, we could demonstrate the behavior type (prevention/detection) by message framing (gain/loss) interaction in the same situation with the same behavioral endpoint. However, the complexity of these studies required them to be conducted in the laboratory, where we recruited college student samples. Clearly, this manuscript was better suited for a journal in social psychology (e.g., *Journal of Personality and Social Psychology, Personality and Social Psychology Bulletin*). Our studies reporting main-effect advantages of gain-framed messages in the promotion of sunscreen use

by beachgoers (Detweiler et al., 1999), or loss-framed messages in the promotion of mammography by telephone company workers (Banks et al., 1995), or for individuals residing in public housing developments and attending community clinics (Schneider, Salovey, Apanovitch, et al., 2001), were better suited for journals at the intersection of social psychology and public health (e.g., *Health Psychology, American Journal of Public Health*). Finally, as part of a larger study promoting Pap testing to prevent cervical cancer, we discovered that many women reported receiving Pap tests inaccurately, confusing any gynecological procedure with a Pap smear (Pizarro, Schneider, & Salovey, 2002). The findings from that study were not theoretically motivated but of practical significance to public health professionals, so we published them in a community health journal (*Journal of Community Medicine*).

The differences in the scientific traditions of social psychology and public health can present problems for those psychologists working on health behavior research. The incentive structure in traditional academic organizations (promotion, awards, grants, graduate student collaborators) often favors scientists working from a disciplinary perspective, especially those whose work is considered central to the mission of that discipline. Young scientists seeking tenure in a psychology department must gain the respect of more senior psychologists and publish in the journals valued by them, for example. However, many universities have become more respectful of interdisciplinary studies, or, at a minimum, favor individuals who can speak to multiple academic audiences. Moreover, psychologists whose primary appointments are in schools of medicine or public health may find that their colleagues expect to see their work influencing a different kind of audience. For the hybrid social-health psychologist, it can be difficult to earn quickly a strong reputation in multiple disciplines. Early in a career, a scientist may be forced to choose one professional identity over another. We shall return to this dilemma later in the chapter.

## CHALLENGE #2: TESTING YOUR QUESTION

Designing a study such that one minimizes threats to internal and external validity can be difficult under the best of circumstances. This challenge can be quite salient when attempting to study social psychological phenomena in health-relevant settings. Not only is one faced with the difficulties of figuring out how to isolate and test the construct of interest, but one also must overcome many obstacles that constrain the design of an ideal study.

The following example may elucidate some of these challenges. Kelly and his colleagues (1991) conducted a study that demonstrated the important role played by popular opinion leaders in gay bars when they advocate safer sex behaviors. These investigators asked bartenders in Biloxi, Mississippi, to identify men who were influential among the people who frequented the bar. These men were then trained to speak to other bar patrons about the use of condoms. This social influence intervention led to increased self-reported condom use among the men in the bar.

When designing this study, Kelly and his colleagues were presented with a number of methodological challenges. First, it was not possible to assign people to an opinion leader intervention versus a comparison condition at an individual level of analysis. The trained peers could not systematically speak to some men in the bar while purposefully ignoring others (based on, say, a flip of a coin). Therefore, to provide a control group, Kelly and his colleagues randomly assigned different towns in Mississippi to this intervention or a control condition. The safer sex behavior of men in Biloxi, where opinion leaders were trained in the intervention, was compared to the behavior of men in two other Mississippi towns, where the intervention was not implemented.

Other methodological compromises had to be made. For instance, the researchers were also limited in the manner by which they could operationalize the key ingredients of their intervention. Safer sex behaviors offer a particularly difficult challenge because they usually happen (or fail to happen) behind closed doors and, at times, in potentially embarrassing situations. The opinion leaders in this study could *talk* about their safer sex behavior; they couldn't demonstrate it, as might be done if trying to promote, say, moderate drinking. In addition, the study had to rely on self-report of condom use during sexual activities because the researchers could not observe the behavior.

As this example shows, flexibility and compromise are important for any researcher conducting studies on health behavior. Although field-based experiments offer an excellent way to test a theory in a real world environment, the cleanliness of laboratory experiments often does not survive the noise of the field. Some have argued that the trade-off is one between rigor and meaningfulness (for opposing points of view on this issue, compare Neisser, 1978, with Banaji & Crowder, 1989). Although this is no doubt an oversimplification, the maximization of rigor at all costs is likely to compromise the meaningfulness of findings. Ideally, social-health psychologists move between laboratory and field settings in order to capitalize on the advantages of each.

We have used an integrated laboratory-field strategy for more than a decade in research on prospect theory and health behavior. For example, as a precursor to the research on promoting two different kinds of mouth rinses, several members of our laboratory invented a disease called the *letrolisus* virus and then promoted a behavior described as detecting or preventing the disease (Rothman, Martino, et al., 1999, Experiment 1). As expected, gain-framed messages tended to be more effective in encouraging the prevention behavior, and loss-framed messages better in encouraging the detection behavior (at least among participants high in need for cognition, that is, those individuals who like to think deeply about things). Because the experiment was conducted in a laboratory, we were able to control many variables, especially prior knowledge of and expectations about the illness domain, and there was no problem assigning participants randomly to detection/prevention and gain-frame/loss-frame conditions. The experiment thus represented an ideal test of our prospect theory–based predictions (gain facilitates prevention; loss facilitates detection), but it offered little in the way of practical public health recommendations. Not only were people choosing to protect themselves from a fictitious disease, but they did so in a highly artificial setting (using a pencil-and-paper scale administered in a psychology laboratory), and the key dependent variable was a rating of one's *intentions* to engage in the fictitious health behaviors at that.

To acquire a better sense of how prospect theory can be applied in more ecologically relevant contexts, we have also recruited samples from vulnerable populations to participate in field experiments. These experiments involve a series of practical hurdles that are largely absent from those conducted in the laboratory. We first must gain access to a relevant population of community residents (a point to which we return later in the chapter). Then we must recruit a very large number of participants, because the impact of the manipulation can be weakened by the distractions of the natural setting, the fact that many of the target behaviors occur infrequently, and because often they must be measured dichotomously. However, it is worth the effort, we believe, as these field experiments provided the opportunity to test the robustness and utility of our approach.

For instance, we recently completed a study promoting HIV-antibody testing among low-income women living in public housing (Apanovitch, McCarthy, & Salovey, 2003). Initially, we expected that loss-framed messages generally would be more effective than

gain-framed messages in promoting this detection behavior. However, we discovered that many participants were confident they had not been exposed to HIV and, thus, assumed that they would test negative for antibodies to the virus. For them, the test was seen as having a certain outcome and, consistent with the theory, they were more persuaded to be tested by gain-framed messages. In contrast, individuals who felt they might test positive for HIV antibodies viewed the procedure as a behavior with uncertain outcomes and were more persuaded by loss-framed messages. If we had conducted this experiment in the laboratory with college students, we might never have observed this unexpected (and important) interaction because there likely would have been insufficient variability in perceptions of HIV risk and the uncertainty of the HIV-antibody test outcome.

Although moving between laboratory and field setting may allow some methodological challenges to be addressed, a few simply cannot be resolved, and traditional standards may need to be compromised. This problem is particularly acute when selecting appropriate dependent variables for measurement. As in the Kelly and colleagues (1991) barroom opinion leader study described earlier, many health behaviors are carried out at a later time out of sight of the experimenter. Thus, researchers must find other ways to assess outcomes.

Many investigators, ourselves included, are sometimes forced to rely on self-reported health behaviors as primary outcome measures (e.g., Apanovitch et al., 2003; Schneider, Salovey, Apanovitch, et al., 2001). Whenever there is an opportunity to validate self-reported behavior against some other source of data, this should be done. Some self-reported health behavior data are actually quite reliable, such as mammography (King, Rimer, Trock, Balshem, & Engstrom, 1990), but other behaviors, such as Pap testing, may not be (Pizarro et al., 2002). Increasingly, investigators are collecting biomarker data as a way of complementing findings based on self-report. So, for instance, if samples are large enough, the effectiveness of an intervention promoting safer sex behaviors can be assessed not just through self-reported condom use but also by observing a reduction in the incidence of any sexually transmitted disease in the targeted population.

Some researchers also try to use outcome measures that serve as a proxy for the actual dependent variable of interest. For example, when we conducted an experiment comparing the effectiveness of gain versus loss-framed messages in promoting sunscreen use on a public beach, we gave participants coupons that could be redeemed for free sunscreen samples later in the day (Detweiler et al., 1999). In this experiment, the outcome measure was the number of coupons redeemed rather than actual sunscreen use. It was not feasible to ask research assistants to monitor beachgoers' behavior to see who applied sunscreen. Although proxy behaviors offer an improvement over self-report data (in that participants do not have to recall information), they still are not as valid as assessing the actual dependent variable of interest.

## CHALLENGE #3: ETHICAL ISSUES

The protection of research participants through responsible collection of data and dissemination of findings is a consideration in any study, but these issues become paramount in health behavior research, especially when it involves the recruitment of individuals from vulnerable populations. In particular, social-health psychologists must take care in designing appropriate comparison and control groups and in determining when responsibility to participants outweighs fidelity to the experimental treatment. They also must ensure that their projects are perceived by the targeted population as making a meaningful contribution to their community rather than as an opportunity for scientific exploitation.

When designing an appropriate comparison or control group in a health behavior study, investigators must remember that it usually is unethical to assign people to an experience that does not at least meet the standard of care normally available. Participants cannot receive medical or psychological treatments that are thought to be less effective than what would be available generally outside the study. This requirement often means that experiments rely on a large number of participants in order to have adequate power to obtain significant effects; the difference in efficacy between the standard of care and the experimental intervention is likely to be smaller than the difference in efficacy between no treatment and the tested intervention.

Social-health psychologists conducting field research with individuals from vulnerable populations can face situations in which experiments need to be terminated prematurely because of ethical considerations. If preliminary analyses suggest that an intervention condition is leading to poorer health outcomes than the standard of care, the experiment may need to be stopped. An excellent example comes from recent medical research on hormone replacement therapy for women. At the start of a major study of the effects of estrogen and progestin supplements, the prevailing belief was that the supplements would benefit postmenopausal women by reducing calcium depletion in the bones, a major cause of hip fractures. However, the research was terminated after only 5 years when the investigators observed increases in the occurrence of breast cancer, coronary heart disease, pulmonary embolism, and stroke among women taking estrogen and progestin (Women's Health Initiative, 2002). The emerging results suggested that the harm to participants was greater than the benefits; therefore, the study had to be stopped.

Investigators must also decide how to proceed if, in the process of the study, they notice behaviors that can harm participants. For instance, research assistants from our lab have observed individuals injecting heroin; do we intervene in some way? Would it make a difference if the syringes appeared not to be sterile? These kinds of dilemmas can be difficult for researchers because they may affect the conduct and outcome of the experiment. However, one must always remember that the well-being and dignity of the participants are the top priorities. It is best to consider the kinds of ethical dilemmas that could arise when planning the study and to discuss them with a representative from an institutional review board (IRB) before proposing the study more formally to the IRB. (For a more thorough discussion of ethical concerns in research design, see Kazdin, 1998, and Kimmel, Chapter 3, this volume.)

## Relationship With the Community

A final ethical issue concerns the establishment and maintenance of a relationship with the community from which investigators draw their samples. Enrolling participants in complex health behavior studies often requires the assistance of community leaders who want to see that their efforts bring rewards to the people they serve, not just to the research team. To that end, it is vitally important that health behavior researchers maintain regular contact with community liaisons and find ways to give something back to the community. For the research of the Health, Emotion, and Behavior Laboratory, we conduct focus groups and enlist community advisers to help design our research protocols and materials. These procedures not only offer the benefit of keeping community partners involved and invested in the work but also ensure that our materials are understandable to the sample population and that the research protocol maximizes our chances for successful data collection. We have frequent meetings with community advisers and other stakeholders in our research both prior to the start of a new study and at various points along the way. We occasionally sponsor parties, barbecues, and picnic lunches as ways to invite community members

to provide input to our team about their needs and reactions to our research efforts.

Community members develop deep resentment when investigators "use" them to collect their data but then, when the study has ended, leave nothing behind in the community. We often look for ways to give something back to our community collaborators. At a minimum, these could be health communication resources such as videotapes, posters, and brochures, along with public presentations of our findings. When we work at community-based clinics and agencies, we try to work out an arrangement whereby audiovisual and computer equipment used in the study can remain at the site permanently after the study has ended. Recently, we completed a project investigating whether the acquisition of computer literacy by parents of Head Start children would have a positive impact on their understanding of cancer prevention behaviors (by making various Web-based resources available to them). For this experiment, we built two Community Technology Centers, located them in Head Start programs, and then helped raise funds to sustain the centers after the grant supporting the research project had ended. Also, in this project, every participant who received computer training "graduated" with a refurbished computer to take home at no cost (Salovey, Mowad, et al., 2002).

Gaining access to communities involves first developing a partnership with community leaders and other gatekeepers. Social-health psychologists conducting field experiments should never assume that the potential scientific gain itself is sufficient inducement to encourage community collaboration. Community leaders often have felt the sting of past exploitation by well-meaning but self-absorbed researchers, and they are reluctant to engage in new scientific collaborations without assurances that there are immediate advantages to participating. Investigators should feel challenged to think creatively about inducements for community collaboration that are not limited to monetary payments to individual participants.

## PROFESSIONAL DEVELOPMENT

Mentorship and training experiences can equip the aspiring social-health psychologist to deal with the challenges involved in conducting health behavior research in the field and laboratory. We provide here a brief review of some of the kinds of training experiences available at the graduate and postdoctoral levels, as well as a glimpse into various employment options available to a person choosing to study at the intersection of health and social psychology.

### *Graduate School*

Given the relatively short duration of graduate training (often about 5 years), it is helpful for a student to be mindful of the need to engage in meaningful research right from the start of graduate school. Students can learn to appreciate the challenges involved in health behavior research by taking courses in departments in addition to psychology (e.g., public health, epidemiology, medical sociology) and by working with multiple mentors across subdisciplinary and disciplinary boundaries. This approach to graduate education allows students to develop a knowledge base drawing on multiple fields, learn to communicate with investigators from various theoretical traditions, and make connections with colleagues in other disciplines. It is often quite helpful to gain exposure to the expectations, methods, and problems of concern to investigators in health-related fields other than psychology. Graduate programs that emphasize a flexible training model (rather than a rigid set of required courses) and a funding policy that allows students to collaborate with multiple mentors (rather than one that encourages indentured servitude) are the kinds of educational settings in which one is more likely to develop the knowledge base and tools needed to conduct health behavior research. However, even students who find themselves in less flexible training programs can find ways to obtain mentorship across the traditional interfield boundaries, such as by asking "outsiders" to serve on dissertation committees.

### *Postdoctoral Training*

Postdoctoral fellowships offer a wonderful opportunity to gain exposure to health behavior research after completing a social psychology (or other) graduate program. There are numerous postdoctoral positions, many funded by NIH training and research grants, available in health psychology, public health, or medical school settings, and postdoctoral compensation has been rising considerably. In some cases, these positions may include opportunities for study in a related, nonpsychological field such as epidemiology or biostatistics. Graduate students can also write their own proposals for postdoctoral training, identifying a mentor and an institutional setting in advance and applying for relevant funding from the NIH. The positions provide young investigators the opportunity to develop knowledge and skills, as well as a more programmatic approach to research itself. For students who plan careers in medical schools (or other settings where grant money is necessary for survival), the experience of having written proposals as a postdoctoral fellow provides a leg up.

### *Employment*

Following graduate school and, usually, postdoctoral training, there are a variety of opportunities for social-health psychologists. For the academically inclined, one may choose to work in a "traditional" department of psychology where he or she likely will teach as well as conduct research. A psychologist focusing on health behavior can also choose to work in schools of medicine or public health. Positions not in departments of psychology may involve a more interdisciplinary and collaborative approach to research. There are usually (but not always) fewer teaching obligations, but there may be stronger expectations on faculty members to support their research (and their own salaries) with grant money.

Another option for students wishing to conduct health behavior research is a position in a government agency such as the National Institutes of Health (NIH), Centers for Disease Control and Prevention (CDC), or National Institute for Occupational Safety and Health (NIOSH). Many young scientists are not aware of the intramural research jobs available in this sector. Often government laboratories are well supported, and investigators can focus on research questions without undue concern about generating external grant funds. Finally, health behavior researchers can choose to work in the private sector in either for-profit industry settings or at various kinds of think tanks and policy centers such as the RAND Corporation. Many such positions involve substantial research components and an expectation that one will continue to publish in academic journals.

## INTEGRATING SOCIAL PSYCHOLOGY AND HEALTH BEHAVIOR

Although the study of social psychological principles and health behavior presents a set of unique challenges, it also offers an exciting array of rewards. Social psychology theory and public health research each contribute to the other; in fact, the National Institutes of Health have developed research funding streams explicitly to foster collaboration between these two fields. Many of the experiments we have presented establish the value of social psychological theory for understanding health behavior, but the study of health behavior can also influence the development of knowledge in social psychology. Studies in the health domain can stimulate thinking that leads to further theory building. For example, research with breast cancer patients showed

that positive, yet illusory, beliefs about the illness were associated with better mental health (Taylor, 1983). This set of findings led Taylor and Brown (1988) to develop a theory of positive illusions, which argues that people often hold unrealistically charitable views of themselves that prove adaptive.

Attribution theory in social psychology has also been refined through the study of health behavior. For instance, blaming oneself for an illness or injury is seen as likely to be detrimental to well-being, but the evidence actually is mixed. Therapists treating paralyzed accident victims reported better coping among those who blamed themselves for their condition than among those who gave a situational explanation or who did not have any clear attribution (Bulman & Wortman, 1977; Silver & Wortman, 1980). However, self-blame was not related to adjustment among women coping with breast cancer (Taylor, Lichtman, & Wood, 1984), and negative consequences were observed among women who blamed themselves after an abortion (Major & Cozzarelli, 1992; Major, Mueller, & Hildebrandt, 1985). These differences may be a product of different types of self-blame. If a person believes that his or her *character* led to a negative health outcome, then recovery may be impeded because such an explanation reduces hope; in contrast, assigning blame to one's *actions* may provide a sense of control over future events that leads to adaptive behavior changes (Timko & Janoff-Bulman, 1985).

We hope that this chapter has provided a sense of the numerous research opportunities available to aspiring social-health psychologists. Even though a young scientist may have to make some difficult choices concerning academic positions and training, it is possible to integrate the theories and skills of social psychology and the practical problem of understanding and influencing health behavior to the benefit of both disciplines and to the betterment of the public's health.

**REFERENCES**

Albarracín, D., Johnson, B. T., Fishbein, M., & Muellerleile, P. A. (2001). Theories of reasoned action and planned behavior as models of condom use: A meta-analysis. *Psychological Bulletin, 127,* 142-161.

Apanovitch, A. M., McCarthy, D., & Salovey, P. (2003). Using message framing to motivate HIV testing among low-income, ethnic minority women. *Health Psychology, 22,* 60-67.

Argyris, C., Putnam, R., & McLain, D. (1985). *Action science.* San Francisco: Jossey-Bass.

Banaji, M. R., & Crowder, R. G. (1989). The bankruptcy of everyday memory. *American Psychologist, 44,* 1185-1193.

Banks, S. M., Salovey, P., Greener, S., Rothman, A. J., Moyer, A., Beauvais, J., et al. (1995). The effects of message framing on mammography utilization. *Health Psychology, 14,* 178-184.

Bulman, R. J., & Wortman, C. B. (1977). Attributions of blame and coping in the "real world": Severe accident victims react to their lot. *Journal of Personality and Social Psychology, 35,* 351-363.

Catania, J. A., Kegeles, S. M., & Coates, T. J. (1990). Towards an understanding of risk behavior: An AIDS risk reduction model (ARRM). *Health Education Quarterly, 17,* 53-72.

Detweiler, J. B., Bedell, B. T., Salovey, P., Pronin, E., & Rothman, A. J. (1999). Message framing and sunscreen use: Gain-framed messages motivate beach-goers. *Health Psychology, 18,* 189-196.

Fishbein, M., Trafimow, D., Middlestadt, S. E., Helquist, M., Francis, C., & Eustace, M. A. (1995). Using a KAPB survey to identify determinants of condom use among sexually active adults from St. Vincent and the Grenadines. *Journal of Applied Social Psychology, 25,* 1-20.

Kahneman, D., & Tversky, A. (1979). Prospect theory: An analysis of decision under risk. *Econometrica, 47,* 263-292.

Kazdin, A. E. (1998). *Research design in clinical psychology* (3rd ed.). Needham Heights, MA: Allyn and Bacon.

Kelly, J. A., St. Lawrence, J. S., Diaz, Y. E., Stevenson, L. Y., Hauth, A. C., Brasfield, T. L., et al. (1991). HIV risk behavior reduction following intervention with key opinion leaders of population. *American Journal of Public Health, 84,* 1918-1922.

King, E., Rimer, B. K., Trock, B., Balshem, A., & Engstrom, P. (1990). How valid are mammography self-reports? *American Journal of Public Health, 80,* 1386-1388.

Lerman, C., Narod, S., Schulman, K., Hughes, C., Gomez-Caminero, A., Bonney, G., et al. (1996). BRCA1 testing in families with heredity breast-ovarian cancer: A prospective study of patient decision making and outcomes. *Journal of the American Medical Association, 275,* 1885-1892.

Lewin, K. (1946). Action research and minority problems. *Journal of Social Issues, 2,* 34-46.

Major, B., & Cozzarelli, C. (1992). Psychosocial predictors of adjustment to abortion. *Journal of Social Issues, 48,* 121-142.

Major, B., Mueller, P., & Hildebrandt, K. (1985). Attributions, expectations, and coping with abortion. *Journal of Personality and Social Psychology, 48,* 585-599.

Meyerowitz, B. E., & Chaiken, S. (1987). The effect of message framing on breast self-examination attitudes, intentions, and behavior. *Journal of Personality and Social Psychology, 52,* 500-510.

National Advisory Mental Health Council, Behavioral Science Workgroup. (2000). *Translating behavioral science into action* (NIH Publication No. 00-4699). Bethesda, MD: National Institutes of Health.

Neisser, U. (1978). Memory: What are the important questions? In M. M. Gruneberg, P. E. Morris, & R. N. Sykes (Eds.), *Practical aspects of memory* (pp. 3-24). London: Academic Press.

Pizarro, J., Schneider, T. R., & Salovey, P. (2002). A source of error in self-reports of Pap test utilization. *Journal of Community Medicine, 57,* 351-356.

Prochaska, J. O., DiClemente, C. C., & Norcross, J. C. (1992). In search of how people change: Applications to addictive behaviors. *American Psychologist, 47,* 1102-1114.

Rothman, A. J., Martino, S. C., Bedell, B. T., Detweiler, J. B., & Salovey, P. (1999). The systematic influence of gain- and loss-framed messages on interest in and use of different types of health behavior. *Personality and Social Psychology Bulletin, 25,* 1355-1369.

Rothman, A. J., & Salovey, P. (1997). Shaping perceptions to motivate healthy behavior: The role of message framing. *Psychological Bulletin, 121,* 3-19.

Sadava, S. W. (1997). Applied social psychology: An introduction. In S. W. Sadava & D. R. McCreary (Eds.), *Applied social psychology* (pp. 1-9). Upper Saddle River, NJ: Prentice Hall.

Salovey, P., Mowad, L., Edlund, D., Pizarro, J., Williams, P., & Moret, M. E. (2002). *Community technology centers for Head Start parents and families: Bridging the digital divide by increasing computer and health literacy* (Final report, subcontract N02-CO-01040–75, National Cancer Institute). Bethesda, MD: National Institutes of Health.

Salovey, P., Rothman, A. J., & Rodin, J. (1998). Health behavior. In D. T. Gilbert, S. T. Fiske, & G. Lindzey (Eds.), *The handbook of social psychology* (4th ed., Vol. 2, pp. 633-683). New York: McGraw-Hill.

Schneider, T. R., Salovey, P., Apanovitch, A. M., Pizarro, J., McCarthy, D., Zullo, J., et al. (2001). The effects of message framing and ethnic targeting on mammography use among low-income women. *Health Psychology, 20,* 256-266.

Schneider, T. R., Salovey, P., Pallonen, U., Mundorf, N., Smith, N. F., & Steward, W. T. (2001). Visual and auditory message framing effects on tobacco smoking. *Journal of Applied Social Psychology, 31,* 667-682.

Silver, R. L., & Wortman, C. B. (1980). Coping with undesirable life events. In J. Garber & M. E. P. Seligman (Eds.), *Human helplessness: Theory and applications* (pp. 279-340). New York: Academic Press.

Taylor, S. E. (1983). Adjustment to threatening events: A theory of cognitive adaptation. *American Psychologist, 38,* 1161-1173.

Taylor, S. E. (1984). The developing field of health psychology. In A. Baum, S. E. Taylor, & J. E. Singer (Eds.), *Handbook of psychology and health* (Vol. 4, pp. 1-22). Hillsdale, NJ: Lawrence Erlbaum.

Taylor, S. E., & Brown, J. D. (1988). Illusion and well-being: A social psychological perspective on mental health. *Psychological Bulletin, 110,* 193-210.

Taylor, S. E., Lichtman, R. R., & Wood, J. V. (1984). Attributions, beliefs about control, and adjustment to breast cancer. *Journal of Personality and Social Psychology, 46,* 489-502.

Thompson, S. C., Anderson, K., Freedman, D., & Swan, J. (1996). Illusions of safety in a risky world: A study of college students' condom use. *Journal of Applied Social Psychology, 26,* 189-210.

Timko, C., & Janoff-Bulman, R. (1985). Attributions, vulnerability, and psychological adjustment: The case of breast cancer. *Health Psychology, 4,* 521-544.

Tversky, A., & Kahneman, D. (1981). The framing of decisions and the psychology of choice. *Science, 211,* 453-458.

Weinstein, N. D., Rothman, A. J., & Sutton, S. R. (1998). Stage theories of health behavior: Conceptual and methodological issues. *Health Psychology, 17,* 290-299.

Women's Health Initiative. (2002). Risks and benefits of estrogen plus progestin in healthy postmenopausal women: Principal results from the Women's Health Initiative randomized controlled trial. *Journal of the American Medical Association, 288,* 366-368.

## CHAPTER 21

# Research Methods of Micro Organizational Behavior

LEIGH THOMPSON

*Kellogg School of Management, Northwestern University*

MARY KERN

*Kellogg School of Management, Northwestern University*

DENISE LEWIN LOYD

*Kellogg School of Management, Northwestern University*

Micro organizational behavior (micro OB) and social psychology have shared a strong and fruitful relationship that has been gaining in strength for many years. There are several reasons for social psychologists and micro OB researchers to better understand this blossoming bond between the two fields. First, micro OB is a close theoretical and empirical cousin to social psychology. Micro OB methods rely on many principles of social psychology while exhibiting some important differences. Second, micro OB research has been dramatically on the rise. The behavioral side of management has taken center stage as

businesses look beyond the numbers to issues such as leadership and motivation to understand successful organizations. Finally, social psychologists and micro OB researchers inform one another's research. There is ample room for fruitful collaboration between social psychologists and micro OB researchers, and a better understanding of micro OB helps make this collaboration easier.

The purpose of this chapter is to provide the reader with a top-down tour of the key theoretical, empirical, and methodological questions in micro OB research and how they are addressed from a design standpoint. We begin by conceptualizing where micro OB

AUTHORS' NOTE: All authors contributed equally to the writing of this chapter. Thompson is listed as first author in keeping with the norms of this volume. The authors would like to thank Dawn Iacobucci for her help in statistical analysis.

falls within the general field of organizational behavior (OB). We follow with a brief comparison of micro OB to social psychology. Next, we trace the development of a micro OB research project employing an experimental methodology. We then discuss the three most common types of methodologies in micro OB research, focusing on two primary considerations: the research site (classroom, field, or laboratory) and the nature of the research design (correlational, experimental, or qualitative). In that section, we also identify some of the most important methodological challenges faced by researchers in the field. Finally, we attempt to dispel some of the more common myths held about micro OB research.

## RELATIONSHIP OF MICRO OB TO ORGANIZATIONAL RESEARCH

Within fields that focus on organizational phenomena, micro OB is closest to human resources (HR) and organizational development (OD). All three areas examine individual and group behavior within organizations. HR and OD are concerned with organizational concepts, models, and interventions, and are more applied and focused in their scope. Micro OB, in contrast, generally relies on a more multidisciplinary approach that leads to more theoretical, rather than practical, contributions to the organizations literature.

OB examines the behavior of individuals, groups, organizations, and groups of organizations using psychological, sociological, and economic theoretical perspectives. Just as social psychology research can be parsed into intra-individual processes (attitudes; cognition) and interpersonal processes, OB usually is parsed into macro and micro factions. Macro OB draws more heavily from sociological theories and examines organizational issues with less emphasis on the individual actors and more on structure, rules, and

institutions. Micro OB, which is the focus of this chapter, draws more heavily from psychological theories with greater attention to individual, dyadic, and group processes.

## COMPARISON OF MICRO OB TO SOCIAL PSYCHOLOGY

A cursory review of the textbooks used in micro OB and social psychology reveal some important similarities as well as differences between micro OB and its close cousin, social psychology. We recently conducted a small-scale analysis of the chapters in four leading OB textbooks—*Understanding and Managing Organizational Behavior* (George & Jones, 2002), *Organizational Behavior* (Hellriegel, Slocum, & Woodman, 2001), *Organizational Behavior* (McShane & Von Glinow, 2000), and *Organization Behavior: A Management Challenge* (Stroh, Northcraft, & Neale, 2002)—and four leading social psychology textbooks—*Social Psychology* (Aronson, Wilson, & Akert, 1999), *Social Psychology* (Brehm, Kassin, & Fein, 2002), *Social Psychology* (Myers, 1999), and *Social Psychology* (Taylor, Peplau, & Sears, 2000). The analysis revealed that micro OB and social psychology researchers cover many of the same topic areas; however, they often do so with different levels of emphasis. Three areas of high emphasis for both fields were perceptions, attitudes, and team and group behavior. There were four notable areas of varying emphasis. First, micro OB focuses more heavily on power and politics than social psychology. Second, micro OB examines learning more than does social psychology. Third, micro OB examines leadership more than does social psychology. Finally, and perhaps most important, micro OB stresses outcome and performance measures that have organizational relevance (e.g., joint gains in negotiation or team quality in decision making), whereas social psychology places more emphasis on process or outcome measures at an individual level.

## The Key Factor Distinguishing Micro OB From Social Psychology

The key distinction between micro OB and social psychology research is the emphasis on organizational context. The organizational context, we argue, is (or should be) present in most studies of micro OB. The nature of the context (in terms of theoretical modeling and empirical operationalizations) can take one of three forms. The researcher can choose to operationalize the context as a key independent variable or a key dependent variable, or it can be omnipresent. This decision is based largely on the research question, the design and setting of the study, and the researcher's objective interest. These three features are not mutually exclusive and may be challenging to tease apart. The critical factor for micro OB researchers is that the organization be present in some component of the research.

### Key Independent Variable

In many studies, some feature of the larger business organization or context is manipulated or varied across conditions. For example, Phillips (1999) manipulated independent variables including whether the team leader received feedback about a subordinate's prior judgments. Durham, Knight, and Locke (1997) varied the role of the leader (whether a "coordinator" or "commander") in the team.

### Key Dependent Variable

In this type of research, the main dependent variable is how the individual makes an organizationally relevant decision or how the organization itself responds. Makiney and Levy's (1998) investigation of factors affecting supervisors' performance judgments is an example of this use of organizational context.

As another example, Arunachalam and Dilla (1995) examined accuracy and performance of negotiators in small group negotiations.

### Omnipresence

In many studies, the larger organization context is an omnipresent part of the situation. This omnipresence need not be explicit: It may instead be implied. Explicit omnipresence exists in micro OB studies conducted within the organization. An example of this is Sutton's (1991) study of norms of expressed emotions at work, in which the data were collected within a bill collection organization. Implied omnipresence is used in studies set in the laboratory or classroom. Using an organizational setting in these cases largely has the effect of lending situational realism to the context for the reader and experimental realism to the situation for the research participant. One example of this use of context is Weingart, Bennett, and Brett's (1993) study of the effects of issue consideration and motivational orientation on group negotiation process and outcome. The task was a multi-issue group negotiation in which each participant was a representative of a store that was interested in opening a joint market. These two examples show how the organizational context can both be operationalized as independent and/or dependent variables and be omnipresent simultaneously.

## RESEARCH PROJECT DEVELOPMENT IN MICRO OB

The development of a research project in micro OB is similar to that in social psychology in many ways, and consequently, this section may seem familiar to social psychologists. Nevertheless, we felt it appropriate to highlight key differences between micro OB and social psychology and to assist those less familiar with the process in general. The steps

**Table 21.1**   Model of the Development of a
Research Project in Micro OB

| Step | Task |
| --- | --- |
| 1 | Problem in real world stimulates unresolved question |
| 2 | Researcher reformulates the real world problem into a testable research question |
| 3 | Researcher consults theory to derive hypotheses |
| 4 | Researcher devises study to test hypotheses |
| 5 | Data analysis and results |
| 6 | Conclusions: theoretical and prescriptive |
| 7 | Application |

involved in the development of a micro OB research project are outlined in Table 21.1. We discuss each step in general terms, and to further illustrate their progress we walk through each step using an example from an article published in *Organizational Behavior and Human Decision Processes* (*OBHDP*), Thompson and Hastie's (1990) study of social perceptions in negotiation.

In their study, Thompson and Hastie (1990) addressed how misperceptions of another party's interests in negotiation can lead to suboptimal outcomes. We selected this particular work as our example for three primary reasons. First, it is representative of the most common methodology used in micro OB research, the laboratory experiment. Second, it has been identified as one of the ten most highly cited articles published in *OBHDP* (one of the top micro OB journals) between 1988 and 1997 (Weber, 1998). Finally, because one of us was the author, we could dig deeper than the published article to understand the research process. In this article, the organizational context takes on the role of the key dependent variable. The variables examined are a performance measure

(joint gains in the negotiation) and a process measure (judgment error).

## Step 1: Problem in Real World Stimulates Unresolved Question

Often in micro OB, a problem in an organization ("the real world") intrigues a researcher, who then wants to better understand it. Thompson and Hastie were interested in studying negotiations because of the overwhelming qualitative evidence that most people view negotiation as a "fixed–pie" enterprise, such that one party's interests are directly opposed to another party's interests (Fisher & Ury, 1981). Additionally, negotiations are important to business students, employers, and employees for three main reasons. First, people regularly engage in negotiations in personal and business contexts. Second, casual observations indicate that many people find negotiating a challenging endeavor. Third, even seasoned negotiators may fail to optimize outcomes in a negotiating situation. Thompson and Hastie (1990) noticed that when people negotiate in organizational contexts, they often reach inefficient solutions that are not satisfying to either party. The researchers wanted to understand if poor outcomes result from fixed-pie perceptions.

## Step 2: Researcher Reformulates the Real World Problem Into a Testable Research Question

Through a process of refining the possible answers to the question, the researcher formulates a testable research question. Thompson and Hastie (1990) refined their initial question of whether misunderstandings between negotiating parties lead to suboptimal outcomes. Their research question evolved into whether accurate judgment of the other party's position leads to "more mutually beneficial negotiation outcomes" (Thompson & Hastie, 1990, p. 100).

## Step 3: Researcher Consults Theory to Derive Hypotheses

The researcher then examines existing literature and determines the theories that relate to the research question. This process also helps the researcher to operationalize the independent and dependent variables. Thompson and Hastie (1990) built on the negotiation research literature that used the behavioral decision theory perspective. This perspective emphasizes negotiators as decision makers who analyze and judge the behavior of their negotiation partner to predict future events and consequences of the negotiation. Thompson and Hastie hypothesized (a) that more accurate judgments of the other party's priorities (relative importance of an issue) should lead to more mutually beneficial negotiation outcomes and (b) that more accurate judgments of the other party's preferences for specific issues might reveal some areas in which negotiators have purely compatible interests and therefore lead to more mutually beneficial negotiation outcomes.

## Step 4: Researcher Devises Study to Test Hypotheses

The development of the study is a crucial step, and there are two critical elements, the research setting and the design. Common research settings in micro OB are the classroom, field, and laboratory, with the laboratory being the most frequently used (Thompson, Loyd, & Kern, 2003). Common research designs in micro OB are correlational, experimental, and qualitative. The design and setting are determined by many factors, including whether the researcher intends to make causal statements and the access the researcher has to potential participants. (These issues will be discussed in

further detail in the following section, dealing specifically with methodology.) Thompson and Hastie (1990) utilized the laboratory experiment, in which participants are brought to a controlled environment and subjected to various conditions driven by the research question. Thompson and Hastie tested their hypotheses using two experiments, one related to each hypothesis.

In Study 1, Thompson and Hastie measured negotiators' judgment of the other parties' priorities for the negotiated issues to understand whether accurate judgment leads to better outcomes. Participants were undergraduate students assigned to either a buyer or seller role in a negotiation for a car. They negotiated on four issues: financing, tax, warranty, and delivery date. The roles were designed such that the buyer and seller had opposing priorities (i.e., if the seller wanted low financing, the buyer wanted high financing). Dyads were created by pairing buyers and sellers and placing them into one of three conditions: judgment (judge the other party's interests before, during, and after negotiation), think aloud (talk aloud spontaneously about the negotiation before, during, and after negotiation), and control (no interruption of the negotiation). Following the negotiation, all participants completed a questionnaire and made judgments about the preferences of their negotiation partner.

In Study 2, Thompson and Hastie examined judgments of interest compatibility (i.e., do negotiators recognize when their interests are purely compatible with those of the other party?). The participants were MBA students who assumed the roles of buyer and seller in a car negotiation. The negotiation was more complex, and negotiators were given more time to negotiate. Most notably, as in Study 1, the task concerned potential for a mutually beneficial agreement. Of the eight total issues, four differed in importance to the negotiators, two were compatible (they shared priorities), and two were incompatible (their priorities were opposed). In this study, participants prepared by reading their role materials and then engaged in a face-to-face negotiation with the other party, without any interruption. Following the negotiation, they were asked to complete judgment accuracy measures that assessed their insight into the opponent's interests and preferences.

### Step 5: Data Analysis and Results

The statistical tools used by micro OB researchers and social psychologists to analyze data are primarily the same, however, the lenses through which these researchers view data differ substantially. Whereas micro OB uses a magnifying glass to examine more behavioral phenomena often involving a real world analog, social psychology often uses a microscope to investigate cognitive, affective, and behavioral processes, many of which may occur out at a preconscious level.

Thompson and Hastie (1990) examined group outcomes (joint profits) as well as individual outcomes. They found support for both of their main hypotheses. Recall that the key prediction was that insight into the opposing party's true interests would lead to more effective negotiation performance, as measured by the profitability of deals made. As predicted in Study 1, negotiators who were less accurate in their judgments of the other party's preferences had lower joint outcomes at the end of the negotiation. Study 2 revealed that a large percentage of negotiators do not recognize when their interests are completely compatible with those of the other party and consequently often settle for inefficient outcomes. Thompson and Hastie referred to this as the "incompatibility effect."

### Step 6: Conclusions: Theoretical and Prescriptive

When drawing conclusions, outlining the practical applications of the research is acutely important in micro OB. Whereas practical issues often appear as an afterthought in other fields, in micro OB they are central. *OBHDP*'s online information for authors states that the journal editors "place a premium on articles that make fundamental contributions to *applied* [italics added] psychology and at the same time are anchored in phenomena relevant to organizations" (*Organizational Behavior and Human Decision Processes*, 2002, ¶2). In contrast, only one of the three independently edited sections of the *Journal of Personality and Social Psychology* (JPSP) mentions interest in research with applications to applied psychology (Journal of Personality and Social Psychology, n.d., ¶4).

Thompson and Hastie's work provides empirical support for some of the theoretical predictions of negotiation researchers using behavioral decision theories. In addition, their work provides possible prescriptions for negotiators. Observing that negotiators who learned more about the other party's interests early in the negotiation fared better during the negotiation, Thompson and Hastie concluded that negotiators should seek information from the other party early in the negotiation to improve their outcomes.

### Step 7: Application

In micro OB, the turnaround time between the publication of an article and the practical application of its content is rather short. The three primary audiences for the information gleaned from micro OB research are scholars, practitioners, and students. Scholars learn of the research through their social networks, academic conferences, and journals. Practitioners may read about the research in the popular press or may hear of the work at industry conferences. They can then incorporate the suggestions into their organizational practices. Students generally are exposed to the findings when they are incorporated into the curriculum of business school OB classes.

For example, negotiations research commonly is disseminated via teaching modules in negotiation courses. The students then take that information and incorporate it into their other classes, workplaces, and personal lives.

We have discussed in detail the research development process in micro OB, specifically as it relates to the laboratory experiment methodology. This methodology, however, is only one of several used in micro OB. Next, we will discuss in more detail the common methodologies in micro OB and some of the challenges they pose for researchers.

## COMMON METHODOLOGIES IN MICRO OB RESEARCH

We recently conducted a thorough review of micro OB research methodologies in articles published in the 5-year period from 1996 to 2000, in the field's leading journal, *OBHDP* (Thompson, Loyd, et al., 2003). Our analysis of the micro OB literature revealed that like social psychology, lab research is most common (63%), followed by classroom research (12%) and then field research (6%) (Thompson, Loyd, et al., 2003). Most studies (66%) used between 26 and 150 participants, and the majority of participants (85%) were students (Thompson, Loyd, et al., 2003). Our analysis of these 263 articles (which included 497 studies/experiments) could be loosely categorized along two different dimensions: setting (classroom, field, or laboratory) and design (correlation, experimental, or qualitative).

### Setting

Setting refers to where the research takes place. The classroom setting is most often the physical classroom where the participants (i.e., the students) interact as a class. In addition, the classroom setting can be extended to virtual classrooms or even to data collected as part of a homework assignment outside class. The classroom is a natural setting for the students that also can be manipulated by the researcher. However, this control has restrictions, such as when the class is held and the quantity and demographics of the student population.

The field setting is a natural setting in which data are collected, and in micro OB the field normally refers to an organization. This setting has the least amount of control in that the groups and relationships observed exist outside the research study and often cannot be manipulated. The field, however, is not contrived and provides the opportunity to examine phenomena as they are experienced in their real setting.

The laboratory setting is a controlled yet contrived environment. It is a location that has been created specifically for the purpose of collecting data. In the lab, participants are acutely aware that they are being observed and are part of an experiment, thereby reflecting the less natural setting.

### Design

Design refers to the degree of control the researcher has and the kinds of conclusions that can be drawn from the data. Like social psychology, micro OB uses standard correlational and experimental designs. Correlational design is concerned with relationships between variables rather than causality. (See Mark and Reichardt, Chapter 12, this volume, for further discussion of correlational design.) The classic experimental design involves random assignment to conditions. Using the experimental design allows the researcher to draw causal conclusions. (Haslam and McGarty, Chapter 11, this volume, should be referred to for more extensive discussion of the experimental design methodology.) Unlike social psychology, however, micro OB also uses a qualitative approach, albeit rarely.

**Table 21.2** Methodologies in Micro OB Research

| | Setting | | |
|---|---|---|---|
| Design | Classroom | Field | Laboratory |
| Correlational | Correlational studies conducted in classroom | Correlational studies conducted in organization | Correlational studies conducted in lab |
| Experimental | Experiments in classes that use random assignment | Field experiments | Classic lab experiments |
| Qualitative | Qualitative study in a classroom | Qualitative study in an organization | Qualitative study in a lab |

Qualitative design is primarily descriptive in nature, and it draws from sociology for its methods. The researcher uses a case notes approach to document observations of the phenomenon of interest. There are no measurements or statistics, and no attempt at manipulation is made. Rather, qualitative research involves passive observation wherein the researcher engages in inductive inference (Glaser & Strauss, 1967).

These two dimensions, setting and design, can be crossed resulting in the nine methodologies identified in Table 21.2. Although each of the nine methodologies is distinct (i.e., each design could theoretically occur in each setting), some are more common than others. It would be convenient to have an algorithm that indicated which setting or design was appropriate to test a specific hypothesis, but we have no such luxury. In truth, there is considerable variation among researchers, who might choose different methodologies to study the same phenomena. We organize our discussion by focusing on the research setting and the methodological challenges posed to the researcher. Researchers need to consider all these factors when choosing which methodology is best for their particular research question. For purposes of exposition, we discuss each setting (i.e. classroom, field, and lab) separately, and the most common designs (i.e., correlational,

experimental, qualitative) within the discussion of setting.

### Classroom Setting

The use of the classroom as a setting for data collection has become increasingly common in micro OB research (Thompson, Loyd, et al., 2003). Business school classrooms provide fertile ground for theory testing and exploratory research. The experiment is the most often used design in the classroom setting, whereas qualitative and correlational designs are more rare.

A frequently cited example of the classroom setting and experimental design methodology is Gruenfeld, Mannix, Williams, and Neale's (1996) study of the effects of member familiarity and information distribution on group decision making. In this study, the organizational context is evident in both the key independent and dependent variables. The data were collected as part of an introductory organizational behavior business school course. The researchers drew on the benefits of the classroom setting in two main ways. First, because decision making is an integral part of most introductory OB courses, the research is directly tied to the course content, thereby remaining faithful to the course and leveraging off the already engaged students. Second, the basis for group composition in this study was member familiarity. There were three, three-person group conditions: groups in which all members were strangers, groups in which all members were familiar, and groups with two familiar members and one stranger. It is natural in the classroom setting for certain students to be familiar with one another and for others to have little or no contact, so the researchers capitalized on this naturally occurring classroom phenomenon. The experiment involved groups making a decision about the most likely suspect in a murder mystery. Gruenfeld et al. (1996) also manipulated the information in the groups such that information was either fully shared or partially shared. They found that groups composed of all strangers were more likely to select the correct suspect when the information was fully shared, but groups composed of all familiar members or two familiar members and one stranger were more likely to identify the correct suspect when the information was only partially shared.

There are a number of advantages for the micro OB researcher using the classroom setting for data collection. First, the data generally are easy to collect. The logistics are easy to manage because the class has a regular time and place for meeting. Second, the participants are highly engaged and involved in the activity. This engagement is due in part to the research topic being directly related to the course material. Finally, there is the potential for a feedback loop from students to researcher (i.e., professor) (Argyris, 1976). The professor often debriefs the students explicitly, and this provides an opportunity to obtain critical feedback from the students, which can then be used to further refine the study.

There are two primary challenges to researchers using the classroom setting. First, the research question may be compromised somewhat by the demands of the classroom. For example, the classroom may limit the ability to do extensive process observations,

and deception in the classroom can be problematic. Second, the classroom creates more concern with contamination of conditions (Cook & Campbell, 1979). The researcher may find it more difficult in the classroom setting to keep the various conditions hidden from the participants, both because of issues of physical proximity and because of the engagement and interest of the participants. (See Cook and Groom, Chapter 2, this volume, for further discussions of threats to validity.)

## Field Setting

The field setting is less frequently used in micro OB. Moreover, it decreased in popularity in empirical articles published in *OBHDP*, from 27% in 1976–1980 to only 6% in 1996–2000 (Thompson, Loyd, et al., 2003). The field setting is most often paired with qualitative or correlational designs. The use of an experimental design in the field is quite rare in micro OB.

A classic example of a micro OB study using the field setting and qualitative design methodology is Sutton's (1991) examination of norms of expressing emotions at work using a sample of bill collectors. In this study, Sutton engaged the organizational context with explicit omnipresence. Using a theory of expressed emotions, Sutton's study examined coping mechanisms and organizational rewards for controlling emotions at work. Sutton used seven qualitative methods to obtain data: interaction with an informant, training as a bill collector, working as a bill collector, conducting focus group interviews, conducting interviews with supervisors, directly observing the work behavior of bill collectors responsible for collecting overdue credit card payments, and reviewing written materials about the corporation (e.g., mission statements, financial reports). Sutton analyzed the data by reviewing and summarizing the data and extracting themes related to norms of expressed emotion in the organization. He found that collectors in this organization are "selected, socialized, and rewarded for following the general norm of conveying urgency (high arousal with a hint of irritation) to debtors" (Sutton, 1991, p. 245).

MacKenzie, Podsakoff, and Fetter's (1991) examination of an insurance firm is an example of the field setting and correlational design methodology. They examined how "organizational citizenship behaviors" (OCBs) and objective performance affect managerial performance evaluations as much as by surveying insurance agency managers about agents' OCB behaviors and productivity. They also obtained objective measures of agents' performance from company records. Using primarily confirmatory factor analysis (CFA), they found that the performance evaluations were affected as much by OCBs as by objective performance.

The greatest advantages to the researcher using the field setting are the high external validity and the fact that participants usually are highly motivated and engaged. The field is a natural setting in which interactions are not contrived. This lack of manipulation lends a high degree of external validity to data collected in this environment. Researchers must be aware, however, that their presence can change the nature of this atmosphere and must take steps to be as unobtrusive as possible. For some, this means becoming a part of the setting (i.e., an employee); for others, this means making observations from an unobserved vantage point. In an effort to gain access, the researcher may emphasize the knowledge the organization can gain through the research results. The research participants (e.g., executives, managers, employees) generally are motivated to participate for the same reasons.

Obtaining access to the field site, however, can be a challenge for the researcher. This can be managed in a number of ways. First, some large corporations sponsor grants for researchers to enter their organizations and conduct research. These grants, however, are not easy to obtain, and the organization itself may have a research agenda into which the experimenter's own topic must fall. One company that has made a corporation-wide effort to invite scholars into their field is Citigroup (www.citigroup.com). For several years, Citigroup placed a call for proposals and awarded grants to researchers that would allow scholars access to several types of organizational data. Contact sometimes can be established through former students or other business associates. Sutton (1991) noted that he obtained access after a former student was hired as a management trainee at the bill collecting organization. Another popular route for gaining access is via a business relationship between the company and the scholar. It is very common for business school professors to offer consulting and training services to companies, and part of this training and consulting may involve obtaining access to company employees.

## Laboratory Setting

The laboratory setting is, by far, the most common setting for micro OB research, and the experiment is the most common design within the lab setting. Pure qualitative or correlational laboratory research tends to be quite rare. However, laboratory studies that utilize the experimental design often report descriptive observational data to support their claims and add to the richness of the research.

A classic example of the micro OB lab experiment is Staw's (1976) work on escalation of commitment. Staw incorporated the organization as both an implied omnipresent condition and as a key independent variable. In this investigation, undergraduate business students played the role of a financial vice president for the "Adams and Smith Company" making a decision about the allocation of funds for a research and development project. The participant had to select which one of two divisions should receive additional funding. Staw manipulated the perceived level of personal responsibility into "high responsibility" (participant makes an initial decision) and "low responsibility" (other makes initial decision). Staw also manipulated the consequences of the initial allotment of resources such that the department that received funding improved its performance (positive consequences) or did not improve its performance (negative consequences). Staw found an interaction between the decision consequences and the level of personal responsibility such that "individuals committed the greatest amount of resources to a previously chosen course of action when they were personally responsible for negative consequences" (Staw, 1976, p. 27).

In the discussions of the field and classroom settings, we articulated many of the challenges researchers encounter; however, in the laboratory setting, we see no real differences between micro OB and social psychology in relation to their methods and challenges. The laboratory is a setting with which social psychologists are intimately familiar, so we will not address the methodological challenges here. We will, however, conclude the chapter by challenging some commonly held assumptions about micro OB that we consider to be myths.

## CONCLUSION

Earlier, we made the point that there is an ongoing relationship between social psychology and micro OB. Increasingly, many young social psychologists have been joining business schools and bringing their backgrounds and knowledge to bear on the kinds of questions raised in micro OB research. Although this increased interaction has made the business school environment more transparent to

social psychologists, some myths about the enterprise remain. We will discuss three of the major myths here.

The first myth is that business schools are not a place where behavioral research is conducted, but rather a place where only formal, theoretical modeling is done. We believe this myth exists for two primary reasons. First, when people think about business school research, they think first and foremost about model-based, normative research (such as formal, theoretical modeling). The prominence of finance, accounting, and strategy departments within many business schools fuels this perception. Second, in a typical psychology department, the ratio of faculty to laboratory space approaches 1:1. In business schools, there may not be a dedicated behavioral lab, and if one exists, it is most likely shared space. In fact, contrary to the myth, behavioral research does take place in micro OB. Micro OB researchers conduct behavioral studies both within laboratories and classrooms.

The second myth is that micro OB research is not as theoretical as research done in social psychology. Although micro OB is more concerned with the applicability of research than is social psychology, the research is grounded in theory. Micro OB researchers have made strong theoretical contributions to the literature in many areas, including decision making, negotiations, and groups and teams.

The third myth is that teaching is more difficult in micro OB than in psychology. There is an image of MBA students as a den of hungry wolves, lying in wait to devour the professor, who dares not discuss research and is limited to bulleted take-away points. The truth is that micro OB courses, including those on negotiations and managing groups and teams, are among the most popular in business schools. One reason for this is the use of experiential learning exercises (often created for research purposes) that engage the students.

The close theoretical and empirical relationship between micro OB and social psychology reveals itself in many ways. Increasingly, teams of collaborators composed of micro OB faculty and social psychologists are engaged in joint research. Frequently, in the course of collaboration, a question arises as to where to place the research article. More often than not, the manuscript could just as easily appear in a micro OB journal as in a social psychology journal. Some of the factors that might be considered when making such decisions include the career aspirations of the researchers (if a young PhD student in social psychology desires to enter the business school market, it behooves him or her to publish in the field) and the proportion of OB and social psychology citations in the articles (if the balance is tipped toward more social psychological studies, then the article might find a more comfortable home in a psychology journal).

Our belief is that the methodological quality of micro OB research is made stronger by virtue of its connection to social psychological research. Many of the most important theoretical and methodological advances in micro OB research can be traced directly to social psychological theory and methods. For example, the intense focus on cognitive processes, biases, and judgment that began in social-cognitive psychology continues as a major area of research in micro OB. Recently, micro OB has moved decidedly to the study of affective and emotional processes, again following the theoretical lead of social psychology.

A critic might argue that micro OB research is simply diluted social psychological research. We disagree. As noted in our introduction, micro OB research has distinguished itself from its tremendously innovative and rigorous cousin, social psychology, in several important ways. Probably among the most important of these distinctions is the strong presence of the organization in micro OB studies. Even in the most controlled laboratory experiments in micro OB, there is a clear sense that the individual is part of an organizational system or that a key variable has organizational relevance, thus creating meaningful analogs to real work contexts. Additionally, micro OB research, with its applied focus, suggests thoughtful prescriptions for organizations.

Our conjecture is that the most distinctive feature of micro OB research (i.e., its incorporation of the organizational context) may very well be the one least explored by social psychological research. In the spirit of Brewer's (1991) theory of optimal distinctiveness, we believe that micro OB research has achieved an equilibrium. Micro OB is similar enough to its cousin, social psychology, to share in a "social category" of research, yet micro OB has differentiated itself in its focus and motivations. Micro OB and social psychology exist as two close cousins, yet micro OB has left its ancestral home and has firmly established roots in its own fertile soil.

## REFERENCES

Argyris, C. (1976). Single-loop and double-loop models in research on decision making. *Administrative Science Quarterly, 21,* 363-375.

Aronson, E., Wilson, T., & Akert, R. (1999). *Social psychology* (3rd ed.). Upper Saddle River, NJ: Prentice Hall.

Arunachalam, V., & Dilla, W. N. (1995). Judgment accuracy and outcomes in negotiation: A causal modeling analysis of decision-aiding effects. *Organizational Behavior and Human Decision Processes, 61,* 289-304.

Brehm, S. S., Kassin, S. M., & Fein, S. (2002). *Social psychology* (5th ed.). Boston: Houghton Mifflin.

Brewer, M. B. (1991). The social self: On being the same and different at the same time. *Personality and Social Psychology Bulletin, 17,* 475-482.

Cook, T. D., & Campbell, D. T. (1979). *Quasi-experimentation: Design and analysis issues for field settings.* Boston: Houghton Mifflin.

Durham, C. C., Knight, D., & Locke, E. A. (1997). Effects of leader role, team-set goal difficulty, efficacy, and tactics on team effectiveness. *Organizational Behavior and Human Decision Processes, 72,* 203-231.

Fisher, R., & Ury, W. (1981). *Getting to yes.* Boston: Houghton Mifflin.

George, J., & Jones, G. (2002). *Understanding and managing organizational behavior* (3rd ed.). Upper Saddle River, NJ: Prentice Hall.

Glaser, B. G., & Strauss, A. L. (1967). *The discovery of grounded theory: Strategies for qualitative research.* London: Weidenfeld and Nicholson.

Gruenfeld, D. H., Mannix, E., Williams, K. Y., & Neale, M. A. (1996). Group composition and decision making: How member familiarity and information distribution affect process and performance. *Organizational Behavior and Human Decision Processes, 67,* 1-15.

Hellriegel, D., Slocum, J. W., Jr., & Woodman, R. W. (2001). *Organizational behavior* (9th ed.). Mason, OH: South-Western/Thomson Learning.

Journal of Personality and Social Psychology, Description of Content. (n.d.). *Journal description.* Retrieved March 3, 2002, from http://www.apa.org/journals/psp/description.html

MacKenzie, S. B., Podsakoff, P. M., & Fetter, R. (1991). Organizational citizenship behavior and objective productivity as determinants of managerial evaluations of salespersons' performance. *Organizational Behavior and Human Decision Processes, 50,* 123-150.

Makiney, J. D., & Levy, P. E. (1998). The influence of self-ratings versus peer ratings on supervisors' performance judgments. *Organizational Behavior and Human Decision Processes, 74,* 212-228.

McShane, S., & Von Glinow, M. A. (2000). *Organizational behavior.* New York: Irwin/McGraw-Hill.

Myers, D. G. (1999). *Social psychology* (6th ed.). New York: McGraw-Hill.

*Organizational Behavior and Human Decision Processes.* (2002, January 11). *Information for authors.* Retrieved March 3, 2002, from http://www.academicpress.com/www/journal/ob/obifa.htm

Phillips, J. M. (1999). Antecedents of leader utilization of staff input in decision-making teams. *Organizational Behavior and Human Decision Processes, 77,* 215-242.

Staw, B. M. (1976). Knee-deep in the big muddy: A study of escalating commitment to a chosen course of action. *Organizational Behavior and Human Decision Processes, 16,* 27-44.

Stroh, L. K., Northcraft, G. B., & Neale, M. A. (2002). *Organization behavior: A management challenge* (3rd ed.). Mahwah, NJ: Lawrence Erlbaum.

Sutton, R. I. (1991). Maintaining norms about expressed emotions: A case of bill collectors. *Administrative Science Quarterly, 36,* 245-268.

Taylor, S. E., Peplau, L. A., & Sears, D. O. (2000). *Social psychology* (10th ed.). Upper Saddle River, NJ: Prentice Hall.

Thompson, L., & Hastie, R. (1990). Social perception in negotiation. *Organizational Behavior and Human Decision Processes, 47,* 98-123.

Thompson, L., Loyd, D. L., & Kern, M. C. (2003). *Classroom research: Bridging pedagogy and research.* Unpublished manuscript, Kellogg School of Management, Northwestern University.

Weber, E. (1998). From performance to decision processes in 33 years: A history of organizational behavior and human decision processes under James C. Naylor. *Organizational Behavior and Human Decision Processes, 76,* 209-222.

Weingart, L., Bennett, R., & Brett, J. (1993). The impact of issues and motivational orientation on group negotiation process and outcome. *Journal of Applied Psychology, 78,* 504-517.

## CHAPTER 22

# Conducting Social Psychological Research in Educational Settings
## "Lessons We Learned in School"

JUDITH M. HARACKIEWICZ

*University of Wisconsin–Madison*

KENNETH E. BARRON

*James Madison University*

Some people become social psychologists because they want to change the world, and others enter the field because they are captivated by theoretical issues and basic research. The social activist depends on basic research, and the basic researcher often tries to extend theory and research into the real world. The trade-offs between basic and applied research are particularly salient in the area of education, because most of us are educators who are trying to change the world through our teaching. It makes sense that those of us doing research in the areas of social cognition, social influence, motivation, and group behavior (to name just a few topics with obvious educational implications) would see and appreciate the applications of our basic research to education. It also makes sense that some of us would want to understand the educational process more deeply.

Sometimes we end up collecting data in educational settings out of convenience, because students in our classes can be a captive population (at least when we can gain access to those populations). The most obvious example is the reliance on students in introductory psychology classes who earn extra credit in their classes in exchange for participation in research. In other cases, researchers begin by studying basic phenomena in the laboratory but then extend their research to include studies conducted in classes and become more focused on educational issues over time. For example, Rosenthal studied self-fulfilling prophecy effects in a number of different settings, beginning with basic experimental studies, then extended his work to include social interaction studies, rat labs, the workplace, and the classroom. It was his experimental demonstration of expectancy effects in an elementary school, reported in *Pygmalion in the Classroom* (Rosenthal & Jacobsen, 1966), that opened up a new line of educational research into the dynamics of teacher-pupil interactions (Rosenthal, 1987, 1991). As another example, Lepper, Greene, and Nisbett (1973) conducted a classic experimental study of self-perception and intrinsic motivation with preschool children in a university nursery school, then went on to conduct experimental studies of rewards and token economies in elementary school classrooms (Greene, Sternberg, & Lepper, 1978). Over time, Lepper has become more involved in educational policy, contributing articles on the importance of microcomputers in education (Lepper, 1985; Lepper & Gurtner, 1989).

Our own research concerns the effects of goals on motivation and performance, and we are interested in the goals that individuals set for themselves as well as the goals that can be suggested or assigned to individuals by other people. In particular, we have been interested in a class of goals known as achievement goals, which concern a person's reasons for engaging in an achievement-oriented activity. For example, people can pursue mastery goals, with a focus on learning and skill development, or performance goals, with a focus on performing well relative to others. Many theorists have adopted what we will term the *mastery goal perspective*, arguing that mastery goals are optimal for motivation and performance, whereas performance goals should have deleterious consequences (Ames, 1992; Dweck, 1986).

Our work on achievement goals started in the early 1990s. We began by using laboratory paradigms to examine the effects of experimentally manipulated mastery and performance goals on intrinsic motivation. One of the activities that we used was pinball games, and we had students play pinball under a mastery or performance goal. Contrary to the mastery goal perspective, our initial findings suggested that performance goals have some positive effects, especially for some individuals. These goals seemed to challenge our participants and get them excited about playing pinball. On the other hand, mastery goals proved optimal for other individuals and in other situations, and our findings suggested that goal effects might be more complex than implied by the mastery goal perspective (Harackiewicz & Elliot, 1993).

Over time, as we continued to document, replicate, and extend these experimental effects (see Harackiewicz, Barron, & Elliot, 1998, for a review), we too became interested in the educational implications of our findings and sought to extend our findings to educational issues. We would like to share our experiences as we made the transition from an experimental, laboratory-based research program to one that involved correlational studies of achievement goals conducted in college classrooms as well as longitudinal studies of college students' progression through their tertiary education. We should note that we haven't actually moved very far—from our labs in the basement to the lecture halls on the first floor of our building—but it has been a major transition for us, and we hope that our experience will inspire others to travel even farther. In addition, we will try to retrace our steps and discuss issues that a researcher can expect to face when moving into an educational setting.

## MOVING OUT OF THE LAB AND INTO THE CLASSROOM: CHOOSING THE SETTING

The first challenge that we faced was choosing the educational setting to study. Education is a lifelong process, and a researcher might be interested in programs ranging from preschool through graduate school, or from vocational training to adult education programs. In our own research, we were interested in extending our experimental work with college students to the real world of college education, so it made sense to conduct our studies in university lecture halls. Moreover, when we reviewed the achievement goal literature, we discovered that most researchers had worked in elementary and junior high settings, and we were surprised to find that not much goals research was being done in college settings. We therefore decided to focus on the college environment. We then decided to focus on a particular academic discipline—one in which we had some expertise and access—and decided to start our new program of research in introductory psychology classes.

The choice of educational setting has a number of implications for research design and procedures. Researchers may encounter logistical challenges in gaining access to appropriate populations. To start, a researcher needs to discuss research possibilities with educational administrators and must obtain permission to contact teachers and conduct research in that setting. The success of a project can depend on the cooperation of teachers and other staff who work with the students that the researcher wants to study, and it is critical to establish a good working relationship with them. Of course, the researcher will need to obtain the informed consent of the students themselves, and whenever research is conducted with minors, consent from parents or guardians must be obtained. This important requirement can pose logistical problems in terms of distributing and collecting consent forms. It is also important to check on the legal definition of a minor with the local institutional review board, because these legal definitions can vary in different parts of the country. For example, even with a study in a college setting, many entering college freshmen still may be under the legal age required for adult status and may require special consent procedures. Addressing all these logistical issues will take time, and our best advice is to plan ahead—really far ahead!

If a researcher only has experience studying students at his or her own university, it may seem daunting to gain access to participants outside the university. However, we can offer a few suggestions for getting started. To find preschool or elementary educational settings, we recommend talking with colleagues who already work with children (e.g., in developmental psychology or language research) for possible leads (see Pomerantz, Ruble, & Bolger, Chapter 18, this volume). They may have already established contacts and the precedent for conducting research at a particular school. Personal contacts can be invaluable; perhaps a teacher or administrator can facilitate access to a school. For example, the first author's mother was an English teacher in a public high school, and she allowed her daughter to collect her dissertation data in her classroom. Alternatively, we recommend contacting school superintendents and/or principals at individual schools to inquire about the possibilities for research and about the protocol to follow at the various institutions. Public schools in university towns are often besieged with requests from researchers and must limit access. One final tip is that it is sometimes easier to collect data in private schools, where there may be fewer researchers petitioning for access and less bureaucracy to negotiate. Of course, one possible downside of this strategy is that private schools may represent more specialized populations, limiting the generalizability of findings.

Even at the researcher's own university, access to students should not be taken for granted. It is important to discuss research possibilities with the chair of a department and the instructors of the courses in which the researcher hopes to collect data. The study needs to be approved by institutional review boards, and students must give their informed consent. To access academic records, explicit permission from students is required, and these issues should be discussed with the institutional review board. For example, once we became interested in studying achievement goals in introductory psychology classes, we discussed our plans with the chair of our department and the instructors of the class. In some projects, we collected data from students who participated in our research outside the actual classroom for extra credit, as part of the departmental research participation program. In other projects, we collected data in classes with the permission of instructors. In our longitudinal studies, we discussed access to student records with the university registrar's office. Each study required a different negotiation with departmental administrators and instructors.

## MOVING INTO THE CLASSROOM: CHOOSING A DESIGN

The next challenge we confronted was deciding what kind of research design would be adequate for testing our hypotheses about goal effects, and what kind of design might be feasible in this research context. It was clear what our independent variable was: achievement goals. But how should we study their effects in a college classroom? As we mentioned earlier, goals can be self-set or externally suggested; for example, a teacher might recommend that students try to master a new math technique, or students might adopt a mastery goal as they learn new math skills. Theorists have argued that self-set and external achievement goals should have similar effects, and many have discussed these types of goals interchangeably. We suspect that there are important differences between these types of goals, however, and think it is important to study goals from both perspectives. If we examine the goals that students freely adopt in college classes, with correlational designs, we can learn a lot about relationships between motivational variables and performance in real world contexts. If we manipulate external goals, as we did in the lab, we can learn a lot about causal effects. From a theoretical perspective, both correlational and experimental designs were appropriate for testing our hypotheses.

From a practical perspective, however, it seemed important to begin our educational research with correlational designs. First, and understandably, educators are much more willing to let researchers come into their classes and administer questionnaires than they are to allow researchers to come in and manipulate features of the educational environment. Leaving the lab means giving up control and working within real world constraints. It is not impossible to conduct an experimental study in classrooms (in fact, the research programs of Rosenthal and Lepper discussed at the beginning of this chapter are both good examples), but it takes a very special relationship with educators to gain the access and control necessary to conduct true experiments in classrooms. Second, even if social psychological researchers could gain access and the ability to manipulate educational factors, they should not rush to conduct intervention studies that might have unanticipated or deleterious effects on students' learning or performance. We believe that it is more feasible and ethically responsible to begin with observational and correlational methods in an educational setting and learn as much as possible about the environment before implementing experimental designs. Of course, our ultimate goal may be to change the world by improving education, and experimental intervention studies will be essential sooner or later. We simply recommend that they come later in a program of research, and only when ethically appropriate. Some research topics may never be ethical to study experimentally, and non-experimental designs may be the only choices available (see Mark & Reichardt, Chapter 12, this volume).

## MOVING INTO THE CLASSROOM: CHOOSING MEASURES

Once we decided to conduct survey studies in college classes and measure our independent variable (students' self-reported achievement goals), our next challenge was to choose appropriate dependent variables and select educational variables that tapped the theoretical constructs in which we were most interested. Our research questions have centered on how goals affect motivation and performance, and in the lab, we have examined performance in terms of pinball scores, and we have measured intrinsic motivation with both self-report questionnaires and behavioral measures. When we moved to the college classroom, we had to decide how to measure motivation and performance in this context. One great advantage of our new research context was the ability to study real world variables with longitudinal designs. We measured students' goals at the beginning of their introductory courses, and we collected outcome measures over the course of the semester. The obvious measure of performance in academic settings is grades, and they provide fairly objective measures of students' success in a course. We obtained final grades directly from departmental records (with the consent of students and instructors). When we measured performance in courses taken later, we obtained grades from students' transcripts obtained through university offices (again, with the consent of students). However, in addition to performance, we consider interest to be a critically important educational outcome (Dewey, 1913; Harackiewicz, Barron, & Elliott, 1998; Jackson, 1968; Maehr, 1976). Nicholls (1979) argued that interest, especially when it endures beyond a particular educational experience, is a particularly significant marker of success in education because it can fuel lifelong learning, and we concur. It was therefore important to design measures of academic interest for our research.

Dependent variables measured in the laboratory are sometimes artificial or abstract, but conducting research in educational settings allows a researcher to measure outcome variables in terms of significant real world outcomes. The theoretical constructs are the same, but these operationalizations can give more weight to our theories. We can also measure outcome variables that span much greater time periods than the typical laboratory research paradigm permits. For example, in our pinball research, we would surreptitiously observe participants to measure how long they played pinball when left alone for 5 minutes at the end of the study, on the assumption that their decision to return to the game reflected their intrinsic interest in the pinball game. When measuring intrinsic motivation in educational settings, we have collected behavioral measures of continued interest by following students throughout their entire undergraduate careers to measure the number of additional psychology courses that they have taken (e.g., Harackiewicz, Barron, Tauer, & Elliot, 2002). This measure, which we coded from academic transcripts, reflects a student's continuing interest in psychology and corresponds to our free-choice measure of pinball interest because college students are free to choose their courses, just as our research participants are free to choose whether to play more pinball when left alone. Thus, our choice of outcome measures has been dictated by our theoretical interests, influenced by our laboratory work, and colored by our consideration of what educational outcomes are important to educators.

## MOVING INTO THE CLASSROOM: IMPLICATIONS AND METHODOLOGICAL TRADE-OFFS

In our longitudinal classroom goal studies, we continued to find positive effects for both performance and mastery goals, challenging the mastery goal hypothesis (Harackiewicz, Barron, Carter, Lehto, & Elliot, 1997; Harackiewicz, Barron, Tauer, Carter, Elliot, 2000; Harackiewicz, Barron, Tauer, & Elliot, 2002). Students who adopted performance goals attained higher grades in the course, whereas students who adopted mastery goals reported more interest and took more psychology courses over the course of their undergraduate careers. Most theorists would have predicted that students pursuing only mastery goals would have been the most successful. However, we found that students who adopted both types of achievement goals were best off—they were more likely to be interested in the class *and* to perform well. Thus, the results of our lab and classroom studies, along with results emerging from other investigations (see Harackiewicz, Barron, Pintrich, Elliot, & Thrash, 2002, for a review), led us to adopt a *multiple goal perspective*, in which we have argued that the evidence to date warrants a major revision of achievement goal theory (Barron & Harackiewicz, 2000; Harackiewicz, Barron, & Elliot, 1998; Harackiewicz, Barron, Pintrich, et al., 2002). Our ideas have been controversial, and many issues remain unresolved. We are engaged in ongoing discussions with researchers in the field (Kaplan & Middleton, 2002; Midgley, Kaplan, & Middleton, 2001), but we will not go into the complexities of this debate here. Rather, we hope to illustrate methodological issues raised by our research on this topic as we have moved from the lab to the classroom (and back again), and to discuss several trade-offs that became salient in our journey. These trade-offs can be considered in term of three types of validity: external, internal, and construct validity (Campbell & Stanley, 1963; Cook & Campbell, 1979).

The classic issue when deciding whether to conduct research in the lab or in the real world of education involves the trade-off between external and internal validity. External validity involves evaluating whether or not the results of a particular study can be generalized to other people, places, or times, and internal validity involves evaluating whether or not cause-and-effect relationships have been established between variables. Of course, the only research design that permits clear and unambiguous cause-and-effect statements involves experimental methods.

Designing a laboratory experiment that is high in both external and internal validity has been the topic of great debate (e.g., Mook, 1983; Sears, 1986) and has been labeled "the dilemma of the social psychologist" (Aronson, Wilson, & Brewer, 1998). Our field tends to rely on experimental methodology to answer cause-and-effect questions, and these studies often lack external validity. Our own laboratory studies were no exception. Despite documenting causal goal effects in our lab, we were not in a strong position to argue that our initial experimental results were relevant and generalizable to education. Of course, we believed that our findings were relevant because our manipulations mirror the kinds of goals that teachers might set for their students as they begin an interesting learning task. But could we really make the case for educational relevance based on experimental goal manipulations for pinball games? How would the general public and policy makers (school boards, legislators, etc.) view our results, and did this open us up to easy criticism from skeptical colleagues? We were studying basic motivational processes that should operate in educational settings, but it still seemed a big jump to educational implications. Our college classroom research added important evidence for the external validity of our work.

We could not make a straightforward case for external validity, however, because our experimental findings from the lab did not line up directly with our correlational findings in the classroom. Both paradigms revealed beneficial effects of both mastery and performance goals, and no one single goal proved optimal in either the lab or classroom setting, thereby providing support for the multiple goal perspective. However, the specific pattern of findings was different across our experimental and correlational studies. Because of numerous differences between these research paradigms (type of activity—pinball versus academic coursework; importance of activity—leisure activity versus academic work; type of goal—manipulated versus measured), it is impossible to determine what was responsible for the different results between paradigms. A similar point was raised by Middleton and Midgley (1997), two of our colleagues in educational psychology, who noted the difficulties of comparing experimental laboratory results with those obtained in the classroom. Their comments concerned differences between an experimental study by Elliot and Harackiewicz (1996) and their own classroom study:

> The results from our study in the field lead us to some different conclusions than those of Elliot and Harackiewicz (1996) in the laboratory. Contrasting methodologies may account for the differences. Elliot and Harackiewicz conducted experimental studies with college-aged students using puzzle-like tasks; whereas our study focuses on an academic setting, specifically the mathematics classroom, with middle school students. (Middleton & Midgley, 1997, p. 715)

Concluding that different results may be due to the methodology employed is less than satisfying when trying to come to a conclusion about debates in the achievement goal literature or any area of educational research, but this highlights the theoretical and applied significance of the methodological choices that we make.

## MOVING BACK TO THE LAB

To address the discrepant pattern of findings between our early experimental studies and classroom work, we returned to the lab, where we could create a learning context and control for many of the differences between previous studies. We (Barron & Harackiewicz, 2001) conducted two studies back in the lab but used both correlational and experimental methods to study the effects of self-set and assigned goals. To accomplish this, we had students take part in an academic learning activity (rather than the pinball or other leisure/game activities that we had used in the past). Specifically, participants were taught new methods for solving everyday math problems. These methods outlined simple strategies to add, subtract, multiply, and divide mentally rather than having to rely on more traditional strategies of working out problems with a calculator or paper and pencil. Then participants' achievement goals for the session were either measured via self-report (Study 1) or manipulated, such that participants were randomly assigned to one of three conditions: mastery only, performance only, or both goals (Study 2).

In Study 1, when students reported their level of achievement goals for the learning session, we replicated the pattern found in our college classroom studies (e.g., Harackiewicz, Barron, Carter, et al., 1997, Harackiewicz, Barron, Tauer, Carter, et al., 2000; Harackiewicz, Barron, Tauer, & Elliot, 2002). Specifically, mastery goals were the sole predictor of *interest* in the math activity, whereas performance goals were the sole predictor of *performance* on the math problems, providing further support for the multiple goal perspective. We found the same pattern of effects in a 45-minute learning session that we found in a semester-long college course, suggesting that our laboratory-based learning program was relatively high in external validity and might even be a good paradigm to use for intervention studies.

When goals were experimentally manipulated and assigned to participants in Study 2, we found a different pattern of effects. On interest outcomes, no single goal was optimal for all participants. Instead, the effects of assigned goals were moderated by personality characteristics of the participant, specifically their general achievement orientation. These results replicated our previous findings based on pinball (e.g., Harackiewicz & Elliot, 1993) and suggest that our experimental findings generalize to important learning activities as well as leisure activities. Thus, once again, we found that mastery and performance goals both can have positive effects (in this case, different goals were beneficial in promoting interest for different people).

In sum, both studies revealed that mastery and performance goals can each promote important outcomes relevant to education, but that the patterns differed depending on whether goals were self-set (Study 1) or assigned (Study 2). When goals were assigned, a more complex relationship involving achievement goals and individual differences was found. Thus, the benefits of self-set goals observed in Study 1 could not be reproduced simply by assigning goals in Study 2. Because we took careful steps to control for other variables that have made previous comparisons between correlational and experimental goal studies difficult (e.g., differences in type of task, type of environment, or age of population), we were now in a better position to conclude that the differences observed across Study 1 and Study 2 involved the origin of the goal. One lesson that we learned from this pair of studies was that we should not equate self-set and manipulated goals, and our theoretical analysis has become more careful and nuanced as a result. Thus, with careful methodological work, it is possible to integrate correlational and experimental methods to learn more about the nature of goal effects.

## BACK TO THE CLASSROOM: VALIDITY ISSUES REVISITED

There is no doubt that moving out of the lab and into an educational setting can have a number of advantages. First and foremost is the obvious benefit of generalizing results to important real world issues and establishing external validity. In addition, classroom research can be convenient (especially if conducted with students at the researcher's own university) and relatively easy to implement. Researchers also can obtain large samples of participants, aiding both external validity and statistical power. For example, we have been able to collect data in samples ranging from a few hundred to 3,000 student participants, yielding considerable statistical power to test our theoretical ideas. Although access to larger samples can be seductive, we have found it especially important to consider the statistical versus meaningful significance of our findings in our large-scale classroom studies. It is also important to remind ourselves that our larger sample sizes do not guarantee external validity, and that we need to be very careful about generalizing our classroom findings. For example, although our college classroom studies have more external validity than our lab research, we have only scratched the surface of the external validity question. Studying goal dynamics in introductory college courses certainly does not address all external validity concerns. Rather, it raises a host of related questions about how far these educational results might generalize. Will the same results generalize to upper-level college courses, classes in other majors, or classes in other types of schools (e.g., small liberal arts colleges)? Will the same relationships generalize to elementary, junior high, and high school students? These are some of questions that we are trying to address in our current research.

So far, we have focused on the trade-offs between external and internal validity and the theoretical progress made as a result of going back and forth between the lab and the real world. We turn now to construct validity, and we would like to highlight how research in classroom settings has informed our work with theoretical constructs in the context of the mastery versus multiple goal debate. Construct validity entails evaluating whether one has successfully measured or manipulated the theoretical constructs of interest. The early achievement goal literature is replete with different measures and labels used to capture the different types of achievement goal construct. Moreover, as we have noted, some researchers discussed goal manipulations and questionnaire measures interchangeably. However, our transition from the lab to the college classroom forced us to think more carefully about goals and about what we really mean by a goal. Our questions about goal origin effects, discussed above, actually are questions about construct validity. For example, is a goal something that can be manipulated directly? Do we assume that individuals all accept and adopt externally suggested goals? Is receiving a performance goal manipulation ("We suggest that you try to outperform other students on these problems") equivalent to endorsing a performance goal on a questionnaire ("It is important for me to do better than other students in this class")?

It is important to recognize the theoretical implications of our methodological choices and to temper our conclusions accordingly. For example, early research was based on a dichotomous model that pitted mastery goals against performance goals. Similarly, some researchers used forced-choice questionnaire measures of self-adopted goals that forced individuals to choose between one goal and the other. In both cases, these research designs failed to offer an adequate test of multiple goal effects. When researchers have measured goals independently on separate scales, they have consistently found that mastery and performance goals are uncorrelated or positively correlated (see Hidi & Harackiewicz, 2000, for review). Thus, rather than pursuing one goal to the exclusion of the other, students are just as likely to report pursuing both goals. Thus, careful questionnaire design has led to a clearer theoretical picture of goals as independent constructs (Finney, Pieper, & Barron, in press).

Our understanding of goal dynamics has deepened as a result of measuring these constructs in real world settings. A major benefit

of conducting studies in large college classes is that we have been able to survey numerous items to tap particular constructs, and then evaluate the underlying structure of our theoretical constructs through exploratory and confirmatory factor analysis. As a result, we have a better understanding of the constructs that we hope to manipulate in the lab and can design more effective experimental manipulations of these constructs. Thus, experimental manipulations can be informed by careful construct validation work conducted in the field.

In addition to considering the construct validity of our goal measures and manipulations (i.e., our independent variables), it is also important to consider the construct validity of our outcome measures (i.e., our dependent variables). For example, goal theorists have argued that researchers should examine a variety of educational outcomes and should consider both adaptive (e.g., academic performance) as well as maladaptive outcomes (e.g., cheating). In other words, by exploring a wider range of outcome variables, we may discover benefits and potential costs associated with pursuing a particular goal or combination of goals as we carefully think through and debate the mastery goal versus multiple goal perspectives. The richness of the real world setting of a classroom provides researchers ample opportunity to consider a wide range of potential outcome variables in addition to performance—such as study strategies, level of processing, effort, self-handicapping, and cheating—in order to gain a fuller understanding of goal effects (Butler, 2000; Midgley et al., 2001).

In our own work, we broadened our conceptual definition of academic success to include interest as well as academic performance. By using a multifaceted definition of success, we were able to document that different achievement goals were linked to different aspects of academic success. If we had used a narrower measure of success, we might have drawn very different conclusions. For example, if we had considered only interest, we would have concluded that mastery goals are optimal and inferred strong support for the mastery goal hypothesis. In contrast, if we had considered only grades, we would have concluded that performance goals are optimal and would have claimed no support for either the mastery goal or multiple goal perspective. Instead, by considering both outcomes as important educational outcomes, we acquired a better understanding how both goals can predict positive outcomes in college education.

## LESSONS WE LEARNED IN SCHOOL

As we noted at the beginning of this chapter, we are certainly not the first social psychologists to leave the lab to test theory in a classroom setting, and we hope we are not the last! We have tried to show how much we have learned from moving between the lab and field, and how this has helped us address the current debate in achievement goal theory. We would like to conclude with a summary of three lessons that we have learned along the way.

### Lesson #1: The Importance of Using Multiple Research Methodologies in Multiple Settings

By using a range of research designs (in particular, correlational, experimental, and quasi-experimental designs) and by moving between the lab and field, we have gained a deeper appreciation for the strengths and weaknesses of different research methodologies and the conclusions that our work allows us to draw. In other words, we have moved beyond a "textbook" understanding of the pros and cons of particular methods to a firsthand appreciation of the unique benefits of each type of design. A social psychologist needs many methodological tools and cannot rely solely on experimental designs. We hope that

the examples from our own work show how different research methodologies can complement each other, and how comparisons between them can also generate new ideas for future research.

We hope it is clear that moving into the classroom to conduct research does not dictate a particular research approach, nor does it necessarily limit methodological choices. We have been interested in whether we can promote interest with externally assigned goals, and we have been interested in whether students' goals predict academic success over the course of their undergraduate careers. As a result, our work in educational settings has been predominantly correlational, whereas our laboratory work has been predominantly experimental, but we have also conducted correlational designs in lab settings, as discussed earlier (Barron & Harackiewicz, 2001), and we are currently planning some experimental studies to be conducted in classrooms. We believe that the choice of educational research design should be based primarily on the theoretical questions. If we are trying to answer a causal question about how to promote interest, or a question about the effectiveness of an educational intervention, then of course we need experimental methods. If our research question is descriptive or predictive in nature, however, and we are interested in the predictors of optimal motivation in college, then non-experimental designs are appropriate.

In addition to theoretical considerations, we have come to appreciate the importance of practical and ethical issues. On practical grounds, it is important to consider potential limitations or barriers that may be encountered when conducting research in an educational setting (e.g., the amount of access and the degree of control). Thus, a researcher may decide that he or she is limited to a particular design by the constraints faced. Or, it may be more practical and advantageous to begin with a non-experimental approach that allows the researcher to become knowledgeable about a particular sample and develop good working relationships with school administrators and teachers before trying to implement an experimental design in a classroom. Finally, it is important to consider ethical issues because manipulating some educational variables or giving/withholding a particular intervention could be inappropriate.

Furthermore, although we have not gone into detail about the statistical procedures used in our different research designs, it is important to note that diverse methods require diverse statistical analyses. As a result, we have also gained a deeper appreciation for the benefits of using different statistical techniques to address our research questions (such as factor analysis, multiple regression, path analyses, moderation/mediation, hierarchical linear modeling, and latent growth modeling), and we have enjoyed learning new techniques to analyze our increasingly complex research designs. Other chapters in this volume (West, Biesanz, & Kwok, Chapter 13; Gonzalez & Griffin, Chapter 14) provide overviews of the variety of statistical procedures available to researchers working with complex, real world data.

Finally, our horizons have broadened as a result of working in educational settings. We have been exposed to new colleagues in different academic disciplines who have a lot to contribute to our understanding of motivation and performance. For example, we have broadened our reading beyond social psychological journals to include a number of educational research publications (e.g., *Journal of Educational Psychology, Contemporary Educational Psychology,* and *Educational Psychologist*), and we have begun attending a wider range of conferences (e.g., the American Educational Researchers Association annual conference). As a result, we have found new outlets in which to share and present our work, and we publish our goals work in both social psychological and educational journals,

depending on our focus (see Salovey & Steward, Chapter 20, this volume, for a similar discussion in the health domain). In sum, our theoretical analyses have been enriched by our use of multiple methodologies and exposure to new academic disciplines.

## Lesson #2: Dealing With the Dilemma of the Social Psychologist

Our initial decision to move out of the laboratory setting into an academic setting (as well as our subsequent decision to move back and forth between these environments) has been well rewarded. We have gained new insights into goal dynamics, and we have improved the construct, external, and internal validity of our work. Social psychologists who are interested in educational issues have a number of real world environments available in which to test and verify their ideas, some of which are as close as the classroom outside their office door or perhaps found at the high school on the way home from work. Although Aronson et al. (1998) noted that it is nearly impossible to design an experiment that is high in both internal and external validity, our work in classroom settings has helped us establish external validity for our work. More important, our classroom work inspired us to bring the classroom back into the laboratory, and we were able to design a laboratory paradigm with greater external validity than many of our earlier experiments (Barron & Harackiewicz, 2001). We think we are closer to balancing internal and external validity in the same study, as well as balancing them across different lines of research. This is an ongoing challenge.

## Lesson #3: Increasing the Credibility and Valuation of Research

We also realized that beyond strengthening the external validity of our work, the benefits of moving out of the lab into an educational setting can also affect the perceived credibility of our work. Consider our earlier example in which educational psychologists (Middleton & Midgley, 1997) discussed the differences between Elliot and Harackiewicz's (1996) achievement goal findings based on an experimental, laboratory paradigm using leisure activities and their own correlational findings in middle school math classes. Which research study is more likely to be valued and considered informative? In particular, which study would the general public and policy makers weight more heavily? Although our lab research with pinball and other leisure activities afforded a tightly controlled experimental design that was high in internal validity, it obviously can be critiqued on its external validity. In contrast, Middleton and Midgley's classroom research, although higher in external validity, was correlational and can be critiqued on its internal validity. In their study, as in our own classroom studies, we have been unable to evaluate causal relationships. In our own work, we have been quick to note this limitation and do not claim that adopting a performance goal causes students to perform better in their class. Instead, we recognize the possibility that students who have a history of performing well in classes might be more likely to adopt performance goals and continue performing well. Similarly, students who are initially interested in a course topic might be more likely to

adopt mastery goals and remain interested in the topic. It is important to document these important relationships, but it would be a mistake to formulate policy on the basis of correlational findings.

Policy makers interested in interventions should weight studies high in internal validity, but they may not attend to studies unless they are also high in external validity. When researchers are attentive to both internal and external validity issues, they can increase the credibility and potential utility of their work. A number of psychologists have made strong cases for the benefits of staying in the controlled environment of the lab, despite critiques of limited external validity. For example, Mook (1983) argued in defense of external *invalidity* and strongly defended research paradigms that may lack direct real world linkages. He suggested that not all research is designed to address external validity, nor should it be. We agree. However, for others to value and appreciate the significance of our work (whether they are colleagues from different academic disciplines, policy makers, or the general public), we also need to consider what data they will find most compelling. In the final analysis, we need to consider our own goals for our science: If we do care about policy and changing the world, we must attend to concerns about external validity, but without losing the fierce commitment to internal validity that defines us as experimental social psychologists.

## REFERENCES

Ames, C. (1992). Classrooms: Goals, structures, and student motivation. *Journal of Educational Psychology, 84*, 261-271.

Aronson, E., Wilson, T. D., & Brewer, M. B. (1998). Experimentation in social psychology. In D. Gilbert & S. Fiske (Eds.), *The handbook of social psychology* (4th ed., pp. 99-142). New York: McGraw-Hill.

Barron, K. E., & Harackiewicz, J. M. (2000). Achievement goals and optimal motivation: A multiple goals approach. In C. Sansone & J. M. Harackiewicz (Eds.), *Intrinsic and extrinsic motivation: The search for optimal motivation and performance* (pp. 229–254). San Diego: Academic Press.

Barron, K. E., & Harackiewicz, J. M. (2001). Achievement goals and optimal motivation: Testing multiple goal models. *Journal of Personality and Social Psychology, 80,* 706-722.

Butler, R. (2000). What learners want to know: The role of achievement goals in shaping information seeking, learning and interest. In C. Sansone & J. M. Harackiewicz (Eds.), *Intrinsic and extrinsic motivation: The search for optimal motivation and performance* (pp. 162-195). San Diego: Academic Press.

Campbell, D. T., & Stanley, J. C. (1963). *Experimental and quasi-experimental designs for research.* Chicago: Rand McNally.

Cook, T. D., & Campbell, D. T. (1979). *Quasi-experimentation.* Chicago: Rand McNally.

Dewey, J. (1913). *Interest and effort in education.* Cambridge, MA: Riverside.

Dweck, C. S. (1986). Motivational processes affecting learning. *American Psychologist, 41,* 1040-1048.

Elliot, A. J., & Harackiewicz, J. M. (1996). Approach and avoidance achievement goals and intrinsic motivation: A mediational analysis. *Journal of Personality and Social Psychology, 70,* 461-475.

Finney, S., Pieper, S., & Barron, K. E. (in press). Examining the psychometric properties of the Achievement Goal Questionnaire in a more general academic context. *Educational and Psychological Measurement.*

Greene, D., Sternberg, B., & Lepper, M. R. (1976). Overjustification in a token economy. *Journal of Personality and Social Psychology, 34,* 1219-1234.

Harackiewicz, J. M., Barron, K. E., Carter, S. M., Lehto, A. T., & Elliot, A. J. (1997). Determinants and consequences of achievement goals in the college classroom: Maintaining interest and making the grade. *Journal of Personality and Social Psychology, 73,* 1284-1295.

Harackiewicz, J. M., Barron, K. E., & Elliot, A. J. (1998). Rethinking achievement goals: When are they adaptive for college students and why? *Educational Psychologist, 33,* 1-21.

Harackiewicz, J. M., Barron, K. E., Pintrich, P. R., Elliot, A. J., & Thrash, T. M. (2002). Revision of achievement goal theory: Necessary and illuminating. *Journal of Educational Psychology, 94,* 562-575.

Harackiewicz, J. M., Barron, K. E., Tauer, J. M., Carter, S. M., & Elliot, A. J. (2000). Short-term and long-term consequences of achievement goals in college: Predicting continued interest and performance over time. *Journal of Educational Psychology, 92,* 316-330.

Harackiewicz, J. M., Barron, K. E., Tauer, J. M., & Elliot, A. J. (2002). Predicting success in college: A longitudinal study of achievement goals and ability measures as predictors of interest and performance from freshman year through graduation. *Journal of Educational Psychology, 94,* 638-645.

Harackiewicz, J. M., & Elliot, A. J. (1993). Achievement goals and intrinsic motivation. *Journal of Personality and Social Psychology, 65,* 904-915.

Hidi, S., & Harackiewicz, J. M. (2000). Motivating the academically unmotivated: A critical issue for the 21st century. *Review of Educational Research, 70,* 151-179.

Jackson, P. W. (1968). *Life in classrooms.* New York: Holt, Rinehart & Winston.

Kaplan, A., & Middleton, M. J. (2002). "Should childhood be a journey or a race?": A response to Harackiewicz et al. *Journal of Educational Psychology, 94,* 646-648.

Lepper, M. R. (1985). Microcomputers in education: Motivational and social issues. *American Psychologist, 40,* 1-18.

Lepper, M. R., Greene, D., & Nisbett, R. E. (1973). Undermining children's intrinsic interest with extrinsic reward: A test of the "overjustification" hypothesis. *Journal of Personality and Social Psychology, 28,* 129-137.

Lepper, M. R., & Gurtner, J. (1989). Children and computers: Approaching the twenty-first century. *American Psychologist, 44,* 170-178.

Maehr, M. L. (1976). Continuing motivation: An analysis of a seldom considered educational outcome. *Review of Educational Research, 46,* 443-462.

Middleton, M. J., & Midgley, C. (1997). Avoiding the demonstration of lack of ability: An underexplored aspect of goal theory. *Journal of Educational Psychology, 89,* 710-718.

Midgley, C., Kaplan, A., & Middleton, M. (2001). Performance-approach goals: Good for what, for whom, under what circumstances, and at what cost? *Journal of Educational Psychology, 93,* 77-86.

Mook, D. G. (1983). In defense of external invalidity. *American Psychologist, 38,* 379-387.

Nicholls, J. G. (1979). Quality and equality in intellectual development. *American Psychologist, 34,* 1071-1084.

Rosenthal, R. (1987). "Pygmalion" effects: Existence, magnitude, and social importance. *Educational Researcher, 16,* 37-41.

Rosenthal, R. (1991). Teacher expectancy effects: A brief update 25 years after the Pygmalion experiment. *Journal of Research in Education, 1,* 3-12.

Rosenthal, R., & Jacobsen, L. (1966). *Pygmalion in the classroom.* New York: Holt, Rinehart & Winston.

Sears, D. O. (1986). College sophomores in the laboratory: Influence of a narrow data base on social psychology's view of human nature. *Journal of Personality and Social Psychology, 51,* 515-530.

# Name Index

# Subject Index

# About the Editors

**Carol Sansone,** PhD (1984, Columbia University), is Professor of Psychology at the University of Utah. Her research examines the process through which people regulate their interest and motivation in day-to-day life, using social and nonsocial means. She is interested in how this process might differ as a function of person characteristics (such as gender) and across the life span, as well as in the applications of this work to selection of and persistence in math and science careers and to online learning. She is a Fellow of the Society of Personality and Social Psychology, has served on the editorial boards of a number of journals in social psychology and personality (including the *Journal of Personality and Social Psychology* and *Journal of Experimental Social Psychology*), and has served as consulting reviewer or on grant panels for a number of national and international granting agencies. She edited a special issue of the *Journal of Experimental Social Psychology* on "New Directions in Intrinsic Motivation and Creativity" (1999) and the book (with J. M. Harackiewicz as coeditor) *Intrinsic and Extrinsic Motivation: The Search for Optimal Motivation and Performance* (Academic Press, 2000). Other recent publications have appeared in the journals *Developmental Psychology, Journal of Experimental Social Psychology, Journal of Personality, Psychological Inquiry,* and *Sex Roles.*

**Carolyn C. Morf,** PhD (1994, University of Utah), formerly Assistant Professor of Psychology at the University of Toronto, is currently Chief of the Personality and Social Cognition Program in the Division of Neuroscience and Basic Behavioral Science at the National Institute of Mental Health (NIMH). In this role, she works closely with researchers in developing and refining their grant ideas and applications, and makes funding decisions in the areas of personality, social cognition, and other social processes broadly construed. In addition, she promotes understudied and/or new and emerging areas of research through the development of program announcements, workshops, and other initiatives. She continues to pursue her own research interests as well, which revolve around understanding the self-regulatory processes—both intrapersonal and interpersonal—through which individuals construct and maintain their desired psychological identities and conceptions of themselves. Her work is at the interface of self and personality research, in that she has been studying these processes in individuals who are high in narcissism. Recent publications include a target article on narcissism in

*Psychological Inquiry* (2001, with Frederick Rhodewalt) and a keynote chapter in the *Handbook of Self and Identity* (2003, with Walter Mischel). In addition to the strong interest in methods shown in her roles as researcher and grant officer, she also has a long history of teaching beginning and advanced statistics and methods courses for graduate and undergraduate students at both the University of Utah and the University of Toronto, and she has served on a regular basis as a methodological and statistical consultant for a range of governmental and private organizations.

**A. T. Panter,** PhD (1989, New York University), is an Associate Professor of Psychology and a member of the L. L. Thurstone Psychometric Laboratory at the University of North Carolina, Chapel Hill. She also serves as a senior technical consultant at The Measurement Group. Her work involves developing research designs and data-analytic strategies for applied health problems, such as HIV/AIDS and nicotine dependence in adolescence. Her publications are in measurement and test theory, multivariate data modeling, program evaluation design, and individual differences (especially personality). She has received awards from her university and the American Psychological Association (APA; Division 5: Evaluation, Measurement, and Statistics) for her innovative approaches to teaching statistics and quantitative methodology to undergraduate and graduate students. She regularly consults with federal agencies on grant review, serves on national committees and editorial boards in social/personality psychology and quantitative methods, and is a Fellow of the APA. She is a coeditor of three volumes on program evaluation and measuring outcomes for HIV/AIDS multisite projects, is a coauthor of an online knowledge base for HIV/AIDS care, and is currently coediting a compendium of innovative methods for teaching statistics in the behavioral sciences.

# About the Contributors

**Kenneth E. Barron** is an Assistant Professor at James Madison University. He received his PhD in social/personality psychology from the University of Wisconsin in 1999. His research interests include motivation, goals, psychological well-being, and assessment. His recent publications appear in the *Journal of Educational Psychology, Journal of Personality and Social Psychology, Educational and Psychological Measurement*, and *Educational Psychologist*.

**Gary G. Berntson** is a Professor of Psychology, Psychiatry and Pediatrics, and a member of the Neuroscience Program faculty at The Ohio State University. His research interests are interdisciplinary and span many fields, including psychology, behavioral neuroscience, psychophysiology, and psychoneuroimmunology. A common theme in much of his research relates to levels of functional organization in neurobehavioral systems. He has published more than 150 scientific articles; among his recent publications are the *Handbook of Psychophysiology* and *Foundations in Social Neuroscience*.

**Jeremy C. Biesanz** is an Assistant Professor of Psychology at the University of Wisconsin–Madison. He received his AB from Cornell University and his PhD from Arizona State University, and he recently completed a postdoctoral research fellowship in longitudinal methodology at the University of North Carolina at Chapel Hill. His primary research interests include personality structure, assessing accuracy in person perception, and quantitative models for assessing stability and change.

**Michael H. Birnbaum** is currently Professor of Psychology and director of the Decision Research Center at California State University, Fullerton. He previously served as Assistant, Associate, and Full Professor at the University of Illinois, Urbana–Champaign (1974–1988). He earned his PhD at UCLA with Allen Parducci in 1972. His research interests include social psychology, judgment and decision making, research methodology, psychophysics, and mathematical psychology. He has published more than 100 scholarly works, including three books, two of which deal with psychological research via the World Wide Web. Recent articles feature results that rule out cumulative prospect theory in favor of his configural weight models of risky decision making.

**Niall Bolger,** New York University, is currently using electronic diary methods to study dyadic adjustment processes in close relationships. He is also interested in statistical models for the analysis of intensive repeated-measures data. His recent work has appeared in *Annual Review of Psychology* (Vol. 54), *Psychological Methods, Journal of Personality, Journal of Personality and Social Psychology, Journal of Marriage and the Family*, and *Handbook of Social Psychology* (4th ed.).

**John T. Cacioppo** is the Tiffany and Margaret Blake Distinguished Service Professor at the University of Chicago, where he is the director of the Social Psychology Program and codirector of the Institute for Mind and Biology. His research concerns affect, emotion, and social behavior, with an emphasis on integrating biological, behavioral, and social levels of analysis. Among his recent book publications are the *Handbook of Psychophysiology* and *Foundations in Social Neuroscience.*

**P. Niels Christensen** is an Assistant Professor of Psychology at San Diego State University. His research centers on the motivational properties of self-evaluations for both group and dyadic processes. He investigates these domains using a wide array of data-analytic techniques, including the social relations model, multilevel modeling, and of course, quantitative synthesis. His recent work has appeared in the *Journal of Personality and Social Psychology* and the *Personality and Social Psychology Bulletin.*

**Thomas D. Cook** is the John Evans Professor of Sociology, Psychology, Education and Social Policy at Northwestern University. He has a BA from Oxford University and a PhD from Stanford University. He has been awarded the Myrdal Prize for Science of the American Evaluation Association, the Donald T. Campbell Prize for Innovative Methodology of the Policy Studies Association, and a Distinguished Scientist Award from the American Psychological Association. He is a Fellow of the American Academy of Arts and Sciences and a Margaret Mead Fellow of the Academy of Political and Social Science, as well as being a trustee of the Russell Sage Foundation. His interests are in social science methodology, evaluation, educational change, and the social contexts of adolescence.

**Leandre R. Fabrigar** is an Associate Professor of Psychology at Queen's University, Ontario, Canada. His primary research interests fall within the domains of attitudes, persuasion, social influence, quantitative methods, and psychological measurement. These interests include the role of affect and cognition in persuasion, the impact of attitude structure on attitudinal processes, and applications of attitude theory to understanding political and consumer behavior. Other research interests include the influence of questionnaire design features (e.g., question order and question format) on the measurement of psychological constructs and methodological issues in the application of statistical methods (e.g., factor analysis and structural equation modeling) to psychological research. His recent work has appeared in *Personality and Social Psychology Bulletin, Psychological Methods,* and the *Journal of Personality and Social Psychology.*

**Susan T. Fiske,** Professor of Psychology, Princeton University, studies social cognition (that is, how people make sense of each other), and she wrote an early book on the topic. She currently investigates emotional prejudices toward different kinds of out-groups. Pity, contempt, envy, and pride appear at cultural, interpersonal, and even neural levels. Her perspective on developing a research program comes partly from kibitzing on other people's work, in her roles editing the *Annual Review of Psychology* and the *Handbook of Social Psychology* (4th ed.). She has also learned by reviewing social psychology for an advanced text, organized around five core motives that promote social survival, *Social Beings: Social Psychology From the Perspective of Core Motives* (2003).

**Richard Gonzalez** is Professor of Psychology at the University of Michigan. He also has joint appointments in marketing and in statistics at the University of Michigan. His research interests include judgment and decision-making processes, group dynamics, research methods, and mathematical psychology. His recent publications include articles in the *Journal of Personality*, *Psychometrika*, and *Psychological Methods*.

**Dale Griffin** is an Associate Professor of Marketing at the Graduate School of Business, Stanford University. His research interests include consumer decision making, forecasting by individuals and groups, the measurement of positive illusions, and research methods for studying interdependence. His recent publications include articles in the *Journal of Personality and Social Psychology* and chapters in *Heuristics and Biases: The Psychology of Intuitive Judgment* and two volumes of the *Blackwell Handbook of Social Psychology*.

**Carla Groom** is a postdoctoral fellow in the Psychology Department of the University of Texas, Austin. She has a BA in natural sciences from Cambridge University and a PhD in social psychology from Northwestern University. She has published in the fields of social identity, acculturation, social cognition, and the influence of individual differences on language and cognitive processes. Her current projects focus on language, gender, and health. Methodological innovation and critique are ongoing themes in her work.

**Judith M. Harackiewicz** is a Professor of Psychology at the University of Wisconsin–Madison. She received her PhD from Harvard University in 1980. Her research interests include interest and intrinsic motivation, achievement goals, and competition. Her recent publications appear in the *Journal of Personality and Social Psychology*, *Journal of Educational Psychology*, *Educational Psychologist*, and *Review of Educational Research*.

**S. Alexander Haslam** is Professor of Social Psychology at the University of Exeter. He studied at the University of St. Andrews, Emory University, and Macquarie University, and his previous appointment was at the Australian National University. He is a former associate editor of the *British Journal of Social Psychology* and is currently editor of the *European Journal of Social Psychology*. His most recent book is *Psychology in Organizations: The Social Identity Approach*.

**Rick H. Hoyle** is Professor and Chair of the Department of Psychology at the University of Kentucky. He also serves as Director of Methodology and Statistics at the Center for Prevention Research and as Director of the Methodology and Statistics Core at the Kentucky Institute for AIDS Research. He has served as associate editor of the *Journal of Personality* since 1996 and recently completed a term as associate editor of the *Journal of Personality and Social Psychology*. His primary research interests are self-esteem processes, personality and social influences on drug and alcohol use, and statistical modeling of complex associations in social science data. His book projects include *Selfhood: Identity, Esteem, Regulation*; *Structural Equation Modeling: Concepts, Issues, and Applications*; *Statistical Strategies for Small Sample Research* (Sage, 1999); and *Research Methods in Social Relations*.

**Mary Kern** is a doctoral student in management and organizations at the Kellogg School of Management, Northwestern University. Her research interests include multiparty negotiations, the formation of norms in competitive groups, and work-family conflict. She has worked in the professional services industry as both a human resources and an audit professional. She holds a BBA in accounting and computer applications from the University of Notre Dame and an MS in human resources from Loyola University.

**John F. Kihlstrom** received his PhD in personality and experimental psychopathology from the University of Pennsylvania in 1975. His 1987 *Science* article on "The Cognitive Unconscious" is often credited with sparking a revival of widespread interest in unconscious mental life. He has held teaching positions at Harvard, Wisconsin, Arizona, and Yale, and he is now Professor in the Department of Psychology at the University of California, Berkeley, and a member of both the Institute for Cognitive and Brain Sciences and the Institute for Personality and Social Research.

**Allan J. Kimmel** is Professor of Marketing at the French business school ESCP-EAP (Paris), where he serves as director of the marketing major (English track) program and coordinator of marketing courses for the MBA program. He is a returning visiting professor at Université Paris IX-Dauphine (Paris) and has also taught at the Solvay Business School, Université Libre de Bruxelles (Belgium). He received an MA and PhD in social psychology from Temple University. In addition to ethics, his research and writing focus on rumors, consumer behavior, and cross-cultural marketing. He recently served as guest editor for a special issue of *Psychology & Marketing* on "Deception in Marketing Research and Practice." His most recent book is *Rumor Control: A Manager's Guide to Understanding and Combating Rumors*.

**Laura A. King** is an Associate Professor, Department of Psychological Sciences, University of Missouri, Columbia. Her research interests focus on goals, stories, memory, well-being, and personality development. Adopting Pennebaker's disclosive writing paradigm for a variety of different aspects of life (including life dreams and identifying the positive in negative experiences), her work has examined how writing about life experience may affect well-being and self-regulation. Her work also involves collecting accounts of life experience from a variety of samples who have experienced major life changes. She has served as an associate editor of *Personality and Social Psychology Bulletin* as well as the *Journal of Personality and Social Psychology*.

**Oi-Man Kwok** is a doctoral student in the quantitative psychology program at Arizona State University. He received his BA at National Taiwan University and his MA at the Chinese University of Hong Kong. His primary quantitative research interests include methods for estimating statistical power in multilevel modeling and the impact of partial measurement invariance. He is also interested in the application of these methods in both clinical and cross-cultural research.

**Tyler S. Lorig** is the Ruth Parmly Professor at Washington and Lee University, where he is chair of the Neuroscience Program and a member of the Psychology Department. His research is concerned with understanding the neurophysiological basis of cognition and its evolution. His recent work includes a chapter in *Signals and Perception: The Fundamentals of Human Sensation* and an article in press for the *Journal of Personality and Social Psychology*.

**Denise Lewin Loyd** is a doctoral student in management and organizations at the Kellogg School of Management, Northwestern University. Her research interests include the effects of group composition on information sharing in groups, the impact of risk of categorization on individual decision making, and work-family conflict. She holds dual BS degrees in civil engineering and architectural engineering from the University of Miami and an MS in civil and environmental engineering from the Massachusetts Institute of Technology.

**Melvin M. Mark** is Professor of Psychology at The Pennsylvania State University. He is currently editor of the *American Journal of Evaluation*. His interests include methodology, program and policy evaluation (including the study of social psychological processes in the context of evaluation), the functions and consequences of affective states, methods of principled discovery, and systematic values inquiry. His latest book (with Gary Henry and George Julnes) is *Evaluation: An Integrated Framework for Understanding, Guiding, and Improving Policies and Programs*, and he is coeditor of the forthcoming *Handbook of Evaluation*.

**Geoffrey Maruyama** is Professor of Educational Psychology and Assistant Vice President for Multicultural and Academic Affairs at the University of Minnesota. His research has included school desegregation, social influence processes in schools, and performance of low-income students living in public housing. He has directed a research, evaluation, and assessment office in a school district, evaluating a range of school programs and reform activities, and worked with urban schools on programs for students from underrepresented groups and on university partnership activities around preK-12 diversity programs. He has authored two books (*Basics of Structural Equation Modeling* and *Research in Educational Settings*) and numerous articles.

**Craig McGarty** is a Reader in Psychology at The Australian National University. His research interests include collective guilt, stereotype formation, and public opinion. He is the author of *Categorization and Social Psychology* and, with Alex Haslam, *Doing Psychology*; he also edited *The Message of Social Psychology* and coedited, with Vincent Yzerbyt and Russell Spears, *Stereotypes as Explanations: The Formation of Meaningful Beliefs About Social Groups*.

**Joan G. Miller** is an Associate Professor of Psychology at the New School University. Her current research examines cultural influences on interpersonal motivation, theory of mind, social support exchange, rules of reciprocity, and moral judgment. Her recent publications include articles in *Psychological Bulletin*, *Psychological Science*, and the *Journal of Experimental Social Psychology* as well as chapters in *The Nebraska Symposium on Motivation: Cross-Cultural Differences in Perspectives on the Self* (Vol. 49), *Blackwell Handbook of Social Psychology: Vol. 1. Intrapersonal Processes*, *The Handbook of Culture and Psychology*, and the *Comprehensive Handbook of Psychology: Vol. 5. Personality and Social Psychology*.

**Howard C. Nusbaum** is Professor of Psychology and Chair of the Department of Psychology at the University of Chicago. His research focuses on the psychological and neurophysiological mechanisms that mediate spoken language use and on cognitive mechanisms of learning and attention. Recent publications investigate the cognitive effects of gesturing while speaking, the cortical lateralization of emotional and syntactic intonation, and perceptual learning of nonnative phonetic categories.

**Eva M. Pomerantz** teaches at the University of Illinois, Urbana–Champaign. The key goal of her research is to examine integrative models of the complex processes involved in the development of self-regulation. Her work is guided by the idea that children's environments and their own characteristics interact to influence their self-regulation. In this vein, she explores the contribution of central aspects of children's environment (e.g., parents' practices, peer relations, culture) in conjunction with children's characteristics (e.g., achievement histories, gender, self-views). Her research has appeared in *Personality and Social Psychology Review*, the *Journal of Personality and Social Psychology*, *Child Development*, *Developmental Psychology*, and the *Journal of Educational Psychology*.

**Charles S. Reichardt** is a Professor of Psychology at the University of Denver. His interests are in the logic (as opposed to the mathematics) of research methods, statistics, and program evaluation. Many of his best articles and chapters on research methods are coauthored with either Harry Gollob or Mel Mark. He has published three books (two of which concern the interplay between qualitative and quantitative research), all coedited with either Tom Cook, Sharon Rallis, or Will Shadish.

**Jorgianne Civey Robinson** is a second-year graduate student in the social psychology doctoral program at the University of Kentucky. Her research focuses on the influence of evaluations of physical appearance on self-regulation and self-esteem.

**Diane N. Ruble**, who teaches at New York University, focuses her research on children's acquisition of knowledge about social categories and its implications for children's identity development, choices, and behaviors. One major focus concerns when and how children's growing knowledge about gender influences their gender-typed preferences and behaviors across the preschool and early school years. She is also examining the development of children's perceptions of themselves and others in terms of stable characteristics, such as personality traits and areas of competence, and some of the antecedents and consequences of this development. Among her recent publications are articles in *Child Development, Personality and Social Psychology Review*, and *Psychological Bulletin*, as well as chapters in the *Handbook of Social Psychology* (4th ed.), *Handbook of Child Psychology* (4th ed.), and *Review of Personality and Social Psychology*.

**Peter Salovey** is the Dean of the Graduate School of Arts and Sciences and Chris Argyris Professor of Psychology at Yale University. He also serves as Professor of Epidemiology and Public Health; Director of the Health, Emotion, and Behavior Laboratory; and Deputy Director of the Center for Interdisciplinary Research on AIDS (CIRA). His research concerns the assessment and validity of emotional competencies, as well as the role of emotion and health communication in motivating health behaviors relevant to preventing cancer and HIV/AIDS. His recent books include *The Wisdom in Feeling: Psychological Processes in Emotional Intelligence* (with Lisa Feldman Barrett) and *Key Readings in the Social Psychology of Health* (with Alexander Rothman).

**Yuichi Shoda** is an Associate Professor of Psychology at the University of Washington. His research focuses on higher-order consistency in social behavior (stable individual differences in the way social behavior changes across situations and over time), identifying and analyzing psychological features of situations; perception of personal coherence and consistency, computational models of personality as an associative network of cognitions and affects, and self-regulatory processes. His work has been published in such journals as *Psychological Review, Science, Journal of Personality and Social Psychology, Personality and Social Psychology Bulletin, Personality and Social Psychology Review, Social Cognition, Journal of Personality*, and *Developmental Psychology*.

**Wayne T. Steward** is a postdoctoral fellow at the Center for AIDS Prevention Studies, University of California, San Francisco (UCSF). His current research interests lie at the intersection of psychology, public health, and policy making. He works with the UCSF AIDS Policy Research Center on the development and implementation of policies that promote structural changes to reduce HIV transmission. His recent publications include articles in the *Journal of Applied Social Psychology* and *American Psychologist* and a chapter in *Handbook of Affect and Social Cognition*.

**Leigh Thompson** is the J. Jay Gerber Distinguished Professor of Dispute Resolution & Organizations in the Kellogg School of Management at Northwestern University. Her research focuses on negotiation, team creativity, and learning. In 1991, she received a multiyear Presidential Young Investigator award from the National Science Foundation for her research on negotiation and conflict resolution, and she has been funded continuously by that agency. In 1994–1995, she was a Fellow at the Center for Advanced Study in the Behavioral Sciences in Stanford, California. She has published more than 65 research articles and chapters and has authored 4 books: *The Mind and Heart of the Negotiator (2nd ed.)*, *Shared Knowledge in Organizations* (with David Messick and John Levine), *Making the Team*, and *The Social Psychology of Organizational Behavior: Essential Reading*. She is a member of the editorial boards of several journals.

**Duane T. Wegener** is an Associate Professor of Psychological Sciences at Purdue University. His primary research interests include attitudes and persuasion, effects of mood and emotion on information processing and judgment, biases and bias correction in social judgment, and use of quantitative methods in psychological research. He is a past associate editor of *Personality and Social Psychology Bulletin* and received the 2001 Distinguished Scientific Award for an Early Career Contribution to Psychology (in social psychology) from the American Psychological Association. His work has appeared in the *Journal of Experimental Social Psychology* and in *The Handbook of Social Psychology* (4th ed.), among other publications.

**Stephen G. West** is Professor of Psychology at Arizona State University. His primary research interests are in the design and statistical analysis of field research, personality research, and the development and evaluation of theory-based preventive interventions. He is currently editor of *Psychological Methods* and is past editor of the *Journal of Personality*. He received the 2000 Henry A. Murray award from the Society for Personality and Social Psychology for distinguished contributions to the study of lives. He is the (co-)author or (co-)editor of 12 volumes, beginning with *A Primer of Social Psychological Theories* and including, most recently, *Applied Multiple Regression/Correlation Analysis for the Behavioral Sciences* (3rd ed.).

**Wendy Wood** is a Professor of Psychology and Associate Vice President for Research at Texas A&M University. Her primary research interests are in attitudes and social influence and in sex differences in behavior. She learned research synthesis techniques when her first academic job did not have a research participant pool and she was unable to conduct the large questionnaire studies that she had used in graduate school. Research synthesis was then new to psychology and offered more in the way of promise than substance. She now uses both research synthesis and primary experiments in her research. Recent publications include articles in *Psychological Bulletin*, the *Journal of Personality and Social Psychology*, and the *Annual Review of Psychology*.